Adventuring with Books

Adventuring with Books

A Booklist for Pre-K–Grade 6

Ninth Edition

Mary Jett-Simpson, Editor,
and the Committee on the Elementary School Booklist
of the National Council of Teachers of English

National Council of Teachers of English
1111 Kenyon Road, Urbana, Illinois 61801

NCTE Editorial Board: Donald R. Gallo, Richard Lloyd-Jones, Raymond J. Rodrigues, Dorothy S. Strickland, Brooke Workman, Charles Suhor, ex officio, Michael Spooner, ex officio

Staff Editors: Jane M. Curran, David A. Hamburg

Book Design: Tom Kovacs for TGK Design

NCTE Stock Number 00783-3020

Library of Congress Cataloging in Publication Data

National Council of Teachers of English. Committee on the Elementary
   School Booklist.
      Adventuring with books: a booklist for pre-K–grade 6 / Mary Jett-
   Simpson, editor, and the Committee on the Elementary School
   Booklist of the National Council of Teachers of English. — 9th ed.
         p.   cm.
      ISBN 0-8141-0078-3   ISSN 1045-7488
      1. Bibliography—Best books—Children's literature.   2. Children's
   literature—Bibliography.   3. Elementary school libraries—Book
   lists.   4. Libraries, Children's—Book lists.   I. Jett-Simpson,
   Mary, 1938– II. Title.
   Z1037.N346   1989
   [PN1009.A1]
   011.62—dc20   89–12906
                                                                         CIP

Contents

Foreword

The National Council of Teachers of English is proud to publish four different booklists, renewed on a regular rotation in its Booklist Series. The four are *Adventuring with Books* (pre-K through grade 6), *Your Reading* (middle school/junior high), *Books for You* (senior high), and *High Interest/Easy Reading* (junior/senior high reluctant readers). Conceived as resources for teachers and students alike, these volumes reference thousands of the most recent children's and young adults' trade books. The works listed cover a wide range of topics, from preschool ABC books to science fantasy novels for high school seniors; from wordless picture books to nonfiction works on family stresses, computers, mass media.

Each edition of an NCTE booklist is compiled by a group of professional teachers and librarians, under leadership appointed by the NCTE Executive Committee. Working for most of three or four years with new books submitted regularly by publishers, the committee members review, select, and annotate the hundreds of works to be listed in their new edition. The members of the committee that compiled this volume are listed on the committee page.

Of course, no single book is right for everyone or every purpose, so inclusion of a work in this booklist is not necessarily an endorsement from NCTE. However, it is an indication that, in the view of the professionals who make up the booklist committee, the work in question is worthy of teachers' and students' attention, perhaps for its informative, perhaps its aesthetic qualities. On the other hand, exclusion from an NCTE booklist is not necessarily a judgment on the quality of a given book or publisher. Many factors—space, time, availability of certain books, publisher participation—may influence the final shape of the list.

We hope that you will find this booklist useful and that you will collect the other booklists in the NCTE series. We feel that these volumes contribute substantially to our mission of helping to improve instruction in English and the language arts. We think you'll agree.

Michael Spooner
NCTE Senior Editor for Publications

Introduction

The 1989 edition of *Adventuring with Books* is an annotated list of books selected for their merit and potential for use in the classroom and at home. Literary and artistic quality were the primary criteria for book selection, as well as judged appeal to children and accuracy of presentation. As in the previous edition, notable books from the past have been recognized in lists appended to each major chapter of the booklist.

The approximately 8,000 titles considered for inclusion in this publication were submitted by publishers in response to a request from the NCTE Director of Publications for children's books published in the United States between 1985 and 1988. Of these, some 1,800 were selected for annotation in this book. A few reissues were included because they appear in a new format with new illustrations. In recent years, many books have gone out of print soon after publication; consequently, some books on this list may be available from publishers for only a limited period, but they should be available in libraries.

Teachers, who are part of the national trend toward making children's books a central component of reading, language arts, and content-area classes, will find this a useful reference volume as they build units of instruction. The annotations, organization of contents, additional booklists, and subject index are designed to assist teachers in developing units around topics, subjects, themes, authors, illustrators, and genres, and to link with content study to extend, enrich, and humanize the information.

The table of contents reflects the categories this committee felt would be most useful to teachers, librarians, and media specialists. Books are categorized by genre and subcategories which highlight books with a specific focus or which meet particular instructional needs. Additionally, six new features have been included: (1) a chapter for the very young, Books for Babies and Toddlers; (2) general grade-level designations: primary (K–3) and intermediate (4–6), which indicate that the books will probably be of most interest to students within those grades (however, younger or older children might enjoy books in the opposite grade level); (3) a subject index for locating additional topics or for cross-reference; (4) an illustrator index; (5) a complete listing of award-winning books and sources of other useful booklists; and (6) a listing of books, annotated in this volume, which are particularly strong in some curriculum dimension of the language arts and which would be especially useful in teaching with literature.

Format of This Book

Each book entry is similar to the one presented below. A brief description of the elements contained in the book entry follows.

11.80   Taylor, Mildred D. **The Friendship.** Illustrated by Max Ginsburg. Dial Books for Young Readers, 1987. Ages 8–11.

    Set in rural Mississippi during the Depression, this short story is narrated by Cassie Logan and her brother, who have appeared in previous books by Mildred D. Taylor. It focuses on a confrontation between an elderly black man and a white store owner. The strong characterization and poignant pen-and-ink drawings make this book a good starter for discussion of racial injustice. *ALA Notable Children's Book*, *Boston Globe–Horn Book Award*, and *Coretta Scott King Award* (for writing).

1.   *The annotation number* identifies the chapter and the book's placement within that chapter according to subcategory and alphabetical order.

2.   *The bibliographic information* includes the author's complete name, followed by the title of the book, the illustrator, the publisher, and the date of publication. Publishers' addresses are listed in the Directory of Publishers, which begins on page 496.

3.   *The interest age range of the book* reflects the booklist committee's judgment about the age range of children who would be interested in either hearing the book read aloud or reading it on their own.

4.   *A brief story summary or content description* is included, along with critical statements where appropriate.

5.   *Curriculum connection statements* are made when the book contains a particularly strong feature for making curriculum ties. These include (a) ties with such content areas as science, social studies, art, and music; (b) structural ties, such as strong characterization and setting, rich use of language, exceptional illustrations, predictable plot structure in books for beginners,

and strong story structure; and (c) classroom activities, such as group story sharing, story theatre, creative drama, storytelling, and models for writing.

6. *Book awards* are included to pinpoint books considered to be exceptional in some way. See chapter 21: Book Awards and Booklists, starting on page 471, for descriptions of the awards included in this book.

Mary Jett-Simpson
University of Wisconsin–
Milwaukee

1 Books for Babies and Toddlers

Board Books

1.1 Bohdal, Susi. **Bobby the Bear.** Illustrated by the author. North-South Books, 1986. Ages 2–4. (Picture book)

Finely drawn illustrations, detailed and richly colored, tell of a world of patched and well-loved toys, including a bear named Bobby.

1.2 Bohdal, Susi. **Harry the Hare.** Illustrated by the author. North-South Books, 1986. Ages 2–5. (Picture book)

Harry the Hare is the patched and beloved playmate of Bobby the Bear, both of which are animated only in a child's imagination. Detailed evocative illustrations of a child's nursery toys are brilliantly colored and beautiful to behold.

1.3 Hill, Eric. **Spot at Play.** Illustrated by the author. G. P. Putnam's Sons/Ventura Books/Little Spot Board Books, 1985. Ages 2–5. (Picture book)

In a tiny book, just right for a preschooler's small hands, Spot the puppy jumps rope and finds other ways to amuse himself. The full-color illustrations in this book and other books in the series will stimulate questions and conversations during the read-aloud time.

1.4 Hill, Eric. **Spot at the Fair.** Illustrated by the author. G. P. Putnam's Sons/Ventura Books/Little Spot Board Books, 1985. Ages 2–5. (Picture book)

Brightly colored illustrations depict Spot the puppy riding a roller coaster and on a merry-go-round and discovering other fun things to do at a fair.

1.5 Hill, Eric. **Spot Looks at Colors.** Illustrated by the author. G. P. Putnam's Sons/Ventura Books/Little Spot Board Books, 1985. Ages 2–5. (Picture book)

A multicolored beachball helps introduce Spot the puppy to all the colors in the world around him. As he explores, he finds objects in the primary colors.

1.6   Hill, Eric. **Spot Looks at Shapes.** Illustrated by the author. G. P. Putnam's Sons/Ventura Books/Little Spot Board Books, 1985. Ages 2–5. (Picture book)

Illustrations in bold, bright colors show Spot the puppy learning to recognize the many shapes in his environment.

1.7   Hill, Eric. **Spot on the Farm.** Illustrated by the author. G. P. Putnam's Sons/Ventura Books/Little Spot Board Books, 1985. Ages 2–5. (Picture book)

Spot the puppy meets a pig, a horse, a cow, and other animals when he visits a farm.

1.8   Hill, Eric. **Spot's First Words.** Illustrated by the author. G. P. Putnam's Sons/Ventura Books/Little Spot Board Books, 1985. Ages 2–5. (Picture book)

Preschoolers will learn some basic vocabulary terms along with Spot the puppy in this tiny book.

1.9   Hoban, Tana. **1, 2, 3.** Photographs by the author. Greenwillow Books, 1985. Ages 1–3. (Picture book)

Clear, colorful photographs of familiar objects illustrate a counting book for the youngest child. Each board page includes a bright red numeral, a number word, and a corresponding array of dots to be counted.

1.10   Hoban, Tana. **What Is It?** Photographs by the author. Greenwillow Books, 1985. Ages 1–3. (Picture book)

Infants and parents will delight in this board book's excellent full-color photographs of familiar objects placed one to a page with no text. A first book for children to identify such everyday objects as a cup, a spoon, keys, and a shoe.

1.11   Krementz, Jill. **Katharine Goes to Nursery School.** Photographs by the author. Random House, 1986. Ages 2–4. (Picture book)

A sturdy board book with colored photographs that depict Katharine, a toddler, and her activities at nursery school: playing, listening, singing, painting, washing, eating, and resting.

1.12   Lynn, Sara. **Clothes.** Illustrated by the author. Macmillan/Aladdin Books, 1986. Ages 2–4. (Picture book)

Items of clothing are drawn in bold colors on each page of this board book. The word printed underneath the object can help the young child with early concepts about reading. Each book in this series about familiar objects in a baby's life clearly depicts the objects in bold colors accompanied by the appropriate caption. The simplicity and clarity of the books should serve to stimulate oral language.

1.13   Lynn, Sara. **Food.** Illustrated by the author. Macmillan/Aladdin Books, 1986. Ages 2–4. (Picture book)

Such food-related objects as a bib, a tomato, and a slice of cheese are depicted in bright colors in this book.

1.14   Lynn, Sara. **Home.** Illustrated by the author. Macmillan/Aladdin Books, 1986. Ages 2–4. (Picture book)

Preschoolers will recognize the everyday objects shown in this book. The name of each object appears underneath.

1.15   Lynn, Sara. **Toys.** Illustrated by the author. Macmillan/Aladdin Books, 1986. Ages 2–4. (Picture book)

Familiar toys appear one to a page in this book for preschoolers about familiar objects.

1.16   McCue, Lisa. **Corduroy on the Go.** Illustrated by the author. Viking Kestrel, 1987. Ages 2–4. (Picture book)

Each double page of this small cardboard book features Don Freeman's lovable bear, Corduroy, engaged in a form of locomotion, such as a swing, waterskis, or scooter. The words paired with the activity will help a child acquire some sight words.

1.17   Pfister, Marcus. **Where Is My Friend?** Illustrated by the author. North-South Books, 1986. Ages 2–5. (Picture book)

A porcupine searching for a friend finds such likely candidates as a cactus, a brush, and a pincushion. When the porcupine finally finds a prickly friend, the young reader or listener will discover what a happy ending is. The tale is just right for a preschooler's sense of humor.

1.18   Roffey, Maureen. **Family Scramble.** Illustrated by the author. E. P. Dutton, 1987. Ages 3–6. (Picture book)

Scramble the pages and learn how many different things each character can do. Because the cardboard pages are cut in half, the young reader can turn the bottom or top halves of the pages to create new combinations of the fourteen family members engaged in fourteen actions. There are ninety-eight possible combinations, involving such characters as Brother Bill and Grandma. Large print aids the beginning reader.

1.19   Roffey, Maureen. **Fantasy Scramble.** Illustrated by the author. E. P. Dutton, 1987. Ages 3–6. (Picture book)

Fourteen fantasy characters, including a pirate, a witch, and a king, can be mixed and matched to form ninety-eight combinations. Each page is cut in half, so the top part of each character's face can be turned independently of the lower part of the face and the torso.

1.20   Schmid, Eleonore. **Farm Animals.** Illustrated by the author. North-South Books, 1986. Ages 3–5. (Picture book)

This board book is a straightforward animal identification book with minimal text naming the farm animals. The animals are not cute or silly, but pleasantly realistic.

1.21   Wells, Rosemary. **Max's Bath.** Illustrated by the author. Dial Books for Young Readers/Very First Books, 1985. Ages 2–5. (Picture book)

Max, the toddler bunny, returns in this series of small board books for the very young child. In this book, Max needs a bath when much of a messy meal remains on his fur. *ALA Notable Children's Book.*

1.22   Wells, Rosemary. **Max's Bedtime.** Illustrated by the author. Dial Books for Young Readers/Very First Books, 1985. Ages 2–5. (Picture book)

Preschoolers will identify with Max the bunny when he has trouble getting ready for bed and falling asleep. *ALA Notable Children's Book.*

1.23   Wells, Rosemary. **Max's Birthday.** Illustrated by the author. Dial Books for Young Readers/Very First Books, 1985. Ages 2–5. (Picture book)

Max happily unwraps a birthday gift from his sister Ruby, but he is scared by the dragon he finds inside. *ALA Notable Children's Book.*

1.24 Wells, Rosemary. **Max's Breakfast.** Illustrated by the author. Dial Books for Young Readers/Very First Books, 1985. Ages 2–5. (Picture book)

Max the rabbit wants strawberries for breakfast, but first he must eat his egg. Max tries hiding the egg and then himself, and his sister Ruby ends up eating the egg.

1.25 Ziefert, Harriet. **Lewis Said, Lewis Did!** Illustrated by Carol Nicklaus. Random House, 1987. Ages 2–4. (Picture book)

This large-sized board book is for a toddler who wants to handle big books without risk of tearing them. Bright, cheery illustrations show Lewis the lion making good on his promises to build a house, fly an airplane, row a boat, and other grand achievements. A beginning reader could read this to a younger child.

1.26 Ziefert, Harriet. **Nicky's Friend.** Illustrated by Richard Brown. Viking Kestrel, 1986. Ages 2–4. (Picture book)

This small cardboard book for very young children has a word or two per page and reaches the satisfying conclusion that everyone likes Nicky the cat and vice versa.

1.27 Ziefert, Harriet. **Nicky's Noisy Night.** Illustrated by Richard Brown. Viking Penguin/Puffin Books/Lift the Flap Books, 1986. Ages 2–6. (Picture book)

When Nicky the cat is unable to get to sleep because of night noises, his mother helps remedy the problem.

1.28 Ziefert, Harriet. **Nicky's Picnic.** Illustrated by Richard Brown. Viking Penguin/Puffin Books/Lift the Flap Books, 1986. Ages 2–6. (Picture book)

Nicky's adventure in the meadow is enhanced by the other animals that he meets on the way.

1.29 Ziefert, Harriet. **No, No Nicky.** Illustrated by Richard Brown. Viking Kestrel, 1986. Ages 2–4. (Picture book)

Nicky the cat reappears in this colorful cardboard book that warns against possible dangers around the house. Children learn along with Nicky about the right things and the wrong things to play with.

1.30　　Ziefert, Harriet. **Where's the Cat?** Illustrated by Arnold Lobel. Harper and Row, 1987. Ages 1–4. (Picture book)

At the end of this small board book, after washing, jumping, and drinking milk, the fat gray cat disappears out the door. The young reader must lift the flap to find out where the cat has gone. A short, sweet, and simple account of what a cat does.

1.31　　Ziefert, Harriet. **Where's the Dog?** Illustrated by Arnold Lobel. Harper and Row, 1987. Ages 1–4. (Picture book)

This small, short board book features a floppy pup that comes into the house wet, drinks from its bowl, and chases a rubber ball. The best part, though, is when the dog hides at the end of the book, and the child must lift the flap to find the pup.

1.32　　Ziefert, Harriet. **Where's the Guinea Pig?** Illustrated by Arnold Lobel. Harper and Row, 1987. Ages 1–4. (Picture book)

A small child can follow a guinea pig going about its normal routine of eating and playing in this small board book. At the end of the book, the guinea pig escapes from its hutch and goes . . . where? The child must lift the flap to find out.

1.33　　Ziefert, Harriet. **Where's the Turtle?** Illustrated by Arnold Lobel. Harper and Row, 1987. Ages 1–4.

A small, baby-sized board book with few pages has a surprise lift-the-flap ending. A turtle does all the usual turtle things—it eats, swims, and hides in its shell—and then disappears for its nap at the end of the book.

Nursery Rhymes

1.34　　Brown, Marc. **Hand Rhymes.** Illustrated by the author. E. P. Dutton, 1985. Ages 2–6. (Picture book)

Fourteen easy-to-read rhymes are presented line-by-line in large print. Each line of text has a small drawing showing how to make the accompanying hand motion. Humorous full-color illustrations surround each hand rhyme, filling the pages with things to see, to hear, and to do.

1.35 Brown, Marc, compiler. **Play Rhymes.** Illustrated by the author. E. P. Dutton, 1987. Ages 3 and younger. (Picture book)

Twelve finger plays for the youngest child are fully illustrated, with small black-and-white insets depicting the motions for each line. Six of the rhymes are songs, and the music appears at the end of the book. Included are such familiar and basic rhymes as "Teddy Bear," "Duke of York," and "John Brown's Baby." The soft, colorful illustrations are appropriate for small children. Also available is Marc Brown's *Finger Rhymes*.

1.36 dePaola, Tomie. **Hey Diddle Diddle, and Other Mother Goose Rhymes.** Illustrated by the author. G. P. Putnam's Sons/Sandcastle Books, 1988. Ages 2–6. (Picture book)

This beautifully illustrated paperback book contains over forty favorite Mother Goose rhymes. It is an ideal book to read aloud to the preschool child.

1.37 dePaola, Tomie. **Tomie dePaola's Mother Goose.** Illustrated by the author. G. P. Putnam's Sons, 1985. Ages 3–8. (Picture book)

This Mother Goose collection is a delight page after page for its design, content, and illustrations. The selection of rhymes includes a satisfying combination of familiar and unfamiliar, each with a bright illustration. The presentation of poems on the page is varied and interesting: some verses are framed with lines, some are placed within decorative borders, some appear on two-page spreads, some are grouped in clusters. An index of first lines is included. *Children's Choice.*

1.38 Galdone, Paul. **Three Little Kittens.** Illustrated by the author. Clarion Books, 1986. Ages 3–8. (Picture book)

Paul Galdone demonstrates his raffish charm and energetic freshness in watercolors enhanced by strokes in ink. His illustrations contain lots of scratchy details, but they never draw attention from the main action in the pictures. Appealing without becoming cloying, the artwork provides a fine way to introduce this popular rhyme to young listeners and readers.

1.39   Hawkins, Colin, and Jacqui Hawkins. **Old Mother Hubbard.**
Illustrated by the authors. G. P. Putnam's Sons, 1985. Ages
3–8. (Picture book)

Old Mother Hubbard peering into her cupboard is perfect material for a lift-the-flap book. Little children will enjoy opening the cupboard door and many other flaps to find out what
silly thing the dog does next. The humor in this contemporary
version with the bright cartoonlike illustrations will not be
lost on the adults reading it, either.

1.40   Lubin, Leonard B. **This Little Pig: A Mother Goose Favorite.**
Illustrated by the author. Lothrop, Lee and Shepard Books,
1985. Ages 3–8. (Picture book)

This well-known old rhyme is fleshed out to book length with
full-color, full-page illustrations. In detail-crammed pictures
that are quasi-historical, elaborately garbed pigs, ducks, and
frogs, weighted down under eighteenth-century ruffles, bows,
and perukes, act out the standard verse, but also extend it.
The book is one to be shared with children because the visual
style may not be immediately appealing.

1.41   Manning, Paul. **Boy.** Illustrated by Nicola Bayley. Macmillan/
Merry-Go-Rhymes Books, 1988. Ages 2–5. (Picture book)

In simple verse, the daily adventures of a small boy are recounted, from waking in the morning till bedtime. An exquisitely colored illustration, rich in detail, accompanies each
line of the poem in this tiny book. Other books in the series
are similar in format and style.

1.42   Manning, Paul. **Clown.** Illustrated by Nicola Bayley. Mac-
millan/Merry-Go-Rhymes Books, 1988. Ages 2–5. (Picture
book)

Preschoolers will enjoy the antics of a clown during his performance in a circus. Detailed illustrations help convey the
mood of a circus.

1.43   Manning, Paul. **Cook.** Illustrated by Nicola Bayley. Mac-
millan/Merry-Go-Rhymes Books, 1988. Ages 2–5. (Picture
book)

A squirrel bakes a chocolate cake and shares it with friends.

1.44   Manning, Paul. **Fisherman.** Illustrated by Nicola Bayley. Macmillan/Merry-Go-Rhymes Books, 1988. Ages 2–5. (Picture book)

A rhyming text tells of a fisherman who encounters rough weather, but who returns home safe and sound.

1.45   Parkinson, Kathy, illustrator. **The Farmer in the Dell.** Albert Whitman, 1988. Ages 3–5. (Picture book)

Each line of the numerous verses of this familiar song is cheerfully illustrated. The artist builds up to a hilarious, chaotic scene in the kitchen once the dog is taking the rat and the rat is taking the cheese.

1.46   Pearson, Tracey Campbell. **Sing a Song of Sixpence.** Illustrated by the author. Dial Books for Young Readers, 1985. Ages 4–6. (Picture book)

Hilarious watercolor illustrations accompany the text of this traditional nursery rhyme. It is hard to tell who is more mischievous—the birds or the children. The children, however, contribute more than their share to the devilment. Excellent illustrations in an average-sized book help make this a good sing-along/read-aloud book. *Children's Choice.*

1.47   Pooley, Sarah, compiler. **A Day of Rhymes.** Illustrated by the compiler. Alfred A. Knopf/Borzoi Books, 1987. Ages 3–6. (Picture book)

Rhymes with which preschoolers are well familiar are gloriously assembled in a rousing, happy collection. Children will want to skip, jump, clap, and sing along. Bright, buoyant illustrations accompany the fifty-five favorite rhymes.

1.48   Prelutsky, Jack, compiler. **Read-Aloud Rhymes for the Very Young.** Illustrated by Marc Brown. Alfred A. Knopf/Borzoi Books, 1986. Ages 2–7. (Picture book)

Over 150 authors are represented in a rollicking, happy-go-lucky book filled with Marc Brown's merry drawings, which match the verses perfectly. Jack Prelutsky has chosen poems that are appropriate for small children's sense of rhythm and rhyme. Rose Fyleman, Dorothy Aldis, Karla Kuskin, Maurice Sendak, Laura E. Richards, and Walter de la Mare are a few of the poets represented. This outstanding collection is recommended for purchase by parents, teachers, and librarians.

1.49   Voake, Charlotte, illustrator. **Over the Moon: A Book of Nursery Rhymes.** Clarkson N. Potter, 1985. Ages 3–7. (Picture book)

Over one hundred nursery rhymes, riddles, and lullabies are included in this title, with jolly black-and-white scratch drawings, many of them over watercolors. The complete text is given for many of the rhymes, such as "Little Bo Peep" and "Pussycat, Pussycat." The book is an excellent resource for the teacher as well as fun for sharing with young children.

1.50   Winter, Jeanette. **Come Out to Play.** Illustrated by the author. Alfred A. Knopf/Borzoi Books, 1986. Ages 4–8. (Picture book)

Imaginative, full-color, double-page paintings illustrate the rhyme "Girls and boys, come out to play, the moon is shining bright as day. . . ." It is presented as dream sequences set on a city street lined with apartments. A small elfin character reminiscent of the Pied Piper calls the children with his violin music.

Other Books

1.51   Allen, Pamela. **Fancy That!** Illustrated by the author. Orchard Books, 1988. Ages 2–6. (Picture book)

In a book of bright, colorful illustrations and large print, Mother Hen hatches six eggs to accompanying barnyard sounds.

1.52   Anderson, Peggy Perry. **Time for Bed, the Babysitter Said.** Illustrated by the author. Houghton Mifflin, 1987. Ages 2–6. (Picture book)

Kids and small frogs will go through the wildest antics to avoid going to bed. Be warned that this book may pass on some new ideas. The comical pictures carry the story with an easy-to-read text of few words that lilts along in rhyme.

1.53   Anno, Mitsumasa. **Anno's Peekaboo.** Illustrated by the author. Philomel Books, 1987. Ages 1–2. (Picture book)

A baby plays a game of peekaboo with this book, as hand-shaped pages are flipped over pictures of various interesting faces. Peekaboo at Santa, a bunny, Mama, a clown! There is no text; the game is all.

1.54 Asch, Frank. **Oak and Wild Apples.** Illustrated by the author. Holiday House, 1988. Ages 3–7. (Picture book)

A fawn and a calf meet in a pasture and learn about each other's lives in the forest and the pasture. When they are away from their mothers at night, both reach a decision.

1.55 Beisert, Heide Helene (retold by Naomi Lewis). **My Magic Cloth: A Story for a Whole Week.** Illustrated by the author. North-South Books, 1986. Ages 2–5. (Picture book)

Each day of the week Tom takes his magic cloth with him as he plays during the day and as he dreams during the night, with the dream becoming an extension of his daytime activities. The full-color illustrations flesh out the text in a book that will be useful in encouraging children to use their imaginations.

1.56 Bond, Michael. **Paddington at the Zoo.** Illustrated by David McKee. G. P. Putnam's Sons, 1985. Ages 3–5. (Picture book)

This is Paddington in "lap book" format. Here the story does not have the length to build up in humor and slapstick, but it is fun reading nonetheless. Paddington takes six marmalade sandwiches to the zoo, where they are all promptly eaten by someone or something else. The illustrations are nicely done in crayon and watercolor. *Children's Choice.*

1.57 Bradman, Tony. **Look Out, He's behind You!** Illustrated by Margaret Chamberlain. G. P. Putnam's Sons/Lift-the-Flap Books, 1988. Ages 2–6. (Picture book)

Movable flaps conceal portions of the illustrations in this amusing, exciting retelling of "Little Red Riding Hood."

1.58 Burton, Marilee Robin. **Tail, Toes, Eyes, Ears, Nose.** Illustrated by the author. Harper and Row, 1989. Ages 3–6. (Picture book)

Very young children will hone their observational skills through this inviting participation story. Flat bright colors applied to simple shapes show animal tails, toes, eyes, ears, and noses. On the following page, the entire animal is revealed. Beginning readers will start to recognize the words used repeatedly to label animal body parts.

1.59 Caple, Kathy. **The Purse.** Illustrated by the author. Houghton Mifflin, 1986. Ages 2–5. (Picture book)

Katie spends all her money on a new "grown-up" purse to replace the old Band-Aid box she uses for her coins. Now her empty purse does not give that satisfying clinkety-clink when shaken. Katie figures out a way to remedy the situation very nicely all by herself. Softly drawn watercolors give little Katie much expression and character.

1.60 Carlstrom, Nancy White. **The Moon Came Too.** Illustrated by Stella Ormai. Macmillan, 1987. Ages 3–6. (Picture book)

In this story in rhyme, a little girl who is going to her grandmother's house plans what she must take along: a fuzzy bear, a windup truck, a puzzle, a fishing pole, hats (one for climbing trees, one for fishing), and so on. The soft watercolors perfectly capture the tone of the author's cumulative poem.

1.61 Chorao, Kay. **The Baby's Story Book.** Illustrated by the author. E. P. Dutton, 1985. Ages 2–4. (Picture book)

Fifteen retellings of traditional tales, many of which are familiar and popular folktales, are illustrated with gentle pastel paintings and are presented in a style accessible to toddlers and well suited for family sharing. Included are "The Gingerbread Boy," "The Little Red Hen," and "The Lion and the Mouse."

1.62 Cleary, Beverly. **Janet's Thingamajigs.** Illustrated by DyAnne DiSalvo-Ryan. Dell/Young Yearling Special Books, 1987. Ages 2–4. (Picture book)

Twins Janet and Jimmy pick up on their mother's use of the term *thingamajig.* Janet finds many items of interest to her (a red bead, pretty leaf, smooth stone) which she will not share with her brother. She keeps her thingamajigs in paper bags inside her crib, where her brother cannot reach them. Then one day a change happens in their lives. For readers who enjoy the twins, *The Growing-up Feet* will also be of interest.

1.63 Cooney, Nancy Evans. **Donald Says Thumbs Down.** Illustrated by Maxie Chambliss. G. P. Putnam's Sons, 1987. Ages 3–6. (Picture book)

Thumb-suckers who want to kick the habit will be heartened and encouraged by Donald's determination to stop. The text is respectful, sympathetic, and realistic in approach, offering sound insights to children who share Donald's problem. Parents will be reassured as well. Bright, cosy illustrations support the text's tone of warmth and acceptance.

1.64   Dale, Penny. **Bet You Can't.** Illustrated by the author. J. P. Lippincott, 1987. Ages 2–7. (Picture book)

The illustrations of a black brother and sister cleaning their room at bedtime look real, and the highly believable facial expressions and body language of the children help make this a very enjoyable book. The simple text and story line are a perfect match.

1.65   Davidson, Amanda. **Teddy in the Garden.** Illustrated by the author. Holt, Rinehart and Winston, 1986. Ages 4–6. (Picture book)

The very young child or emergent reader will relate to the bright pictures and simple one-line text depicting Teddy and his friends in a beautiful garden. A frisky puppy steals Teddy's hat, and the adventure begins. Searching for the hat leads the friends to many discoveries, including a new friend.

1.66   Denton, Kady MacDonald. **Granny Is a Darling.** Illustrated by the author. Margaret K. McElderry Books, 1988. Ages 3–6. (Picture book)

Everyone says that "Granny is a darling," and Billy does too in this tender, loving, and humorous story about her visit to his home. He shares his room and his fear of the dark with Granny, who helps him solve his problem. *Children's Choice.*

1.67   Dodds, Siobhan. **Charles Tiger.** Illustrated by the author. Little, Brown/Joy Street Books, 1987. Ages 2–5. (Picture book)

This simple, repetitive story of a tiger's quest for his lost roar is a lap book that will soon have a listening toddler joining in the telling. The story ends with a joke that even little ones will enjoy. The gentle, cheery illustrations of the tiger and the other animals contain enough humor to prevent too much sweetness.

1.68   Dodds, Siobhan. **Elizabeth Hen.** Illustrated by the author. Little, Brown/Joy Street Books, 1987. Ages 2–5. (Picture book)

A young child is introduced to the animals of the barnyard as Elizabeth Hen makes the rounds to announce the arrival of her egg. A toddler could probably guess the "surprise" ending. The animals are drawn with humor and sweetness.

1.69   Gay, Michel. **Little Shoe.** Illustrated by the author. Macmillan, 1986. Ages 3–5. (Picture book)

A little shoe looks everywhere for her sister in a house prepared for Christmas, but she has no success. Finally, the big brother shoe offers to help look. This is a slight story in a small format. The watercolor illustrations are adequate.

1.70   Gay, Michel. **Take Me for a Ride.** Illustrated by the author. Viking Penguin/Puffin Books, 1987. Ages 1–3. (Picture book)

A favorite childhood pastime, stroller riding, becomes the vehicle for this gentle fantasy. Little Teddy gives some friendly woodland animals a ride in his stroller and then is treated to an exciting ride in return, ending up safe with Mom. Soft, unfussy watercolor illustrations are easily comprehensible to the stroller set.

1.71   Gillham, Bill. **And So Can I!** Photographs by the author. G. P. Putnam's Sons, 1987. Ages 2–5. (Picture book)

"This dog can wade . . . and so can I!" sets the pattern of the book. An animal doing something interesting is shown in a full-page photograph on the left page. A child doing the same thing appears on the right page. Because the sentences match the photographs, learning and practicing sight words is facilitated for the beginning reader.

1.72   Gillham, Bill. **Can You See It?** Photographs by Fiona Horne. G. P. Putnam's Sons/Look and Talk Books, 1986. Ages 2–5. (Picture book)

The Look and Talk Books are designed for adults to share with young children to stimulate thought and language. Action photographs, organized in two-page sets, encourage children to look for differences between the pictures, to search for something hidden, to work out where something belongs, and to see the possibilities for creative play. In this book, children are shown a particular object in one photograph and then must find the same object in an adjoining photograph.

1.73 Gillham, Bill. **What Can You Do?** Photographs by Fiona Horne. G. P. Putnam's Sons/Look and Talk Books, 1986. Ages 2–5. (Picture book)

Photographs and a brief, rhythmic text present a variety of objects and experiences and then suggest possibilities for creative play based on these objects or experiences.

1.74 Gillham, Bill. **What Happens Next?** Photographs by Jan Siegieda. G. P. Putnam's Sons, 1985. Ages 2–5. (Picture book)

Turn each page to find paired photographs showing a sequence of cause and effect. A minimal text repeatedly asks, "What happens next?" Small children will enjoy reading this as a game or simply talking about the familiar objects and activities.

1.75 Gillham, Bill. **What's the Difference?** Photographs by Fiona Horne. G. P. Putnam's Sons/Look and Talk Books, 1986. Ages 2–5. (Picture book)

Paired photographs are similar but not identical, giving readers the opportunity to find and discuss the differences between pictures.

1.76 Gillham, Bill. **Where Does It Go?** Photographs by Fiona Horne. G. P. Putnam's Sons/Look and Talk Books, 1986. Ages 2–5. (Picture book)

In this book, readers are to look first at photographs of various items and to decide where those objects belong. Solutions are presented in accompanying photographs.

1.77 Graham, Bob. **The Red Woolen Blanket.** Illustrated by the author. Little, Brown, 1987. Ages 3–5. (Picture book)

A red woolen blanket is wrapped around Julia when she is born, and it becomes her constant companion throughout early childhood. Her dependence on the blanket decreases, as does the size of the blanket. Both diminishments are handled with humor enough to reassure young blanket-toters that this is a natural part of growing up.

1.78 Graham, Thomas. **Mr. Bear's Chair.** Illustrated by the author. E. P. Dutton, 1987. Ages 2–5. (Picture book)

When Mrs. Bear's chair breaks, Mr. Bear makes her a new one, step by step. A surprise ending and simple, richly colored illustrations showing a warm, rustic setting add to the book's appeal. *Children's Choice.*

1.79　Gretz, Susanna, and Alison Sage. **Teddy Bears Take the Train.** Illustrated by Susanna Gretz. Four Winds Press, 1987. Ages 3–7. (Picture book)

In another in a series of Teddy Bear books, the teddy bears take a train ride to visit Uncle Jerome. The book, while not extraordinary, will appeal to younger readers interested in trains. The characters are believable, and each has a distinct personality. Watercolor illustrations make effective use of white space. Care is taken to make the bears expressive and interesting.

1.80　Hague, Kathleen. **Out of the Nursery, Into the Night.** Illustrated by Michael Hague. Henry Holt, 1986. Ages 3–5. (Picture book)

In rhyme the author recounts the dreams of some teddy bears and admonishes listeners to dream their own dreams. The illustrations are fanciful and imaginative full-color paintings with lots to look at in each dream sequence.

1.81　Hall, Derek. **Polar Bear Leaps.** Illustrated by John Butler. Alfred A. Knopf/Sierra Club, 1985. Ages 3–5. (Picture book)

A baby polar bear faces danger when a small ice floe breaks away, carrying him away from his mother, but he jumps to safety. Delicately colored, precise watercolors enhance the simple text.

1.82　Harmer, Juliet. **The Little Go-to-Sleep Book.** Illustrated by the author. Margaret K. McElderry Books, 1986. Ages 3–5. (Picture book)

To soothe a reluctant baby at bedtime, the mother describes how various living creatures go to sleep—the frog on wet lily leaves, mice in warm nests under the floorboards, and the fish with a night-light. Full-page color drawings of each animal combine realism with wistful imagination.

1.83　Harper, Anita. **Just a Minute!** Illustrated by Susan Hellard. G. P. Putnam's Sons, 1987. Ages 2–7. (Picture book)

A young kangaroo discovers that everyone has a different meaning for "just a minute" in this funny story for even the youngest child.

1.84 Hayes, Susan. **This Is the Bear.** Illustrated by Helen Craig. J. B. Lippincott, 1986. Ages 2–4. (Picture book)

Inadvertently carted away to the dump, a stuffed bear awaits rescue by its owner. Told in the catchy rhythm of "This Is the House That Jack Built," the read-aloud story with its half-page drawings and large print will delight young children.

1.85 Hill, Eric. **Spot Goes to the Beach.** Illustrated by the author. G. P. Putnam's Sons, 1985. Ages 2–5. (Picture book)

The beginning reader is invited to learn something unexpected about Spot the puppy's trip to the beach by folding back part of the picture on each page and peeking underneath. Simple text printed in huge letters accompanies the full-page illustrations.

1.86 Hill, Eric. **Spot Goes to the Circus.** Illustrated by the author. G. P. Putnam's Sons, 1986. Ages 2–6. (Picture book)

"Fetch your ball, Spot," says the pup's father. Where should he look for it? Each page has a flap to peek behind to see where Spot will look. Using huge print and one simple sentence for each two-page illustration, the text is for the beginning reader. Also available in Spanish as *Spot Va al Circo.*

1.87 Hill, Eric. **Spot's Big Book of Words.** Illustrated by the author. G. P. Putnam's Sons/Ventura Books, 1988. Ages 2–6. (Picture book)

Large, cheerful, brightly colored drawings illustrate vocabulary words selected around twelve themes, such as breakfast time, farm life, winter play, and birthdays. Each theme is presented in a two-page spread with a paragraph that presents a story about Spot and his friends.

1.88 Hill, Eric. **Spot's First Easter.** Illustrated by the author. G. P. Putnam's Sons/Ventura Books, 1988. Ages 2–6. (Picture book)

A simple text, large print, heavy paper, and movable parts make this story about Spot's first Easter a perfect book for the careful young child.

1.89 Hines, Anna Grossnickle. **All by Myself.** Illustrated by the author. Clarion Books, 1985. Ages 3–5. (Picture book)

This is a reassuring book for the young child who is in transition between dependence on parents and independence. The little girl in the story does not want to wear diapers to bed anymore. Through gentle encouragement from her mother and her own persistence, she finally manages to stay dry at night. Simple drawings on each page show a loving relationship between mother and toddler.

1.90 Hines, Anna Grossnickle. **It's Just Me, Emily.** Illustrated by the author. Clarion Books, 1987. Ages 2–6. (Picture book)

This is a repetitive story with Emily hiding and pretending to be various creatures and Mother guessing what the creatures are. Each time Emily reveals, "It's just me . . . Emily." The book has satisfying color illustrations to enhance the fun.

1.91 Hoopes, Lyn Littlefield. **Mommy, Daddy, Me.** Illustrated by Ruth Lercher Bornstein. Harper and Row/Charlotte Zolotow Books, 1988. Ages 3–5. (Picture book)

Soft shades of green and lavender illustrate this quiet story of a little boy and his parents on a canoe trip to an island. The succinct rhyming text describes their day's adventure.

1.92 Howell, Lynn, and Richard Howell. **Winifred's New Bed.** Illustrated by the author. Alfred A. Knopf/Borzoi Books, 1985. Ages 2–4. (Picture book)

Winifred outgrows her crib, so she gets a new bed. The bed is very big, so Winifred adds her animal friends one by one, with hilarious results. Printed on heavy stock to withstand wear and tear, this cumulative story has a format similar to Eric Carle's *Very Hungry Caterpillar*. It is excellent for reading aloud, counting, or individual perusal.

1.93 Hughes, Shirley. **When We Went to the Park.** Illustrated by the author. Lothrop, Lee and Shepard Books, 1985. Ages 3–5. (Picture book)

Multiethnic watercolor and pen-and-ink illustrations elaborate upon a counting-book narrative of a little girl's trip to the park with her grandfather. The small format is helped by the detailed illustrations. This is an excellent concept book and lap book.

1.94   Keller, Holly. **Geraldine's Big Snow.** Illustrated by the author. Greenwillow Books, 1988. Ages 3–5. (Picture book)

After Geraldine the pig puts her new sled by the door, it seems an endless wait for the first snow. Full-page watercolor illustrations show what she does to keep busy until the snow finally comes. Each page contains from one to four simple sentences.

1.95   Kightley, Rosalinda. **The Farmer.** Illustrated by the author. Macmillan, 1987. Ages 2–6. (Picture book)

Bold shapes and bright colors all the way to the edge of the page bring plenty of visual energy. The illustrations depicting the activities of a farmer and his family are accompanied by a simple rhyming text, making the book fun to read over and over again.

1.96   Kightley, Rosalinda. **The Postman.** Illustrated by the author. Macmillan, 1987. Ages 2–6. (Picture book)

The postman makes stops all over town: at businesses, schools, the ice cream van, and, finally, home. There is much for a young child on a lap to point to on each page. The illustrations are bright, bold, and cheerful. The simple rhyming text is similar to a nursery rhyme, likely to be memorized before many readings.

1.97   Kilroy, Sally. **Grandpa's Garden.** Illustrated by the author. Viking Kestrel, 1986. Ages 2–5. (Picture book)

The several books in this series for toddlers by Sally Kilroy let youngsters experience simply detailed daily events. Each book features different children as main characters. In this book the children visit Grandpa and help out in his garden.

1.98   Kilroy, Sally. **Market Day.** Illustrated by the author. Viking Kestrel, 1986. Ages 2–5. (Picture book)

Young readers and listeners will learn about going to the market and perhaps will make comparisons to their own shopping expeditions. Colorful illustrations support the easy text.

1.99   Kilroy, Sally. **On the Road.** Illustrated by the author. Viking Kestrel, 1986. Ages 2–5. (Picture book)

Sally Kilroy's brief text and colorful illustrations tell the story of a bus trip to town.

1.100   Kilroy, Sally. **What a Week!** Illustrated by the author. Viking Kestrel, 1986. Ages 2–5. (Picture book)

A fun-filled week is depicted in a simple text and cartoon-style illustrations. The book is sized to fit a child's small hands.

1.101   Kitamura, Satoshi. **Lily Takes a Walk.** Illustrated by the author. E. P. Dutton, 1987. Ages 3–5. (Picture book)

On her walk, a small girl is busy admiring the scenery while her dog fends off imagined monsters and other dangers. Full-color illustrations enhance the few sentences of text per page and provide a humorous perspective on the dog's view of the walk.

1.102   Kline, Suzy. **Don't Touch!** Illustrated by Dora Leder. Albert Whitman, 1985. Ages 2–6. (Picture book)

In his curiosity to squeeze, smash, and pound, Dan hears lots of grown ups say, "Don't Touch!" Finally he finds something he can touch. Young children will be able to relate easily to this well-illustrated story.

1.103   Kline, Suzy. **Oops!** Illustrated by Dora Leder. Albert Whitman, 1988. Ages 3–6. (Picture book)

It is not just five-year-olds who go "Oops!" Even grownups have their klutzy moments, as this book gently and humorously reminds us. The illustrations depict a happy family in homey detail and bright color. There will be many times when this will be just the book for the moment.

1.104   Lester, Alison. **Clive Eats Alligators.** Illustrated by the author. Houghton Mifflin, 1986. Ages 3–5. (Picture book)

This book is not just to be read—it is to be played with. We meet seven different children and learn about their individual food preferences, pets, clothing, and bedtime rituals. After learning about the characters' choices for breakfast and dressing, readers try to predict what these characters might choose for pets, play spaces, and lunch.

1.105   Lloyd, David. **Duck.** Illustrated by Charlotte Voake. J. B. Lippincott, 1988. Ages 2–5. (Picture book)

A young boy calls all animals "duck" and all vehicles "truck." His grandmother gives him some kind, nurturing assistance that helps him in his oral language development.

1.106 McPhail, David. **The Dream Child.** Illustrated by the author. E. P. Dutton/Unicorn Books, 1985. Ages 3–6.

In a gently lyrical bedtime story, the Dream Child and Tame Bear sail away in a winged boat to a mystical moonlit land occupied by a welcoming kingdom of creatures. The mesmerizing prose is effectively depicted in the evocative full-page misty watercolors.

1.107 Martin, Bill, Jr., and John Archambault. **Here Are My Hands.** Illustrated by Ted Rand. Henry Holt, 1987. Ages 2–6. (Picture book)

This read-aloud rhyming picture book for the young child deals with parts of the body and their functions, such as "hands for catching and throwing" and "skin that bundles me in." *Children's Choice.*

1.108 Monrad, Jean. **How Many Kisses Good Night.** Illustrated by Eloise Wilkin. Random House, 1986. Ages 2 and under. (Picture book)

A 1949 verse is illustrated with delicate, sweet drawings of a small girl and mother at bedtime. The pages are sturdier than those in most picture books. Toddlers will enjoy the book as a finger play for bedtime.

1.109 Morgan, Michaela. **The Monster Is COMING!** Illustrated by Sue Porter. Harper and Row, 1987. Ages 1–4. (Picture book)

This lift-the-flap book is uncomplicated enough to permit small hands to manipulate it over and over again, which they will. The simple story of a little girl being chased by a huge, furry, just-a-little-scary monster leads to a funny surprise ending. The text is meant to be read aloud with great expression, and after one reading a preschooler will be able to "read" it all alone.

1.110 Morgan, Michaela. **Visitors for Edward.** Illustrated by Sue Porter. E. P. Dutton, 1987. Ages 3–6. (Picture book)

Edward imagines lots of possibilities when he overhears his parents' conversation about a surprise in the morning. How delighted he is when he discovers what his surprise is the next day.

1.111   Mueller, Virginia. **Monster and the Baby.** Illustrated by Lynn
Munsinger. Albert Whitman, 1985. Ages 3–5. (Picture book)

Baby is crying, so Monster gives him one red block, but Baby
does not stop crying. Humorously drawn full-page illustrations show what Monster keeps trying next until a happy resolution is achieved. The single sentences on each page are
easy to read.

1.112   Mueller, Virginia. **A Playhouse for Monster.** Illustrated by
Lynn Munsinger. Albert Whitman, 1985. Ages 3–5. (Picture
book)

Monster puts a Keep Out! sign on his playhouse, but he has a
special problem when a friend shows up. Young children
should relate to the conflict between proud ownership and
sharing. The full-page drawings add to the humor of the story.

1.113   Narahashi, Keiko. **I Have a Friend.** Illustrated by the author.
Margaret K. McElderry Books, 1987. Ages 2–5. (Picture
book)

A small boy is accompanied by an unnamed friend throughout
the day until nightfall, when his shadow disappears. A haunting, poetic quality is found in both illustrations and text,
which ends by naming the child's mysterious friend this way:
"He is yesterday's night left behind for the day." The watercolor illustrations, with their vivid color and bold, flowing
shapes, dominate each page.

1.114   Newton, Laura P. **William the Vehicle King.** Illustrated by
Jacqueline Rogers. Bradbury Press, 1987. Ages 2–6. (Picture
book)

Young William begins to play with his cars, and soon his entire bedroom rug is turned into an extensive motorway with
emergency vehicles, construction equipment, roads, bridges,
towers, and many, many different cars. A playful cat follows
William's progress with interest. Watercolor illustrations are
warm and fuzzy like the rug in the room.

1.115   Oxenbury, Helen. **Tom and Pippo and the Washing Machine.**
Illustrated by the author. Macmillan/Aladdin Books/Pippo
Books, 1988. Ages 1–3. (Picture book)

Full-color illustrations depict the everyday adventures of a
toddler, his pet monkey, Pippo, and his parents. Large print

and simple words make the books in this series perfect for a beginning reader to share with a younger brother or sister. In this book, Pippo goes into the washing machine after he plays in the mud with young Tom.

1.116 Oxenbury, Helen. **Tom and Pippo Go for a Walk.** Illustrated by the author. Macmillan/Aladdin Books/Pippo Books, 1988. Ages 1–3. (Picture book)

Tom and his pet monkey, Pippo, go for a walk and manage to find a mud puddle.

1.117 Oxenbury, Helen. **Tom and Pippo Make a Mess.** Illustrated by the author. Macmillan/Aladdin Books/Pippo Books, 1988. Ages 1–3. (Picture book)

Young Tom tries to help his father paint a room. When he makes a mess, Tom blames it on Pippo, his toy monkey.

1.118 Oxenbury, Helen. **Tom and Pippo Read a Story.** Illustrated by the author. Macmillan/Aladdin Books/Pippo Books, 1988. Ages 1–3. (Picture book)

When Tom's father gets tired as he reads to Tom and his toy monkey, Pippo, Tom takes over and "reads" to Pippo.

1.119 Riddell, Chris. **Ben and the Bear.** Illustrated by the author. J. B. Lippincott, 1986. Ages 2–5. (Picture book)

Ben and the Bear spend the afternoon together in a variety of exciting, funny adventures. The large type and simple illustrations work well together.

1.120 Rockwell, Anne, and Harlow Rockwell. **My Baby-Sitter.** Illustrated by the authors. Macmillan/My World Books, 1985. Ages 2–5. (Picture book)

Here is a positive narrative of the activities of a small boy and his sitter while his parents are out. This small book has large print and warm, colorful watercolor illustrations. It is a nice addition to books dealing with a child's maturing in self-reliance and self-confidence.

1.121 Roffey, Maureen. **I Spy at the Zoo.** Illustrated by the author. Four Winds Press/I Spy Books, 1988. Ages 2–5. (Picture book)

A little boy, a little girl, and their parents tour the zoo. Readers finish the sentences by saying what they "spy" in the illustrations of the zoo. All ages and several ethnic groups are included in these brightly colored illustrations.

1.122   Roffey, Maureen. **I Spy on Vacation.** Illustrated by the author. Four Winds Press/I Spy Books, 1988. Ages 2–7. (Picture book)

Young children as well as beginning readers can spy something different to look at and talk about on each page of this book depicting a seashore vacation.

1.123   Roffey, Maureen. **Look, There's My Hat!** Illustrated by the author. G. P. Putnam's Sons, 1985. Ages 3–5. (Picture book)

"Look, there's my hat!" says the girl pointing to her mother, who is wearing a hat. Because the shape of the mother's face has been cut out, turning the page transfers the hat to the child's head. "Oops, no! It's Mommy's." The text invites the young reader to see what happens each time the girl claims something. Beginning readers are aided by a spare text printed in huge letters.

1.124   Shannon, George. **Oh, I Love!** Illustrated by Cheryl Harness. Bradbury Press, 1988. Ages 2–5. (Picture book)

This book is based on the North American folksong known as "My Little Rooster" or "The Barnyard Song." It is a lullaby that repeats the sounds made by a little girl's favorite toys—a rooster, a pig, chicks, a goose, and a lamb. A wise choice for reading aloud to the youngest child.

1.125   Sheldon, Dyan. **I Forgot.** Illustrated by John Rogan. Four Winds Press, 1988. Ages 2–5. (Picture book)

Young Jake has a lot to remember, so please excuse him if once in awhile he forgets a thing or two. The reader follows Jake around town as he gathers together presents for his mother's birthday, which he did not forget. Illustrations are colorful and uncluttered enough to use during a group story time.

1.126   Stoddard, Sandol. **Bedtime for Bear.** Illustrated by Lynn Munsinger. Houghton Mifflin, 1985. Ages 3–5. (Picture book)

Small Bear resists bedtime with excuse after excuse. When all attempts at reason fail, Big Bear rocks Small Bear, a cozy solution to the universal bedtime dilemma.

1.127 Sutherland, Harry A. **Dad's Car Wash.** Illustrated by Maxie Chambliss. Atheneum, 1988. Ages 3–6. (Picture book)

For John, taking a bath is more fun when he pretends he is at Dad's car wash. Bright, humor-filled illustrations show Dad with sponge in hand as he scrubs John's "wheels," "hubcaps," "axles," and "roof." Children will enjoy the imaginative comparison of child to car. *Children's Choice.*

1.128 Taylor, Judy. **My Cat.** Illustrated by Reg Cartwright. Macmillan, 1988. Ages 2–6. (Picture book)

Beginning readers will be able to find pleasure in this story with simple text and illustrations that tell the life story of a little boy's cat, from the time it was a kitten until it had kittens of its own.

1.129 Taylor, Judy. **My Dog.** Illustrated by Reg Cartwright. Macmillan, 1988. Ages 2–6. (Picture book)

A little girl describes her dog's adventures with a basket, a bone, a ball, another dog, a bath, and a dream in this book with simple text and illustrations.

1.130 Titherington, Jeanne. **Big World, Small World.** Greenwillow Books, 1985. Ages 2–4. (Picture book)

A simple story of a child shopping with her mother is told as both Mama's story and little Anna's, with two separate lines of text on each page. A child can explore the differing points of view of a big person and a small one in the full-page, finely drawn illustrations, which are subtly shaded in hazy pastels.

1.131 Tsutsui, Yoriko. **Anna's Secret Friend.** Illustrated by Akiko Hayashi. Viking Kestrel, 1987. Ages 2–6. (Picture book)

When her family moves to a new home, young Anna is lonely until someone begins to leave small presents—first flowers and then a letter at the front door. Could this be a new friend? It is, and she wants to be friends with Anna. The warm, soft illustrations and simple text are perfect for lap reading or group story times.

1.132 van der Beek, Deborah. **Superbabe!** Illustrated by the author. G. P. Putnam's Sons, 1988. Ages 2–6. (Picture book)

Here is a loving, slightly exaggerated account of the trials of living with a Superbabe, from the point of view of the older sister. The illustrations capture exactly the way a one-year-old body moves, with all the squirms, evasive actions, and single-minded attempts to alter the environment. Older siblings and parents will find this book an amusing distraction, especially if they live with a Superbabe. The text is in bouncy verse.

1.133 Wahl, Jan. **Humphrey's Bear.** Illustrated by William Joyce. Henry Holt, 1987. Ages 3–6. (Picture book)

Although his father thinks Humphrey is too old to sleep with a toy, each night Humphrey and his bear embark on an imaginative dream voyage. Illustrations rich in color surprise the viewer with unexpected perspectives. *Children's Choice.*

1.134 Ward, Cindy. **Cookie's Week.** Illustrated by Tomie dePaola. G. P. Putnam's Sons, 1988. Ages 2–4. (Picture book)

Cookie the kitten creates as much havoc in a household as a toddler. Each day of the week brings a new disaster, shown closeup in splashy, bright illustrations. A toddler might enjoy comparing mishaps while learning the days of the week.

1.135 Watanabe, Shigeo. **It's My Birthday!** Illustrated by Yasuo Ohtomo. Philomel Books/I Love Special Days Books, 1988. Ages 2–5. (Picture book)

On Bear's fourth birthday, he and his family go through the family photo album and talk about their memories of his birth, his babyhood, and his previous birthdays.

1.136 Weiss, Nicki. **Barney Is Big.** Illustrated by the author. Greenwillow Books, 1988. Ages 3–4. (Picture book)

In a book designed for the child who will soon be going to nursery school, a young boy and his mother talk about what he was like as a baby and how much he has grown since then.

1.137 Wells, Rosemary. **Forest of Dreams.** Illustrated by Susan Jeffers. Dial Books for Young Readers, 1988. Ages 3–5. (Picture book)

The reader is taken through the forest with two young girls as they discover all that God has provided for them.

1.138 Wells, Rosemary. **Max's Christmas.** Illustrated by the author. Dial Books for Young Readers, 1986. Ages 3–6. (Picture book)

Max the bunny and his big sister Ruby eagerly await the arrival of Santa on Christmas Eve. After Ruby puts Max to bed, he sneaks downstairs in hopes of seeing Santa. Large watercolor illustrations add to the humor in this simple story. *ALA Notable Children's Book.*

1.139 Winthrop, Elizabeth. **Shoes.** Illustrated by William Joyce. Harper and Row, 1986. Ages 3–5. (Picture book)

A bouncy, sing-along rhyme categorizes all sorts of shoes, but the best footgear of all turns out to be plain old unshod feet. The one line of text per page is highlighted by bright, warm illustrations.

1.140 Yektai, Niki. **What's Missing?** Illustrated by Susannah Ryan. Clarion Books, 1987. Ages 3–5. (Picture book)

The girl flies through the air toward her mother, and the text asks, "What's missing?" The slide is. Turn the page and find it drawn in. Every other page presents an event with some part of the picture missing. The repetitive pattern and large print invite the beginning reader to learn some sight words.

1.141 Zemach, Margot. **Hush, Little Baby.** Illustrated by the author. E. P. Dutton/Unicorn Books, 1987. Ages 2–5. (Picture book)

Tempera paintings, which Margot Zemach originally imagined while she lived in London, accompany this familiar folk lullaby.

1.142 Ziefert, Harriet. **Where's the Halloween Treat?** Illustrated by Richard Brown. Viking Penguin/Puffin Books/Lift the Flap Books, 1985. Ages 2–6. (Picture book)

A simple chant is combined with flaps that lift to reveal mysterious and strange characters to young trick-or-treaters. The format, combined with bold and colorful illustrations, makes this a holiday read-aloud that invites audience participation.

1.143   Zinnemann-Hope, Pam. **Find Your Coat, Ned.** Illustrated by Kady MacDonald Denton. Margaret K. McElderry Books, 1987. Ages 2–6. (Picture book)

Where did you put your raincoat, Ned? The reader follows an energetic young boy as he goes from place to place to locate his coat. Large print and a simple text make this an appropriate book for a young child as well as a beginning reader.

1.144   Zinnemann-Hope, Pam. **Let's Go Shopping, Ned.** Illustrated by Kady MacDonald Denton. Margaret K. McElderry Books, 1986. Ages 2–6. (Picture book)

Dad and Ned take along Fred the dog when they go shopping for Ned's new sweater—with disastrous results. This is a happy romp for young readers, full of rhythmic prose and wonderful watercolor illustrations.

1.145   Zinnemann-Hope, Pam. **Let's Play Ball, Ned.** Illustrated by Kady MacDonald Denton. Margaret K. McElderry Books, 1987. Ages 2–6. (Picture book)

Large print, a simple text, and action-filled illustrations make this story of Ned, his dad, his dog, and a ball perfect for the young reader.

1.146   Zinnemann-Hope, Pam. **Time for Bed, Ned.** Illustrated by Kady MacDonald Denton. Margaret K. McElderry Books, 1986. Ages 3–6. (Picture book)

A rambunctious young boy is summoned by his mother to go to bed in this hilarious story. The flowing crayon and watercolor illustrations blend with the simple text to create a delightful read-aloud book for preschool audiences or a read-alone book for beginning readers. Also to be enjoyed is *Let's Go Shopping, Ned.*

1.147   Zolotow, Charlotte. **Sleepy Book.** Illustrated by Ilse Plume. Harper and Row, 1986. Ages 2–5. (Picture book)

Information about where familiar as well as less familiar creatures sleep is presented in simple, poetic text. The book, originally published in 1958, has been reissued with new illustrations, which are beautiful full-page color drawings depicting the resting environment chosen by each of the thirteen animals, birds, and insects. The last page shows a boy and girl in their cozy beds.

Recommended Books Published before 1985

Ahlberg, Janet, and Allan Ahlberg. *Peek-a-Boo!* Viking Press, 1981. 2–4.

Asch, Frank. *Just Like Daddy*. Parent's Magazine Press, 1981. 3–5.

Atkinson, Allen. *Mother Goose's Nursery Rhymes*. Alfred A. Knopf, 1984. 3–6.

Bayley, Nicola. *Nicola Bayley's Book of Nursery Rhymes*. Alfred A. Knopf, 1977. 3–6.

Boynton, Sandra. *Moo Baa La La La*. Simon and Schuster, 1982. 2–4.

Brown, Margaret Wise. *Goodnight Moon*. Illustrated by Clement Hurd. Harper and Row, 1947. 3–5.

Burningham, John. *The Cupboard*. Thomas Y. Crowell, 1975. 2–4.

Carle, Eric. *The Very Hungry Caterpillar*. Philomel Books, 1981. 3–6.

Chorao, Kay, comp. *The Baby's Lap Book*. E. P. Dutton, 1977. 3–6.

De Angeli, Marguerite. *Marguerite De Angeli's Book of Nursery and Mother Goose Rhymes*. Doubleday, 1954. 3–6.

Eastman, P. D. *Are You My Mother?* Beginner Books, 1960. 3–5.

Fujikawa, Gyo. *Mother Goose*. Grosset and Dunlap, 1968. 2–4.

Hill, Eric. *Spot's First Walk*. G. P. Putnam's Sons, 1981. 2–4.

Lindgren, Barbro. *Sam's Cookie*. Illustrated by Eva Eriksson. William Morrow, 1982. 2–4.

Omerod, Jan. *101 Things to Do with a Baby*. Lothrop, Lee and Shepard Books, 1984. 2–4.

Oxenbury, Helen. *Shopping Trip*. Dial Books for Young Readers, 1982. 3–5.

Rockwell, Harlow. *My Nursery School*. Greenwillow Books, 1976. 3–5.

Sendak, Maurice. *One Was Johnny: A Counting Book*. Harper and Row, 1962. 4–7.

Tudor, Tasha. *A Is for Annabelle*. Henry Z. Walck, 1954. 5–7.

———. *Mother Goose*. David McKay, 1944. 3–7.

Udry, Janice May. *A Tree Is Nice*. Illustrated by Marc Simont. Harper and Row, 1956. 3–6.

Watanabe, Shigeo. *Where's My Daddy?* Illustrated by Yasuo Ohtomo. Philomel Books, 1982. 3–6.

Wells, Rosemary. *Max's First Word*. Dial Books for Young Readers, 1979. 3–6.

———. *Max's Bath*. Dial Books for Young Readers, 1985. 3–6.

2 Basic Concept Books

ABC Books

2.1 Bove, Linda. **Sign Language ABC with Linda Bove.** Illustrated by Tom Cooke; photographs by Anita and Steve Shevett. Random House/Children's Television Workshop, 1985. Ages 6–9. (Picture book)

Sesame Street characters team up with Linda Bove to introduce the letters of the alphabet and seventy-five useful words in sign language. Photographs and drawings assist young children in duplicating the words and sentences.

2.2 Folsom, Marcia, and Michael Folsom. **Easy as Pie: A Guessing Game of Sayings.** Illustrated by Jack Kent. Clarion Books, 1985. Ages 7–10. (Picture book)

Letters of the alphabet are introduced with old sayings such as ''M—Stubborn as a Mule'' and ''D—Dark as a Dungeon.'' The format can be useful as a stimulus for children to think up their own sayings. Jack Kent's cartoon art is utilitarian.

2.3 Fowler, Richard. **Mr. Little's Noisy ABC.** Illustrated by the author. Grosset and Dunlap, 1987. Ages 4–8. (Picture book)

Mr. Little experiences many noisy, zany adventures marked by each letter of the alphabet, from A (Ahhh!) to Z (Zoom!). For H, Mr. Little is colorfully arrayed as a happy harlequin hooting ''Ha, ha, ha.''

2.4 Gardner, Beau. **Have You Ever Seen . . . ? An ABC Book.** Illustrated by the author. Dodd, Mead, 1986. Ages 3–6. (Picture book)

Have you ever seen an octopus eating oatmeal or a unicorn under an umbrella? You will in this ABC book, in which a similar witty invention accompanies each letter of the alphabet. Bold color graphics will amuse the young child, while the question on each page provides opportunities to find words in the text that contain the letter being presented. *Children's Choice*.

2.5 Geisert, Arthur. **Pigs from A to Z.** Illustrated by the author. Houghton Mifflin, 1986. Ages 2–8. (Picture book)

Detailed etchings of the efforts of seven piglets to build a tree house are interesting in themselves, but each picture also contains a puzzle. The whole book is an alphabet hide-and-seek game with the letters hidden in each drawing. The piglets also hide from the reader, adding to the complexity and fun. There is appeal here not only for children just learning letter shapes, but also for older children and adults who enjoy puzzles.

2.6 Hawkins, Colin, and Jacqui Hawkins. **Busy abc.** Illustrated by the authors. Viking Kestrel, 1987. Ages 4–6. (Picture book)

A romp through the alphabet with children doing what comes naturally—asking, banging, crawling, crying, dancing, and so on. Several descriptive words are usually suggested for each one-page lower-case letter. Stuffed animals, children, dogs, cats, and rabbits offer their own dialogue concerning their activities on each page. Illustrations are expressive and full of action with uncluttered backgrounds for even the youngest listener to enjoy.

2.7 Hughes, Shirley. **Lucy and Tom's a.b.c.** Illustrated by the author. Viking Penguin/Puffin Books, 1987. Ages 4–7. (Picture book)

This is an alphabet book, but it is also a catalog of all those things most important to toddlers Lucy and Tom. There is much to see and talk about in the detailed, richly colored illustrations, which evoke the happy, familiar tumble of family life.

2.8 Kitamura, Satoshi. **What's Inside: The Alphabet Book.** Illustrated by the author. Farrar, Straus and Giroux, 1985. Ages 3–8. (Picture book)

This is an imaginative ABC book with secret boxes, cans, and containers that hide the next-page letter items. The vivid, full-color, intricate illustrations should have children engrossed.

2.9   MacDonald, Suse. **Alphabatics.** Illustrated by the author. Bradbury Press, 1986. Ages 5–8. (Picture book)

This is an alphabet book that takes the shapes of the letters and makes them play, to the reader's delight. The letters' shapes are twisted, turned, and transformed into surprising new things. All this is done in bright, bold color on lots of white paper. The book is not just for those who are learning the alphabet, but for anyone who enjoys design in action. *Caldecott Honor Book.*

2.10   McPhail, David. **David McPhail's Animals A to Z.** Illustrated by the author. Scholastic/Hardcover Books, 1988. Ages 2–6. (Picture book)

The author-illustrator provides a one-page drawing for each letter of the alphabet in which an animal is the main focus but which also includes several other items beginning with the same letter. For example, for the letter L a lion peers at a ladybug sitting on a lemon, and for F a hungry fox is about to fry a fish on an outdoor fire just as a frog is about to hit the fox on the head with a flute. Good use of color and attractive animals will keep everyone going over and over each picture. The animals are identified at the back of the book.

2.11   Neumeier, Marty, and Byron Glaser. **Action Alphabet.** Illustrated by the authors. Greenwillow Books, 1985. Ages 3–8. (Picture book)

If you cross concrete poetry with the alphabet, this book is what you get. Each letter illustrates itself with a pictorial charade of a representative word. For example, the letter *A*, for *acrobat*, balances on a high wire. Each turn of the page offers a new letter in upper and lower case and a clever and amusing surprise.

2.12   Owen, Annie. **Annie's abc.** Illustrated by the author. Alfred A. Knopf/Borzoi Books, 1987. Ages 3–6. (Picture book)

Young children will enjoy identifying each letter of the alphabet and the accompanying items beginning with that letter.

2.13   Potter, Beatrix. **Peter Rabbit's ABC.** Illustrated by the author. Frederick Warne, 1987. Ages 2–4. (Picture book)

With new full-color reproductions of Beatrix Potter's illustrations and quotes from her books, the publishers have devised a beautifully designed alphabet book.

2.14   Van Allsburg, Chris. **The Z Was Zapped: A Play in Twenty-Six Acts.** Illustrated by the author. Houghton Mifflin, 1987. Ages 2–5. (Picture book)

In a twenty-six act production, something happens to each letter of the alphabet, something dramatic, nasty, and definitely alphabetical. Each letter appears on stage in a marvelously executed black-and-white line-and-shade drawing, and readers can determine what has happened to each: A was in an avalanche, B was badly bitten, C was cut to ribbons, and so on through the alphabet.

Colors

2.15   Gundersheimer, Karen. **Colors to Know.** Illustrated by the author. Harper and Row, 1986. Ages 2–6. (Picture book)

A teeny-tiny person helps introduce thirteen color words. The format can be used easily with even the youngest child.

2.16   McMillan, Bruce. **Growing Colors.** Photographs by the author. Lothrop, Lee and Shepard Books, 1988. Ages 2–5. (Picture book)

Photographs illustrate the colors found in nature, including green peas, yellow corn, red potatoes, and purple beans. Each fruit or vegetable has been given a shower to enhance its color, but some appear in colors that are not customary.

2.17   Peek, Merle. **Mary Wore Her Red Dress, and Henry Wore His Green Sneakers.** Illustrated by the author. Clarion Books, 1985. Ages 3–7. (Picture book)

In this book based on the lyrics of an old folksong, Katy Bear's birthday party provides the backdrop for a parade of colors. Each animal guest arrives dressed in a different hue.

Pencil and crayon illustrations detail the festivities in this pattern story. The repetition of words encourages immediate language participation.

2.18   Samton, Sheila White. **Beside the Bay.** Illustrated by the author. Philomel Books, 1987. Ages 3–5. (Picture book)

Flat full-color illustrations with a rhyming text on the opposite page serve to teach a child the colors. The scenes all take place beside the bay.

2.19   Serfozo, Mary. **Who Said Red?** Illustrated by Keiko Narahashi. Margaret K. McElderry Books, 1988. Ages 3–6. (Picture book)

Simple color concepts, bright illustrations featuring a glorious red, and abundant use of adjectives make this book attractive and inviting as well as useful.

Counting Books

2.20   Ayleswood, Jim. **One Crow: A Counting Rhyme.** Illustrated by Ruth Young. J. B. Lippincott, 1988. Ages 2–6. (Picture book)

First in summer and then in winter, the author uses verse to introduce animals around the farm. The reader will see puppies, kittens, horses, pigs, hens, sheep, cows, squirrels, and a crow as well as children on the farm and will learn the numbers from 1 to 10. The large print makes this a good book for the younger reader.

2.21   Boon, Emilie. **1 2 3, How Many Animals Can You See?** Illustrated by the author. Orchard Books, 1987. Ages 3–5. (Picture book)

This simple counting book has easily recognizable animals. The charcoal and color-blended illustrations perfectly complement the large print and simple text.

2.22   Conran, Sebastian. **My First 1, 2, 3 Book.** Illustrated by the author. Macmillan/Aladdin Books, 1988. Ages 3–9. (Picture book)

The numbers 1 through 20, 30, 40, 50, 60, 100, 1,000, and 1,000,000 are introduced in this brightly illustrated counting book designed for use with the younger child.

2.23   Crews, Donald. **Bicycle Race.** Illustrated by the author. Greenwillow Books, 1985. Ages 4–6. (Picture book)

An exciting bicycle race helps readers learn to recognize numerals on the helmets of the riders. This counting book is different in that the numbers are not in sequence as the riders race along and change their order. Donald Crews's full-color illustrations are crisp and graphic. The suspense that number 9 creates before winning the race provides a plot for this book of numbers.

2.24   de Brunhoff, Laurent. **Babar's Counting Book.** Illustrated by the author. Random House, 1986. Ages 2–6. (Picture book)

The three children of Babar and Celeste count to 10 with their friend Pom in this jolly, full-color counting book. Numerals are clear as each page portrays the number of animals to be counted. The last pages depict counting by 10 to 20—and a certificate that is signed by Babar for learning to count to 20.

2.25   de Regniers, Beatrice Schenk. **So Many Cats!** Illustrated by Ellen Weiss. Clarion Books, 1985. Ages 3–5. (Picture book)

This imaginative story tells, in rhyme, how twelve cats came to live with a family. The illustrations, done in watercolor and pen-and-ink, complement the story quite nicely. Preschoolers will enjoy the repetitiveness, the colorful illustrations, and the humor.

2.26   Fowler, Richard. **Mr. Little's Noisy 1 2 3.** Illustrated by the author. Grosset and Dunlap, 1987. Ages 3–8. (Picture book)

In this counting book from 1 to 100, Mr. Little has a noisy dream where he hears such sounds as three trains tooting, eighteen crickets clicking, twenty ducks quacking, and fifty mice squeaking, only to be awakened by one noise.

2.27   Giganti, Paul, Jr. **How Many Snails? A Counting Book.** Illustrated by Donald Crews. Greenwillow Books, 1988. Ages 2–9. (Picture book)

A young child takes a walk and is asked to look for general as well as specific details in each picture: yellow flowers with black centers, red fish with open mouths, and starfish with five arms on rocks.

2.28   Gray, Catherine. **One, Two, Three, and Four: No More?** Illustrated by Marissa Moss. Houghton Mifflin, 1988. Ages 4–8. (Picture book)

Animals act out rhyming verses that deal with the numbers 1 through 4 in various mathematical relationships.

2.29   Hague, Kathleen. **Numbears: A Counting Book.** Illustrated by Michael Hague. Henry Holt, 1986. Ages 3–5. (Picture book)

Let's count from 1 to 12 in lilting rhymes about winsome little bears, who are pictured in full-page antique-like illustrations. There is much to discover and discuss and count in the busy life of these active little furry friends.

2.30   Hughes, Shirley. **Lucy and Tom's 1.2.3.** Illustrated by the author. Viking Kestrel, 1987. Ages 3–6. (Picture book)

Counting goes on all one Saturday as we follow young Lucy and Tom and their parents. In this narrative, the numbers are not highlighted but are talked about within the story. Activities are ordinary everyday happenings that will interest both boys and girls. The day ends with a family birthday party for Grandma. Other math concepts mentioned are pairs, odd and even numbers, comparing sizes, and number progression.

2.31   Inkpen, Mick. **One Bear at Bedtime.** Illustrated by the author. Little, Brown, 1987. Ages 3–7. (Picture book)

A little boy introduces readers to the numbers from 1 through 10 as he gets ready for bed. We see four giraffes who sit in the bath, six snakes who unwind the toilet paper, and a monster with ten heads who takes forever to say good night. This is a fine book to share at bedtime with a young child.

2.32   Kitchen, Bert. **Animal Numbers.** Illustrated by the author. Dial Books, 1987. Ages 3–5. (Picture book)

Lifelike color drawings show a mother animal and the appropriate number of baby animals crawling on, lying against, or swimming in a large number on each page. Counting proceeds from one baby kangaroo to ten puppies, but the numbers 15, 25, 50, 75, and 100 also are included with the corresponding number of animal offspring. Facts about each animal pictured are given at the end of the book.

2.33   Margolin, Harriet. **Busy Bear's Closet.** Illustrated by Carol Nicklaus. Grosset and Dunlap, 1985. Ages 2–4. (Picture book)

Brightly colored illustrations on heavy paper show Busy Bear counting as he empties out his closet: ten balls, nine toys, eight shoes, and so on.

2.34   Ockenga, Starr, photographer (text by Eileen Doolittle). **World of Wonders: A Trip through Numbers.** Houghton Mifflin/Floyd Yearout Books, 1988. All ages.

Toy lovers of all ages will be intrigued by this counting book with detailed photographs of subjects associated with the numbers one through twelve. A key to each photograph will help the reader unlock the mysteries found on each page.

2.35   Rees, Mary. **Ten in a Bed.** Illustrated by the author. Little, Brown/Joy Street Books, 1988. Ages 2–6. (Picture book)

Children may be familiar with this counting rhyme where one child falls out of bed, and the littlest child continues to "Roll over! Roll over!" until everyone is out of bed. The fun will be enjoyed even more in this humorously illustrated version.

2.36   Wadsworth, Olive A. **Over in the Meadow: A Counting-Out Rhyme.** Illustrated by Mary Maki Rae. Viking Kestrel, 1985. Ages 2–5. (Picture book)

A new brightly colored version of this old counting rhyme. Lush greens and blues make a continuous backdrop for the stylized shapes that form the animals and their settings. The pictures are alive with color and movement.

Other Concepts

2.37   Barton, Byron. **Airplanes.** Illustrated by the author. Thomas Y. Crowell, 1986. Ages 3–6. (Picture book)

Each book in a series on transportation covers a particular vehicle and explains its purpose. Bold, vivid illustrations provide much eye appeal for the young child. In this book, the author looks at airplanes and what they do.

2.38   Barton, Byron. **Boats.** Illustrated by the author. Thomas Y. Crowell, 1986. Ages 3–6. (Picture book)

Boats and their purposes are introduced by a brief, simple text with brightly colored illustrations.

2.39   Barton, Byron. **Trains.** Illustrated by the author. Thomas Y. Crowell, 1986. Ages 3–6. (Picture book)

A brief text and bold, simply drawn illustrations introduce a passenger train, freight train, and electric train and depict people riding on and working on trains.

2.40   Barton, Byron. **Trucks.** Illustrated by the author. Thomas Y. Crowell, 1986. Ages 3–6. (Picture book)

This small book examines different kinds of trucks and what they do. A spare commentary complements the brightly colored drawings.

2.41   Benjamin, Alan. **Rat-a-Tat, Pitter Pat.** Photographs by Margaret Miller. Thomas Y. Crowell, 1987. Ages 2–5. (Picture book)

Black-and-white photographs, often of children, illustrate familiar sounds. Double-page spreads feature such rhyming words as *whack* and *quack*, *slurp* and *burp*, and *munch* and *crunch*. The book's format invites listeners to think of other examples of sound words.

2.42   Demi. **Demi's Opposites: An Animal Game Book.** Illustrated by the author. Grosset and Dunlap, 1987. Ages 3–8. (Picture book)

Children will be drawn to the large, two-page, carefully illustrated animals and the humorous verse used to show familiar as well as not-quite-so-familiar opposites: curly/straight, inside/outside, alike/different, right side up/upside down.

2.43   Ekker, Ernst A. **What Is beyond the Hill?** Illustrated by Hilde Heyduck-Huth. J. B. Lippincott, 1986. Ages 3–5. (Picture book)

Dreamy soft pastel scenes portray what is beyond the hill, the mountain, the stars. With each new view the question is asked, "Does the world stop here?" The final spread says, "And the stars go on forever." A book for sharing with the very young.

2.44 Girard, Linda Walvoord. **Jeremy's First Haircut.** Illustrated by Mary Jane Begin. Albert Whitman, 1986. Ages 2–4. (Picture book)

Snip, snap—oops! What could be more traumatizing than a child's first haircut, especially when Mom's the barber? Colorful drawings capture the fun and frustration of this all-important first event. Very young children will be soothed and comforted while witnessing Jeremy's metamorphosis from a "little, little boy" to a "big, little boy."

2.45 Gundersheimer, Karen. **Shapes to Show.** Illustrated by the author. Harper and Row, 1986. Ages 2–6. (Picture book)

As they play with their toys, two mice discover twelve different shapes in this small book for even the youngest child.

2.46 Hoban, Tana. **Is It Larger? Is It Smaller?** Photographs by the author. Greenwillow Books, 1985. Ages 3–6. (Picture book)

Tana Hoban's colorful photographs illustrate animals and objects in larger and smaller sizes in this beautiful book with no text.

2.47 Hooper, Meredith. **Seven Eggs.** Illustrated by Terry McKenna. Harper and Row, 1985. Ages 3–5. (Picture book)

What animal will hatch from each of the seven eggs? By flipping each page, the reader can see who it is, and that animal then joins in watching for the next egg to hatch. An ostrich, a frilled lizard, and a barn owl are among the babies pictured.

2.48 Hughes, Shirley. **Bathwater's Hot.** Illustrated by the author. Lothrop, Lee and Shepard Books, 1985. Ages 3–5. (Picture book)

This is a warm, realistic look at family activities and the concept of opposites: "bathwater's hot, seawater's cold." The small size restricts this to a lap book. The crayon-and-ink illustrations show such activities as a father washing the children and add a great deal to the text.

2.49 Hughes, Shirley. **Noisy.** Illustrated by the author. Lothrop, Lee and Shepard Books, 1985. Ages 3–5. (Picture book)

Crayon-and-ink illustrations perfectly complement this story of the different kinds of noises a little girl hears and makes. Some are loud, like a pan banging, and some are soft, like rain. A lap book suitable for preschool listeners.

2.50   Isadora, Rachel. **I Hear.** Illustrated by the author. Greenwillow Books, 1985. Ages 2–4. (Picture book)

Baby's first sounds are captured by the bold-lettered text and
delicate full-colored illustrations, creating an aura of warmth
and tenderness. Parent and child will enjoy sharing this early
concept read-aloud book.

2.51   Isadora, Rachel. **I See.** Illustrated by the author. Greenwillow
Books, 1985. Ages 2–4. (Picture book)

A simple concept book for toddlers. A little girl spends a day
from morning to bedtime seeing objects and doing things.
Every page contains two sentences, such as "I see my spoon.
I eat." The first sentence always begins with "I see. . . ."
Soft pastel illustrations accompany the simple text, which is
large enough for young children beginning to read. An excellent first book for small children.

2.52   Isadora, Rachel. **I Touch.** Illustrated by the author. Greenwillow Books, 1985. Ages 2–4. (Picture book)

Intended to please the littlest of children, this book is not too
big to hold on a lap with a baby. The illustrations are large
two-page spreads with soft lines and warm colors. The text is
minimal and repetitive; "I touch . . ." begins each page with
a different experience in touching.

2.53   Kandoian, Ellen. **Under the Sun.** Illustrated by the author.
Dodd, Mead, 1987. Ages 4–7. (Picture book)

Molly asks her mother where the sun goes when she goes to
bed. Her mother responds by introducing various children or
animals watching the sun set as the Earth turns. A boy on a
Mississippi River houseboat, a girl on the Great Plains, a
Rocky Mountain elk, a gull in San Francisco, children of the
Pacific Ocean, a young Japanese girl, a Chinese Panda, a
camel in the Mongolian Desert, and a boy in eastern Russia
all watch the sun set. Finally, the day begins again, and Molly
watches the sun rise. Illustrations are pen and watercolor,
with minimal color introduced.

2.54   Linn, Margot. **A Trip to the Dentist.** Illustrated by Catherine
Siracusa. Harper and Row, 1988. Ages 3–7. (Picture book)

A child's first visit to the dentist might be eased if this book is
read before the appointment. This is a lap book designed to

encourage discussion. The instruments, chair, and procedures used by the dentist are previewed in a series of "guessing games" on each page. Open the flaps for a preview of a dental examination.

2.55   Linn, Margot. **A Trip to the Doctor.** Illustrated by Catherine Siracusa. Harper and Row, 1988. Ages 3–7. (Picture book)

This is just the book to read to a small child before a visit to the doctor. Dialogue is encouraged as the child is asked to guess what he or she is likely to find at the doctor's office. The pages then open up to reveal a reassuring scene illustrating a typical visit and the various instruments used for a medical examination.

2.56   Rogers, Fred. **Going to Day Care.** Photographs by Jim Judkis. G. P. Putnam's Sons/First Experience Books, 1985. Ages 2–5. (Picture book)

In this excellent book, Mister Rogers explores the probable feelings of a child when leaving parents for the day for the first time. The full-color photographs depict typical events that happen at a day-care center.

2.57   Rogers, Fred. **Going to the Doctor.** Photographs by Jim Judkis. G. P. Putnam's Sons/First Experience Books, 1986. Ages 2–4. (Picture book)

A child's visit to a doctor is presented in simple, direct language and bright, full-color photographs. Mister Rogers helps reassure youngsters by describing typical procedures during a medical examination. The presentation is interracial and nonsexist. *Outstanding Science Trade Book for Children.*

2.58   Rogers, Fred. **Going to the Hospital.** Photographs by Jim Judkis. G. P. Putnam's Sons/First Experience Books, 1988. Ages 3–6. (Picture book)

This is another title in this series of books dealing with first-time experiences that may be troubling both to children, who do not know what to expect, and to parents, who are not sure how to help their children. This book explains typical procedures during a hospital stay. It emphasizes that being in the hospital is not a punishment and that people go to a hospital to receive special care until they are well enough to go home. The book encourages children to ask questions in advance of going to the hospital and while they are there and to talk about their feelings. *Outstanding Science Trade Book for Children*.

2.59   Rogers, Fred. **Going to the Potty.** Photographs by Jim Judkis. G. P. Putnam's Sons/First Experience Books, 1986. Ages 2–5. (Picture book)

Using simple, direct language and bright, full-color photographs, the much-loved television host discusses how children learn to use the toilet when eliminating waste products from their bodies. The honest, reassuring treatment of the topic will serve as a discussion starter between adults and children. The presentation is interracial and nonsexist.

2.60   Rogers, Fred. **Making Friends.** Photographs by Jim Judkis. G. P. Putnam's Sons/First Experience Books, 1987. Ages 3–6. (Picture book)

Mister Rogers explains what it means to be a friend, and discusses some of the easy and difficult aspects of friendship. He offers his commonsense advice without talking down to children and encourages them to express their feelings. Full-color photographs of friends add further warmth to the book.

2.61   Rogers, Fred. **Moving.** Photographs by Jim Judkis. G. P. Putnam's Sons/First Experience Books, 1987. Ages 3–6. (Picture book)

Moving to a new home can be stressful for children, whether it is a move across town or a move across the country. Mister Rogers explains the process of moving a household and describes the uncertainty, sadness, and excitement of moving. He states that friendships remain after a move, though in a different form, and also encourages children to say hello to new friends and places.

2.62   Rogers, Fred. **The New Baby.** Photographs by Jim Judkis. G. P. Putnam's Sons/First Experience Books, 1985. Ages 3–5. (Picture book)

Mister Rogers helps ease the situation for the older child with a new sibling. The full-color photographs on each page follow a black family and a white family during the preparations for a new baby and after its arrival. The text is brief but one to share with the older child who may be feeling displaced. *ALA Notable Children's Book*.

2.63 Rogers, Fred. **When a Pet Dies.** Photographs by Jim Judkis. G. P. Putnam's Sons/First Experience Books, 1988. Ages 3–6. (Picture book)

When a pet dies, the whole family feels the loss. Mister Rogers briefly explains death and encourages children to discuss their feelings of sadness, loneliness, and perhaps anger and frustration. He emphasizes that these feelings will not last and that love shared with a pet remains within us even after the pet dies.

2.64 Roy, Ron. **Whose Hat Is That?** Photographs by Rosmarie Hausherr. Clarion Books, 1987. Ages 4–8. (Picture book)

Who wears a snug helmet that buckles under the chin? Turn the page and find a black-and-white photograph of jockeys in a race. The text explains the purpose of the jockey's helmet. Eighteen different hats are presented, including a beekeeper's and a surgeon's.

2.65 Simon, Norma. **Children Do, Grownups Don't.** Illustrated by Helen Cogancherry. Albert Whitman, 1987. Ages 3–8. (Picture book)

Children will be fascinated by the contrasts in this book, comparing children's and grownups' ideas and activities. For instance, "Kids like to play outdoors, even on drizzly days," while "Grownups would rather stay inside and be clean, warm and dry." The book also covers the different ideas on eating, bubble gum, tub toys, baldness, teeth, strength, clothes, valentines, birthday gifts, mailboxes, sleeping, worries, and more. The illustrations are realistic, colorful, and full of expression.

2.66 Wells, Tony. **Puzzle Doubles.** Illustrated by the author. Macmillan/Aladdin Books, 1987. Ages 2–5. (Picture book)

This puzzle book asks a child to look closely at two nearly (but not quite) identical illustrations to spot the differences between them. The illustrations are bright, with lots of lines and bold shapes. Answers are provided, but they could best be ignored to prevent turning play into work.

2.67 Wolff, Ashley. **A Year of Beasts.** Illustrated by the author. E. P. Dutton, 1986. Ages 2–5. (Picture book)

A sister and brother experience the joys of changing seasons marked by their month-to-month traditional activities and the appearance of animals common to the season. The vitality of the children and animals is projected by linoleum-block prints accented in bright washes. Companion to *A Year of Birds*.

2.68 Yektai, Niki. **Bears in Pairs.** Illustrated by Diane deGroat. Bradbury Press, 1987. Ages 2–6. (Picture book)

Forty-eight whimsically colorful bears in juxtaposed pairs cavort through the pages on their way to Mary's tea party. There, each can be plainly identified in the festive assembled group of toys. The repetitive, rhyming text is easy enough for beginning readers.

2.69 Ziefert, Harriet. **All Clean!** Illustrated by Henrik Drescher. Harper and Row, 1986. Ages 3–6. (Picture book)

Bright, flashy illustrations and a simple text are the components of a series of books about animals for preschoolers. This book explains that dogs shake, elephants shower, hippos soak, and lions lick, all in the name of cleanliness.

2.70 Ziefert, Harriet. **All Gone!** Illustrated by Henrik Drescher. Harper and Row, 1986. Ages 3–6. (Picture book)

In this book from a series about animals, the author explains how hungry animals eat—mice gnaw, kangaroos graze, anteaters snack, and chimps feast.

2.71 Ziefert, Harriet. **Bear All Year: A Guessing-Game Story.** Illustrated by Arnold Lobel. Harper and Row, 1986. Ages 3–5. (Picture book)

The reader is asked to guess what Bear is wearing for each seasonal activity, and then the page flips open to reveal the answer. This quietly understated book invites the child's participation and knowledge. It contains delightful crayon and watercolor illustrations. Other titles in this series are *Bear Gets Dressed*, *Bear Goes Shopping*, *Bear's Busy Morning*. All of these books exhibit the same uniqueness, imagination, and fun, coupled with wonderful illustrations.

2.72 Ziefert, Harriet. **Cock-A-Doodle-Do!** Illustrated by Henrik Drescher. Harper and Row, 1986. Ages 3–6. (Picture book)

Preschoolers will enjoy mimicking the sounds that various animals make, including hoots, honks, meows, bow-wows, and cock-a-doodle-dos, in this book from a series about animals.

2.73   Ziefert, Harriet. **Run! Run!** Illustrated by Henrik Drescher. Harper and Row, 1986. Ages 3–6. (Picture book)

A fourth book in this series about animals introduces preschoolers to some of the things that animals do— baboons leap, cheetahs streak, and warthogs scurry. Brightly colored illustrations accompany the spare text.

Recommended Books Published before 1985

Anno, Mitsumasa. *Anno's Alphabet: An Adventure in Imagination.* Thomas Y. Crowell, 1975. 4–7.
———. *Anno's Counting Book.* Harper and Row, 1977. 4–7.
Azarian, Mary. *A Farmer's Alphabet.* David R. Godine, 1981. 6–8.
Barrett, Peter, and Susan Barrett. *The Circle Sarah Drew.* Scroll Press, 1973. 5–8.
Bayer, Jane. *A, My Name Is Alice.* Illustrated by Steven Kellogg. Dial Books for Young Readers, 1984. 5–8.
Brown, Marcia. *All Butterflies.* Charles Scribner's Sons, 1974. 4–7.
———. *Listen to a Shape.* Franklin Watts, 1979. 5–8.
Burningham, John. *ABCDEFGHIJKLMNOPQRSTUVWXYZ.* Bobbs-Merrill, 1964. 3–5.
Crews, Donald. *We Read: A to Z.* Greenwillow Books, 1984. 3–6.
de Brunhoff, Laurent. *Babar's Book of Color.* Random House, 1984. 3–5.
Eichenberg, Fritz. *Ape in a Cape: An Alphabet of Odd Animals.* Harcourt, Brace and World, 1952. 4–7.
Emberley, Ed. *Ed Emberley's ABC.* Little, Brown, 1978. 5–7.
———. *Green Says Go.* Little, Brown, 1968. 4–6.
Feelings, Muriel. *Jambo Means Hello: Swahili Alphabet Book.* Illustrated by Tom Feelings. Dial Press, 1974.
———. *Moja Means One: Swahili Counting Book.* Illustrated by Tom Feelings. Dial Press, 1971. 5–8.
Hoban, Tana. *Circles, Triangles and Squares.* Macmillan, 1974. 3–6.
———. *Is it Red? Is it Yellow? Is it Blue?* Greenwillow Books, 1978. 3–6.
———. *Look Again.* Macmillan, 1971. 5–8.
———. *Over, Under and Through, and Other Spatial Concepts.* Macmillan, 1973. 3–6.

Jensen, Virginia Allen. *Catching: A Book for Blind and Sighted Children with Pictures to Feel as Well as to See*. Philomel Books, 1983. 3–7.

Lionni, Leo. *Little Blue and Little Yellow*. Astor-Honor, 1959. 3–6.

Lobel, Arnold. *On Market Street*. Illustrated by Anita Lobel. Greenwillow Books, 1981. 3–6.

Maestro, Betsy, and Giulio Maestro. *Around the Clock with Harriet: A Book about Telling Time*. Crown, 1984. 4–7.

Miles, Miska. *Apricot ABC*. Illustrated by Peter Parnall. Little, Brown, 1969. 4–7.

Munari, Bruno. *ABC*. World, 1960. 4–7.

Newberry, Clare Turlay. *The Kittens' ABC*. Harper and Row, 1965. 3–6.

Pienkowski, Jan. *Shapes*. Simon and Schuster, 1981. 3–5.

Sendak, Maurice. *One Was Johnny: A Counting Book* (in *The Nutshell Library*). Harper and Row, 1962. 3–6.

Testa, Fulvio. *If You Take a Pencil*. Dial Books for Young Children, 1982. 4–6.

Tudor, Tasha. *A Is for Annabelle*. Henry Z. Walck, 1954. 4–7.

Watson, Clyde. *Applebet: An ABC*. Illustrated by Wendy Watson. Farrar, Straus and Giroux, 1982. 4–6.

Watanabe, Shigeo. *I Can Take a Walk*! Illustrated by Yasuo Ohtomo. Philomel Books, 1984. 3–5.

Wildsmith, Brian. *Brian Wildsmith's ABC*. Franklin Watts, 1963. 3–5.

3 Wordless Picture Books

3.1   Amoss, Berthe. **What Did You Lose, Santa?** Harper and Row, 1987. Ages 3–7. (Picture book)

In this wordless Christmas picture book, Santa and Mrs. Claus search for the missing banner for Santa's sleigh ride. The banner proclaims, "Peace on Earth."

3.2   Collington, Peter. **The Angel and the Soldier Boy.** Alfred A. Knopf/Borzoi Books, 1987. Ages 4–8. (Picture book)

A little girl falls asleep with two tiny dolls on her pillow who come to life as soon as her eyes close. A rowdy gang of pirate raiders kidnap the soldier doll and take him to their tiny model ship. The angel doll is brave and resourceful enough to restore order before the little girl awakens. The whole adventure is drawn in exquisite detail with no text.

3.3   Drescher, Henrik. **The Yellow Umbrella.** Bradbury Press, 1987. Ages 3–8. (Picture book)

This textless lap book tells the story of two hapless monkeys, a mother and her child, who are trapped in a most unhappy zoo. The fortuitous arrival of a yellow umbrella sets them off on an adventure that changes their lives completely. This simple story is enhanced by the pen-and-ink drawings and, of course, the yellow umbrella throughout.

3.4   Goodall, John S. **Little Red Riding Hood.** Margaret K. McElderry Books, 1988. All ages. (Picture book)

Full-page and half-page watercolor illustrations retell this classic tale with a mouse as the main character. On the way to her grandmother's house, the mouse meets animals as well as the wicked wolf himself.

3.5   Goodall, John. **Naughty Nancy Goes to School.** Margaret K. McElderry Books, 1985. Ages 5–8. (Picture book)

Naughty Nancy Mouse is reluctant to start school. Once there, she amuses herself and her classmates by living up to her name. Nancy's antics end with a redeeming, heroic deed. This wordless picture book has detailed watercolor illustrations with some half-page masks.

3.6   Goodall, John. **Paddy to the Rescue.** Margaret K. McElderry Books, 1985. Ages 5–9. (Picture book)

The familiar character Paddy the pig launches on a suspenseful wordless adventure pursuing a robber rat who has just stolen a mistress pig's jewels. Watercolor double-page spreads continue the action. Half-page illustrations appear between each double spread, heightening the drama. Against all odds, Paddy persistently tracks the scoundrel, triumphantly bringing him to justice.

3.7   Hoban, Tana. **Look! Look! Look!** Greenwillow Books, 1988. Ages 2–8. (Picture book)

Full-color photographs of familiar objects are first seen through a cutout hole and then in their entirety as the reader turns the page in this carefully planned, shiny-paper picture book. The book is designed as a guessing game, where the clue is a first look at a small part of the whole.

3.8   McCully, Emily Arnold. **The Christmas Gift.** Harper and Row, 1988. Ages 3–7. (Picture book)

A loving mouse family celebrates Christmas in traditional American fashion, including a trip to Grandma and Grandpa's house. When a prized new toy is accidentally broken, Grandpa saves the day by retrieving an old electric train from the attic. Cheerful line-and-wash paintings depict the holiday festivities and familial warmth, support, and comfort in this completely wordless picture book.

3.9   McCully, Emily Arnold. **First Snow.** Harper and Row, 1985. Ages 4–8. (Picture book)

A mouse family loads the old red pickup with sleds and skates for a winter outing. Scarves and hats are bright against the big blobs of inviting white snow in this wordless picture book. Children will discover one timid little mouse who learns to brave the big hill on a sled. Varying perspectives and action that spills off the page keep the simple story interesting.

3.10   McCully, Emily Arnold. **New Baby.** Harper and Row, 1988. Ages 3–6. (Picture book)

The youngest mouse child feels lonely, neglected, and sad when a new baby arrives. Whimsical watercolor illustrations empathetically tell this story without words.

3.11   McCully, Emily Arnold. **School.** Harper and Row, 1987. Ages 4–6. (Picture book)

It is autumn, and a family of mice children head off to school in this story without words. Only the youngest mouse child remains home with its mother, but before long it, too, ventures off surreptitiously to the one-room schoolhouse to join its siblings. The understanding teacher allows the visitor to join in the class activities, after which Mom appears to take her young mouse home. The brightly colored illustrations offer a sense of early fall and back-to-school time.

3.12   Munro, Roxie. **Christmastime in New York City.** Dodd, Mead, 1987. Ages 5–8. (Picture book)

This book, by the author-illustrator of *The Inside-Outside Book of New York City*, is a delightful look at Manhattan's special places—such as Rockefeller Center, the Lord and Taylor store windows, the New York Public Library, and Times Square—during the Christmas season. The last page of this picture book is devoted to a short history of each scene depicted earlier. There is one error—the herald angels in Rockefeller Center were there much earlier than the 1981 date given by the author.

3.13   Prater, John. **The Gift.** Viking Penguin/Puffin Books, 1987. Ages 5–9. (Picture book)

When a large, mysterious package arrives, two young children are more curious about the box than its contents. As they jump inside, the children are launched on a wondrous, magical voyage. This spectacular wordless picture book brings a flight of fancy to vivid life in brightly colored illustrations. The imaginative story is a natural for stimulating both oral and written language.

3.14   Saltzberg, Barney. **The Yawn.** Atheneum, 1985. Ages 2–8. (Picture book)

One child's yawn is passed on throughout the day until it travels full circle in this wordless pen-and-ink book. Another planet catches the yawn, too, in this fun-filled adventure.

3.15   Tafuri, Nancy. **Have You Seen My Duckling?** Viking Penguin/ Puffin Books, 1986. Ages 3–6. (Picture book)

Early one morning, one duckling leaves the nest and hides. On each set of pages, while the mother unsuccessfully looks for the duckling in a new place, the young reader can find it partially hidden. The story is told entirely through the full-page color drawings; the only text is the repeated question, "Have you see my duckling?" *Caldecott Honor Book.*

3.16   Tafuri, Nancy. **Rabbit's Morning.** Greenwillow Books, 1985. Ages 1–3. (Picture book)

Luminous double-page watercolors portray a rabbit's sun-showered morning walk through a countryside filled with flowers and inhabited by many feathered and furry friends. The large vivid paintings and nearly wordless text make this a perfect choice for the animal-loving toddler.

Intermediate

3.17   Dupasquier, Philippe. **The Great Escape.** Houghton Mifflin, 1988. Ages 6–11. (Picture book)

An escaped prisoner leads police on a madcap chase in this wordless book filled with action-packed, humorous illustrations. The slapstick plot moves along at high speed through frames arranged in comic-strip style. Loads of detail on every page and a double-twist ending make this book appealing to children who may consider themselves too old for picture books.

3.18   Wiesner, David. **Free Fall.** Lothrop, Lee and Shepard Books, 1988. Ages 8–12. (Picture book)

When a boy falls asleep with his book on his chest, his dreams transport him to fantasy lands and adventure far from his bedroom. The final page will send the reader back to the beginning of the picture story to meet the visual challenge of finding how items from the boy's room were transformed to accompany him on the adventure. *Caldecott Honor Book.*

Recommended Books Published before 1985

Alexander, Martha. *Bobo's Dream*. Dial Press, 1970. 4–6.

Anno, Mitsumasa. *Anno's Britain*. Philomel Books, 1982. 7–10.

————. *Anno's Journey*. Philomel Books, 1978. 7–10.

Bang, Molly. *The Grey Lady and the Strawberry Snatcher*. Four Winds Press, 1980. 4–7.

Briggs, Raymond. *The Snowman*. Random House, 1978. 3–6.

Carle, Eric. *Do You Want to Be My Friend?* Thomas Y. Crowell, 1971. 3–6.

de Groat, Diane. *Alligator's Toothache*. Crown, 1977. 4–8.

dePaola, Tomie. *Flicks*. Harcourt Brace Jovanovich, 1979. 4–8.

————. *Sing, Pierrot, Sing: A Picture Book in Mime*. Harcourt Brace Jovanovich, 1983. 4–7.

Goodall, John. *Creepy Castle*. Atheneum, 1975. 4–8.

Hutchins, Pat. *Changes, Changes*. Macmillan, 1971. 3–5.

Keats, Ezra Jack. *Psst! Doggie*. Franklin Watts, 1973. 3–6.

Krahn, Fernando. *The Mystery of the Giant Footprints*. E. P. Dutton, 1977. 5–8.

————. *Robot-Bot-Bot*. E. P. Dutton, 1979. 4–7.

Mayer, Mercer. *Bubble, Bubble*. Parents Magazine Press, 1973. 5–8.

————. *Frog Goes to Dinner*. Dial Press, 1974. 4–7.

Spier, Peter. *Peter Spier's Rain*. Doubleday, 1982. 3–7.

Turkle, Brinton. *Deep in the Forest*. E. P. Dutton, 1976. 4–6.

Ungerer, Tomi. *Snail, Where Are You?* Harper and Row, 1962. 4–7.

Ward, Lynd. *The Silver Pony*. Houghton Mifflin, 1973. 7–10.

Winter, Paula. *The Bear and the Fly*. Crown, 1976. 5–8.

4 Language and Reading

Easy-Reading Books

4.1   Alexander, Sue. **Witch, Goblin, and Ghost Are Back.** Illustrated by Jeanette Winter. Pantheon Books/I Am Reading Books, 1985. Ages 5–8.

Witch, Goblin, and Ghost are together again for five activities—a winter day, painting, making fudge, a day in the meadow, and a raft trip. Each episode is told as a separate story. The friends discover that they need not always enjoy the same activities to be friends. Humorous black-and-white illustrations add to the fun of this easy-to-read book.

4.2   Baker, Barbara. **Digby and Kate.** Illustrated by Marsha Winborn. E. P. Dutton, 1988. Ages 5–8. (Picture book)

Digby the dog and his friend Kate the cat experience the ups and downs and gives-and-takes of friendship in short, humorous, easy-to-read stories. Bright, cheerful watercolor illustrations on every page complement the text.

4.3   Berenstain, Stan, and Jan Berenstain. **The Berenstain Bears Get Stage Fright.** Illustrated by the authors. Random House/First Time Books, 1986. Ages 5–8. (Picture book)

Brother is confident, but Sister is scared when they both contemplate being in the school play. During the actual performance their feelings are reversed, and Sister cues Brother when he is gripped with stage fright.

4.4   Berenstain, Stan, and Jan Berenstain. **The Berenstain Bears Go Out for the Team.** Illustrated by the authors. Random House/First Time Books, 1986. Ages 5–8.

Brother and Sister Bear enjoy playing baseball with their neighborhood friends in Farmer Ben's back meadow. Sister Bear is the rules expert and also a terrific batter. When Papa

Bear talks Brother and Sister into trying out for the big-league team, pressure builds for everyone in the family as tryout day approaches.

4.5 Bucknall, Caroline. **The Three Little Pigs.** Illustrated by the author. Dial Books for Young Readers, 1987. Ages 3–6. (Picture book)

In this easy-reading, rhyming version of the traditional story of the three pigs, Caroline Bucknall has created simple, expressive, and colorful illustrations for even the youngest child to enjoy. Instead of being eaten by the wolf, each pig runs helter-skelter to the next strongest house, and all three enjoy wolf stew together.

4.6 Bulla, Clyde Robert. **The Chalk Box Kid.** Illustrated by Thomas B. Allen. Random House/Stepping Stone Books, 1987. Ages 5–8. (Picture book)

A new home, a new school, and boorish Uncle Max sharing his room make Gregory's life a bit hard to take. An abandoned chalk factory and some imagination open a world of acceptance and friendship that the boy has not dared to expect. This moving story of one child's artistic vision is another in a series designed for the newly independent reader.

4.7 Cameron, Ann. **Julian's Glorious Summer.** Illustrated by Dora Leder. Random House/Stepping Stone Books, 1987. Ages 5–8. (Picture book)

How can Julian admit he is afraid of bicycles when his friend Gloria can already ride her new bike with no hands? To save face, he tells a little fib instead, which mushrooms into a major whopper. The Stepping Stone series continues to prove that humor, family love, and action can coexist with simple vocabulary and short chapters.

4.8 Chorao, Kay. **Ups and Downs with Oink and Pearl.** Illustrated by the author. Harper and Row/I Can Read Books, 1986. Ages 5–9. (Picture book)

Three appealing, well-illustrated stories involve two piglets and their adventures with a super-fizz soda, a mail-order movie projector, and a witch. The pig tales are certain to delight the young reader.

4.9   Christian, Mary Blount. **April Fool.** Illustrated by Diane
            Dawson. Macmillan/Aladdin Books/Ready-to-Read Books,
            1986. Ages 5–8. (Picture book)

            The people of medieval Gotham trick their annoying king into
            leaving them in peace. Seth proves the value of dreaming by
            coming up with the silly, but effective, idea that drives off the
            king. Some say this may have been the beginning of our own
            April Fool's Day. The illustrations in this short, amusing
            book help explain the text, which consists of a limited vocab-
            ulary.

4.10   Christian, Mary Blount. **Go West, Swamp Monsters!** Illus-
            trated by Marc Brown. Dial Books for Young Readers, 1985.
            Ages 6–8. (Picture book)

            A hilariously funny book for beginning readers. Four swamp
            monster children are "acting as bad as children!" and are de-
            nied supper until they learn to behave "like monsters!" The
            cartoonlike illustrations in color add to the slapstick humor.

4.11   Christian, Mary Blount. **The Toady and Dr. Miracle.** Illus-
            trated by Ib Ohlsson. Macmillan/Ready-to-Read Books, 1985.
            Ages 6–8.

            Luther is a young pioneer boy who is commandeered by Dr.
            Miracle to be a toady, or assistant, for his medicine show.
            Luther saves the day for the locals by outwitting the wily
            charlatan. There are amusing two-color cartoonlike illustra-
            tions.

4.12   Coerr, Eleanor. **Chang's Paper Pony.** Illustrated by Deborah
            Kogan Ray. Harper and Row/I Can Read Books, 1988. Ages
            5–8.

            This easy-to-read chapter book is engaging and informative
            historical fiction, illuminating events in the American West
            during the 1850s. Chinese immigrants Chang and his grand-
            father prepare food at a California mining camp during the
            Gold Rush. There they must face the prejudice of the gold-
            crazed miners. Chang dreams of owning a pony. Honesty,
            hard work, and a good friend help him realize his dream and
            make a home in his new land.

4.13   Coerr, Eleanor. **The Josefina Story Quilt.** Illustrated by Bruce
            Degen. Harper and Row/I Can Read Books, 1986. Ages 5–8.

A young girl makes a patchwork quilt that gives details of the family's trip west in the 1800s. Two patches tell of Josefina, her pet hen, and the exciting times the two have on the trip. The illustrations work well with the easy-to-read text.

4.14 Cole, Joanna. **Hungry, Hungry Sharks.** Illustrated by Patricia Wynne. Random House/Step into Reading Books, 1986. Ages 5–9.

Using an easy-to-read vocabulary and format, Joanna Cole describes different kinds of sharks, their eating habits, and other information of interest to children. She begins with the statement that sharks were alive at the time of the dinosaurs and ends with a prediction that sharks will be alive as long as there are oceans, which stimulates new ways of thinking about these great creatures. The colored pencil drawings support the text on each page.

4.15 Cole, Joanna. **The Missing Tooth.** Illustrated by Marylin Hafner. Random House/Step into Reading Books, 1988. Ages 5–8. (Picture book)

Robby and Arlo are alike in so many ways: they like to eat and do the same things, and they even have teeth missing in the same place. But one day something changes, and their friendship suffers. Brightly colored illustrations help convey the story.

4.16 Collins, Meghan. **The Willow Maiden.** Illustrated by László Gál. Dial Books for Young Readers/Pied Piper Books, 1988. Ages 6 and up. (Picture book)

Enter the mystical world of people who only emerge from the Willow Tree on Midsummer's Eve. Here is a beautifully written, original fairy tale with softly colored watercolors that reflect the enchantment of the text and haunt the memory.

4.17 Cross, Molly. **Wait for Me!** Illustrated by Joe Mathieu. Random House/Children's Television Workshop/Sesame Street Start-to-Read Books, 1987. Ages 2–7. (Picture book)

Elmo is just too young and too small to keep pace with his older and bigger friends from Sesame Street. He feels lonely until Grover's grandfather invites him along on a trip to the zoo. Grandpa likes to walk slowly and to look around at life.

They share a pleasant afternoon at the zoo, and Grandpa has to promise Grover that he can come along the next time Grandpa and Elmo decide to visit the zoo.

4.18   Cushman, Doug. **Aunt Eater Loves a Mystery.** Illustrated by the author. Harper and Row/I Can Read Books, 1987. Ages 4–7. (Picture book)

Aunt Eater sees mysteries everywhere: in switched luggage on a train, in shadows on a wall, and in puzzling mailbox notes. When a real mystery comes along, she becomes a detective and proves her mettle in a manner that beginning readers will applaud. This is another successful book in a series of easy-reading books.

4.19   de Brunhoff, Laurent. **Babar and the Ghost: An Easy-to-Read Version.** Illustrated by the author. Random House/Step into Reading Books, 1986. Ages 6–9.

When Babar's children bring home a ghost to be a secret friend, lots of tricks get played until Babar has to step in. The book uses simple vocabulary and from two to fifteen lines of print per page. *Children's Choice.*

4.20   Dennis, Lynne. **Raymond Rabbit Goes Shopping.** Illustrated by the author. E. P. Dutton, 1987. Ages 2–4. (Picture book)

Anticipating a new pair of shoes, Rabbit accompanies his mother on a shopping trip. Young children will relate to his experience of realizing he has followed the wrong mother around the store. Full-page color illustrations support the simple text.

4.21   Donnelly, Judy. **Tut's Mummy: Lost . . . and Found.** Illustrated by James Watling. Random House/Step into Reading, 1988. Ages 7–10.

Hidden treasures, secret tombs, and a mummy are captivating topics for the beginning reader. This book describes the burial of the pharaoh Tutankhamen and the discovery of his tomb by archeologists more than three thousand years later.

4.22   Dubowski, Cathy East, and Mark Dubowski. **Cave Boy.** Illustrated by the authors. Random House/Step into Reading Books, 1988. Ages 5–7. (Picture book)

Large print and simple text convey the story of how Harry solves the dilemma of giving Chief Grump something on his birthday that he has not seen before. *Children's Choice.*

4.23 Dubowski, Cathy East, and Mark Dubowski. **Pretty Good Magic.** Illustrated by the authors. Random House/Step into Reading Books, 1987. Ages 6–9. (Picture book)

Presto the magician attempts to show his town, Forty Winks, a really great trick. Surprisingly, the hat-and-rabbit trick works better than expected and amazes the entire town.

4.24 Ehrlich, Amy. **Buck-Buck the Chicken.** Illustrated by R. W. Alley. Random House/Step into Reading Books, 1987. Ages 5–9. (Picture book)

Buck-Buck, Nancy's most extraordinary chick, likes to swing, dress in doll clothes, ride in a buggy, and play games—until one day an event happens that changes her life.

4.25 Elliott, Dan. **Grover Learns to Read.** Illustrated by Normand Chartier. Random House/Children's Television Workshop/ Sesame Street Start-to-Read Books, 1985. Ages 3–7. (Picture book)

Young readers will enjoy this book about Grover in which he does not tell his mother that he can read so that she will continue to read to him. Jim Henson's Muppets are the characters that help Grover in a crisis.

4.26 Gage, Wilson. **Mrs. Gaddy and the Fast-Growing Vine.** Illustrated by Marylin Hafner. Greenwillow Books/Read-Alone Books, 1985. Ages 5–7. (Picture book)

Mrs. Gaddy's new plant has the growing power of Jack's beanstalk. When all of her efforts to control the wild vine fail, she buys a ravenous goat. But then she must face a new dilemma—controlling the goat's uncontrollable appetite. Pen-and-ink drawings visually portray Mrs. Gaddy's rib-tickling antics.

4.27 Hautzig, Deborah. **Happy Birthday, Little Witch.** Illustrated by Marc Brown. Random House/Step into Reading Books, 1986. Ages 5–8.

Little Witch worries that her friends will not come to her birthday party. The colorful, humorous illustrations are well matched to the text in this book for the beginning reader.

4.28 Hayes, Geoffrey. **The Secret of Foghorn Island.** Illustrated by the author. Random House/Step into Reading Books, 1988. Ages 6–9. (Picture book)

Otto and Uncle Tooth set out on an adventure to investigate a number of recent shipwrecks and come in contact with dangerous Sid Rat.

4.29 Hayward, Linda. **Hello, House!** Illustrated by Lynn Munsinger. Random House/Step into Reading Books, 1988. Ages 4–7. (Picture book)

This book is based upon one of the "Tales of Uncle Remus." Brer Wolf hides in Brer Rabbit's house so that he can catch the rabbit upon his return, but once again Brer Rabbit outsmarts the wolf. *Children's Choice.*

4.30 Hayward, Linda. **Noah's Ark.** Illustrated by Freire Wright. Random House/Step into Reading, 1987. Ages 4–6. (Picture book)

Here is an easy-to-read version of the Old Testament story of Noah and his family and how they build their ark so that they and each animal species can be saved from the flood.

4.31 Hoban, Lillian. **Arthur's Loose Tooth.** Illustrated by the author. Harper and Row/I Can Read Books, 1985. Ages 5–9. (Picture book)

Once again Lillian Hoban uses Arthur and Violet to teach a lesson in a delightful manner. Arthur wants to prove that he has "THE POWER" and is a fearless chimp, while his sister Violet readily admits that she is afraid of the dark. When Arthur's tooth becomes loose, he is afraid to pull it out. Violet, with the help of the baby-sitter, is able to overcome her fear, and soon Arthur is able to face his fear, too. The story is greatly enhanced by the illustrations.

4.32 Hoban, Lillian. **The Case of the Two Masked Robbers.** Illustrated by the author. Harper and Row/I Can Read Books, 1986. Ages 4–7. (Picture book)

Raccoon twins Arabella and Albert are determined to find out who stole Mrs. Turtle's eggs. There are spooky noises and shadowy characters to be dealt with as the duo gathers clues. The cozy illustrations are just scary enough to be intriguing in this easy-to-read mystery.

4.33 Hoff, Syd. **Barney's Horse.** Illustrated by the author. Harper and Row/Early I Can Read Books, 1987. Ages 4–7. (Picture book)

Few words are needed to tell about the love between Barney the peddler and his horse. This beginning-reading book skillfully depicts that trusting relationship and allows children to learn a bit about an earlier time, while it maintains a controlled vocabulary. Syd Hoff's characteristic illustrations exhibit the same economy of expression.

4.34 Hooker, Ruth. **Sara Loves Her Big Brother.** Illustrated by Margot Apple. Albert Whitman, 1987. Ages 2–6. (Picture book)

Sara rather overdoes her devotion to her big brother. She loves him to the point where he scarcely seems to have a moment to himself, but the two conclude their day with a mutual declaration of love. The delightful pictures are done with colored pencils and add to the dynamic feeling of this relationship.

4.35 Hopkins, Lee Bennett, compiler. **More Surprises.** Illustrated by Megan Lloyd. Harper and Row/Charlotte Zolotow Books/I Can Read Books, 1987. Ages 5–7.

Thirty-five poems in an easy-to-read format tell of school, brothers, caterpillars, loose teeth, good books, and other things of interest to beginning readers. The playfulness of the rhythm and rhyme is repeated in the brightly colored illustrations on each page.

4.36 Hutchins, Pat. **The Tale of Thomas Mead.** Illustrated by the author. Greenwillow Books/Mulberry Books, 1988. Ages 5–8. (Picture book)

Thomas Mead cannot read. "Why should I?" he asks as he encounters disaster after disaster due to his failure to understand the written word. Beginning readers will enjoy Thomas's hilarious misadventures and rejoice with him as he discovers the delights of reading. Humorous cartoonlike illustrations accompany the easy-to-read text.

4.37 Krensky, Stephen. **Lionel at Large.** Illustrated by Susanna Natti. Dial Books for Young Readers/Easy-to-Read Books, 1986. Ages 6–8.

The beginning reader will enjoy five stories about Lionel and his adventures when his sister loses a snake (which Lionel is afraid of) in his room, when he sleeps overnight at a friend's house (and gets a little homesick), and when he decides not to eat green beans, but ends up eating them anyway. Each story is complete in itself, and there are full-color illustrations on each page.

4.38 Kuskin, Karla. **Something Sleeping in the Hall.** Illustrated by the author. Harper and Row/Charlotte Zolotow Books/I Can Read Books, 1985. Ages 5–8.

These humorous easy-to-read poems about animals will be enjoyable reading for the youngest readers. Simple illustrations seem well suited to the text.

4.39 Lerner, Sharon. **Follow the Monsters!** Illustrated by Tom Cooke. Random House/Children's Television Workshop/Step into Reading Books, 1985. Ages 4–7. (Picture book)

The large print and controlled vocabulary are important features in this series of beginning-reading books, but the real value is the appeal of the stories. This story, in rhyme, is about a parade of monsters bumbling their way to Sesame Street.

4.40 Levinson, Nancy Smiler. **Clara and the Bookwagon.** Illustrated by Carolyn Croll. Harper and Row/I Can Read Books, 1988. Ages 6–9.

The story of how Mary Lemist Titcomb began the first book-mobile in the area surrounding Hagerstown, Maryland, is an exciting success story told in the controlled vocabulary and text layout of a beginning-reading book. The horse-drawn bookwagon brought library books to the farm families in the region.

4.41 Lewis, J. Patrick. **The Tsar and the Amazing Cow.** Illustrated by Friso Henstra. Dial Books for Young Readers, 1988. Ages 5–9. (Picture book)

In this book, beautifully illustrated by a Dutch artist, an old peasant couple in Russia are restored to their youth by drinking the milk of their faithful cow. Other extraordinary events happen which take the couple to the Tsar and restore their earlier losses.

4.42   Lexau, Joan M. **The Dog Food Caper.** Illustrated by Marylin Hafner. Dial Books for Young Readers/Easy-to-Read Books, 1985. Ages 5–9.

Willy Nilly needs to solve the problem of dog food appearing in strange places so he asks a witch, Miss Happ, to help solve the mystery. Attractive pencil, colored ink, and watercolor illustrations seem perfect with this easy-to-read mystery.

4.43   Little, Emily. **David and the Giant.** Illustrated by Hans Wilhelm. Random House/Step into Reading Books, 1987. Ages 4–7. (Picture book)

This is a simplified retelling of the Old Testament story of David, the shepherd boy, whose faith in God helps him overcome the giant Goliath.

4.44   Little, Emily. **The Trojan Horse: How the Greeks Won the War.** Illustrated by Michael Eagle. Random House/Step into Reading, 1988. Ages 7–10. (Picture book)

Emily Little retells the story of how Greek soldiers used a wooden horse to win the Trojan War. A pronunciation guide for the difficult names is included in this easy-reading book.

4.45   Luttrell, Ida. **Tillie and Mert.** Illustrated by Doug Cushman. Harper and Row/I Can Read Books, 1985. Ages 4–8. (Picture book)

When Tillie the skunk and Mert the field mouse get together, many inventive ideas turn everyday occurrences into happy occasions. In three short stories they learn about garage-sale bargains, the price of fame, and the value of cooperation. Simple, tricolored drawings harmoniously blend with the simplicity of these easy-reading stories.

4.46   McCully, Emily Arnold. **The Grandma Mix-up.** Illustrated by the author. Harper and Row/I Can Read Books, 1988. Ages 6–8. (Picture book)

Pip is perplexed when two very different grandmas come to baby-sit, each with her own way of doing things. Finally, the child takes charge and lets the grandmas know just how things are done when Pip's parents are home. All three can then relax and enjoy themselves until Pip's parents return from their trip. The full-color illustrations support the beginning-reading vocabulary and text layout.

4.47   McKissack, Patricia. **Monkey-Monkey's Trick: Based on an African Folk Tale.** Illustrated by Paul Meisel. Random House/Step into Reading, 1988. Ages 5–9. (Picture book)

In this retelling of an African folktale, Monkey-Monkey is tricked by a greedy hyena. When he discovers the trick being played on him, he decides on a plan to save himself.

4.48   Marshall, Edward. **Four on the Shore.** Illustrated by James Marshall. Dial Books for Young Readers/Easy-to-Read Books, 1985. Ages 4–7.

In this companion to *Three by the Sea*, three children try to outdo each other's scary stories, hoping to drive away pesky tagalong Willie. In a zesty turnaround, it is Willie's story that sends them running for cover.

4.49   Marshall, James. **Fox on the Job.** Illustrated by the author. Dial Books for Young Readers/Easy-to-Read Books, 1988. Ages 4–7. (Picture book)

Fox wants to earn money for a new bicycle, but he cannot hold a job until he finds one thing he's really good at. Children will enjoy feeling more adept than foolish Fox. The simply written short chapters and James Marshall's characteristically wacky illustrations will be inviting to those who are learning to read.

4.50   Marshall, James. **Three up a Tree.** Illustrated by the author. Dial Books for Young Readers/Easy-to-Read Books, 1986. Ages 6–8. (Picture book)

Up in their tree house, Lolly, Spider, and Sam compete to see who can tell the best story. Beginning readers should be amused by the three stories within a story, with their humor involving such characters as a friendly monster, a chicken on the run, and a doll. Several other books in this series feature the same three characters.

4.51   Marzollo, Jean. **Soccer Sam.** Illustrated by Blanche Sims. Random House/Step into Reading Books, 1987. Ages 5–9. (Picture book)

Marco arrives in the United States from Mexico for an extended stay with his cousin Sam. His verbal skills and confidence are bolstered by his athletic ability and his willingness to teach others how to play soccer.

4.52   Milton, Joyce. **Dinosaur Days.** Illustrated by Richard Roe. Random House/Step into Reading Books, 1985. Ages 5–9. (Picture book)

An easy-to-read book on a popular topic depicts the prehistoric lives of eleven different dinosaurs, their environments, eating habits, and unusual characteristics. Lively, colorful drawings breathe life into these amazing creatures. Large type, pronunciations, and elementary vocabulary reinforce the simplified format for the young reader.

4.53   Muschg, Hanna. **Two Little Bears.** Illustrated by Kathi Bhend-Zaugg. Bradbury Press, 1986. Ages 4–9. (Picture book)

Two little bear cubs grow up in a cave with their mother, who teaches them survival skills in the forest. This book, based on fact and simply illustrated with line drawings, is a welcome departure from the usual books for beginning readers.

4.54   Nixon, Joan Lowery. **If You Were a Writer.** Illustrated by Bruce Degen. Four Winds Press, 1988. Ages 8–10. (Picture book)

Never has the writing process been so accessible to young children and seemed such an exciting activity, within the reach of all. As a mother explains the craft of being a writer, the affection between her and her daughters is made explicit throughout the warmly welcoming illustrations. Try this book, and put the techniques in practice using Chris Van Allsburg's *The Mysteries of Harris Burdick.*

4.55   O'Connor, Jane. **Lulu Goes to Witch School.** Illustrated by Emily Arnold McCully. Harper and Row/I Can Read Books, 1987. Ages 4–8. (Picture book)

Lulu likes everything about witch school, except know-it-all Sandy. Young readers will relish the witchy turnarounds, where a black spidery dress and a haglike teacher named Miss Slime are considered beautiful. The cheery drawings enhance this early reading book.

4.56   O'Connor, Jane. **Sir Small and the Dragonfly.** Illustrated by John O'Brien. Random House/Step into Reading, 1988. Ages 5–9. (Picture book)

Large print and simple text are components of this beginning-reading series. In this book, Sir Small from the town of Pee Wee attempts to save a lady in distress. Will his plan work?

4.57 O'Connor, Jane. **The Teeny Tiny Woman.** Illustrated by R. W. Alley. Random House/Step into Reading Books, 1986. Ages 3–7. (Picture book)

The extremely simple vocabulary and the large print effectively retell a familiar folktale about a teeny tiny woman and her maneuverings in a miniature world. Animated full-page drawings colorfully depict her suspenseful encounter with an intruder. Intended for the very young reader, the repetitive pattern invites prediction. *Children's Choice.*

4.58 O'Connor, Jim, and Jane O'Connor. **The Ghost in Tent 19.** Illustrated by Charles Robinson. Random House/Stepping Stone Books, 1988. Ages 6–9. (Picture book)

Danny can sense things that just might happen in the future, and he has exciting, and sometimes scary, dreams. At camp, he and his friends have the usual adventures, but they also are called by the ghost of Captain Blood's son to help him join his famous father. The short sentences and controlled vocabulary help make this adventure mystery an easy-reading first chapter book. *Children's Choice.*

4.59 Oechsli, Kelly. **Mice at Bat.** Illustrated by the author. Harper and Row/I Can Read Books, 1986. Ages 6–9. (Picture book)

Two mice teams play a zany game of baseball long after the fans have gone home from the ballpark. Many surprises are included in this beginning reader. This is an imaginative, funny story that will hold the listener's and reader's attention.

4.60 Osborne, Mary Pope. **Mo to the Rescue.** Illustrated by DyAnne DiSalvo-Ryan. Dial Books for Young Readers/Easy-to-Read Books, 1985. Ages 5–7. (Picture book)

This easy-to-read book includes four short stories featuring Mo, the good-hearted beaver who is sheriff of a community of animals. Brightly colored watercolor illustrations suit the cheery humor of the stories.

4.61 Phillips, Joan. **Lucky Bear.** Illustrated by J. P. Miller. Random House/Step into Reading, 1986. Ages 4–6. (Picture book)

This beginning-reading book contains limited vocabulary, large print, and colorful illustrations. Lucky Bear moves from one adventure to another in this story until he finds a home.

4.62 Phillips, Joan. **My New Boy.** Illustrated by Lynn Munsinger. Random House/Step into Reading Books, 1986. Ages 5–6. (Picture book)

This paperback is written from the dog's point of view and is a beginning-to-read book that gives some criteria for dog care as preferred by a canine. The winsome full-color illustrations give reading clues to fledgling readers, who are also aided by the large print and simple vocabulary.

4.63 Phillips, Joan. **Tiger Is a Scaredy Cat.** Illustrated by Norman Gorbaty. Random House/Step into Reading Books, 1986. Ages 4–7. (Picture book)

A tiger who is such a scaredy cat that he fears mice turns out to be the hero of this simple story with a satisfying ending. The vocabulary is controlled, the sentences are short and repetitive, and the print is large; best of all, the story is interesting for a beginning reader. The full-page illustrations are a dramatic plus. *Children's Choice.*

4.64 Polushkin, Maria. **Kitten in Trouble.** Illustrated by Betsy Lewin. Bradbury Press, 1988. Ages 2–7. (Picture book)

Cartoonlike pictures with a watercolor wash illustrate the troublesome kitten's antics as it pounces again and again. The predictable pattern of the kitten's prancing makes this useful as a story lead for beginning writers.

4.65 Polushkin, Maria. **Who Said Meow?** Illustrated by Ellen Weiss. Bradbury Press, 1988. Ages 3–5. (Picture book)

Hearing a kitten's meow, a puppy looks everywhere to find out who is making that noise. He asks a bee, a dog, and other animals while the kitten stays out of sight. A few sentences per page and uncomplicated full-page color illustrations make this an easy-to-read book.

4.66 Rappaport, Doreen. **The Boston Coffee Party.** Illustrated by Emily Arnold McCully. Harper and Row/I Can Read Books, 1988. Ages 6–10. (Picture book)

This historical fiction for beginning readers is based on a true incident during the American Revolutionary War, as recorded by Abigail Adams in a letter to her husband, John Adams. Strong women plotted a way to show their displeasure with a merchant's high price for sugar in the 1760s.

4.67 Robins, Joan. **Addie Meets Max.** Illustrated by Sue Truesdell. Harper and Row/Early I Can Read Books, 1985. Ages 5–8. (Picture book)

Addie stubbornly announces to her mother that she will never befriend her new neighbor—a boy named Max. A "near-fatal" bike collision with Max seemingly cements Addie's hostile feelings. This true-to-life childhood dilemma is depicted humorously by cartoonlike characters in an easy-to-read book.

4.68 Rylant, Cynthia. **Henry and Mudge: The First Book of Their Adventures.** Illustrated by Suçie Stevenson. Bradbury Press, 1987. Ages 6–8. (Picture book)

Henry loves Mudge as much as a boy can love his dog. Skillfully written in beginning reader's vocabulary, each episode will ring true to children who love pets.

4.69 Rylant, Cynthia. **Henry and Mudge in Puddle Trouble: The Second Book of Their Adventures.** Illustrated by Suçie Stevenson. Bradbury Press, 1987. Ages 6–8. (Picture book)

A beginning reader's vocabulary is used expertly in each humorous, heartwarming, springtime episode about Henry and his dog, Mudge. Their adventures include playing in puddles, admiring the first crocus, and watching the new kittens next door.

4.70 Rylant, Cynthia. **Henry and Mudge in the Green Time: The Third Book in Their Adventures.** Illustrated by Suçie Stevenson. Bradbury Press, 1987. Ages 6–10. (Picture book)

Henry and his dog and best friend, Mudge, enjoy a picnic, the sprinkler, and an exciting hike in this beginning-to-read celebration of summertime fun.

4.71 Rylant, Cynthia. **Henry and Mudge in the Sparkle Days: The Fifth Book of Their Adventures.** Illustrated by Suçie Stevenson. Bradbury Press, 1988. Ages 4–7. (Picture book)

The comforting warmth of familial love infuses these adventures of a little boy and his big dog. Newly independent readers will enjoy the three short stories in this book, Rylant's fifth about Henry and Mudge. She proves it is possible to use simple language and yet write with feeling. This is a fitting companion to Arnold Lobel's Frog and Toad books or to Bernard Wiseman's books about Morris and Boris. *Children's Choice.*

4.72 Saunders, Susan. **The Daring Rescue of Marlon the Swimming Pig.** Illustrated by Gail Owens. Random House/Stepping Stone Books, 1987. Ages 5–8. (Picture book)

When Hartley and Justin learn their favorite attraction at the Aquarama, a swimming pig, is about to be sold for bacon, they become pignappers. Before their adventure, they had no idea how much food a growing pig could eat. It does not take them long to realize they are in serious trouble. Another in the Stepping Stone series, this hilarious book will keep kids turning the pages.

4.73 Schwartz, Alvin. **All of Our Noses Are Here, and Other Noodle Tales.** Illustrated by Karen Ann Weinhaus. Harper and Row/I Can Read Books, 1985. Ages 6–9.

This collection of five stories about silly people can be enjoyed by the beginning reader. Humorous illustrations add to the folklore from America, India, Japan, Korea, and the *Arabian Nights.*

4.74 Seymour, Peter. **What's at the Beach?** Illustrated by David A. Carter. Holt, Rinehart and Winston, 1985. Ages 3–6. (Picture book)

Answers to ''What's in the basket?'' ''What's inside the shell?'' and six other similarly direct questions are provided by cleverly designed and brilliantly colored, but fragile, pop-up illustrations. The repetition of a familiar sentence structure and the obvious clues in the illustrations make this book suitable for very early reading experiences.

4.75 Shreve, Susan. **Lily and the Runaway Baby.** Illustrated by Sue Truesdell. Random House/Stepping Stone Books, 1987. Ages 6–9.

When Lily, the middle child, begins to feel overlooked by her busy family, she decides to run away. Just in case they do not notice her absence, she takes the baby with her. This humorous paperback with short chapters is perfect for newly independent readers. Lighthearted illustrations set the tone.

4.76 Standiford, Natalie. **The Best Little Monkeys in the World.** Illustrated by Hilary Knight. Random House/Step into Reading Books, 1987. Ages 6–8.

While Judy, the baby-sitter, talks to her friends all night on the phone, two little monkeys, Marvin and Mary, do as they please—make banana shakes, leave the kitchen a disaster, let the bubble bath overflow, and watch horror movies on TV, to end the perfect night. Then, while the baby-sitter is asleep, Marvin and Mary clean up the entire house before their parents return to find them sleeping peacefully.

4.77 Thaler, Mike. **Hippo Lemonade.** Illustrated by Maxie Chambliss. Harper and Row/I Can Read Books, 1986. Ages 5–7. (Picture book)

Hippo shares a variety of adventures with animal friends, including making a wish, selling lemonade, and telling a scary story in this humorous book. The illustrations add further humor to the easy-to-read text.

4.78 Thaler, Mike. **Pack 109.** Illustrated by Normand Chartier. E. P. Dutton, 1988. Ages 4–7. (Picture book)

A pack of forest scouts tries to earn different merit badges in each of five short chapters. Children will chuckle at the group's ineptness and rejoice at the scouts' hard-won triumphs. This inviting story proves that controlled-vocabulary books do not have to be dull to do their job.

4.79 Thomson, Pat. **My Friend Mr. Morris.** Illustrated by Satoshi Kitamura. Delacorte Press/Share-a-Story Books, 1987. Ages 4–7.

The Share-a-Story series is meant to be a duet between parent and child, with the child's page easier to read than the parent's page. The story of Mr. Morris will delight Amelia Bedelia fans who relish Peggy Parrish's plays on words. Readers will enjoy the silliness of running shorts where the shorts do the running and a hat band which would need an especially big hat. Pat Thomson's free-flowing imaginative zaniness is matched by Satoshi Kitamura's whimsical illustrations.

4.80 Van Leeuwen, Jean. **More Tales of Amanda Pig.** Illustrated by Ann Schweninger. Dial Books for Young Readers/Easy-to-Read Books, 1985. Ages 5–8. (Picture book)

Amanda and her pig family have five new adventures involving noisy cousins who come to visit and stuffed animals that are given a bath. The illustrations, done with carbon pencils, colored pencils, and watercolor washes, will appeal to young readers.

4.81 Van Leeuwen, Jean. **Oliver, Amanda, and Grandmother Pig.** Illustrated by Ann Schweninger. Dial Books for Young Readers/Easy-to-Read Books, 1987. Ages 4–7.

Amanda, Oliver, and Grandmother Pig learn that each person's special needs help make life more pleasant as they figure out ways they can help each other. The warmth of the story shines through the beginning-to-read controlled vocabulary and short sentences.

4.82 Viorst, Judith. **The Good-Bye Book.** Illustrated by Kay Chorao. Atheneum, 1988. Ages 3–6. (Picture book)

A young boy tries every way possible to avoid staying home with the baby-sitter—including begging, bargaining, and threatening. As usual, Judith Viorst accurately captures the thoughts, feelings, and voice of a disgruntled child. Humorous pastel drawings are an apt complement to the spirited text. *Children's Choice.*

4.83 Whelan, Gloria. **Silver.** Illustrated by Stephen Marchesi. Random House/Stepping Stone Books, 1988. Ages 6–9. (Picture book)

Nine-year-old Rachel is given the runt of the litter when Ruff, Rachel's father's prized lead sled dog, has puppies. Rachel vows to take extra special care of Silver and to race just like her father. The land of Alaska is described vividly in this controlled-vocabulary first chapter book. *Children's Choice.*

4.84 Yep, Laurence. **The Curse of the Squirrel.** Illustrated by Dirk Zimmer. Random House/Stepping Stone Books, 1987. Ages 5–8.

Beware the full moon, when Shag the giant squirrel haunts the forest. A hilarious spoof of the horror story genre, this book is easy to read and is divided into short chapters. Those children who enjoyed the Bunnicula books of James Howe will rejoice to learn that the power of garlic once again defeats the power of darkness.

4.85   Yolen, Jane. **Commander Toad and the Dis-Asteroid.** Illustrated by Bruce Degen. Coward-McCann, 1985. Ages 6–9.

Spaceship Commander Toad and his crew of Star Warts are famous for keeping the galaxies safe. In this mission, they rush to save a flooded, bird-inhabited asteroid from destruction. Colorful characters, snappy text, silly humor, and a combination of three-color drawings and black-and-white sketches make this series a sure winner among the easy-reader set.

4.86   Yolen, Jane. **Commander Toad and the Intergalactic Spy.** Illustrated by Bruce Degen. Coward-McCann, 1986. Ages 6–9.

In another punny, funny story for beginning readers, Commander Toad is looking for his cousin, Agent 007½, whose real name is Tip Toad. Of course, to catch the cousin, the Commander sends him "through the tulips" in this story that is great for reading aloud.

4.87   Yolen, Jane. **Commander Toad and the Space Pirates.** Illustrated by Bruce Degen. Coward-McCann, 1987. Ages 6–9.

Beginning readers will enjoy Commander Toad's adventures in outer space as he and his fearless crew encounter a mean, green space pirate. The easy-to-read humor-filled prose lilts along rhythmically.

4.88   Ziefert, Harriet. **Harry Takes a Bath.** Illustrated by Mavis Smith. Viking Kestrel/Hello Reading Books, 1987. Ages 4–8. (Picture book)

Written for the beginning reader, this playful story of Harry Hippo and his adventures taking a bath will delight the youngest reader. *Children's Choice.*

4.89   Ziefert, Harriet. **Jason's Bus Ride.** Illustrated by Simms Taback. Viking Kestrel/Hello Reading Books, 1987. Ages 4–8. (Picture book)

Colorful illustrations and an easy-reading text go together well in this story of Jason's bus ride in the city. He is the only one who is able to solve the problem of a dog that will not move away from the front of the bus.

4.90 Ziefert, Harriet. **Mike and Tony: Best Friends.** Illustrated by Catherine Siracusa. Viking Kestrel/Hello Reading Books, 1987. Ages 4–8. (Picture book)

Mike and Tony do everything together—they eat, walk, and play together—until they have a fight. The simple text makes the story one for the beginning reader.

4.91 Ziefert, Harriet. **A New House for Mole and Mouse.** Illustrated by David Prebenna. Viking Kestrel/Hello Reading Books, 1987. Ages 4–8. (Picture book)

Mole and Mouse move into a new home and must try out everything—the piano, washtub, mixer, bathtub, clock, bed, and doorbell. The bold illustrations and the easy-reading text are appropriate for beginning readers.

4.92 Ziefert, Harriet. **Nicky Upstairs and Down.** Illustrated by Richard Brown. Viking Kestrel/Hello Reading Books, 1987. Ages 4–8. (Picture book)

New readers will enjoy the simple text and colorful illustrations of this story about Nicky the kitten. One day when Nicky's mother asks, "Nicky, where are you?" and she does not get a reply, she must look all over for him. Where can he be?

4.93 Ziefert, Harriet. **Say Good Night!** Illustrated by Catherine Siracusa. Viking Kestrel/Hello Reading Books, 1987. Ages 4–8. (Picture book)

The youngest reader will find out what's good about "good morning" (seeing and smelling) and "good night" (seeing, hearing, and feeling).

4.94 Ziefert, Harriet. **So Sick!** Illustrated by Carol Nicklaus. Random House/Step into Reading Books, 1985. Ages 5–8. (Picture book)

For the brief time a new reader benefits from controlled-vocabulary books, it is nice to have especially inviting ones. This book has large print, simple vocabulary, engaging illustrations, and an amusing story of Lewis, who is first sick himself and then plays doctor.

History of Language

Intermediate

4.95   Fisher, Leonard Everett. **Symbol Art: Thirteen** ☐s ○s △s
            from around the World. Illustrated by the author. Four Winds
            Press, 1985. Ages 9–13. (Picture book)

            Another elegant volume by Leonard Everett Fisher explores
            in clear graphics and few words, symbols that are used in
            such areas as astronomy, magic, music, shorthand, and
            weather forecasting. In an attempt to be complete in particu-
            lar categories, some pages contain more symbols than easily
            fit on the page, but interested young readers will be glad for
            all the information presented.

4.96   Perl, Lila. **Blue Monday and Friday the Thirteenth.** Illustrated
            by Erika Weihs. Clarion Books, 1986. Ages 10–12.

            Lila Perl presents the cultural and linguistic origins of the
            names of the days of the week and explains the superstitions
            connected with them. This unusual reference book will serve
            curious readers well.

4.97   Sperling, Susan Kelz. **Murfles and Wink-a-Peeps: Funny Old
            Words for Kids.** Illustrated by Tom Bloom. Clarkson N. Pot-
            ter, 1985. Ages 10–12.

            For that very limited audience of kids genuinely interested in
            words, this quirky collection of more than sixty old words
            will make engrossing reading. The pattern of presentation in-
            cludes a question using each word, a definition of the word,
            and another sentence linking the now-defined word to another
            word. These obsolete words are useful in teaching the con-
            cept that language changes.

Jokes, Riddles, and Puns

Intermediate

4.98   Adler, David A. **The Dinosaur Princess, and Other Prehistoric
            Riddles.** Illustrated by Loreen Leedy. Holiday House, 1988.
            Ages 6–10. (Picture book)

            "Why did Brachiosaurus have such a long neck?" "Because
            his head was so far from the rest of him." This is just one of

the numerous riddles and jokes about dinosaurs and cave dwellers. There is only one joke per page, but each one is a gem. Each has an accompanying black-and-white line drawing to bring the punch line home.

4.99 Adler, David A. **The Purple Turkey, and Other Thanksgiving Riddles.** Illustrated by Marylin Hafner. Holiday House, 1986. Ages 6–9. (Picture book)

Both original and well-worn riddles relating to the Pilgrims, turkeys, cranberries, and corn are found in this holiday book. The format features one joke per page, with humorous pen-and-ink cartoon-style drawings in which characters sometimes supplement the joke by spouting dialogue.

4.100 Adler, David A. **Remember Betsy Floss, and Other Colonial American Riddles.** Illustrated by John Wallner. Holiday House, 1987. Ages 8–10. (Picture book)

Colonial life and the American Revolution are the subject of this illustrated collection of really hilarious riddles. *Children's Choice.*

4.101 Adler, David A. **The Twisted Witch, and Other Spooky Riddles.** Illustrated by Victoria Chess. Holiday House, 1985. Ages 6–9. (Picture book)

Young children will have many laughs with these riddles and accompanying illustrations about ghosts, witches, vampires, werewolves, and other scary creatures, especially at Halloween.

4.102 Bernstein, Joanne E., and Paul Cohen. **Grand-Slam Riddles.** Illustrated by Meyer Seltzer. Albert Whitman, 1988. Ages 7–10. (Picture book)

This fine, cartoon-style illustrated collection of riddles and jokes about baseball players, teams, and other aspects of the game of baseball should appeal to young children who are interested in the sport.

4.103 Bernstein, Joanne E., and Paul Cohen. **Happy Holiday Riddles to You!** Illustrated by Meyer Seltzer. Albert Whitman, 1985. Ages 6–9.

One hundred riddles about religious and secular holidays are presented in this book designed especially for the younger reader. Black-and-white illustrations have been brightened with orange to add zip to the text.

4.104　Rosenbloom, Joseph. **The Funniest Knock-Knock Book Ever!** Illustrated by Hans Wilhelm. Sterling, 1986. Ages 4–9.

Open the door to Eddie ("Eddie-body home?"), Anita ("Anita tell some knock-knock jokes"), and other visitors. This hysterical, full-color collection of over forty knock-knock jokes will tickle even the youngest joke lover.

4.105　Swann, Brian. **A Basket Full of White Eggs.** Illustrated by Ponder Goembel. Orchard Books, 1988. Ages 6–8.

Fourteen riddles from as many places around the world challenge the reader with more than guessing the answer. The language tickles the imagination, and the full-color paintings offer details of the geography of the country and its culture, as well as the answer to the riddle. The riddles are organized to move the reader through a typical day from sunrise to night time.

Language Play

Primary

4.106　Hawkins, Colin, and Jacqui Hawkins. **Jen the Hen.** Illustrated by the authors. G. P. Putnam's Sons, 1985. Ages 4–8.

This humorously illustrated flip-the-page rhyming story follows the format of the author's previous tale, *Pat the Cat*. In this book, different key words ending in *-en* are created with a new consonant with each turn of the cutaway pages. The simple story is enhanced by cartoon-bubble comments from two caterpillars who follow Jen. This book will be enjoyed as a read-aloud book and by beginning readers. Other titles in this format are *Mig the Pig*, *Fog the Dog*, and *Zug the Bug*.

Intermediate

4.107　Moscovitch, Rosalie. **What's in a Word? A Dictionary of Daffy Definitions.** Illustrated by Andy Myer. Houghton Mifflin, 1985. Ages 10–13.

Definitions that make no sense, except for the sounds when said aloud, will tickle children's funny bones. For example: "Balsam: Cry a Little," is a definition based on words; in contrast, "Kidnap" is defined by an illustration that shows a little goat dozing at the feet of a larger one. Two to four words are defined on each page, including such common words as *cabinet*, but more often the terms include uncommon words like *bulwark*. The conventional definitions are given at the end of the book.

4.108 Terban, Marvin. **Guppies in Tuxedos: Funny Eponyms.** Illustrated by Giulio Maestro. Clarion Books, 1988. Ages 9–12.

Marvin Terban introduces young readers to eponyms, words that come from people's names. Arranged in categories ranging from food to measurements, the origins of one hundred words are explained and illustrated by Giulio Maestro's clever cartoons that further supplement the text. Although the text is relatively simple, readers of all ages will enjoy this clever approach to etymology. *Children's Choice.*

4.109 Terban, Marvin. **Mad as a Wet Hen! And Other Funny Idioms.** Illustrated by Giulio Maestro. Clarion Books, 1987. Ages 7–12. (Picture book)

Idioms can be amusing and sometimes confusing to elementary-aged children. This reference book, with a multitude of demonstrative illustrations, is a fun and informative sourcebook for children interested in finding out the source of various idioms, such as *in the pink*, *red tape*, and *apple of his eye*. The more than one hundred idioms are arranged in categories and cross-referenced as well, which makes this language book particularly useful.

Vocabulary

Primary

4.110 Heller, Ruth. **A Cache of Jewels, and Other Collective Nouns.** Illustrated by the author. Grosset and Dunlap, 1987. Ages 4–9. (Picture book)

Such collective nouns as a *bevy* of beauties and a *muster* of peacocks are the subject in this picture book. Large, detailed illustrations in vivid color will invite commentary from read-

ers. Each illustration of multiples is accompanied by its re-
spective collective noun, and the rhyming text is supplemented by a short section at the end of the book giving
additional information. The only regret is that there seem to
be too few collective nouns illustrated.

4.111   Wyllie, Stephen. **There Was an Old Woman.** Illustrated by
Maureen Roffey. Harper and Row, 1985. Ages 4–8. (Picture
book)

The little old woman cannot sleep at night because of the
noisy mouse who lives in her thatched roof. She buys a marmalade cat who gets rid of the mouse and takes up residence
in the roof, but the old woman still cannot sleep because of
the noise. The add-on pattern of the story continues and is
complemented by bright full-page illustrations. Certain vocabulary words are written on flaps that readers can lift to view
the picture underneath as a confirmation of the meaning of
the words.

Writing

Primary

4.112   Ahlberg, Janet, and Allan Ahlberg. **The Jolly Postman; or,
Other People's Letters.** Illustrated by the authors. Little,
Brown, 1986. Ages 6–10.

The Jolly Postman delivers letters to favorite characters from
folktales and fairy tales. Each letter, card, or invitation is
tucked into an envelope bound into the book, and its message
is appropriate for the particular folk character. Children will
enjoy intercepting the mail to get a peek into the private lives
of the familiar characters. Part of the fun is guessing who are
the receivers and senders. *Notable Children's Trade Book in
the Language Arts.*

Intermediate

4.113   Benjamin, Carol Lea. **Writing for Kids.** Thomas Y. Crowell,
1985. Ages 9–12.

In brief enough compass to hold students' attention and using
an enthusiastic, supportive tone, the author gets kids started
writing and talks about the process itself. She suggests how to

get ideas for writing and explains how to work from the sentence to the paragraph to the finished story or essay. She is suitably eclectic, acknowledging that writers work in many different ways.

4.114 Mabery, D. L. **Tell Me about Yourself: How to Interview Anyone from Your Friends to Famous People.** Lerner Publications, 1985. Ages 9–12.

Here is a useful tool for language arts teachers interested in helping children understand that not all reports have to be based on library research. Seven brief chapters move chronologically from an exposition of what an interview is, through the steps in preparing for and conducting an interview, to a final chapter on applying the material acquired in an interview. A glossary of terms is included.

4.115 Martin, Bill, Jr., and John Archambault. **Listen to the Rain.** Illustrated by James Endicott. Henry Holt, 1988. Ages 7–12. (Picture book)

The sounds of the rain in all its moods are mirrored in onomatopoetic language which cries out to be read aloud. Drenched pastels complete a striking presentation, and although the curricular applications are obvious, the book deserves to be shared primarily as a work of art and language.

Recommended Books Published before 1985

Adkins, Jan. *Letterbox: The Art and History of Letters.* Walker, 1981. 8–11.

Amon, Aline. *Talking Hands: Indian Sign Language.* Doubleday, 1968. 8–10.

Brewton, Sara, et al., comps. *My Tang's Tungled and Other Ridiculous Situations: Humorous Poems.* Illustrated by Graham Booth. Thomas Y. Crowell, 1973. 8–12.

Brown, Marc. *Finger Rhymes.* E. P. Dutton, 1980. 3–6.

Charlip, Remy. *Arm in Arm: A Collection of Connections, Endless Tails, Reiterations, and Other Echolalia.* Parents Magazine Press, 1969. 6 and up.

Charlip, Remy, and Mary Beth. *Handtalk: An ABC of Finger Spelling and Sign Language.* Illustrated by George Ancona. Four Winds Press, 1980. 6–12.

de Regniers, Beatrice Schenk. *It Does Not Say Meow, and Other Animal Riddle Rhymes.* Illustrated by Paul Galdone. Clarion Books, 1972. 4–7.

Fischer, Leonard Everett. *Alphabet Art: 13 ABC's from around the World.* Four Winds Press, 1978. 9–12.

Greenfield, Howard. *Books: From Writer to Reader.* Thomas Y. Crowell, 1976. 10 and up.

Gwynne, Fred. *The King Who Rained.* Windmill Books, 1970. 7–9.

Leach, Maria. *Riddle Me, Riddle Me, Ree.* Illustrated by William Wiesner. Viking Press, 1970. 9–12.

Lobel, Arnold. *Days with Frog and Toad.* Harper and Row, 1979. 4–8.

———. *Grasshopper on the Road.* Harper and Row, 1978. 4–8.

———. *Mouse Soup.* Harper and Row, 1977. 4–8.

Maestro, Betsy, and Giulio Maestro. *On the Go: A Book of Adjectives.* Crown, 1979. 3–6.

Maestro, Giulio. *What's a Frank Frank? Tasty Homograph Riddles.* Clarion Books, 1984. 7–10.

Marshall, Edward. *Three by the Sea.* Illustrated by James Marshall. Dial Books for Young Readers, 1981. 4–7.

Minarik, Else Holmelund. *A Kiss for Little Bear.* Illustrated by Maurice Sendak. Harper and Row, 1968. 4–8.

Parish, Peggy. *Amelia Bedelia.* Illustrated by Fritz Siebel. Harper and Row, 1963. 4–8.

Patz, Nancy. *Moses Supposes His Toeses Are Roses, and Seven Other Silly Old Rhymes.* Harcourt Brace Jovanovich, 1983. 5–8.

Pomerantz, Charlotte. *The Piggy in the Puddle.* Illustrated by James Marshall. Macmillan, 1974. 4–6.

Rand, Ann, and Paul Rand. *Sparkle and Spin.* Harcourt, Brace and World, 1957. 5–8.

Schwartz, Alvin. *The Cat's Elbow and Other Secret Languages.* Illustrated by Margot Zemach. Farrar, Straus and Giroux, 1982. 8–12.

Seuss, Dr. *Horton Hears a Who!* Random House, 1954. 5–8.

Steig, William. *c d b!* Simon and Schuster, 1968. 8 and up.

Udry, Janice May. *Thump and Plunk.* Illustrated by Ann Schweninger. Harper and Row, 1981. 4–7.

Van Allsburg, Chris. *The Mysteries of Harris Burdick.* Houghton Mifflin, 1984. 9–12.

Wood, Audrey. *The Napping House.* Illustrated by Don Wood. Harcourt Brace Jovanovich, 1984. 3–6.

5 Poetry

Primary

5.1   Bauer, Caroline Feller, editor. **Snowy Day: Stories and Poems.** Illustrated by Margot Tomes. J. B. Lippincott, 1986. Ages 4–8.

The wonders of winter's white are explored through stories and poems by recognized authors, easy recipes and crafts, snow trivia, and complementary black-and-white sketches. A bibliography of "snow-theme" books is appended. *Children's Choice.*

5.2   Chorao, Kay. **The Baby's Good Morning Book.** Illustrated by the author. E. P. Dutton, 1986. Ages 2–6. (Picture book)

Brightly hued, full-color illustrations in watercolors, colored pencils, and ink create joyous wake-up images to accompany twenty-six short poems and rhymes by such poets as Eleanor Farjeon, Walter Crane, A. A. Milne, Gertrude Stein, and William Wordsworth.

5.3   dePaola, Tomie, compiler. **Tomie dePaola's Book of Poems.** Illustrated by the compiler. G. P. Putnam's Sons, 1988. Ages 5–12.

Strong rhythms, playful language, images children understand, and subjects children care about are found in these eighty-six poems. This collection, of interest at all times of the year and for some special occasions, includes poets as varied as Robert Louis Stevenson, Dorothy Aldis, X. J. Kennedy, and David McCord, as well as a few poems from non-English-speaking cultures. The illustrations show children of various cultures and provide fine visual accompaniment to this collection, which will be important for all primary and preschool classrooms. The illustrations are varied in mood and color to fit each particular poem.

5.4   Livingston, Myra Cohn, compiler. **New Year's Poems.** Illustrated by Margot Tomes. Holiday House, 1987. Ages 4–8.

This collection of old and new poems celebrates the New Year. Well-done illustrations complement this fine anthology. Included are "January One" by David McCord, "Beginning a New Year Means" by Ruth Whitman, and "The Bell Hill," a poem of Cornish superstitions about New Year's Day by Julia Fields.

Intermediate

5.5   Hopkins, Lee Bennett, compiler. **Click, Rumble, Roar: Poems about Machines.** Photographs by Anna Held Audette. Thomas Y. Crowell, 1987. Ages 8–12.

Included are eighteen poems about such machinery as an automated car wash, parking-lot lift, garbage truck, subway train, lawnmower, washing machine, and calculator, with a black-and-white photograph accompanying each poem. Works by Myra Cohn Livingston, Eve Merriam, Leland B. Jacobs, David McCord, and eight other contemporary poets are presented. *Children's Choice.*

5.6   Janeczko, Paul B., compiler. **This Delicious Day.** Orchard Books, 1987. Ages 9–12.

Sixty-five poems, including works by Arnold Adoff, Karla Kuskin, William Stafford, and Valerie Worth, provide nourishment for the senses, evoking memories of daily experiences or sharpening the senses to become aware of events most often ignored. Most of the poems convey the images using precise words and distinctive arrangements rather than using the rhythms and rhymes typical of poems used in elementary school. Teachers will want to read these poems aloud to encourage students to savor the sounds and to strengthen their responses.

5.7   Livingston, Myra Cohn, compiler. **Poems for Jewish Holidays.** Illustrated by Lloyd Bloom. Holiday House, 1986. Ages 10–12.

Sixteen commissioned poems offer images of twelve Jewish holidays, including Yom Kippur, Purim, and Shabbat. The poems evoke personal responses and memories, but the emotions stirred are universal. The book is elegant in design, and the black-and-white illustrations heighten the impact of emotion and the depth of reflection.

5.8 Livingston, Myra Cohn, compiler. **Thanksgiving Poems.** Illustrated by Stephen Gammell. Holiday House, 1985. Ages 9–12.

Sixteen poems, including Indian songs, traditional hymns, and original works by contemporary poets, explore Thanksgiving themes. Thanksgiving is viewed as a holiday, as a time for customs and symbols, and as a personal expression of joy, caring, and gratefulness. Finely executed pencil drawings, with blue and brown washes, illustrate each poem.

All Ages

5.9 Chapman, Jean, compiler. **Cat Will Rhyme with Hat: A Book of Poems.** Illustrated by Peter Parnall. Charles Scribner's Sons/Books for Young Readers, 1986. All ages.

Sixty elegant poems, many pertaining to cats, appear in a slim volume celebrating language, with pencil sketches decorating the sections. The poems roll off the tongue in this delightful and witty collection. Elizabeth Coatsworth, Eleanor Farjeon, T. S. Eliot, and J.R.R. Tolkien are represented in this collection of poems selected from books that are no longer in print.

5.10 de Regniers, Beatrice Schenk, Eva Moore, Mary Michaels White, and Jan Carr, compilers. **Sing a Song of Popcorn: Every Child's Book of Poems.** Illustrated by Marcia Brown, Leo and Diane Dillon, Richard Egielski, Trina Schart Hyman, Arnold Lobel, Maurice Sendak, Marc Simont, and Margot Zemach. Scholastic, 1988. All ages.

This splendid collection contains 128 poems by such renowned poets as Robert Louis Stevenson, Robert Frost, Emily Dickinson, Vachel Lindsay, Edward Lear, Ogden Nash, A. A. Milne, and Carl Sandburg and by such contemporary favorites as David McCord, Eve Merriam, Langston Hughes, Myra Cohn Livingston, Shel Silverstein, and John Ciardi. Illustrations to accompany the poems are by nine Caldecott Medal artists. The book is perfect to be read by one child alone, to be shared with a friend or parent, or to be used in a classroom of children. Revised edition of *Poems Children Will Sit Still For. ALA Notable Children's Book.*

5.11   Hopkins, Lee Bennett, compiler. **Creatures.** Illustrated by
Stella Ormai. Harcourt Brace Jovanovich, 1985. Ages 6–12.

Witches, elves, mermaids, ghosts, and dracula vines—these
are just a few of the many magical and supernatural creatures
featured in eighteen rhyming poems. The poems begin with
the well-known characters and move to those whose prime
reason for being might be to scare. The comforting Cornish
litany that keeps us from things that go bump in the night
completes the experience, bringing the reader back to safe
ground. Full-page pen-and-ink illustrations complement each
poem.

5.12   Larrick, Nancy, compiler. **Cats Are Cats.** Illustrated by Ed
Young. Philomel Books, 1988. All ages.

"If you've lived with a cat, you have come under the spell."
So begins Nancy Larrick's collection of cat poems which,
along with Ed Young's illustrations, will cast a spell on the
reader. Such poets as Eve Merriam, T. S. Eliot, John Ciardi,
and Jane Yolen introduce moonlight cats, cats strayed and
lost, elegant cats, and alley cats in this exquisite integration
of poems and art. The book could be the foundation for a
readers theatre production featuring cats.

5.13   Livingston, Myra Cohn, compiler. **Cat Poems.** Illustrated by
Trina Schart Hyman. Holiday House, 1987. Ages 5–12.

This book celebrates all that collectively comprises the
essence of cathood: cats hunting, washing, sleeping, and
playing. The details of the nineteen poems, written by such
well-known poets as John Ciardi, Elizabeth Coatsworth, and
Valerie Worth, are each expanded by the black-and-white
drawings.

5.14   Livingston, Myra Cohn, compiler. **Poems for Mothers.** Illustrated by Deborah Kogan Ray. Holiday House, 1988. All
ages.

Twenty poems from a variety of cultures and time periods
present ideas about mothers, the essential person whom we
all treasure but sometimes overlook. These fresh looks at
mothers' jobs, responsibilities, and love for their families enrich and strengthen children's appreciation of their mothers.

Individual Poets

Primary

5.15   Brown, Ruth. **Ladybug, Ladybug.** Illustrated by the author. E. P. Dutton, 1988. Ages 2–8. (Picture book)

This extended, beautifully illustrated version of the familiar "Ladybug, ladybug, fly away home . . ." poem can be enjoyed over and over by even the youngest child.

5.16   Coleridge, Sara. **January Brings the Snow: A Book of Months.** Illustrated by Jenni Oliver. Dial Books for Young Readers, 1986. Ages 3–6.

"January brings the snow, Makes our feet and fingers glow," while "February brings the rain, Thaws the frozen lake again." Every month has its own couplet that describes a special characteristic of that time of year. Each two-page watercolor illustration captures a cherished memory of the month.

5.17   de Regniers, Beatrice Schenk. **This Big Cat and Other Cats I've Known.** Illustrated by Alan Daniel. Crown, 1985. Ages 5–10.

A wide variety of poems—sad, funny, thoughtful, rollicking, short, and long—celebrate cats. Soft watercolor wash illustrations in shades of black and gray convincingly portray the many moods of cats.

5.18   de Regniers, Beatrice Schenk. **The Way I Feel . . . Sometimes.** Illustrated by Susan Meddaugh. Clarion Books, 1988. Ages 6–10. (Picture book)

Eleven poems suggest the variety and depth of emotion felt by boys and girls, beginning with feeling mean and nasty and finally feeling all right after all. Full-color drawings highlight each emotion.

5.19   Dragonwagon, Crescent. **Half a Moon and One Whole Star.** Illustrated by Jerry Pinkney. Macmillan, 1986. Ages 5–8. (Picture book)

Full-color watercolor illustrations accompany a poem to lull Susan to sleep. It is a poem itemizing the night sounds of animals, a ship in the harbor, a musician on his way to his night job, and morning glories closing tightly to "conceal their blueness through the night," and ending with "Yes sleep, Susan, sleep." *Coretta Scott King Award* (for illustrations).

5.20   Fisher, Aileen. **The House of a Mouse.** Illustrated by Joan Sandin. Harper and Row/Charlotte Zolotow Books, 1988. Ages 3–7.

This collection of poems is exactly like the subject itself: small, trim, sweet. The poems should be read aloud in a tiny voice because all are about mice. A young listener on a lap will appreciate the flowing rhythm and rhyme and the direct images. The delicately colored drawings of mice and their world are appealing.

5.21   Fisher, Aileen. **When It Comes to Bugs.** Illustrated by Chris and Bruce Degen. Harper and Row, 1986. Ages 5–10.

This book will capitalize on children's fascination with creeping, crawling things of all sorts. No one is a more masterful writer of the kind of traditionally rhymed, rhythmic poems that are included here than is Aileen Fisher. The scratchboard drawings are enriched with color overlays.

5.22   Greenfield, Eloise. **Under the Sunday Tree.** Illustrated by Amos Ferguson. Harper and Row, 1988. Ages 5–10. (Picture book)

The bold, bright, primitive-style paintings immediately attract a reader's attention with their vibrancy, energy, and good spirits. The accompanying poems turn out to be a perfect match, creating images just as alive. Poems and illustrations offer a loving glimpse of life in the Bahamas, but they are really about special moments all of us share: a girl dreaming, boys fishing, a policeman directing traffic. *ALA Notable Children's Book* and *Coretta Scott King Honor Book* (for illustrations).

5.23   Hooper, Patricia. **A *Bundle* of Beasts.** Illustrated by Mark Steele. Houghton Mifflin, 1987. Ages 7–10.

Twenty-five clever poems about animals in groups are presented with gusto. From a *drift* of hogs to a *sleuth* of bears, the names of the groups are authentic. The poet's imagination takes over from there, and fun is the result. Black-and-white sketches accent the humor of the poetry.

5.24   Hubbell, Patricia. **The Tigers Brought Pink Lemonade.** Illustrated by Ju-Hong Chen. Atheneum, 1988. Ages 6–9. (Picture book)

Entirely about animals, these poems show variety in form and meter. The placement of text and artwork also varies, giving the book an inviting, informal appearance.

5.25   Krauss, Ruth. **Big and Little.** Illustrated by Mary Szilagyi. Scholastic/Hardcover Books, 1987. Ages 5–7. (Picture book)

The love that enables big things to encompass little things with warmth and security is the message given in each line of this reassuring poem. The full-color illustrations completely fill each page.

5.26   Lear, Edward. **The Owl and the Pussycat.** Illustrated by Lorinda Bryan Cauley. G. P. Putnam's Sons, 1986. Ages 5–8. (Picture book)

The famous verse by Edward Lear is pleasantly illustrated in full color. Large bold type and minimal text on each page make this picture book available to a young reader who reads well. Illustrations are primarily scenic, with a lush sea and with an owl and cat that have character. Recommended for the primary grades.

5.27   Lear, Edward. **The Owl and the Pussycat.** Illustrated by Paul Galdone. Clarion Books, 1987. Ages 3–6. (Picture book)

The owl and pussycat set sail on the *H.M.S. Nonsense*, and the rest is history. Paul Galdone's watercolors are lovely and full of fun. The large-sized text and large format make the book appropriate for story hour.

5.28   Lear, Edward. **The Owl and the Pussycat.** Illustrated by Claire Littlejohn. Harper and Row/Poetry Pop-Up Books, 1987. Ages 3–8. (Picture book)

This familiar poem receives fresh treatment with full-page color drawings and elaborate, imaginative pop-ups on every other page.

5.29   Little, Lessie Jones. **Children of Long Ago.** Illustrated by Jan Spivey Gilchrist. Philomel Books, 1988. Ages 5–8.

Seventeen poems focus on the everyday events of children who lived in the early 1900s. Readers discover that they share many of the emotions of those long-ago children, even if the daily tasks are sometimes quite different. Full-color illustrations accompany each poem.

5.30   Livingston, Myra Cohn. **Celebrations.** Illustrated by Leonard Everett Fisher. Holiday House, 1985. Ages 5–10.

Myra Cohn Livingston and Leonard Everett Fisher collaborate again, this time to present a brilliant panorama of American holidays. Martin Luther King Day, Labor Day, Passover, and thirteen others are celebrated through imaginative original verse and vivid acrylic paintings, richly reproduced by a special laser scanning technique. The poems can easily serve as models for writing. A delight for all!

5.31   Livingston, Myra Cohn. **Higgledy-Piggledy: Verses and Pictures.** Illustrated by Peter Sis. Margaret K. McElderry Books, 1986. Ages 4–9. (Picture book)

In verse, the author describes all the positive characteristics of Higgledy-Piggledy, who takes out the garbage, drinks healthful juices, and saves every penny, only to end each praise by wishing him bad luck. Carefully illustrated, the verses will delight the youngest readers.

5.32   Lobel, Arnold. **Whiskers and Rhymes.** Illustrated by the author. Greenwillow Books, 1985. Ages 5–9.

Arnold Lobel is up to his usual high standard here with his witty verse and pleasantly detailed pictures. Among other characters, he introduces readers to the old woman who stitches the sun to the highest hill, and to Clara, whose curls were scared into standing up like a picket fence. These are not commonplace characters, but rather exceptional or even eccentric in the tradition of those Mother Goose characters from whom they descend. *Children's Choice.*

5.33   Merriam, Eve. **Blackberry Ink.** Illustrated by Hans Wilhelm. William Morrow, 1985. Ages 6–10.

The poems in this collection feature an impressive variety of both form (different rhyme schemes and line lengths) and topic (real and fantasy). Included are serious poems, such as "Cat's Tongue," and nonsense verse, such as "I'm sweet, Says the beet." Eve Merriam's ability to observe aspects of daily life, such as the common tendency to save new things instead of using them, is as sharp as in previous collections of her poems. The accompanying watercolors are fresher because of the generous use of white space. *Children's Choice.*

5.34   Merriam, Eve. **You Be Good and I'll Be Night: Jump-on-the-Bed Poems.** Illustrated by Karen Lee Schmidt. Morrow Junior Books, 1988. Ages 3–9. (Picture book)

This lively collection of whimsically illustrated poems is especially for the active, exuberant young child.

5.35   Nerlove, Miriam. **I Made a Mistake.** Illustrated by the author. Margaret K. McElderry Books, 1985. Ages 5–9.

Engaging rhymed couplets based on a jump-rope rhyme combine with delightful drawings to expand the concept in the title. "I went to the laundry to wash my socks, I made a mistake . . ." (turn the page) "and washed a fox." The same adventuresome, contemporary child is seen in a new situation with each couplet, undaunted by the creatures previously encountered.

5.36   Prelutsky, Jack. **Tyrannosaurus Was a Beast: Dinosaur Poems.** Illustrated by Arnold Lobel. Greenwillow Books, 1988. Ages 4–10. (Picture book)

This carefully, colorfully illustrated collection features fourteen humorous dinosaur poems about Tyrannosaurus, Brachiosaurus, Leptopterygius, Stegosaurus, Deinonychus, Ankylosaurus, Diplodocus, Coelophysis, Triceratops, Corythosaurus, Allosaurus, Iguanodon, Quetzalcoatlus, and Seismosaurus.

5.37   Stevenson, Robert Louis. **Block City.** Illustrated by Ashley Wolff. E. P. Dutton, 1988. Ages 3–6. (Picture book)

The classic rhyme about a young child's self-created kingdom of blocks is enlivened with bold-toned wash and linoleum-block paintings. The poem, with its subject of creative play, is as appealing and relevant today as it was when first published generations ago.

5.38   van Vorst, M. L. **A Norse Lullaby.** Illustrated by Margot Tomes. Lothrop, Lee and Shepard Books, 1988. Ages 3–8. (Picture book)

First published in the *St. Nicholas Magazine* in 1897, this Norse poem tells of a mother and children who await the father's return one winter evening. The illustrations add a wonderful quality to the book.

5.39 Westcott, Nadine Bernard. **The Lady with the Alligator Purse.** Illustrated by the author. Little, Brown/Joy Street Books, 1988. Ages 3–9. (Picture book)

This illustrated version of the old jump-rope rhyme/nonsense verse begins "Miss Lucy had a baby, His name was Tiny Tim, She put him in the bathtub, To see if he could swim. . . ." *Children's Choice.*

Intermediate

5.40 Adoff, Arnold. **Sports Pages.** Illustrated by Steve Kuzma. J. B. Lippincott, 1986. Ages 9–12. (Picture book)

Poetry without rhyme describes real and imagined experiences of young male and female athletes. Each poem authentically captures a particular sport and evokes feelings sure to be recognized by anyone who is or dreams of being an athlete.

5.41 Browning, Robert (revised by Terry Small). **The Pied Piper of Hamelin.** Illustrated by the reviser. Harcourt Brace Jovanovich/Gulliver Books, 1988. Ages 8–12.

Revised to remove some of Robert Browning's obscure syntax and vocabulary, this version of the Middle Ages legend is highly readable. The black pen-and-ink drawings on the left-hand page detail the verse appearing on the opposite page, making this a book to linger over.

5.42 Coltman, Paul. **Tog the Ribber; or, Granny's Tale.** Illustrated by Gillian McClure. Farrar, Straus and Giroux, 1985. Ages 10–12. (Picture book)

Descended from Lewis Carroll's "Jabberwocky," this rich language—which must be read aloud to be appreciated—is visually dressed with illustrations of minute, engaging complexity. The poem describes strange creatures, shown by the artist in elaborate framed illustrations that sometimes escape the frame and that always beckon the eye to look more deeply to understand the fantasy. *ALA Notable Children's Book.*

5.43   de Regniers, Beatrice Schenk. **A Week in the Life of Best Friends, and Other Poems of Friendship.** Illustrated by Nancy Doyle. Scholastic, 1988. Ages 10–13.

Nine poems explore the joys, frustrations, and exuberance of friendship. The simple black-and-white line drawings heighten the whimsy of each poem. Students might respond to the direct honesty of these poems by writing some of their own.

5.44   Frost, Robert. **Birches.** Illustrated by Ed Young. Henry Holt, 1988. Ages 8–12. (Picture book)

The dreaming and the drama of Robert Frost's poem "Birches" are conveyed in a picture-book format. Each image is supported with a painting in muted browns, blues, greens, and yellows. The illustrations invite readers to stretch their imaginations and to contemplate their own personal meanings for Frost's words.

5.45   Kennedy, X. J. **The Forgetful Wishing Well: Poems for Young People.** Illustrated by Monica Incisa. Margaret K. McElderry Books, 1985. Ages 8–12.

With subtle twists of words, X. J. Kennedy's seventy poems spark the reader's imagery and tickle the funny bone. Growing pains, curious people and creatures, and wonders of the natural world are some of the topics in this collection of realistic and fanciful poems. Eight pen-and-ink drawings challenge the imagination.

5.46   Lewis, Claudia. **Long Ago in Oregon.** Illustrated by Joel Fontaine. Harper and Row/Charlotte Zolotow Books, 1987. Ages 8–12.

Seventeen poems reflect upon the places, people, and simple events of a young girl's life in an Oregon town during 1917 and 1918. The soft pencil drawings magnify the emotions recreated by each poem.

5.47   Livingston, Myra Cohn. **Earth Songs.** Illustrated by Leonard Everett Fisher. Holiday House, 1986. Ages 10–14.

Myra Cohn Livingston's celebration of the Earth through poetic text is fully complemented by Leonard Everett Fisher's acrylic illustrations. Water, land and all its formations, time and change, and Earth as one part of all the universe can be found in these pages. Enjoyable by themselves, the poems may also suggest writing and illustration activities to children. *Notable Children's Trade Book in the Language Arts.*

5.48   Livingston, Myra Cohn. **Sea Songs.** Illustrated by Leonard Everett Fisher. Holiday House, 1986. Ages 10–14.

This collection of poems honoring the sea evokes images of cresting waves, mermaids, and sunken ships. The poems are a bit more difficult than those in *Earth Songs*. Bold acrylic illustrations accompany the poems.

5.49   Livingston, Myra Cohn. **Space Songs.** Illustrated by Leonard Everett Fisher. Holiday House, 1988. Ages 10–14.

The heavens above us and outer space are the focus of this collection of evocative poems and full-color paintings done in acrylics. This is another in a series of poetry books paying tribute to the natural world.

5.50   Longfellow, Henry Wadsworth. **Paul Revere's Ride.** Illustrated by Nancy Winslow Parker. Greenwillow Books, 1985. Ages 9–12.

Longfellow's classic poem is dramatized with rich illustrations that add to the excitement of an important event in American history. The map, historical framework, and glossary are valuable concomitant resources.

5.51   Merriam, Eve. **Halloween ABC.** Illustrated by Lane Smith. Macmillan, 1987. Ages 8–12. (Picture book)

D is for demon, E is for elf, and F is for fiend in this collection of twenty-six Halloween poems, one for each letter of the alphabet. The scary, surprising, and spooky poems are perfectly complemented by the illustrations.

5.52   Simmie, Lois. **Auntie's Knitting a Baby.** Illustrated by Anne Simmie. Orchard Books, 1988. Ages 8–12.

Lois Simmie has created fifty-two clever poems that center on frustrations, fears, anxieties, and excitable events in our growing-up years. Interspersed throughout the collection are poems about Auntie's baby-to-be. The poems are humorous to adults and children alike.

5.53   Stevenson, Robert Louis (compiled by Michael Hague). **The Land of Nod, and Other Poems for Children.** Illustrated by the compiler. Henry Holt, 1988. Ages 9–12. (Picture book)

Michael Hague has selected thirty classic poems by Robert Louis Stevenson and presents these timeless poems in picture-book format with contemporary illustrations.

5.54 Turner, Ann. **Street Talk.** Illustrated by Catherine Stock. Houghton Mifflin, 1986. Ages 8–12.

This collection of poems about city life and experiences is best if read aloud to children. Neither the topics nor the imagery will attract the casual reader, despite the interesting vocabulary and figures of speech. In "Grandma," for example, we learn she knows all there is to know, including "the smell of magnolias so thick you could cut a dress out of it." *Notable Children's Trade Book in the Language Arts.*

5.55 Worth, Valerie. **Small Poems Again.** Illustrated by Natalie Babbitt. Farrar, Straus and Giroux, 1986. Ages 9–14.

Subjects ranging from jacks to the library to a heron become tightly written images seen anew. This collection of twenty-five exquisite, delicate poetic observations is decorated with pen-and-ink line drawings. *ALA Notable Children's Book* and *Notable Children's Trade Book in the Language Arts.*

All Ages

5.56 Carroll, Lewis. **The Walrus and the Carpenter.** Illustrated by Jane Breskin Zalben. Henry Holt, 1986. Ages 5–12.

The complete nonsense poem of the oyster-eating walrus and the carpenter is introduced as Tweedledee and Tweedledum introduce it to Alice in the classic tale *Through the Looking Glass.* The book ends with the exchange between Alice and Tweedledee and Tweedledum. Watercolor and ink illustrations are surprisingly realistic looking.

5.57 de la Mare, Walter (compiled by Catherine Brighton). **The Voice.** Illustrated by the compiler. Delacorte Press, 1986. All ages. (Picture book)

Catherine Brighton's lush, medieval-style illustrations enhance the thirteen de la Mare poems that range from "The Cupboard" to "Asleep" and that illustrate the range of the poet's style and subjects. Poems describe quiet scenes from daily life and imaginary happenings. This book would be excellent at any level of instruction, from the library story hour to a classroom studying the literary techniques of poetry.

5.58   Esbensen, Barbara Juster. **Words with Wrinkled Knees: Animal Poems.** Illustrated by John Stadler. Thomas Y. Crowell, 1986. Ages 6–12.

The words are better than the illustrations in this volume of nearly two dozen poems about such disparate animals as elephants and mosquitoes. The author, who also wrote the earlier *A Celebration of Bees* (about helping children write poetry), here shows her fine ear for the nuances of language. These poems both sound good and look good; children should look at the arrangement of the free verse on the page while they listen to the movement of the sounds.

5.59   Fleischman, Paul. **I Am Phoenix: Poems for Two Voices.** Illustrated by Ken Nutt. Harper and Row/Charlotte Zolotow Books, 1985. All ages.

The world of birds is presented through fifteen sensitive poems and unusual black-and-white drawings. These poems capture the essence of flight and the sounds and songs of selected birds. The poems in this unique book are designed to be read aloud as duets or savored in reading alone.

5.60   Fleischman, Paul. **Joyful Noise: Poems for Two Voices.** Illustrated by Eric Beddows. Harper and Row/Charlotte Zolotow Books, 1988. All ages.

In a companion volume to *I Am Phoenix*, the author celebrates insects in poetry. Each poem, which describes various attributes of a particular insect, is designed to be read aloud by two readers at once, with the two separate parts meshing as in a musical duet. Playful pencil illustrations reinforce the lively spirit of the poems. *ALA Notable Children's Book* and *Newbery Medal.*

5.61   Fleischman, Paul. **Rondo in C.** Illustrated by Janet Wentworth. Harper and Row/Charlotte Zolotow Books, 1988. All ages. (Picture book)

As a young piano student plays Beethoven's Rondo in C at her recital, we learn through the poetic text and the delicate pastel illustrations how each person in her audience responds to this evocative music. The book invites listening experiences with this and other musical masterpieces.

5.62 Giovanni, Nikki. **Spin a Soft Black Song.** Rev. ed. Illustrated by George Martins. Hill and Wang, 1985. All ages.

The revised edition of this book includes a wide variety of poetry about topics that are real in the lives of children. Poems tell about warm and loving relationships, sad and happy times, and important things. Surprise endings often generate chuckles. Abundant black-and-white illustrations depict black individuals in realistic settings.

5.63 Livingston, Myra Cohn. **There Was a Place, and Other Poems.** Margaret K. McElderry Books, 1988. All ages.

Myra Cohn Livingston's poems speak to children about the complexity of human relationships. While offering no solutions, the poems address the feelings children have about death, divorce, and separation. The patterns of the poems are strong models for children's writing.

5.64 Ryder, Joanne. **Inside Turtle's Shell, and Other Poems of the Field.** Illustrated by Susan Bonners. Macmillan, 1985. All ages.

Forty-one short, unrhymed poems create a subtle, continuous narrative chronicling a day in the meadow. "Black snake/ slides up/stealing/the sitting rock's/sun." "At the tip of the pond/muskrat stops,/swallowing/the coldness,/the brightness/ of stars." Soft black-and-white drawings extend each poem visually, evoking realistic elements of nature. Distinctive page layouts give contrast and variety to a collection of poems for sampling or reading aloud without interruption. *Outstanding Science Trade Book for Children.*

5.65 Thayer, Ernest Lawrence (with additional text by Patricia Polacco). **Casey at the Bat: A Ballad of the Republic, Sung in the Year 1888.** Illustrated by Patricia Polacco. G. P. Putnam's Sons, 1988. All ages.

Ernest Lawrence Thayer's story poem of Casey, published originally in 1888, comes to life in modern form. Patricia Polacco, through additional text at the beginning and end of this classic poem and through illustrations that are full of color, movement, humor, and jaunty postures, places Casey on a Little League field and surprises the reader with a twist at the end of her narrative.

Recommended Books Published before 1985

Adoff, Arnold. *Black Is Brown Is Tan*. Illustrated by Emily Arnold McCully. Harper and Row, 1973. 6–9.

———. *Eats: Poems*. Illustrated by Susan Russo. Lothrop, Lee and Shepard Books, 1979. 8–12.

———. *Make a Circle, Keep Us In: Poems for a Good Day*. Illustrated by Ronald Himler. Delacorte Press, 1975. 6–9.

Arbuthnot, May Hill, and Shelton Root, Jr., comps. *Time for Poetry*, 3d ed. Illustrated by Arthur Paul. Scott, Foresman, 1968. 5–12.

Bodecker, N. M. *It's Raining, Said John Twaining*. Macmillan, 1977. 4–8.

———. *Snowman Sniffles, and Other Verse*. Atheneum, 1983. 8–10.

Causley, Charles. *Figgie Hobbin*. Illustrated by Trina Schart Hyman. Walker, 1973. 8–12.

Ciardi, John. *I Met a Man*. Illustrated by Robert Osborn. Houghton Mifflin, 1961. 5–8.

———. *You Read to Me, I'll Read to You*. Illustrated by Edward Gorey. Harper and Row, 1961. 5–9.

Cole, William, ed. *Poem Stew*. Illustrated by Karen Ann Weinhaus. J. B. Lippincott, 1981. 8–12.

Dunning, Stephen, Edward Lueders, and Hugh Smith, comps. *Reflections on a Gift of Watermelon Pickle, and Other Modern Verse*. Lothrop, Lee and Shepard Books, 1967. 10–12.

Frost, Robert. *Stopping by Woods on a Snowy Evening*. Illustrated by Susan Jeffers. E. P. Dutton, 1978. 7–12.

Hopkins, Lee Bennett, comp. *A Song in Stone: City Poems*. Photographs by Anna Held Audette. Thomas Y. Crowell, 1983. 7–9.

Kennedy, X. J., and Dorothy M. Kennedy, eds. *Knock at a Star: A Child's Introduction to Poetry*. Illustrated by Karen Ann Weinhaus. Little, Brown, 1982. 8–12.

Kuskin, Karla. *Any Me I Want to Be*. Harper and Row, 1972. 6–9.

Lee, Dennis. *Garbage Delight*. Illustrated by Frank Newfeld. Houghton Mifflin, 1978. 8–10.

Livingston, Myra Cohn, ed. *Callooh! Callay! Holiday Poems for Young Readers*. Illustrated by Janet Stevens. Atheneum, 1978. 9–12.

———. *Listen, Children, Listen: An Anthology of Poems for the Very Young*. Illustrated by Trina Schart Hyman. Harcourt Brace Jovanovich, 1972. 6–10.

Lobel, Arnold. *The Book of Pigericks: Pig Limericks*. Harper and Row, 1983. 7–10.

McCord, David. *Every Time I Climb a Tree*. Illustrated by Marc Simont. Little, Brown, 1967. 5–9.

Merriam, Eve. *It Doesn't Always Have to Rhyme*. Illustrated by Malcolm Spooner. Atheneum, 1964. 9–12.

Moore, Lilian. *Sam's Place*. Illustrated by Talivaldis Stubis. Atheneum, 1973. 6–12.

Nash, Ogden. *Custard and Company: Poems*. Selected and illustrated by Quentin Blake. Little, Brown, 1980. 8–12.

O'Neil, Mary. *Hailstones and Halibut Bones*. Illustrated by Leonard Weisgard. Doubleday, 1961. 5–8.

Prelutsky, Jack. *It's Valentine's Day*. Illustrated by Vossi Abolafia. Greenwillow Books, 1983. 4–8.

———. *The New Kid on the Block*. Illustrated by James Stevenson. Greenwillow Books, 1984. 8–12.

———, comp. *The Random House Book of Poetry for Children*. Illustrated by Arnold Lobel. Random House, 1983. 4 and up.

Silverstein, Shel. *Where the Sidewalk Ends: Poems and Drawings*. Harper and Row, 1974. 8–12.

Viorst, Judith. *If I Were in Charge of the World, and Other Worries: Poems for Children and Their Parents*. Illustrated by Lynne Cherry. Atheneum, 1981. 8–12.

Worth, Valerie. *Small Poems*. Illustrated by Natalie Babbitt. Farrar, Straus and Giroux, 1972. 8–10.

6 Classics

Primary

6.1   Barrie, J. M. **Peter Pan.** Illustrated by Michael Hague. Henry
Holt, 1987. Ages 7–11.

This wonderful classic is given new life through Michael
Hague's beautiful full-page artwork filled with fairies, timeless characters, and unforgettable scenes. The child in all of
us is transported back to that time of wonder and make-
believe. This title should be included in all elementary school
library or classroom collections.

6.2   Collodi, Carlo (translated by Francis Wainwright). **The Adventures of Pinocchio.** Illustrated by the translator. Henry
Holt, 1986. Ages 5–10. (Picture book)

In this classic tale by Carlo Collodi, beautifully retold by
Francis Wainwright, an exuberant puppet tries hard to be
good, but the insatiable desire for excitement and adventure
causes him to get into all kinds of trouble. Children will love
the colorful illustrations.

6.3   Kipling, Rudyard. **The Elephant's Child.** Illustrated by Tim
Raglin. Alfred A. Knopf/Borzoi Books/Book and Cassette
Classic Series, 1986. Ages 6–10. (Picture book)

In a rendition close to the original version in Rudyard Kipling's *Just So Stories*, a young elephant becomes overly curious about what the crocodile eats for dinner and ends up with
a long trunk. Each page is generously illustrated with softly
colored illustrations imbued with the humor inherent in the
story. The accompanying cassette, with its intriguing musical
arrangement and excellent narration by Jack Nicholson, enhances the literary experience, although the book and cassette each stands on its own merits. The book is available
separately.

6.4 Potter, Beatrix. **Further Tales from Beatrix Potter.** Illustrated by the author. Frederick Warne, 1987. Ages 3–8. (Picture book)

Beatrix Potter's tales of Benjamin Bunny, Jeremy Fisher, Tom Kitten, and Pigling Bland are told in the original form in this reissue of a classic. New reproductions of Potter's original artwork have a detail and clarity not seen in earlier editions.

Intermediate

6.5 Collodi, Carlo (translated by E. Harden). **The Adventures of Pinocchio.** Illustrated by Roberto Innocenti. Alfred A. Knopf/ Borzoi Books, 1988. Ages 9–12.

Roberto Innocenti's illustrations invoke a somber retelling of the story of the legendary puppet, first published as a serial in 1882. The meticulous drawings convey sympathy for the original unsentimental spirit of Carlo Collodi's tale, set in Innocenti's native Italy.

6.6 Lofting, Hugh. **The Voyages of Dr. Dolittle.** Centenary ed. Illustrated by the author. Delacorte Press, 1988. Ages 9–12.

This revised edition retains most of the text, illustrations, and appeal of the original book, while the racially offensive passages and drawings found in the first edition have been removed. Some previously unpublished illustrations by Hugh Lofting have been added. Also available is *The Story of Dr. Dolittle*, which will be followed by revised editions of six other Dr. Dolittle books.

6.7 Sandburg, Carl. **Rootabaga Stories: Part One.** Illustrated by Michael Hague. Harcourt Brace Jovanovich, 1988. Ages 9–11.

Michael Hague illustrates each humorous short story with one full-color, full-page plate. The warmth of the illustrations enlivens this edition of the 1920 Sandburg classic.

7 Traditional Literature

Fables

Primary

7.1 Berrill, Margaret. **Chanticleer.** Illustrated by Jane Bottomley. Raintree Children's Books/Raintree Stories, 1986. Ages 4–7. (Picture book)

Barbara Cooney's Caldecott-winning version of this fable, *Chanticleer and the Fox*, is still the standard against which every other edition must be measured. However, this adaptation from Chaucer's *Canterbury Tales* will appeal to a younger audience, as the full-page illustrations are bright and boldly colored. Yellows and reds are used to maximum effect in the ageless tale of the trickster tricked and the vain upended.

7.2 Bierhorst, John. **Doctor Coyote: A Native American Aesop's Fables.** Illustrated by Wendy Watson. Macmillan, 1987. Ages 7–9.

Based on an early copy of Aesop's fables that found its way to Mexico, these fables were put into the Aztec language by a sixteenth-century Indian scribe who made Coyote the main character. Coyote is the well-known trickster who travels from place to place trying to outsmart everyone else while often outsmarting himself. The illustrations are full of humor and details of life in the southwestern United States.

7.3 Castle, Caroline. **The Hare and the Tortoise.** Illustrated by Peter Weevers. Dial Books for Young Readers, 1985. Ages 6–10. (Picture book)

Aesop would be proud to read this version of his famous fable about the tortoise and the hare. Such extra characters as a badger, frog, and mole are added to enhance the lesson that is given through this story. Beautiful illustrations help bring this age-old fable to life. *Children's Choice.*

7.4   Hague, Michael, compiler. **Aesop's Fables.** Illustrated by the compiler. Holt, Rinehart and Winston, 1985. Ages 5–11.

In this new collection, thirteen of Aesop's most well known fables are presented. High-quality, colorful, detailed illustrations are sure to catch the eye of young and older readers alike.

7.5   Lionni, Leo. **It's Mine!** Illustrated by the author. Alfred A. Knopf/Borzoi Books, 1986. Ages 6–8. (Picture book)

Leo Lionni's brilliant collage art and minimal text tell of three frogs who constantly shout, ''It's mine!'' until a disastrous flood makes them realize the beauty of living together and the importance of sharing.

7.6   Stevens, Janet. **The Town Mouse and the Country Mouse.** Illustrated by the author. Holiday House, 1987. Ages 4–7. (Picture book)

In this adaptation of the Aesop fable, a town mouse and a country mouse exchange visits and discover each is better suited to its own environment. The illustrations are oversized and easy to follow. *Children's Choice.*

7.7   Wallner, John. **City Mouse–Country Mouse, and Two More Mouse Tales from Aesop.** Illustrated by the author. Scholastic, 1987. Ages 5–8. (Picture book)

Two familiar tales and a less familiar one are told in an easy-to-read text. Full-page watercolor drawings are uncluttered in their development of the story line.

Folksongs and Ballads

Primary

7.8   Domanska, Janina, illustrator. **Busy Monday Morning.** Greenwillow Books, 1985. Ages 4–8. (Picture book)

This picture-book adaptation of a rural folksong features a father and son readying their hay for feed. Their week of day-by-day tasks is recounted in rhythmic patterned verse illustrated with multicolored pastels featuring simple lines and large forms that emphasize the warm humility of the Slavic peasant tradition.

7.9 Koontz, Robin Michal, illustrator. **This Old Man: The Counting Song.** Dodd, Mead, 1988. Ages 2–6. (Picture book)

Here is a cleverly illustrated version of the well-known counting song about "this old man." Included are a copy of the music and suggestions for playing the counting song.

7.10 Sewall, Marcia, illustrator. **Animal Song.** Little, Brown/Joy Street Books, 1988. Ages 2–6. (Picture book)

This adaptation of the 1939 version of "Animal Song" contains the music, five verses of the song, and illustrations of the animals gathering for the crow's birthday. Four pages of animal illustrations are presented in alphabetical order, and the reader is asked to find the animals in the story.

7.11 Sewall, Marcia, illustrator. **Ridin' That Strawberry Roan.** Viking Kestrel, 1985. Ages 5–7. (Picture book)

This picture book is a lively rendition of an old cowboy song about a foolhardy bronco-buster who meets his match in a horse called Strawberry Roan. Humorous illustrations, done in pen-and-ink and watercolor, complement the text. This is a fun participatory book that provides a brief peek at a previous era in American history.

Folktales and Fairy Tales

Primary

7.12 Aardema, Verna. **Bimwili and the Zimwi: A Tale from Zanzibar.** Illustrated by Susan Meddaugh. Dial Books for Young Readers, 1985. Ages 5–7. (Picture book)

Bimwili, the tagalong little sister, goes to the seashore with her two older sisters. There she finds a shell but then leaves it behind. When she must go back alone to retrieve it, she encounters the Zimwi and trouble. The illustrations are rich in color and texture and are quite suited to the text. The story reads and tells well, and the author's choice of words and phrases reflects the tale's origin in Zanzibar.

7.13 Aardema, Verna. **Princess Gorilla and a New Kind of Water: A Mpongwe Tale.** Illustrated by Victoria Chess. Dial Books for Young Readers, 1987. Ages 6–9. (Picture book)

Princess Gorilla wants to marry someone who loves her, but her father is determined to find her a husband who is strong and brave. What better way to do it than a test, but what sort of test? King Gorilla finds a barrel of vinegar which has fallen from a trader's wagon; tasting it, he decides that whoever can drink the entire barrel of this new kind of water will win his daughter's hand in marriage. This West African folktale lends itself to creative dramatization.

7.14 Bennett, Jill. **Teeny Tiny.** Illustrated by Tomie dePaola. G. P. Putnam's Sons, 1986. Ages 4–6.

Tomie dePaola's characteristically lumpy figures lower the fright factor in this familiar repetitive English ghost story, making it perhaps more appropriate for younger children than Paul Galdone's version, *The Teeny-Tiny Woman*, or such variants as *Tailypo* by Joanna Galdone. *Children's Choice.*

7.15 Brett, Jan. **Goldilocks and the Three Bears.** Illustrated by the author. Dodd, Mead, 1987. Ages 3–8. (Picture book)

Richly colored, lavishly detailed paintings flesh out this retelling of a favorite fairy tale. Intricately decorated borders, plump animated bears, and a braided Goldilocks in embroidered frocks make this a fresh and distinguished version of an ever-popular story.

7.16 Bryan, Ashley. **The Cat's Purr.** Illustrated by the author. Atheneum, 1985. Ages 7–10.

Cat and Rat are friends until Cat receives a small drum as a gift from his uncle and refuses to let Rat play it. What happens when Rat schemes to play the drum and gets caught leads to an explanation of why the animals are not friends today and why cats purr. This West Indian folktale, originally from Africa, is illustrated with simple pencil drawings on each page.

7.17 Carey, Valerie Scho. **The Devil and Mother Crump.** Illustrated by Arnold Lobel. Harper and Row, 1987. Ages 7–9. (Picture book)

Mother Crump is so mean that she never gives anything to anyone without expecting something back. She is so mean that she even bests the devil at meanness and wins three wishes. With those three wishes, this feisty woman beats

Death, so that when she dies, even old Lucifer will not have her. Arnold Lobel's rhythmic black-and-white drawings touched with color match the flow of the text in this variant of a Jack tale.

7.18 Dee, Ruby. **Two Ways to Count to Ten: A Liberian Folktale.** Illustrated by Susan Meddaugh. Henry Holt, 1988. Ages 6–9. (Picture book)

The leopard, king of the jungle, wishes to choose a successor who is clever as well as wise. King Leopard challenges all the animals to throw a spear high enough so they can count to ten before it lands on the ground. One clever animal is able to meet the challenge in this Liberian folktale.

7.19 de Gerez, Toni. **Louhi, Witch of North Farm.** Illustrated by Barbara Cooney. Viking Kestrel, 1986. Ages 5–8. (Picture book)

This Finnish folktale of a mischievous witch who steals and hides the sun and the moon is dramatized in richly colored double-page paintings. The rustic warmth of the village eases into the icy blues and grays of winter and erupts into the vibrant hues of spring after the sun and moon are returned, emphasizing the narrative tension. The tale is from Finland's epic poem, the *Kalevala*.

7.20 Delaney, A. **The Gunnywolf.** Illustrated by the author. Harper and Row, 1988. Ages 3–8. (Picture book)

A little girl lives at the edge of a woods into which she has never ventured because of the Gunnywolf who lives there. One day she is tempted into the deep, dark woods by flowers that she sees blooming nearby. As she sings the alphabet song, the Gunnywolf appears, and a chase begins. Will the little girl be saved? Will she ever go back in the woods again? *Children's Choice.*

7.21 Demi. **The Hallowed Horse.** Illustrated by the author. Dodd, Mead, 1987. Ages 4–10. (Picture book)

Illustrations heavily influenced by traditional Indian art are well matched to this intriguing Indian folktale about a magical horse much sought after by a king to protect his kingdom from the evil Kaliya, the multiheaded snake. The horse is raised by a lowly potter who loves him dearly. The king's astrologers locate the two of them, and the story unfolds. Children will treasure the detailed and highly decorative illustrations. The story should be especially appealing to horse lovers.

7.22   dePaola, Tomie. **Tomie dePaola's Favorite Nursery Tales.** Illustrated by the author. G. P. Putnam's Sons, 1986. Ages 3–8.

The large format, the bordered pages, and the dominance of the illustrations make this a book with much visual appeal. The selection of tales offers variety; included are fairy tales, fables, poetry, and tales from other lands. Some are short, some long, some familiar, some not. The authors are noted, but not the particular translation or version used. "The Three Little Pigs," for example, is offered in a sanitized version. A good first collection. *Children's Choice.*

7.23   Eisen, Armand. **Goldilocks and the Three Bears.** Illustrated by Lynn Bywaters Ferris. Alfred A. Knopf/Borzoi Books/ Ariel Books, 1987. Ages 2–6. (Picture book)

This is the old German story of Goldilocks in a new adaptation, told in a conversational tone with dialogue used to make the story more immediate. The moralizing of some versions has been cut. The illustrations are the book's glory, exquisitely detailed and glowingly colored, making the little house irresistible to both Goldilocks and the reader. Each page is bordered in Old World folk designs that echo the story.

7.24   Eisen, Armand. **Little Red Riding Hood.** Illustrated by Lynn Bywaters Ferris. Alfred A. Knopf/Borzoi Books/Ariel Books, 1988. Ages 3–8. (Picture book)

This is a retelling of the traditional story of the little girl who goes to visit her ill grandmother with a basket full of food. The book is beautifully illustrated with twenty watercolor paintings.

7.25   Forest, Heather. **The Baker's Dozen: A Colonial American Tale.** Illustrated by Susan Gaber. Harcourt Brace Jovanovich/Gulliver Books, 1988. Ages 4–7. (Picture book)

The origin of the term *baker's dozen* is recounted in this tale of a New England baker famous for his St. Nicholas cookies. An old woman curses the success of the greedy baker. To redeem himself, he returns to the practice of a thirteen-count dozen, and other bakers follow his example of generosity. Bright bordered watercolors adorn this morality tale suitable for holiday fare or as a general read-aloud book.

7.26   Galdone, Paul. **Rumpelstiltskin.** Illustrated by the author. Clarion Books, 1985. Ages 4–9.

This classic retelling of an age-old Brothers Grimm tale portrays Rumpelstiltskin as a jolly old man whose evil nature is only gradually revealed. The colorful full-page illustrations provide animation throughout, enhancing characterization.

7.27   Grifalconi, Ann. **The Village of Round and Square Houses.** Illustrated by the author. Little, Brown, 1986. Ages 4–9. (Picture book)

A young girl in a small village in the Cameroons listens to Gran'ma Tika tell the story of why the men live in square houses, while the women live in round houses. "Each one has a place to be apart, and a time to be together," says Gran'ma. Respect for the wisdom of experience of the elders figures prominently in a boldly illustrated story of change and continuity. *Caldecott Honor Book* and *Notable Trade Book in the Field of Social Studies.*

7.28   Grimm, Jacob, and Wilhelm Grimm (retold by Bernadette Watts). **The Elves and the Shoemaker.** Illustrated by the reteller. North-South Books, 1986. Ages 7–9. (Picture book)

This book is useful for the comparison it makes possible with the earlier Adrienne Adams version of the same tale. The oversized page allows for a pleasantly open appearance; the white of the generous margins sets off the watercolor and ink line drawings effectively. The amount of detail shown in the pictures does not overwhelm the simple tale.

7.29   Grimm, Jacob, and Wilhelm Grimm (adapted by Anthea Bell). **The Golden Goose.** Illustrated by Dorothée Duntze. North-South Books, 1988. Ages 6–11. (Picture book)

Highly stylized illustrations dominate this retelling of the familiar tale from the Brothers Grimm. Dorothée Duntze varies her format, sometimes using a double-page spread, sometimes using three panels on a page to highlight key incidents in this story of the youngest son who proves that he is not a simpleton after all.

7.30 Grimm, Jacob, and Wilhelm Grimm (retold by Bernadette Watts). **Snow White and Rose Red.** Illustrated by the reteller. North-South Books, 1988. Ages 6–9. (Picture book)

The traditional Brothers Grimm story of the two sisters who are opposites in many ways, but who have a cozy and happy life together with their poor mother, is retold and illustrated with lavish, detailed illustrations in earth tones, befitting a story in a woodland setting. The eye will want to linger over the double-page spreads, particularly the depictions of the girls' encounters with the feisty dwarf and the bear-prince. This is a good book for reading aloud.

7.31 Haley, Gail E. **Jack and the Bean Tree.** Illustrated by the author. Crown, 1986. Ages 6–10. (Picture book)

This Appalachian folktale, recounted in a slight mountain dialect, is a variant of "Jack and the Beanstalk" told by Poppyseed, a mountain storyteller. Brilliant illustrations, highly stylized, tell the tale of Jack's triumph over the giant, with an especially scary perspective of the giant climbing down the stalk.

7.32 Haley, Gail E. **Jack and the Fire Dragon.** Illustrated by the author. Crown, 1988. Ages 8–10. (Picture book)

This Appalachian version of an oral traditional folktale has bright linocut illustrations. It tells of Jack's adventures with the monster known as Fire Dragaman. Can he fight the monster and rescue the captives?

7.33 Hastings, Selina. **The Man Who Wanted to Live Forever.** Illustrated by Reg Cartwright. Henry Holt, 1988. Ages 7–9. (Picture book)

Bodkin loves life and goes to stay with the Old Man of the Mountain, who is to live as long as the mountain endures. One day Bodkin becomes curious about his old home and goes on a journey. This tale of a man who would cheat death—and its surprise ending—will pleasantly haunt children. The illustrations contain an appropriately rustic quality, as well as an aura of eeriness well in keeping with the story.

7.34 Hastings, Selina. **Peter and the Wolf.** Illustrated by Reg Cartwright. Henry Holt, 1987. Ages 3–6. (Picture book)

Selina Hastings retells the famous Russian fairy tale of the impish boy, Peter, who disregards his grandfather's warnings and captures the wolf to save his friends. The full-color illustrations make this famous fairy tale unique.

7.35   Hodges, Margaret. **Saint George and the Dragon: A Golden Legend.** Illustrated by Trina Schart Hyman. Little, Brown, 1984. Ages 6–10.

Trina Schart Hyman's romantic illustrations complement this retelling of the traditional tale from Edmund Spenser's *Faerie Queene*. George, the Red Cross Knight, tenaciously works for three days to slay the dragon that has been terrorizing the countryside and to win the hand of the princess. In doing so, he earns his name, Saint George of Merry England.

7.36   Hogrogian, Nonny. **The Cat Who Loved to Sing.** Illustrated by the author. Alfred A. Knopf/Borzoi Books, 1988. Ages 5–9. (Picture book)

Nonny Hogrogian's spritely retelling of this Armenian cumulative folktale is enhanced by warm, detailed watercolor illustrations. The singing cat is a jaunty fellow who makes a series of trades, only to end with a mandolin—just the thing for a cat of his musical talents.

7.37   Hogrogian, Nonny. **The Glass Mountain: Retold from the Tale by the Brothers Grimm.** Illustrated by the author. Alfred A. Knopf/Borzoi Books, 1985. Ages 6–10. (Picture book)

Handmade marbleized papers by the author-illustrator frame the lush, handsome illustrations that retell the story "The Raven." A princess is changed into a raven and beseeches a young man to rescue her. After he fails the first test, he is determined to save her, but he must climb a glass mountain to reach her. Three disgruntled brothers provide the invisible cloak, the horse that can climb the mountain, and a stick that will open any door, enabling the young man to rescue the princess. The two live happily ever after, of course.

7.38   Ishii, Momoko (translated by Katherine Paterson). **The Tongue-Cut Sparrow.** Illustrated by Suekichi Akaba. E. P. Dutton/Lodestar Books, 1987. Ages 5–9. (Picture book)

This is a refreshing Japanese folktale of an old man and his greedy wife. The clean and simple text makes good use of repetition and is spiced with several onomatopoeic Japanese words that children will love to chant. Suekichi Akaba has used traditional Japanese techniques— ink and brush, color used sparingly in a decorative fashion, stylized figures—and the pages are even printed to resemble rice paper. Children will enjoy experiencing this book many times. *Children's Choice.*

7.39 Ivimey, John W. **The Complete Story of the Three Blind Mice.** Illustrated by Paul Galdone. Clarion Books, 1987. Ages 3–8. (Picture book)

How did the three blind mice get into such a fix? Maintaining the rhyme patterns of the original song, the author tells how three bold mice become the three cold mice and then the three hungry mice before arriving at the farmer's house. Full-page illustrations detail their adventure.

7.40 Kellogg, Steven. **Chicken Little.** Illustrated by the author. William Morrow, 1985. Ages 4–8. (Picture book)

Chicken Little and his feathered friends, alarmed that the sky seems to be falling, become easy prey for hungry Foxy Loxy when he poses as a police officer in hopes of tricking them into his truck. The visual jokes, puns, and silly details in Steven Kellogg's colorful illustrations enliven this modernized retelling of an old favorite story. *Children's Choice.*

7.41 Langton, Jane. **The Hedgehog Boy: A Latvian Folktale.** Illustrated by Ilse Plume. Harper and Row, 1985. Ages 8–10.

In this Latvian transformation tale, a princess honors a promise made by her father and marries a prickly hedgehog boy. She inadvertently causes him to fall ill, but nurses him back to health. Then she finds the hedgehog boy transformed into a handsome young man.

7.42 Lee, Jeanne M. **Toad Is the Uncle of Heaven: A Vietnamese Folk Tale.** Illustrated by the author. Holt, Rinehart and Winston, 1985. Ages 5–9. (Picture book)

A quickly identifiable story pattern and the triumph of a small but plucky hero make this Vietnamese tale, which explains why toads croak before it rains, particularly appealing. The journey of the toad and his friends to the King of Heaven and the challenges they face when they arrive are highlighted by vibrant and expressive two-page illustrations. *Children's Choice.*

7.43   Littledale, Freya. **Peter and the North Wind.** Illustrated by Troy Howell. Scholastic/Hardcover Books, 1988. Ages 4–7. (Picture book)

This retelling of a Norse tale features the three trials and the triumph of good over evil, a standard folklore motif. The innocence of the small boy and the fair treatment he receives from the North Wind are contrasted with the sly greed of the innkeeper. Troy Howell's illustrations have a sweet, enchanted, elfin quality reminiscent of artwork by Maxfield Parrish or Jessie Wilcox Smith.

7.44   Littledale, Freya. **The Twelve Dancing Princesses: A Folk Tale from the Brothers Grimm.** Illustrated by Isadore Seltzer. Scholastic/Easy-to-Read Folktale Series, 1988. Ages 5–9. (Picture book)

This original paperback version of a Brothers Grimm tale retells the story of twelve princesses who dance holes in their shoes each night. Through wit and magic, a clever soldier discovers the secret of their nighttime adventures. The retelling is graceful, faithful to original sources, and enhanced by dramatic, vividly colored illustrations.

7.45   Marshall, James. **Goldilocks and the Three Bears.** Illustrated by the author. Dial Books for Young Readers, 1988. Ages 3–8. (Picture book)

The traditional German story is set in a Victorian home with the three bears going out for a ride on their bicycle while their porridge cools. They return and are not happy to find an intruder in their home. Hilarious illustrations make this a great book for any collection. *ALA Notable Children's Book* and *Caldecott Honor Book.*

7.46   Marshall, James. **Red Riding Hood.** Illustrated by the author. Dial Books for Young Readers, 1987. Ages 4–6. (Picture book)

The old German story of Red Riding Hood's encounter with the wolf is retold tongue-in-cheek as a spoof. Bright full-page illustrations add goofy humor that should appeal to new readers who may consider themselves too sophisticated for the traditional nursery tale. *Children's Choice.*

7.47 Meyers, Odette. **The Enchanted Umbrella.** Illustrated by Margot Zemach. Harcourt Brace Jovanovich/Gulliver Books, 1988. Ages 5–8. (Picture book)

In this French folktale, the enchanted umbrella brings helpful magic, but only to the right person—young Patou, the loving apprentice to an umbrella maker. When the old man dies, Patou's future is in doubt, but he eludes danger and secures his fortune, all because of the umbrella. Margot Zemach's comical illustrations develop both the plot and the setting in this tale of familiar motifs. The book includes a short history of the umbrella.

7.48 Morimoto, Junko, illustrator. **The Inch Boy.** Viking Kestrel, 1986. Ages 3–9. (Picture book)

Although he is only one inch tall, Issunboshi sets sail in a rice-bowl boat, bound for Kyoto. He dreams of becoming a famous samurai serving a noble lord. His dream comes true, and his first day of active duty is filled with excitement. The colorful and comical illustrations greatly enhance the book.

7.49 Morimoto, Junko, illustrator. **Mouse's Marriage.** Viking Kestrel, 1986. Ages 8–10.

Mouse parents searching for the most powerful husband for their daughter approach the sun, the clouds, the wind, and a stone. Pleasantly understated though vibrantly colored, full-page illustrations face pages of text in this variation of the old Aesop fable "The Wind and the Sun." The perspectives of the illustrations will attract viewers' attention: looking between the buildings, up to the clouds, down on the wedding feast.

7.50 Morris, Ann. **The Little Red Riding Hood Rebus Book.** Illustrated by Ljiljana Rylands. Orchard Books, 1987. Ages 5–8. (Picture book)

Bright little pictures replace some of the words in this book, but a rebus dictionary in the back of the book helps in figuring out the missing words. This book is not suitable for reading aloud or as a lap book, but it would be appropriate for use as a puzzle by young readers just for fun. First and second graders will appreciate the possibilities of inventing silly substitutions for some of the words.

7.51   Osborne, Mary Pope. **Beauty and the Beast.** Illustrated by
Winslow Pinney Pels. Scholastic, 1987. Ages 5–10. (Picture
book)

Mary Pope Osborne retells the classic story of the beautiful
woman and the ugly beast in a simple but literate style that is
enhanced by the soft pastel illustrations.

7.52   Oxenbury, Helen. **The Helen Oxenbury Nursery Story Book.**
Illustrated by the author. Alfred A. Knopf/Borzoi Books,
1985. Ages 5–9.

This colorfully illustrated collection of ten well-known fairy
tales in large print is suitable for the youngest reader. Included are "Goldilocks and the Three Bears," "The Elves
and the Shoemaker," and "Little Red Riding Hood."

7.53   Perrault, Charles (retold by Amy Ehrlich). **Cinderella.** Illustrated by Susan Jeffers. Dial Books for Young Readers, 1985.
Ages 6–10. (Picture book)

This retelling by Amy Ehrlich is accompanied by colored ink
illustrations in Susan Jeffers's usual, highly detailed style,
which once again create formally posed tableaux. There is
much to delight the eye in this familiar tale, and readers might
enjoy comparing it with other versions of the tale.

7.54   Perrault, Charles (translated by Diane Goode). **Cinderella.** Illustrated by the translator. Alfred A. Knopf/Borzoi Books,
1988. Ages 6–10. (Picture book)

Diane Goode's illustrations capture the magical transforma-
tions in Charles Perrault's version of this classic tale: the
mice to horses, the lizard to a coachman, and Cinderella's
ball gown back to rags as the clock strikes midnight. Facial
expressions are of special interest, too, even though this Cinderella is not as conventionally beautiful as in other editions.

7.55   Pevear, Richard. **Mister Cat-and-a-half.** Illustrated by Robert
Rayevsky. Macmillan, 1986. Ages 8–11. (Picture book)

This is a crisp retelling of an old Ukrainian tale about a wolf,
bear, boar, and hare, friends who try to woo the attractive
Mistress Fox, who decides to wed the well-fed Mister Cat-
and-a-half. The repetitive tale moves swiftly to its logical, humorous dinner-party ending, accompanied by Robert

Rayevsky's naturalistic drawings, sharpened with ink lines. His use of crosshatching to create three-dimensional drawings is particularly effective.

7.56   Pevear, Richard. **Our King Has Horns!** Illustrated by Robert Rayevsky. Macmillan, 1987. Ages 6–10. (Picture book)

Here is a finely told folktale from the Soviet republic of Georgia, in which an unfortunate barber must keep secret the fact that his newest customer—the king—has horns. Robert Rayevsky carefully uses the white space on each page to set off his rich, earthy colors. He shows particular wit in his characters' facial expressions and eyes. Colored-pen and watercolor illustrations are a perfect complement to the sometimes-fantastic twists to this story line.

7.57   Philip, Neil. **Drakestail Visits the King: A Magic Lantern Fairy Tale.** Illustrated by Henry Underhill. Philomel Books, 1986. Ages 6–9. (Picture book)

An old French fairy tale is smoothly retold by the author to accompany colored illustrations reproduced from Victorian magic lantern slides. Drakestail swallows his friends who wish to accompany him to visit the king. Each friend then rescues Drakestail from the king's efforts to kill him until, finally, Drakestail is king. This tale lends itself to creative dramatics.

7.58   Phillips, Mildred. **The Sign in Mendel's Window.** Illustrated by Margot Zemach. Macmillan, 1985. Ages 8–10. (Picture book)

In a folktale set in the very small Russian town of Kosnov, Mendel, the butcher, and his wife, Molly, put a sign in their shopwindow offering to rent half their space. A well-dressed stranger rents the space, overhears Mendel counting the money in his cash box, and summons two policemen from the city. The stranger accuses Mendel of stealing his money and names the exact amount in the cash box. With the help of his neighbors and his wife, Mendel wins the day. Margot Zemach's full-color illustrations are an integral part of the text.

7.59   Rogasky, Barbara. **The Water of Life: A Tale from the Brothers Grimm.** Illustrated by Trina Schart Hyman. Holiday House, 1986. Ages 5–9.

This beautiful tale from the Brothers Grimm involves a sick king and his son's search for the water of life that will cure his father. As in many fairy tales, good conquers evil, and the youngest son is rewarded for his good deeds. The illustrations beautifully enhance the well-known tale.

7.60   Ross, Tony. **Lazy Jack.** Illustrated by the author. Dial Books for Young Readers, 1986. Ages 4–8. (Picture book)

The tale of Lazy Jack, who can never do anything right but who makes a sad princess laugh, is given humorous treatment in full-page watercolor drawings bound to make the reader laugh. *Children's Choice.*

7.61   Saunders, Susan. **The Golden Goose.** Illustrated by Isadore Seltzer. Scholastic/Hardcover Books, 1988. Ages 5–8. (Picture book)

Simpleton finds the golden goose and, eventually, the love of his life, a princess, in this version of the tale by the Brothers Grimm, retold in a lively style that will appeal to even the youngest of readers or listeners. Isadore Seltzer's humorous illustrations add to the hilarity of Simpleton and his quest for the hand of the lovely princess.

7.62   Shute, Linda. **Clever Tom and the Leprechaun: An Old Irish Story.** Illustrated by the author. Lothrop, Lee and Shepard Books, 1988. Ages 5–8. (Picture book)

In this traditional Irish folktale, Tom believes he has tricked a leprechaun into leading him to hidden gold, but when Tom returns to the spot to begin digging for treasure, it is obvious that the leprechaun is the clever one. Bright, mildly comical watercolors are an apt complement to this playful read-aloud tale. Informative source notes are appended.

7.63   Snyder, Dianne. **The Boy of the Three-Year Nap.** Illustrated by Allen Say. Houghton Mifflin, 1988. Ages 6–10. (Picture book)

This is an adaptation of a Japanese trickster tale in which lazy Taro, who seems to spend years napping, wins a wife and riches through a clever ruse. The story is lively and amusing, but the illustrations are an immediate attraction. The line-and-ink drawings of Japanese landscapes and everyday life are vibrantly colored and expressive. *ALA Notable Children's Book* and *Caldecott Honor Book.*

7.64   Steptoe, John. **Mufaro's Beautiful Daughters: An African Tale.** Illustrated by the author. Lothrop, Lee and Shepard Books, 1987. Ages 4–9. (Picture book)

Two beautiful sisters—one vain, the other kind—compete for the king's attention when he announces he is looking for a wife. Brilliant full-color pen-and-ink watercolor paintings illustrate this Cinderella tale. John Steptoe skillfully uses light and color to give emotional power to illustrations rich in detail about a specific region in Zimbabwe. *ALA Notable Children's Book, Caldecott Honor Book, Children's Choice,* and *Coretta Scott King Award* (for illustrations).

7.65   Uchida, Yoshiko. **The Two Foolish Cats.** Illustrated by Margot Zemach. Margaret K. McElderry Books, 1987. Ages 5–8. (Picture book)

This tale, suggested by a Japanese folktale, illustrates a problem of justice: how can the spoils of the hunt be equitably divided? Two foolish and quarreling cats bring such a dilemma before an old monkey judge, who makes peace in a surprising way. Margot Zemach's watercolor paintings with their bold black lines are dramatic in content, nicely complementing the story. The story could be read aloud or even dramatized in the classroom.

7.66   Vernon, Adele. **The Riddle.** Illustrated by Robert Rayevsky and Vladimir Radunsky. Dodd, Mead, 1987. Ages 5–9. (Picture book)

This is a riddle story in which the wisdom of a king is topped by that of a lowly, but clever, charcoal maker. Every two pages form a double-page spread bordered in red with illustrations that are rich in color, but muted and formal, to suit this old Catalan tale. Aside from the fine illustrations, the text could stand alone as an engaging and amusing read-aloud story.

7.67   Waddell, Martin. **The Tough Princess.** Illustrated by Patrick Benson. Philomel Books, 1986. Ages 4–8. (Picture book)

Here is a fairy tale story with a contemporary approach. A princess rejects conventional life and goes off on adventures with a fairy, a goblin, dragons, and serpents before she reaches the Enchanted Castle.

7.68   Watts, Bernadette. **Goldilocks and the Three Bears.** Illustrated by the author. North-South Books, 1988. Ages 3–9. (Picture book)

The traditional German story of Goldilocks is retold with bright, warm, and appealing illustrations suitable for even the youngest child.

7.69   Westwood, Jennifer. **Going to Squintum's: A Foxy Folktale.** Illustrated by Fiona French. Dial Books for Young Readers, 1985. Ages 3–6. (Picture book)

In this cumulative tale, a fox leaves a bag at a neighbor's house with the admonition, "Don't look in the bag!" But each neighbor cannot resist, and when the creature in the bag escapes, the neighbor has to put something else into the bag. The fox gets his comeuppance in the end when he decides to eat the boy in the bag and discovers it's a dog instead. Bright primitive figures, reminiscent of American primitive art, decorate the pages. The bold art with the fox on every page will entertain youngsters. *Children's Choice.*

7.70   Wiesner, David, and Kim Kahng. **The Loathsome Dragon.** Illustrated by David Wiesner. G. P. Putnam's Sons, 1987. Ages 8–10. (Picture book)

Romantic illustrations placed in double-page spreads emphasize the fairy tale qualities of this retelling of an old English story with its lovely enchanted princess, hero prince, and cursed dragon. Read this dramatic tale aloud or have children act it out.

7.71   Winter, Jeanette. **The Magic Ring: A Tale by the Brothers Grimm.** Illustrated by the author. Alfred A. Knopf/Borzoi Books, 1987. Ages 6–10. (Picture book)

Jeanette Winter simply but effectively retells this classic Brothers Grimm tale of a young girl who is left in the enchanted woods and who is eventually rescued by a prince. Colorful, imaginative illustrations sustain the surreal quality of this charming story of love and trust.

7.72   Yolen, Jane. **The Emperor and the Kite.** Illustrated by Ed Young. Philomel Books, 1988. Ages 3–8. (Picture book)

Using richly colored and intricate paper cutouts set against a plain white background, Ed Young amply complements this sensitively told story from China of how the youngest and most insignificant daughter of the emperor uses her kite to save him. This is a fine example of how a little goes a long way.

7.73 Zelinsky, Paul O. **Rumpelstiltskin.** Illustrated by the author. E. P. Dutton, 1986. Ages 6–10. (Picture book)

Panoramic full-color endpapers of the terrain introduce this version of the Brothers Grimm tale, followed by architectural details framing the title page. All lead into the story itself, in which text is interspersed among full-page and nearly full-page illustrations. Paul O. Zelinsky varies distances in interesting fashion: some of the illustrations are closeups, others show far-distant vistas. Light quality also attracts attention, varying from the full light of day to the luminous darkness in the night scenes. *Caldecott Honor Book.*

Intermediate

7.74 Bryan, Ashley. **Lion and the Ostrich Chicks, and Other African Folk Tales.** Illustrated by the author. Atheneum, 1986. Ages 8–12.

This is a collection of four folktales retold from the Hausa, Angolan, Masai, and Bushman people of Africa. The stories are well written and will be easy to read aloud or tell. The story of the "Foolish Boy" who is smart enough to outsmart Ananse the Spider is the best of the four. The illustrations by the author, which are done in black-and-white and in orange, red, and black woodcuts, enhance the stories. *Coretta Scott King Award* (for writing).

7.75 Cleaver, Elizabeth. **The Enchanted Caribou.** Illustrated by the author. Atheneum, 1985. Ages 8–12. (Picture book)

Unusual shadow-puppetlike illustrations, simple and blocky in nature, accompany the spare text in this retelling of an old Inuit tale. There is an interesting parallel with the Snow White tale, where an intruder comes in and combs the female character's hair. Instructions for how to transform the story into a shadow-theater presentation are included at the end of the book.

7.76   Climo, Shirley. **Someone Saw a Spider: Spider Facts and Folktales.** Illustrated by Dirk Zimmer. Thomas Y. Crowell, 1985. Ages 10–14.

Brief factual pages, poetry, and longer folktales (from nine different cultures) alternate to reveal various aspects of arachnids for the curious. The "Extras and Explanations" section offers additional details, and a three-page bibliography is conveniently divided into subsections: facts, fiction, and beliefs. Though most of the tales have been translated from other languages, their distinctive folk flavors have been retained. Read aloud one or two of the tales to motivate individual readers to finish the book. *Notable Children's Trade Book in the Field of Social Studies* and *Outstanding Science Trade Book for Children.*

7.77   Crossley-Holland, Kevin. **British Folk Tales.** Orchard Books, 1987. Ages 10–12.

Kevin Crossley-Holland retells fifty-five familiar and unfamiliar British tales representing the major types of folktales, including fairy tales, ghost stories, and heroic adventures. Included are a pronunciation guide, a list of sources, and notes for each of the tales. An excellent reference.

7.78   Garner, Alan. **A Bag of Moonshine.** Illustrated by Patrick James Lynch. Delacorte Press, 1986. Ages 8–12.

Ideal for reading aloud, these twenty-two short stories are English and Welsh versions of tales widely known in other forms from different sources. Versions of Aesop's "The Wind and the Sun," of the Brothers Grimm tale "Clever Elsie," and of the Rumpelstiltskin name-guessing motif will serve useful curriculum purposes as teachers encourage children to compare and contrast tales, noting both language and plot differences. Both full-color and black-and-white illustrations, suitably quirky, accompany the tales. *ALA Notable Children's Book.*

7.79   Grimm, Wilhelm (translated by Ralph Manheim). **Dear Mili.** Illustrated by Maurice Sendak. Farrar, Straus and Giroux/ Michael di Capua Books, 1988. Ages 7–12. (Picture book)

Wilhelm Grimm wrote this tale in a letter to a little girl in 1816, but it was not discovered until 1983. A mother sends her little girl into the woods for three days to save her from the ravages of war. The girl is given shelter by an old man, St. Joseph, who lives in the woods. She stays for what she thinks is three days, but actually thirty years pass. When the girl returns home and is reunited with her mother, the tale tragically ends. *Children's Choice.*

7.80   Hamilton, Virginia. **The People Could Fly: American Black Folktales.** Illustrated by Leo and Diane Dillon. Alfred A. Knopf/Borzoi Books. 1985. Ages 10–13.

This annotated collection of twenty-four tales contains the variety, grit, sly humor, and spirit of black American stories. Included are folktales of animals, fantasy, and the supernatural. The style reflects the oral traditions of the tales, which read aloud easily. The black-and-white illustrations inform, inspire, amuse, and frighten the reader. A cassette containing twelve of the stories features James Earl Jones and Virginia Hamilton using their strong voices to create the despair, humor, and beliefs found in the stories. *ALA Notable Children's Book, Coretta Scott King Award* (for writing) and *Honor Book* (for illustrations), and *Notable Children's Trade Book in the Field of Social Studies.*

7.81   Hooks, William H. **Moss Gown.** Illustrated by Donald Carrick. Clarion Books, 1987. Ages 6–12. (Picture book)

Expressive full-page watercolor illustrations enhance this romantic Southern fairy tale about a girl whose two evil sisters are favored over her and who is banished from her father's plantation. Children will recognize elements of "Cinderella" in the tale, while teachers can point out corollaries to *King Lear.*

7.82   Laroche, Michel. **The Snow Rose.** Illustrated by Sandra Laroche. Holiday House, 1986. Ages 8–11. (Picture book)

Share this book with children, who will enjoy its elegant quasi-silhouettes, enriched with pleasantly intense watercolor, decorating every page of this fairly complex tale. Read it aloud in a small group, so children can hear the sounds of the formal language and yet be close enough to study the detailed illustrations in this tale of the troubadour who tries to win the hand of a princess.

7.83   Lester, Julius. **The Tales of Uncle Remus: The Adventures of Brer Rabbit.** Illustrated by Jerry Pinkney. Dial Books for Young Readers, 1987. Ages 5–11.

This is the kind of book that an eleven year old would like to read and a younger child would like to hear read aloud. The hilarious adventures of Brer Rabbit, as retold by storyteller Julius Lester, are presented again in a voice that is at once contemporary and timeless. *Coretta Scott King Award* (for writing).

7.84   Martin, Eva. **Tales of the Far North.** Illustrated by László Gál. Dial Books for Young Readers, 1986. Ages 8–12.

The twelve stories in this collection come from the French and English folklore traditions of Canada. These folktales are clearly and economically told and would be excellent for reading aloud. Each story has a single, highly detailed, colored-pencil illustration of a seminal scene from the text. The illustrations are muted and slightly flat in perspective, obtained by using short pencil strokes. As with many folktales, these stories can be violent at times. But it is not senseless violence, and it often provides an interesting insight into the time period. Kings, princes, princesses, witches, giants, and other popular folk figures abound. In the end, sly, mischievous heroes often win out over evil and greed.

7.85   Mayer, Marianna. **Aladdin and the Enchanted Lamp.** Illustrated by Gerald McDermott. Macmillan, 1985. Ages 10–12.

In this retelling of an old Arabian story, Aladdin, with the help of a genie from a magic lamp, is able to outsmart the evil sorcerer in many adventures and to win the hand of a princess. Elegant watercolor and pastel-pencil illustrations accompany the tale.

7.86   Riordan, James. **The Woman in the Moon, and Other Tales of Forgotten Heroines.** Illustrated by Angela Barrett. Dial Books for Young Readers, 1985. Ages 9–12.

Strong, proud, capable women are featured in these traditional tales, thus uniting the modern concept of female equality with an ancient storytelling tradition. Similar to Rosemary Minard's *Womenfolk and Fairy Tales* or Ethel J. Phelps's *Maid of the North: Feminist Folk Tales from around the World*, the book is appropriate for storytelling or reading aloud.

7.87 Sadler, Catherine Edwards. **Heaven's Reward: Fairy Tales from China.** Illustrated by Cheng Mung Yun. Atheneum, 1985. Ages 9–12.

Six Chinese tales from several time periods, representing different schools of thought ranging from Confucianism to communism, are retold here in spare language. Their minimal characterization and setting make them typical of folk literature. Animals often move the plots ahead: tigers carrying people to heaven and huge birds carrying characters on long journeys distinguish these tales. The author provides useful additional material representing oriental cultures, though it is probably of interest only to determined readers.

7.88 Schmid, Eleonore (adapted by Anthea Bell). **Cats' Tales: Feline Fairy Tales from around the World.** Illustrated by the author. North-South Books, 1985. Ages 8–12.

Varied images of cats are contained in this book: positive, as in "The Tale of the Cats" from Italy; neutral, as in "Cats Will Be Cats" from Vietnam; and negative, as in "Two Cats and a Loaf" from India. The tales are collected from twenty different countries. The elegant text pages, with their imaginative use of decorative lines, designs, and text placement, set off the full-page, full-color illustrations effectively.

7.89 Schwartz, Alvin. **Gold and Silver, Silver and Gold: Tales of Hidden Treasure.** Illustrated by David Christiana. Farrar, Straus and Giroux, 1988. Ages 8–12.

The author has unearthed a fascinating collection of true stories and folklore dealing with buried treasure. There are chapters on pirates, treasure maps and codes, famous searches, and haunted treasures. Some treasures have been found, such as the golden rabbit buried by Kit Williams, who left clues to its location in his picture book *Masquerade*. Other treasures are still waiting. This book may inspire some searches. Notes and sources are given.

7.90 Schwartz, Alvin. **Tales of Trickery from the Land of Spoof.** Illustrated by David Christiana. Farrar, Straus and Giroux, 1985. Ages 9–14.

April Fools' Day brings out the trickster in almost everyone, but few have gone to the same lengths as those in the more than twenty preposterous episodes described by folk-humor scholar Alvin Schwartz. Extensive notes, reliable source documentation, and a list of related readings earmark all of Schwartz's books, and here they provide the background necessary for knowing that such pranks have occurred.

7.91   Schwartz, Alvin. **Telling Fortunes: Love Magic, Dream Signs, and Other Ways to Learn the Future.** Illustrated by Tracey Cameron. J. B. Lippincott, 1987. Ages 8–12.

Alvin Schwartz, noted scholar of folklore, sayings, and traditions, describes various methods people use to predict the future. In a light vein, Schwartz presents sayings, games, brief astrology descriptions, and many other ways to tell fortunes. Notes and a bibliography are appended. The author points out to the reader in an epilogue that the future and the methods used for predicting it can encourage the reader to think of possibilities that lie ahead and that predicting the future is fun if not taken too seriously.

7.92   Shannon, George. **Stories to Solve: Folktales from around the World.** Illustrated by Peter Sis. Greenwillow Books, 1985. Ages 8–11.

These short, intriguing puzzles in folktale form will challenge inquisitive children and help develop their thinking skills. Some of the stories are very easy to solve; others take more involved thinking. Taken from eleven different countries, with sources indicated in endnotes, the tales are told without elaboration, but they are interesting, nonetheless. Black pointilistic ink drawings by Peter Sis decorate the pages.

7.93   Stockton, Frank R. **The Bee-Man of Orn.** Illustrated by Maurice Sendak. Harper and Row, 1985. Ages 8–11.

This is a reprint of the cherished tale of the Bee-Man who was very content living among the bees and eating their honey. One day a Junior Sorcerer appears, challenging the Bee-Man to find out what he was transformed from. Whimsical pastel illustrations by Maurice Sendak help tell the adventures the two encounter.

7.94   Weiss, Jaqueline Shachter. **Young Brer Rabbit, and Other Trickster Tales from the Americas.** Illustrated by Clinton Arrowwood. Stemmer House/Barbara Holdridge Books, 1985. Ages 8–11.

An assortment of silhouettes, pen-and-ink sketches, and watercolors decorates this entertaining collection of fifteen Brer Rabbit tales from the Afro-American culture of Central and South America and the Caribbean. The humorous selections are ideal for reading aloud, storytelling, and comparative study of traditional literature.

7.95 Williams-Ellis, Anabel. **Tales from the Enchanted World.** Illustrated by Moira Kemp. Little, Brown, 1987. Ages 10–13.

Including Russian, African, Chinese, British, and German tales, this collection of stories delights with its variety. Some tales are familiar, others little known, but all are good, "tellable" stories. Black-and-white line drawings, along with some in color, make this book visually attractive as well. References and notes are included.

7.96 Yolen, Jane. **The Sleeping Beauty.** Illustrated by Ruth Sanderson. Alfred A. Knopf/Borzoi Books/Ariel Books, 1986. Ages 9–12. (Picture book)

Great care was taken by Ruth Sanderson to paint extraordinarily old-looking paintings to accompany Jane Yolen's retelling of a much-loved fairy tale. Twelve fairies present the princess with thoughtful, enduring gifts, while the thirteenth fairy gives her a curse.

Myths and Legends

Primary

7.97 Chaikin, Miriam. **Exodus.** Illustrated by Charles Mikolaycak. Holiday House, 1987. Ages 7–10. (Picture book)

Miriam Chaikin retells the ancient story of Exodus, of Moses leading the Israelites out of Egypt and slavery. Charles Mikolaycak's colorful illustrations enhance the text by adding details of life 3,000 years ago.

7.98 Climo, Shirley. **King of the Birds.** Illustrated by Ruth Heller. Thomas Y. Crowell, 1988. Ages 4–7. (Picture book)

Long ago when the Earth was young, the birds squabbled and fought from morning until night. They needed a ruler who would bring order out of chaos. This universal myth of their search for a king is illustrated in vibrant full color and reveals that thinking skills will match the strength of the mighty.

7.99   Cohen, Caron Lee. **The Mud Pony: A Traditional Skidi Pawnee Tale.** Illustrated by Shonto Begay. Scholastic/Hardcover Books, 1988. Ages 4–8. (Picture book)

In this retelling of a Pawnee legend, the spirit of Mother Earth comes to a boy in the shape of a horse made from clay. The clay horse comes to life, carrying the boy to victory over enemies and to successful buffalo hunts. When the grown boy becomes chief and has his own strength, the horse returns to Mother Earth. Misty color illustrations add to the mythical quality of the story. Sources for the tale are given.

7.100   Connolly, James. **Why the Possum's Tail Is Bare, and Other Northern American Indian Nature Tales.** Illustrated by Andrea Adams. Stemmer House/Barbara Holdridge Books, 1985. Ages 7–12.

What makes this collection of legends stand heads above others is the fact that the author gives a brief history of all the North American tribes represented in these stories. In addition, each legend is preceded by background information on each of the stories. The Iroquois, Cherokee, Ojibway, Micmac, Sioux, Blackfoot, Cree, and Chinook tribes are represented, with each story reflecting each tribe's diversity. The succinct, well-written tales are excellent for telling or reading aloud. The black-and-white pen-and-ink illustrations are an excellent accompaniment to the text. This is an outstanding collection of folktales as well as a fine addition to Native American lore. *Notable Children's Trade Book in the Field of Social Studies.*

7.101   dePaola, Tomie. **The Legend of the Indian Paintbrush.** Illustrated by the author. G. P. Putnam's Sons, 1988. Ages 4–8. (Picture book)

Through the use of stylized watercolors, Tomie dePaola captures the spirit of traditional Native American art while still demonstrating his own individual style. He presents an account of how the wildflower Indian paintbrush got its name. According to this legend, Little Gopher becomes an artist and is able to bring the vivid colors of the sunset down to Earth. Both the text and the illustrations are uncluttered and quite accessible. Children unfamiliar with Native American folklore will find this a good introduction.

7.102 dePaola, Tomie. **The Miracles of Jesus.** Illustrated by the author. Holiday House, 1987. Ages 6–12. (Picture book)

Twelve miracles performed by Jesus Christ are fully illustrated in this adaptation from the New Testament. Included are Christ's calming of a storm, walking on water, and raising the dead to life.

7.103 dePaola, Tomie. **The Parables of Jesus.** Illustrated by the author. Holiday House, 1987. Ages 6–12. (Picture book)

Tomie dePaola retells seventeen parables used by Jesus Christ in his teachings in this beautifully illustrated book. "The Good Samaritan," "The Lost Sheep," and "The Prodigal Son" are included. The illustrations were inspired by Romanesque art.

7.104 Fussenegger, Gertrud (translated by Anthea Bell). **Noah's Ark.** Illustrated by Annegert Fuchshuber. J. B. Lippincott, 1987. Ages 4–7. (Picture book)

Dramatic full-color paintings, with a tapestrylike flatness of perspective, enhance the calm and measured re-creation of this ageless Biblical story. Children will understand the uncompromising relationship of wickedness and retribution, but they will also be cheered by the joyful message of hope after the turbulence and turmoil of the flood.

7.105 Goble, Paul. **The Great Race of the Birds and Animals.** Illustrated by the author. Bradbury Press, 1985. Ages 6–10. (Picture book)

In the mythology of the Cheyenne and the Sioux, humans assumed domination over the rest of creation by winning the "Great Race." This is the story of that race, which was won by cleverness in the end, thus determining that humans would eat buffalo, not the other way around. The language is written as if it were spoken. Paul Goble's illustrations give visual brilliance and symbolic weight to the straightforward text. Includes references.

7.106 Goble, Paul. **Her Seven Brothers.** Illustrated by the author. Bradbury Press, 1988. Ages 5–9. (Picture book)

Tender and mystical, this Cheyenne legend of the origin of the Big Dipper constellation is illustrated in Caldecott-winner Paul Goble's familiar style. The bold colors are offset by refreshing areas of white space, producing an uncluttered feeling of openness appropriate to the Great Plains. *Children's Choice.*

7.107   Goble, Paul. **Iktomi and the Boulder: A Plains Indian Story.** Illustrated by the author. Orchard Books, 1988. Ages 6–10.

Iktomi, a Plains Indian trickster, gets caught under a boulder and tricks some bats into helping him get free. In traditional style, the listeners are invited to comment about Iktomi's behavior at appropriate points in this legend which explains why the Great Plains are covered with small stones. The brightly colored illustrations are reflective of Plains Indian art. *ALA Notable Children's Book.*

7.108   Heine, Helme. **One Day in Paradise.** Illustrated by the author. Margaret K. McElderry Books, 1986. Ages 3–7. (Picture book)

This tender portrayal of the sixth day of Creation depicts God as a bewhiskered gardener-artist and Adam and Eve as children to whom he gave the gift of Paradise. The softly luminous watercolors are an appropriate tribute to the beauty of the Earth.

7.109   Hirsch, Marilyn. **Joseph Who Loved the Sabbath.** Illustrated by Devis Grebu. Viking Kestrel, 1986. Ages 4–8. (Picture book)

This Jewish folktale tells of hard-working, humble Joseph, who uses what little resources he has to celebrate the Sabbath, despite the ridicule of his wealthy, selfish employer, Sorab. In genuine folktale form, good is rewarded and greed punished when a prophetic dream comes true, leaving Sorab's wealth to Joseph. The spare rhythmic text and subtle humor make this well suited for reading aloud. Line-and-wash paintings accent the Middle-Eastern setting.

7.110   Hogrogian, Nonny. **Noah's Ark.** Illustrated by the author. Alfred A. Knopf/Borzoi Books, 1986. Ages 4–9. (Picture book)

This version of the story of Noah's ark suits the biblical tale in its simplicity and grace. The story begins with the Creation and then follows the generations of people who descend from Adam and Eve. God floods the world to destroy the wickedness of these people, but he saves Noah's family and a pair from each animal species in an ark. Delicate lines and gentle color in the illustrations suit the retelling.

7.111 Hutton, Warwick. **Adam and Eve: The Bible Story.** Illustrated by the author. Margaret K. McElderry Books, 1987. Ages 6–12. (Picture book)

The author has selected the King James Version of the Bible as the text and produced watercolor paintings to retell the story of the creation of Adam and Eve in the Garden of Eden and their subsequent disobedience.

7.112 Hutton, Warwick. **Moses in the Bulrushes.** Illustrated by the author. Margaret K. McElderry Books, 1986. Ages 5–11. (Picture book)

The story unfolds as the pharaoh decrees that all boy babies born to Hebrew women shall be destroyed. One woman bravely decides to keep her son away from danger. Watercolor paintings accompany this Bible story of Moses from infancy to adulthood.

7.113 Lattimore, Deborah Nourse. **The Prince and the Golden Ax: A Minoan Tale.** Illustrated by the author. Harper and Row, 1988. Ages 4–8. (Picture book)

A Minoan prince from the ancient island of Thera challenges the power of the Goddess Diktynna, who wields a golden double-bladed ax. Despite the help of his wiser sister, the boy's arrogance leads to destruction. The illustrations are reminiscent of remaining Minoan art and architecture. A class studying ancient mythology will be interested in this tale from preclassical times, when goddesses were still supreme.

7.114 Mayer, Mercer. **The Pied Piper of Hamelin.** Illustrated by the author. Macmillan, 1987. Ages 6–10. (Picture book)

In this new interpretation of the Pied Piper legend, conflict between the rats and townspeople of Hamelin is given new emphasis as the rats are personified. The striking illustrations accent the drama, while the colorful text is captivating when read aloud.

7.115 Osborne, Mary Pope. **Pandora's Box.** Illustrated by Lisa Amoroso. Scholastic/Hello Reader Books, 1987. Ages 5–9. (Picture book)

Curious Pandora peeks into a beautiful golden box given her
by Zeus, thereby releasing all the world's miseries. Simply
but faithfully retold, this story introduces beginning readers
to Greek mythology. Whimsical line drawings, shaded in two
colors, show a classical Greek setting. Background information and a pronunciation guide are included in this paperback.

7.116 Weil, Lisl. **Pandora's Box.** Illustrated by the author. Atheneum, 1986. Ages 7–10. (Picture book)

The coming of trouble and the dawn of hope in the world are
retold in the familiar myth about Pandora, who is unable to
resist the temptation of a mysterious box. Lisl Weil's stylized
earth-tone watercolor paintings, reminiscent of ancient Gre-
cian art, are appropriate to the tale. *Notable Children's Trade
Book in the Field of Social Studies.*

Intermediate

7.117 Baskin, Hosie, and Leonard Baskin. **A Book of Dragons.** Illustrated by Leonard Baskin. Alfred A. Knopf/Borzoi Books,
1985. Ages 9–12.

Vibrant, fierce, imaginative full-color paintings of many different types of dragons from many mythologies and liter-
atures appear opposite the text defining and describing each
dragon. Included are St. George's dragon, the Hydra, and
Smaug from *The Hobbit.* According to the jacket, the dark
and dreadful dragons symbolize terror, luck, fortune, and fortitude.

7.118 Cooper, Susan. **The Selkie Girl.** Illustrated by Warwick Hutton. Margaret K. McElderry Books, 1986. Ages 8–11.

The legend of a lonely man who takes the skin of a beautiful
Selkie woman in hopes of capturing her for his bride is recounted in flowing prose. The Selkie lives the life of a human
wife and mother until her children discover the hidden
sealskin, allowing her to return to the sea. Watercolor paintings, primarily in blues and greens, evoke the power and mystery of the sea implied in the tale.

7.119 Curry, Jane Louise. **Back in the Beforetime: Tales of the California Indians.** Illustrated by James Watts. Margaret K.
McElderry Books, 1987. Ages 9–12.

Twenty-two tales retell the events of the Creation of the world based on a variety of California Indian legends. James Watts's black-and-white drawings are rich in details that reflect each legend.

7.120 De Armond, Dale. **Berry Woman's Children.** Greenwillow Books, 1985. Ages 8–12.

The use of black, white, and red make the design of this book immediately striking. Woodcut engravings of the animals of Inuit legend—the raven, polar bear, crab, and others—stand out in a black-line frame. On the facing page a spare retelling of a myth featuring that animal, also line framed, begins with the initial letter in dark red. The book is beautiful to look at and is also useful for the study of Inuit culture and folklore. Includes a short glossary.

7.121 Gerstein, Mordicai. **Tales of Pan.** Illustrated by the author. Harper and Row, 1986. Ages 9–12. (Picture book)

Thirteen amusing tales from Greek mythology capture the spirit of Pan, the goat-legged, horned god of "noisy confusion." Mordicai Gerstein's lively four-color pen-and-ink line drawings are controlled yet joyful and spontaneous. The humor will appeal to intermediate readers willing to read or listen to a teacher reading sophisticated picture books.

7.122 Hamilton, Virginia. **In the Beginning: Creation Stories from around the World.** Illustrated by Barry Moser. Harcourt Brace Jovanovich, 1988. Ages 10–13.

Twenty-five creation myths from various cultures are told in styles appropriate to the source. Notes accompanying each story help the reader understand the culture and the story. Wonderful full-color paintings appear at the beginning of each story. Because some of the stories are complex, this collection will find readership among more mature readers and as a read-aloud collection for upper elementary and older children. *ALA Notable Children's Book* and *Newbery Honor Book.*

7.123 Hastings, Selina. **Sir Gawain and the Loathly Lady.** Illustrated by Juan Wijngaard. Lothrop, Lee and Shepard Books, 1985. Ages 9–12.

"What is it women most desire?" While searching for the answer to this question, King Arthur meets the ugliest living thing ever, who knows the answer to the riddle. But in order to get the answer, Sir Gawain must agree to marry the woman. The illustrations are boldly done in bright color, in the style of illuminated manuscripts. An excellent book to use for any age level when studying the Arthurian legends.

7.124 Heyer, Marilee. **The Weaving of a Dream: A Chinese Folktale.** Illustrated by the author. Viking Kestrel, 1986. Ages 8–10.

Elegantly mannered illustrations decorate this legend of a woman so enamored with a painting portraying a palace and its wondrous gardens that she weaves a tapestry of the palace. The tapestry blows away, and the youngest of her three sons perseveres in his travels to retrieve the weaving, barely saving her life. Based on a Chinese tale, the traditional story will strike a familiar echo for children. Although not appealing to all children, the illustrated tale will be enjoyed by fairy tale aficionados.

7.125 Houston, James. **The Falcon Bow: An Arctic Legend.** Illustrated by the author. Margaret K. McElderry Books, 1986. Ages 9–12.

Kungo returns to his adoptive parents in this sequel to *The White Archer*, but he soon sets out to help his starving coastal Inuit people. A hazardous journey to the inland Indian tribe reunites him with his sister and reconciles the two groups, who are both starving. An exciting story of survival against the elements.

7.126 Jaffrey, Madhur. **Seasons of Splendour: Tales, Myths and Legends of India.** Illustrated by Michael Foreman. Atheneum, 1985. Ages 8–12.

The richly diverse folklore and mythology of India is captured in resonant prose suitable for reading aloud or retelling. The arrangement of the twenty-two tales follows the Hindu calendar of festivals. Each section is introduced by the author's childhood recollections, which give a sense of Indian customs and traditions. Numerous stylized watercolors convey the majestic mysticism that the tales present. *Notable Children's Trade Book in the Field of Social Studies*.

7.127 Lewis, Richard. **In the Night, Still Dark.** Illustrated by Ed Young. Atheneum, 1988. Ages 9–12.

This poem is an adaptation drawn from a traditional Hawaiian creation chant, *The Kumulipo*. The creation of living things is boldly proclaimed with quiet naming of the creatures and striking full-color illustrations, beginning with the simple creatures in darkness and ending with the complex creatures at daybreak.

7.128 Low, Alice. **The Macmillan Book of Greek Gods and Heroes.** Illustrated by Arvis Stewart. Macmillan, 1985. Ages 9–12.

Pleasantly open pages with wide margins and a large, easily readable typeface with generous spacing between lines make this a book easy to read aloud. Full-color, full-page and half-page illustrations alternate with smaller, black-ink line drawings. The text of these Greek myths is simple, yet natural sounding. A brief afterword explains the context of the stories.

7.129 Mayo, Gretchen Will. **Star Tales: North American Indian Stories about the Stars.** Illustrated by the author. Walker, 1987. Ages 8–12.

These fourteen Indian legends about the stars, from various North American tribes, are retold as two- to four-page tales that make good read-aloud selections. A brief commentary on the constellation introduces each tale and is accompanied by an ink drawing that represents the artwork of the tribe. Shaded pencil drawings convey the feeling and action of the tales. A listing of the sources for each tale is included.

7.130 Monroe, Jean Guard, and Ray A. Williamson. **They Dance in the Sky: Native American Star Myths.** Illustrated by Edgar Stewart. Houghton Mifflin, 1987. Ages 10 and up.

This book is a useful reference for teachers or storytellers interested in Native American folktales and lore, specifically myths about the stars, including the Milky Way and such constellations as the Big Dipper. Detailed introductions to each story not only add interest to the story, but describe Native American culture and lore. The stories themselves are wonderfully "tellable," even to young audiences. Beautiful black-and-white pencil sketches illustrate the legends. Included are a bibliography, glossary, index, and recommended further reading.

7.131   Osborne, Will, and Mary Pope Osborne. **Jason and the Argonauts.** Illustrated by Steve Sullivan. Scholastic, 1988. Ages 10–12.

The authors retell the classic story of Jason, one of the most important Greek heroes. Basing their account on various retellings of the legend, the Osbornes present a lively and lucid story of Jason and his heroic adventures. Steve Sullivan's black-and-white sketches add to the story line. This would make an important addition to any collection of Greek legends and myths.

7.132   O'Shea, Pat. **Finn Mac Cool and the Small Men of Deeds.** Illustrated by Stephen Lavis. Holiday House, 1987. Ages 9–11.

Aided by the eight Small Men of Deeds, Finn Mac Cool, the tallest, wisest, and bravest man in Ireland, solves the mystery of who has been stealing the giant king's children. Black-and-white sketches enliven this entertaining hero tale. *ALA Notable Children's Book.*

7.133   Perl, Lila. **Don't Sing Before Breakfast, Don't Sleep in the Moonlight: Everyday Superstitions and How They Began.** Illustrated by Erika Weihs. Clarion Books, 1988. Ages 7–10.

This account of superstitions examines what humanity has believed through the ages and, more importantly, why these beliefs have taken hold. Students might use the book more as a browser or a reference book than as a book that they want to read from cover to cover. It leads naturally into a study of word and phrase origins, and it might be a good spinoff to a writing activity in which children imagine and defend the origin of one of these customs and then contrast their versions with the version in the book.

7.134   Philip, Neil. **The Tale of Sir Gawain.** Illustrated by Charles Keeping. Philomel Books, 1987. Ages 9–12.

Using the traditional sources of the Arthurian legends from Chaucer and Malory to T. H. White, Neil Philip has compiled the stories of Sir Gawain and arranged them in an unusual but traditional retelling. Sir Gawain, Arthur's nephew, lies wounded and tells his story to a young squire, recounting the adventures of King Arthur and his knights, his own battle with the Green Knight, his marriage, and the fall of Camelot.

7.135   San Souci, Robert D. **The Enchanted Tapestry.** Illustrated by
László Gál. Dial Books for Young Readers, 1987. Ages 5–12.

Long ago in China, a poor widow works at her loom to support her three grown sons. After she labors for over one year
on a very special tapestry, the family is devastated when it is
stolen. The mother falls ill with grief and sends her sons to retrieve the precious tapestry. It is the youngest son who eludes
the evil sorcerers, crosses the icy sea and the flaming mountains, and reaches the gold palace of the fairies of Sun Mountain. Once retrieved, the cloth magically changes their lives
into the very vision of the widow's dream.

7.136   Segal, Lore. **The Book of Adam to Moses.** Illustrated by
Leonard Baskin. Alfred A. Knopf/Borzoi Books, 1987. Ages
8 and up.

The ancient Hebrew writings of the first five books of Moses
are translated here in clear and elegant modern English, making them wonderfully accessible to young people. Yet there is
nothing childish about this new version. The stories of the
Creation, the Flood, the Tower of Babel, Abraham, Jacob,
Joseph, Moses, and others are powerful and dramatic, especially when read aloud. The stark black-and-white drawings
do not prettify the stories, but add intensity to the drama. An
outline of the stories, with Biblical chapters and verses noted,
is included.

Tall Tales

Primary

7.137   Aylesworth, Jim. **Shenandoah Noah.** Illustrated by Glen
Rounds. Holt, Rinehart and Winston, 1985. Ages 6–9. (Picture book)

Recluse Shenandoah Noah shuns all work until one day when
he has no choice. After getting fleas from his hounds, he must
bathe and wash his clothes, which means splitting wood and
making a fire. The smoke from his fire signals trouble to his
kin in the distant valley. They come to investigate, with surprising results. Humorous pen-and-ink sketches shaded with
gold add to the enjoyment of this tale.

7.138   Cohen, Caron Lee. **Sally Ann Thunder Ann Whirlwind Crockett.** Illustrated by Ariane Dewey. Greenwillow Books, 1985. Ages 5–8.

Sally Ann Thunder Ann Whirlwind Crockett, wife of Davy Crockett, is one woman who is ready for any challenge. Wearing a beehive for a hat, a bearskin dress, and a snake for a belt and carrying a bowie knife for a toothpick, Sally Ann turns the tables on that ornery Mike Fink and sets his teeth to rattling.

7.139   Kellogg, Steven. **Johnny Appleseed: A Tall Tale.** Illustrated by the author. William Morrow, 1988. Ages 4–9. (Picture book)

Steven Kellogg recounts the life of John Chapman, better known as Johnny Appleseed, describing his love of nature, his kindness to animals, his physical fortitude, and his widespread planting of apple trees. Exquisite, detailed illustrations accompany the text, and the alert reader will spot Pinkerton in an apple orchard. *Children's Choice.*

7.140   Rounds, Glen. **Washday on Noah's Ark.** Illustrated by the author. Holiday House, 1985. Ages 7–9. (Picture book)

A fresh, new twist on the story of Noah and his ark is told with Glen Rounds's usual flair for tall tales. Noah builds an ark because the weather reports predict heavy rains. Mrs. Noah has a huge load of wash after forty days and nights on the ark. She ingeniously uses a kite and a variety of snakes for a clothesline, and by the forty-first night her family is clean and shining. Pastel colors brighten the familiar rough ink drawings of Rounds.

Intermediate

7.141   Dewey, Ariane. **Laffite the Pirate.** Illustrated by the author. Greenwillow Books, 1985. Ages 7–12. (Picture book)

Jean Laffite is a tall-tale-type character who embodies the daring roguish ways of pirates. This book blends fact and fantasy into a humorous story of adventure that should appeal to the mature but slow reader, as well as a younger reader. Colorful action-packed illustrations on each page add to the humor of this book.

Recommended Books Published before 1985

Aardema, Verna. *Why Mosquitoes Buzz in People's Ears: A West African Tale Retold.* Illustrated by Leo and Diane Dillon. Dial Books for Young Children, 1975. 4–7.

Aesop. *Three Aesop Fox Fables.* Retold and illustrated by Paul Galdone. Clarion Books, 1971. 5–8.

Aliki. *The Twelve Months: A Greek Folktale Retold.* Greenwillow Books, 1978. 5–8.

Asbjørnsen, Peter C., and J. E. Moe. *The Three Billy Goats Gruff.* Illustrated by Marcia Brown. Harcourt, Brace and World, 1957. 5–7.

Bang, Molly. *Wiley and the Hairy Man: Adapted from an American Folk Tale.* Macmillan, 1976. 6–9.

Bider, Djemma. *The Buried Treasure.* Illustrated by Debby L. Carter. Dodd, Mead, 1982. 6–9.

Brown, Marcia. *Once a Mouse: A Fable Cut in Wood.* Charles Scribner's Sons, 1961. 5–9.

Bryan, Ashley. *Beat the Story Drum, Pum, Pum.* Atheneum, 1980. 5–9.

———. *Walk Together Children: Black American Spirituals.* Macmillan, 1981. 8–12.

Cauley, Lorinda Bryan. *Jack and the Beanstalk.* G. P. Putnam's Sons, 1983. 5–8.

Chase, Richard, ed. *Grandfather Tales: American-English Folk Tales.* Illustrated by Berkeley Williams, Jr. Houghton Mifflin, 1948. 8–10.

Colum, Padraic. *The Golden Fleece and the Heroes Who Lived before Achilles.* Illustrated by Willy Pogany. Macmillan, 1962. 10–12.

Cooper, Susan. *The Silver Cow: A Welsh Tale Retold.* Illustrated by Warwick Hutton. Atheneum, 1983. 5–8.

D'Aulaire, Ingri, and Edgar Parin D'Aulaire. *Book of Greek Myths.* Macmillan, 1962. 8–12.

De Beaumont, Madame. *Beauty and the Beast.* Illustrated by Diane Goode. Bradbury Press, 1978. 7–9.

dePaola, Tomie. *The Clown of God.* Harcourt Brace Jovanovich, 1978. All ages.

———. *The Legend of the Bluebonnet: An Old Tale of Texas.* G. P. Putnam's Sons, 1983. 6–9.

———. *The Prince of the Dolomites: An Old Italian Tale Retold.* Harcourt Brace Jovanovich, 1980. 6–9.

———. *Strega Nona: An Old Tale Retold*. Prentice-Hall, 1975. 4–8.

de Regniers, Beatrice Schenk. *May I Bring a Friend?* Illustrated by Beni Montresor. Atheneum, 1964. 4–8.

Domanska, Janina. *King Krakus and the Dragon*. Greenwillow Books, 1979. 5–8.

Emberley, Barbara. *Drummer Hoff*. Illustrated by Ed Emberley. Prentice-Hall, 1967. 6–9.

Farjeon, Eleanor. *The Silver Curlew*. Illustrated by Ernest H. Shepard. Viking Press, 1954. 8–12.

Fleischman, Sid. *McBrooom Tells a Lie*. Illustrated by Walter Lorraine. Little, Brown, 1976. 7–9.

French, Fiona. *The Blue Bird*. Henry Z. Walck, 1972. 5–8.

Gág, Wanda. *Gone Is Gone; Or, The Story of a Man Who Wanted to Do Housework*. Coward-McCann, 1935. 5–8.

———. *Millions of Cats*. Coward McCann, 1928. 4–7.

Galdone, Paul. *The Three Bears*. Clarion Books, 1972. 5–7.

Goble, Paul. *Buffalo Woman*. Bradbury Press, 1984. 6–8.

Grimm, Jacob, and Wilhelm Grimm. *The Juniper Tree, and Other Tales from Grimm*. Translated by Lore Segal and Randall Jarrell. Illustrated by Maurice Sendak. Farrar, Straus and Giroux, 1973. 8–10.

———. *Snow White*. Translated by Paul Heins. Illustrated by Trina Schart Hyman. Little, Brown, 1974. 5–8.

———. *Snow White and the Seven Dwarfs: A Tale from the Brothers Grimm*. Translated by Randall Jarrell. Illustrated by Nancy Ekholm Burkert. Farrar, Straus and Giroux, 1972. 5–8.

Haley, Gail E. *A Story, a Story: An African Tale Retold*. Atheneum, 1970. 5–8.

Hastings, Selina. *Sir Gawain and the Green Knight*. Illustrated by Juan Wijngaard. Lothrop, Lee and Shepard Books, 1981. 8–10.

Haviland, Virginia. *Favorite Fairy Tales Told in India*. Illustrated by Blair Lent. Little, Brown, 1973. 8–10.

Hirsch, Marilyn. *Could Anything Be Worse? A Yiddish Tale Retold*. Holiday House, 1974. 6–8.

Hodges, Margaret. *Saint George and the Dragon: A Golden Legend Adapted from Edmund Spenser's "Fairie Queene."* Illustrated by Trina Schart Hyman. Little, Brown, 1984. 7–10.

Hogrogian, Nonny. *The Contest*. Greenwillow Books, 1976. 5–8.

Hyman, Trina Schart. *Sleeping Beauty*. Little, Brown, 1977. 7–9.

Jacobs, Joseph. *English Fairy Tales*, 3d ed. Illustrated by John D. Batten. Dover, 1967. 8–11.

Jameson, Cynthia. *The Clap Pot Boy: Adapted from a Russian Tale.* Illustrated by Arnold Lobel. Coward, McCann and Geoghegan, 1973. 5–8.

Keats, Ezra Jack. *John Henry: An American Legend.* Pantheon Books, 1965. 5–8.

Kellogg, Steven. *Paul Bunyan: A Tall Tale Retold.* William Morrow, 1984. 5–8.

Lang, Andrew (edited by Brian Alderson). *The Blue Fairy Book,* rev. ed. Illustrated by John Lawrence. Viking Press, 1978. 7–9.

Langstaff, John. *Frog Went A-Courtin'.* Illustrated by Feodor Rojankovsky. Harcourt, Brace and World, 1955. 5–8.

Lee, Rika. *Legend of the Milky Way.* Holt, Rinehart and Winston, 1983. 5–8.

Lesser, Rika. *Hansel and Gretel.* Illustrated by Paul O. Zelinsky. Dodd, Mead, 1984. 5–8.

Lester, Julius. *The Knee-High Man, and Other Tales.* Illustrated by Ralph Pinto. Dial Books for Young Readers, 1972. 5–8.

Lobel, Arnold. *Fables.* Harper and Row, 1980. 8–10.

———. *Ming Lo Moves the Mountain.* Greenwillow Books, 1982. 6–10.

Lurie, Alison. *The Heavenly Zoo: Legends and Tales of the Stars.* Illustrated by Monika Beisner. Farrar, Straus and Giroux, 1980. 9–12.

McDermott, Gerald. *Anansi the Spider.* Henry Holt, 1972. 7–10.

———. *Arrow to the Sun: A Pueblo Indian Tale.* Viking Press, 1974. 5–8.

McKinley, Robin. *Beauty: A Retelling of the Story of Beauty and the Beast.* Harper and Row, 1978. 10–12.

Minard, Rosemary, ed. *Womenfolk and Fairy Tales.* Illustrated by Suzanna Klein. Houghton Mifflin, 1975. 8–12.

Mosel, Arlene. *The Funny Little Woman.* Illustrated by Blair Lent. E. P. Dutton, 1972. 5–7.

Ness, Evaline. *Tom Tit Tot.* Charles Scribner's Sons, 1965. 6–9.

Nic Leodhas, Sorche. *Thistle and Thyme: Tales and Legends from Scotland.* Illustrated by Evaline Ness. Holt, Rinehart and Winston, 1962. 9–12.

Perrault, Charles (translated by Marcia Brown). *Cinderella; Or, The Little Glass Slipper.* Illustrated by the translator. Charles Scribner's Sons, 1954. 5–8.

Pyle, Howard. *The Merry Adventures of Robin Hood of Great Renown in Nottinghamshire.* Charles Scribner's Sons, 1976. 10–12.

Ransome, Arthur. *The Fool of the World and the Flying Ship: A Russian Tale Retold.* Illustrated by Uri Shulevitz. Farrar, Straus and Giroux, 1968. 5–8.

Schwartz, Alvin. *Scary Stories to Tell in the Dark: Collected from American Folklore.* Illustrated by Stephen Gammell. J. B. Lippincott, 1981. 9–11.

———. *Whoppers: Tall Tales and Other Lies Collected from American Folklore.* Illustrated by Glen Rounds. J. B. Lippincott, 1975. 9–11.

Sherlock, Philip M. *Anansi the Spider Man: Jamaican Folk Tales.* Illustrated by Marcia Brown. Thomas Y. Crowell, 1954. 9–11.

Shulevitz, Uri. *The Treasure.* Farrar, Straus and Giroux, 1978. 6–9.

Singer, Isaac Bashevis. *Zlateh the Goat, and Other Stories.* Translated from the Yiddish by the author and Elizabeth Shub. Illustrated by Maurice Sendak. Harper and Row, 1966. 8–10.

Sleator, William. *The Angry Moon.* Illustrated by Blair Lent. Little, Brown, 1981. 5–8.

Spier, Peter. *Noah's Ark.* Doubleday, 1977. 5–8.

Steptoe, John. *The Story of Jumping Mouse: An American Indian Tale Retold.* Lothrop, Lee and Shepard Books, 1984. 5–8.

Stevenson, James. *"Could Be Worse!"* Greenwillow Books, 1977. 4–7.

Wildsmith, Brian. *The Hare and the Tortoise: Based on the Fable by La Fontaine.* Oxford University Press, 1966. 5–8.

Wolkstein, Diane. *The Red Lion: A Tale of Ancient Persia Retold.* Illustrated by Ed Young. Thomas Y. Crowell, 1977. 5–8.

Yolen, Jane. *The Emperor and the Kite.* Illustrated by Ed Young. Philomel Books, 1967. 6–10.

Zemach, Harve. *Duffy and the Devil: A Cornish Tale Retold.* Illustrated by Margot Zemach. Farrar, Straus and Giroux, 1973. 7–9.

8 Fantasy

Adventure and Magic

Primary

8.1   Aiken, Joan. **The Moon's Revenge.** Illustrated by Alan Lee. Alfred A. Knopf/Borzoi Books, 1987. Ages 6–10. (Picture book)

In his wish to be the maker of enchanted fiddle music, Sep offends the moon and has to pay a price for this magic. Alan Lee's atmospheric illustrations portray both the fantastic and the frightening aspects of this tale, where the cause of the danger is also the salvation from it. *Children's Choice.*

8.2   Dahan, André. **My Friend the Moon.** Illustrated by the author. Viking Kestrel, 1987. Ages 5–7. (Picture book)

In this imaginative picture book, a man makes friends with the moon. When the moon falls in the water, the man rescues him and takes him home. There they discover they both like chocolate pudding. The illustrations, done in crayon and watercolor, extend the succinct text.

8.3   Lyon, David. **The Runaway Duck.** Illustrated by the author. Lothrop, Lee and Shepard Books, 1985. Ages 4–8. (Picture book)

Sebastian ties Egbert, his toy duck, to the bumper of his father's car. Before Sebastian can intercede, Egbert goes sailing off and lands in a stream headed to the ocean. Egbert is then attacked by a shark, discovered on a deserted island by a castaway, and eventually returned to Sebastian.

8.4   McKissack, Patricia C. **Mirandy and Brother Wind.** Illustrated by Jerry Pinkney. Alfred A. Knopf/Borzoi Books, 1988. Ages 8–11. (Picture book)

How Mirandy manages to get Brother Wind to help her win the junior cakewalk is told with dialogue in dialect and bright, detailed illustrations. This lighthearted story will introduce some black folk customs and entertainments of earlier days to its middle-grade audience. *ALA Notable Children's Book*, *Caldecott Honor Book*, and *Coretta Scott King Award* (for illustrations).

8.5 Schroeder, Binette. **Flora's Magic House.** Illustrated by the author. North-South Books, 1986. Ages 7–10.

Innovative full-color artwork illustrates this imaginative fantasy. A magic box uses scissors to fashion a paper house, plane, and boat when circumstances dictate. When the paper boat starts to sink, Flora, Humpty Dumpty, and Magic Box are rescued by Robert Bird and taken back to their garden.

8.6 Steig, William. **Brave Irene.** Illustrated by the author. Farrar, Straus and Giroux, 1986. Ages 4–8. (Picture book)

The dressmaker's daughter battles snow, cold, and wind to deliver an evening gown to the duchess in time for the ball. Plucky Irene is a wonderfully determined character in a funny, melodramatic story. The black line drawings with full-color watercolor washes blanket pages with soft white snow against gray skies, truly evoking a sense of winter. *Notable Children's Trade Book in the Language Arts.*

8.7 Waddell, Martin. **Alice the Artist.** Illustrated by Jonathan Langley. E. P. Dutton, 1988. Ages 4–7. (Picture book)

When Alice changes her painting to suit each passerby, she is unsatisfied with the result. This gentle lesson in artistic integrity makes its point using simple language and uncluttered illustrations. Alice's declaration, "I'm doing it my own way, this time!" and her remark, as she gazes at the finished painting, "I like it!" will be satisfying to children.

8.8 Yorinks, Arthur. **Company's Coming.** Illustrated by David Small. Crown, 1988. Ages 5–8. (Picture book)

Laconic understatement is in delicious contrast to the wildness of this extraterrestrial tale, imaginatively illustrated by David Small. Alarmist Moe and motherly Shirley, who believes the way to the aliens' hearts is through their stomachs, look as though they will fly off the page into reality. Children will enjoy the plot surprises and the spoof of classic alien encounter films. *ALA Notable Children's Book.*

8.9 Yorinks, Arthur. **Hey, Al.** Illustrated by Richard Egielski. Farrar, Straus and Giroux, 1986. Ages 4–7. (Picture book)

Al, a janitor, and his faithful dog, Eddie, leave their mundane lives behind for a taste of paradise and find there is a price to pay. Richard Egielski's excellent use of color and shading shows the contrasts between Al's dreary one-room apartment and a fantastic paradise populated by exotic birds. *ALA Notable Children's Book.*

Intermediate

8.10 Agee, Jon. **The Incredible Painting of Felix Clousseau.** Illustrated by the author. Farrar, Straus and Giroux, 1988. Ages 7–12. (Picture book)

The brief, straightforward telling of this preposterous story of paintings coming alive and the blocky outlined figures in the dark-toned illustrations, which jest art fashions, blend to form a book to be enjoyed as a make-believe story for the very young and as a humorous spoof for the more mature and sophisticated reader. *ALA Notable Children's Book.*

8.11 Aiken, Joan. **Dido and Pa.** Delacorte Press, 1986. Ages 10–14.

Dido Twite returns in yet-another high-paced adventure story, this time centering around the coronation of King Richard and the plot to kidnap him and replace him with a double. Dido discovers old friends, once thought lost, and they conspire to restore the rightful king to the throne.

8.12 Alexander, Lloyd. **The Illyrian Adventure.** E. P. Dutton, 1986. Ages 11–13.

Vesper Holly sets out on a quest to find traces of the legendary kingdom of Illyria so that she can restore her deceased father's academic reputation. Many exciting adventures await her and her guardian in this mythical European kingdom of magical warriors and rebel forces trying to assassinate the king. The book is representative of Lloyd Alexander's excellent writing. *ALA Notable Children's Book* and *Children's Choice*.

8.13   Bauer, Marion Dane. **Touch the Moon.** Illustrated by Alix Berenzy. Clarion Books, 1987. Ages 9–11.

Jennifer dreams of owning a horse and is disappointed with her birthday gift, a tiny china horse. Quickly Jennifer finds herself on a thrilling ride on the palomino named Moonseeker. Imagination and reality blend, and Jennifer learns that she shares her father's dream of riding Moonseeker. She begins to understand that a dream shared strengthens both the imagination and the reality of important things in life.

8.14   Carroll, Lewis. **Alice's Adventures in Wonderland.** Illustrated by Anthony Browne. Alfred A. Knopf/Borzoi Books, 1988. Ages 8–12.

The dreamlike, surreal quality of Alice's visit to Wonderland is captured beautifully in Anthony Browne's detailed, finely drawn illustrations. The reader will discover the interplay between the illustrations and text and between one illustration and another. Everything starts looking familiar after a while, as in a dream. It is hard to imagine an Alice other than John Tenniel's, but this one is equally quiet, observant, and unflappable.

8.15   Carroll, Lewis. **Alice's Adventures in Wonderland.** Illustrated by Michael Hague. Holt, Rinehart and Winston, 1985. Ages 10–13. (Picture book)

This edition joins a growing company of visualizations of Lewis Carroll's popular adventure tale. Michael Hague has produced expectable illustrations. Naturalistic, they are washed in pleasant sepia tones and made easy to understand because of their complete, "readable" details. Justin Todd's version depicts a more distanced, restrained Alice and environment, while S. Michelle Wiggins's version shows an agitated, jumbled environment and characters. Each edition is valuable in its own way: comparisons and contrasts are possible because all three books illustrate primarily the same scenes.

8.16 Gormley, Beatrice. **The Ghastly Glasses.** Illustrated by Emily Arnold McCully. E. P. Dutton, 1985. Ages 9–11.

Andrea, a young girl in need of glasses, mistakenly visits a psychic researcher who prescribes a special pair of glasses for her. The special powers seem minute at first, but later progress to something more serious. The theme emphasizes that the power to change things could make them worse.

8.17 Kennedy, Richard. **Amy's Eyes.** Illustrated by Richard Egielski. Harper and Row, 1985. Ages 10–12.

This unusual story involves dolls being changed into humans or animals, a bawdy down-to-the-sea-in-ships tale of a hunt for pirates' gold, and a Victorian melodrama with sophisticated adult humor, topped off with snatches from Mother Goose. The book lacks the depth and character growth of Richard Adams's *Watership Down*, but it is fun to read. It is a perfect read-aloud tale. The characters, for all their uniqueness, are believable, as is the plot, taken within the realm of fantasy. The length (over four hundred pages) will limit this title to a child who enjoys reading and who hates to come to the end of a story. *ALA Notable Children's Book* and *Children's Choice*.

8.18 McGowen, Tom. **The Magician's Apprentice.** E. P. Dutton/ Lodestar Books, 1987. Ages 9–12.

Tigg, a pickpocket apprenticed to an enchanter, sets out with his master in search of hidden knowledge from the ancient days of magic. The adventure plot and the boy's metamorphosis from a street urchin to a confident, trustworthy, and intellectually curious companion are interesting and believable.

8.19 Winthrop, Elizabeth. **The Castle in the Attic.** Illustrated by Trina Schart Hyman. Holiday House, 1985. Ages 8–12.

Mrs. Phillips, a much-loved nanny, gives young William a toy castle that sets off a series of fantasy adventures. William must solve a riddle, venture through the forest, and battle to break the spell of the Wizard Alastor. As William faces the challenges on his quest, he also resolves a personal dilemma. *Children's Choice*.

Characters

Animals

Primary

8.20 Asch, Frank. **Bear Shadow.** Illustrated by the author. Prentice-Hall, 1985. Ages 2–6. (Picture book)

Bear is fishing, only to have his shadow scare the big fish. He determines to eliminate the shadow, but it changes direction during the day. The simple illustrations are in blue, green, and brown. This is a good story and humorous to those children who know the secret of the sun. *Children's Choice.*

8.21 Barklem, Jill. **The High Hills.** Illustrated by the author. Philomel Books, 1986. Ages 5–8. (Picture book)

This beautifully illustrated book is reminiscent of works by Beatrix Potter and Kenneth Grahame. Jill Barklem's illustrations are done in muted tones and are extremely detailed and intricate. The illustrations carry the story about a young mouse that becomes absorbed in a book he is reading about explorers. When the opportunity for adventure comes along, he is prepared.

8.22 Bellows, Cathy. **Four Fat Rats.** Illustrated by the author. Macmillan, 1987. Ages 5–7. (Picture book)

Four fat rats are pushed out of their nest into the wide world to seek their fortune. They find it by taking over, in succession, the rabbits' hole, the squirrels' tree, and the cows' barn. They meet their match, however, when they invade the little yellow house. This has elements of Leo Lionni's *Frederick*, "Goldilocks and the Three Bears," and "The Fisherman and His Wife" combined in one humorous tale. It could be used as a prelude to the longer, more complex folktales. Pen-and-ink and watercolor illustrations nicely complement the text.

8.23 Blaustein, Muriel. **Lola Koala and the Ten Times Worse Than Anything.** Illustrated by the author. Harper and Row, 1987. Ages 4–8. (Picture book)

Two young sisters visiting their grandma come to realize that although each of them has things she is afraid of, they both are brave in different ways. Lola is timid about scary movies and high places, which do not worry her sister. Big sister is terrified of amusement park rides, so Lola comforts her. Illustrations are large, cartoonlike and colorful, much like James Stevenson's illustrations.

8.24 Bond, Michael. **Paddington at the Palace.** Illustrated by David McKee. G. P. Putnam's Sons/Paddington Books, 1986. Ages 3–7. (Picture book)

Paddington Bear visits Buckingham Palace to see the changing of the guard. Mr. Gruber, with his camera, teaches Paddington and his young reader friends about respect for property. Small children can empathize with the whimsical little bear's problems and applaud his solutions.

8.25 Bond, Michael. **Paddington Cleans Up.** Illustrated by David McKee. G. P. Putnam's Sons/Paddington Books, 1986. Ages 3–7. (Picture book)

Leaving Paddington Bear alone worries Mrs. Brown. If she only knew what was happening in her kitchen while she was gone! Paddington's problems with the vacuum cleaner will leave the reader a bit shocked, but dear, lovable Paddington muddles through another episode.

8.26 Bottner, Barbara. **Zoo Song.** Illustrated by Lynn Munsinger. Scholastic, 1987. Ages 3–8. (Picture book)

To counterattack Gertrude the hippo's constant singing, Herman the lion, her immediate neighbor, takes up the violin, courtesy of a passing musician. Another neighbor, Fabio the bear, accepts a little girl's gift of red tap shoes and begins to dance. The zoo is in an uproar as all three practice on their own. Eventually they reach harmony and a rhythm that is music to *their* ears. Soft colored-pencil illustrations are unfussy and pleasing.

8.27 Boujon, Claude. **Bon Appétit, Mr. Rabbit!** Illustrated by the author. Margaret K. McElderry Books, 1987. Ages 3–8. (Picture book)

In this English translation of a French tale, a rabbit does not like to eat carrots. He decides to see if his neighbors like something better than carrots. But when he learns what the fox eats, he decides that carrots are not so bad. *Children's Choice.*

8.28   Boujon, Claude. **The Cross-Eyed Rabbit.** Illustrated by the author. Margaret K. McElderry Books, 1988. Ages 5–8. (Picture book)

Three rabbit brothers live together in a burrow. One night while two of the brothers are out in the woods, they are discovered by a hungry fox. The third brother, who is visually impaired, is able to save them in an amusing way in this translation of a French tale.

8.29   Brady, Susan. **Find My Blanket.** Illustrated by the author. J. B. Lippincott, 1988. Ages 3–5. (Picture book)

Although Sam Mouse loves to snuggle in his bed with his blanket, he is afraid that he is missing the fun shared by the rest of his family after he goes to bed. He devises a plan to change that. The quiet, unassuming text is perfectly complemented by soft watercolor illustrations; together they relate a story that will be familiar to young children. Due to unfortunate stitching, the story ends with one of the mice hiding in the binding.

8.30   Brandenberg, Franz. **Otto Is Different.** Illustrated by James Stevenson. Greenwillow Books, 1985. Ages 5–6. (Picture book)

A very active young octopus is inquisitive about his physical appearance. Why can't he be like everyone else? Through his daily activities he finds that he has a definite advantage in being different. He realizes that by having eight arms he can get dressed faster, be an asset to his team in sports, and thoroughly enjoy more hugs from his family.

8.31   Brimner, Larry Dane. **Country Bear's Good Neighbor.** Illustrated by Ruth Tietjen Councell. Orchard Books, 1988. Ages 4–9. (Picture book)

Colored-pencil drawings illustrate this tale of Country Bear, who borrows apples, sugar, eggs, flour, walnuts, cinnamon, butter, and milk from his neighbor and returns the ingredients in quite a different form in a surprise gesture of neighborliness.

8.32   Brown, Marc. **D.W. All Wet.** Illustrated by the author. Little, Brown/Joy Street Books, 1988. Ages 3–7. (Picture book)

Arthur's younger sister, D.W., complains bitterly when their aardvark family goes to the beach for the day. It is not until Arthur plays a trick on D.W. that she discovers the joys of splashing, floating, dipping, squirting, and dunking.

8.33   Bucknall, Caroline. **One Bear in the Picture.** Illustrated by the author. Dial Books for Young Readers, 1988. Ages 4–6. (Picture book)

All Ted Bear has to do is stay spotless all day for the school picture. But one catastrophe leads to another, and he is very dirty by the time the photographer is done. Though Ted thinks he has fooled his mother, it is not for long. Bright colored-pencil drawings of the winsome bear and his friends accompany the rhyming text.

8.34   Bunting, Eve. **Happy Birthday, Dear Duck.** Illustrated by Jan Brett. Clarion Books, 1988. Ages 4–7. (Picture book)

Duck's animal friends give him swimming paraphernalia for his birthday, and although pleased to be remembered, he is puzzled about what to do with the items since the setting of this story is a desert. The mystery of the gifts is finally solved with the arrival of the last gift—a swimming pool. Lively and bright illustrations combine with the rhyming text to make this a pleasurable read-aloud book for preschoolers.

8.35   Bunting, Eve. **The Mother's Day Mice.** Illustrated by Jan Brett. Clarion Books, 1986. Ages 5–9. (Picture book)

Little Mouse and his brothers set off to find Mother's Day presents. Jan Brett's detailed illustrations of the mice and their environment bring a special charm to the story of the mice's search, while her clever use of proportion emphasizes the real-life dangers the tiny mice face. Eve Bunting's text ends on a safe and positive note as Little Mouse presents his mother with lasting gifts: a song and his love.

8.36   Burton, Marilee Robin. **Oliver's Birthday.** Illustrated by the author. Harper and Row, 1986. Ages 2–5. (Picture book)

Will his friends remember Oliver the ostrich's birthday? Will they sing for him and bring surprises? This colorful picture book with few words will answer those questions.

8.37 Byrd, Robert. **Marcella Was Bored.** Illustrated by the author. E. P. Dutton, 1985. Ages 5–7. (Picture book)

Marcella the cat is bored with her home, her life, everything—until she becomes lost in the woods. This is a quiet story with heavy moral overtones. The colored pen-and-ink illustrations add a great deal to the book.

8.38 Caple, Kathy. **The Biggest Nose.** Illustrated by the author. Houghton Mifflin, 1985. Ages 5–7. (Picture book)

After being ridiculed for having the biggest nose in school, a humiliated Eleanor the elephant knots her trunk. Neither she nor frantic family members can undo the knot until Eleanor sneezes a sneeze powerful enough to untwist her trunk. The direct, amusing story is perfectly paired with uncluttered, subtle-toned watercolors.

8.39 Caple, Kathy. **Harry's Smile.** Illustrated by the author. Houghton Mifflin, 1987. Ages 4–8. (Picture book)

Harry determines he will no longer smile because he finds his photograph unbecoming. When he writes to his pen pal, Wilma, that he can no longer be her pen pal and tells Sam, his friend, that he will no longer smile, the two friends hit on the solution that makes Harry smile again. Watercolor illustrations depict Harry as a dog, Wilma a rabbit, and Sam a cat. This is a satisfying story for the preschooler, and the text is simple enough for beginning readers.

8.40 Carle, Eric. **The Very Busy Spider.** Illustrated by the author. Philomel Books, 1985. Ages 3–6. (Picture book)

Each of the farm animals asked the spider to come away and leave her task, but to each, "The spider didn't answer. She was very busy spinning her web." The illustrations are typical of Eric Carle—done in collage, watercolor, and crayon. In addition, the spider, her web, and a fly are raised and can be felt. The book is a perfect blend of repetitive story and illustrations for sighted and visually handicapped preschoolers, as well as a good introduction to animals and their sounds.

8.41 Carlson, Nancy. **Louanne Pig in Making the Team.** Illustrated by the author. Viking Penguin/Puffin Books, 1986. Ages 4–6. (Picture book)

Animals are cast in this story with a twist. Louanne Pig decides to try out for the cheerleading squad, while her friend Arnie tries to make the football team. Each day as they practice, they discover that Louanne is better at tackling and throwing the football, and Arnie is better at cartwheels and split jumps. This is a not-too-obvious approach to breaking sexual stereotypes. The illustrations are childlike and fun.

8.42 Carlson, Nancy. **Louanne Pig in Witch Lady.** Illustrated by the author. Carolrhoda Books, 1985. Ages 4–8. (Picture book)

Four animal friends are afraid of an old lady who lives in a house on top of the hill. When they try to run through her yard, Louanne Pig twists her ankle and is left behind. The witch turns out to be a friendly, fascinating old woman. The spooky story with its cheerful drawings will satisfy the beginning reader.

8.43 Carlson, Nancy. **Loudmouth George and the New Neighbors.** Illustrated by the author. Viking Penguin/Puffin Books, 1986. Ages 5–7. (Picture book)

A new family of pigs moves in next door to the rabbits. George the rabbit does not want to join the fun at first, but he later changes his mind.

8.44 Carlstrom, Nancy White. **Jesse Bear, What Will You Wear?** Illustrated by Bruce Degen. Macmillan, 1986. Ages 5–7. (Picture book)

The repetitive rhyme asks Jesse Bear what will he wear. His answers, also in rhyme, make a charming picture book. The watercolors evoke an era of times past—of rose-covered trellises, white picket fences, iron stoves, and a bathtub with feet. This is a warm, enjoyable family story with which the picture-book crowd can identify. *Children's Choice.*

8.45 Carrick, Carol. **What Happened to Patrick's Dinosaurs?** Illustrated by Donald Carrick. Clarion Books, 1986. Ages 4–8. (Picture book)

"Where did all the dinosaurs go?" Fact and fantasy intertwine as young Patrick's vivid imagination counters the scientific explanation given by his older brother, Hank. Donald Carrick's spectacular full-color illustrations project Patrick's visions of the dinosaurs, and Carol Carrick's text captures the freshness of a small boy's imagination. *ALA Notable Children's Book.*

8.46   Castle, Caroline. **Herbert Binns and the Flying Tricycle.** Illustrated by Peter Weevers. Dial Books for Young Readers, 1987. Ages 6–9. (Picture book)

Watercolor paintings support this picture-book story of a small inventor mouse who delights almost all his friends. Three jealous animals want to spoil his latest invention by stealing its pin. Will they be successful?

8.47   Cazet, Denys. **Frosted Glass.** Illustrated by the author. Bradbury Press, 1987. Ages 4–7. (Picture book)

Gregory the dog is a daydreamer, often out of synch with the rest of his school class. He has a chance to shine when his imaginative artwork is recognized and prominently displayed. *Children's Choice.*

8.48   Cazet, Denys. **Great-Uncle Felix.** Illustrated by the author. Orchard Books, 1988. Ages 4–7. (Picture book)

Sam, a young rhinoceros, wants to impress a visiting relative, but when things do not go as planned, he is crestfallen. Children whose confidence needs a boost will enjoy Great-Uncle Felix's warmth and understanding and will better appreciate the meaning of friendship.

8.49   Cherry, Lynne. **Who's Sick Today?** Illustrated by the author. E. P. Dutton, 1988. Ages 4–6. (Picture book)

Animals that are sick in bed, visit a doctor, or stay in a hospital are introduced in rhyme. Readers will meet a small fox with chicken pox, whales on a scale, a chimp with a limp, llamas in pajamas, and young stoats with sore throats in this colorfully illustrated book for young children. *Children's Choice.*

8.50   Chorao, Kay. **Cathedral Mouse.** Illustrated by the author. E. P. Dutton, 1988. Ages 4–8. (Picture book)

A mouse escapes from a pet shop and takes refuge in a great cathedral, where he finds a friend and a home. The illustrations of a winsome little mouse wandering around the vast, imposing cathedral are especially fetching. The colored-pencil and ink drawings contrast the cold, gray stonework of the building with the tenderness and warmth of the characters. The story stands alone as a good read-aloud tale, too.

8.51 Christelow, Eileen. **Olive and the Magic Hat.** Illustrated by the author. Clarion Books, 1987. Ages 5–8. (Picture book)

While wrapping a new top-hat for their father's birthday, Olive and Otis Opossum accidently push it out the window. Magically it lands on Mr. Foxley's head as he passes by. Colorful double-page drawings illustrate the ensuing comedy of errors as the children try to retrieve the hat. Primary-grade children will enjoy reading this book for themselves. *Children's Choice.*

8.52 Christopher, Matt. **The Dog That Pitched a No-Hitter.** Illustrated by Daniel Vasconcellos. Little, Brown, 1988. Ages 7–10.

After the beginning-reading books have been mastered, and before chapter books are comfortable, young readers sometimes have a problem finding enjoyable reading. Books such as this one solve that difficulty. Mike and his dog, Harry, share a love of sports and a secret: ESP.

8.53 Coxe, Molly. **Louella and the Yellow Balloon.** Illustrated by the author. Thomas Y. Crowell, 1988. Ages 3–7. (Picture book)

When Louella Pig is taken to the circus by her mother, Patricia Pig, she wanders off to retrieve her balloon. Patricia frantically hunts for Louella all over the circus until she locates Louella in a most unusual predicament.

8.54 Craig, Helen. **Susie and Alfred in the Night of the Paper Bag Monster.** Illustrated by the author. Alfred A. Knopf/Borzoi Books, 1985. Ages 3–7. (Picture book)

Whimsical watercolors illustrate the efforts of pigs Susie and Alfred to create unusual Halloween costumes. Disaster and a quarrel ensue, but the two friends learn that cooperation leads to success.

8.55 Dabcovich, Lydia. **Mrs. Huggins and Her Hen Hannah.** Illustrated by the author. E. P. Dutton, 1985. Ages 3–7. (Picture book)

The companionship between Mrs. Huggins and her pet hen is warmly developed in simple text and large, detailed color illustrations that show the two of them sharing such daily activities as shearing the sheep, planting the garden, and sitting by the fire. How Mrs. Huggins becomes consoled after the death of her pet brings a surprise ending that gently instructs the young child about the ongoing life cycle. *Children's Choice*.

8.56   Damjan, Mischa. **The Fake Flamingos.** Illustrated by Józef Wilkoń. North-South Books, 1987. Ages 4–8. (Picture book)

Discontented as a stork, Click decides to become a pink flamingo, but becoming a *red* flamingo is not in her plans. This simple fable gently suggests that it is better to be yourself than to pretend to be something you are not. The large, textured illustrations will make this a popular choice for story hour.

8.57   Da Rif, Andrea. **Thomas in Trouble.** Illustrated by the author. Margaret K. McElderry Books, 1987. Ages 5–9.

Thomas—for Trouble—gets into trouble by throwing a baseball through a window, talking in class, and dropping a quart of milk and three eggs, and he is sent to his room. When he decides to run away from home, he has some exciting adventures that get him into trouble once again.

8.58   Day, Alexandra. **Frank and Ernest.** Illustrated by the author. Scholastic/Hardcover Books, 1988. Ages 7–11. (Picture book)

Ernest, an elephant, and Frank, a bear, run a business of minding other people's businesses when they are on vacation. When the two friends are asked to operate a diner, they prepare by researching the special diner language. Children will enjoy figuring out this special language—"Paint a bow-wow red, Frank, and I need a nervous pudding."

8.59   Delton, Judy. **A Birthday Bike for Brimhall.** Illustrated by June Leary. Carolrhoda Books/On My Own Books, 1985. Ages 5–9.

It is easy to empathize with Brimhall the bear as he offers excuses instead of admitting that he does not know how to do something—in this case, ride a bike. The book's pattern of predictability and Brimhall's eventual triumph will please young readers. Expressive black-and-white illustrations enhance the text.

8.60   Deming, A. G. **Who Is Tapping at My Window?** Illustrated by Monica Wellington. E. P. Dutton, 1988. Ages 5–8. (Picture book)

When asked, "Who is tapping at my window?" each animal responds, "It is not I." Young readers can respond to the repetition and rhythm of this old verse or can use the picture clues to find the answer to the question. Illustrations fill each page with clean lines, shapes, and colors.

8.61   Dubanevich, Arlene. **Pig William.** Illustrated by the author. Bradbury Press, 1985. Ages 4–6. (Picture book)

In this sequel to *Pigs in Hiding*, William's incessant dawdling causes him to miss the school picnic, but as usual he creates his own fun and is soon joined by his siblings after rain drowns their picnic plans. Brightly colored cartoon drawings and humorous balloon-captioned dialogue offer unlimited child appeal.

8.62   Duke, Kate. **Seven Froggies Went to School.** Illustrated by the author. E. P. Dutton, 1985. Ages 4–7.

Large, brightly colored, animated pictures catch the antics of the seven froggies at school. Master Bullfrog "from his seat on the log . . . teaches the wisdom of the bog." The lively illustrations are appealing and make the book appropriate for reading aloud or for beginning readers. The text is adapted from a song the author's grandmother learned as a child. *Children's Choice.*

8.63   Duke, Kate. **What Would a Guinea Pig Do?** Illustrated by the author. E. P. Dutton, 1988. Ages 4–8. (Picture book)

What if a guinea pig wanted to clean up its house, bake a cake, or be like somebody else? The author responds to these questions with many silly suggestions that will delight the youngest reader.

8.64   Dunbar, Joyce. **A Cake for Barney.** Illustrated by Emilie Boon. Orchard Books, 1987. Ages 4–8. (Picture book)

Barney the bear attempts to eat a delicious cake with five cherries on it. But each time he is ready to take a bite, he is interrupted, in turn, by a wasp, mouse, crow, squirrel, and fox, who each want part of it. When a big bear wants the cake, a turn of events takes place, and Barney learns to stand up for himself in a nonviolent way.

8.65   Duvoisin, Roger. **Petunia the Silly Goose Stories.** Illustrated by the author. Alfred A. Knopf/Borzoi Books, 1987. Ages 4–7. (Picture book)

Petunia the goose learns valuable lessons about herself and others in this reissue of five favorite stories, some of which no longer appear in print in separate editions.

8.66   Eagle, Mike. **The Marathon Rabbit.** Illustrated by the author. Holt, Rinehart and Winston, 1985. Ages 6–9. (Picture book)

A rabbit running in a city marathon? The note on his sweat-shirt says that is what he wants to do. The rabbit is allowed in the race, and he easily pulls ahead of the people and wins. A sentence or two on each page and full-color drawings convey accurate details of a marathon despite the intrusion of a rabbit in racing togs.

8.67   Ehrlich, Amy. **Bunnies All Day Long.** Illustrated by Marie H. Henry. Dial Books for Young Readers, 1985. Ages 4–8. (Picture book)

The mischievous antics of Larry, Harry, and Paulette Bunny will strike a chord of recognition with children who experience similar problems with parents, siblings, and teachers. Delicate watercolor vignettes humorously depict daily events described by the smoothly flowing story line.

8.68   Ernst, Lisa Campbell. **The Rescue of Aunt Pansy.** Illustrated by the author. Viking Kestrel, 1987. Ages 3–5. (Picture book)

In this enjoyable story, a nice cat is given a new toy for his birthday. How he acquires a new friend with this toy makes for a quietly amusing story, which is enhanced with double-page and half-page illustrations in pen-and-ink and acrylics.

8.69   Foreman, Michael. **Cat and Canary.** Illustrated by the author. Dial Books for Young Readers/Pied Piper Books, 1987. Ages 4–8. (Picture book)

The friendship between a cat and canary leads to an unexpected solution to Cat's dilemma when, tangled in a kite string, he is whisked up over Manhattan. Stunning full-page watercolor illustrations, with their perspectives of skyscrapers from Cat's eyes, complement the rich language of the text, making this a story to be read aloud over and over. All the story-map parts are here.

8.70 Fox, Mem. **Hattie and the Fox.** Illustrated by Patricia Mullins. Bradbury Press, 1987. Ages 2–6. (Picture book)

While the other animals do not appear to be interested when Hattie the hen sights danger, they soon discover that she is telling the truth. Illustrations using tissue paper and crayon in a collage technique greatly enhance this adventure.

8.71 Fuchshuber, Annegert. **The Cuckoo-Clock Cuckoo.** Illustrated by the author. Carolrhoda Books, 1988. Ages 4–7. (Picture book)

Magical things happen at the witching hour of midnight, and when a curious cuckoo leaves his clock, he is unable to return for twenty-four hours. The same view of a street is shown throughout the day, with a clock face counting the hours. A lengthy text, crowded illustrations, and times of day that are not on the hour make this a possible choice for a child whose sense of time is quite secure.

8.72 Graham, Thomas. **Mr. Bear's Boat.** Illustrated by the author. E. P. Dutton, 1988. Ages 4–7. (Picture book)

Mr. Bear is a confident and patient builder as he uses information from books to construct a sailboat. Even a crowded sea and a brief stay on a sand dune do not spoil Mr. and Mrs. Bear's outing in this full-color picture book.

8.73 Gretz, Susanna. **Roger Takes Charge!** Illustrated by the author. Dial Books for Young Readers, 1987. Ages 4–6. (Picture book)

Bossy pig Flo gets her comeuppance when Roger takes charge. Lively watercolor illustrations convey the range of emotions from dismay to delight as Roger and his little brother Nelson see Flo get a taste of her own medicine. *Children's Choice.*

8.74   Harper, Anita. **It's Not Fair!** Illustrated by Susan Hellard.
            G. P. Putnam's Sons, 1986. Ages 5–7.

Children with younger siblings will be able to relate to this
story of an older sister who has to come to terms with her
feelings about her baby kangaroo brother. While he is an in-
fant, she says it's not fair that he gets special treatment. But
as he begins to grow up, she realizes that there are many
things she does that he cannot do. Bold ink-and-wash drawings complement the simple, straightforward text.

8.75   Harper, Anita. **What Feels Best?** Illustrated by Susan Hellard.
            G. P. Putnam's Sons, 1988. Ages 4–8. (Picture book)

A young kangaroo doing things all alone begins to realize that
it would be much more fun to do things with someone else.
Many emotions are introduced, and readers might want to
discuss these feelings.

8.76   Henkes, Kevin. **Chester's Way.** Illustrated by the author.
            Greenwillow Books, 1988. Ages 5–9. (Picture book)

Chester, a young mouse, does things in his own way. He develops special friendships and learns that even the closest of
friends can have their own interests and abilities that make
them truly unique. Charming watercolor and pen-and-ink illustrations enhance the story. *ALA Notable Children's Book.*

8.77   Heuck, Sigrid. **Who Stole the Apples?** Illustrated by the au-
            thor. Alfred A. Knopf/Borzoi Books, 1986. Ages 3–5. (Picture
            book)

A pony lives in a clearing near an apple tree that supplies his
apples. One day he discovers all the apples missing. With the
help of a teddy bear, he sets out to find the apples. This
charming cumulative story is told using pictographs, which
are beautifully drawn in acrylics. A good book for storytelling.

8.78   Holabird, Katharine. **Angelina and Alice.** Illustrated by
            Helen Craig. Clarkson N. Potter, 1987. Ages 3–6. (Picture
            book)

Angelina and her new school chum Alice love to dance and
do gymnastics together. One terrible day Alice walks off and
leaves a brokenhearted Angelina behind. Mr. Hopper, the

sports teacher, announces that the school is going to put on a gymnastics show for the village. Angelina and Alice team up again and perform brilliantly for the crowd. Full-color illustrations enhance the story.

8.79 Howard, Jane R. **When I'm Sleepy.** Illustrated by Lynne Cherry. E. P. Dutton, 1985. Ages 3–5. (Picture book)

With detail reminiscent of Nancy Ekholm Burkert and fuzzy animals recalling Garth Williams, Lynne Cherry's watercolor and pen-and-ink illustrations perfectly capture the mood of a little girl as she imagines sleeping in various places with various animals. Large print and illustrations make this perfect for preschoolers and naptime reading.

8.80 Isenberg, Barbara, and Susan Wolf. **Albert the Running Bear Gets the Jitters.** Illustrated by Diane deGroat. Clarion Books, 1987. Ages 5–8.

When Albert the marathon-winning bear meets his greatest challenge in Boris, a huge bully bear, he is overcome with anxiety. Friends help him cope with the pressure. Of course, Albert not only wins the race, but he also wins Boris's respect and friendship. Sportsmanship, fear, and stress control are examined in a lighthearted text and cartoon-style watercolors. An appended note suggests ways children may cope with stressful situations. *Children's Choice.*

8.81 Janosch (translated by Edite Kroll). **The Old Man and the Bear.** Illustrated by the author. Bradbury Press, 1987. Ages 6–9. (Picture book)

In this sensitive story, an old man lives alone in a house near a village. Each winter he takes his savings to purchase singing birds in the market and then sets them free. One cold winter, when the aging man becomes frail and hungry, he is helped by a bear who, in turn, helps one of the old man's birds after his death.

8.82 Jenkin-Pearce, Susie. **Bad Boris and the New Kitten.** Illustrated by the author. Macmillan, 1987. Ages 5–8.

Maisie's life with Boris the elephant changes when a stray kitten joins them. Trying to get Maisie's attention, Boris attempts the same stunts as the kitten, but gets into trouble. This story will appeal to anyone who has ever had to cope with the arrival of a new brother or sister.

8.83 Johnston, Tony. **Whale Song.** Illustrated by Ed Young. G. P. Putnam's Sons, 1987. Ages 3–7.

Ed Young's magnificent paintings show the size, beauty, and movement of whales. The illustrations and text blend beautifully to create a powerful song-story using numbers as the whale song rather than as a counting book.

8.84 Korth-Sander, Irmtraut (translated by Rosemary Lanning). **Will You Be My Friend?** Illustrated by the author. North-South Books, 1986. Ages 3–5. (Picture book)

Peter the pig wants a friend, so he leaves his parents in the farmyard and sets out in search of a friend. It is not as easy as he imagined, but he manages. This is a quiet book, but one that will evoke a great deal of empathy among the preschool set. Acrylic and crayon drawings are nicely done and capture the mood of the story.

8.85 Kroll, Steven. **Don't Get Me in Trouble!** Illustrated by Marvin Glass. Crown, 1987. Ages 4–7. (Picture book)

A friendship between dogs Mickey and Jake, reminiscent of that in Arnold Lobel's Frog and Toad books, and the humor in the scattery, windblown illustrations will attract children. The story pattern, containing an unexpected turn of events, may spark children's own writing.

8.86 Latimer, Jim. **Going the Moose Way Home.** Illustrated by Donald Carrick. Charles Scribner's Sons, 1988. Ages 6–8. (Picture book)

In this collection of good-humored short tales, fantasy is accepted as commonplace. The book focuses on an unusual moose who shares his root beer with cows, helps smaller animals get across a toll bridge, and mistakes a train for a female moose. Children will enjoy the atmosphere of friendship and will find the varied page layout and short chapters conducive to independent reading.

8.87 Leedy, Loreen. **The Bunny Play.** Illustrated by the author. Holiday House, 1988. Ages 4–8. (Picture book)

Comical bug-eyed bunnies cavort through a production of "Little Red Riding Hood," providing a clear and simple explanation of what goes on behind the scenes in a theater. The brief, easy-to-read text will enable children to stage their own plays, from tryouts to final performance. A glossary of theater terms is included.

8.88 Lindgren, Astrid (translated by Barbara Lucas). **I Don't Want to Go to Bed.** Illustrated by Ilon Wikland. R and S Books, 1988. Ages 4–8. (Picture book)

"I don't want to go to bed!" screams five-year-old Larry. He always has one more excuse at bedtime. One day his neighbor, Aunt Lottie, lets Larry look through her strange and wonderful glasses. Bright, detailed illustrations accompanying the text take Larry and the young reader to animal families at bedtime. Larry's mother is in for a surprise!

8.89 Lindsay, Elizabeth. **A Letter for Maria.** Illustrated by Alex de Wolf. Orchard Books, 1988. Ages 3–8. (Picture book)

Bear cannot write a letter so he paints a picture letter for his friend Maria, who is in the hospital. A tender, loving story for the young child.

8.90 Lionni, Leo. **Nicolas, Where Have You Been?** Illustrated by the author. Alfred A. Knopf/Borzoi Books, 1987. Ages 4–7. (Picture book)

When the birds take all the red, ripe, juicy berries, the mice are left with only the dry, tart ones and a very mean attitude toward the birds. Nicolas, in attempting to outsmart the birds, lands in a predicament that teaches (but does not preach) that "one bad bird doesn't make a flock." Beautifully illustrated in collage, this title can be used with several age levels.

8.91 Lucas, Barbara. **Sleeping Over.** Illustrated by Stella Ormai. Macmillan/Lucas Evans Books, 1986. Ages 3–8. (Picture book)

Froggie Green is spending the night with his friend Bitty Bear. Somehow he just cannot fall asleep in a strange bed. Then he comes up with the perfect solution. The illustrations are beautiful in color and detail.

8.92 McCarthy, Ruth. **Katie and the Smallest Bear.** Illustrated by Emilie Boon. Alfred A. Knopf/Borzoi Books, 1985. Ages 3–5. (Picture book)

The smallest bear who lives at the zoo is lonely because he has no playmate—until Katie comes along. They go to the park, play, eat lunch, and have a lovely time together. A warm, imaginative story, this will be excellent for reading aloud or telling. The illustrations in crayon and watercolor perfectly match the text.

8.93   McPhail, David. **Emma's Pet.** Illustrated by the author. E. P. Dutton, 1985. Ages 3–5. (Picture book)

Emma the bear wants a pet. The fish that she brings home is too slippery, and the frog tries to take a bath with her mother. But Emma finds a cuddly pet in an unexpected place. The full-page color illustrations on each page capture the range of Emma's feelings as she searches for the right pet.

8.94   McPhail, David. **Emma's Vacation.** Illustrated by the author. E. P. Dutton, 1987. Ages 3–5. (Picture book)

The bear family—Emma, her mother, and her father—are on vacation. They take in all the Disney-like hoopla, which tires Emma to the point where she opts for just enjoying the natural delights near their cottage. There are full-color illustrations to augment the story.

8.95   Maestro, Betsy. **Dollars and Cents for Harriet.** Illustrated by Giulio Maestro. Crown/Money Concept Books, 1988. Ages 3–6. (Picture book)

Harriet the elephant does various chores to earn enough money for a kite. In the process, the reader learns how many pennies, nickels, dimes, quarters, and half dollars it takes to make a dollar.

8.96   Majewski, Joe. **A Friend for Oscar Mouse.** Illustrated by Maria Majewska, 1988. Ages 4–7. (Picture book)

Oscar the house mouse and Alfie the field mouse have a fine time exploring, playing, and rescuing each other from danger. Children will enjoy the pleasant, low-key story of their friendship and the large illustrations. The flowers look as though they might be pickable, and the mice look pettable, but there is also a natural quality to the illustrations that saves them from being saccharine.

8.97 Marushkin, Fran. **Little Rabbit's Baby Brother.** Illustrated by Diane deGroat. Crown, 1986. Ages 4–8. (Picture book)

Little Rabbit discovers what it is like to become a big sister in this tender yet funny story with beautiful illustrations. Her questions are ones that many children ask their parents at the birth of a new sibling.

8.98 Marshall, James. **George and Martha Round and Round.** Illustrated by the author. Houghton Mifflin, 1988. Ages 4–9. (Picture book)

George and Martha, two hippo friends, enjoy each other's company despite the ups and downs in their friendship. In this book, one of several about the hippos, they have adventures involving a loud clock, a boat ride, painting a picture, the attic, and a surprise.

8.99 Marshall, James. **Wings: A Tale of Two Chickens.** Illustrated by the author. Viking Kestrel, 1986. Ages 6–8. (Picture book)

James Marshall's wacky story is played out by two very different friends, Harriet and Winnie. These portly poultry encounter the expected fox, this time in a chicken costume. Funny, skin-of-the-teeth escapes are resolved, in the end, by Harriet's determination to rescue her friend.

8.100 Marshall, James. **Yummers Too: The Second Course.** Illustrated by the author. Houghton Mifflin, 1986. Ages 5–8. (Picture book)

Once again Emily Pig and her friend Eugene star in a hilarious story. Emily cannot resist eating three popsicles from Eugene's popsicle wagon. But Emily has no money, and her efforts to earn some produce a gleeful, funny adventure. James Marshall's comic illustrations add to the fun.

8.101 Martin, Bill, Jr., and John Archambault. **Barn Dance!** Illustrated by Ted Rand. Henry Holt, 1986. Ages 5–10. (Picture book)

What does the owl mean by "There's magic in the air"? A boy creeps outside to find out. What he discovers—a barn dance in full swing—proves there is magic. This story-poem with its barn-dance rhythms should be read aloud. Full-page pictures convey a love of country life.

8.102   Mathers, Petra. **Maria Theresa.** Illustrated by the author. Harper and Row, 1985. Ages 5–7. (Picture book)

Maria Theresa is unlike other hens in Signora Rinaldo's chicken coop. She seems to want more, and so one day, when Signora Rinaldo inadvertently leaves open the door of the coop, Maria Theresa flies—several stories down to the street—and joins the circus. The imaginative text is enhanced by the detailed and humorously drawn watercolors.

8.103   Miller, Moira. **Oscar Mouse Finds a Home.** Illustrated by Maria Majewska. Dial Books for Young Readers, 1985. Ages 4–10. (Picture book)

Oscar Mouse thinks his attic home is too crowded and noisy, so he sets out to explore the house for a perfect place of his own. This predictable story will be useful as a model for writing. Full-color illustrations in watercolors, inks, and crayons accompany the text. *Children's Choice.*

8.104   Miller, Moira. **The Proverbial Mouse.** Illustrated by Ian Deuchar. Dial Books for Young Readers, 1987. Ages 5–7. (Picture book)

The title for this beautifully illustrated and written picture book stems from the fact that a proverb summarizes each set of rhymes. Little mouse is hungry: his tum is empty, his toes are empty, and his tail is empty, so he sets off in the toy shop to rectify the situation. The book can be used on many levels—poetry, picture story, or proverbs.

8.105   Modesitt, Jeanne. **Vegetable Soup.** Illustrated by Robin Spowart. Macmillan, 1988. Ages 4–7. (Picture book)

Children reluctant to try new foods will feel right at home with Elsie and Theodore, rabbits whose move to a new home has left the cupboard bare. Friends are found who introduce fresh culinary delights, which the rabbits at first are hesitant to try. The story ends with vegetable soup being enjoyed by everyone. Softly rounded figures in hazy, textured paintings will entice young readers.

8.106   Moers, Herman (translated by Rosemary Lanning). **Hugo the Baby Lion.** Illustrated by Józef Wilkoń. North-South Books, 1986. Ages 4–6. (Picture book)

While hunting for the first time, Hugo the lion painfully encounters a cactus, mistakenly pokes his head in a crocodile's mouth, and falls into the river, but the cub's final, gentle triumph is warmly reassuring. The full-color paintings are filled with humor, especially Hugo's facial expressions.

8.107   Moore, Lilian. **I'll Meet You at the Cucumbers.** Illustrated by Sharon Wooding. Atheneum/Jean Karl Books, 1988. Ages 6–10.

Adam, a country mouse, is invited to visit his pen pal, Amanda, who lives in the city. At first fearful of city life, Adam finds excitement, adventure, and new friends in this quickly paced first read-alone chapter book. Adam teaches his friends about poetry by reciting his own poems as well as those of famous poets.

8.108   Morgan, Michaela. **Edward Loses His Teddy Bear.** Illustrated by Sue Porter. E. P. Dutton, 1988. Ages 3–6. (Picture book)

Edward wakes up to discover his teddy bear is missing. With the help and encouragement of his mother and his own wild imagination, he is able to locate his lost toy.

8.109   Novak, Matt. **Rolling.** Illustrated by the author. Bradbury Press, 1986. Ages 3–7. (Picture book)

Fearful of thunder, the animals of the forest race for shelter. Soon the rolling thunder subsides, and the animals are led safely home by a new and comforting "rolling" sound. Animated full-page drawings capture this tale's drama and enhance the simplified vocabulary. Children will readily identify with the theme of this story.

8.110   Numeroff, Laura Joffe. **If You Give a Mouse a Cookie.** Illustrated by Felicia Bond. Harper and Row, 1985. Ages 5–8. (Picture book)

One thing leads to another in this lighthearted book describing the consequences of offering a cookie to a mouse. The fun is in the anticipation of the mouse's outrageous yet quite logical requests. Too much telling would spoil the joke, so illustrations dominate and provide much of the humor.

8.111   Oakley, Graham. **The Diary of a Church Mouse.** Illustrated by the author. Atheneum, 1987. Ages 7–10. (Picture book)

This new entry in the Church Mice series is filled with the same wit and good humor that have characterized the other books. Humphrey the mouse's eventful diary chronicles the adventures of the mice, Sampson the cat, and the other inhabitants of Wortlethorpe Church. The story serves as a natural tie-in to creative writing.

8.112   Oppenheim, Joanne. **You Can't Catch Me!** Illustrated by Andrew Shachat. Houghton Mifflin, 1986. Ages 4–8. (Picture book)

This read-aloud tale recounts the adventures of a mischievous fly—and his most surprising final encounter. The smug retort of the fly as he eludes his animal pursuers is repeated throughout the story as in "The Gingerbread Boy." Imaginative full-page paintings enhance the fly's escapades, and the clever pattern provides an easy story structure for student authors.

8.113   Panek, Dennis. **Ba Ba Sheep Wouldn't Go to Sleep.** Illustrated by the author. Orchard Books/Lucas Evans Books, 1988. Ages 5–8. (Picture book)

Like many young children, Ba Ba Sheep feels that staying awake and playing is better than going to sleep. The little sheep stays up all night, but he finds that the following day is not as enjoyable because he is so tired. Dennis Panek shows through his humorous illustrations and story line that lack of sleep can cause a b-a-a-a-d day.

8.114   Peet, Bill. **Zella, Zack and Zodiac.** Illustrated by the author. Houghton Mifflin, 1986. Ages 5–8. (Picture book)

The theme of one good turn deserves another is explored in verse. Zella the zebra raises Zack, an abandoned ostrich chick. Later Zack, as an adult, rescues Zella's colt, Zodiac, from certain death. The colorful and expressive cartoon illustrations enliven the appealing story.

8.115   Potter, Beatrix. **The Complete Adventures of Tom Kitten and His Friends.** Illustrated by the author. Viking Penguin/Puffin Books, 1986. Ages 3–8. (Picture book)

All five of Beatrix Potter's stories about naughty kittens Tom and his sisters and their mother's friend Ribby are included in this volume: *The Tale of Tom Kitten, The Tale of Samuel*

Whiskers, The Tale of Ginger and Pickles, The Story of Miss Moppet, and *The Tale of the Pie and the Patty Pan.* The stories appear in full, accompanied by all of the original color illustrations in this large, paper edition.

8.116 Potter, Beatrix. **The Tale of Jemima Puddle-Duck, and Other Farmyard Tales.** Illustrated by the author. Frederick Warne, 1986. Ages 4–9. (Picture book)

The tales of Jemima Puddle-Duck, Mr. Jeremy Fisher, Mrs. Tiggy-Winkle, and Pigling Bland are gathered here with the original illustrations and in the original text. Although the single-title lap books are wonderful, this larger-format anthology will be useful for larger groups of picture-book or read-aloud audiences.

8.117 Pryor, Ainslie. **The Baby Blue Cat and the Dirty Dog Brothers.** Illustrated by the author. Viking Kestrel, 1987. Ages 4–8. (Picture book)

In this story about differences and tolerance, Baby Blue Cat would rather romp in the mud with the Dirty Dog Brothers than play quiet, clean games with his siblings. The dogs, on the other hand, decide it is also fun to take a bath, as Baby Blue Cat must. This quiet story is fun while it teaches that it is all right to be different. Colorful illustrations done in crayon and pen-and-ink make this a good picture book for young readers.

8.118 Quackenbush, Robert. **Mouse Feathers.** Illustrated by the author. Clarion Books, 1988. Ages 4–7. (Picture book)

Maxine Mouse babysits her two nephews, and calamity follows catastrophe when a pillow fight gets out of hand. Hilarity ensues, resulting in a bad case of "mouse feathers" and two chastened rodent rabble-rousers. Robert Quackenbush's fast-paced story is well matched by his flyaway illustrations.

8.119 Rayner, Mary. **Mrs. Pig Gets Cross, and Other Stories.** Illustrated by the author. E. P. Dutton, 1987. Ages 4–8.

This collection of six stories centers around Mary Rayner's now-familiar pig family. Unlike the three others in this series, this book has fewer illustrations to match the sometimes-lengthy stories. The main theme is life around the house, but the first and last stories are also titillating adventures. The watercolors are broad and straightforward, amusing in their interpretation of pigs as people. This would make a good read-aloud book.

8.120   Rockwell, Anne. **Come to Town.** Illustrated by the author. Thomas Y. Crowell, 1987. Ages 3–5. (Picture book)

Although many of the illustrations are quite busy, preschool and kindergarten youngsters will easily recognize and relate to the bears as they visit the school, the supermarket, and the library. Anne Rockwell invites the children to think and participate.

8.121   Rockwell, Anne. **First Comes Spring.** Illustrated by the author. Thomas Y. Crowell, 1985. Ages 4–7. (Picture book)

When spring comes to town, what does Bear Child wear? What is everyone doing? Bright full-page illustrations show lots of activity, like putting up birdhouses, making mud pies, and plowing fields. Turn the page, and each activity is separated from the others and clearly labeled. Each season's special characteristics are noted with simple text.

8.122   Root, Phyllis. **Moon Tiger.** Illustrated by Ed Young. Holt, Rinehart and Winston, 1985. Ages 7–9. (Picture book)

Jessica Ellen, like many older sisters, is punished for not taking care of her younger brother. She creates a Moon Tiger to take her away from this unpleasant situation. With the tiger, she travels from the cold north to the tropics of Africa, and when she returns, she feels much better about her brother. Soft-colored illustrations, combined with the story, carry the reader into fantasyland.

8.123   Round, Graham. **Hangdog.** Illustrated by the author. Dial Books for Young Readers, 1987. Ages 3–9. (Picture book)

Hangdog is a kind, gentle, polite dog, but no one notices him and he has no friends. Because of his loneliness, he decides to leave home in a makeshift boat in search of a friend. A surprise awaits him at the distant shore.

8.124   Schaffer, Libor (translated by Rosemary Lanning). **Arthur Sets Sail.** Illustrated by Agnès Mathieu. North-South Books, 1987. Ages 4–8. (Picture book)

The land of the aardvarks and the land of the rosy-pink pigs have always been separated by ocean until Arthur the adventurous aardvark sets sail and introduces the two. It takes a while for the spirit of tolerance to make good neighbors of them, a struggle that is ours as well. This is a morality tale, but gently told. Reading the book aloud may lead to much thinking and discussing. Delicate full-page illustrations add to the reflective quality of the book.

8.125 Schumacher, Claire. **Tim and Jim.** Illustrated by the author. Dodd, Mead, 1987. Ages 4–8. (Picture book)

Tim and Jim are two cats who look very much alike. Lucky Tim lives in a cozy house and is well cared for, but he is desperate for a friend. Jim is a street cat and longs for a good home. One day Tim runs off to find a friend and becomes lost. Jim, his look-alike, is mistakenly returned to the owner of the warm, cozy home. When Tim finds his way home again, his owner is surprised, but pleased and happy to have two cats who need each other and her.

8.126 Selkowe, Valrie M. **Spring Green.** Illustrated by Jeni Crisler Bassett. Lothrop, Lee and Shepard Books, 1985. Ages 4–7. (Picture book)

It's spring! Everyone is going to the woodchuck's party. There's a prize for whoever brings the best green thing. Danny the duck searches in vain for something original and green, or does he? Bright, animated, full-page illustrations help tell the tale of Danny's quest.

8.127 Singer, Marilyn. **Archer Armadillo's Secret Room.** Illustrated by Beth Lee Weiner. Macmillan, 1985. Ages 5–8.

When Archer Armadillo's family moves to a new burrow, Archer runs away to his secret place in the old burrow and plans to live there alone. His unhappy feelings will be familiar to children who have had to move. Archer's problem is resolved when he learns that someone does care about him after all.

8.128 Sis, Peter. **Rainbow Rhino.** Illustrated by the author. Alfred A. Knopf/Borzoi Books, 1987. Ages 4–7. (Picture book)

Rhino is happy with his life and his three friends, the rainbow birds: one blue, one red, and one yellow. One day they all go for a walk, and each bird discovers a new, more colorful place in which to live. However, danger lurks everywhere, and the birds are happy to return to the quiet, safe life with Rhino. The sparse illustrations are done in subdued colors.

8.129   Stadler, John. **Snail Saves the Day.** Illustrated by the author. Thomas Y. Crowell, 1985. Ages 3–8. (Picture book)

Detailed, humorous, full-color illustrations tell the story and portray the emotions as two football teams face each other in Animal Bowl I. Readers see two stories unfold on alternate pages: a snail preparing to go to the game and his teammates getting beaten as each down progresses. Very beginning readers can use the pictures to read the short sentence captions.

8.130   Stadler, John. **Three Cheers for Hippo!** Illustrated by the author. Thomas Y. Crowell, 1987. Ages 4–7. (Picture book)

In this very easy-to-read story, Hippo decides to take Pig, Dog, and Cat up in his airplane for a parachuting lesson. Pig and Dog are thrilled, but Cat is terrified. Trouble appears in the form of three hungry alligators waiting down below to gobble up the jumpers. Hippo steps in and saves the day. Drawn in large, cartoonlike boxes, the illustrations are full of action. Three to four words of text for each picture appear below in another box. *Children's Choice.*

8.131   Stanley, Diane. **A Country Tale.** Illustrated by the author. Four Winds Press, 1985. Ages 5–9.

In this story about cats in a Victorian setting, divisive Mrs. Snickers, a visitor from the city, causes Cleo to feel discontented with herself and to reject Lucy, her country friend. The story is resolved as Cleo learns a universal lesson—the importance of being oneself. Remarkably detailed colored-ink illustrations show how much an illustrator can extend a story by adding supportive information in visual format.

8.132   Stehr, Frédéric. **Quack-Quack.** Illustrated by the author. Farrar, Straus and Giroux/Sunburst Books, 1988. Ages 3–7. (Picture book)

Hatching while its mother is away from the nest, a duckling assumes that the first animal it sees, a frog, is its mother. The frog takes the duck from one animal to another in an effort to find the true mother. Very reminiscent of P. D. Eastman's *Are You My Mother?*, this book is illustrated with full-page colored-pencil drawings. The simple text integrated with the pictures provides strong story structure for the young reader.

8.133 Steig, William. **Solomon the Rusty Nail.** Illustrated by the author. Farrar, Straus and Giroux, 1985. Ages 5–9. (Picture book)

Solomon the rabbit discovers he can turn himself into a rusty nail in this well-written, attractively illustrated adventure story. Solomon's magic trick surprises some and mystifies others as he meets a cruel cat and is held captive until an unlikely event happens in this read-aloud story.

8.134 Stepto, Michele. **Snuggle Piggy and the Magic Blanket.** Illustrated by John Himmelman. E. P. Dutton, 1987. Ages 2–5. (Picture book)

Snuggle Piggy has a magic blanket dotted with animals who come to life when Aunt Daisy is not watching. The rich, full-color watercolors are vibrant but simple, executed with a good deal of humor and warmly complementing this appealing tale. This would make a fine bedtime story.

8.135 Stevenson, James. **Are We Almost There?** Illustrated by the author. Greenwillow Books, 1985. Ages 4–8. (Picture book)

Larry and Harry, two lively pups, beg their parents to take them to the beach, but their constant squabbling in the car threatens to end the trip quickly. The pups decide to get along and stop the fighting, and the whole family has a great day at the beach. Each page is divided into cartoon panels, and the humorous story is told entirely through dialogue balloons.

8.136 Stevenson, Suçie. **I Forgot.** Illustrated by the author. Orchard Books, 1988. Ages 4–8. (Picture book)

Arthur Peter Platypus, Jr., has great difficulty remembering things, such as names of the oceans, mathematical equations, and even everyday events. He tries various techniques to aid his memory: he practices, he ties string on his flippers, he writes notes, and he places rubber bands on his wrist, but nothing works. Finally an event occurs that breaks the pattern. Watercolor illustrations help carry the story along.

8.137 Stoeke, Janet Morgan. **Minerva Louise.** Illustrated by the author. E. P. Dutton, 1988. Ages 3–5. (Picture book)

Minerva Louise is an endearing hen who loves her farmyard, but she is quite eager to tour the farmhouse with the red curtains. What follows is as delightful a story as "The Little Red Hen," but without all the disastrous consequences. Brightly colored illustrations carry the amusing story.

8.138   Tejima. **Fox's Dream.** Illustrated by the author. Philomel
Books, 1987. Ages 6–8. (Picture book)

A fox wanders through the forest in winter and has a vision
about the changes the seasons bring and about the birth of a
family. The story is told in strong woodcuts and spare text.
The illustrations clearly delineate the reality of the fox's
habitat from that of his dream. *ALA Notable Children's
Book.*

8.139   Testa, Fulvio. **Wolf's Favor.** Illustrated by the author. Dial
Books for Young Readers, 1986. Ages 3–7. (Picture book)

Stylized full-color paintings adorn a contemporary tale of
kindness. Wolf's simple favor for Porcupine sets off a chain
reaction of good deeds among the animals. Pleased with the
results, Wolf decides to continue the chain and not to make a
meal of a grazing lamb. Well suited for family or group sharing.

8.140   Thaler, Mike. **In the Middle of the Puddle.** Illustrated by
Bruce Degen. Harper and Row, 1988. Ages 3–7. (Picture
book)

When a rainstorm comes, Fred the frog and Ted the turtle are
astonished to see their puddle turn first into a pool, then a
pond, a lake, and, finally, a sea. With the appearance of the
sun, the water regresses to their comfortable puddle again.
The easy-to-read text is supported with full-color illustrations.

8.141   Tyler, Linda Wagner. **Waiting for Mom.** Illustrated by Susan
Davis. Viking Kestrel, 1987. Ages 5–9. (Picture book)

Watercolor illustrations accompany this story of a hippo waiting for his mother to pick him up after school. He asks several questions that many young readers may ask themselves as
he patiently awaits his mother's arrival, and at last she appears, after being stuck in traffic. *Children's Choice.*

8.142   Van Allsburg, Chris. **Two Bad Ants.** Illustrated by the author. Houghton Mifflin, 1988. Ages 4–8. (Picture book)

The closeup views of the ants' adventures provide the humor
in this story of two ants who stay behind to eat sugar from
the sugar bowl. The language is suggestive of great adventure
tales, and the dangers of the yard and the kitchen setting are
presented from the ants' perspective in both words and illustrations. *Children's Choice.*

8.143   Velthuijs, Max. **A Birthday Cake for Little Bear.** Illustrated by the author. North-South Books, 1988. Ages 4–8. (Picture book)

It is Little Bear's birthday, and Little Pig bakes a wonderful cake with whipped cream and strawberries. As the friends sample generously, a catastrophe seems imminent. How does the party turn out? The reader may be surprised by the events in this warm, friendly, and caring book with its simple, direct text and illustrations, and even a recipe.

8.144   Vernon, Tannis. **Little Pig and the Blue-Green Sea.** Illustrated by the author. Crown, 1986. Ages 4–6. (Picture book)

Little Pig is headed to market, but en route he takes a detour and ends up on the high seas, in a "wooden box filled with life jackets." He loves the sea, so this is a perfect solution for him. The text is well written, the story flows, and the text and wash watercolors are perfectly blended. There is just enough humor to carry this beautifully executed book.

8.145   Vincent, Gabrielle. **Feel Better, Ernest!** Illustrated by the author. Greenwillow Books, 1988. Ages 3–6. (Picture book)

Ernest the bear has the flu, so little Celestine the mouse nurses, cajoles, and charms him back to health. The mouse-child and bear-adult characters are so lovingly presented that a reader accepts the truth of their relationship and is warmed by it. The lightly colored line and watercolor drawings are richly expressive and perfectly capture the emotional content of the simple story.

8.146   Waber, Bernard. **Funny, Funny Lyle.** Illustrated by the author. Houghton Mifflin, 1987. Ages 6–8. (Picture book)

Lyle the crocodile is so happy that his mother, Felicity, has come to live with him in the Primms' house. Felicity loves life. But Lyle worries about robbers and that his mother will be sent away after she inadvertently gets herself in big trouble. There is also a new addition to the Primm family in the house on East 88th Street—a new baby.

8.147   Weiss, Leatie. **My Teacher Sleeps in School.** Illustrated by Ellen Weiss. Viking Penguin/Puffin Books, 1986. Ages 4–8.

The children in Mrs. Marsh's class think she lives at school, and gather the evidence to prove it. Humorous illustrations picturing elephants in human roles and a satisfying ending in which Mrs. Marsh reveals where she really lives provide a delightful answer to a question many young children may have.

8.148   Wells, Rosemary. **Hazel's Amazing Mother.** Illustrated by the author. Dial Books for Young Readers, 1985. Ages 3–6. (Picture book)

When she gets lost, Hazel is set upon by three bullies who take her doll, toss it around until it becomes a rag, and ride the doll's buggy into the pond. Hazel's mother gets caught up in a wind, lands on the very tree under which this is happening, and makes everything right by demanding reparation. The fully dressed and strongly developed animal characters in this very funny book are illustrated in full color.

8.149   Wells, Rosemary. **Shy Charles.** Illustrated by the author. Dial Books for Young Readers, 1988. Ages 3–6. (Picture book)

Black-ink and watercolor illustrations help extend the story in verse of an extremely shy mouse. Ballet lessons, football practice, and special treats do not seem to help him gain confidence, but when a real emergency arises, Charles surprises everyone by rescuing his baby-sitter.

8.150   West, Colin. **"Hello, Great Big Bullfrog!"** Illustrated by the author. J. B. Lippincott, 1987. Ages 4–7. (Picture book)

A large bullfrog feels he is big in this easy-to-read tale. Then he meets other animals who are much bigger than he is, which makes him feel small. His confidence returns when he meets a bumblebee.

8.151   West, Colin. **"Not Me!" Said the Monkey.** Illustrated by the author. J. B. Lippincott, 1987. Ages 4–7. (Picture book)

A mischievous monkey gets into trouble with the other animals in the jungle when he denies his action in this fun-filled book meant for the young reader as well as the young listener.

8.152   West, Colin. **"Pardon?" Said the Giraffe.** Illustrated by the author. Harper and Row/Harper Trophy Books, 1986. Ages 3–7. (Picture book)

"What's it like up there?" the frog asks the giraffe, but the giraffe's head is so far above the frog that he cannot hear. The frog develops a solution to this dilemma, with humorous results. Only a few lines of print are on each page; the drawings are simple line drawings. The story lends itself to predicting and to following the repeated pattern.

8.153 Whelan, Gloria. **A Week of Raccoons.** Illustrated by Lynn Munsinger. Alfred A. Knopf/Borzoi Books, 1988. Ages 5–8.

Mr. Twerkle copes with the mischief of five raccoons by trapping them and transporting them, one by one on successive days, to the piney woods. The raccoons help each other as they set out for a return to the Twerkles, but each one happily finds an even better place to live. The cumulative nature of the plot and the detailed illustrations offering a bird's-eye view of the setting make an appealing combination.

8.154 Wildsmith, Brian. **Give a Dog a Bone.** Illustrated by the author. Pantheon Books, 1985. Ages 5–8. (Picture book)

This amusing, frustrating adventure story involves a stray dog and her attempt to get a bone. Many surprises are found within this beautifully illustrated tale.

8.155 Wildsmith, Brian. **Goat's Trail.** Illustrated by the author. Alfred A. Knopf/Borzoi Books, 1986. Ages 3–7. (Picture book)

In this cumulative tale, a wild mountain goat sets out to investigate noises emanating from the valley. En route, other animals join his entourage, and pandemonium ensues. Lively full-color spreads combined with cutout windows that allow the reader to anticipate the story make this an excellent choice for audience participation.

8.156 Wilhelm, Hans. **Oh, What a Mess.** Illustrated by the author. Crown, 1988. Ages 5–7. (Picture book)

Most of the time Franklin the pig is alone. He wants to invite friends over, but his home and his family are always too messy. However, Franklin's talent as a painter changes all that. The humorous text and accompanying watercolors should provide a great deal of enjoyment.

8.157 Wilhelm, Hans. **Tyrone the Horrible.** Illustrated by the author. Scholastic/Hardcover Books, 1988. Ages 5–8. (Picture book)

Boland is the victim of constant trouble caused by bully
Tyrone until little Boland uses his brain to get the best of
Tyrone. The full-color illustrations make the dinosaurs whim-
sical and charming—except Tyrone, the Tyrannosaurus.

8.158   Wiseman, Bernard. **Dolly Dodo.** Illustrated by the author.
Scholastic, 1987. Ages 5–9. (Picture book)

Dolly, a forgetful dodo bird, gets some help from her friends
for her poor memory. This silly book will bring many laughs
from its young readers.

8.159   Wood, Audrey. **Detective Valentine.** Illustrated by the author. Harper and Row, 1987. Ages 4–8. (Picture book)

The great Detective Valentine has his work cut out for him
when the Snow Queen's crown is stolen and his own hats
begin to disappear. Suspects abound; chases and accusations
ensue. It is the mayor who has stolen the crown, and for a
good reason. Detective Valentine unveils a plan to save the
contest to everyone's satisfaction. Illustrations—full of action, color, and snow—help convey the action.

8.160   Yeoman, John. **The Bear's Water Picnic.** Illustrated by Quentin Blake. Atheneum, 1987. Ages 3–7. (Picture book)

A quiet picnic is what Bear has in mind. The middle of the
lake seems like a good place until the tranquil setting is destroyed by friendly, but raucous, frogs. Frogs and picnickers
finally make their peace, but only after a near disaster. This
warm-hearted, amusing tale with a lesson in cooperation will
be enjoyed most as a lap book so that the listener does not
miss the comical illustrations.

8.161   Ziefert, Harriet. **Lewis the Fire Fighter.** Illustrated by Carol
Nicklaus. Random House, 1986. Ages 4–7. (Picture book)

Lewis the lion decides to play firefighter alone in his sister's
room when she refuses to join him. His misadventures in-
doors help turn the story around to an outdoor, rainy-day
playtime with Kate.

Intermediate

8.162   Conly, Jane Leslie. **Racso and the Rats of NIMH.** Illustrated
by Leonard Lubin. Harper and Row, 1986. Ages 8–11.

In this sequel to Newbery Award–winner *Mrs. Frisby and the Rats of NIMH* by Robert C. O'Brien, author Jane Leslie Conly has borrowed her father's premise (rats with laboratory-induced longevity and intelligence) but little else. The threat to Thorn Valley and the rat colony's ingenious solution to its problems are hers alone. Children will enjoy the details of the rats' lives, the danger and adventure, and the characters, particularly rascal Racso. *Children's Choice* and *Notable Children's Trade Book in the Field of Social Studies.*

8.163 Howe, James. **Nighty-Nightmare.** Illustrated by Leslie Morrill. Avon Books/Camelot Books/Jean Karl Books, 1988. Ages 8–10.

When the Monroe family plans to go camping on St. George's Eve, the family cat, Chester, is concerned since this is the one night of the year when evil spirits lurk in the woods. Despite Chester's warnings, the camping trip takes place, and everyone begins to wonder if the legends are true. Chester and the family's two dogs eventually save the Monroes, but not without some hilarious hair-raising adventures. This is another in the series about Bunnicula, the vampire rabbit. *Children's Choice.*

8.164 King-Smith, Dick. **Babe the Gallant Pig.** Illustrated by Mary Rayner. Crown, 1985. Ages 9–12.

A piglet arrives at the sheep farm destined to become ham and bacon, but instead he becomes a "sheep-pig." When the pig is suspected of killing sheep, an aging sheepdog proves the pig's innocence. The black-and-white drawings add to the charm of the story. *ALA Notable Children's Book, Children's Choice,* and *England's 1984 Guardian Award for Excellence.*

8.165 Kirby, Mansfield. **The Secret of Thut-Mouse III; or, Basil Beaudesert's Revenge.** Illustrated by Mance Post. Farrar, Straus and Giroux, 1985. Ages 8–12.

The ancient feud between cat and mouse is given new sparkle in this animal fantasy, which gently satirizes the narrow-mindedness of the subject specialists. Museum residents Basil Beaudesert and his nephew, Danny, are two clever mice who plot to convince Pa-Ti-Paw, a menacing Siamese cat, that mice were very powerful in ancient Egypt. Their brilliant scheme has consequences that go far beyond their original intentions. The illustrations—blurry, detailed pastels—and inventive page design add to the book's charm.

8.166   Lively, Penelope. **A House Inside Out.** Illustrated by David Parkins. E. P. Dutton, 1988. Ages 8–11.

This view of life from the perspective of a dog, mouse, and bug takes readers behind the scenes of a house to prove there is more going on than the owners know. Mice lead heroic lives of danger, spiders are intrepid web-weavers, and pill bugs prove their worth in herculean climbs. Beginning writers will enjoy the unusual perspective: an everyday object can be the basis of a story. The short chapters make the book appropriate for reading aloud.

8.167   Murphy, Jim. **The Last Dinosaur.** Illustrated by Mark Alan Weatherby. Scholastic/Hardcover Books, 1988. Ages 8–12. (Picture book)

What caused the dinosaurs to disappear from the Earth? What might have occurred during those final days of the dinosaurs? The author and illustrator of this fictional account give their interpretation of what might have happened to these great beasts. *Children's Choice.*

8.168   Pierce, Meredith Ann. **Birth of the Firebringer.** Four Winds Press, 1985. Ages 10–12.

Aljan the unicorn vanquishes a deadly foe and comes to maturity in this compelling fantasy. The author maintains the reader's belief in her created world through her consistent portrayal of the characters and their conflicts. This would be a good transition book for the child who reads only realistic animal stories and who is not yet ready for Richard Adams's *Watership Down,* William Horwood's *Duncton Wood,* or Walter Wangerin's *Book of the Dun Cow.*

8.169   Wrightson, Patricia. **Moon-Dark.** Illustrated by Noela Young. Margaret K. McElderry Books, 1987. Ages 10–12.

The Bandicoot War starts slowly; even the ranger who cares for the land and the animals is only aware of some trouble brewing. The ancient magic of Australia and the mystical dark of the moon are needed to restore balance. The author presents the story through the eyes of the fisherman's dog, Blue, without humanizing him completely. This skillful treatment might be useful in teaching writing.

Humans with Special Powers

Primary

8.170 Arnold, Tim. **The Winter Mittens.** Illustrated by the author. Margaret K. McElderry Books, 1988. Ages 7–10.

Addie finds a small silver box which contains a worn pair of mittens. She has no use for the box, but does need the mittens, so she keeps them, ignoring her conscience. When Addie finds her mittens control the snow, and she enjoys the power of that control, disaster threatens. The book could be effectively combined with *The Stranger* by Chris Van Allsburg or *The Winter Wren* by Brock Cole, additional books about human interaction with the seasons.

Intermediate

8.171 DeFelice, Cynthia C. **The Strange Night Writing of Jessamine Colter.** Macmillan, 1988. Ages 9–12.

For fifty years Jessamine Colter's calligraphy has enriched the lives of the townspeople as she prepares announcements of birth, marriage, and death. One night she reads what she has written, and realizes the event recorded has not yet taken place. She is able to predict the future. This is a wise book and a subtle one. The eternal truths which fill it will linger with young readers, in a manner reminiscent of Natalie Babbitt's *Tuck Everlasting*.

8.172 Haas, Dorothy. **The Secret Life of Dilly McBean.** Bradbury Press, 1986. Ages 10–13.

Dilloway McBean is not like other boys. An orphan, he has been raised by the Commercial Chemical and Corn Trust and Savings Bank, and he is magnetic. The first condition has made him independently lonely, and the second—controlling his magnetic force—has made him strong. Dilly's life is abruptly interrupted when he is kidnapped by a madman who plans to control the world with a computer.

Other Make-Believe Characters

Primary

8.173 Boswell, Stephen. **King Gorboduc's Fabulous Zoo.** Illustrated
by Beverley Gooding. E. P. Dutton, 1986. Ages 7–9. (Picture
book)

A unicorn, griffin, dodo, and baby mammoth live in the king's
private zoo. When the king becomes dissatisfied, he sends his
soldiers out to find an additional creature, a dragon. What
happens next is quite an imaginative event in this beautifully
illustrated book.

8.174 Denton, Terry. **Felix and Alexander.** Illustrated by the author. Houghton Mifflin, 1988. Ages 4–7.

Felix, a resourceful toy dog, sets out through the city to find
his missing owner, Alexander. Offbeat watercolor illustrations make the night-dark streets eerie and frightening in contrast to the bright, cheery comfort of home. The two friends
are happily reunited, and through a Hansel-and-Gretel-like
twist, they return home.

8.175 Elzbieta. **Dikou and the Mysterious Moon Sheep.** Illustrated
by the author. Thomas Y. Crowell, 1988. Ages 3–8. (Picture
book)

This is an enchanting and fantastic story, unique in many
ways. It is not clear exactly what the main characters in the
story are, but we recognize them as a mother, father, and
small boy. Each page draws the reader further and further
into the story, where he or she finds an odd but appealing
bedtime tale, written in expressive prose that is supported by
illustrations in pastels and watercolors.

8.176 Gedin, Birgitta (translated by Elisabeth Dyssegaard). **The Little House from the Sea.** Illustrated by Petter Pettersson.
R and S Books, 1988. Ages 5–10.

This little house is personified. It stands alone on an island in
the sea, wondering what lies beyond the horizon and vaguely
remembering its past life as a boat. It was built, we learn,
from a ship's timbers. A poetic text and lovely impression-
istic illustrations in watercolor work together to make this an
unusually thoughtful and provocative book.

8.177 Goffstein, M. B. **Artists' Helpers Enjoy the Evenings.** Illustrated by the author. Harper and Row/Charlotte Zolotow Books, 1987. Ages 4–8. (Picture book)

Spare stories, illustrated in pastels, reveal the distinct personalities of five artists' crayons—Blanc, Noir, Gris, Bistre, and Sanguine—as they share adventures after dark. An introductory page translates the crayons' French color names and provides a pronunciation guide.

8.178 Lyon, George Ella. **Father Time and the Day Boxes.** Illustrated by Robert Andrew Parker. Bradbury Press, 1985. Ages 6–9. (Picture book)

In a tall-tale narrative with elegant illustrations, the story of Father Time is told: "Minute-ticks, hour-tocks don't bother Father Time. Years don't fret him either. 'Mind days,' he says, 'and years follow.'" Full-color watercolors by an eminent painter expand the imaginative text about how each day Father Time takes a packet from the 365 packets he keeps in a vault in the clouds, and tosses it down to Earth.

8.179 Martin, C.L.G. **The Dragon Nanny.** Illustrated by Robert Rayevsky. Macmillan, 1988. Ages 5–9. (Picture book)

Fired by the king because she has gotten old, Nanny Nell Hannah seems fated to become dragon food. Instead, in a bargain for her life, she takes on the care of two baby dragons. When they learn to love humans before they learn to breathe fire, trouble begins. Feisty Nanny Nell Hannah is a gem, and Robert Rayevsky takes full advantage of the incongruities of dragons in diapers. *Children's Choice.*

8.180 Peet, Bill. **Jethro and Joel Were a Troll.** Illustrated by the author. Houghton Mifflin, 1987. Ages 4–9. (Picture book)

Jethro and Joel, a large, two-headed, turnip-eating troll that is good and bad, start trouble in the town only to discover that they can be helpful as royal architects and master castle builders.

8.181 Root, Phyllis. **Soup for Supper.** Illustrated by Sue Truesdell. Harper and Row, 1986. Ages 5–10. (Picture book)

A wee small woman tricks a giant into returning the vegetables he has stolen from her garden. They form an unlikely friendship over her pot of vegetable soup. Color illustrations are humorous in detailing the feisty character of the woman and the inept efforts of the giant.

8.182   Van Allsburg, Chris. **The Stranger.** Illustrated by the author. Houghton Mifflin, 1986. Ages 8–10.

Once again, Chris Van Allsburg does it. He takes the common occurrence of fall and tinges it with a touch of fantasy. Farmer Bailey hits a stranger with his car, causing the stranger to lose his memory. Slowly, as signs of fall occur around the farm, the man begins to remember. Younger children may have a problem identifying the stranger as Jack Frost, but they will enjoy the striking pictures. *Notable Children's Trade Book in the Language Arts.*

8.183   Winthrop, Elizabeth. **Maggie and the Monster.** Illustrated by Tomie dePaola. Holiday House, 1987. Ages 4–7. (Picture book)

Every night a monster with big hairy feet crashes around Maggie's room, sighing and grumbling and making lots of noise. "What do you want?" Maggie finally asks, only to find out the monster is looking for its mother. Mother is found in the broom closet, and a loving reunion takes place. There is peace at last, so Maggie can go to sleep. *Children's Choice.*

Intermediate

8.184   Alcock, Vivien. **Ghostly Companions: A Feast of Chilling Tales.** Delacorte Press, 1987. Ages 10 and up.

Deliciously chilling tales of wicked aunts, haunted typewriters, and scissors coming to life are offered in this compilation of ten ghost stories set in England for young readers. The protagonists are children or young adults who must summon courage to face the unknown in order to save themselves and others from disaster or a ghastly destiny. The taut writing will pull readers into each story and keep them there until the end.

8.185   Banks, Lynne Reid. **The Fairy Rebel.** Illustrated by William Geldart. Doubleday, 1988. Ages 8–12.

Tiki, a rebellious fairy who is in trouble for breaking the rule against wearing jeans, risks the wrath of the Fairy Queen by trying to fulfill the wish of Jan and Charlie to have a child. This modern fairy tale of magic, suspense, and adventure is accompanied by black-and-white illustrations.

8.186 Charnas, Suzy McKee. **The Bronze King.** Houghton Mifflin, 1985. Ages 11–14.

New York City is threatened when one of the city's guardians, a massive statue, disappears from Central Park. Tina and Joel, with the help of the wizard Paavo, fight an epic battle against the forces of evil and gain a costly victory. Some rough language may signal an older audience.

8.187 Hildick, E. W. **The Ghost Squad and the Ghoul of Grünberg.** E. P. Dutton/Ghost Squad Books, 1986. Ages 10–12.

This is the fourth in the Ghost Squad series about the ghosts of four young people, all killed in violent accidents, and two living members; yet, Hildick keeps the story fresh by introducing imaginative "facts" about ghostdom as this suspenseful story unfolds. The fast-moving plot begins with the squad's surveillance of and by a mysterious stranger and leads to a hunt for a Nazi war criminal. Interesting characters and consistency to the author's rules for what is possible in a ghost world combine to keep the story credible.

8.188 Hildick, E. W. **The Ghost Squad Flies Concorde.** E. P. Dutton/Ghost Squad Books, 1985. Ages 10–13.

In this adventure, the Ghost Squad travels to England while investigating a con artist who is courting Jack's mother for the insurance money she received after her son's death.

8.189 Hunter, Mollie. **The Mermaid Summer.** Harper and Row/ Charlotte Zolotow Books, 1988. Ages 10–13.

Mermaids have been characters of folklore for years and in most stories are portrayed as being gentle and admired by fishermen. Yet in a small town in Scotland, a mermaid exhibits strong powers to get what she desires. Two adventurous young people try to discover the mermaid's weakness and dissolve her curse upon their grandfather and her plans to destroy the town in this exciting read-aloud book.

8.190 McGraw, Eloise. **The Trouble with Jacob.** Margaret K. McElderry Books, 1988. Ages 9–12.

"Somebody's got my bed," says Jacob, the strange boy who disappears suddenly and who can only be seen by certain people. When Andy Peterson says he will help the boy, he does not realize how unusual his quest will be, nor how much courage will be required to right old wrongs.

8.191   Windsor, Patricia. **How a Weirdo and a Ghost Can Change Your Life.** Illustrated by Jacqueline Rogers. Delacorte Press and Dell/Yearling Books, 1986. Ages 9–12.

Sick in bed with strep throat and deserted by her best friend, Martha now has to put up with Teddy the Windbag when he brings her the school assignments. Everyone in her class thinks he is weird, but Martha may be changing her mind. After teaching her how to use a Ouija board, Teddy introduces her to some enterprising ghosts who enjoy being detectives. Before she knows it, Martha is caught up in some peculiar mysteries.

Children's Imagination and Dreams

Primary

8.192   Adoff, Arnold. **Flamboyan.** Illustrated by Karen Barbour. Harcourt Brace Jovanovich, 1988. Ages 9–12. (Picture book)

A joyous evocation of island life, this story, told in poetic language, sets a dream flight sequence in the frame of a realistic story of a day in the life of young Flamboyan, who was named after the tree whose red blossoms are the same color as her hair. Bold, high-intensity, full-page watercolor and gouache paintings in their consciously primitive forms and saturated color reflect the influence of painter Henri Matisse.

8.193   Berger, Barbara Helen. **When the Sun Rose.** Illustrated by the author. Philomel Books, 1986. Ages 4–9. (Picture book)

An enchanting but mysterious new companion enters the playhouse of an imaginative little girl. Their friendship develops until it is time for the visitor to leave. Will she come again? By viewing the contents slowly, children will experience the mysterious and magical mood created by the radiant acrylic paintings. Multiple themes allow enjoyment by readers on many levels.

8.194 Bohdal, Susi (translated by Anthea Bell). **The Magic Honey Jar.** Illustrated by the author. North-South Books, 1987. Ages 6–9. (Picture book)

Julian, who has been attacked by the Flu Goblin, is read to from a book about the *Arabian Nights.* As he drifts off to sleep, he becomes part of a mystery about a honey jar and the loss of its magic powers. The illustrations enhance the simple beauty of this special story.

8.195 Craven, Carolyn. **What the Mailman Brought.** Illustrated by Tomie dePaola. G. P. Putnam's Sons, 1987. Ages 5–7. (Picture book)

When William is sick, the mailman brings him various gifts. The mailman appears as different creatures, and the gifts are appropriate for each mailman. The reader is left wondering who the mailman is and whether the events really happened. Tomie dePaola's illustrations have a clean white look with soft bright colors, appropriate for a sickroom, and are varied and imaginative to match the wonderment of the story.

8.196 Drescher, Henrik. **Look-Alikes.** Illustrated by the author. Lothrop, Lee and Shepard Books, 1985. Ages 3–9. (Picture book)

A full-color adventure of the imagination offers new possibilities to think about and new things to see with each re-reading of the book. Henrik Drescher moves outside of artistic conventions while creating unique ways for readers to participate with Buster and Rudy in the fun of moving from day to night in more than one dimension of the universe. A handsome and conceptually exciting book.

8.197 Faulkner, Matt. **The Amazing Voyage of Jackie Grace.** Illustrated by the author. Scholastic/Hardcover Books, 1987. Ages 5–8. (Picture book)

A young boy's imagination takes him on a wondrous adventure full of storms, cutthroat pirates, and battles—all while taking a bath. Illustrations are exaggerated pen and watercolor caricatures using cartoon captions in place of text.

8.198 Fields, Julia. **The Green Lion of Zion Street.** Illustrated by Jerry Pinkney. Margaret K. McElderry Books, 1988. Ages 7–10. (Picture book)

Bright watercolors and pencil illuminate this fantasy tale about a lion monument that comes alive in the minds of schoolchildren on a cold, fog-enveloped morning. This imaginative story in rhyme can be used to stimulate writing or with drama or choral groups.

8.199   Gray, Nigel. **A Balloon for Grandad.** Illustrated by Jane Ray. Orchard Books, 1988. Ages 4–8. (Picture book)

The loss of a balloon stimulates Sam and his father to imagine the adventures his balloon might have on its way to visit his grandfather who lives in Egypt. Jane Ray's illustrations complement the story.

8.200   Haseley, Dennis. **My Father Doesn't Know about the Woods and Me.** Illustrated by Michael Hays. Atheneum, 1988. Ages 7–9. (Picture book)

Paintings, so light-filled they seem to glow from within, and a graceful, image-laden text tell the story of a boy and his father walking through the woods. Children who experience their journey will henceforth find all forests enchanted, as they enter a magical world of limitless possibilities. The curricular applications of the book are legion, but the affective benefits are probably more important and longer lasting.

8.201   Jonas, Ann. **The Trek.** Illustrated by the author. Greenwillow Books, 1985. Ages 5–9. (Picture book)

An elegantly designed picture book tells the story of a small girl who teams up with a classmate to brave a jungle and desert on the trek to school. Cleverly camouflaged in the drawings are jungle animals—the hedge is a flock of sheep, the park trees are elephants. Children will spend hours poring over the pastel pictures, trying to find the hidden animals, which are identified at the end of the book. The book offers endless possibilities for class discussion.

8.202   Laurencin, Geneviève (translated by Andrea Mernan). **I Wish I Were.** Illustrated by Ulises Wensell. G. P. Putnam's Sons, 1987. Ages 4–7. (Picture book)

A small boy dreams he is an animal with special abilities to help him handle life's difficulties. If he were a sheep, for instance, he would not have to dress in so many clothes in the winter. If he were a monkey, he could play tricks on two overbearing aunts. Eventually he decides being an animal would be fun as long as he could return to being himself whenever he wanted.

8.203 Morgan, Michaela. **Edward Gets a Pet.** Illustrated by Sue Porter. E. P. Dutton, 1987. Ages 3–6. (Picture book)

Edward goes to a pet store with his mother to select a pet. His imagination wanders each time she suggests a pet. A cuddly creature like a cute little hamster makes him envision an ape and a bear, and other common pets suggest images of other wild animals.

8.204 Morgan, Michaela. **Edward Hurts His Knee.** Illustrated by Sue Porter. E. P. Dutton, 1988. Ages 4–8. (Picture book)

Edward falls and skins his knee as he walks to Grandma's house with his mother. He is given a bandage, which helps a little, but his mother needs to encourage him the remainder of the walk. He imagines himself getting to Grandma's in a variety of ways, such as by stretcher and by satellite, ending up with a marvelous tale to tell Grandma.

8.205 Nolan, Dennis. **The Castle Builder.** Illustrated by the author. Macmillan, 1987. Ages 4–7. (Picture book)

A boy builds a sandcastle and lets his imagination soar, becoming a tamer of dragons and a conqueror of knights, but he finds his castle cannot stand up to the inexorable power of the sea. The grainy illustrations, composed of minute hand-drawn dots of black ink, are a splendid match.

8.206 Nunes, Susan. **Coyote Dreams.** Illustrated by Ronald Himler. Atheneum, 1988. Ages 7–10. (Picture book)

This book has a far different character from the work of Byrd Baylor and Peter Parnall, but the spirit is the same. Both author-illustrator teams share a respect for nature and an ability to depict wide-open spaces and waking dreams. In this easy-reading story, coyotes come at night and bring the desert to a suburban garden, and after they depart, the dreams linger on. Coyotes came— or did they?

8.207 Oram, Hiawyn. **In the Attic.** Illustrated by Satoshi Kitamura. Holt, Rinehart and Winston, 1985. Ages 3–5. (Picture book)

In this simple story of the imagination, a bored young boy climbs the ladder of his toy fire truck to an attic of enchanted make-believe, but he is finally enticed back to reality by his empty stomach. Double-page bold watercolors, featuring blue and lavender hues, enhance the fantastical motif.

8.208 Paige, Rob. **Some of My Best Friends Are Monsters.** Illustrated by Paul Yalowitz. Bradbury Press, 1988. Ages 5–7. (Picture book)

Children's vivid imaginations create monsters which, in most cases, can be very frightening. The narrator in this book creates several other uses for monsters. They can play with you and also help other members of your family with their work. Most of all they can keep you company when you are alone in the dark. Who says that monsters have to be bad? This book proves that they can be useful to have around.

8.209 Renberg, Dalia Hardof. **Hello, Clouds!** Illustrated by Alona Frankel. Harper and Row, 1985. Ages 3–7. (Picture book)

The imagination of a young child interacts with the ethereal-like illustrations of cloud formations. The simplicity of softly colored clouds ranging in shape from dragons to bubblebaths, enhanced by few sentences, will capture the fancy of the reader.

8.210 Ross, Tony. **Oscar Got the Blame.** Illustrated by the author. Dial Books for Young Readers, 1988. Ages 4–7. (Picture book)

When anything happens in Oscar's home, such as mud around the house, the dog dressed in Dad's things, or frogs in Granny's slippers, Oscar is blamed. He claims that his friend Billy is to blame, but no one can see Billy except Oscar—until one day. *Children's Choice.*

8.211 Ryder, Joanne. **The Night Flight.** Illustrated by Amy Schwartz. Four Winds Press, 1985. Ages 4–8. (Picture book)

In her dream, a stone lion comes to life and carries Anna on an adventure through the familiar park, now turned into a nighttime jungle. The dreamlike quality of the imaginative and poetic text is heightened by richly colored drawings against stark black backgrounds.

8.212   Say, Allen. **A River Dream.** Illustrated by the author. Houghton Mifflin, 1988. Ages 6–9. (Picture book)

A gift from his uncle, a personal fly box for fishing supplies, takes Mark on a trip that is part reality and part dream. We observe places and events changing as Mark goes fishing with his uncle. What will become of the fish he has caught in this carefully illustrated, touching story?

8.213   Sharmat, Marjorie Weinman. **Go to Sleep, Nicholas Joe.** Illustrated by John Himmelman. Harper and Row, 1988. Ages 4–6. (Picture book)

Children will find the premise of this book quite amusing: a boy dressed in pajamas flies about the world on his top sheet and puts adults to bed as though he were the adult and they were the children. The text is full of humor accurately geared to younger readers. The bright, largely solid color illustrations in watercolors and pen-and-ink may owe a debt to Maurice Sendak, but they still stand on their own. *Children's Choice.*

8.214   Stanley, Diane. **Birdsong Lullaby.** Illustrated by the author. William Morrow, 1985. Ages 4–8.

With her mother's encouragement, a young girl fantasizes about the wonderful things she could do if only she were a bird.

Humor

Primary

8.215   Allard, Harry. **Miss Nelson Has a Field Day.** Illustrated by James Marshall. Houghton Mifflin, 1985. Ages 4–8. (Picture book)

The football team at Horace B. Smedley School is just pitiful. The coach has a nervous breakdown and is replaced by Coach Swamp, a woman who toughens up the team and gets it winning. In a surprise ending, Coach Swamp turns out to be none other than the gentle teacher Miss Nelson. Colored cartoonlike illustrations add a further zany note. *Children's Choice.*

8.216 Blake, Quentin. **The Story of the Dancing Frog.** Illustrated by the author. Alfred A. Knopf/Borzoi Books, 1985. Ages 7–9.

A mother tells her son of Aunt Gertrude's adventurous life with George the dancing frog in this witty, lighthearted example of a tall tale. Line-and-wash cartoon-style drawings animate the text's tongue-in-cheek humor.

8.217 Blundell, Tony. **Joe on Sunday.** Illustrated by the author. Dial Books for Young Readers, 1987. Ages 5–8. (Picture book)

When Joe goes to bed Sunday night, he is a little boy, but when his mother looks in Monday morning, there is a "piggy in Joe's bed"! Thereafter, on each succeeding morning, there is a different "creature" in Joe's bed: a lion, mouse, monkey, monster, and king. Cartoonlike illustrations reminiscent of those by Stan and Jan Berenstain convey the imaginative slapstick humor of the text. Children could be encouraged to imagine other creatures which Joe could become.

8.218 Bradman, Tony. **Dilly the Dinosaur.** Illustrated by Susan Hellard. Viking Kestrel, 1987. Ages 7–10.

The mischievous doings of Dilly the Dinosaur are narrated by his often-exasperated older sister in this amusing book about family life with a demanding younger brother. Older siblings will relate to these four stories, each with four to six rough pen-and-ink illustrations.

8.219 Burningham, John. **John Patrick Norman McHennessy—The Boy Who Was Always Late.** Illustrated by the author. Crown, 1987. Ages 5–9. (Picture book)

The stuffy tutor, pedantic in flowing academic gown, never believes the excuses given by John Patrick to explain his tardiness. One day the teacher, like Margot Zemach's judge, has reason to know that the boy is telling the truth. Children will enjoy the neat plot reversal and will want to write pattern stories. *Children's Choice*.

8.220 Burningham, John. **Where's Julius?** Illustrated by the author. Crown, 1986. Ages 5–7. (Picture book)

Each time a tantalizing meal is prepared for the Troutbeck family, Julius is off on some exotic adventure in places like Egypt, Peru, Tibet, or Russia, and his mother or father must put his meal on a tray and take it to him. This hilarious story is chockfull of imagination and fun; it is typical John Burningham. As always, the illustrations in wax crayon are quite appropriate to the story and add to the humor.

8.221 Cole, Babette. **Princess Smartypants.** Illustrated by the author. G. P. Putnam's Sons, 1987. Ages 4–7. (Picture book)

Not wishing to marry any of her royal suitors, Princess Smartypants devises difficult tasks at which they all fail until Prince Swashbuckle turns up. He is able to accomplish all the princess's tasks, so she is forced to kiss him and turn him into a frog to get rid of him. Finally, she reaches her goal—to be left to herself.

8.222 Cole, Babette. **The Trouble with Gran.** Illustrated by the author. G. P. Putnam's Sons, 1987. Ages 5–8. (Picture book)

Gran is an alien who turns the senior citizen trip into a real fantasy trip, to the concern of everyone except the seniors. Full-color cartoonlike illustrations add to the craziness.

8.223 Cole, Babette. **The Trouble with Grandad.** Illustrated by the author. G. P. Putnam's Sons, 1988. Ages 4–8. (Picture book)

When Grandad's gigantic vegetables win all the prizes, a jealous competitor gives him a trick tomato plant that grows taller than the police station. Now the whole town is angry at Grandad. Through a series of whacky events, he arrives at a solution to please everyone. The humorous, full-page, brightly detailed watercolor illustrations are accompanied by one sentence of text per page.

8.224 Coleridge, Ann. **The Friends of Emily Culpepper.** Illustrated by Roland Harvey. G. P. Putnam's Sons, 1987. Ages 4–7. (Picture book)

This book will appeal most to a child with a really wicked sense of humor. Elderly Miss Culpepper delights in having guests so much that she wants to preserve them —miniaturized and in jars, that is. The illustrations are as dryly funny as the text.

8.225 Delacre, Lulu. **Nathan's Fishing Trip.** Illustrated by the author. Scholastic/Hardcover Books/Lucas Evans Books, 1988. Ages 4–6. (Picture book)

In this story it seems quite natural that a mouse should take an elephant out on his first fishing trip. After several humorous mishaps, they do indeed manage to catch a fish in an unconventional way. But in the end, Nathan and Alexander decide that peanut butter for supper is preferable to the pretty rainbow trout. The delicate watercolor illustrations are lovely and add drama and humor to a simple tale.

8.226   Demarest, Chris L. **No Peas for Nellie.** Illustrated by the author. Macmillan, 1988. Ages 4–7. (Picture book)

"No peas, no dessert," says Dad, so Nellie begins to fantasize about the things she would rather eat. These include a furry spider, a slimy salamander, and a hairy warthog. Most of the humor comes from the slapdash illustrations, which depict Nellie, armed with cutlery and salt shaker, chasing these hapless creatures, whose frightened faces reflect their dismay.

8.227   Geringer, Laura. **A Three Hat Day.** Illustrated by Arnold Lobel. Harper and Row/Harper Trophy Books, 1987. Ages 5–8. (Picture book)

Text and illustrations combine to tell the engaging and humorous story of the eccentric R. R. Pottle, his passion for hats, and the happy ending in his quest for the woman of his dreams. The comic full-color illustrations enhance the rich vocabulary of the telling. *ALA Notable Children's Book.*

8.228   Graves, Robert. **The Big Green Book.** Illustrated by Maurice Sendak. Macmillan, 1985. Ages 4–8. (Picture book)

Jack lives with his prim and proper aunt and uncle, who give him very little freedom to do what little boys like to do. Luckily, he finds a big green book of magic in the attic, which enables him to turn into anything he likes and to appear and disappear at will. This proves very useful in easing his situation. Maurice Sendak's illustrations make this delightfully ridiculous story plausible.

8.229   Greene, Carol. **The Insignificant Elephant.** Illustrated by Susan Gantner. Harcourt Brace Jovanovich, 1985. Ages 5–7. (Picture book)

"Humber lived with a herd of other elephants in the Royal Coconut Grove around the Pearlish Palace of the Proud Pasha

Pusha of Rabbidum.'' But because he is so insignificant, no one ever notices him—and that is why he is chosen to spy for the Head of the Pearlish Palace Guards. This is a funny story of an unlikely hero. Susan Gantner's colored illustrations, done in watercolor and pen-and-ink, enhance the story and add to the humor. They are reminiscent of the illustrations in Laurent de Brunhoff's Babar books.

8.230 Heller, Nicholas. **An Adventure at Sea.** Illustrated by the author. Greenwillow Books, 1988. Ages 4–8. (Picture book)

Harold bids his brother and sister to join him aboard his cardboard-box ship. He then takes charge of their adventure, transforming everyday backyard occurrences into hair-raising experiences on the high seas. The realistic full-color view of the backyard is contrasted with Harold's imaginary scene on every two-page spread.

8.231 Hutchins, Pat. **The Very Worst Monster.** Illustrated by the author. Greenwillow Books, 1985. Ages 4–7. (Picture book)

In a humorous twist of the predictable sibling-rivalry story, monster Hazel is so jealous when her baby brother is hailed as the worst monster in the world that she becomes determined to outdo his dastardly deeds. Bright watercolors, both silly and grotesque, convey the ironic fun featuring a Hazel literally green with envy.

8.232 Joyce, William. **George Shrinks.** Illustrated by the author. Harper and Row, 1985. Ages 4–8. (Picture book)

George wakes up to find that he has mysteriously shrunk to the size of a mouse, but he obediently follows the written directions left by his parents. Young children will be able to enjoy the humor of the story, which would be good for reading aloud.

8.233 Karlin, Nurit. **The Tooth Witch.** Illustrated by the author. J. B. Lippincott, 1985. Ages 3–7. (Picture book)

After six hundred years of work, the once-exciting job of collecting baby teeth has become painfully boring for the tooth witch. Abra Cadabra, her impish new assistant, takes over, bringing a fresh approach with happy surprises. Bold blue-and-black drawings enhance this simple tale of one of childhood's popular visitors—the tooth fairy.

8.234 Kellogg, Steven. **Best Friends.** Illustrated by the author. Dial Books for Young Readers, 1986. Ages 6–9. (Picture book)

Louise and Kathy are the best of friends. They do everything together until Louise goes away for the summer. Kathy is desperately lonely and is furious when Louise writes she is having a good time. But Louise returns with presents and tells her friend she has been lonely, too. Steven Kellogg's exuberant illustrations, pleasingly crowded with wonderful detail, make this an outstanding picture book. Another excellent contribution to children's literature from this prolific author-illustrator. *Children's Choice.*

8.235 Kellogg, Steven. **Prehistoric Pinkerton.** Illustrated by the author. Dial Books for Young Readers, 1987. Ages 5–8. (Picture book)

Pinkerton the Great Dane is up to his old tricks, managing to bring down a diplodocus in his search for a bone to chew on. The hilarious illustrations complement the text. Together, they form another enjoyable romp for reading aloud or alone.

8.236 King-Smith, Dick. **Farmer Bungle Forgets.** Illustrated by Martin Honeysett. Atheneum, 1987. Ages 4–8. (Picture book)

Halfway through this book, children will probably start laughing aloud each time Farmer Bungle forgets his wife's instructions. The brisk, simple text moves this story along a fairly predictable path, which in this case makes things all the more funny. The colored pencil illustrations are comical and full of visual jokes that many young readers are sure to enjoy. This would be a fine story to share with a group of children.

8.237 Komaiko, Leah. **Earl's Too Cool for Me.** Illustrated by Laura Cornell. Harper and Row, 1988. Ages 5–9. (Picture book)

A humorous story and illustrations depict Earl, a young boy who does all kinds of cool things, such as riding on the Milky Way, growing a rose from his fingernails, and driving to China in an egg-roll car.

8.238 Kudrna, C. Imbior. **To Bathe a Boa.** Illustrated by the author. Carolrhoda Books, 1986. Ages 4–7. (Picture book)

In this hilarious story, a little boy wants to give his pet boa a bath, but the snake has other ideas and hides from him. The search for the boa is written in rhyme. The illustrations, done in pen-and-ink and crayon, continue the humor. Young children will appreciate this very imaginative story.

8.239 Lester, Helen. **It Wasn't My Fault.** Illustrated by Lynn Munsinger. Houghton Mifflin, 1985. Ages 4–7. (Picture book)

When accidents happen to Murdley Gurdson, they are usually his fault—until one day, when a hilarious set of circumstances leads him to wonder if it is his fault that a bird has laid an egg on his head. Murdley and humorously drawn animals are depicted in full-page drawings.

8.240 Lloyd, David. **The Sneeze.** Illustrated by Fritz Wegner. J. B. Lippincott, 1986. Ages 4–8. (Picture book)

Three characters, a man, a girl and a dog, engage in a series of events in which the reader is asked an ongoing series of questions, starting with "Who wore the hat? Did the man wear the hat? Did the girl wear the newspaper? Did the dog wear the suitcase?" The reader turns the page to find out the answers and to encounter the next set of nonsense questions, which move the story forward. The illustrations and text invite the reader to participate in telling the story.

8.241 McEwan, Jamie. **The Story of Grump and Pout.** Illustrated by Sandra Boynton. Crown, 1988. Ages 5–8. (Picture book)

Two argumentative monsters encounter a cobbler who offers a solution to their miseries. Humor in the events that lead toward resolution of the monsters' difficulties is developed primarily through Sandra Boynton's customary cheerful, humorous illustrations. *Children's Choice.*

8.242 McGovern, Ann. **Eggs on Your Nose.** Illustrated by Maxie Chambliss. Macmillan, 1987. Ages 2–6. (Picture book)

When a little boy begins to eat fried eggs by himself, the eggs end up all over the room, all over the house—eggs on the floor, eggs on the door, eggs everywhere! The simple rhymes and joyously colorful full-page illustrations will have children laughing as they follow the egg trail everywhere.

8.243 McKee, David. **Two Monsters.** Illustrated by the author. Bradbury Press, 1986. Ages 5–7. (Picture book)

In this story, one monster lives on the west side of the mountain, and a second monster lives on the east. Because of this, when one sees the sunrise, the other sees night arriving. This leads to some unpleasantness between the two monsters, but it will make for some great fun for readers. The watercolors, though not overpowering, add a lot to the humor.

8.244   Madsen, Ross Martin. **Perrywinkle and the Book of Magic Spells.** Illustrated by Dirk Zimmer. Dial Books for Young Readers/Easy-to-Read Books, 1986. Ages 6–8.

Perrywinkle and his pet talking crow, Nevermore, get into hilarious trouble when they discover a book of magic spells. Perrywinkle learns, for example, that a novice wizard should not "spell" at school. The word w-a-t-e-r-f-a-l-l almost drowns his class! When all goes wrong for Perrywinkle, a special friend brings out his most magical qualities.

8.245   Matthews, Ellen. **Debugging Rover.** Illustrated by Arthur Thompson. Dodd, Mead, 1985. Ages 8–10.

Justin finds that a home computer/robot named Rover can be both a bother and a help. For example, Rover gives reminders to do homework and then helps with math assignments. When Justin's gerbil runs away, there is a malfunction in the robot, yet Rover helps find the gerbil. A mystery develops in this book for those who like computers and fantasy.

8.246   Mayer, Mercer. **There's an Alligator under My Bed.** Illustrated by the author. Dial Books for Young Readers, 1987. Ages 4–7. (Picture book)

In this sequel to *There's a Nightmare in My Closet*, this time the boy disposes of his nightmare himself because his parents refuse to believe that there is an alligator under his bed. He lures the alligator to the garage with food and snacks and slams the door, leaving his father to hassle with the problem in the morning. There are full-color, full-page realistic illustrations. An imaginative, humorous book.

8.247   Mayer, Mercer. **Whinnie the Lovesick Dragon.** Illustrated by Diane Dawson Hearn. Macmillan, 1986. Ages 5–7. (Picture book)

Full of imagination and humor, this wonderful picture book revolves around the attempt of Whinnie the dragon to win the heart of Alfred the knight. All he ever does, however, is whack her, causing her to fly off in humiliation. Of course, he thinks he has frightened her off. It takes a wizard to sort things out. The illustrations are colorful, lively, full of humor, and busy.

8.248 Murphy, Jill. **Five Minutes' Peace.** Illustrated by the author. G. P. Putnam's Sons, 1986. Ages 3–5. (Picture book)

Mrs. Large, an elephant, wants just five minutes' peace from her three offspring, so she loads a tray with food and sets off for the bathroom. She is looking forward to a hot bath, a cup of tea, and solitude. She is not alone long until, one by one, all the children come join her. There is imaginative humor in this portrait of family life. The large, colorful illustrations capture the flavor of the story and evoke a great deal of sympathy for poor Mrs. Large.

8.249 Myers, Bernice. **Sidney Rella and the Glass Sneaker.** Illustrated by the author. Macmillan, 1985. Ages 5–8.

The youngest of Mr. and Mrs. Rella's three boys is Sidney, who wants to be on the football team with his two older brothers. With the aid of his fairy godfather, Sidney Rella makes the team, wins the game, and is paired up with his glass sneaker by the coach. Cartoonlike illustrations add to the mirthful fantasy showing that fame and fortune go to those who have fairy godfathers to do their chores and provide the talent. The spoof could work a little reverse psychology.

8.250 Nordqvist, Sven (translated by Angela Barnett-Lindberg). **The Hat Hunt.** Illustrated by the author. R and S Books, 1988. Ages 6–9. (Picture book)

Translated from the Swedish, this story tells of Grandpa, who loses his beloved hat. His search for the hat brings him in contact with his highly unusual friends and neighbors, who are better depicted through the book's colorful and detailed illustrations than in the text. Most significant, however, is the insight the book provides into the sometimes capricious memory of the elderly.

8.251 Oram, Hiawyn. **Jenna and the Troublemaker.** Illustrated by Tony Ross. Henry Holt, 1986. Ages 5–8. (Picture book)

In his usual, delightful way, Tony Ross illustrates Hiawyn Oram's story of a little girl who is loaded with troubles but the worst is—freckles! She is befriended by a troublemaker who collects all her friends' troubles. Jenna selects the lightest load and discovers that it is her own. A lighthearted story with flowing prose that will be fun to read aloud and share with young children.

8.252 Parrish, Peggy. **Amelia Bedelia Goes Camping.** Illustrated by Lynn Sweat. Greenwillow Books/Read-Alone Books, 1985. Ages 5–8. (Picture book)

Amelia Bedelia's humorous misinterpretations of oral directions will be enjoyed by the youngest reader. This early reading book takes Amelia Bedelia and her family on a camping trip that has many laughs as Amelia Bedelia carefully and literally follows instructions to hit the road, pitch a tent, and row a boat. *Children's Choice.*

8.253 Pinkwater, Daniel. **Aunt Lulu.** Illustrated by the author. Macmillan, 1988. Ages 6–9. (Picture book)

Aunt Lulu's life as a librarian in Alaska is unusual. She and her fourteen sled dogs—Melvin, Louise, Phoebe, Willie, Norman, Hortense, Bruce, Susie, Charles, Teddie, Neddie, Eddie, Freddie, and Sweetie-Pie—take books to the miners. However, when Aunt Lulu gets fed up with the frozen wastes, life in Parsippany, New Jersey, beckons. But what does she do with fourteen Alaskan sled dogs? Aunt Lulu's solution to her dilemma is novel, to say the least, and will produce nonstop chuckles.

8.254 Pinkwater, Daniel. **The Frankenbagel Monster.** Illustrated by the author. E. P. Dutton, 1986. Ages 7–10.

Harold Frankenbagel, creator of exotic bagels, outdoes himself with the Glimville Bagelunculus, a night-roaming monster. In this zany plot, Frankenbagel seeks the help of Professor Von Sweeney in stopping the monster by planning to eat it—"Bagels always go stale just before you're ready to eat them." Full of puns and illustrated with full-color computer-generated artwork.

8.255 Purdy, Carol. **Iva Dunnit and the Big Wind.** Illustrated by Steven Kellogg. Dial Books for Young Readers, 1985. Ages 4–8. (Picture book)

The story of pioneer Iva Dunnit and her six children braving the elements on the prairie is comical, but there is a lesson to be learned. Iva, who prides herself on having children who "stay put," is relieved to see them "using their wits" when she gets caught in the Big Wind. The book is greatly enhanced with the entertaining full-color illustrations.

8.256 Ross, Tony. **Super Dooper Jezebel.** Illustrated by the author. Farrar, Straus and Giroux, 1988. Ages 4–9. (Picture book)

Jezebel is perfect in every way—she never gets dirty; she cleans up after the cat; she puts away all her things; she is the best at everything; and she always takes her medicine. But then something shocking changes her life.

8.257 Rusling, Albert. **The Mouse and Mrs. Proudfoot.** Illustrated by the author. Prentice-Hall, 1985. Ages 4–8. (Picture book)

In this cumulative story, Mrs. Proudfoot and her daughter, Miranda, are frightened by a mouse. They send for various animals in succession to deal with the problem. Multicolored cartoonlike illustrations are opposite each page of text.

8.258 Simmonds, Posy. **Lulu and the Flying Babies.** Illustrated by the author. Alfred A. Knopf/Borzoi Books, 1988. Ages 6–9. (Picture book)

Lulu is reluctant to visit the local art museum with her father and brother Willy. What awaits her is a flying romp through the museum and in and out of various works of art. She is accompanied on this magical tour by two polite baroque cherubs who come to life from a painting and a sculpture right in front of Lulu's eyes. *Children's Choice.*

8.259 Small, David. **Imogene's Antlers.** Illustrated by the author. Crown, 1986. Ages 4–6. (Picture book)

Imogene awakens one morning to discover that during the night she has grown a set of very, very large antlers. How she and her family cope make this a delightfully funny and imaginative story that has an even funnier climax. The paperback format and busy illustrations do not lend themselves to being presented as a picture book. It is better for reading aloud or reading alone.

8.260 Spurr, Elizabeth. **Mrs. Minetta's Car Pool.** Illustrated by Blanche Sims. Atheneum, 1985. Ages 6–10. (Picture book)

The neighborhood children never get to school on Fridays, when Mrs. Minetta drives the carpool. Magically, the car heads elsewhere—to the beach, the mountains, or an amusement park. Whimsical pen-and-ink drawings, colored and black-and-white, add to the fun.

8.261   Stanley, Diane. **The Good-Luck Pencil.** Illustrated by Bruce Degen. Four Winds Press, 1986. Ages 6–8. (Picture book)

Mary Ann finds a magic pencil that writes a fabulous biography for her school assignment. But a problem arises when the pencil's fiction becomes reality, and Mary Ann finds that she is eager to get back to her own real life. Cartoon drawings illustrate the text.

8.262   Stevenson, James. **Emma.** Illustrated by the author. Greenwillow Books, 1985. Ages 6–8. (Picture book)

Two nasty old witches tease young Emma, who yearns to fly on a broom as they do. A comic contest of wits ensues, with Emma and her friends clear winners. The story is told comicbook style, which should appeal to children who prefer their dialogue in bubbles.

8.263   Stevenson, James. **That Dreadful Day.** Illustrated by the author. Greenwillow Books, 1985. Ages 5–7. (Picture book)

After Mary Ann and Louie complain about their miserable first day of school, Grandpa recalls his own first-day traumas as he faced the evil tyranny of grinch-ish Mr. Smeal. James Stevenson's now-familiar watercolor cartoon drawings are sure to provoke as many giggles as the text does.

8.264   Stevenson, James. **We Hate Rain!** Illustrated by the author. Greenwillow Books, 1988. Ages 3–8. (Picture book)

When Mary Ann and Louie come in to complain about playing in the rain, Grandpa regales them with a tall tale about the time when he was a boy and it rained so hard that the neighbors visited by boat, floating through the living room. The only way to rid the house of the water was to pull the plug in the bathtub. Cartoons in comic-strip format depict a mustached little boy (Grandpa) and his family. This is hilarious fare for reading aloud.

8.265   Talbott, Hudson. **We're Back! A Dinosaur's Story.** Illustrated by the author. Crown, 1987. Ages 5–9. (Picture book)

Here is a totally weird story that kids will love. Seven dinosaurs participate in a product test of Brain Grain, an IQ enhancer, and win a sightseeing trip to the twentieth century, resulting in much excitement and hilarity. Toothy heroes and a feisty professor, who is anything but absent-minded, are depicted with an exuberance that just matches this flaky tall tale. *Children's Choice.*

8.266 Tusa, Tricia. **Maebelle's Suitcase.** Illustrated by the author. Macmillan, 1987. Ages 3–7. (Picture book)

Comical crayon and watercolor illustrations and a lively text tell of Maebelle, a 108-year-old hatmaker and bird lover who uses her unusual talents to help her feathery friend Binkle fly south for the winter.

8.267 Wood, Audrey. **Elbert's Bad Word.** Illustrated by Audrey and Don Wood. Harcourt Brace Jovanovich, 1988. Ages 5–7. (Picture book)

During an elegant garden party, a bad word (resembling a furry creature) flies into young Elbert's mouth. At the first opportune moment, the word creature jumps into the crowd, bigger and uglier than before. Washing Elbert's mouth with soap is not enough, so a wizard feeds Elbert powerful, but good, words that send the ugly creature scurrying. Stylized energetic watercolors are an apt complement to this absurd and amusing cautionary tale. *Children's Choice.*

Intermediate

8.268 Aiken, Joan. **Mortimer Says Nothing.** Illustrated by Quentin Blake. Harper and Row/Charlotte Zolotow Books, 1985. Ages 9–11.

This fourth volume in a series of adventures about Arabel Jones and her pet raven, Mortimer, continues with four separate stories filled with slapstick humor and exaggerated characters. In the midst of preparations for the visit of Mrs. Jones's Kitchen Club, Mortimer stymies a bird researcher trying to record his "Nevermore" call. In other stories, Arabel outwits a visiting relative, accompanies the family on a trip to Wales, and mysteriously disappears after a prank phone call. Quentin Blake's cartoon drawings further detail these wacky episodes.

8.269 Hughes, Dean. **Theo Zephyr.** Atheneum, 1987. Ages 9–12.

When Theo Zephyr arrives, all of Brad's wildest daydreams come true. This is not surprising: Theo is Brad's own creation, a fantasy come to life. When Theo looks good, Brad's archenemy, a bright, athletic boy named Gil, looks bad. This should make Brad happy, but he is terrified that people will discover Theo's origin, and he is beginning to understand that his thoughts about Gil are unworthy. *Children's Choice.*

8.270 Macaulay, David. **Why the Chicken Crossed the Road.** Illustrated by the author. Houghton Mifflin, 1987. Ages 8 and up. (Picture book)

The antic-filled, cumulative pattern of this picture book will appeal to intermediate readers. A chick crosses the road on the book's first page, causing a chain reaction of growing proportions. Calm seems to be restored by the book's end. But in the final pages, it seems the pattern might be repeated. Vibrant, zany illustrations enhance the book's humor.

8.271 McInerney, Judith Whitelock. **Judge Benjamin: The Superdog Gift.** Illustrated by Leslie Morrill. Holiday House, 1986. Ages 8–10.

Judge Benjamin, a beloved 200-pound St. Bernard, narrates his fifth adventure as a member of the lively O'Riley family. Christmas holiday activities are the backdrop for his new mate's efforts to rescue an elderly woman. Preparation for their first litter of puppies is told with a sense of humor that will delight middle-grade fans of Judge Benjamin.

8.272 Marney, Dean. **The Computer That Ate My Brother.** Houghton Mifflin, 1985. Ages 8–10.

Harry Smith receives a most unusual computer for his twelfth birthday, one that has a mind of its own. Harry's loathsome brother, Roger, and Imogene S. Cuniformly, a retired math teacher and previous owner of the contentious computer, figure in the hilarious outcome of Dean Marney's whimsical fantasy.

8.273 Richler, Mordecai. **Jacob Two-Two and the Dinosaur.** Illustrated by Norman Eyolfson. Alfred A. Knopf/Borzoi Books, 1987. Ages 8–10.

In this sequel to *Jacob Two-Two and the Hooded Fang*, Jacob has turned eight and has acquired a baby lizard, some sixty-five million years old, that grows into a dinosaur. Dippy is declared a menace, and the two escape to the wilderness. A tall tale with slapstick humor.

8.274   Roberts, Willo Davis. **The Magic Book.** Atheneum, 1986. Ages 9–11.

When twelve-year-old Alex goes to a used-book sale and finds that a book of magic spells falls mysteriously into his hands, he is sure a spell will help him deal with Norman, the class bully. Young readers will enjoy the spells that Alex and his friends try, as well as the unexpected twist on the bully hex.

8.275   Tapp, Kathy Kennedy. **The Scorpio Ghosts and the Black Hole Gang.** Harper and Row, 1987. Ages 9–12.

This is a lively and humorous ghost story narrated by Ryan, one of the four children whose family has just purchased an old schoolhouse in the cornfields of Wisconsin with the intention of renovating it for their new home. What had promised to be a dull summer turns into great adventure as Ryan and his siblings encounter two ghosts traveling in a ghost bookmobile, caught in a haunt pattern that only the children can help break.

Literary Folk Literature

Primary

8.276   Andersen, Hans Christian (adapted by Alan Benjamin). **The Nightingale.** Illustrated by Beni Montresor. Crown, 1985. Ages 6–10. (Picture book)

This new translation of Hans Christian Andersen's classic story of the emperor and the nightingale omits much of the detail of the original, but it leaves us with a smooth text that begs to be read aloud. The illustrations, however, are the book's glory. They are dramatic in structure and brilliantly colored in dusky rich tones.

8.277   Andersen, Hans Christian (adapted by Anthea Bell). **The Old House.** Illustrated by Jean Claverie. North-South Books, 1986. Ages 6–10. (Picture book)

Children may be unfamiliar with this tale in which a little boy befriends a lonely old man. The illustrations offer a well-defined sense of place and time. Read the book together with Hans Christian Andersen's "The Steadfast Tin Soldier" since both tales feature a soldier character.

8.278   Andersen, Hans Christian. **The Princess and the Pea.** Illustrated by Dorothée Duntze. North-South Books, 1985. Ages 5–10. (Picture book)

Designs swirl, patterns abound, and pastels pervade every page in this highly stylized, two-dimensional rendition of the improbable old tale. These are royal personages, including the bedraggled princess with water "oozing out of her shoes." Illustrations capably evoke a distinctly different time and place.

8.279   Andersen, Hans Christian (translated by Anthea Bell). **The Snow Queen.** Illustrated by Bernadette Watts. North-South Books, 1987. Ages 3–10. (Picture book)

Pastels and a gentle wash are combined to illustrate Anthea Bell's version of Hans Christian Andersen's classic tale of the Snow Queen. The pages are large, and the illustrations make full use of the space available. Children can come back again and again to find new things among the many details. The translation is appealing and should provide good material for story time. *Children's Choice.*

8.280   Andersen, Hans Christian (retold by Marianna Mayer). **The Ugly Duckling.** Illustrated by Thomas Locker. Macmillan, 1987. Ages 5–10. (Picture book)

A retelling of Hans Christian Andersen's tale of a bird who thinks he is an ugly duckling but who grows into a beautiful swan is illustrated with oil paintings done in the style of the Dutch masters. This is a fine story for reading aloud.

8.281   Andersen, Hans Christian (translated by Anne Stewart). **The Ugly Duckling.** Illustrated by Monika Laimgruber. Greenwillow Books, 1985. Ages 6–9. (Picture book)

Anne Stewart's rendition of this Hans Christian Andersen tale matches the author's usual, complex vocabulary with Monika Laimgruber's complex illustrations, which are spaced interestingly in different places on the page and which show, though do not extend, the text. The artist uses myriad small black lines overlaid on the color to add definition.

8.282 Aylesworth, Jim. **Hanna's Hog.** Illustrated by Glen Rounds. Atheneum, 1988. Ages 4–8. (Picture book)

Hanna Brodie tends a big garden and raises chickens, bees, and a prize pig. She is well able to manage everything in her mountain setting but her shiftless neighbor, Kenny Jackson. When Hanna's hog is missing, she knows she has to do something about light-fingered Kenny. And when Hanna is through with him, Kenny will not even visit his outhouse without taking along his rifle. Children will applaud Hanna's pluck and resourcefulness.

8.283 Bang, Molly. **The Paper Crane.** Illustrated by the author. Greenwillow Books, 1985. Ages 4–9. (Picture book)

In this modern retelling of an old story, a man and his young son own and operate a small roadside restaurant desperately in need of customers. One day a long-time traveler appears and pays for his meal with a folded paper crane. It comes to life and dances for all the customers, who flock to the restaurant to see the bird. When prosperity has returned, so does the traveler, who rides away on the crane, never to return. The illustrations are splendid photographs of detailed, three-dimensional paper-cutout dioramas.

8.284 Barber, Antonia. **The Enchanter's Daughter.** Illustrated by Errol Le Cain. Farrar, Straus, and Giroux, 1988. Ages 7–11. (Picture book)

Here is a book of great beauty, both in theme and illustration. The enchanter and the girl he calls his daughter live in isolation in the "cold white land at the top of the world." He provides her with every comfort, but she longs for companionship and love. In a story that can be taken as a parable, the young girl discovers the marvels of the rest of the world through books and later gains her freedom through wit and courage. Errol Le Cain's illustrations are superb—sophisticated and "other worldly."

8.285 de Marolles, Chantal. **The Lonely Wolf.** Illustrated by Eleonore Schmid. North-South Books, 1986. Ages 5–9.

This is a morality tale about a cold, hungry, little wolf who is turned away at three different doors before he is taken in and fed by a woodsman who hears him howl. Later the other three feel remorse for the wolf and go out looking for him. All get together in the woodsman's hut. The illustrations are in full color and have a Slavic appearance.

8.286   Gerstein, Mordicai. **The Mountains of Tibet.** Illustrated by the author. Harper and Row, 1987. Ages 7 and up. (Picture book)

A Tibetan woodcutter dies and is given the choice of going to heaven or living another life anywhere in the universe. The choice for reincarnation is beautifully depicted in the illustrations and language of this adaptation of the *Tibetan Book of the Dead*.

8.287   Haugaard, Erik Christian. **Prince Boghole.** Illustrated by Julie Downing. Macmillan, 1987. Ages 6–9. (Picture book)

Here is a literary folktale laced with gentle humor. Set long ago in the kingdom of Munster on the isle of Eire, the story tells of Princess Orla and the three princes who set out to win her hand. The descriptive and rhythmic text is accompanied by finely detailed, full-color illustrations.

8.288   Lionni, Leo. **Six Crows: A Fable.** Illustrated by the author. Alfred A. Knopf/Borzoi Books, 1988. Ages 4–8. (Picture book)

Six crows seek the assistance of an owl to help settle an argument about who should have the rights to a crop of wheat. Through compromise they are able to settle the argument peacefully.

8.289   MacDonald, George (adapted by Anthea Bell). **Little Daylight.** Illustrated by Dorothée Duntze. North-South Books, 1987. Ages 4–10. (Picture book)

This finely illustrated book makes use of double-page spreads and decorative insets to accompany a captivating tale of a princess cursed to spend her days asleep and nights awake, though only when the moon is still present. The images are the most striking feature of this book and should easily draw children's interest. The story is good for reading aloud.

8.290   McKissack, Patricia C. **Flossie and the Fox.** Illustrated by Rachel Isadora. Dial Books for Young Readers, 1986. Ages 5–10. (Picture book)

Young Flossie, on an errand to deliver eggs to a neighbor, takes a shortcut through the woods, where she outwits a sly, thievish fox. This high-spirited tale begs to be read aloud. The illustrations are warm, dappled, and lush; best of all, they capture the humor of the story and the twinkle in Flossie's eye. *Notable Children's Trade Book in the Language Arts.*

8.291   Mahy, Margaret. **Seventeen Kings and Forty-Two Elephants.** Illustrated by Patricia MacCarthy. Dial Books for Young Readers, 1987. Ages 3–5. (Picture book)

A perfect blend of illustrations (batik on silk) and rhyming text with nonsensical words describes the journey of seventeen kings and their forty-two elephants during a wild, wet night. Children will enjoy this imaginative tale.

8.292   Noble, Trinka Hakes. **Meanwhile Back at the Ranch.** Illustrated by Tony Ross. Dial Books for Young Readers, 1987. Ages 6–10. (Picture book)

Written in the tradition of the tall tale, Rancher Hicks drives to Sleepy Gulch looking for something to happen, leaving his wife, Elna, home to mind the ranch. While Hicks is hanging out at the barber shop, the amazing events of Elna's day begin with a phone call telling her she has just won a brand-new wall-to-wall frost-free super-cool refrigerator with a built-in automatic food maker. And that is just the beginning. The wacky illustrations are a perfect contrast for the deadpan style of the story.

8.293   Ross, Tony. **Stone Soup.** Illustrated by the author. Dial Books for Young Readers, 1987. Ages 4–7. (Picture book)

In a hilarious twist to an old tale, a little red hen tricks a wolf into doing many chores for her while fixing him stone soup. After vacuuming, chopping down a tree, and cleaning the chimney, he is given all the soup. Now too full to eat her, he runs away. Wacky, colorful illustrations are on each page. *Children's Choice.*

8.294   Walter, Mildred Pitts. **Brother to the Wind.** Illustrated by Leo and Diane Dillon. Lothrop, Lee and Shepard Books, 1985. Ages 7–10. (Picture book)

This is not a true African folktale, although it has all the ingredients of one. Emeke wishes to fly like a bird. With the help of Good Snake, and by performing three tasks, he does just that. A subtle combination of folktale and contemporary kite flying makes this a well-told story. However, it is the excellent watercolors in beautiful hues of blues, greens, and mauve that put this book above the ordinary.

8.295 West, Colin. **The King of Kennelwick Castle.** Illustrated by Anne Dalton. J. B. Lippincott, 1986. Ages 4–8. (Picture book)

In this cumulative read-aloud story, we learn about a young boy bringing a birthday gift to the King of Kennelwick Castle from the Queen of Spain. The end of the tale reveals a most-welcome surprise. The structure of "This Is the House That Jack Built" is the pattern for the book.

8.296 Wood, Audrey. **King Bidgood's in the Bathtub.** Illustrated by Don Wood. Harcourt Brace Jovanovich, 1985. Ages 5–10. (Picture book)

King Bidgood prefers to do everything in his bath: go to battle, eat lunch, fish, and dance along with whomever he can get to join him in this whimsical tub frolic. Only the young page knows what to do to stop the nonsense— pull the plug, glub, glub, glub. The intricate humorous illustrations provide the detail of every event down to the tiniest bubble. The repeated pattern of the story will invite the reader to join in the reading and to predict what will happen next. *ALA Notable Children's Book* and *Caldecott Honor Book*.

8.297 Wright, Jill. **The Old Woman and the Willy Nilly Man.** Illustrated by Glen Rounds. G. P. Putnam's Sons, 1987. Ages 5–8. (Picture book)

Full-color drawings illustrate this Arkansas folktale. The Old Woman cannot get any sleep because her shoes start dancing by themselves. When all else fails, she consults the mean old Willy Nilly Man for his help. Storytellers everywhere will be using this book.

Intermediate

8.298 Aiken, Joan. **The Last Slice of Rainbow, and Other Stories.** Illustrated by Alix Berenzy. Harper and Row/Charlotte Zolotow Books, 1988. Ages 9–12.

Joan Aiken looks at the common things that fill our lives and makes us think about them in an exciting new way in these nine adventures filled with children, fairies, and spirits.

8.299   Andersen, Hans Christian (retold by Richard Hess). **The Snow Queen.** Illustrated by the reteller. Ages 8–12.

According to tradition, when one breaks a mirror, one has seven years of bad luck. In this retelling of Hans Christian Andersen's tale, Kai gets a piece of the wicked demon's broken mirror in his eye. Not only does he have bad luck, but he also loses his feelings of love and friendliness. Because of his lack of warmth and love toward others, the Snow Queen takes Kai to her ice castle. Only the devotion of his friend Gerda and the warmth of her tears can melt Kai's cold heart. She sets out on a perilous but magical journey to find Kai and return him to his home. Articulate yet soft illustrations give the book that magical aura of a tale written many years ago.

8.300   Andersen, Hans Christian (translated by Naomi Lewis). **The Snow Queen.** Illustrated by Angela Barrett. Henry Holt, 1988. Ages 8–12. (Picture book)

After the Snow Queen abducts Kai, his dear friend Gerda embarks on an adventure filled with danger and magic in order to find him. The translation (originally done in 1968) flows beautifully and is enhanced by stunning, detailed illustrations in muted tones. The reader of this exquisitely designed book will become absorbed in this story of enchantment, where goodness ultimately triumphs.

8.301   Day, David. **The Emperor's Panda.** Illustrated by Eric Beddows. Dodd, Mead, 1986. Ages 8–10.

In an enchanting story set in ancient China, Kung, a young shepherd boy, becomes emperor with the help of Master Panda, a wise, magical creature. The plot is filled with good versus evil and impossible tasks fulfilled. The illustrations, done in charcoal and pen-and-ink, perfectly complement the story and help set the tone.

8.302   Pittman, Helena Clare. **The Gift of the Willows.** Illustrated by the author. Carolrhoda Books, 1988. Ages 9–12. (Picture book)

The life of a Japanese potter becomes intertwined with the growth and survival of three willow trees. As the years bring him challenges from nature, he observes the willows and eventually reaches a peaceful view of life. Full-page color illustrations beautifully complement the moods of the characters and the special feelings for the trees. *Children's Choice.*

8.303 Prusski, Jeffrey. **Bring Back the Deer.** Illustrated by Neil Waldman. Harcourt Brace Jovanovich/Gulliver Books, 1988. Ages 8–12. (Picture book)

Based on the style of Native American legends, this story tells of a young brave's first deer hunt. On his journey he learns the ways of his people and comes to recognize his inner strength. The dramatic paintings bring his search for identity to life.

8.304 Spirin, Gennady, illustrator. **The Enchanter's Spell: Five Famous Tales.** Dial Books for Young Readers, 1987. Ages 8 and up. (Picture book)

Literary fairy tales from five diverse cultures are presented in an exquisitely designed volume. Included are George Macdonald's "Little Daylight," Alexander Pushkin's "The Princess and the Seven Brothers," E.T.A. Hoffmann's "Nutcracker," Miguel de Cervantes's "The Beautiful Kitchen Maid," and Hans Christian Andersen's "The Emperor's New Clothes." The reader will feel compelled to pore over Gennady Spirin's rich, lavish paintings, which enrich these varied tales of enchantment.

Modern Fairy Tales

Intermediate

8.305 Hunter, Mollie. **The Three-Day Enchantment.** Illustrated by Marc Simont. Harper and Row/Charlotte Zolotow Books/ Knight of the Golden Plain Books, 1985. Ages 9–12.

Magically a boy is transformed into Sir Dauntless, a fearless knight. He sets out to free Dorabella, his damsel in distress, and his adventures to reach her call for much courage and ingenuity.

8.306 Snyder, Zilpha Keatley. **The Changing Maze.** Illustrated by Charles Mikolaycak. Macmillan, 1985. Ages 9–12.

Haunting pencil and watercolor drawings enhance this suspenseful, well-written story of Hugh, a shepherd. His black lamb wanders off into a magical green-thorn maze with paths that constantly shift and change. A treasure in the center of the maze could alter his life forever. What will Hugh do—take the treasure or save his lamb?

8.307 Vande Velde, Vivian. **A Hidden Magic.** Illustrated by Trina Schart Hyman. Crown, 1985. Ages 9–12.

This contemporary fairy tale follows the lively adventures of a plain but plucky princess who risks her safety to rescue her bewitched prince charming. With the help of an offbeat sorcerer, she saves the prince but refuses his offer of marriage—realizing that she could never be stuck with anyone so stuck on himself. The unique, witty parody provides a study of folktale structure, feminist literature, and pure entertainment.

Other Worlds and Times

Intermediate

8.308 Hughes, Monica. **Sandwriter.** Henry Holt, 1985. Ages 10–12.

Princess Antia is caught in an intrigue she cannot unravel. Her determination and will make her face decisions based on the values of greed and power or cooperation and respect. The setting for this fantasy adventure, the desert island of Roshan, is evocative of the geography of the Middle Eastern countries, and readers will probably make some associations and insights into today's world, too.

8.309 Macaulay, David. **Baaa.** Illustrated by the author. Houghton Mifflin, 1985. Ages 10 and up. (Picture book)

"There is no record of when the last person disappeared. The only person who could have recorded when the last person disappeared was the last person to disappear." But the sheep survive, find the deserted houses and supermarkets of the people, and learn to speak and eventually to read by watching videos. The sheep generally acquire the habits and customs of humans—with one notable exception. David Macaulay's examination of society in briefly captioned pen-and-ink drawings may be called "wit with a bite" by some and gallows humor by others.

8.310 Service, Pamela F. **Tomorrow's Magic.** Atheneum/Jean Karl Books, 1987. Ages 11–13.

In this sequel to *The Winter of Magic's Return*, in which Heather, Welly, and Earl succeed in bringing King Arthur back to the throne in a future era, Arthur is now trying to unite a post-holocaust Britain. Earl is revealed as Merlin, who became a teenager because of a spell. Merlin and Heather struggle to find their magic in time to defeat Arthur's relentless enemy, Morgan La Fay. Far from a standard saga of good versus evil, this is a multifaceted tale of human growth and fantasy adventure.

8.311   Slote, Alfred. **The Trouble on Janus.** Illustrated by James Watts. J. B. Lippincott, 1985. Ages 10–12.

In this fourth story about Jack and his robot buddy, Danny One, the two masquerade as each other and as Janus's young king when they go to the planet Janus to learn about its trouble. Economical and simple language is used to tell a straightforward but involved plot that will appeal to children just beginning to read science fantasy stories.

Supernatural Tales

Primary

8.312   Cohen, Daniel. **America's Very Own Ghosts.** Illustrated by Alix Berenzy. Dodd, Mead, 1985. Ages 7–10.

In short, simple sentences, Daniel Cohen tells the stories of nine American ghosts. The subject matter and Alix Berenzy's powerful black-and-white illustrations will appeal to readers of all ages. *Children's Choice.*

8.313   Mayer, Mercer. **There's Something in My Attic.** Illustrated by the author. Dial Books for Young Readers, 1988. Ages 3–8. (Picture book)

There's a nightmare in the attic, and the girl sneaks upstairs to capture it one night. Finding it holding her teddy bear, she lassos it and pulls it downstairs for her parents to see. Full-page pen-and-ink and watercolor drawings depict a determined girl and a huge but not-so-scary nightmare to delight young readers who have heard noises at night and wondered about them.

8.314 Sherrow, Victoria. **There Goes the Ghost.** Illustrated by Megan Lloyd. Harper and Row, 1985. Ages 5–9. (Picture book)

A rich farming family living in the colonial period matches wits with a ghost who inhabits their jewel of a house. Vivid, animated pictures depict the mischief instigated by the hobgoblin as it causes pewter mugs to clatter amidst showers of toads. As a read-aloud story, the book is imaginative and open-ended.

Intermediate

8.315 Bedard, Michael. **A Darker Magic.** Atheneum, 1987. Ages 10–14.

Sometimes a door opens from the normal, real, everyday world to another, darker dimension, and evil is let loose upon the unsuspecting. That is what happened in 1936, when Miss Potts was a girl. Now, fifty years later, it seems as though the same dark pied piper is exercising his malevolent influence upon the town, and only Emily Endicott can avert tragedy.

8.316 Brittain, Bill. **Dr. Dredd's Wagon of Wonders.** Illustrated by Andrew Glass. Harper and Row, 1987. Ages 8–11.

Fans of Bill Brittain's *Devil's Donkey* and *The Wish Giver* will relish this sequel. Exciting action and short, cliffhanger chapters involve the reader as the stalwart town of Coven Tree battles Dr. Dredd's fearsome magic. Andrew Glass provides misty, evocative drawings to enhance the scary tale, sure to appeal to followers of John Bellairs.

8.317 Cohen, Daniel. **Phone Call from a Ghost: Strange Tales from Modern America.** Illustrated by David Linn. Dodd, Mead, 1988. Ages 9–12.

Daniel Cohen retells thirteen (of course!) tales of possibly supernatural happenings in modern America. These tales, some of which have been investigated by authorities, report strange happenings in urban and suburban locations. Cohen's position as an editor for *Science Digest* magazine adds to the credibility of his retelling of such happenings as a warning from an Ouija board and ghosts associated with the crash of Flight 401 in Miami. David Linn's eerie black-and-white drawings add to the mood of these supernatural tales.

8.318 Dunlop, Eileen. **The House on the Hill.** Holiday House, 1987. Ages 10–12.

Philip gradually grows close to his unsmiling great-aunt Jane as he and his cousin Susan set out to solve the mysteries that Jane's old mansion holds. When they are confronted by the ghost that occupies the empty second-floor room, they find the key to the mystery that has shrouded Jane. Philip learns that caring about someone gives him a sense of self-worth. *ALA Notable Children's Book.*

8.319 Gorog, Judith. **No Swimming in Dark Pond, and Other Chilling Tales.** Philomel Books, 1987. Ages 9–12.

Evil, external and impersonal, is terrifying; but the most insidious terror is that which arises out of one's own thoughts, fears, and actions. Thirteen creepy short stories will be enjoyed by those who liked Daniel Cohen's *The Headless Roommate, and Other Tales of Terror.*

8.320 Hearne, Betsy. **Eli's Ghost.** Illustrated by Ronald Himler. Margaret K. McElderry Books, 1987. Ages 9–11.

Eli finds his long-lost mother and is happy living in her swamp home, away from his cold, unloving father, who may receive his own just desserts in the form of a shrewish wife. Eli encounters the ghosts of friends from earlier days, and his own ghost is released prematurely when he has a brush with death. Eli's ghost is of a prankish turn of mind and gets into much mischief. Simple, spare prose tells a sweet story of friendship and love.

8.321 Russell, Jean, editor. **Supernatural Stories: Thirteen Tales of the Unexpected.** Orchard Books, 1987. Ages 10–12.

Tales of ghosts, of dolls becoming real, and of powers that consume people's lives are several of the thirteen well-sculpted short stories that weave a sense of anticipation and suspense, leaving the reader wondering, with a slight shiver, Can that really be? Readers will rush on to the next story assured of meeting memorable characters and of pushing the limits of reality just a little farther than they ever expected.

8.322 Sobol, Donald J. **The Amazing Power of Ashur Fine.** Macmillan, 1986. Ages 10–12.

Sixteen-year-old Ashur Fine's life is totally changed the day the zoo's ancient elephant chooses to bestow on Ashur a Power. A cat-and-mouse chase ensues as Ashur tries to find and bring to justice the person who mugged Aunt Ruth, with whom Ashur lives. Often trapped in life-threatening situations, Ashur learns the special effects and limitations of the Power in this tongue-in-cheek, fast-reading, high adventure story.

8.323   Vivelo, Jackie. **A Trick of the Light: Stories to Read at Dusk.** G. P. Putnam's Sons, 1987. Ages 9–11.

These short stories are filled with chills of a pleasant variety. Jackie Vivelo has the twin gifts of making readers care about her characters within a short span of time and of creating plots that build steadily to surprising conclusions.

Recommended Books Published before 1985

Alexander, Lloyd. *The High King*. Holt, Rinehart and Winston, 1968. 10 and up.

Allard, Harry. *Miss Nelson Is Back*. Illustrated by James Marshall. Houghton Mifflin, 1982. 6–9.

Andersen, Hans Christian. *The Wild Swans*. Retold by Amy Ehrlich. Illustrated by Susan Jeffers. Dial Books for Young Readers, 1981. 5–8.

Atwater, Richard, and Florence Atwater. *Mr Popper's Penguins*. Illustrated by Robert Lawson. Little, Brown, 1938. 8–10.

Babbitt, Natalie. *Tuck Everlasting*. Farrar, Straus and Giroux, 1975. 10 and up.

Barrett, Judi. *Cloudy with a Chance of Meatballs*. Illustrated by Ron Barrett. Atheneum, 1978. 4–7.

Bellairs, John. *The House with a Clock in Its Walls*. Illustrated by Edward Gorey. Dial Books for Young Readers, 1973. 9–12.

Bond, Michael. *A Bear Called Paddington*. Illustrated by Peggy Fortnum. Houghton Mifflin, 1960. 6–9.

Boston, L. M. *The Children of Green Knowe*. Illustrated by Peter Boston. Harcourt, Brace, and World, 1955. 9–11.

Bright, Robert. *Georgie*. Doubleday, 1944. 4–7.

Burningham, John. *Mr. Gumpy's Outing*. Holt, Rinehart and Winston, 1971. 3–6.

Burton, Virginia Lee. *Mike Mulligan and His Steam Shovel*. Houghton Mifflin, 1939. 4–7.

Coombs, Patricia. *Dorrie and the Wizard's Spell*. Lothrop, Lee and Shepard Books, 1968. 5–8.

Cooper, Susan. *The Dark Is Rising*. Atheneum, 1973. 10 and up.

Cresswell, Helen. *A Game of Catch*. Illustrated by Ati Forberg. Macmillan, 1977. 7–9.

Dahl, Roald. *James and the Giant Peach*. Illustrated by Nancy Elkholm Burkert. Alfred A. Knopf, 1961. 9–11.

dePaola, Tomie. *Georgio's Village*. G. P. Putnam's Sons, 1982. 4–8.

de Regniers, Beatrice Schenk. *May I Bring a Friend?* Atheneum, 1964. 4–8.

Dickinson, Peter. *The Devil's Children*. Little, Brown, 1970. 10 and up.

Dunlop, Eileen. *Elizabeth, Elizabeth*. Illustrated by Peter Farmer. Holt, Rinehart and Winston, 1977. 10 and up.

Eager, Edward. *Half-Magic*. Illustrated by N. M. Bodecker. Harcourt, Brace and World, 1954. 9–11.

Erickson, Russell E. *A Toad for Tuesday*. Illustrated by Lawrence DiFiori. Lothrop, Lee and Shepard Books, 1974. 7–9.

Farmer, Penelope. *The Summer Birds*. Harcourt, Brace and World, 1962. 9–11.

Gág, Wanda. *Millions of Cats*. Coward-McCann, Franklin, 1928. 4–7.

Garner, Alan. *The Weirdstone of Brisingamen*. Franklin Watts, 1961. 9–11.

Grahame, Kenneth. *The Wind in the Willows*. Illustrated by Ernest H. Shepard. Charles Scribner's Sons, 1958 (originally published in 1908). 9–11.

Gramatky, Hardie. *Little Toot*. G. P. Putnam's Sons, 1939. 4–7.

Hoover, H. M. *The Rains of Eridan*. Viking Press, 1977. 10 and up.

Howe, Deborah, and James Howe. *Bunnicula: A Rabbit-Tale of Mystery*. Illustrated by Alan Daniel. Atheneum, 1979. 8–10.

Jones, Diana Wynne. *Witch Week*. Greenwillow Books, 1982. 9–11.

Karl, Jean. *Beloved Benjamin Is Waiting*. E. P. Dutton, 1978. 9–11.

Kessler, Leonard. *Kick, Pass, and Run*. Harper and Row, 1966. 4–7.

Key, Alexander. *Escape to Witch Mountain*. Illustrated by Leon B. Wisdom, Jr. Westminster Press, 1968. 8–10.

Kraus, Robert. *Leo the Late Bloomer*. Illustrated by Jose Aruego. Abelard-Schuman, 1971. 6–9.

Krensky, Stephen. *The Witching Hour*. Illustrated by A. Delaney. Atheneum, 1981. 9–11.

Langton, Jane. *The Fledgling*. Harper and Row, 1980. 9–11.

Lawson, Robert. *Rabbit Hill*. Viking Press, 1944. 8–10.

Leaf, Munro. *The Story of Ferdinand*. Viking Press, 1936. 4 and up.

LeGuin, Ursula K. *A Wizard of Earthsea*. Illustrated by Ruth Robbins. Parnassus Press, 1968. 11 and up.

L'Engle, Madeleine. *A Wrinkle in Time*. Farrar, Straus and Giroux, 1962. 9 and up.

Lewis, C. S. *The Lion, The Witch and the Wardrobe*. Illustrated by Pauline Baynes. Macmillan, 1950. 9–11.

Lindgren, Astrid. *Pippi Longstocking*. Illustrated by Louis S. Glanzman. Viking Press, 1950. 8–10.

Lionni, Leo. *Swimmy*. Pantheon Books, 1963. 5–7.

Lobel, Arnold. *Frog and Toad Are Friends*. Harper and Row, 1970. 4–8.

———. *Ming Lo Moves the Mountain*. Greenwillow Books, 1982. 6–10.

McCaffrey, Anne. *Dragonsong*. Atheneum, 1976. 11 and up.

McCloskey, Robert. *Make Way for Ducklings*. Viking Press, 1969. 4–8.

MacDonald, George. *The Light Princess*. Illustrated by Maurice
Sendak. Farrar, Straus and Giroux, 1977. 7–9.

McKillip, Patricia A. *The Riddle-Master of Hed*. Atheneum, 1976. 11
and up.

McKinley, Robin. *The Blue Sword*. Greenwillow Books, 1982. 11 and
up.

Mahy, Margaret. *The Haunting*. Atheneum, 1982. 10 and up.

Minarik, Else Holmelund. *Little Bear*. Illustrated by Maurice Sendak.
Harper and Row, 1957. 6–8.

Norton, Andre. *The Wraiths of Time*. Atheneum, 1976. 10 and up.

Norton, Mary. *The Borrowers*. Illustrated by Beth and Joe Krush.
Harcourt, Brace and World, 1953. 8–10.

Oakley, Graham. *The Church Mouse*. Atheneum, 1972. 4–8.

O'Brien, Robert. *Mrs. Frisby and the Rats of NIMH*. Illustrated by
Zena Bernstein. Atheneum, 1971. 8–11.

Pearce, Philippa. *Tom's Midnight Garden*. Illustrated by Susan
Einzig. J. B. Lippincott, 1959. 8–11.

Peck, Richard. *The Ghost Belonged to Me*. Viking Press, 1975. 9–12.

Pope, Elizabeth Marie. *The Perilous Gard*. Illustrated by Richard
Cuffari. Houghton Mifflin, 1974. 11 and up.

Potter, Beatrix. *The Tale of Peter Rabbit*. Frederick Warne, 1902.
4–7.

Rey, H. A. *Curious George*. Houghton Mifflin, 1941. 4–7.

Rodgers, Mary. *Freaky Friday*. Harper and Row, 1972. 9–12.

Selden, George. *The Cricket in Times Square*. Illustrated by Garth
Williams. Farrar, Straus and Giroux, 1960. 8–10.

Sendak, Maurice. *Nutshell Library*. Harper and Row, 1962. 3–8.

———. *Outside Over There*. Harper and Row, 1981. 6–8.

———. *Where the Wild Things Are*. Harper and Row, 1963. 4–8.

Seuss, Dr. *The 500 Hats of Bartholomew Cubbins*. Random House,
1938. 5–9.

———. *Horton Hatches the Egg*. Random House, 1940. 5 and up.

Sharp, Margery. *The Rescuers*. Illustrated by Garth Williams. Little,
Brown, 1959. 7–10.

Smith, Robert Kimmel. *Chocolate Fever*. Illustrated by Gioia Fiam-
menghi. Coward, McCann and Geoghegan, 1971. 9–11.

Snyder, Zilpha Keatley. *The Headless Cupid*. Illustrated by Alton
Raible. Atheneum, 1971. 9–11.

Steig, William. *The Amazing Bone*. Farrar, Straus and Giroux, 1976.
4–7.

———. *Doctor De Soto*. Farrar, Straus and Giroux, 1982. 5–8.

———. *Sylvester and the Magic Pebble*. Simon and Schuster, 1969.
4–7.

Stolz, Mary. *Cat in the Mirror*. Harper and Row, 1975. 9–12.

Tolkien, J.R.R. *The Hobbit; or, There and Back Again*. Houghton Mifflin, 1938. 10 and up.

Turkle, Brinton. *Do Not Open*. E. P. Dutton, 1981. 6–9.

Van Allsburg, Chris. *Jumanji*. Houghton Mifflin, 1981. 6–9.

———. *The Wreck of the Zephyr*. Houghton Mifflin, 1983. 7–10.

White, E. B. *Charlotte's Web*. Illustrated by Garth Williams. Harper and Row, 1952. 8–10.

Williams, Jay. *Everyone Knows What a Dragon Looks Like*. Illustrated by Mercer Mayer. Four Winds Press, 1976. 4–7.

Williams, Jay, and Raymond Abrashkin. *Danny Dunn and the Homework Machine*. Illustrated by Ezra Jack Keats. Wittlesey House, 1958. 8–10.

———. *Morris Tells Boris Mother Moose Stories and Rhymes*. Dodd, Mead, 1979. 4–7.

Zion, Gene. *Harry the Dirty Dog*. Illustrated by Margaret Bloy Graham. Harper and Row, 1956. 4–7.

9 Science Fiction

9.1 Willis, Jeanne. **The Long Blue Blazer.** Illustrated by Susan Varley. E. P. Dutton, 1987. Ages 5–8. (Picture book)

A new boy arrives at school and refuses to take off his long blue blazer. When his mother is late picking him up, the boy says it is because she has a long way to come. Children will enjoy this literally far-out science fiction tale involving friendship and a happy surprise ending. The book will appeal to fans of Edward Marshall's *Space Case. Children's Choice.*

Intermediate

9.2 Asimov, Janet, and Isaac Asimov. **Norby Finds a Villain.** Walker, 1987. Ages 10–14.

Sixth in a series, this book features intergalactic time-jumping as robot Norby, teenage Jeff, and their female counterparts, Pera and Rinda, try to stop Ing the Ingrate, who holds the fate of the universe in his unsteady hands. The book jackets for the series are designed to appeal to a younger audience than would be attracted to the content.

9.3 Chetwin, Grace. **Out of the Dark World.** Lothrop, Lee and Shepard Books, 1985. Ages 10–12.

When eighth-grader Meg begins dreaming about a boy whose mind is trapped inside a computer program, she uses a hypnotic trance to summon the sorceress Morgan le Fay to help her free the boy.

9.4 Christopher, John. **When the Tripods Came.** E. P. Dutton, 1988. Ages 9–12.

This is a prequel to the popular Tripods trilogy. The story is told by an adolescent boy, Laurie, who witnesses the arrival of the gigantic hemisphere from outer space and who reacts with horror as the towering Tripods relentlessly proceed to dominate the world. Deftly written, with believable characters, the story contains the action and suspense which mark John Christopher's previous three Tripods novels.

9.5 DeWeese, Gene. **The Dandelion Caper.** G. P. Putnam's Sons, 1986. Ages 10–13.

Shortly after their adventure with "tourists" from another planet (in *Blacksuits from Outer Space*), logical Calvin and intuitive Kathy set off to investigate new extraterrestrial beings. This time the aliens are evil, but Dandelion, an unusual cat, comes to their rescue. The book is entertaining and well paced, and reading the earlier *Blacksuits* is not a prerequisite to enjoying this book.

9.6 Fradin, Dennis Brindell. **How I Saved the World.** Dillon Press/Gemstone Books, 1986. Ages 8–12.

If you came from another planet to conquer Earth, you would want to be inconspicuous, blending into the culture until you were ready to strike. How better than to use television to learn about the culture? The ruse is working, but then Shelley and Uncle Myron become suspicious. The newcomers are simply too nice. Their speech and mannerisms seem vaguely familiar, something like reruns from the 1950s.

9.7 Hoover, H. M. **Orvis.** Viking Kestrel, 1987. Ages 10–13.

Born and bred in outer space, young Toby and her friend Thaddeus attend a boarding school on Earth in the far distant future. Accidentally they discover Orvis, an ancient but highly intelligent robot, and resolve to save him from his fate of obsolescence. Escaping from the boarding school in search of finding a home for Orvis thrusts the two friends into danger in the inhospitable wilderness that much of Earth has become. Orvis protects the children, and they in turn teach him about feelings and friendship. The concept of artificial intelligence is explored in this skillfully written and exciting novel for better readers.

9.8 Jacobs, Paul Samuel. **Born into Light.** Scholastic/Hardcover Books, 1988. Ages 11–13.

The reader is immediately drawn into this science fiction story written in the form of the reminiscences of an old man, Roger Westwood. Using descriptive language and a storytelling style, Roger recounts the unusual appearance of "wild children" seventy-five years ago. Two of these children were adopted and raised by the Westwood family, but only Roger seemed to guess the true nature of these exceptional extraterrestrial beings. This is a fascinating story, beautifully told, for better readers.

9.9 Karl, Jean E. **Strange Tomorrow.** E. P. Dutton, 1985. Ages 11–14.

Two separate times are linked by two different young women, each named Janie. The earlier Janie struggles to maintain life in a complex underground government shelter. The later Janie belongs to one of several diverse communities attempting to create the sustenance for a new civilization's survival.

9.10 Kurtz, Katherine. **The Legacy of Lehr.** Walker/Byron Preiss Books/Millennium Books, 1986. Ages 12 and up.

Murder is never nice, but it is truly terrifying in the closed world of an interstellar space vehicle, especially when the killer may be an animal gifted with psychic powers. This unusual blend of ancient legends and modern technologies will be enjoyed by experienced readers.

9.11 McIntyre, Vonda N. **Barbary.** Houghton Mifflin, 1986. Ages 10–14.

Streetwise orphan Barbary must adapt to new people and situations in order to remain on the research station *Einstein*, where she is to live with a new family. Through the escapades of Barbary and her new sister, Heather, a fascinating picture of life on a space station is presented. Strong female characters prevail.

9.12 Service, Pamela F. **A Question of Destiny.** Atheneum, 1986. Ages 11–13.

What would you do if your dad were running for president and you accidentally discover that his top adviser has no past? Worse, on the man's calculator is a set of symbols that appear not to be from this planet. The book contains adventure, mystery, and suspense.

9.13 Service, Pamela F. **Stinker from Space.** Charles Scribner's Sons, 1988. Ages 8–11.

When his spaceship crashes, alien Tsynq Yr must make a quick switch. His current body is mortally wounded, and he needs another without delay. Unfortunately, the only body available belongs to a skunk. Pursued by the evil Zarnk, his spaceship beyond repair, and in unfamiliar terrain, Tsynq Yr fears that his return home to the Sylon Confederacy is impossible.

9.14 Wilkes, Marilyn Z. **C.L.U.T.Z. and the Fizzion Formula.** Illustrated by Larry Ross. Dial Books for Young Readers, 1985. Ages 8–11.

Rodney Pentax, his fluffy pink dog, Aurora, and the robot C.L.U.T.Z. find themselves involved in shady goings-on at GalactiCola. Someone is trying to sabotage the plant, steal the Fizzion formula, or take over the world. Readers of Alfred Slote's "boy-and-his-robot" books will enjoy the world of Rodney and C.L.U.T.Z.

9.15 Yolen, Jane, Martin H. Greenberg, and Charles G. Waugh, eds. **Dragons and Dreams: A Collection of New Fantasy and Science Fiction Stories.** Harper and Row, 1986. Ages 10–14.

Inventive plots, imaginative characters, and writing of a uniformly high quality make this a distinctive anthology. Some of the most well respected names of fantasy and science fiction writing are here, including Patricia A. McKillip and Diana Wynne Jones. These are satisfying short stories, but every one contains ideas which deserve expansion.

Recommended Books Published before 1985

Cameron, Eleanor. *The Wonderful Flight to the Mushroom Planet.* Illustrated by Robert Henneberger. Little, Brown, 1954. 7–9.
Christopher, John. *The Lotus Caves.* Macmillan, 1969. 10 and up.
———. *The White Mountains.* Macmillan, 1967. 10 and up.
Engdahl, Sylvia Louise. *Enchantress from the Stars.* Illustrated by Rodney Shackell. Atheneum, 1970. 11 and up.
Hoover, H. M. *This Time of Darkness.* Viking Press, 1980. 11 and up.
Marshall, Edward. *Space Case.* Illustrated by James Marshall. Dial Books for Young Readers, 1980. 4–8.
Pinkwater, Daniel M. *Fat Men from Space.* Dodd, Mead, 1977. 8–10.

Slobodkin, Louis. *The Space Ship under the Apple Tree*. Macmillan, 1952. 7–9.
Yolen, Jane. *Commander Toad and the Planet of the Grapes*. Illustrated by Bruce Degen. Coward, McCann and Geoghegan, 1982. 4–7.

10 Contemporary Realistic Fiction

Adventure

Primary

10.1   Martin, Bill, Jr., and John Archambault. **Up and Down on the Merry-Go-Round.** Illustrated by Ted Rand. Henry Holt, 1988. Ages 4–8. (Picture book)

The magical sights and sounds of merry-go-rounds are captured in rollicking rhyme and energetic, bright, watercolor illustrations. Text and pictures are beautifully integrated in this read-aloud book.

10.2   Oechsli, Helen. **Fly Away!** Illustrated by Kelly Oechsli. Macmillan, 1988. Ages 4–8. (Picture book)

A young child describes to her teddy bear the sights, sounds, and feelings of her first airplane trip. Young readers will share her delight as she finally rushes to grandparents' outstretched arms in this sprightly text with bright, cheerful illustrations. The book conveys accurate concepts through the eyes of a child.

Intermediate

10.3   George, Jean Craighead. **Water Sky.** Harper and Row, 1987. Ages 10 and up.

Lincoln Noah Stonewright steps from a plane in Barrow, Alaska, into another world. This is a hard-to-put-down story which, on the surface, is a gripping adventure narrative about whaling, but which encompasses multiple levels of meaning. This book should not be missed. It could be used, along with a book like Sheila Garrigue's *Eternal Spring of Mr. Ito*, for exploring the beauties other cultures have to offer. Included are a glossary and an explanatory topographical pen drawing.

10.4   Greer, Gery, and Bob Ruddick. **This Island Isn't Big Enough for the Four of Us!** Thomas Y. Crowell, 1987. Ages 10–13.

Camping, hiking, and adventure are three criteria that two teenage boys set for a fun-filled vacation. Their anticipation of living on a deserted island is shattered when they encounter girl inhabitants. Initially the girls antagonize them, which brings about a series of revengeful pranks. The book has an easy readability level, but it will be of high interest to young adolescents.

10.5   Kingman, Lee. **The Luck of the Miss L.** Houghton Mifflin, 1986. Ages 8–11.

A New England setting and a tale of summer boat racing provide the foundation for this exciting story of competition, responsibility, self-discipline, and conquering fear. Alec's overconfidence about an upcoming race turns to overwhelming fear after a potentially fatal accident. Fast-paced adventure, thematic texture, and interesting relationships between characters make this a good choice for reluctant and skilled readers.

10.6   Lindbergh, Anne. **The Worry Week.** Illustrated by Kathryn Hewitt. Harcourt Brace Jovanovich, 1985. Ages 10–12.

By trickery, Allegra and her two sisters are left alone for a week at their family's summer house on a Maine island. Allegra's survival skills are put to a test as they search for food and a mysterious treasure hidden in the house.

10.7   Myers, Walter Dean. **Ambush in the Amazon.** Viking Penguin/Puffin Books, 1986. Ages 9–12.

Teenage brothers Chris and Ken Arrow are attacked by a legendary swamp monster while camping in the Amazon. Together with Tarya, an intelligent girl of the jungle, they save themselves and her village from a great evil. An exciting adventure story with an exotic setting in which the author treats the natives with respect.

10.8   Paulsen, Gary. **Hatchet.** Bradbury Press, 1987. Ages 9–13.

This is a gripping story of survival. Brian Robeson's bitter memories of his parents' divorce suddenly are interrupted when the pilot of his plane suffers a fatal heart attack. Brian, the only passenger, manages to crash-land the plane and then must spend fifty-four days alone in the Canadian wilderness. Gary Paulsen uses the events of those days to convince the reader of Brian's growing confidence in himself in this contemporary coming-of-age story. *ALA Notable Children's Book* and *Newbery Honor Book.*

Animals

Primary

10.9 Bonsall, Crosby. **The Amazing, the Incredible Super Dog.** Illustrated by the author. Harper and Row, 1986. Ages 5–9. (Picture book)

A young girl tells her cat about the incredible tricks her dog can do in this funny story that has many surprises. The full-color illustrations add much to this story, which will be enjoyed by young readers over and over. *Children's Choice.*

10.10 Brett, Jan. **Annie and the Wild Animals.** Illustrated by the author. Houghton Mifflin, 1985. Ages 4–8. (Picture book)

Deep, rich colors, elaborate details, and intricate lines in the illustrations contribute to the successful development of this story. Each illustration is framed by a border containing tiny pictures that foreshadow the plot. Readers will discover long before Annie the happy outcome of her search for her lost cat. *Children's Choice.*

10.11 Brown, Ruth. **Our Cat Flossie.** Illustrated by the author. E. P. Dutton, 1986. Ages 3–7. (Picture book)

Flossie the cat is most appealing in this beautifully illustrated book about cats and their daily pursuits. Young and old catlovers will particularly enjoy it.

10.12 Brown, Ruth. **Our Puppy's Vacation.** Illustrated by the author. E. P. Dutton, 1987. Ages 3–5. (Picture Book)

Cornwall, England, is the setting for this picture story of a Labrador's first vacation with its four-children family. Richly detailed full-page paintings follow the puppy through its first day, from the beach to the farmyard. A few words of text are integrated into the story told by each picture. *Children's Choice.*

10.13   Carlson, Nancy. **Arnie and the Stolen Markers.** Illustrated by the author. Viking Kestrel, 1987. Ages 4–8. (Picture book)

Arnie sees a set of markers at the store that he just has to have. However, he has spent all of his money, so he steals the markers. This problem is resolved in a humorous but believable manner without moralizing. The acrylic and pen-and-ink illustrations add substance to the text. This book, suitable for reading aloud to younger children and for older children to read to themselves, would be a useful addition to units on ethics. *Children's Choice.*

10.14   Carter, Anne. **Bella's Secret Garden.** Illustrated by John Butler. Crown/It's Great to Read Books, 1987. Ages 3–7. (Picture book)

Bella, a young rabbit, discovers the tenderness of a child when she happens to be discovered in a place where she is not wanted.

10.15   Carter, Anne. **Ruff Leaves Home.** Illustrated by John Butler. Crown/It's Great to Read Books, 1986. Ages 4–7. (Picture book)

Ruff the young fox goes out to explore the unknown world alone. His exciting adventures are beautifully illustrated in full color.

10.16   Cazet, Denys. **A Fish in His Pocket.** Illustrated by the author. Orchard Books, 1987. Ages 5–8. (Picture book)

A deceptively simple picture book examines the difficult issues of accidents, death, and responsibility. Russell Bear accidentally causes the death of a small fish from a neighborhood pond. Overcome by guilt, he spends a miserable day contemplating how to make amends. Finally, he decides to make a paper boat and to return the fish to its pond. Animal characters and pastel watercolors help soften this very complex message.

10.17   Kanao, Keiko. **Kitten up a Tree.** Illustrated by the author. Alfred A. Knopf/Borzoi Books, 1987. Ages 3–6. (Picture book)

In this simple story, a curious kitten gets stuck in a tree until it is rescued by the mother cat. The unusual vertical format and sparse illustrations help convey the story.

10.18   Little, Jean. **Lost and Found.** Illustrated by Leoung O'Young. Viking Kestrel, 1985. Ages 7–9.

Lucy, new in town and lonely, meets a small lost dog and wants to take him home. Although she is disappointed when the rightful owner is found, Lucy chooses another dog and succeeds in making new friends. The simple text has short chapters, for those just beyond beginning readers.

10.19   Locker, Thomas. **The Mare on the Hill.** Illustrated by the author. Dial Books for Young Readers, 1985. Ages 5–10. (Picture book)

Thomas Locker's beautiful paintings make this a book that will be read and reread. The paintings, reminiscent of earlier masters, depict the changing seasons with a beautiful simplicity that will speak to all. The story is a simple one of a mistreated horse and two young boys who come to love her.

10.20   McNulty, Faith. **The Lady and the Spider.** Illustrated by Bob Marstall. Harper and Row, 1986. Ages 4–8. (Picture book)

Gentle, soft-toned pictures and economical text are blended into a hymn to nature that will foster the desire to live in harmony with the small things of the Earth, to recognize beauty in the world about us, and to respect the rights of the creatures that share our planet. The story concerns a woman who finds a spider in her head of lettuce but who saves it by returning it to the garden. The book could enhance a science unit or be used for quiet small group sharing.

10.21   Pizer, Abigail. **Harry's Night Out.** Illustrated by the author. Dial Books for Young Readers, 1987. Ages 5–8. (Picture book)

In shades of blue, author-illustrator Abigail Pizer conveys the story of Harry the cat during one night of adventures. Cat lovers young and old will recognize that Harry is not as lazy as he appears, for his nighttime adventures give him good reason to sleep all day.

10.22   Samuels, Barbara. **Duncan and Dolores.** Illustrated by the author. Bradbury Press, 1986. Ages 4–7. (Picture book)

Dolores learns that cats are not easy to befriend. Duncan warms up to her only after she learns to respect his unique nature. Line and watercolor illustrations, reminiscent of children's drawings, add humor to the tale. *Children's Choice.*

10.23   Schwartz, Amy. **Oma and Bobo.** Illustrated by the author. Bradbury Press, 1987. Ages 5–9. (Picture book)

Alice gets Bobo the dog from the pound as a birthday gift. At the urging of her grandmother, Oma, she takes him to dog obedience school to learn how to sit up, roll over, and fetch. The story, illustrated in pen-and-ink with watercolor wash and pencil, has a few surprises. *ALA Notable Children's Book.*

10.24   Simon, Norma. **Oh, That Cat!** Illustrated by Dora Leder. Albert Whitman, 1986. Ages 4–8. (Picture book)

Max, a mischievous cat, does what he likes all day long. He hides, plays, purrs, naps, and teases in very catlike ways. Halftone illustrations catch his essence and that of his middle-class minority family.

10.25   Tejima. **Owl Lake.** Illustrated by the author. Philomel Books, 1987. Ages 3–6. (Picture book)

In breathtaking two-page woodcuts, Tejima depicts the night-life of an owl family. As darkness settles on their lake, they fly in search of food. The simple text and dramatic pictures of the owls in flight provide a glimpse of nature that should fascinate children. The book won the Japanese prize for outstanding picture books in 1983. *ALA Notable Children's Book.*

10.26   Tyler, Linda Wagner. **When Daddy Comes Home.** Illustrated by Susan Davis. Viking Kestrel, 1986. Ages 4–6. (Picture book)

Here is a warm family story of a young hippo and his dad. Although they don't have much time together, they spend their special time doing fun things. The illustrations are nicely done in watercolor wash.

10.27   Wilhelm, Hans. **I'll Always Love You.** Illustrated by the author. Crown, 1985. Ages 3–7. (Picture book)

A young boy's grief over the death of his dog is eased by the fact that he had told her every night, "I'll always love you." He knows that someday he will have another pet, and he will tell it every night, "I'll always love you." Watercolor illustrations enhance the text.

Intermediate

10.28   Hall, Lynn. **Danger Dog.** Charles Scribner's Sons, 1986. Ages 10–12.

Although the initial premise—that parents would let their child attempt to "deprogram" an attack dog—is a bit far-fetched, and although David's devotion to Max, a Doberman pinscher, is perhaps too intense to be believable, readers will not mind. They will be completely absorbed in the contest of wills between David and his Doberman.

10.29   Martin, Ann M. **Me and Katie (the Pest).** Illustrated by Blanche Sims. Holiday House, 1985. Ages 7–10.

Ten-year-old Wendy suffers through the successes of her accomplished younger sister, Katie. She feels that she is a failure at everything and that her parents don't understand what a true pest her sister is. When Wendy discovers she likes horses and is a natural at riding, she is dismayed that Katie wants to learn, too. She is sure Katie will outshine her. But it is Wendy who wins a prize for her riding and Katie who decides she does not want to take riding lessons. Realistic situations and good characterization throughout the text enhance this horse story.

10.30   Morrison, Dorothy Nafus. **Whisper Again.** Atheneum, 1987. Ages 10–13.

In order to meet financial demands, the Chambers arrange to lease part of their Oregon ranch to a children's camp. This sequel to *Whisper Goodbye* deals with Stacey's resistance to this idea and her special relationship with one of the campers.

10.31   Rogers, Jean. **The Secret Moose.** Illustrated by Jim Fowler. Greenwillow Books, 1985. Ages 7–9.

It is spring, and the snow is melting in Fairbanks, Alaska, when Gerald secretly follows the trail of an injured moose. He reads books about caring for her and discovers a baby moose. Eventually, both animals return to the wild. Short chapters, expressive drawings, and a realistic portrayal of wilderness living make this appealing to young animal lovers.

10.32   Rylant, Cynthia. **Every Living Thing.** Illustrated by S. D. Schindler. Bradbury Press, 1985. Ages 10–12.

Cynthia Rylant uses her soft technique in bringing together people and the animals that soon become their pets. These people give an animal a home and, as a result, lead more meaningful lives. A retired schoolteacher and a collie find happiness with each other. A young boy is encouraged to be a winner by the loving friendship of a pet turtle. These short stories with loving messages are easy to read . . . and remember.

10.33   Springer, Nancy. **A Horse to Love.** Harper and Row, 1987. Ages 9–11.

Although there is plenty of horse lore to hold the interest of the most rabid fanatic, this is no mere horse lover's dream fantasy, but an honest, loving portrayal of human and animal relationships. Realistic character portrayals and problem resolution give depth to this novel and raise it far above the average tale of girl-loves-horse.

10.34   Whitmore, Arvella. **You're a Real Hero, Amanda.** Houghton Mifflin, 1985. Ages 9 and up.

Amanda defies a town law in order to keep a promise she made to her dying grandmother. While in her father's office— he is Prairie Bend's doctor—she accidentally learns an alarming secret about Virginia Thornhill. Amanda also learns that her pet rooster has been stolen and is being used in cock fights. As she deals with these issues, Amanda is courageous and determined and learns the value of loyalty and perseverance.

10.35   Williams, Barbara. **Mitzi and the Elephants.** Illustrated by Emily Arnold McCully. E. P. Dutton, 1985. Ages 8–10.

In this book, the fourth of a series, eight-and-a-half-year-old Mitzi wants a pet of her very own. She hopes to get a free St. Bernard puppy from her friend if her stepfather will build a fence. Instead, she meets Ed, the elephant keeper at the zoo, and makes friends with two large elephants. Amusing adventures occur before her wish comes true.

Appreciation of Nature

Primary

10.36 Ormondroyd, Edward. **Johnny Castleseed.** Illustrated by Diana Thewlis. Houghton Mifflin/Parnassus Press, 1985. Ages 4–8.

Until a day at the beach opens his eyes, Evan thinks he is being teased when his dad talks about Johnny Castleseed. Surely he has the name wrong. Full-color watercolor drawings portray a sunny day—perfect for building sandcastles. Use this book with Barbara Cooney's *Miss Rumphius* to foster a love of and respect for the beauty of the Earth.

10.37 Parnall, Peter. **Apple Tree.** Illustrated by the author. Macmillan, 1987. Ages 5–8. (Picture book)

The battered old apple tree grows and makes its seasonal changes from spring to winter while sustaining the lives of many creatures: bumblebees, ants and bugs, chickadees, robins, woodpeckers, nuthatches, deer, and mice. Suffering the cold, the tree knows the robins and spring will come again. Peter Parnall depicts the interdependence of tree and animals in words as well as through his gentle illustrations.

10.38 Parnall, Peter. **Winter Barn.** Illustrated by the author. Macmillan, 1986. Ages 6–9. (Picture book)

This account of the unceasing life within an old barn during a Maine winter reads like poetry. Parnall's familiar spare illustrations of weathered wood and animals burrowing against the cold are enhanced by the carefully chosen descriptions, thus creating a totally believable world, filled with lyrical delights and palpable dangers. *Notable Children's Trade Book in the Field of Social Studies* and *Outstanding Science Trade Book for Children.*

10.39 Ryder, Joanne. **Step into the Night.** Illustrated by Dennis Nolan. Four Winds Press, 1988. Ages 7–10. (Picture book)

Soft-edged, three-dimensional watercolors illuminate this hymn to the night in which a child imagines the lives of animals in the night. The evocative text combines science and poetry, expanding the definitions of both. Because the small night creatures are treated respectfully, but without sentiment, the result is a kind of realistic mystery children will eagerly explore. Dennis Nolan's technique in *The Castle Builder* was completely different, making him an intriguing illustrator to study.

Intermediate

10.40   Baylor, Byrd. **I'm in Charge of Celebrations.** Illustrated by Peter Parnall. Charles Scribner's Sons, 1986. Ages 8–12. (Picture book)

In poetic text, Coyote Day describes some of the events from the past year that she chooses to celebrate. She marks her encounter with a young coyote trotting through the brush and heralds the Time of Falling Stars, a day in August when the sky went wild. Special characteristics of life in the Southwest desert are almost mystically illustrated on each page.

10.41   George, Jean Craighead. **One Day in the Woods.** Illustrated by Gary Allen. Thomas Y. Crowell, 1988. Ages 8–10.

Rebecca plans an expedition to the Teatown Woods of New York to find the ovenbird. During this expedition, she discovers the other wonders of the woods. Jean Craighead George describes the relationship of the plants and animals through a charming narrative. Black-and-white drawings enhance the text. An index helps readers looking for specific information.

Ethnic, Racial, and Religious Groups

Primary

10.42   Andrews, Jan. **Very Last First Time.** Illustrated by Ian Wallace. Margaret K. McElderry Books, 1986. Ages 6–9. (Picture book)

Striking illustrations help make this a special book about Eva, an Inuit girl. Although she has gone beneath the ice with her mother, looking for mussels, she has never gone alone before. As she explores the world beneath the ice by herself for the first time, it becomes a fantastic new place for her. *Children's Choice, Notable Children's Trade Book in the Field of Social Studies,* and *Notable Children's Trade Book in the Language Arts.*

10.43 Brown, Tricia. **Hello, Amigos!** Illustrated by Fran Ortiz. Henry Holt, 1986. Ages 5–9. (Picture book)

A brief first-person narrative accompanied by marvelous black-and-white photographs describes Frankie Valdez's seventh birthday. Details of contemporary Hispanic family life abound in the universal story of a special day in a child's life. A glossary is included at end.

10.44 Caines, Jeannette. **I Need a Lunch Box.** Illustrated by Pat Cummings. Harper and Row, 1988. Ages 4–8. (Picture book)

Colors, the days of the week, and a young child's imagination are emphasized in this picture book. A young black boy wishes that he could have a lunch box like his older sister, even though he does not yet attend school.

10.45 Chang, Heidi. **Elaine, Mary Lewis, and the Frogs.** Illustrated by the author. Crown, 1988. Ages 7–9.

Third-grader Elaine, a Chinese American from San Francisco, is apprehensive about moving to a new school in a small Iowa town and wonders whether she will make friends. Initially, eating rice at lunch instead of a sandwich makes her feel out of place. Things get better when she meets boisterous Mary Lewis, however, and together they develop an unusual science project—a flying frog. With larger print and attractive pencil illustrations, this simply told story makes a good read-alone novel for young readers. It could be useful for intercultural understanding and friendship units.

10.46 Daly, Niki. **Not So Fast Songololo.** Illustrated by the author. Margaret K. McElderry Books, 1986. Ages 3–8. (Picture book)

From South Africa comes this realistic story of a boy and his grandmother. Malusi is a little fellow who dawdles in the busy confusion of his big family, but his old grandmother, Gogo, appreciates Malusi's slower pace. The two are good companions as they shop together. Beautiful, bright watercolors capture the expressions of love and delight. *Notable Children's Trade Book in the Field of Social Studies.*

10.47 Martin, Bill, Jr., and John Archambault. **Knots on a Counting Rope.** Illustrated by Ted Rand. Henry Holt, 1987. Ages 6–12. (Picture book)

The authors tell a lyrical story of a Native American grandfather's efforts to help his young grandson, Boy-Strength-of-
Blue-Horses, grow strong and independent despite the boy's
blindness. Vibrant illustrations are ideal complements to the
text, brightening to a full spectrum of colors as the boy's confidence emerges.

Intermediate

10.48   Clifford, Eth. **The Remembering Box.** Illustrated by Donna
Diamond. Houghton Mifflin, 1985. Ages 8–12.

Joshua's visits with his grandmother on the Sabbath help him
understand his Jewish roots as she recalls her past by means
of small objects from her Remembering Box. Later, the love
he shares with her and other family members helps him accept her death. Scattered black-and-white illustrations support this tender story. *Notable Children's Trade Book in the
Field of Social Studies.*

10.49   Kaufman, Stephen. **Does Anyone Here Know the Way to
Thirteen?** Houghton Mifflin, 1985. Ages 10–14.

All Myron Saltz wants for his thirteenth birthday is to be a
Little League superstar and to skip his dreaded bar mitzvah
in the fall. Myron meets two new friends who have been
through their bar mitzvahs already and who encourage him to
ask questions of his elders, to rediscover his Jewishness. Myron gains further strength from his parents, and a little extra
batting practice with a high school baseball player shoots Myron right up to stardom with his team. By the time of his bar
mitzvah, Myron has undergone tremendous personal and religious growth.

10.50   Myers, Walter Dean. **Scorpions.** Harper and Row, 1988. Ages
11–13.

Twelve-year-old Jamal lives in Harlem and is trying to make
sense of his life in an adult world. His life is beset with problems—he has trouble with his schoolwork and with the principal; his brother Randy is serving a prison term for robbery;
his mother is working long hours trying to support the family
and to raise money to appeal Randy's conviction; Randy is
pressuring Jamal to take over his position as leader of the
Scorpions gang; and there is the ever-present temptation of

drugs. Jamal tries to assume leadership of the Scorpions, but he finds that some members refuse to accept him. His status improves when he finds a gun, but it leads to a tragedy that nearly destroys his friends' lives as well as his own. This contemporary city story, which "tells it like it is," is provocative for readers on the outside and inside. *Newbery Honor Book.*

10.51 O'Dell, Scott. **Black Star, Bright Dawn.** Houghton Mifflin, 1988. Ages 9–12.

When Bright Dawn's father is injured, she and her lead dog, Black Star, take her father's place in the famous dog sled race across Alaska, the Iditarod. Along the way she gains self-confidence and insight into the Eskimo culture. Although Bright Dawn loses the race, she wins the respect of her fellow sledders.

10.52 Paterson, Katherine. **Park's Quest.** E. P. Dutton/Lodestar Books, 1988. Ages 11 and up.

In this poignant tale of family relationships, Park's search for knowledge about his father, who was killed in Vietnam, takes him to his grandfather's farm in Virginia and leads inexorably to new insights into his family relationships and into his own inner self. *Children's Choice.*

10.53 Wilkinson, Brenda. **Not Separate, Not Equal.** Harper and Row, 1987. Ages 9–12.

From the author of the Ludell books, this book describes the struggle for integration by blacks in a small southern town in the mid-sixties. The story is told from the viewpoint of the six students who were chosen to integrate Pineridge High. The author speaks of the strengths and weaknesses of both races, as she gives today's readers an excellent glimpse of what black-white relations were like two decades ago. This will be useful as supplementary reading to units on American history and social studies or will be just good reading.

Human Relationships

Death

Primary

10.54 Joosse, Barbara M. **Better with Two.** Illustrated by Catherine Stock. Harper and Row, 1988. Ages 7–9.

When her elderly neighbor's old dog, Max, dies, young Laura is sad, too. She is able to make Mrs. Brady feel better by sharing in the swinging and "elevenses" that Max and Mrs. Brady used to share.

10.55   Jukes, Mavis. **Blackberries in the Dark.** Illustrated by Thomas B. Allen. Alfred A. Knopf/Borzoi Books, 1985. Ages 6–9.

In this touching story, Austin and his grandmother share their grief on his first trip to visit her after his grandfather's death. They become closer after several attempts to share one of his grandfather's favorite activities—fly-fishing.

10.56   Le Tord, Bijou. **My Grandma Leonie.** Illustrated by the author. Bradbury Press, 1987. Ages 4–7. (Picture book)

Pastel watercolors illustrate this poignant story of the loss of a beloved grandmother. The minimal text and the illustrations convey this loving relationship.

10.57   Porte, Barbara Ann. **Harry's Mom.** Illustrated by Yossi Abolafia. Greenwillow Books/Read-Alone Books, 1985. Ages 5–9. (Picture book)

Harry was only one year old when his mother died, so he has no memories of her. He loves to hear how brave and wonderful she was from his understanding father, his loving grandparents, and Aunt Rose. A warm, caring book about coping with the death of one parent.

10.58   Taha, Karen T. **A Gift for Tía Rosa.** Illustrated by Dee deRosa. Dillon Press/Gemstone Books, 1986. Ages 7–9. (Picture book)

Tía Rosa has taught Carmela how to knit, but she dies before Carmela can knit a gift for her. Carmela is crushed and refuses to believe that Tía Rosa has died. The characters are realistically portrayed, and the author handles the difficult subject of death with compassion, without becoming maudlin. The watercolor illustrations depict a quiet dignity in joy as well as sorrow.

Intermediate

10.59   Little, Jean. **Mama's Going to Buy You a Mockingbird.** Viking Kestrel, 1984. Ages 11–13.

The Talbot family—Jeremy, his sister, and their parents—find their lives change dramatically when Mr. Talbot becomes terminally ill with cancer. How this family deals with the father's disease and death makes for an extremely moving and powerful story, although the book does begin rather slowly. The characters are well drawn and quite believable.

10.60 Martin, Ann M. **With You and without You.** Holiday House, 1986. Ages 10–12.

When seventh-grader Liza O'Hara learns that her father is dying of heart disease, she and her family make his last months memorable. After he dies, their lives change, and Liza, like the others, has trouble coping with the changes. She eventually adjusts to her loss and finds new self-confidence. The book provides a sensitive and realistic portrayal of the grieving process.

Disabilities

Primary

10.61 Charlip, Remy, and Mary Beth Miller. **Handtalk Birthday: A Number and Story Book in Sign Language.** Photographs by George Ancona. Four Winds Press, 1987. Ages 4–8. (Picture book)

While demonstrating the sign language for many words and lots of numbers (with which children will enjoy experimenting), this book also shows a surprise party for a hearing-impaired woman. The color photographs of Mary Beth Miller give her vibrant facial expressions plenty of play. Care is taken in these photos to reduce detail through the use of dark backgrounds and colorful costumes, which focuses attention on action and objects. This book has a joyful quality that many children will find irresistible. *Children's Choice.*

10.62 Hamm, Diane Johnston. **Grandma Drives a Motor Bed.** Illustrated by Charles Robinson. Albert Whitman, 1987. Ages 5–8. (Picture book)

Using straightforward narration and brown/orange drawings, this picture book tells of a boy's visit with his ailing grandmother, who is now confined to bed and wheelchair. Despite the grim details—Grandma's frustrations, the room's unpleasant odors, throwaway diapers—this is ultimately a picture of family love and support exemplified by Grandpa's backrubs and nibbling on Grandma's ear.

10.63   Stanek, Muriel. **My Mom Can't Read.** Illustrated by Jacqueline Rogers. Albert Whitman, 1986. Ages 6–7. (Picture book)

While learning how to read, a first grader discovers that her mother is illiterate. She confides in her teacher, who helps them both obtain lessons at a community center, where they joyfully learn to read together. The soft black-and-white pencil illustrations enhance this touching story.

Intermediate

10.64   DeClements, Barthe. **Sixth Grade Can Really Kill You.** Viking Kestrel, 1985. Ages 8–12.

Helen fears that lack of improvement in her reading may leave her stuck in the sixth grade forever, until a good teacher recognizes her reading problem. Barthe DeClements, a school psychologist, writes books that focus on realistic problems that children encounter at various grade levels. Highly recommended as a read-aloud book.

10.65   Dixon, Jeanne. **The Tempered Wind.** Atheneum, 1987. Ages 10–12.

Gabriella, an adolescent dwarf living in the years just following World War II, is forced to live a deprived existence, at first passed between a string of aunts and finally shipped off to Montana, where she faces life as a chore girl, never having done housework in her life. Jeanne Dixon paints a vivid picture of a young woman striving not only for independence, but also for simple acceptance in a time when these were nearly impossible goals for a physically different person. This first-person narrative is not afraid to show its characters at their best—and worst. This is a truthful book, one that effectively shows the attitudes of a particular time period.

10.66   Gould, Marilyn. **The Twelfth of June.** J. B. Lippincott, 1986. Ages 9–12.

Finding ways to cope with the challenges of sixth grade brings Janis and Barney even closer together in this sequel to *Golden Daffodils*. In addition to the usual sixth-grade routines, and to his approaching bar mitzvah, Barney is busy trying to reform the gang called the Cobras. Janis is surprised when she reacts with newly discovered and intense emotions. Her mother worries about her daughter's cerebral palsy, and Janis worries about her grandmother's stroke. All the worry and effort pay off as Janis and Barney surprise each other and come to an exciting new place in their friendship.

10.67 Hansen, Joyce. **Yellow Bird and Me.** Clarion Books, 1986. Ages 9–12.

A young girl's determination to visit a close friend who has moved away helps her develop a strong relationship with a new friend. Doris and Bird James Towers experience many humorous and serious situations together. Doris discovers that Bird's antics in the classroom are a coverup for his reading disorder—dyslexia. Sequel to *The Gift Giver.*

10.68 Levinson, Marilyn. **And Don't Bring Jeremy.** Illustrated by Diane deGroat. Holt, Rinehart and Winston, 1985. Ages 9–11.

The plot in this first-person narrative is similar to, but not as well executed as, that in Babbis Friis Boasted's *Don't Take Teddy.* Adam's thirteen-year-old brother, Jeremy, is learning disabled, which Adam thinks is interfering with his own ability to make friends in their new town. The characters are honestly and sensitively portrayed.

10.69 Rabe, Berniece. **Margaret's Moves.** Scholastic/Apple Paperbacks, 1988. Ages 9–11.

Spunky nine-year-old Margaret finds her wheelchair inadequate after seeing a special basketball game whose players have lightweight sports models. Family dynamics are portrayed realistically with Margaret, an especially spunky heroine.

Divorce

Primary

10.70 Girard, Linda Walvoord. **At Daddy's on Saturdays.** Illustrated by Judith Friedman. Albert Whitman, 1987. Ages 5–9. (Picture book)

In this beautifully illustrated book, Katie feels several confused emotions when her parents are divorced. She discovers that she can maintain a positive, loving relationship with both parents even though they live apart.

Intermediate

10.71   Bates, Betty. **The Great Male Conspiracy.** Holiday House, 1986. Ages 10–13.

When Maggie's brother-in-law leaves her sister and brand-new baby, Maggie decides that all males are rotten. She even throws her father into that batch for a while. This is a well-handled plot of an increasingly familiar story. The characters are believable and have depth. Although things work out in the end, it is not a pat ending. This book should have appeal as a story and possibly as an aid to problem relationships.

10.72   Fox, Paula. **The Moonlight Man.** Bradbury Press, 1986. Ages 11–13.

The Moonlight Man is Catherine Ames's father, divorced from her mother for longer than Catherine can remember. Catherine and her father spend a month together in Nova Scotia, where she learns that much of her mother's mistrust and fear of her father is well founded. As with other Paula Fox novels, this one is tightly woven, with the plot taking unexpected turns. The reader feels Catherine's anger, fear, and apprehension as her father's drinking reaches alarming proportions; but Catherine also experiences a sense of security from the quiet hours that she and her father spend together. The setting is beautifully sketched; the characters are three-dimensional and quite believable. This is a special book for a special reader. *ALA Notable Children's Book* and *Notable Children's Trade Book in the Field of Social Studies.*

10.73   Ruby, Lois. **Pig-Out Inn.** Houghton Mifflin, 1987. Ages 11–14.

Dovi's mother has drifted around the country from one job to another. Now Dovi is hoping that they will stay in one place so she can go to the same school for two years. Dovi sees a lot of different characters come and go, but nothing really surprises her until nine-year-old Tag is left by his father at the diner where her mother works. Dovi finds out that Tag has been kidnapped by his father and becomes involved in the parents' custody battle.

Everyday Life

Primary

10.74 Aseltine, Lorraine. **First Grade Can Wait.** Illustrated by Virginia Wright-Frierson. Albert Whitman, 1988. Ages 4–5. (Picture book)

Luke is supposed to go to first grade next year, but he is afraid that he cannot learn or do all the things that will be expected of him. The problem is resolved in a very reassuring and realistic manner. The illustrations are multiracial and done in sepia tones. This title will work well with four and five year olds with similar problems.

10.75 Baisch, Cris. **When the Lights Went Out.** Illustrated by Ulises Wensell. G. P. Putnam's Sons, 1987. Ages 4–8. (Picture book)

While Sally and her sister Melanie are playing one day, the lights go out. It is too dark to continue playing inside, so they take a trip to the bakery and then play ghost until their mother comes home. "It is a blackout," they learn at the bakery. But "where do you think the electricity's gone?" the sisters wonder. Maybe it has gone to Paris, France, or the moon, or to eat ice cream, they giggle. The warm illustrations enhance this small reading treat.

10.76 Bang, Molly. **Delphine.** William Morrow, 1988. Illustrated by the author. Ages 3–6. (Picture book)

Delphine goes to the post office to pick up a gift that awaits her from her grandmother. Brightly colored illustrations show her conquering numerous perils, while the text quietly tells the reader that Delphine is afraid of the bicycle that she knows awaits her. This book could initiate a discussion of fear and bravery, especially with children just old enough to learn to ride a two-wheeler.

10.77 Bauer, Caroline Feller. **Midnight Snowman.** Illustrated by Catherine Stock. Atheneum, 1987. Ages 4–8. (Picture book)

A young girl from a mild climate has always wished for snow, and one evening her wish comes true. With her parents' permission, she and her friends go outside at night to build a snowman. Pretty soon all the neighbors have joined the children, and they manage to build a really large, strange-looking snowman. Watercolor illustrations are full of splashes of color and the excitement of the unusual evening. *Children's Choice.*

10.78   Baum, Arline, and Joseph Baum. **Opt: An Illusionary Tale.** Illustrated by the author. Viking Kestrel, 1987. Ages 6–8. (Picture book)

Full-color illustrations present common optical illusions within the context of the Kingdom of Opt's preparations for the young prince's birthday party. The brief text focuses the reader's attention on the illusions and asks questions pertinent to the illusion's success. The explanations for the illusions fill the last eight pages of the book. *Children's Choice.*

10.79   Birdseye, Tom. **Airmail to the Moon.** Illustrated by Stephen Gammell. Holiday House, 1988. Ages 5–8. (Picture book)

When Ora Mae Cotton of Crabapple Orchard looses her tooth in the middle of her spaghetti, she hurries right to bed to dream about what she can get with the money the tooth fairy will bring. But when morning comes, she discovers the tooth is gone. Pulling on her overalls and baseball cap, she sets out to find the culprit, yelling, "Some crook stole my tooth. And when I catch 'em I'm gonna open up a can of gotcha and send 'em airmail to the moon!" The humorous illustrations, down-home language, and Ora Mae combine to make a jolly tale. *Children's Choice.*

10.80   Blegvad, Lenore. **Anna Banana and Me.** Illustrated by Erik Blegvad. Margaret K. McElderry Books, 1985. Ages 3–8. (Picture book)

A small boy tries to keep up with his sometimes-playmate, Anna Banana, as they play in the park, a city apartment, and a playground. Her fearlessness inspires him to face his own fears. Multicolored realistic pictures add to the playful feeling of the book. *Children's Choice.*

10.81   Brandenburg, Franz. **The Hit of the Party.** Illustrated by Aliki. Greenwillow Books, 1985. Ages 5–9. (Picture book)

Kate and Jim are fighting over whose costume will be the hit of the party when Cheeks the hamster is discovered missing. Before Cheeks can be found, he chews off the colorful tail feathers of Jim's rooster costume. Jim is so happy about finding his pet that he still wants to go to the party, even as a hen, and both Kate and Jim are the hits of the party. Colorful Aliki illustrations are large, clear, and bright enough for large group storytelling.

10.82   Brinckloe, Julie. **Fireflies!** Illustrated by the author. Macmillan, 1985. Ages 6–8.

Julie Brinckloe conveys a time of wonder for children and a nostalgic, bittersweet story for adults. In this simple, first-person narrative, a young boy sees fireflies outside just before dinner. Hastily eating supper, he joins his neighborhood friends and catches a jarful of fireflies. Then the boy realizes that he must release the fireflies or they will die. Pencil drawings are brightened with pastel blue and yellows.

10.83   Brinckloe, Julie. **Playing Marbles.** Illustrated by the author. William Morrow, 1988. Ages 8–10. (Picture book)

As three children enjoy a game of marbles, a little girl displays her playing skills. The rules of the game are also explained, which should be of interest to those who are unfamiliar with the game.

10.84   Carlstrom, Nancy White. **Wild Wild Sunflower Child Anna.** Illustrated by Jerry Pinkney. Macmillan, 1987. Ages 4–7. (Picture book)

Vibrantly alive, Anna embraces nature, determined to wring every last drop of joy from the sunny day. She delights in pretending; first as the captain of a fine ship and then as a bright green frog, Anna romps, unfettered, as free as the verse and the sun-splashed paintings that chronicle her day.

10.85   Caseley, Judith. **Molly Pink.** Illustrated by the author. Greenwillow Books, 1985. Ages 5–7. (Picture book)

Molly can sing "as clear as a bell," and she does everywhere—except in front of her family. The watercolor illustrations enhance the text of this realistic and believable book. The small size prohibits its use with a large group.

10.86   Chevalier, Christa. **Spence Is Small.** Illustrated by the author. Albert Whitman, 1987. Ages 4–7. (Picture book)

This is a humorously illustrated story about too-small Spencer, who just cannot reach his box of crayons on top of the refrigerator no matter what maneuvers he tries. He discovers, however, that he is just the right size to retrieve his mother's lost earring from under the couch. "We are both just right," says Spence's mother. Pen illustrations with an apricot wash support the story.

10.87 Cohen, Miriam. **Liar, Liar, Pants on Fire!** Illustrated by Lillian Hoban. Greenwillow Books, 1985. Ages 5–8. (Picture book)

Natural dialogue, a realistic situation, and a satisfying resolution of a single problem are becoming trademarks of this series, which relates the growth of a multiethnic classroom of children with distinct personalities. Readers will feel warmly about Jim and the new boy, Alex, who wants only to belong.

10.88 Cohen, Miriam. **Starring First Grade.** Illustrated by Lillian Hoban. Greenwillow Books, 1985. Ages 5–7. (Picture book)

Jim saves the day for the first-grade play when Paul gets stage fright. Young readers will be able to relate to this incident and to identify with the children in the class.

10.89 Conford, Ellen. **A Job for Jenny Archer.** Illustrated by Diane Palmisciano. Little, Brown/Springboard Books, 1988. Ages 6–8.

The indubitable Jenny Archer goes full speed ahead in her efforts to earn money so that she can buy her mother a birthday present. Putting her own house up for sale brings her efforts to a rapid halt, but it does not dampen her enthusiasm. Readers will find that the short chapters, the large, open typeface, and the wide spacing between lines make this first read-alone chapter book move quickly. *Children's Choice.*

10.90 Dantzer-Rosenthal, Marya. **Some Things Are Different, Some Things Are the Same.** Illustrated by Miriam Nerlove. Albert Whitman, 1986. Ages 4–7. (Picture book)

This book is especially for the youngster who is shy about going to new places. As the title says, some things are different at another's house, and that's what Josh discovers when he visits Stephen. "But when he comes home, he's happy to be back where everything is the same."

10.91 Davis, Gibbs. **Katy's First Haircut.** Illustrated by Linda Shute. Houghton Mifflin, 1985. Ages 5–8. (Picture book)

Katy loves having the longest hair in her class, but it becomes a lot of trouble. She decides to get a haircut. Then Katy regrets her decision, especially when she is mistaken for a boy. At school she hides under a hat until it tumbles off during art class. An understanding teacher congratulates Katy for having the courage to make such a big decision, and all the children cheer for her. The gentle characters in this book are represented in illustrations that reflect their warmth.

10.92 Dragonwagon, Crescent. **Margaret Ziegler Is Horse-Crazy.** Illustrated by Peter Elwell. Macmillan, 1988. Ages 7–10. (Picture book)

Teased for being "horse-crazy," Margaret is sure she will prove herself at horseback-riding camp. Her fantasy of triumph on a wild stallion is soon squelched by a slow, fat horse which steps on her foot. Margaret's true triumph is facing her disappointment. Pen-and-ink illustrations bring out the humor in this short novel for a newly independent reader who may be a little horse-crazy, too. *Children's Choice.*

10.93 Duncan, Lois. **Wonder Kid Meets the Evil Lunch Snatcher.** Illustrated by Margaret Sanfilippo. Little, Brown/Springboard Books, 1988. Ages 6–8.

Shy and skinny Brian Johnson and his new friend, Robbie, plot a clever effort to stop Matt Gordon, the school bully and lunch stealer. The plans have problems at every step, but good triumphs in spite of the troubles. Each chapter is seven pages long, and the open typeface and wide spacing between lines will not tire young readers.

10.94 Dupasquier, Philippe. **Dear Daddy. . . .** Illustrated by the author. Bradbury Press, 1985. Ages 5–8. (Picture book)

Sophie writes touching letters to her father, who is thousands of miles away at sea on a cargo ship. Sophie's letters are a warm commentary of family life through all seasons. Bright, detailed illustrations depict two worlds: Sophie, busy at home on the top portion of the page, and her father, shown on board ship on the bottom half of the page. The two appear together in a final, warm scene reuniting the family.

10.95 Fife, Dale H. **Rosa's Special Garden.** Illustrated by Marie DeJohn. Albert Whitman, 1985. Ages 5–8. (Picture book)

The Carlos family is busily working together to plant a back-yard garden, but because four-year-old Rosa is too little to join them, she must be content with her own tiny plot. The eventual use to which she puts her garden provides the story with a surprising yet satisfying conclusion.

10.96 Gould, Deborah. **Brendan's Best-Timed Birthday.** Illustrated by Jacqueline Rogers. Bradbury Press, 1988. Ages 6–8. (Picture book)

Illustrations of oil pastels, watercolors, and colored pencils highlight this exciting birthday story. Brendan's newly ac-quired digital watch with a stopwatch adds enjoyment to the wonderful event.

10.97 Graham, Bob. **First There Was Frances.** Illustrated by the author. Bradbury Press, 1985. Ages 5–8. (Picture book)

Frances lives alone in the city. She is joined, one by one, by people and animals and eventually must move to the country. Illustrations work well with the amusing tale.

10.98 Havill, Juanita. **Jamaica's Find.** Illustrated by Anne Sibley O'Brien. Houghton Mifflin, 1986. Ages 4–8. (Picture book)

Jamaica does not feel right about her decision to keep a worn, stuffed dog she finds in the park. Her actions and feelings should be familiar to young readers as she eventually returns the toy and finds its owner. Full-page watercolor illustrations add warmth and sensitivity to the story line, which is well de-veloped. *Children's Choice.*

10.99 Hazen, Barbara Shook. **Fang.** Illustrated by Leslie Holt Mor-rill. Atheneum, 1987. Ages 3–7. (Picture book)

To protect himself from scary things, a young boy chooses a large, fierce-looking dog as a pet and names him Fang. But looks are deceiving. Fang is more afraid than the boy, who must now be brave enough for both of them.

10.100 Henkes, Kevin. **A Weekend with Wendell.** Illustrated by the author. Penguin Viking/Puffin Books, 1987. Ages 4–8. (Picture book)

While his family is away, Wendell spends a weekend with Sophie's family and makes everyone's life miserable. The humorous text is enhanced by equally humorous watercolors. This title will simultaneously teach young children tolerance and self-assuredness. *Children's Choice.*

10.101 Heyduck-Huth, Hilde. **The Starfish.** Illustrated by the author. Margaret K. McElderry Books/Treasure Chest Stories, 1987. Ages 5–9. (Picture book)

One lone starfish has varying adventures as it passes from hand to hand. Then Anna, a young girl, finds the starfish and places it in her treasure chest.

10.102 Heyduck-Huth, Hilde. **The Strawflower.** Illustrated by the author. Margaret K. McElderry Books/Treasure Chest Stories, 1987. Ages 5–9. (Picture book)

One strawflower, separated from the bouquet, is tossed to the winds in a snow storm, becoming the center of attention in a snowman family. After serving a variety of functions, the strawflower finds itself on Anna's Christmas tree and, finally, in her treasure chest.

10.103 Hines, Anna Grossnickle. **Bethany for Real.** Illustrated by the author. Greenwillow Books, 1985. Ages 5–8. (Picture book)

Childhood is depicted here as the incarnation of imagination, where children fall easily into "pretend" and where the suspension of belief is wholehearted. The dialogue is terse, real, childlike. This could be used with Miriam Cohen's *Liar, Liar, Pants on Fire!* (10.87) to spark a discussion of what is real.

10.104 Hines, Anna Grossnickle. **Don't Worry, I'll Find You.** Illustrated by the author. E. P. Dutton, 1986. Ages 4–7. (Picture book)

Sarah's special doll, Abigail, accompanies Sarah when she goes with her mother on a shopping excursion to the mall. Sarah's affection for Abigail provides the basis for this endearing story, as finding Sarah some new clothes is not all that is discovered on this memorable mother-daughter outing.

10.105 Hutchins, Pat. **The Doorbell Rang.** Illustrated by the author. Greenwillow Books, 1986. Ages 3–8. (Picture book)

A large platter of freshly baked cookies gets smaller and smaller as the doorbell rings and successive groups of neighborhood children enter the kitchen in need of a snack. Each double-page spread cleverly places the door just off the right-hand edge of the page, so that the reader's attention is drawn to it. *ALA Notable Children's Book, Children's Choice,* and *Notable Children's Trade Book in the Language Arts.*

10.106 Kline, Suzy. **Herbie Jones.** Illustrated by Richard Williams. G. P. Putnam's Sons, 1985. Ages 7–9.

Herbie and his friend scheme to get out of their reading group, which is the lowest in third grade. Funny and true-to-life depictions of childhood concerns are presented. *Children's Choice.*

10.107 Kline, Suzy. **Herbie Jones and the Class Gift.** Illustrated by Richard Williams. G. P. Putnam's Sons, 1987. Ages 7–10.

When third-grader Herbie Jones and his best friend, Raymond, are sent to pick up the ceramic owl that is to be the gift for their teacher, troubles ensue. This third book about Herbie presents real dilemmas and, with its short chapters, is a welcome addition for those making the transition from picture books to longer stories.

10.108 Komaiko, Leah. **I Like the Music.** Illustrated by Barbara Westman. Harper and Row, 1987. Ages 4–9. (Picture book)

Leah Komaiko's appealing story in rhyme is about the difference in musical tastes between a grandmother and granddaughter. It is lively, with a strong beat, and loaded with interesting but contrasting imagery of symphonies and street music. The verse demonstrates Komaiko's skill at wordplay. The line and watercolor illustrations complement the character of the story; they are bright, simple, and childlike, using primarily solid colors.

10.109 Krensky, Stephen. **Lionel in the Fall.** Illustrated by Susanna Natti. Dial Books for Young Readers/Easy-to-Read Books, 1987. Ages 5–8. (Picture book)

Going back to school, a new teacher, raking leaves, and trick-or-treat adventures with Lionel are activities to which most young children can easily relate. The illustrations for this book with chapters were prepared with pencils, colored pencils, and watercolor washes.

10.110 Kroll, Steven. **I Love Spring!** Illustrated by Kathryn E. Shoemaker. Holiday House, 1987. Ages 5–7. (Picture book)

Mark discovers all the things he enjoys about spring—the weather, new puppies, planting, Easter, Passover, outdoor and indoor activities, a parade, and the circus.

10.111 Lasky, Kathryn. **Sea Swan.** Illustrated by Catherine Stock. Macmillan, 1988. Ages 7–10. (Picture book)

This joyful, exuberant tale is a good companion to Barbara Cooney's *Miss Rumphius*. Elzibah Swan, who at age seventy-five decides to take up swimming, has the same indomitable soul and zest for living. Glowing watercolors are the perfect complement to an affirmation of life that reaches across the barriers of age as Elzibah uses letters to share her new pastime with her grandchildren.

10.112 Le Tord, Bijou. **Joseph and Nellie.** Illustrated by the author. Bradbury Press, 1986. Ages 3–7. (Picture book)

Joseph and his wife, Nellie, are commercial fishermen. The spare text and softly muted watercolors tell the simple story of one day in their lives. *Notable Children's Trade Book in the Field of Social Studies.*

10.113 Levine, Abby, and Sarah Levine. **Sometimes I Wish I Were Mindy.** Illustrated by Blanche Sims. Albert Whitman, 1986. Ages 5–7. (Picture book)

A little girl wishes she had all the things her friend Mindy has—such as a big house, a swimming pool, a maid, and "five million toys." Her family shows her that in most cases there is more to life than designer t-shirts and other material objects. The blue and gray illustrations in crayon add to the humor of this book.

10.114 Lovik, Craig. **Andy and the Tire.** Illustrated by Mark Alan Weatherby. Scholastic, 1987. Ages 5–7.

It is Andy's first day in a new school, and he has made friends only with Fuzzy, the class hamster. However, the discovery of a discarded tire changes his life in this warm story, which closely mirrors problems faced by many youngsters. The watercolor illustrations are fun and add greatly to the story.

10.115 McBrier, Michael. **Oliver's Back-Yard Circus.** Illustrated by Blanche Sims. Troll Associates, 1987. Ages 7–10.

Black-and-white illustrations depict Oliver and his friends as they team up to present a backyard circus in order to raise funds for a community animal shelter.

10.116 Major, Beverly. **Playing Sardines.** Illustrated by Andrew Glass. Scholastic/Hardcover Books, 1988. Ages 4–8. (Picture book)

That magic time in a summer evening—after dinner, before baths—is captured here. The illustrations have a fuzzy, violet, twilight glow about them. The story is simply about a game of sardines, a version of hide-and-seek, played by the neighborhood kids. An adult reader will become nostalgic, and a child will have the urge to run outside and find some friends for the game.

10.117 Malone, Nola Langner. **A Home.** Illustrated by the author. Bradbury Press, 1988. Ages 4–8. (Picture book)

Molly experiences the joys and sorrows of moving to a new house. She begins to feel more comfortable when she makes friends with Miranda Marie.

10.118 Mayper, Monica. **After Good-Night.** Illustrated by Peter Sis. Harper and Row, 1987. Ages 4–8. (Picture book)

Nan is the eyes and ears of the quiet house as it settles down for the night. Softly, gently, the spare poetic text lulls the reader in this hymn to sleep and rest. The illustrations, composed of tiny points of black ink on white paper, are dreamy, drifting like smoke. They are as relaxed and evanescent as the mood created by the textual lullaby.

10.119 Neville, Emily Cheney. **The Bridge.** Illustrated by Ronald Himler. Harper and Row, 1988. Ages 5–8. (Picture book)

Little Ben likes to watch big machines at work—bulldozers, backhoes, and other construction equipment. When the old wooden bridge connecting his driveway with the road crashes into the creek below, many of these huge and interesting machines are put to work right at his doorstep. The warm tone of this story, its focus on the little boy's fascination with machinery, and the delicately colorful illustrations, which still capture the power of the machines, combine to produce a book that young children will enjoy.

10.120 O'Donnell, Elizabeth Lee. **Maggie Doesn't Want to Move.** Illustrated by Amy Schwartz. Four Winds Press, 1987. Ages 5–8. (Picture book)

Simon claims it's his baby sister, Maggie, who doesn't want to move. The reader sees via the full-color illustrations that this is not the truth. Finally, when he sees the new neighborhood and the new school, "Maggie" has a change of mind.

10.121 Parker, Kristy. **My Dad the Magnificent.** Illustrated by Lillian Hoban. E. P. Dutton, 1987. Ages 5–8. (Picture book)

After Buddy brags to his boastful friend Alex about the wonderful things his dad does, he has to admit that his dad just works in an office. The reality of the loving quality time Buddy has with his dad each Saturday gives the reader an understanding of how very special his dad really is. Full-color illustrations enhance the story.

10.122 Provensen, Alice, and Martin Provensen. **Shaker Lane.** Illustrated by the authors. Viking Kestrel, 1987. Ages 5–8. (Picture book)

Shaker Lane was once a quiet lane leading to the Herkimer Farm. As the acreage is sold off, the lane becomes inhabited by junked cars, assorted people, and animals. Then the townspeople decide to build a dam and reservoir on the land, and the residents of Shaker Lane move away. The short, succinct text is enhanced by illustrations typical of these authors. This life story of a road could be used as a straight story, as a companion to Virginia Lee Burton's *Little House*, or as an adjunct to a social studies unit on the environment and conservation.

10.123 Ray, Deborah Kogan. **My Dog, Trip.** Illustrated by the author. Holiday House, 1987. Ages 6–9. (Picture book)

When Allie's father brings home a frail orphan puppy, she nurses him to health. Allie is anguished over his disappearance, but she feels compassionate toward the little girl who finds Trip. Sensitive charcoal and pencil illustrations convey warmth and family closeness, while the use of Appalachian mountain dialect adds another element to the spare, touching story.

10.124 Richardson, Jean. **Clara's Dancing Feet.** Illustrated by Joanna Carey. G. P. Putnam's Sons, 1987. Ages 5–8. (Picture book)

This is an engaging story of Clara, who is always dancing. She looks forward to taking dancing lessons, but when she arrives at class, her feet will not move. As her class is performing for parents, Clara overcomes her shyness and becomes a real dancer at last.

10.125 Rockwell, Anne, and Harlow Rockwell. **The First Snowfall.** Illustrated by the authors. Macmillan, 1987. Ages 2–6. (Picture book)

A child's special day in the snow is depicted in bold pencil and watercolor illustrations and a simple text of one sentence every page or two. From shoveling snow and sledding to the cup of cocoa at the end of the day, she delights in each activity of her snowy world. The simple sentence structure and vocabulary can be managed by the beginning reader.

10.126 Ross, Pat. **M & M and the Mummy Mess.** Illustrated by Marylin Hafner. Viking Kestrel, 1985. Ages 6–9.

Mandy and Mimi are so excited to see the museum's exhibit, Mummy Wonders, that they go a week early. Their adventures, as they sneak into the closed exhibit area, are scary for them and fun for the readers. The text gives interesting facts about museums and mummies and is enhanced by humorous illustrations.

10.127 Scheffler, Ursel (translated by Andrea Mernan). **A Walk in the Rain.** Illustrated by Ulises Wensell. G. P. Putnam's Sons, 1986. Ages 3–6. (Picture book)

In his new yellow raincoat and boots, Josh goes for a walk in the rain with his grandmother. All the things they see and appreciate are enhanced by beautiful watercolor paintings.

10.128 Schertle, Alice. **My Two Feet.** Illustrated by Meredith Dunham. Lothrop, Lee and Shepard Books, 1985. Ages 3–8. (Picture book)

This book enumerates the many ways one can be made aware of feet. Included are dancing, going barefoot, walking in mud, walking on sand, getting new shoes, putting on galoshes, and, finally, resting them.

10.129 Schwartz, Amy. **Annabelle Swift, Kindergartner.** Illustrated by the author. Orchard Books, 1988. Ages 4–8. (Picture book)

Annabelle's older sister tries to prepare Annabelle for her first day at school. She learns about geography, counting, colors, and wearing a nametag, but the advice does not always work out as planned. Pen-and-ink illustrations with watercolor wash and pencil accompany this story that has a surprise ending. *ALA Notable Children's Book.*

10.130 Smith, Janice Lee. **The Show-and-Tell War, and Other Stories about Adam Joshua.** Illustrated by Dick Gackenbach. Harper and Row, 1988. Ages 5–8.

Newly independent readers will appreciate the large print, generous margins, and humor-filled drawings that enhance this third collection of short stories about Adam Joshua. These attributes make the book easier to read and will allow children to feel "grown up." Although each story is about life, values, and the maturing process, the tone is always gently humorous, and the lessons are implied, rather than being earnest, heavy-handed, and obvious. *Children's Choice.*

10.131 Soya, Kiyoshi. **A House of Leaves.** Illustrated by Akiko Hayashi. Philomel Books, 1987. Ages 2–5. (Picture book)

Younger children will enjoy this simple story of a young Japanese girl who decides to wait under a bush during a rainstorm. There she is visited by a number of friendly insects. Carefully focused but simple illustrations complement a sparse text. Much is told in the girl's facial expressions alone.

10.132 Stock, Catherine. **Sophie's Bucket.** Illustrated by the author. Lothrop, Lee and Shepard Books, 1985. Ages 2–6. (Picture book)

On her way to the ocean for the first time, little Sophie wonders if she can fit the sea into her new bucket. Not all of it, she finds; but many treasures do fit. This simple tale of a family outing is illustrated in soft watercolors. The youngest children will enjoy recalling their own seaside holidays as they share this book.

10.133 Stolz, Mary. **Storm in the Night.** Illustrated by Pat Cummings. Harper and Row, 1988. Ages 4–8. (Picture book)

Shades of blue and purple brightened by flashes of white accompany this warm story of Thomas and his grandfather and
their special relationship. One stormy night the electricity
goes off, and Thomas's grandfather helps him use his senses
to appreciate life without television. This title would be useful
in a discussion of children's fears. Although the subject matter and picture-book format are suited to younger children,
the lengthy text will appeal to older children in the age range.
Coretta Scott King Honor Book (for illustrations).

10.134 Szilagyi, Mary. **Thunderstorm.** Illustrated by the author.
Bradbury Press, 1985. Ages 4–7. (Picture book)

A little girl and her dog race inside as a thunderstorm approaches. Through full-page illustrations and simple text, the
thunderstorm is depicted vividly. The girl's fear and the comfort she seeks in her home should be familiar experiences to
young children who are uneasy about storms. This read-aloud
book should help ease children's anxiety about being afraid.

10.135 Thomas, Jane Resh. **Wheels.** Illustrated by Emily Arnold Mc-
Cully. Clarion Books, 1986. Ages 4–7. (Picture book)

Colorful line-and-wash paintings illustrate this story of a five-
year-old boy who, with the help of a loving grandfather, must
learn that winning is not everything after he finishes last in
the neighborhood Big Wheel race.

10.136 Williams, Vera B. **Cherries and Cherry Pits.** Illustrated by the
author. Greenwillow Books, 1986. Ages 4–9.

A young girl tells and draws stories about four people she observes in her neighborhood. Each becomes a distinct individual, illustrating—and celebrating—human diversity, although
each one is ultimately linked by common experience. The
child's sense of story, visual and textual, accompanies the
adult's stunning watercolor paintings of a creative child bent
over her work in concentration. Vera B. Williams successful-
ly creates "story" on several levels simultaneously, and yet
another layer will be added to the story-within-a-story when it
is shared with children. *ALA Notable Children's Book.*

10.137 Winthrop, Elizabeth. **Tough Eddie.** Illustrated by Lillian
Hoban. E. P. Dutton, 1985. Ages 5–7. (Picture book)

Eddie wears his cowboy boots and belt to school and feels really tough. At home, he pulls his dollhouse out of the closet and plays with it. How he reconciles these two interests and maintains his friendships makes for a lively and believable story. It is disheartening not to see an integrated classroom depicted in the illustrations. In spite of this flaw, the book is recommended, but not as enthusiastically as it would have been if the children had reflected more of our multiethnic society.

10.138 Ziefert, Harriet. **The Small Potatoes and the Snowball Fight.** Illustrated by Richard Brown. Dell/Yearling Books/Small Potatoes Club Series, 1986. Ages 7–9.

The excitement of the first snow of the season is the focus of this book. Ideas of things to do with snow are presented, along with a safety lesson.

10.139 Zolotow, Charlotte. **Something Is Going to Happen.** Illustrated by Catherine Stock. Harper and Row, 1988. Ages 3–9. (Picture book)

On a cold November morning, each member of a family awakens thinking "Something is going to happen." They go about their morning activities only to discover that indeed something has happened—the first snowfall.

Intermediate

10.140 Bauer, Marion Dane. **On My Honor.** Clarion Books, 1986. Ages 10–12.

When twelve-year-old Joel and his friend Tony go swimming in a treacherous river that they promised never to go near, tragedy occurs. A devastated Joel must confront his guilt and face both sets of parents to explain Tony's drowning, in this powerful novel for preadolescents. *Newbery Honor Book.*

10.141 Boyd, Candy Dawson. **Forever Friends.** Viking Penguin/Puffin Books, 1986. Ages 10–13.

The second published novel by a relatively new black writer who grew up in Chicago concerns sixth-grader Toni's efforts to qualify for a better school. Her struggle to accept the accidental death of her best friend rings with emotional power; authenticity and an upbeat tone mark this family story. Originally published as *Breadsticks and Blessing Places.*

10.142 Cameron, Eleanor. **The Private Worlds of Julia Redfern.** E. P. Dutton, 1988. Ages 11–13.

In this fifth book about Julia, her fifteenth year is filled with jealousy, forgiveness, first love, and explorations of her writing and acting talents. Her devoted Uncle Hugh, her adopted grandmother, and other family members contribute to her dawning awareness of her limits. This is a believable, introspective novel for those who have followed Julia's growth in previous books.

10.143 Clifford, Eth. **I Never Wanted to Be Famous.** Houghton Mifflin, 1986. Ages 9–12.

Ordinary Goodwin "Goody" Tribble has greatness thrust upon him after saving a choking baby. How the thirteen year old copes with publicity and the ambitious plans of his mother to make him even more famous makes entertaining reading. Told in the first person, this is a good read-aloud story.

10.144 Delton, Judy. **Angel's Mother's Wedding.** Illustrated by Margot Apple. Houghton Mifflin, 1987. Ages 8–11.

Fans of Angel O'Leary will enjoy the fourth book in the series, describing her trials and tribulations as her mother prepares to marry Rudy. Changing her last name to Papadopolis and assuring her younger brother, Raggs, that he does not need to wear a bear costume to be the ring "bear" are just two of the amusing happenings in this witty, readable book for middle-grade children.

10.145 Duder, Tessa. **Jellybean.** Viking Kestrel, 1986. Ages 10–12.

Just when Geraldine recognizes her love of music and her longing to be a conductor, a strange man upsets the comfortable but hectic life she shares with her cello-playing mother. Is it a coincidence, or does the man's name, Gerald, bear some meaning from her mother's life before Geraldine's birth? As the story unfolds, Geraldine learns to accept her talents, her mother, Gerald, and even her nickname, Jellybean, and she looks forward to meeting her father.

10.146 Greene, Constance C. **Star Shine.** Viking Kestrel, 1985. Ages 11–12.

Jenny and Mary's star-struck mom joins a traveling summer theater group, and the girls convince their dad that they are old enough to take care of themselves. When a movie company comes to town, eleven-year-old Jenny lands a part as an extra and befriends high school heartthrob Scott Borkowski. Both sisters make discoveries about fame and family relationships.

10.147 Hest, Amy. **Pete and Lily.** Clarion Books, 1986. Ages 10–12.

Twelve-year-old Pete (short for Patricia) lives with her recently widowed mother in the same apartment building as Lily and her divorced father. When the two friends discover that their parents are seeing each other, they take action to stop the romance. In addition, Pete feels abandoned when Lily discovers boys. The book portrays adolescent jealousy and the need to adapt to life's changes.

10.148 Hicks, Clifford B. **The Peter Potts Book of World Records.** Illustrated by Kathleen Collins Howell. Henry Holt, 1987. Ages 9–12.

Peter and his friend Joey attempt to set their own world records in this book from the Peter Potts series. Their projects, duly recorded by Peter, range from the world's largest cotton-candy machine to the "biggest kid parade," with much mischief and unexpected results in-between. In addition to its humorous aspects, this is also a story about Peter's warm and loving family as it prepares to welcome a new baby.

10.149 Holmes, Barbara Ware. **Charlotte Cheetham: Master of Disaster.** Illustrated by John Himmelman. Harper and Row, 1985. Ages 8–10.

Charlotte constantly makes up stories in order to get attention or to get out of trouble. These lies involve her parents, her friends, and the school librarian. Determined to break this bad habit, Charlotte is aided by an understanding family. This lightweight, realistic story could also be helpful as bibliotherapy.

10.150 Honeycutt, Natalie. **The All New Jonah Twist.** Bradbury Press, 1986. Ages 8–10.

Jonah starts third grade having to prove that he is responsible enough to have a pet of his own. Life at home and at school is a struggle, especially with an older brother who is perfect and with the new kid at school, Granville Hicks, who appears to threaten Jonah. The trials of growing up are told with humor and sensitivity.

10.151 Hopper, Nancy J. **The Truth or Dare Trap.** E. P. Dutton, 1985. Ages 10–12.

Megan is thrilled when she finally becomes a member of the in-group. But is it worth the price? She loves being popular and doing all the neat, exciting things Angie comes up with in her Truth or Dare games. However, when Angie asks the group to do illegal things or carry out possibly harmful dares, should Megan draw the line?

10.152 Jukes, Mavis. **Getting Even.** Alfred A. Knopf/Borzoi Books, 1988. Ages 10–12.

Ten-year-old Maggie is taunted by the class bully and adopts her friend Iris's plan to get even. When the girls get caught and Maggie has to face her mother at a time of tense family relationships because of her parents' divorce, a catharsis is reached. Poignant, humorous events contribute to a strong story of school life and growing up. *Children's Choice.*

10.153 Lisle, Janet Taylor. **The Great Dimpole Oak.** Illustrated by Stephen Gammell. Orchard Books, 1987. Ages 9–12.

This contemporary fable centers around an ancient oak that stands in a farmer's field outside a small town. The tree represents different things to the people who rally together to save the historic tree from being cut down. Full-page black-and-white drawings of the oak lend an air of mystery to the story.

10.154 Little, Jean. **Different Dragons.** Illustrated by Laura Fernandez. Viking Kestrel, 1986. Ages 10–12.

We all have different dragons to fight, and Ben Tucker is no different. Ben does not like to admit he is afraid of such things as dogs, darkness, storms, and new people and places. As he spends some time with his aunt and a neighbor girl, he learns to face his fears. He discovers that he *can* slay a dragon when he wants to and that he is not the only dragon slayer around. Young people can relate to Ben's experience and can realize that admission of fear or weakness is half the battle.

10.155 Lowry, Lois. **Rabble Starkey.** Houghton Mifflin, 1987. Ages 10–12.

Twelve-year-old Rabble (short for Parable) Starkey and her mother, Sweet Hosanna, live with the Bigelow family. Rabble's best friend, Veronica Bigelow, is a constant companion while Sweet Hosanna takes care of the Bigelow children. Told in the local Appalachian pattern of speech and seen through Rabble's maturing eyes, the story involves Veronica's homely brother, her mentally ill mother, and her gentle father, plus an elderly cranky neighbor they try to help. Changes do take place as Rabble and Sweet Ho move on with their lives in this novel with strong character development. *Boston Globe–Horn Book Award.*

10.156 McDonnell, Christine. **Just for the Summer.** Illustrated by Diane deGroat. Viking Kestrel, 1987. Ages 8–10.

Fans of Christine McDonnell's characters from *Lucky Charms and Birthday Wishes* will find Lydia spending the summer with her aunts and continuing her adventures with Ivy and Emily. Lydia's father is hospitalized with a serious illness, and she also must cope with a dismal day-camp experience, a day-care program as a money-making scheme, and her fear of learning to swim. These are balanced with her budding artistic talent, summertime games, picnics, and warm family relationships.

10.157 Mauser, Pat Rhoads. **Patti's Pet Gorilla.** Illustrated by Diane Palmisciano. Atheneum, 1987. Ages 7–10.

Patti suddenly finds she is telling her class about her pet gorilla. This realistic tale shows how Patti's lie catches up with her and relays her nervous thoughts along the way. It is a consistent and fairly interesting story. However, the full-page pencil illustrations are disappointing in their cuteness.

10.158 Mills, Claudia. **The One and Only Cynthia Jane Thornton.** Macmillan, 1986. Ages 9–12.

A ten-year-old girl wrestles with her jealousy of her sister's talents and her new interests in writing. Readable and engaging, the novel moves quickly and concerns classroom writing as well as family relationships.

10.159 Naylor, Phyllis Reynolds. **The Agony of Alice.** Atheneum, 1985. Ages 9–11.

Life for Alice, a motherless sixth grader, is in agony as she searches for a female role model. Everything would be fine if her teacher were the glamorous Miss Cole and not the pear-shaped Mrs. Plotkin, who has her students keep a journal. Alice begins to accept herself as her teacher shows kindness and as she learns that physical appearance is not so important. A visit to an aunt and cousin provides further growing-up experiences, and even Alice's brother begins to act like a human being. *ALA Notable Children's Book* and *Children's Choice.*

10.160 Orgel, Doris. **Midnight Soup and a Witch's Hat.** Illustrated by Carol Newsom. Viking Kestrel, 1987. Ages 8–10.

In this sequel to *My War with Mrs. Galloway* and *Whiskers Once and Always*, Becky Suslow goes to visit her divorced dad in Portland, Oregon. It is hard for Becky to share her father with his live-in friend, Rosellen, and her six-year-old daughter, Hope. However, third-grader Becky becomes sensitive to Hope's unrealized dreams and adjusts to the blended family arrangement with the help of understanding adults.

10.161 Park, Barbara. **Almost Starring Skinnybones.** Alfred A. Knopf/Borzoi Books, 1988. Ages 9–12.

This sequel to *Skinnybones* finds Alex Frankovitch starring in a cat food commercial. Now a media star in his own mind, Alex sets his sights on a starring role in the school play, with disastrous (and hilarious) results. Alex is brash and obnoxious, yet strangely likable. The story moves swiftly, with convincing dialogue and realistic characters.

10.162 Robertson, Keith. **Henry Reed's Think Tank.** Viking Kestrel, 1986. Ages 9–13.

Laced with bold but gentle humor, this fifth Henry Reed book is a good candidate for a serial read-aloud story, as well as for a child's private enjoyment. Henry and Midge's adventures as problem-solving entrepreneurs find them in the midst of offbeat, yet believable, situations. Children should be able to relate to the problems and implied lessons, providing that adults resist the temptation to draw these lessons from the story, rather than allowing the story to stand on its own.

10.163 Rocklin, Joanne. **Sonia Begonia.** Illustrated by Julie Downing. Macmillan, 1986. Ages 9–11.

Sonia Begley wants to be more than a baby-sitter and decides, at age eleven, to set up her own business venture. Her house-sitting effort, Sonia's Safety Sentinel Service, receives help from her friend, Jason, and a lonely neighbor, Mrs. Fineberg. Problems arise when a client's house is burglarized, but Sonia is enterprising and continues with family support.

10.164 Roos, Stephen. **The Fair-Weather Friends.** Illustrated by Dee deRosa. Atheneum, 1987. Ages 9–11.

Twelve-year-old Kit, her older brother Derek, and her younger sister Margo always spend summers on an island with their grandmother, who runs a summer theater. Kit looks forward to good times with her summer friend, Phoebe. This year, however, she is shocked to discover that Phoebe, who has just returned from Paris, is more interested in boys, parties, and clothes than in biking and playing in their secret treehouse. This is a poignant story about changing friendships, compromise, and growing up.

10.165 Roos, Stephen. **Thirteenth Summer.** Illustrated by Dee deRosa. Atheneum, 1987. Ages 10–13.

In this second book about New England coastal life on Plymouth Island, year-round resident Pink Cunningham wonders what life would be like if he could attend the same prestigious prep school as his wealthy summer-resident friend, Mackie Vanderbeck. Overcoming his father's resistance to the idea is Pink's greatest challenge. In the self-examination process, the reader shares Pink's changing attitude toward his future and friends. Pink, a maturing thirteen-year-old male protagonist, is portrayed in a sensitive, thoughtful way.

10.166 Shreve, Susan. **How I Saved the World on Purpose.** Illustrated by Suzanne Richardson. Holt, Rinehart and Winston, 1985. Ages 8–10.

In this first-person narrative, nine-year-old Miranda is making big plans to save the world's children. In the meantime, she has to figure a way to outclass her brother and outsmart the class bully. An average formula plot, with adequately drawn characters.

10.167 Shura, Mary Francis. **The Josie Gambit.** Avon Books/Camelot Books, 1988. Ages 10–12.

Twelve-year-old Greg renews his friendship with Josie Nolan's family during a six-month stay with his grandmother. Josie's grandfather taught both of them to play chess, a game which plays an important part in the story as Josie's friend Tory schemes a real-life gambit—a high-risk ploy. Strong characters and relationships and a clever plot contribute to a strong realistic novel demonstrating the value of friendship. *ALA Notable Children's Book.*

10.168 Smith, Doris Buchanan. **Karate Dancer.** G. P. Putnam's Sons, 1987. Ages 10 and up.

Do not be misled by the title of this classy sleeper. It is about much more than karate, and it will appeal to children, and adults, who either laud or denigrate the martial arts. This is a story about a fourteen-year-old artist, Troy Matthews, and his sometimes-conflicting loves in the visual and martial arts. Those looking for examples of vitality in written language will enjoy Doris Buchanan Smith's snappy way with words.

10.169 Stiles, Martha Bennett. **Sarah the Dragon Lady.** Macmillan, 1986. Ages 8–12.

During Sarah's fourth-grade year, she and her mother move to Kentucky because of her mother's job as an illustrator, while her father remains in New York. Young people should be able to relate to the story of Sarah's trials, tribulations, and fun times during this time of separation. At the end the family happily gets together again for a trip to Paris.

10.170 Stolz, Mary. **The Explorer of Barkham Street.** Illustrated by Emily Arnold McCully. Harper and Row, 1985. Ages 10–12.

Martin, a perpetual dreamer, loves to daydream about being on heroic missions to many parts of the world. Some of this teenager's fantasies encompass real-life situations that include a special friend, a pet, and hopes for an exciting family life. But as Martin explores the real world, he realizes that there is more to life than just dreaming about it. He finds that the reality of those dreams requires his participation and understanding.

10.171 Wolkoff, Judie. **In a Pig's Eye.** Illustrated by the author. Bradbury Press, 1986. Ages 9–11.

A true-to-life story of two fourth graders who sometimes are best friends and sometimes are not. The girls keep busy by publishing their own neighborhood newspaper, entering their dogs in a dog show, and dealing with a brother's messy room. The author's illustrations include a map of the neighborhood and a copy of the girls' newspaper.

Family Life

Primary

10.172 Ackerman, Karen. **Song and Dance Man.** Illustrated by Stephen Gammell. Alfred A. Knopf/Borzoi Books, 1988. Ages 5–9.

Grandpa puts on his dancing shoes and stages a show for his grandchildren, showing them some of the songs, dances, and jokes from his vaudeville act. Stephen Gammell's scratchy drawings and use of color celebrate the joyfulness of the occasion. *ALA Notable Children's Book* and *Caldecott Medal.*

10.173 Alexander, Martha. **Even That Moose Won't Listen to Me.** Illustrated by the author. Dial Books for Young Readers, 1988. Ages 5–7. (Picture book)

When nobody believes Rebecca's announcement that there is a moose in the garden, she takes matters into her own hands in this book with a strong story structure. The text, a few sentences per page, reads delightfully like the way a young child would think. The illustrations, made with pencils and watercolor washes, support the story line with just the right amount of detail. *Children's Choice.*

10.174 Arnold, Tedd. **No Jumping on the Bed!** Illustrated by the author. Dial Books for Young Readers, 1987. Ages 3–7. (Picture book)

Jumping on his bed is just what young Walter wants to do, even though he knows he should not. Sure enough, he and his bed crash through the floor. Together they tumble through the apartment building, taking with them an ever-growing number of tenants. Children will be delighted to recognize the story's pattern while still being surprised by Walter's antic adventures and entertained by the humorous and colorful illustrations. *Children's Choice.*

10.175   Buckley, Helen E. **Someday with My Father.** Illustrated by Ellen Eagle. Harper and Row, 1985. Ages 3–6. (Picture book)

A little girl dreams of all the wonderful things she and her father will do together—as soon as her cast comes off. A warm, sensitive story is realistically portrayed in crayon drawings. The story is suitable for reading aloud; the size of the book restricts it to a lap book.

10.176   Byars, Betsy. **Beans on the Roof.** Illustrated by Melodye Rosales. Delacorte Press, 1988. Ages 7–9.

Anna Bean is on the roof, writing a poem for a school contest. Her brother, George, sits on the roof for days and cannot get any ideas. Complications arise when Anna finishes her poem. All the Beans are sure it is the most beautiful poem in the world, but Anna does not win the contest. In the end, George realizes the strength of the bond that his family shares, and Anna realizes that there are more important things than school contests.

10.177   Cameron, Ann. **More Stories Julian Tells.** Illustrated by Ann Strugnell. Alfred A. Knopf/Borzoi Books, 1986. Ages 6–9.

Seven short chapters, each a complete story, continue the everyday adventures of a black family and friends begun in *The Stories Julian Tells.* Frequent charcoal sketches emphasize the narrative's gentle humor and warmth. The subject and format make this a prime choice for reading aloud and for the young reader entering the chapter-book world.

10.178   de Hamel, Joan. **Hemi's Pet.** Illustrated by Christine Ross. Houghton Mifflin/Dorothy Butler Books, 1987. Ages 5–8. (Picture book)

Soft, colored-pencil illustrations beautifully provide a rural school setting for this story of sibling love. When Rata's older brother Hemi needs a pet at school, he takes three-year-old Rata as his "pet." They win potato chips and a red ribbon, which Hemi gives to Rata to keep "forever and ever." This is a loving story that is perfect for reading aloud.

10.179 Dragonwagon, Crescent. **Diana, Maybe.** Illustrated by Deborah Kogan Ray. Macmillan, 1987. Ages 7–10. (Picture book)

Longing to know the stepsister who is only a name, Rosie imagines all the things the two of them could do and share if they lived in the same house. The text describes Rosie's dreams with details and strong emotion supported by the warm and gentle pencil drawings on every other page.

10.180 Drescher, Joan. **My Mother's Getting Married.** Illustrated by the author. Dial Books for Young Readers, 1986. Ages 5–8. (Picture book)

Katy worries that after her mother marries Ben, she will lose the special relationship she and her mother have shared. She changes her mind after her whole class comes to the wedding.

10.181 Engel, Diana. **Josephina the Great Collector.** Illustrated by the author. William Morrow, 1988. Ages 3–6. (Picture book)

Josephina is a joyous, irrepressible collector of anything and everything. She finally drives her tidy sister right out of their shared bedroom. So that the sisters can make peace, Josephina comes up with a creative solution to her "junk" problem. Bright, appropriately cluttered illustrations add humor to the serious business of problem solving.

10.182 Flournoy, Valerie. **The Patchwork Quilt.** Illustrated by Jerry Pinkney. Dial Books for Young Readers, 1985. Ages 5–8. (Picture book)

The daily life of a loving black family is pictured with full-color realistic watercolors. Grandma is using material from everyone's worn-out clothing to make a patchwork quilt of memories. When she gets sick, young Tanya and her mother work on the quilt until Grandma is well enough to get back to it. *Children's Choice* and *Coretta Scott King Award* (for illustrations).

10.183 Galbraith, Kathryn Osebold. **Waiting for Jennifer.** Illustrated by Irene Trivas. Margaret K. McElderry Books, 1987. Ages 4–6. (Picture book)

Mother tells Nan and Thea a secret—there is going to be a new baby in the family. Nan wants to name her Jennifer because she already knows how to spell it. The baby takes forever to come, and when it does arrive, there is a surprise.

This is a warm, realistic, believable family story appropriately illustrated in crayon and pen-and-ink with ethnically diverse characters.

10.184   Gauch, Patricia Lee. **Christina Katerina and the Time She Quit the Family.** Illustrated by Elise Primavera. G. P. Putnam's Sons, 1987. Ages 4–8. (Picture book)

Due to a commotion involving her brother, Christina Katerina decides to quit the family. For four days she lives in an area of the house that she marks off with rope, eats and wears what she chooses, and plays until midnight. Mildred, her mother, asks for a favor. Will she rejoin the family or not?

10.185   Goffstein, M. B. **Our Snowman.** Illustrated by the author. Harper and Row/Charlotte Zolotow Books, 1986. Ages 3–5. (Picture book)

This delightful story is told simply but with originality in text and illustration. A young boy is instructed in the correct way to build a snowman by his older sister. When night falls and the children are concerned that the snowman is lonely, an understanding father goes out with the girl to build a wife for the snowman. "Now they each have company." Full-color pastel pictures illustrate the story.

10.186   Greenfield, Eloise. **Grandpa's Face.** Illustrated by Floyd Cooper. Philomel Books, 1988. Ages 3–5. (Picture book)

Tamika loves her grandfather's kind face, but one day she sees his face turn into a mean face that "could not love." Her grandfather is rehearsing for an acting role, but Tamika fears that his strange face could someday become real. Her grandfather's insight into her fear and the constancy of his love finally reassure her. The expressive faces in the illustrations demonstrate the tenderness between the old man and the little girl. *ALA Notable Children's Book.*

10.187   Hest, Amy. **The Purple Coat.** Illustrated by Amy Schwartz. Four Winds Press, 1986. Ages 4–8. (Picture book)

Once a year, Gabrielle visits Grampa in his New York City tailor shop, where she's fitted for a new coat. Mamma always insists on navy blue, but this time Gabrielle wants purple! Clever and loving Grampa comes up with a satisfying compromise. Colorful illustrations add a nostalgic tone. *ALA Notable Children's Book.*

10.188 Hines, Anna Grossnickle. **Daddy Makes the Best Spaghetti.** Illustrated by the author. Clarion Books, 1986. Ages 3–6. (Picture book)

Done in crayon and pen-and-ink, the illustrations help elaborate this quiet but effective story of how a father helps around the house and especially how he helps with Corey, the young narrator of this charming picture book. The simple text depicts contemporary role models appropriate for this era of working mothers and shared household responsibilities. *Children's Choice.*

10.189 Hines, Anna Grossnickle. **Grandma Gets Grumpy.** Illustrated by the author. Clarion Books, 1988. Ages 3–7. (Picture book)

Here is the patient and fun-loving grandma every child wants, but even she has her limits. When her five grandchildren carry play too far and Grandma gets grumpy, the children suddenly realize that it was Grandma who taught their parents the rules that are so often repeated at home. The fun of the children's adventures and their recognition that their parents were children once, too, will appeal to young listeners. *Children's Choice.*

10.190 Hoffman, Mary. **My Grandma Has Black Hair.** Illustrated by Joanna Burroughes. Dial Books for Young Readers, 1988. Ages 4–7. (Picture book)

The story is rather slim: a little girl lovingly describes her unconventional grandmother. However, it is useful in dispelling stereotypes and allowing children to see beyond labels. The warm relationship is reflected in the realistically casual illustrations. When the girl tells Gran that she is not a bit like the grandmothers depicted in storybooks, her response is, "Well . . . I'm not going to change, so the books'll have to."

10.191 Hurwitz, Johanna. **Russell Rides Again.** Illustrated by Lillian Hoban. William Morrow, 1985. Ages 6–9.

Johanna Hurwitz's stories sweetly capture childlike emotions, the delicious thrill of pretending, and the importance of small events, and are similar to Beverly Cleary's Ramona books. Short episodic chapters make for good reading aloud or alone. This book focuses on Russell as he gets ready to celebrate his sixth birthday and also features Nora, Teddy, and Aldo. Sequel to *Rip-Roaring Russell.*

10.192 Johnston, Tony. **The Quilt Story.** Illustrated by Tomie de-
Paola. G. P. Putnam's Sons, 1985. Ages 5–8. (Picture book)

Folk-art illustrations enhance the story about a handmade
quilt that eases the loneliness of a pioneer girl when she
moves. Generations later, another girl finds the quilt in the attic, and it gives her comfort when her family moves to a new
town. *Children's Choice.*

10.193 Joosse, Barbara M. **Jam Day.** Illustrated by Emily Arnold
McCully. Harper and Row, 1987. Ages 7–10. (Picture book)

Worried with doubts about his kind of family, Ben takes part
in the family's annual berry-picking and jam-making event.
He is reassured to discover that he belongs within a family
filled with love, traditions, stories, and lots of noise.

10.194 Jukes, Mavis. **Like Jake and Me.** Illustrated by Lloyd Bloom.
Alfred A. Knopf/Borzoi Books, 1984. Ages 6–10.

Alex is in awe of his seemingly fearless new stepfather, Jake,
who is a real cowboy and who does not quite know what to
do with a small boy who wants to help. But when a hairy wolf
spider gets lost on Jake, Alex is the brave one who helps him
make the search for it. The growing acceptance and affection
between Jake and Alex bind the family together as everyone
awaits the arrival of twins. *Newbery Honor Book.*

10.195 Kessler, Ethel, and Leonard Kessler. **The Sweeneys from 9D.**
Illustrated by the author. Macmillan, 1985. Ages 6–9. (Picture
book)

The three Sweeney children move to an apartment in the big
city where their mother has a new job, and they must get
used to a new neighborhood, a new school, and being on their
own after school. This clear, sensitive story has a pleasantly
reassuring tone as it deals with real social adjustments.

10.196 Khalsa, Dayal Kaur. **I Want a Dog.** Illustrated by the author.
Clarkson N. Potter, 1987. Ages 3–6. (Picture book)

Young May desperately wants a dog and tries every trick that
she knows to get one, including begging her parents and buying her mother a puppy for *her* birthday, which she has to return to the pet store. May finally settles on getting ready for
dog ownership by pulling a roller skate around on a leash and
by practicing that it is a real puppy. Her parents are im-

pressed, and in a couple of years, May does get a dog of her own. Meanwhile, every other child on the block is practicing with his or her own roller skate on a leash. *ALA Notable Children's Book.*

10.197 Khalsa, Dayal Kaur. **Tales of a Gambling Grandma.** Illustrated by the author. Clarkson N. Potter, 1986. Ages 4–10. (Picture book)

A child's account of her grandmother's life is based on her own observations and Grandma's exaggerations and elaborately embroidered memories. It is the life of a woman who immigrated to the United States from Russia, married a plumber, and gambled to earn extra money. Grandma's unique and delightful character is marvelously portrayed with an original use of point of view, giving her a depth of character rarely seen in a short book. Dayal Kaur Khalsa has chosen an entertaining variety of visual and textual details to bring Grandma's past to life. *ALA Notable Children's Book* and *Notable Children's Trade Book in the Language Arts.*

10.198 Loh, Morag. **Tucking Mommy In.** Illustrated by Donna Rawlins. Orchard Books, 1987. Ages 4–6. (Picture book)

The usual bedtime routine is reversed when an exhausted Mommy falls asleep before her daughters do. They lovingly take care of Mommy until Daddy returns home and puts them to bed. Warm-toned drawings depict a realistic family in a book that emphasizes mutual love and support. *ALA Notable Children's Book.*

10.199 Martin, Bill, Jr., and John Archambault. **The Ghost-Eye Tree.** Illustrated by Ted Rand. Holt, Rinehart and Winston, 1985. Ages 7–9.

This story in rhyme tells of two youngsters who go out to get milk on a dark and windy night. Using their imaginations, Ellie and her brother envision ghosts following them from the ghost-eye tree. Ted Rand's dramatic illustrations greatly enhance the theme of the story, which could be presented as creative drama. *Children's Choice.*

10.200 Martin, Bill, Jr., and John Archambault. **White Dynamite and Curly Kidd.** Illustrated by Ted Rand. Holt, Rinehart and Winston, 1986. Ages 6–12. (Picture book)

Curly Kidd's ride on White Dynamite, the meanest bull of all, is seen through the eyes of his daughter, who looks on with fear and pride as her father drops on the bull in the chute and begins his corkscrew ride. The poetic text is meant to be read aloud. Full-page illustrations capture the excitement of rodeos.

10.201 Pearson, Susan. **Happy Birthday, Grampie.** Illustrated by Ronald Himler. Dial Books for Young Readers, 1987. Ages 5–9. (Picture book)

Martha puts a lot of thought into how to make a birthday card for her blind eighty-nine-year-old Swedish grandfather. Will he be able to "read" her loving message? Carefully done watercolor paintings add much to the sensitivity of this well-written book.

10.202 Pearson, Susan. **My Favorite Time of Year.** Illustrated by John Wallner. Harper and Row, 1988. Ages 4–9. (Picture book)

There are many details in this book, which centers around a small girl and her family. These details evoke a real sense of each season—catching fireflies and going to the beach in summer, finding lost mittens and toys under the melting snow in spring. Because seasons are so tied into what one *does* during specific times of the year, children will find this approach captivating. Lively, detailed watercolors provide a fine accent to the text.

10.203 Polushkin, Maria. **Baby Brother Blues.** Illustrated by Ellen Weiss. Bradbury Press, 1987. Ages 4–8. (Picture book)

A young girl describes a day in the life of her baby brother. Everyone thinks he is adorable, even though terribly messy, but he cannot do any of the things his big sister is capable of—not even feed himself, stand, or play nicely. In the end, though, she decides she does like him after all.

10.204 Rabe, Berniece. **Where's Chimpy?** Photographs by Diane Schmidt. Albert Whitman, 1988. Ages 3–8. (Picture book)

It is bedtime, and Misty cannot settle down until she finds her favorite toy, Chimpy. She and Daddy patiently review the day's activities until they solve the mystery. This cozy reassuring tale features a main character with Down's syndrome, but the disability is totally subordinate to the story; it is only mentioned in a prefatory note. The full-color photographs capture a small slice of family life, with which many children will identify.

10.205 Riggio, Anita. **Wake Up, William!** Illustrated by the author. Atheneum, 1987. Ages 3–6. (Picture book)

This story with little text is told primarily with the slightly colored drawings. Brother, sister, and dog all try unsuccessfully to wake William, who the reader knows is faking it. When he does choose to come alive, he scares everyone, and only Dad's arrival puts an end to the shenanigans.

10.206 Rylant, Cynthia. **Birthday Presents.** Illustrated by Suçie Stevenson. Orchard Books, 1987. Ages 2–6. (Picture book)

A five-year-old girl listens as her mother and father tell her about the special cakes, presents, and love surrounding each of her birthdays, including her birth. The girl is now taking an active part in setting up her next birthday celebration—her sixth birthday. Bright colors and lots of action will keep children looking for new details. *Children's Choice.*

10.207 Rylant, Cynthia. **The Relatives Came.** Illustrated by Stephen Gammell. Bradbury Press, 1985. Ages 6–8. (Picture book)

One momentous summer day a battered, rainbow-colored station wagon delivers an entourage of Virginia relatives of all shapes and sizes. Amidst endless hugging and laughter good times abound, making even the crowded sleeping conditions a memorable event. Colorful animated caricatures depict everyday happenings and turn them into unforgettable memories. *Caldecott Honor Book* and *Children's Choice.*

10.208 Stevenson, Suçie. **Do I Have to Take Violet?** Illustrated by the author. Dodd, Mead, 1987. Ages 4–7. (Picture book)

Elly the rabbit is asked by her mother to care for her younger sister, Violet, when she plans a day at the seashore. What starts out as an unhappy chore for Elly turns out to be a fun-filled day for both girls.

10.209 Vigna, Judith. **I Wish Daddy Didn't Drink So Much.** Illustrated by the author. Albert Whitman, 1988. Ages 6–9. (Picture book)

A young girl's Christmas celebration is disrupted when her al-coholic father becomes drunk and unpleasant. Lisa discovers ways to cope with the situation with the help of her mother and a family friend, a recovering alcoholic. Although this pic-ture book suffers from generalizations and didacticism, it is successful in its purpose—to expose the emotional isolation, instability, and disappointment that children of alcoholics ex-perience. Due to the sensitive topic, the book should be used with the guidance of a qualified adult.

10.210 Warren, Cathy. **Saturday Belongs to Sara.** Illustrated by DyAnne DiSalvo-Ryan. Bradbury Press, 1988. Ages 6–10. (Picture book)

Sara has planned a perfect day at the beach for the special day she will spend with her mother. But her aunt asks them to visit an older woman on the way, and as they visit, it begins to rain. It turns out to be a pleasant day after all, for Mrs. Ivey can play a lively clarinet. A true respect for Sara by the adults makes this story unique and warm. Black-and-white illustrations opposite each page of text will encourage young readers to read the story.

10.211 Wilhelm, Hans. **Let's Be Friends Again!** Illustrated by the au-thor. Crown, 1986. Ages 3–5. (Picture book)

When Little Sister takes Brother's pet turtle to the pond and sets it free, he goes through various stages of anger. He final-ly decides he is only hurting himself and begins making friends with his sister again. *Notable Children's Trade Book in the Field of Social Studies.*

10.212 Yolen, Jane. **Owl Moon.** Illustrated by John Schoenherr. Philomel Books, 1987. Ages 4–9. (Picture book)

A father and daughter walk in the woods on a cold, quiet, moonlit night with the hope that they will catch a glimpse of an owl. Jane Yolen's haunting prose and John Schoenherr's fine pen-and-ink and watercolor paintings capture the wonder and the intimacy of a special occasion. Schoenherr's illustra-tions reflect the light of the full moon on a rural winter night. *Caldecott Medal.*

10.213 Zolotow, Charlotte. **A Rose, a Bridge, and a Wild Black Horse.** Illustrated by Robin Spowart. Harper and Row, 1987. Ages 3–7. (Picture book)

A small boy lists the special things he wants to do for his sister, like capturing a wild black horse and taming it for her to ride. Each wish, stated in simple text of one or two sentences, is illustrated in full-page pastels. The love between brother and sister continues through his final wish—that they explore the world together.

10.214 Zolotow, Charlotte. **Timothy Too!** Illustrated by Ruth Robbins. Houghton Mifflin/Parnassus Press, 1986. Ages 4–8.

Little brother Timothy is a nuisance to big brother John. Timothy always says things twice and follows John everywhere. John resents this until one day Timothy finds a friend his own age. John feels the void. Full-color illustrations enhance the action of the story.

Intermediate

10.215 Alcock, Vivien. **The Cuckoo Sister.** Delacorte Press, 1985. Ages 10–12.

Everyone is shocked when a spikey teenager arrives at the door of a London home with a letter claiming that she is the baby abducted long ago from the family. Kate, once an only child, is consumed with the fear of being replaced, but she also continues to fantasize about the sister this person might be. It is Kate's determination that brings about the family's resolution of this extraordinary situation. *ALA Notable Children's Book.*

10.216 Amoss, Berthe. **The Mockingbird Song.** Harper and Row, 1988. Ages 9–11.

Abandoned by her mother, eleven-year-old Lindy has a problem adjusting to her father's new wife. The problem turns into a crisis when she must move in with an elderly neighbor because her stepmother is expecting a baby. Through her relationships with her relatives, friends, and the neighbor and her maid, Lindy, who is a caring, sensitive girl, learns what her new family really means to her. The setting, New Orleans in the 1930s, adds regional flavor and interest.

10.217 Auch, Mary Jane. **Cry Uncle!** Holiday House, 1987. Ages 9–12.

How does Davey adjust when his great uncle moves in? More than just giving up his room to his uncle, he must come to grips with his uncle's growing old and the resulting strange behaviors. The issue of nursing-home care must be resolved as well.

10.218 Auch, Mary Jane. **Pick of the Litter.** Holiday House, 1988. Ages 9–11.

In this warm, humorous, insightful story, eleven-year-old Catherine (Cat) Corwin, an adopted child and an only child, suddenly finds her life completely changed when her mother gives birth to quadruplet boys. Cat becomes frustrated by being overlooked and runs away. A death in the family brings her home, where she then learns to accept the new situation.

10.219 Bates, Betty. **Ask Me Tomorrow.** Holiday House, 1987. Ages 11 and up.

At sixteen, Paige does not know what he wants, but he knows what he does not want, and that is to take over the family orchard in Maine. When he meets thirteen-year-old Abby, he begins to reevaluate his plans and options, struggling to make sense of life's conflicting obligations. Paige and his family and friends ring true. Even the minor characters are more than one-dimensional, making this a satisfying story to read and remember.

10.220 Branscum, Robbie. **Johnny May Grows Up.** Illustrated by Bob Marstall. Harper and Row, 1987. Ages 9–12.

In this sequel to *The Adventures of Johnny May*, the main character is now eleven years old. Robbie Branscum continues to draw a sympathetic character who is experiencing the universal problems attendant with adolescence. The book's rural Arkansas setting and the interesting characters surrounding Johnny May add special appeal. *Children's Choice*.

10.221 Carris, Joan. **Hedgehogs in the Closet.** Illustrated by Carol Newsom. J. B. Lippincott, 1988. Ages 9–11.

This third book in a series of Howard family adventures finds the Howards leaving Ohio to live in England for two years. Eleven-year-old Nick is unhappy about leaving his friends and school. While struggling to adjust, he shares his thoughts with Spike, his adopted pet hedgehog secretly hidden in his closet. Gradually Nick makes new friends, learns to play rugby, and decides to stay in England. This is a lighthearted, wholesome story of three brothers in a traditional family setting.

10.222 Cleaver, Vera. **Sweetly Sings the Donkey.** J. B. Lippincott, 1985. Ages 10–14.

Fourteen-year-old Lily projects a strong, positive model for readers. Her grit and cleverness provide the strength her entire family needs as they establish a new home in Florida. Characterizations are the strongest aspect of this well-written book as we come to know Lily's impractical father, her whiney mother, and her quarrelsome brothers. *Children's Choice.*

10.223 Conrad, Pam. **Seven Silly Circles.** Illustrated by Mike Wimmer. Harper and Row, 1987. Ages 9–12.

Nicki Bennett struggles with her self-consciousness, knowing that the seven red circles still remain from when she put suction cups on her face. She chooses to stay far away from everyone, but the love and encouragement of family and friends help her overcome her embarrassment.

10.224 Conrad, Pam. **Staying Nine.** Illustrated by Mike Wimmer. Harper and Row, 1988. Ages 8–10.

Her ninth year has been so wonderful that Heather does not want to turn ten. She does agree to a family birthday party with no presents or candles to remind her of getting older, however. Twenty-three-year-old Rosa Rita, an adult with whom Heather identifies, helps nudge Heather toward acceptance of the inevitable in this exuberant story that celebrates growing up. The larger-sized, clear type and attractive pencil illustrations make this volume especially inviting for beginning novel readers.

10.225 Corcoran, Barbara. **A Horse Named Sky.** Atheneum, 1986. Ages 10 and up.

This sensitive, no-nonsense story about growing up in a troubled family avoids the pitfalls of either a phony happy ending or undue pessimism about outcomes. It is the story of Georgia, who moves to Montana with her mother to get away from her alcoholic father and who dreams of owning her own horse. Besides being a rousing good story, the book provides a strong and positive statement about the possibilities for mutual mother-daughter support, the meaning of good friends, and the potential for new beginnings out of adversity.

10.226 Corcoran, Barbara. **I Am the Universe.** Atheneum, 1986. Ages 10–14.

While attempting to write a paper on who she is, eighth-grader Kit weathers the crisis of her mother's headaches and successful brain surgery. She responds to this by assuming responsibility for her siblings at home. Eventually she succumbs to the pressures during a night of petty vandalism. The first-person narration adds to this story of personal growth.

10.227 Fox, Paula. **The Village by the Sea.** Orchard Books, 1988. Ages 9–12.

Because of her father's life-threatening surgery, Emma must spend two weeks in the isolated seashore home of her mean and vindictive aunt. Emma begins her stay with dread, but soon she is absorbed in creating an elaborate sand-castle village with a newfound friend. Paula Fox's masterful use of language brings the characters and the village alive. *ALA Notable Children's Book.*

10.228 Girard, Linda Walvoord. **Adoption Is for Always.** Illustrated by Judith Friedman. Albert Whitman, 1986. Ages 8–12. (Picture book)

Who were her birth parents? Why did they give her up for adoption? As Celia struggles to understand her status in the family, her adoptive parents thoughtfully make her adoption day a family holiday and give her factual information about adoption proceedings, which helps Celia develop feelings of security and acceptance.

10.229 Hahn, Mary Downing. **The Jellyfish Season.** Clarion Books, 1985. Ages 10–14.

Because of her father's unemployment, Kathleen, her mother, and her sisters must spend the summer with detested relatives while her father stays behind seeking a job. Problems grow for Kathleen and her parents as they face an uncertain future. Engrossing situations bring well-crafted characters alive in this realistic story of a family coping with the stress of change.

10.230 Hahn, Mary Downing. **Tallahassee Higgins.** Clarion Books, 1987. Ages 10–13.

Tallahassee adores the unstructured life she lives with her free-spirited mother, Liz. When Liz leaves for California with a new boyfriend, Tallahassee is sent to live with stern relatives in a small town. The trauma forces her to accept unpleasant truths about those she loves most. Sympathetic characters, a fully developed story, and skillful balance of humor and heartache make this book a celebrated addition to the problem-novel genre.

10.231 Jarrow, Gail. **If Phyllis Were Here.** Houghton Mifflin, 1987. Ages 9–12.

Phyllis, Libby's grandmother, wins the lottery and moves to Florida. Libby's whole life has been built around Phyllis's being there when Libby needs her. Now Libby must learn to depend on her parents, which happens after some struggle. And as Libby says in the end, "I still come home to an empty house . . . and I still miss Phyllis. But only sometimes."

10.232 Locker, Thomas. **Family Farm.** Illustrated by the author. Dial Books, 1988. Ages 6–10. (Picture book)

Thomas Locker's exquisitely detailed oil paintings, stylistically reminiscent of the Hudson River School, illustrate routines and concerns of everyday farm life as a contemporary family struggles in the face of hard times. Art appreciation and social studies tie-ins to the book are possible.

10.233 Lowry, Lois. **All about Sam.** Illustrated by Diane deGroat. Houghton Mifflin, 1988. Ages 9–12.

Fans of Anastasia and the Krupnik family will welcome this book, which recounts the first years of her brother Sam's life, uniquely narrated from baby Sam's perspective. The recognizable characters, the humor, and the author's respect for children's concerns found in the earlier books are evident here. Older children will enjoy predicting naive Sam's mishaps. This would make a rollicking read-aloud book for the classroom.

10.234 McDonald, Joyce. **Mail-Order Kid.** G. P. Putnam's Sons, 1988. Ages 8–12.

When Flip's parents adopt a young Korean boy, Flip has problems adjusting to not being the only child. He decides to mail-order a pet—a red fox. It is through Flip's problems with Vickie, his fox, that he finally begins to understand what his new brother is going through. *Children's Choice.*

10.235 Mark, Jan. **Trouble Half-Way.** Illustrated by David Parkins. Atheneum, 1986. Ages 9–12.

Amy, a worrier, is still grieving over her father's death when she is forced to travel with her new stepfather, a long-distance truck driver, through northern England. Through this journey, Amy matures and gains self-confidence. Vivid dialogue, touches of humor, and a glossary explaining British terms add to this story's universal appeal.

10.236 Martin, Ann M. **Ten Kids, No Pets.** Holiday House, 1988. Ages 8–11.

The ten Rosso children, spaced a year apart and named alphabetically, desperately want a pet. A rambunctious and exciting life unfolds for them as their family leaves New York City for fifteen acres, a big farmhouse, and new friends in New Jersey. The children tell their story in the first person, one to a chapter, making this a fine read-aloud choice.

10.237 Mebs, Gudrun (translated by Sarah Gibson). **Sunday's Child.** Dial Books for Young Readers, 1986. Ages 10–12.

Jenny has always lived in an orphanage and has always wanted parents. She is placed in a foster home, but at first her foster mother does not meet Jenny's expectations. Eventually Jenny learns the value of friendship and genuine affection. This book won a German children's book prize.

10.238 Nelson, Theresa. **The 25¢ Miracle.** Bradbury Press, 1986. Ages 10–12.

Elvira's father loses his job and decides that she will have to live with Aunt Darla, a development that Elvira feels she must stop. A trip to the library seems to provide the answer. Miss Ivy, the librarian, is pretty and the mother of two sons who need a father. Elvira plots and plans so that she can have the one thing she wants, a family.

10.239 Nixon, Joan Lowery. **Maggie, Too.** Harcourt Brace Jovanovich, 1985. Ages 10–12.

Margaret's father, an older Hollywood director, is going to marry a twenty-two-year-old starlet. Margaret is angry because she feels that her dad is betraying her mom's memory, so she is sent to her grandmother's house, where family and love reign supreme. In this new environment, she is able to come to grips with her problem.

10.240 Osborne, Mary Pope. **Last One Home.** Dial Books for Young Readers, 1986. Ages 12 and up.

Bailey's world is falling apart. Her mother has a drinking problem and has moved to Miami; her brother, Claude, is going into the army after breaking up with his girlfriend; and her father is marrying Janet. Bailey faces all these problems and more as she struggles with her feelings of loneliness.

10.241 Paterson, Katherine. **Come Sing, Jimmy Jo.** E. P. Dutton/ Lodestar Books, 1985. Ages 9–13.

This touching story set in Appalachia traces a shy young boy's struggle to gain confidence in himself. Katherine Paterson's language is as rhythmic and descriptive as the country music that eleven-year-old Jimmy Jo sings so well. Readers will see the boy gain confidence in his talents as they learn about country music and the nontraditional lifestyle his family leads. *ALA Notable Children's Book* and *Children's Choice.*

10.242 Rocklin, Joanne. **Dear Baby.** Illustrated by Eileen McKeating. Macmillan, 1988. Ages 10–12.

There are so many changes in Farla's life. First her mom marries Charlie; now they are expecting a baby. To help cope with all the changes, Farla writes a series of letters to the unborn baby during the months of her mother's pregnancy. She describes her feelings toward her family, her friends, and her future brother or sister. Joanne Rocklin's tender, funny story will appeal to those preteens who have ever felt uncertain about their place in the family.

10.243 Rylant, Cynthia. **A Blue-Eyed Daisy.** Bradbury Press, 1985. Ages 9–12.

Cynthia Rylant tells of Ellie's eleventh year in fourteen short stories that are grouped loosely by seasons. The writing is distinguished, smooth, and a joy to read. Ellie's warm and loving Appalachian family has fallen on hard times because of her father's mining injury. A best friend, a schoolmate's death, a first kiss, and her father's accident are catalysts for Ellie's maturing. Almost all of the stories can be read independently, making the book excellent for reading aloud to family or classes.

10.244 Sachs, Elizabeth-Ann. **Shyster.** Illustrated by Judith Gwyn Brown. Atheneum, 1985. Ages 9–11.

Not only does Becky have to adjust to her father's departure, but she must learn to accept Arthur, the new man in her mother's life. A tender relationship with a stray cat helps ease this adjustment.

10.245 Sachs, Marilyn. **Fran Ellen's House.** E. P. Dutton, 1987. Ages 9–12.

This sequel to *The Bears' House* finds Fran Ellen and her family reunited after living over a year in separate foster homes. Fran Ellen is disappointed when her three-year-old sister is sent back to her foster home. Italicized dialogue throughout the story describes the rehabilitation of the old Bears' House, the classroom dollhouse with toy bears that serves as Fran Ellen's fantasy, and parallels the acceptance of changes in her own life. *ALA Notable Children's Book.*

10.246 Slote, Alfred. **Moving In.** J. B. Lippincott, 1988. Ages 10–12.

Robby, the eleven-year-old narrator, and his sister, Peggy, are unhappy about their move to Michigan, especially since it looks as though their widowed father is going to marry Ruth Lowenfeld, his new business partner. They plot to foil the romantic plans, which gives the story good-natured humor and a good pace.

10.247 Smith, Doris Buchanan. **Laura Upside-Down.** Viking Penguin/Puffin Books, 1986. Ages 10–13.

Doris Buchanan Smith once again writes about a young girl who is faced with several different problems. Laura thinks best when she is hanging upside-down. She relies on this technique when she must come to grips with religious differences and must gain an understanding of an older woman who has been in a mental institution. With the help of her parents, Laura begins to comprehend her world.

10.248 Smith, Doris Buchanan. **Return to Bitter Creek.** Viking Kestrel, 1986. Ages 10 and up.

Doris Buchanan Smith has written an engrossing novel on modern family relationships. She explores relationships that need mending, Southern family ties, and the tragedy that finally reunites a family torn apart by differences and misunderstandings. Life as seen through the eyes of a twelve year old can be very difficult and hard to comprehend; however, this story provides the reader with clear insights. *ALA Notable Children's Book* and *Notable Children's Trade Book in the Field of Social Studies.*

10.249 Smith, Robert Kimmel. **Mostly Michael.** Illustrated by Katherine Coville. Delacorte Press, 1987. Ages 10–12.

Michael turns eleven years old on April 19, and on that night he makes the first entry in his new diary, a not-so-welcomed gift from his Aunt Helen. The last entry of the book is on December 24, when Michael reflects upon the birth of his baby brother and upon how much has happened to him since the first entry only nine months earlier. By reading all of the entries in-between, the reader can share Michael's side of the excitement, frustrations, challenges, and successes in his life and can appreciate his insights into other characters' perceptions of the same events.

10.250 Strauss, Linda Leopold. **The Alexandra Ingredient.** Illustrated by the author. Crown, 1988. Ages 8–12.

"Alexandra is not exactly perfect" is an understatement as she moves from one dilemma to the next. Alexandra's good intentions cause more trouble than her "perfect" family can understand. When Mike enters her life through the Adopt-a-Grandparent program, he brings new meaning and caring. For Mike, she is a life saver. This is a warm, honest, funny novel about the ups and downs of being an imperfect but lovable eleven year old and about a young-old relationship.

10.251 Sussman, Susan. **Casey the Nomad.** Illustrated by Joelle Shefts. Albert Whitman, 1985. Ages 8–11.

"Naturally rotten" at sports, Casey signs up for the Scouting Olympics because his dad has promised to coach him. Then "Code Man Cooper" is needed by the army, and Casey feels angry and betrayed by his father's prolonged absence.

Casey's relationship with friends and family are well drawn, and the pleasant story will appeal to newly independent readers.

10.252 Talbert, Marc. **Toby.** Dial Books for Young Readers, 1987. Ages 9 and up.

Toby will make you laugh, cry, and applaud. Any child who has experienced the pain of being a scapegoat or of being made fun of will immediately identify with Toby, the son of a "slow" father and brain-damaged mother. His is a universal story of the struggle for understanding and surviving the often-deliberate cruelty of other children and the unthinking cruelty of well-intentioned adults. Adults who work with children could gain great insight into their own effects on children through this poignant story.

10.253 Terris, Susan. **The Latchkey Kids.** Farrar, Straus and Giroux, 1986. Ages 9–11.

This thematically rich novel realistically portrays the effects of mental illness on a family. After her father suffers a siege of serious depression and her mother returns to work, eleven-year-old Callie is given after-school responsibility for her younger brother. A friendship with Chinese-immigrant Nora, also a latchkey child, offers Callie a reprieve from home pressures, but their mischief leads to a crisis.

10.254 Withey, Barbara Hobbs. **The Serpent Ring.** Illustrated by the author. Dillon Press/Gemstone Books, 1988. Ages 10–13.

Before he dies, Jenny's father requests that she live with the mysterious Kesha Kropas, who also had been his guardian. Jenny is apprehensive, but she soon becomes curious enough about this unusual woman to make some important discoveries about her eventful past. Jenny also is instrumental in uniting Kesha with the grandson she has never heard of. The happy ending to this story will please middle-grade readers even though adults may find it a little too pat.

10.255 Wood, Marcia. **The Secret Life of Hilary Thorne.** Atheneum, 1988. Ages 9–11.

Hilary has read books since she was six and is able to invent book fantasies that include *her* in the story. Mole and Rat, Harriet the Spy, Merlin, and Tom Sawyer all are her friends, and at times they get in the way of making friends. When Hilary's family moves to a wonderful new house, it would be perfect except that her father, always her best friend, now spends all his time at work. During Hilary's adjustment to the situation, the reader has the treat of going on several book adventures with her. The bibliography of books Hilary has read is a real bonus.

Friendship

Primary

10.256 Caseley, Judith. **Molly Pink Goes Hiking.** Illustrated by the author. Greenwillow Books, 1985. Ages 6–8. (Picture book)

When Molly Pink and her family go hiking, Molly learns some important lessons about making friends. Her condescending attitude toward Robert, a shy, chubby boy encountered on the trail, is transformed by a heroic episode.

10.257 Eriksson, Eva. *"Victor and Rosalie"* in **Jealousy.** Illustrated by the author. Carolrhoda Books, 1985. Ages 5–7. (Picture book)

While Rosalie has the mumps, Victor makes friends with someone else. The characters involved in this threesome manage to reconcile their differences in an unusual and hilarious way. The succinct text is enhanced by black-and-white pen-and-ink drawings with dashes of yellow thrown in. The careful reader will note that the plot hinges on the word *pigtail* but that the illustrations show ponytails. This inconsistency may have arisen in translating the text into English from the original Swedish.

10.258 Greene, Carol. **The Jenny Summer.** Illustrated by Ellen Eagle. Harper and Row, 1988. Ages 7–9.

This sequel to *Robin Hill* details Robin's summer friendship with a new neighbor, Jenny. An impending divorce forces Jenny to live with her grandmother. Robin then resumes her friendship with Melissa, who was displaced when Jenny moved in. This is a good transition book, with one realistic drawing in each chapter.

10.259 Giff, Patricia Reilly. **Sunny-Side Up.** Illustrated by Blanche Sims. Dell/Yearling Books/Kids of the Polk Street School Series, 1986. Ages 6–10.

It is summer, time for fun! Right? Wrong, there's summer
school, and Beast's best friend, Matthew, is moving. The
boys have many adventures before Matthew has to leave, including trying to fry an egg on the sidewalk. Through it all,
Beast tries to remember to think of something good when
things are not going well.

10.260 Hughes, Shirley. **Moving Molly.** Illustrated by the author.
Lothrop, Lee and Shepard Books, 1988. Ages 5–8. (Picture
book)

Moving from a city apartment to a house with a yard and garden is exciting but lonely for Molly, the preschooler of the
family. Beautiful illustrations and a gentle text present the
warm concept of children on a quest for friends, a universal
experience in every family.

10.261 Komaiko, Leah. **Annie Bananie.** Illustrated by Laura Cornell. Harper and Row, 1987. Ages 5–7. (Picture book)

A friend who moves away is a sad event, but retelling stories
of the good times helps. In a funny, exaggerated rhyming
text, a special friendship is recalled with splashy illustrations
to match.

10.262 Rosner, Ruth. **Arabba Gah Zee, Marissa and Me!** Illustrated
by the author. Albert Whitman, 1987. Ages 5–7. (Picture
book)

Two friends engage in a variety of imaginative after-school
games. Bright, cheerful watercolors portray the playful energy that the text describes. The friendship of the two mothers
parallels that of their children.

10.263 Rylant, Cynthia. **All I See.** Illustrated by Peter Catalanotto.
Orchard Books/Richard Jackson Books, 1988. Ages 7–10.
(Picture book)

Understated prose and evocative double-page watercolors tell
the story of a shy boy's growing friendship with a lakeside
artist. This unique and memorable picture book, a perfect
union of the visual and literary arts, explores and celebrates
the creative potential in all of us. *Children's Choice.*

10.264 Tusa, Tricia. **Stay Away from the Junkyard!** Illustrated by the
author. Macmillan, 1988. Ages 6–9. (Picture book)

When Theodora moves to Jasper, Texas, she is warned by the small town shopkeepers to stay away from Old Man Crampton. Theodora discovers that he not only has treasure in his junkyard, is inventive, and loves children; he has never met the townspeople in the six months he has lived there. This is a jolly tale of an outgoing child who overcomes the small town's fears of someone new and who makes a new friend. Eccentric drawings further enliven the story.

10.265 Waber, Bernard. **Ira Says Goodbye.** Illustrated by the author. Houghton Mifflin, 1988. Ages 5–9.

Ira feels terrible when he learns that his friend Reggie is going to move away. Character development, although brief, is clear through Ira's first-person narration and through the repetitive and clever dialogue. The full-color cartoonlike illustrations reflect the boys' feelings and add to the humor of the book.

Intermediate

10.266 Blume, Judy. **Just as Long as We're Together.** Orchard Books, 1987. Ages 11–13.

Once again, with the use of an easily accessible first-person narrative, Judy Blume shows her characters through their thoughts and feelings—their reactions to typical, but important, events. A large portion of the author's skill lies in her ability to recognize which events would be important to her audience and why. Many readers will identify with circumstances of this story, which revolves around trials and tribulations in a friendship of three early adolescent girls coping with seventh grade, their families, and each other.

10.267 Christian, Mary Blount. **Growin' Pains.** Viking Penguin/Puffin Books, 1987. Ages 10–12.

Twelve-year-old Ginny wonders what is in her future. She wants more than just to live in a dirt-poor Texas town. Ginny develops a friendship with physically impaired Mr. Billy, and it is through this relationship that she gains a better understanding of herself, her mother's attitude, and, finally, her grandparents.

10.268 Gilson, Jamie. **Double Dog Dare.** Illustrated by Elise Primavera. Lothrop, Lee and Shepard Books, 1988. Ages 9–11.

In this fourth Hobie Hanson story, Hobie and his classmates are fifth graders continuing their humorous pranks. His friend Amber's learning disability is handled with dignity, helping readers accept individual talents and abilities. Jealousy, preteen peer-pressure concerns, and boy-girl relationships are handled with sensitivity and humor.

10.269 Gondosch, Linda. **Who's Afraid of Haggerty House?** Illustrated by Helen Cogancherry. E. P. Dutton/Lodestar Books, 1987. Ages 9–12.

This is a good story—told with verve and wit—about loneliness, about how appearances and misconceptions can keep people isolated, and about the ups and downs of friendship. It is the story of a young girl who befriends an old woman who lives in a haunted house while attempting to sell her Christmas cards. Without turning maudlin, Linda Gondosch illustrates how friendships can help us survive and triumph over some of life's trials. What is most endearing about this story is how she does it with often-hilarious humor.

10.270 Greene, Constance C. **Just Plain Al.** Viking Kestrel, 1986. Ages 10–14.

Al is growing up. At fourteen, she is still concerned about her appearance, clothes, and boys, but she is beginning to have room for concern about the world and her place in it. She and her friend Polly are also trying to cope with life in New York City. This book will be especially popular with readers who have followed Al's development in four earlier volumes.

10.271 Hall, Lynn. **Mrs. Portree's Pony.** Charles Scribner's Sons, 1986. Ages 10–12.

In this lovely story of a foster child who falls in love with a thirty-year-old pony and who begins a relationship with a lonely woman whose only daughter owned the pony, Addie fulfills her need to be loved for herself. Beautiful descriptions and strong characterization make this horse story a memorable reading experience.

10.272 Haven, Susan. **Maybe I'll Move to the Lost and Found.** G. P. Putnam's Sons, 1988. Ages 11–14.

The dual demands of friendship and family are explored using the lighthearted humor that has made books by Judy Blume and Paula Danziger so popular. Gilly Miles struggles with her new neighbor's flamboyance, her old friend's jealousy, her attraction to a boy, and her dislike for her divorced father's girlfriend, "Airhead." She comes to understand that while there are no easy answers, there are some pleasant surprises along the way.

10.273 Hines, Anna Grossnickle. **Cassie Bowen Takes Witch Lessons.** Illustrated by Gail Owens. E. P. Dutton, 1985. Ages 8–13.

Fourth-grader Cassie Bowen is horrified when she has to work on an important school project with Agatha, the very unpopular new girl in their class. However, Agatha proves worthy of the friendship, and despite the ridicule and jeering of Cassie's best friend, Cassie and Agatha work out well as a team. Cassie learns a hard lesson about choosing her own friends and deciding what is right and wrong for herself.

10.274 Holmes, Barbara Ware. **Charlotte the Starlet.** Illustrated by John Himmelman. Harper and Row, 1988. Ages 9–11.

In this sequel to *Charlotte Cheetham: Master of Disaster*, Charlotte channels her imagination into writing a book instead of telling lies. When she realizes she is writing junk to earn friendship, she decides to change her ways.

10.275 Keeton, Elizabeth B. **Second-Best Friend.** Atheneum, 1985. Ages 10–13.

Twelve-year-old Henrietta is desperate to be part of the in-crowd, but her outspoken aunt and hand-me-down wardrobe make her less than popular. When a lonely, awkward new girl offers Henrietta a dress for a special party, Henrietta is thrilled until she learns the dress is stolen and she is labeled a thief. Fully realized characters, a vivid setting, a sound story, and thematic richness make this a memorable and valuable book.

10.276 MacLachlan, Patricia. **The Facts and Fictions of Minna Pratt.** Harper and Row/Charlotte Zolotow Books, 1988. Ages 9–12.

For Minna Pratt, a young cellist in search of a vibrato, the weekly music lessons take on new meaning when Lucas completes the quartet. The progress they make in learning Mozart for a competition parallels the growing friendship between

Minna and Lucas. This book is so vivid and resonant with truths that the reader can easily imagine an independent life for its characters beyond the book's ending.

10.277 Radin, Ruth Yaffe. **Tac's Island.** Illustrated by Gail Owens. Macmillan, 1986. Ages 8–10.

Two unlikely companions—one a boy from a Pennsylvania suburb, the other a year-round islander—discover each other's worlds during a summer vacation on a Virginia coastal island. The theme of developing friendship, a quick pace, and frequent dialogue will appeal to reluctant readers.

10.278 Ruckman, Ivy. **This Is Your Captain Speaking.** Walker, 1987. Ages 10–12.

Tom Palmer spends his afternoons at a retirement home where his mother works, and befriends an old sea captain. Together they construct a model ship and discuss tales of the sea. This relationship is rewarding for Tom, whose father died of leukemia when he was four. Tom also misses his brother, a college athlete, although he feels inadequate in comparison. As narrator, Tom comes to terms with death, loss, and self-acceptance.

10.279 Singer, Marilyn. **Lizzie Silver of Sherwood Forest.** Illustrated by Miriam Nerlove. Harper and Row, 1986. Ages 9–11.

For Lizzie, it is difficult to decide when reality should be changed into dreams and when dreams can become reality. Plans on how to become one of Robin Hood's band at the Medieval Faire take up the part of Lizzie's life not devoted to learning to play the harp well enough to be accepted into music boarding school, just like her best friend, Tessa. Troubles abound because of Lizzie's obsession and determination to achieve both goals. Along the way, Lizzie learns about friendships, talents, and change.

10.280 Springstubb, Tricia. **Eunice (The Egg Salad) Gottlieb.** Delacorte Press, 1988. Ages 10–12.

Although published third (after *Which Way to the Nearest Wilderness* and *Eunice Gottlieb and the Unwhitewashed Truth about Life*), this is the first in a trilogy which follows two friends through the years from ten to twelve. Joy's aptitude for gymnastics puts a strain on the friendship because Eunice is a hopelessly inept gymnast and because she vehemently dislikes the rude new gym teacher. The simultaneous problems of her brother and sister are handled with sympathetic good humor, and the adults in the story have more substance than is usual in this genre. Students will want to read the entire series.

10.281 Wild, Elizabeth. **Along Came a Black Bird.** J. B. Lippincott, 1988. Ages 9–12.

Louise Berry has seen Beau Carney shoplifting, so she does not trust him. When his mother's illness causes him to live with Louise's family, his only friend at first is their pet bird, Crowberry. Louise and her sisters learn much about friendship, honesty, and courage in an eventful summer which changes their lives. This is a warm and involving story which should appeal to children who like to read about interesting people.

Humor

Primary

10.282 Brown, Ruth. **The Big Sneeze.** Illustrated by the author. Lothrop, Lee and Shepard Books, 1985. Ages 4–6. (Picture book)

Big, bold pictures enliven this story of the misadventures of the farmer and his animals when he sneezes. The illustrations are done in watercolor and with a humor the picture-book crowd will appreciate. This book will be excellent for reading aloud.

10.283 Himmelman, John. **The Talking Tree; or, Don't Believe *Everything* You Hear.** Illustrated by the author. Viking Kestrel, 1986. Ages 5–8. (Picture book)

When Skylar gets trapped inside an apple tree and calls for help, first one neighbor and then the whole town are convinced that the tree talks. Hilarious illustrations show the reactions of the increasing crowd of participants and Skylar, who begins to enjoy the situation.

10.284 Hurwitz, Johanna. **The Adventures of Ali Baba Bernstein.** Illustrated by Gail Owens. William Morrow, 1985. Ages 7–9.

When David Bernstein changes his name to Ali Baba, life becomes a series of adventures. Gently humorous episodes, filled with likable characters, lead readers through David's ninth year.

10.285 Marshall, James. **The Cut-Ups Cut Loose.** Illustrated by the author. Viking Kestrel, 1987. Ages 5–8. (Picture book)

Joe and Spud are real cutups, but their principal manages to cramp their style. Although the ending is anticlimactic, young readers will enjoy the story as well as the illustrations, which are done in watercolors and look like cartoons.

10.286 Steig, William. **Spinky Sulks.** Illustrated by the author. Farrar, Straus and Giroux/Michael di Capua Books, 1988. Ages 6–9.

Anyone who has ever felt sulky will appreciate Spinky. His sulk lasts for days despite the best efforts of his friends and family to cheer him. When he recovers, it is on his own terms. William Steig's witty illustrations tell us even more about Spinky and his "world-class" bad mood.

10.287 Zemke, Deborah. **The Way It Happened.** Illustrated by the author. Houghton Mifflin, 1988. Ages 4–8. (Picture book)

Sarah tells Bill about an accident she had on her bike. Somehow the message gets all mixed up, and soon another child is blamed for something that never happened!

Intermediate

10.288 Adler, David A. **Eaton Stanley and the Mind Control Experiment.** Illustrated by Joan Drescher. E. P. Dutton/Eaton Stanley Adventure Series, 1985. Ages 9–11.

Eaton Stanley intrigues his friend Brian Newman with his egghead ideas. However, Eaton's science project, a mind-control experiment, gets out of control. The mind he attempts to control is that of their sixth-grade teacher, Mrs. Bellzack. A clever plot and interesting characters are part of this comic story.

10.289 Birdseye, Tom. **I'm Going to Be Famous.** Holiday House, 1986. Ages 10–12.

Fifth-grader Arlo Moore is determined to beat the time listed in the *Guiness Book of World Records* for eating bananas (seventeen of them in less than two minutes). School friends practice breaking other records, and the whole school gets involved with betting. This is a fast-paced story with appeal for middle-grade children wanting a humorous story.

10.290 Byars, Betsy. **The Blossoms and the Green Phantom.** Illustrated by Jacqueline Rogers. Delacorte Press, 1987. Ages 10–12.

This is the third comic novel in the series of the Not-Just-Anybody-Family. Junior is making a balloon, Pap is stuck in a dumpster, and Maggie is learning to do acrobatic tricks. The book celebrates family love and humor. *ALA Notable Children's Book.*

10.291 Gondosch, Linda. **Who Needs a Bratty Brother?** Illustrated by Helen Cogancherry. E. P. Dutton/Lodestar Books, 1985. Ages 8–11.

Kelly's biggest problem is her brother, Ben-the-Brat. A mousetail bookmark and worms in her drinking cup convince Kelly that Ben has got to go! The author knows the things kids do that drive their siblings wild, and she has a good ear for the endless bickering that accompanies these actions.

10.292 Greenwald, Sheila. **Rosy Cole's Great American Guilt Club.** Illustrated by the author. Atlantic Monthly Press, 1985. Ages 8–10.

Rosy is concerned with the preteen preoccupations of having the right clothes and doing or saying the right things. Rosy's Great American Guilt Club idea is her plan to get the things she wants. When the idea folds, her parents help her realize that "being yourself" is most important. Sheila Greenwald's drawings add to the humor and understanding of the simply written text. Sequel to *Give Us a Great Big Smile, Rosy Cole.*

10.293 Herzig, Alison Cragin, and Jane Lawrence Mali. **The Ten-Speed Babysitter.** E. P. Dutton, 1987. Ages 10–14.

Fourteen-year-old Tony's summer job as a mother's helper turns out to involve much more responsibility than he bargained for, as his employer leaves him in charge of her active little boy, Duncan, while she vacations in the Caribbean for a weekend. How Tony copes with the many near-disasters that occur while he and Duncan are on their own makes hilarious reading, especially for reluctant older readers or when read aloud.

10.294 Hollands, Judith. **The Like Potion.** Atheneum, 1986. Ages 8–11.

Eleven-year-old Beverly Trapp's good friend Doris goes away for the summer, so Beverly goes to Play Days at her school every day. She and Jason are the only "regulars," and both love softball. They become good friends. But when school begins, Jason begins to follow snub-nosed, bratty Dina around. Beverly is hurt and bewildered. She and Doris mix up a potion they call a "like" potion, instead of a love potion, for Jason. By mistake, the practice teacher, Mr. Pinehurst, drinks it, with hilarious results.

10.295 Jones, Rebecca C. **Germy Blew It.** E. P. Dutton, 1987. Ages 9–12.

Jeremy Bluett, known to his friends as Germy Blew It, tries to organize a classroom strike to protest the cancellation of his school's field trips. But when Jeremy stays home from school, he misses a chance to be on television. Determined to get himself on TV, he organizes a bubblegum-blowing contest at his house. Complications creep in, and Jeremy blows his moment of glory. The book is filled with good humor, especially for middle-grade readers. *Children's Choice.*

10.296 Klein, Robin. **Hating Alison Ashley.** Viking Kestrel, 1987. Ages 10–12.

Erica Yurken, "Yuk" for short, is the smartest and most popular student in the sixth grade until a new girl, Alison Ashley, arrives. Alison challenges Yuk for her position as the "one genius," so Yuk plans revenge. Through a series of humorous misadventures, Yuk and Alison resolve their differences and grow up just a little bit, too. Yuk also comes to terms with her parents' divorce and her hated last name. *ALA Notable Children's Book.*

10.297 Kline, Suzy. **Herbie Jones and the Monster Ball.** Illustrated by Richard Williams. G. P. Putnam's Sons, 1988. Ages 7–11.

This book captures the dialogue and dilemmas of a third grader so accurately that even an adult reader grins through it.

Herbie Jones cannot get out of playing summer baseball, no matter how bad he is, because his uncle Dwight is the coach. This is only one of the problems that Herbie faces during vacation. Each short chapter finds Herbie in another funny situation as he works things out. A newly independent reader can be lured into longer books with this one.

10.298 Lowry, Lois. **Anastasia Has the Answers.** Houghton Mifflin, 1986. Ages 9–12.

Anastasia is thirteen and as indomitable as ever. An aspiring journalist, she keeps a notebook in which she practices writing about her concerns: friends, love, and life, with herself as the "who" of each story. These journal entries serve as introductions to each of the humorous chapters that make up an entertaining read-aloud book.

10.299 Lowry, Lois. **Anastasia on Her Own.** Houghton Mifflin, 1985. Ages 9–11.

Fifth in the series about Anastasia, this book begins on a seemingly sexist note, with Dad making up an organizational chart for an overly harried Mom, but the chart becomes the hilarious crux of the story as Anastasia tries to run the household during her mother's absence. The characters are adequately portrayed through dialogue and action. The humorous view of family life will prove fun reading.

10.300 Lowry, Lois. **Anastasia's Chosen Career.** Houghton Mifflin, 1987. Ages 10–12.

When Anastasia Krupnik is assigned to write a paper on her future career, she chooses to do her research at Studio Charmante, a modeling school. Anastasia hopes to learn self-confidence and to survive seventh grade. She eventually succeeds at both but not without some hilarious adventures along the way.

10.301 McMullan, Kate. **Great Advice from Lila Fenwick.** Illustrated by Diane deGroat. Dial Books for Young Readers, 1988. Ages 9–12.

Middle-grade students will enjoy the adventures of Lila and her friend Rita as they spend two weeks at a Boy Scout camp where Lila's father is volunteering as the camp doctor. This lighthearted book deals with important, though not critical, concerns of intermediate readers.

10.302 Naylor, Phyllis Reynolds. **Beetles, Lightly Toasted.** Atheneum, 1987. Ages 9–12.

Andy enters the fifth-grade essay contest and finds his imagination is stimulated to creative heights as he competes with his know-it-all cousin. Andy comes up with recipes using some unusual food sources, such as beetles, worms, and grubs, and tests them on unaware friends and family. An excellent companion to Thomas Rockwell's *How to Eat Fried Worms.*

10.303 Park, Barbara. **The Kid in the Red Jacket.** Alfred A. Knopf/ Borzoi Books, 1987. Ages 8–11.

After ten-year-old Howard Jeeter makes a very reluctant move from Arizona to Massachusetts, he is desperate for new friends. Despite her obvious adoration, six-year-old Molly is not his idea of the perfect pal. This humorous and realistic novel of adjustment and self-worth is sure to ring true with young readers. *Children's Choice.*

10.304 Peck, Robert Newton. **Soup on Fire.** Illustrated by Charles Robinson. Delacorte Press, 1987. Ages 8–12.

Children who have read any of Robert Newton Peck's previous books about Soup and Rob will enjoy their latest escapades. In this latest adventure, the two boys scheme to attract the attention of a Hollywood talent scout who is visiting their small Vermont town.

10.305 Peck, Robert Newton. **Soup on Ice.** Illustrated by Charles Robinson. Alfred A. Knopf/Borzoi Books, 1985. Ages 8–12.

Miss Kelly and Miss Boland promise a special surprise at the tree-lighting ceremony on Christmas Eve, but it is Rob and Soup who provide the biggest surprise of all. Readers will enjoy another humorous adventure of growing up in rural Vermont. Each chapter has black-and-white illustrations.

10.306 Roos, Stephen. **My Favorite Ghost.** Illustrated by Dee deRosa. Atheneum, 1988. Ages 10–12.

Derek Malloy needs to come up with a scheme to "get rich quick" when he loses his summer job, so he decides to capitalize on the legends concerning the ghost of Evangeline Coffin. He convinces his friends that he has seen the ghost, and he tries to charge them for a glimpse of her. When his friends discover his ruse, they plan a hilarious revenge. Fun for all.

10.307 Sachar, Louis. **There's a Boy in the Girls' Bathroom.** Alfred A. Knopf/Borzoi Books, 1987. Ages 9–12.

Bradley, the fifth-grade class outcast, learns to like himself and make friends, with the help of a new boy and the school counselor. This humorous story with such details of school life as birthday parties and homework and a catchy title will appeal to middle graders. *Children's Choice.*

10.308 Steiner, Barbara. **Oliver Dibbs to the Rescue!** Illustrated by Eileen Christelow. Macmillan, 1985. Ages 9–12.

Ten-year-old Ollie paints his dog with tiger stripes as the first in a series of sometimes-disastrous moneymaking ventures to raise funds on behalf of wildlife preservation. The book is funny and fast paced, with appealing, spirited illustrations. Ollie proves that in a good cause pluck and a kind heart are what matter.

10.309 Twohill, Maggie. **Bigmouth.** Bradbury Press, 1986. Ages 9–11.

Take one fifth-grade girl who talks too much and does not listen, and you have the beginning of a comedy of errors. Brinny Squill misunderstands a phone message from her father's boss, resulting in her family's making plans to transfer to London in a week. When the error is uncovered, Brinny almost stops talking, which her family and friends try to change. There is plenty of humor for those who see themselves like Brinny.

10.310 Wallace, Bill. **Ferret in the Bedroom, Lizards in the Fridge.** Holiday House, 1986. Ages 9 and up.

Liz's dad, a zoologist, turns their home into a refuge for such animals as a ferret named Fred, lizards that live in the refrigerator, and Bessie, the hawk with a broken wing. Liz's friends convince her that the animals will have to go if Liz hopes to be elected class president. Liz discovers, through a series of hilarious animal antics, the true meaning of friendship, both human and animal.

Mystery

Primary

10.311   Adler, David A. **Cam Jansen and the Mystery at the Monkey House.** Illustrated by Susanna Natti. Viking Kestrel, 1985. Ages 7–9.

Aided by her photographic memory, Cam, her friend Eric, and a new boy, Billy, set out to solve the mysterious disappearance of several monkeys from the zoo. Readers will develop powers of observation and logic as they sort through clues. This tenth adventure is one of a series popular with those wanting transitional books with short chapters and frequent illustrations.

10.312   Adler, David A. **The Fourth Floor Twins and the Fish Snitch Mystery.** Illustrated by Irene Trivas. Viking Kestrel/Fourth Floor Twins Series, 1985. Ages 7–9.

When two sets of apartment-house twins team up to trade jokes and solve mysteries, readers of easy mysteries are treated to short chapters with plenty of action, humor, and drawings. In this first book of the series, the twins set out to see who is stealing the early morning newspapers and observe their neighbors' nephew involved in some strange behavior. *Children's Choice.*

10.313   Adler, David A. **The Fourth Floor Twins and the Fortune Cookie Chase.** Illustrated by Irene Trivas. Viking Kestrel/ Fourth Floor Twins Series, 1985. Ages 7–9.

In the second volume of the series, the fourth-floor twins receive a message in a fortune cookie that warns them to beware of a man in a blue hat. As the story progresses, the twins capture petnappers who steal pets and later collect the reward money.

10.314   Adler, David A. **My Dog and the Birthday Mystery.** Illustrated by Dick Gackenbach. Holiday House/First Mystery Books, 1987. Ages 4–8.

Jenny and her dog are asked to help solve the mystery of Ken's missing bicycle. My Dog, as she calls him, helps her follow up all the clues, and he also follows all her friends. None of the friends remembers that it is her birthday. When they find the missing bicycle, they also find a big birthday surprise in this wonderfully original mystery for beginning readers. *Children's Choice.*

10.315 Adler, David A. **My Dog and the Green Sock Mystery.** Illustrated by Dick Gackenbach. Holiday House, 1986. Ages 6–8.

Can Jenny's rambunctious dog solve the mystery of her friend's missing things? With just enough clues to pull the reader in, the story keeps a lively pace to the end. Full-page color drawings are cartoonlike and funny in this easy-to-read mystery.

10.316 Maccarone, Grace. **The Haunting of Grade Three.** Illustrated by Kelly Oechsli. Scholastic/Lucky Star Books, 1987. Ages 7–9.

During the expansion of the Elmwood school, the third grade moves to temporary quarters in the old Blackwell Mansion. The students set out to prove that the mansion is haunted. This is a better-than-average mystery, although how third graders are allowed to roam around alone at night is never explained. *Children's Choice.*

10.317 Sharmat, Marjorie Weinman. **Nate the Great and the Fishy Prize.** Illustrated by Marc Simont. Coward-McCann, 1985. Ages 5–9.

The prize for the pet contest disappears just an hour before it is needed. Can Nate the Great and his dog Sludge find enough clues to lead them to the prize? Will Sludge win the contest for the smartest pet? How Nate works to unravel the case will keep young readers guessing until the end. This is another in a series of Nate the Great detective stories.

10.318 Sharmat, Marjorie Weinman. **Nate the Great Stalks Stupidweed.** Illustrated by Marc Simont. Coward-McCann, 1986. Ages 6–9.

Oliver the pest begs Nate to locate his missing Superweed when it disappears from a pot on Oliver's porch. Using determination and the companionship of his dog Sludge, Nate impressively accumulates clues in the neighborhood and resolves the problem. Black-and-white or color drawings are on most pages of this easy-to-read book. This is another in a series of Nate the Great detective stories. *Children's Choice.*

Intermediate

10.319 Brittain, Bill. **Who Knew There'd Be Ghosts?** Illustrated by Michele Chessare. Harper and Row, 1985. Ages 8–11.

Overheard conversations and a love for the old Parnell House lead Tommy, Harry, and Books into eerie encounters with two lively ghosts. The talking human head and the wet ring on the floor are only two of the mysteries revealed as the children try to save the house from an unscrupulous antique dealer.

10.320 Christian, Mary Blount. **Merger on the Orient Expressway.** Illustrated by Kathleen Collins Howell. E. P. Dutton/Determined Detectives Series, 1986. Ages 8–10.

The Determined Detectives, Fenton P. Smith and Gerald Grubbs, return to solve their second mystery, this one involving Fenton's mother both as a victim and suspect. White-collar crime is investigated when her company is regularly underbid by a rival construction company. Disguised as typewriter repairmen, the young sleuths discover that smuggled typewriter ribbons are the main evidence in this short, humorous mystery.

10.321 Christian, Mary Blount. **The Mysterious Case Case.** Illustrated by Ellen Eagle. E. P. Dutton/Determined Detectives Series, 1985. Ages 8–10.

The plot is hardly credible, but fledgling mystery buffs will enjoy seeing through the cases of mistaken identity. The rivalry between the Determined Detectives and their feisty nemesis Mae Donna Dockstadter adds a further lighthearted touch. The book is good fare for beginners and for those who enjoy series. Mary Blount Christian's books about Sebastian Super Sleuth are another recommended series.

10.322 Clifford, Eth. **Harvey's Marvelous Monkey Mystery.** Houghton Mifflin, 1987. Ages 8–11.

In this further adventure of Harvey and Nora (who appeared in *Harvey's Horrible Snake Disaster*), the cousins discover a monkey outside Harvey's house along with a man with "alligator eyes." The man mysteriously disappears while the monkey escapes up a tree outside Harvey's window. Hoping to keep the monkey as a pet, the children become involved in a mystery regarding the animal's owner and the identity of the strange man. Intrigue and humor with a lesson in accepting differences in others make this easily read book an enjoyable experience.

10.323 Cross, Gilbert B. **Mystery at Loon Lake.** Atheneum, 1986. Ages 10–12.

A mysterious tunnel in the cliff beyond the swamp intrigues three young people during their summer vacation. They begin with some research at the public library, which leads to a full investigation. Twists and turns in the story create life-threatening situations for these inexperienced detectives.

10.324 Curry, Jane Louise. **The Great Flood Mystery.** Margaret K. McElderry Books, 1985. Ages 9–11.

Unusual characters abound in this mystery based on the legend of some gold coins supposedly buried during the Johnstown Flood of 1889. Gordy and two other sleuths set out to unravel the mystery amid hidden clues, a villain in disguise, and help from Gordy's eccentric Great-Aunt Willi.

10.325 Deleon, Eric. **Pitch and Hasty Check It Out.** Orchard Books/ Richard Jackson Books, 1988. Ages 8–11.

Mystery fans who like fast-paced action and who are willing to go along with a plot that is slightly far-fetched will enjoy this book. Ten-year-old Pitch and his friend, Hasty, discover a parrot-smuggling operation based in the pet store at their local shopping mall. They stow away in a crate of parrots bound for the airport, where the book's eventful climax takes place.

10.326 Eisenberg, Lisa. **Mystery at Snowshoe Mountain Lodge.** Dial Books for Young Readers, 1987. Ages 10–14.

Kate Clancy's first ski trip brings friendship, mystery— and danger. This good-humored tale, told in a flip, breezy, first-person style, is undemanding fare for the mystery monger or reluctant reader.

10.327 Galbraith, Kathryn Osebold. **Something Suspicious.** Margaret K. McElderry Books, 1985. Ages 8–12.

Lizzie and Ivy liven up what could have been a ho-hum summer by tracking a suspicious character. They think he might possibly be the Green Pillowcase Bandit who robbed the bank in a neighboring town. He is, and there is excitement for all. A good mystery story for this age group.

10.328 Haas, Dorothy. **To Catch a Crook.** Clarion Books, 1988. Ages 8–11.

Dorothy Haas effectively mixes mystery and humor in this book featuring the intrepid Gabby O'Brien, a would-be detective. Gabby is trying to be a private eye for Career Day, but her investigations into the reasons behind a number of puzzling disappearances are unproductive until there is a sudden break in the case. The plot is ingenious, and the characters ring true.

10.329 Hahn, Mary Downing. **Wait Till Helen Comes: A Ghost Story.** Clarion Books, 1986. Ages 8–12.

When their mother remarries, Molly and Michael get a new stepsister and move to a converted church with a mysterious graveyard. A series of mysterious and terrifying events leads Michael and Molly to save their stepsister from the ghosts of her past.

10.330 Hildick, E. W. **The Case of the Muttering Mummy.** Illustrated by Blanche Sims. Macmillan/McGurk Mystery Series, 1986. Ages 9–11.

The McGurk Organization gets involved investigating a mystery in the local museum after Joey purchases a replica of an ancient Egyptian cat. Warned by an expert in the field about curses on such cats, McGurk gets suspicious and sets a trap. Fans of the series will enjoy the group's scientific deductions that enable them to solve the mystery.

10.331 Hildick, E. W. **The Case of the Wandering Weathervanes.** Illustrated by Denise Brunkus. Macmillan/McGurk Mysteries, 1988. Ages 9–11.

In this, the eighteenth book of the series, McGurk and his detectives set out to solve the case of the stolen weathervanes. Adults in the community help with their investigations, which involve the discovery that top-secret information is about to be smuggled to agents of another country. Students will learn thinking skills while reading for pleasure by using deductive reasoning to solve the case.

10.332 Howe, James. **What Eric Knew.** Atheneum/Sebastian Barth Mystery Series, 1985. Ages 10–12.

A young group of would-be detectives, under the direction of Sebastian Barth, solve not only one but two mysteries in the quiet little town of Penbroke, Connecticut. As in many mysteries, the usual notes, ghosts, and unexplainable happenings all materialize in this delightful story, the first in a series.

10.333 Hughes, Dean. **Nutty and the Case of the Mastermind Thief.** Atheneum, 1985. Ages 9–11.

In this second book about Freddie "Nutty" Nutsell, part of the school Christmas money collection is missing, and Nutty does not want others to know about it. He and his three best friends turn to an ex-classmate to help solve the puzzle, and they find themselves in hot water many times before discovering the real thief.

10.334 Kehret, Peg. **Deadly Stranger.** Dodd, Mead, 1987. Ages 9–11.

Newcomer Katie Osborne barely forms a friendship with classmate Shannon Lindstrom when Shannon is kidnapped. Katie can identify the kidnapper, and she finds herself being stalked by the stranger. Alternating chapters show the two girls' vantage points. Suspense builds as the stranger is revealed as a victim of mental illness. *Children's Choice.*

10.335 Klein, Robin. **People Might Hear You.** Viking Kestrel, 1987. Ages 11 and up.

Frances, who has spent her life moving from one rented flat to another, is excited about going to a real house to live. At first, Frances trustingly accepts her aunt's marriage to Mr. Tyrell and to the mysterious "temple," with its strange, fanatical beliefs. But as she uncovers the sinister secrets of the temple, she realizes she must escape.

10.336 Naylor, Phyllis Reynolds. **The Bodies in the Bessledorf Hotel.** Atheneum/Bernie Magruder Mystery Series, 1986. Ages 9–11.

While managing the Bessledorf Hotel, Bernie Magruder's father gets bad publicity when two dead bodies disappear from hotel rooms and a corpse from the next-door mortuary gets put in a room. Bernie intercepts a note from his mother's former boyfriend, who turns out to be the perpetrator of the hoax. An appealing comedy-mystery for middle graders.

10.337 Newman, Robert. **The Case of the Indian Curse.** Atheneum, 1986. Ages 10 and up.

Once again Andrew and Sara become involved in a Scotland Yard case, this time involving the mysterious illness of their friend Beasley, a statue of an Indian goddess, and a band of secret murderers. A well-developed plot, breakneck action, and an aura of the supernatural all contribute to an intriguing tale set in the 1890s.

10.338 Newman, Robert. **The Case of the Murdered Players.** Atheneum, 1985. Ages 11 and up.

Inspector Peter Wyatt of Scotland Yard is romantically linked to the well-known London actress, Verna Tillet, but his interest is complicated by the fact that a number of London actresses have recently been murdered. The actress's son, Andrew, and his friend Sara get involved when Verna appears to be the next target. Another in Newman's mystery series set in the 1890s and filled with colorful characters.

10.339 Petersen, P. J. **The Freshman Detective Blues.** Delacorte Press, 1987. Ages 10 and up.

The level of the lake has fallen, due to drought, making Eddie and Jack's trolling for discarded "treasures" an interesting pastime. When they discover a skeleton, they also uncover a dangerous secret that threatens their lives and that reveals secrets about those closest to them. A realistic blend of action and adolescent concerns, this book should interest those who like the novels of Jay Bennett or who enjoyed Willo Davis Roberts's *A View from the Cherry Tree.*

10.340 Roos, Kelley, and Stephen Roos. **The Incredible Cat Caper.** Illustrated by Katherine Coville. Dell/Yearling Books, 1986. Ages 8–11.

Twelve-year-old Jessie manages to smuggle her Siamese cat, Simba, into the Florida condominium where her mother and new stepfather live. Pets are not allowed, and her life is complicated by a "cat burglar" who is robbing apartments in the building. New friends help her solve the mystery and enable her to keep her cat.

10.341 Singer, Marilyn. **A Clue in Code.** Illustrated by Judy Glasser. Harper and Row/Sam and Dave Mystery Series, 1985. Ages 8–10.

Someone has stolen the money for the class trip from the teacher's locked cabinet. It is up to Sam and Dave Bean, twin detectives, to find the culprit. A tightly constructed plot shifts suspicion from one character to another throughout the story to the surprise ending. The moral, "You can't tell a book by its cover," is subtle.

10.342 Singer, Marilyn. **Where There's a Will, There's a Wag.** Illustrated by Andrew Glass. Henry Holt, 1986. Ages 9–12.

Samantha Spayed, an intelligent dog, and Philip Barlowe, her owner, are detectives on the trail of the lost second will of Carlotta Bucks. This is the third in a series involving snappy dialogue and a play on names that should tickle the funny bone. One character is Hugh Dunsay—get it?

10.343 Sobol, Donald J. **Encyclopedia Brown and the Case of the Mysterious Handprints.** Illustrated by Gail Owens. Bantam Books/Skylark Books, 1986. Ages 8–12.

Middle-grade mystery readers will enjoy matching wits with boy detective Encyclopedia Brown. Clues presented in each of ten new cases lead to solutions given correctly at the book's end. *Children's Choice.*

10.344 Vivelo, Jackie. **Beagle in Trouble: Super Sleuth II; Twelve Solve-It-Yourself Mysteries.** G. P. Putnam's Sons, 1986. Ages 8–12.

The familiar "Can you solve this case?" format is given an interesting and instructive twist here. Ellen, one of the book's super sleuths, uses a method of deductive logic that readers can apply to each of twelve mysteries. Sequel to *Super Sleuth.*

10.345 Vivelo, Jackie. **Super Sleuth: Twelve Solve-It-Yourself Mysteries.** G. P. Putnam's Sons, 1985. Ages 8–12.

Readers are invited to join twelve-year-old Ellen as she solves the local mysteries discovered by her boss and partner, Charles Beaghley. Clues are listed and a chart of the suspects is provided for each case, so that the reader can try to solve the mystery. Cases are tied together by the relationship of the two detective agency partners.

10.346   Wright, Betty Ren. **Christina's Ghost.** Holiday House, 1985. Ages 8–11.

Christina and her sister plan to spend their summer vacation with their grandmother, but when she becomes sick, the girls have to split up. Christina has no alternative but to stay with her grumpy bachelor uncle, Ralph, who has volunteered to house-sit a gloomy old house. Feeling sorry for herself, Christina decides to solve the mystery of the ghostly figure of a small boy who reappears mysteriously. Soon uncle and niece are caught up in a thirty-year-old murder mystery and nearly become victims themselves. *Children's Choice.*

New Immigrants

Primary

10.347   Harvey, Brett. **Immigrant Girl: Becky of Eldridge Street.** Illustrated by Deborah Kogan Ray. Holiday House, 1987. Ages 8–10.

The complex topic of immigration is explored as Becky, a Jewish immigrant from Russia, experiences growing up in New York City in 1910. Beautiful illustrations and a glossary of unfamiliar terms make this an essential reference for the study of immigration and its effects on individuals.

Intermediate

10.348   Gilson, Jamie. **Hello, My Name Is Scrambled Eggs.** Illustrated by John Wallner. Lothrop, Lee and Shepard Books, 1985. Ages 10–14.

Harvey Trumble takes his task of Americanizing Tuan seriously when the Nguyen family arrives from Vietnam. Both boys learn as their diverse customs and languages begin to merge. Prejudice surfaces as Quint tries to undermine Harvey's best intentions. The story has many humorous moments, as well as a serious side when Tuan relives the trauma of escaping from his homeland. This is a timely story of adjustment in a new culture.

10.349   Uchida, Yoshiko. **The Happiest Ending.** Margaret K. McElderry Books, 1985. Ages 9–12.

Outspoken twelve-year-old Rinko is determined to save Auntie Hata's daughter from marrying a stranger twice her age. As she plans how to save Teru from the arranged marriage, Rinko gains new insights into the meaning of love and the importance of friends within her Japanese community in California.

Social Issues

Primary

10.350 Stanek, Muriel. **All Alone after School.** Illustrated by Ruth Rosner. Albert Whitman, 1985. Ages 6–9. (Picture book)

Josh needs to stay alone after school while his mother works. He develops self-reliance and helps someone else in the same situation. The illustrations work well with this story of contemporary life.

10.351 Vigna, Judith. **Nobody Wants a Nuclear War.** Illustrated by the author. Albert Whitman, 1986. Ages 4–7.

Young children often have difficulty articulating their fears, especially about forces that even adults have difficulty understanding. Here is a realistic story that can be appreciated by every such child and every adult who tries to reassure children without creating false illusions about life in the nuclear age. *Jane Addams Award.*

Intermediate

10.352 Byars, Betsy. **Cracker Jackson.** Viking Kestrel, 1985. Ages 10–12.

Alma is the only one who calls him Cracker, so he knows who sent the anonymous warning, "Keep away, Cracker, or he'll hurt you." The note confirms his belief that Alma, his favorite baby-sitter, is being beaten by her husband. Domestic violence is handled realistically and sensitively, as Cracker Jackson tries to figure out a way to help Alma. The magnitude of Alma's problem is carefully unfolded as Cracker Jackson, his friend Goat, and, finally, his mother take steps to bring Alma and her baby to a safe place and a new life apart from her violent husband. *ALA Notable Children's Book, Children's Choice,* and *Notable Children's Trade Book in the Field of Social Studies.*

10.353 Doyle, Brian. **Angel Square.** Bradbury Press, 1986. Ages 9–14.

Blatant stereotypes become transformed into real individuals in a wildly unconventional novel concerning a staunch protagonist who matter-of-factly expects to fist-fight his daily way, simultaneously making war and keeping peace with Irish Catholics, French Canadians, and Jews alike. Tommy, a.k.a. "The Shadow," is equally dauntless in his quest for classmate Margot Lane's attention and in his pursuit of the person responsible for neighborhood anti-Semitic acts in this story set in Ottawa in 1945. Humorous, challenging, discussable.

10.354 Shreve, Susan. **Lucy Forever and Miss Rosetree, Shrinks.** Henry Holt, 1987. Ages 9–13.

Lucy and Rosie, best friends, have set up a basement psychiatric office, "Shrinks, Inc." where they imitate Lucy's father, a well-known child psychiatrist. One of his patients, Cinder, a victim of child abuse, appears at their door, and they become involved in her plight. A suspenseful thriller develops with memorable characters and a dramatic ending. *Edgar Allan Poe Award.*

10.355 Taylor, Mildred D. **The Gold Cadillac.** Illustrated by Michael Hays. Dial Books for Young Readers, 1987. Ages 9–11.

Although this is fiction, it is based upon the experiences of the author and her family. The mother of two black girls is angry at their father for trading in their two-year-old Mercury and spending the money they have saved for a new house on a Cadillac. But Mother says she will ride with Father when he decides to drive the car to the South. What follows is the family's harrowing and, for the girls, enlightening trip into the Deep South of the 1950s. This excellent retelling of an aspect of America's less-glorious past will be an appropriate adjunct to a unit dealing with social issues and minorities in the United States.

Sports

Primary

10.356 Christopher, Matt. **The Hit-Away Kid.** Illustrated by George Ulrich. Little, Brown/Springboard Books, 1988. Ages 6–8.

Barry McGee has learned to hit so well that he is the respected hit-away batter for the Peach Street Mudders. But Barry has more to learn about baseball than he realizes. He must decide whether it is more important to win or to play fairly. The short chapters, open typeface, and wide spacing between lines of text make this a successful first read-alone chapter book.

10.357 Kuskin, Karla. **The Dallas Titans Get Ready for Bed.** Illustrated by Marc Simont. Harper and Row/Charlotte Zolotow Books, 1986. Ages 5–8.

A buoyant text and three-color cartoon drawings follow a fictitious professional football team into the locker room for a fun and informative look at postgame victory celebrations and necessary rituals, including early bedtime. The illustrations reveal uniform and equipment details of interest to budding football players.

Intermediate

10.358 Brooks, Bruce. **The Moves Make the Man.** Harper and Row, 1984. Ages 11–13.

Jerome, "the Jayfox," crosses town as the only black student to integrate the biggest white school in Wilmington, North Carolina, and begins to teach Bix Rivers, the sharpest white athlete he has ever seen, how to play basketball. Child readers may well focus simply on the story's events: the basketball details, the encounter between the railroad men and Jerome over his lantern, the amazingly funny interchange in the home ec room over mock apple pie. But it is in Jerome's private reflections, his thinking things out, that Bruce Brooks demonstrates his writing talent so conclusively. This is the kind of work to which teachers should lead students who are interested in sports. *Boston Globe–Horn Book Award* and *Newbery Honor Book.*

10.359 Kelly, Jeffrey. **The Basement Baseball Club.** Houghton Mifflin, 1987. Ages 9–12.

Shooter Carroll, the narrator, and his pals of the McCarthy Roaders baseball team also play basement bowling and board games and try to recruit James Johnson, the new kid, for their baseball team. Instead, John's sister, Olive, joins the team and reveals why John mysteriously refuses to play. Slapstick humor abounds as this likeable group of bullies and heroes face up to their flaws and friendships in a fast-paced story. *Children's Choice.*

10.360 Van Leeuwen, Jean. **Benjy the Football Hero.** Illustrated by Gail Owens. Dial Books for Young Readers, 1985. Ages 8–10.

Fourth grade comes to life as Benjy, of *Benjy and the Power of Zingies*, leads his team toward a hard-fought victory in the Fourth Grade Super Bowl championship. Characters and incidents ring true. The humorous text is enhanced by Gail Owens's drawings.

10.361 Zirpoli, Jane. **Roots in the Outfield.** Houghton Mifflin, 1988. Ages 9–12.

Josh is the worst player on his baseball team and decides to get away for the summer. On his vacation in Wisconsin with his father and stepmother, he discovers a garage full of baseball memorabilia. This discovery leads to a mysterious turn of events. In solving the mystery, Josh solves some of the problems of growing up.

Stories Set in Other Countries

Primary

10.362 Bemelmans, Ludwig. **Madeline: A Pop-up Book Based on the Original by Ludwig Bemelmans.** Illustrated by the author. Viking Kestrel, 1987. Ages 5–8. (Picture book)

Based on the original color illustrations by Ludwig Bemelmans, this new pop-up book depicts a favorite classic in three-dimensional format. Children can open the windows of the old house in Paris and see the twelve little girls in two straight lines as they break their bread, brush their teeth, and go to bed.

10.363 Bonnici, Peter. **The Festival.** Illustrated by Lisa Kopper. Carolrhoda Books, 1985. Ages 5–9.

Arjuna goes through the rituals of manhood while joining in the festival in his Indian village. Well-chosen illustrations complement this read-aloud story.

10.364 Bonnici, Peter. **The First Rains.** Illustrated by Lisa Kopper. Carolrhoda Books, 1985. Ages 5–9.

Arjuna, a young Indian boy, waits for the first rain of the monsoon season to hit his village. New words are presented by the author for clarity. Illustrations complement this read-aloud story.

10.365 Green, Hannah. **In the City of Paris.** Illustrated by Tony Chen. Doubleday, 1985. Ages 6–9.

The airy cadences and wonderful illustrations of this story-poem combine to create a lilting answer to the question, Who *can* "come in" when there are no dogs allowed? The pictures truly make a captivating, imaginative adventure that manages at the same time to poke gentle fun at adult officialdom.

10.366 Lee, Jeanne M. **Bà-Năm.** Illustrated by the author. Henry Holt, 1987. Ages 6–8. (Picture book)

Keung and Nan go with their family to the graveyard to honor their ancestors on Thanh-minh day in Vietnam. They wander away from the family to climb trees and pick fruit and are frightened by Bà-Năm, the grave keeper. Later they are caught alone in a thunderstorm, and it is Bà-Năm who finds Keung and Nan and protects them from harm during the storm. The children return to their family the following morning with their newfound friend. The story is based on the author's own experiences growing up in Vietnam.

10.367 Lessac, Frané. **My Little Island.** Illustrated by the author. J. B. Lippincott, 1984. Ages 5–8. (Picture book)

A young boy travels with his best friend to visit the sunny Caribbean island where he was born. The island is vividly brought to life through brilliant paintings illustrating Caribbean wildlife, plants, people, and customs.

10.368 Montaufier, Poupa (translated by Tobi Tobias). **One Summer at Grandmother's House.** Illustrated by the author. Carolrhoda Books, 1985. Ages 5–7. (Picture book)

Exquisitely drawn, stylized watercolors in muted tones bring alive this quiet story of a little girl's annual visit to her grandmother's house in Alsace. Each page chronicles a separate adventure and custom of everyday life in this Alsatian village and can be read separately as very short chapters.

Intermediate

10.369 Bawden, Nina. **The Finding.** Lothrop, Lee and Shepard Books, 1985. Ages 9–12.

Mystery surrounds the beginnings of young Alex, the foundling who was rescued from the arms of the Sphinx along the Thames River in London. The mystery deepens when a lonely old lady dies and wills her fortune to Alex. Could she be his grandmother? The inheritance produces new problems that Alex tries to solve by running away to the City.

10.370 Berry, James. **A Thief in the Village, and Other Stories.** Orchard Books, 1987. Ages 8–12.

The cultural and geographical flavor of Jamaica is subtly portrayed through a series of short stories about the lives of the villagers and children of the banana and coconut plantations. Told using some of the rhythmic language patterns of the culture, the stories will enrich and enhance study of the area. *ALA Notable Children's Book* and *Coretta Scott King Honor Book* (for writing).

10.371 Fox, Paula. **Lily and the Lost Boy.** Orchard Books, 1987. Ages 10–14.

This loving depiction of the Greek island of Thasos, and of the relationship between Lily, her brother Paul, and the enigmatic Jack, is for readers who like to immerse themselves in the mood and atmosphere of a story, and who enjoy the ebb and flow of language in the hands of a master. Events are compelling, and the characters are finely drawn. Descriptions are lyrical, and the author shows a warm appreciation for the vagaries of human nature, but the questions left unanswered make the book tease the mind like an elusive melody.

10.372 Mohr, Nicholasa. **Going Home.** Dial Books for Young Readers, 1986. Ages 10–13.

Felita lives in New York City, but she has always dreamed of visiting Puerto Rico and her relatives who chose not to move to the United States. When she has the chance to spend the summer in San Juan, she eagerly plans for a chance to prove her independence. Once there, she experiences mixed emotions as her new friends do not readily accept her. Felita must learn to deal with their differences and grow up at the same time. *Notable Children's Trade Book in the Field of Social Studies.*

10.373 Naidoo, Beverley. **Journey to Jo'burg: A South African Story.** Illustrated by Eric Velasquez. J. B. Lippincott, 1985. Ages 10–12.

What is it like to be black in South Africa? Naledi and her nine-year-old brother, Tiro, find out when they brave the dangerous journey to Johannesburg, where Mma, their mother, works as a maid for a white family, so that they can bring her back to the village to care for their sick baby sister. In the city, Naledi and Tiro see the painful struggle for freedom and dignity. Upon returning to their village, Naledi realizes that the struggle is also hers, that she must work to actualize her dream to be a doctor. The book contains a map and a short glossary. *Notable Children's Trade Book in the Field of Social Studies.*

10.374 Nilsson, Ulf (translated by Lone Thygesen Blecher and George Blecher). **If You Didn't Have Me.** Illustrated by Eva Eriksson. Margaret K. McElderry Books, 1987. Ages 9–12.

This lively book spans one summer in the life of a young boy and his baby brother, who are sent to their grandparents' farm while their parents are building a new home. It is an excellent candidate for a serial read-aloud story, with its short chapters covering different episodes of farm life in Sweden. These episodes, ranging from the hilarious to the movingly serious, build to a surprisingly intense climax as the summer ends. *ALA Notable Children's Book* and *Mildred L. Batchelder Award.*

Recommended Books Published before 1985

Alexander, Martha. *When the New Baby Comes, I'm Moving Out.* Dial Press, 1979. 4–7.

Aliki. *The Two of Them.* Greenwillow Books, 1979. 4–7.

Babbitt, Natalie. *Goody Hall.* Farrar, Straus and Giroux, 1971. 9–11.

Baylor, Byrd. *Hawk, I'm Your Brother.* Illustrated by Peter Parnall. Charles Scribner's Sons, 1976. 7–9.

Bellairs, John. *The Treasure of Alpheus Winterborn.* Illustrated by Judith Gwyn Brown. Harcourt Brace Jovanovich, 1979. 8–11.

Bemelmans, Ludwig. *Madeline*. Viking Press, 1939. 4–8.

Blume, Judy. *Tales of a Fourth Grade Nothing*. Illustrated by Ray Doty. E. P. Dutton, 1972. 8–10.

Bond, Nancy. *Country of Broken Stone*. Atheneum, 1980. 10 and up.

Bonsall, Crosby. *The Case of the Hungry Stranger*. Harper and Row, 1963. 4–7.

Brown, Marc. *Arthur's Eyes*. Little, Brown, 1979. 4–7.

Burnford, Sheila. *The Incredible Journey*. Illustrated by Carl Burger. Little, Brown, 1961. 9 and up.

Butler, Beverly. *Light a Single Candle*. Dodd, Mead, 1962. 9 and up.

Byars, Betsy. *The Pinballs*. Harper and Row, 1977. 10 and up.

Cameron, Eleanor. *Room Made of Windows*. Atlantic Monthly Press, 1971. 12 and up.

Carrick, Carol. *The Accident*. Illustrations by Donald Carrick. Seabury Press, 1976. 7–9.

Cleary, Beverly. *Dear Mr. Henshaw*. Illustrations by Paul O. Zelinsky. William Morrow, 1983. 9–12.

———. *Ramona Forever*. Illustrations by Alan Tiegreen. William Morrow, 1984. 7–10.

———. *Ramona Quimby Age 8*. Illustrated by Alan Tiegreen. William Morrow, 1981. 8–10.

Cleaver, Vera, and Bill Cleaver. *Where the Lilies Bloom*. Illustrated by Jim Spanfeller. J. B. Lippincott, 1969. 10 and up.

Clifford, Eth. *The Rocking Chair Rebellion*. Houghton Mifflin, 1978. 10 and up.

Clifton, Lucille. *Amifika*. Illustrated by Thomas DiGrazia. E. P. Dutton, 1977. 4–7.

Corcoran, Barbara. *A Dance to Still Music*. Illustrated by Charles Robinson. Atheneum, 1974. 10 and up.

Cresswell, Helen. *Absolute Zero*. Macmillan, 1978. 10 and up.

Curry, Jane Louise. *The Bassumtyte Treasure*. Atheneum, 1978. 9 and up.

Danziger, Paula. *The Cat Ate My Gymsuit*. Delacorte Press, 1974. 10 and up.

dePaola, Tomie. *Nana Upstairs and Nana Downstairs*. G. P. Putnam's Sons, 1973. 6–8.

Douglass, Barbara. *Good as New*. Illustrated by Patience Brewster. Lothrop, Lee and Shepard Books, 1982. 4–7.

Duncan, Jane. *Brave Janet Reachfar*. Illustrated by Mairi Hedderwick. Seabury Press, 1975. 4–7.

Enright, Elizabeth. *Thimble Summer*. Holt, Rinehart and Winston, 1938. 9–11.

Estes, Eleanor. *The Moffats*. Illustrated by Louis Slobodkin. Harcourt, Brace and World, 1941. 9–11.

Farber, Norma. *How Does It Feel to Be Old?* Illustrated by Trina Schart Hyman. E. P. Dutton, 1979. 8–11.

Fitzgerald, John D. *The Great Brain*. Illustrated by Mercer Mayer. Dial Books for Young Children, 1967. 8–10.

Fitzhugh, Louise. *Harriet the Spy*. Harper and Row, 1964. 9–12.

Freeman, Don. *Mop Top*. Viking Press, 1955. 4–7.

Friedman, Ina R. *How My Parents Learned to Eat*. Illustrated by Allen Say. Houghton Mifflin, 1984. 5–8.

Garfield, James B. *Follow My Leader*. Illustrated by Robert Greiner. Viking Press, 1957. 9–12.

Gates, Doris. *Blue Willow*. Illustrated by Paul Lantz. Viking Press, 1940. 8–10.

George, Jean Craighead. *My Side of the Mountain*. E. P. Dutton, 1959. 9 and up.

Giff, Patricia Reilly. *Loretta P. Sweeney, Where Are You?* Illustrated by Anthony Kramer. Delacorte Press, 1983. 9–11.

Gilson, Jamie. *4B Goes Wild*. Illustrated by Linda Strauss Edwards. Lothrop, Lee and Shepard Books, 1983. 9–11.

Greene, Constance C. *Beat the Turtle Drum*. Illustrated by Donna Diamond. Viking Press, 1976. 10 and up.

———. *A Girl Called Al*. Illustrated by Byron Barton. Viking Press, 1969. 10 and up.

Greenwald, Sheila. *Give Us a Great Big Smile, Rosy Cole*. Little, Brown, 1981. 8–10.

Hamilton, Virginia. *The House of Dies Drear*. Illustrated by Eros Keith. Macmillan, 1968. 10 and up.

Hedderwick, Mairi. *Katie Morag Delivers the Mail*. Bodley Head, 1984. 4–7.

Heide, Florence Parry. *Growing Anyway Up*. J. B. Lippincott, 1976. 11 and up.

Henry, Marguerite. *Misty of Chincoteague*. Illustrated by Wesley Dennis. Rand McNally, 1947. 9–12.

Hinton, S. E. *The Outsiders*. Viking Press, 1967. 10 and up.

Hoban, Russell. *Bedtime for Frances*. Illustrated by Garth Williams. Harper and Row, 1960. 4–7.

Holman, Felice. *Slake's Limbo*. Charles Scribner's Sons, 1974. 11 and up.

Hughes, Shirley. *Alfie Gets in First*. Lothrop, Lee and Shepard Books, 1981. 5–8.

Hunter, Mollie. *A Sound of Chariots*. Harper and Row, 1972. 11 and up.

Hutchins, Pat. *The Mona Lisa Mystery*. Illustrated by Laurence Hutchins. Greenwillow Books, 1981. 7–9.

Irwin, Hadley. *The Lilith Summer*. Feminist Press, 1979. 10 and up.

Isadora, Rachel. *Max*. Macmillan, 1976. 7–9.

Keats, Ezra Jack. *The Snowy Day*. Viking Press, 1962. 3–6.

———. *Whistle for Willie*. Viking Press, 1964. 4–7.

Konigsburg, E. L. *From the Mixed-up Files of Mrs. Basil E. Frankweiler*. Atheneum, 1967. 9–12.

———. *Jennifer, Hecate, Macbeth, William McKinley and Me, Elizabeth*. Atheneum, 1967. 9–12.

L'Engle, Madeleine. *Meet the Austins*. Vanguard Press, 1960. 9–12.

Little, Jean. *Mine for Keeps*. Illustrated by Lewis Parker. Little, Brown, 1962. 9–12.

Livingston, Myra Cohn. *Will I Have a Friend?* Illustrated by Lillian Hoban. Macmillan, 1967. 4–7.

Lowry, Lois. *Anastasia Krupnik*. Houghton Mifflin, 1979. 9–12.

———. *A Summer to Die*. Illustrated by Jenni Oliver. Houghton Mifflin, 1977. 9–12.

McCloskey, Robert. *Blueberries for Sal*. Viking Press, 1948. 4–7.

———. *Make Way for Ducklings*. Viking Press, 1941. 4–8.

———. *One Morning in Maine*. Viking Press, 1952. 5–8.

———. *Time of Wonder*. Viking Press, 1957. 5–8.

Mathis, Sharon Bell. *The Hundred Penny Box*. Illustrated by Leo and Diane Dillon. Viking Press, 1975. 6–9.

Merrill, Jean. *The Pushcart War*. Harper and Row, 1964. 11–13.

Miles, Miska. *Annie and the Old One*. Illustrated by Peter Parnall. Little, Brown, 1971. 7–10.

Miller, Edna. *Mousekin's Close Call*. Prentice-Hall, 1978. 5–8.

Mowat, Farley. *Owls in the Family*. Illustrated by Robert Frankenberg. Little, Brown, 1961. 8 and up.

Ness, Evaline. *Same, Bangs and Moonshine*. Holt, Rinehart and Winston, 1966. 5–8.

Noble, Trinka Hakes. *The Day Jimmy's Boat Ate the Wash*. Illustrated by Steven Kellog. Dial Books for Young Readers, 1980. 6–9.

O'Dell, Scott. *Island of the Blue Dolphins*. Houghton Mifflin, 1960. 10 and up.

Paterson, Katherine. *Bridge to Terabithia*. Illustrated by Donna Diamond. Thomas Y. Crowell, 1977. 8–12.

Politi, Leo. *Song of the Swallows*. Charles Scribner's Sons, 1949. 5–8.

Raskin, Ellen. *Nothing Ever Happens on My Block*. Atheneum, 1966. 4–8.

———. *The Westing Game*. E. P. Dutton, 1978. 10–13.

Rey, H. A. *Curious George*. Houghton Mifflin, 1941. 4–7.

Roberts, Willo Davis. *The View from the Cherry Tree*. Atheneum, 1975. 10 and up.

Robertson, Keith. *Henry Reed, Inc.* Illustrated by Robert Mc-Closkey. Viking Press, 1958. 9–11.

Robinson, Veronica. *David in Silence*. Illustrated by Victor Ambrus. J. B. Lippincott, 1966. 9–11.

Rockwell, Thomas. *How to Eat Fried Worms*. Illustrated by Emily Arnold McCully. Franklin Watts, 1973. 8–10.

Shura, Mary Frances. *The Season of Silence*. Illustrated by Ruth Sanderson. Atheneum, 1976. 9–12.

Slote, Alfred. *Hang Tough, Paul Mather*. J. B. Lippincott, 1973. 9–12.

Smith, Doris Buchanan. *A Taste of Blackberries*. Illustrated by Charles Robinson. Thomas Y. Crowell, 1973. 8–11.

Snyder, Zilpha Keatley. *The Egypt Game*. Illustrated by Alton Raible. Atheneum, 1967. 9–12.

Sobol, Donald. *Encyclopedia Brown, Boy Detective*. Illustrated by Leonard Shortall. Bantam Books, 1978. 8–10.

Southall, Ivan. *Ash Road*. Greenwillow Books, 1965. 9–12.

Spier, Peter. *Bored—Nothing to Do*. Doubleday, 1978. 6–8.

Steptoe, John. *Daddy Is a Monster . . . Sometimes*. Harper and Row, 1980. 5–8.

———. *Stevie*. Harper and Row, 1969. 6–8.

Tobias, Tobi. *Jane, Wishing*. Illustrated by Trina Schart Hyman. Viking Press, 1977. 5–8.

Viorst, Judith. *Alexander and the Terrible, Horrible, No Good, Very Bad Day*. Illustrated by Ray Cruz. Atheneum, 1972. 6–9.

Ward, Lynd. *The Biggest Bear*. Houghton Mifflin, 1952. 4–8.

Williams, Barbara. *Jeremy Isn't Hungry*. Illustrated by Martha Alexander. E. P. Dutton, 1978. 5–8.

Williams, Vera B. *A Chair for My Mother*. Greenwillow Books, 1982. 4–7.

Wittman, Sally. *A Special Trade*. Illustrated by Karen Gundersheimer. Harper and Row, 1978. 4–7.

Yashima, Taro. *Crow Boy*. Viking Press, 1955. 6–12.

Zolotow, Charlotte. *It's Not Fair*. Illustrated by William Pène du Bois. Harper and Row, 1976. 4–7.

———. *My Grandson Lew*. Illustrated by William Pène du Bois. Harper and Row, 1974. 5–8.

———. *William's Doll*. Illustrated by William Pène du Bois. Harper and Row, 1972. 4–7.

11 Historical Fiction

Prehistoric Times

Primary

11.1 Brett, Jan. **The First Dog.** Illustrated by the author. Harcourt Brace Jovanovich, 1988. Ages 4–8. (Picture book)

As Kip, an Ice Age boy, makes his hazardous way back home to his cave, he meets a paleowolf which tags along. The animal is tamed by making a bargain with Kip: he will give Kip protection in exchange for rhino ribs, thus becoming the first dog. The illustrations show a compressed Ice Age landscape with glaciers, plains, and mountains teaming with the wildlife we know only through bones, stones, and cave paintings. This is a book to dream over as a reader imagines what those prehistoric times were like. It is, however, fiction and not to be regarded as science or history.

Intermediate

11.2 Turner, Ann. **Time of the Bison.** Illustrated by Beth Peck. Macmillan, 1987. Ages 8–11.

This story of eleven-year-old Scar Boy and his gift for making pictures would serve as a good introduction to the life of prehistoric people. Soft illustrations lend themselves well to the text. Children will wonder about Scar Boy's future, whether he will find acceptance as an artist, and about the secret of the caves. The book can be read aloud to younger children.

Early Civilization

Intermediate

11.3 Furlong, Monica. **Wise Child.** Alfred A. Knopf/Borzoi Books, 1987. Ages 10–12.

When Wise Child needs a home, no one will take her in but Juniper. Like the rest of the inhabitants of her remote Scottish village in this early Christian era, Wise Child distrusts the young woman's herbal skills and arcane learning. Before long she discovers Juniper's compassionate heart, but she fears that will not save Juniper from the fear-maddened folk who crave a scapegoat. *ALA Notable Children's Book.*

Medieval Times

Primary

11.4   Carrick, Donald. **Harald and the Great Stag.** Illustrated by the author. Clarion Books, 1988. Ages 6–9. (Picture book)

Young Harald, who lives in England during the Middle Ages, loves to hear the stories of the Baron's hunters, particularly of the Great Stag who has eluded them again and again. Harald inadvertently endangers the majestic stag and sets a courageous course to save him. Full-color watercolor illustrations capture the medieval setting and the serious mood of the story.

11.5   Goodall, John S. **The Story of a Main Street.** Illustrated by the author. Margaret K. McElderry Books, 1987. All ages. (Picture book)

This wordless picture history shows the ever-changing scene of an English town center from medieval times to the present. Beautiful watercolor paintings full of many details provide a truly remarkable view of social history in England.

11.6   Skurzynski, Gloria. **The Minstrel in the Tower.** Illustrated by Julek Heller. Random House/Stepping Stone Books, 1988. Ages 6–8.

It is the late twelfth century, and Alice and Roger are sent by their ailing mother to find her brother, Lord Raimond, and to ask his forgiveness. In spite of troubles encountered in the French countryside along the way, Alice finds Lord Raimond's fortress and convinces him that she is his long-lost niece. All ends well for Alice, Roger, their mother, and Lord Raimond, but a few twists add interest to the predictable ending. Short chapters, short sentences, and a controlled vocabulary make this a successful first chapter book.

Intermediate

11.7 Fleischman, Sid. **The Whipping Boy.** Illustrated by Peter Sis. Troll Associates/Troll Books, 1987. Ages 8–12.

The loathsome Prince Brat and his whipping boy, Jemmy, are caught up in a series of adventures and misadventures when the two run away from home and exchange identities for a while. The familiar plot devices of a prince-and-pauper tale are revitalized with tongue-in-cheek humor. Although Sid Fleischman uses a relatively simple vocabulary and simple sentence structure, the text is marked by eloquence, and numerous distinctive black-and-white drawings add to the richness of a fine, episodic novel. *ALA Notable Books for Children* and *Newbery Award*.

11.8 Lasker, Joe. **A Tournament of Knights.** Illustrated by the author. Thomas Y. Crowell, 1986. Ages 8–12.

In this story of life during the age of chivalry, Justin, son of a wealthy knight, competes in his first tournament. Tournaments are described and illustrated, as are weapons and clothes. Children interested in knights, armor, and medieval stories should find this book interesting. Included is a short glossary, as well as annotated pictures of weapons and clothing.

Fifteenth and Sixteenth Centuries

World

Intermediate

11.9 Hilgartner, Beth. **A Murder for Her Majesty.** Houghton Mifflin, 1986. Ages 11–12.

After eleven-year-old Alice Tuckfield witnesses the murder of her father, she decides to go to a friend of the family for help. But as she journeys to Chellisford Hill in England, a mishap occurs. Alice must disguise herself as a boy and take refuge in a boy's dormitory. Her determination, nerves of steel, and sense of humor allow her to live with the boys for a long period of time and also enable her to apprehend her father's killer. This is a good reading supplement for sixteenth-century English history. *Notable Children's Trade Book in the Field of Social Studies*.

Seventeenth and Eighteenth Centuries

United States

Intermediate

11.10 Rinaldi, Ann. **Time Enough for Drums.** Holiday House, 1986. Ages 9–12.

In this stirring book which portrays history accurately, Jemima Emerson grows from a rebellious child to a courageous young woman. Set in Trenton, New Jersey, between 1775 and 1781, during the American Revolution, Jemima's story tells how the war touched the lives of people surrounding her. Readers will catch Ann Rinaldi's enthusiasm for her topic. A bibliography is included.

11.11 Wisler, G. Clifton. **This New Land.** Walker/American History Series for Young People, 1987. Ages 9–12.

Ten-year-old Richard Woodley tells the story of crossing the ocean on the *Mayflower* and settling at Plymouth. The book is characterized by rich details that bring this historical account to life, making it a good supplementary book during a social studies unit on early America. A selected bibliography is included.

World

Primary

11.12 Brighton, Catherine. **Five Secrets in a Box.** Illustrated by the author. E. P. Dutton, 1987. Ages 4–7. (Picture book)

This picture book is a first-person account of how Galileo's eldest daughter, Virginia, amuses herself during the day while her father, who is up all night studying the stars, sleeps. The book is richly illustrated and accurately reproduces life in seventeenth-century Italy. It could be used for pleasure reading or as an adjunct to a science project.

11.13 Hort, Lenny. **The Boy Who Held Back the Sea.** Illustrated by Thomas Locker. Dial Books for Young Readers, 1987. Ages 4–8. (Picture book)

The popular Dutch tale of Hans Brinker and his silver skates is revitalized by luminous paintings, which show the influence of such masters as Rembrandt and Vermeer and which seem to glow from within. The simple story of a boy's courage is made unforgettable by such consummate artistry.

Intermediate

11.14 Calvert, Patricia. **Hadder MacColl.** Viking Penguin/Puffin Books, 1986. Ages 10–13.

Determined to uphold her country's and her family's honor and confused by her beloved brother's rejection of violent means, fourteen-year-old Hadder MacColl disguises herself as a boy and joins the fight to return Bonnie Prince Charlie to the throne in eighteenth-century Scotland. A series of tragedies forces the young warrior to confront her own values in this fast-paced, richly textured look at the contrasting desires for war and peace in society and in human nature.

11.15 Marko, Katherine McGlade. **Away to Fundy Bay.** Walker/ American History Series for Young People, 1985. Ages 10–12.

Caught up in the unrest prior to the American Revolution, Doone Ramsey realizes that he must leave his home in Halifax or be punished for siding with the rebels. His mother and sister work for his Tory uncle, and Doone longs to bring them to a home of their own. He seeks refuge and work in Fundy Bay while he tries to help his family. Strange happenings there convince Doone that all is not well with his mother and sister, and that there is a spy who may be endangering all of them. Is his friend Jake a true friend or an adversary?

Nineteenth Century

United States

Primary

11.16 Goble, Paul. **Death of the Iron Horse.** Illustrated by the author. Bradbury Press, 1987. Ages 5–9. (Picture book)

Cheyenne braves derail and raid a freight train in an act of defiance against white settlers who are encroaching on their land in the 1860s. This story, based on an actual Cheyenne attack on a steam train, is related from the Native American point of view. Flat, vibrant illustrations add authenticity.

11.17   Harvey, Brett. **My Prairie Year: Based on the Diary of Ele-nore Plaisted.** Illustrated by Deborah Kogan Ray. Holiday House, 1986. Ages 7–9.

A young girl narrates her experiences with her family on the frontier prairie of the Dakota Territory. She describes the weekly routine of work and, less often, play and tells how this is affected by the changing of the seasons. The simple narration describes an isolated life of hard work and simple pleasures. Pencil sketches are a perfect match for the text.

11.18   Hiser, Berniece T. **The Adventure of Charlie and His Wheat-Straw Hat: A Memorat.** Illustrated by Mary Szilagyi. Dodd, Mead, 1986. Ages 5–7. (Picture book)

Based on a story told by the author's great-grandfather, this is a warm and humorous story of Appalachia at the time of the Civil War. Charlie goes to a lot of trouble to have a hat, and even more trouble to keep it. The illustrations, in crayon and acrylics, greatly complement the story. The book repro-duces the dialect spoken by the English, Scottish, and Irish settlers in eastern Kentucky. A fine introduction to an aspect of American history. *Children's Choice.*

11.19   Hoguet, Susan Ramsay. **Solomon Grundy.** Illustrated by the author. E. P. Dutton, 1986. Ages 7–9.

Susan Ramsay Hoguet uses this Mother Goose verse to give her readers a glimpse of American history and social life. Her version of Solomon Grundy is the child of English immigrants and becomes a baker in Connecticut. Full-page illustrations provide information about clothing, transportation, architec-ture, and historic events in the nineteenth century. Children will be fascinated by the details in the illustrations. The book contains a historical note at the end.

11.20   Hooks, William H. **Pioneer Cat.** Illustrated by Charles Robin-son. Random House/Stepping Stone Books, 1988. Ages 6–8.

Katie leaves behind a best friend when she and her family begin their move from Missouri to Oregon as part of a wagon train. She finds another best friend in the spunky Rosie. To-gether they face the dangers and excitement of the trip and work together to keep Katie's cat, Snuggs, a secret from the family and others. Short sentences and the controlled vocabu-lary make this an easy first chapter book.

11.21   Johnston, Tony. **Yonder.** Illustrated by Lloyd Bloom. Dial Books for Young Readers, 1988. Ages 4–8. (Picture book)

The illustrations, intense with the colors of the natural world, portray the rural lives and the passage of time. Somewhere, over yonder, in a place that could be any place, a family grows and changes as the seasons change. The gentle, spare text heightens the reader's emotional response.

11.22   Lent, Blair. **Bayberry Bluff.** Illustrated by the author. Houghton Mifflin, 1987. Ages 6–9. (Picture book)

The illustrations, made as cardboard cutouts, highlight this story of an island that grew from a place where people tented on summer holiday to a village where people live year round in elaborately decorated homes. Blair Lent based the story on the real village of Oak Bluff on Martha's Vineyard.

11.23   Nixon, Joan Lowery. **Beats Me, Claude.** Illustrated by Tracey Campbell Pearson. Viking Kestrel, 1986. Ages 5–9. (Picture book)

Claude would be pleased if Shirley would bake him an apple pie, but Shirley's pies are better suited for capturing crooks and con men than for eating. This book is well designed for children just beginning to read chapter books. Three short chapters and the lively illustrations break up the print into nonintimidating blocks. This humorous book is good for reading (and laughing) out loud.

11.24   Nixon, Joan Lowery. **Fat Chance, Claude.** Illustrated by Tracey Campbell Pearson. Viking Kestrel, 1987. Ages 6–9. (Picture book)

The hero and heroine of *If You Say So, Claude* and *Beats Me, Claude* are back again in a prequel that tells the story of their childhoods and their courtship. Shirley had a mind of her own from the start, and Claude, who brought up his two brothers, joins up with Shirley's wagon in the trip to Colorado for gold. Told with the flavor of a tall tale, and illustrated with full-color artwork, this zesty story will captivate youngsters.

11.25   Roop, Peter, and Connie Roop. **Keep the Lights Burning, Abbie.** Illustrated by Peter E. Hanson. Carolrhoda Books/On My Own Books, 1985. Ages 5–11. (Picture book)

Abbie Burgess is one of the brave lighthouse keepers of U.S. history. In 1856, young Abbie assumed responsibility for a lighthouse off the Maine coast during a storm that kept her father away and while illness prevented her mother from maintaining the lamps. The tension and excitement of this actual event are well handled in the short fictionalized account. Each page is illustrated with watercolor paintings, and a historical note precedes the text.

11.26 Steiner, Barbara. **Whale Brother.** Illustrated by Gretchen Will Mayo. Walker, 1988. Ages 6–10. (Picture book)

Omu, an Inuit boy, longs to be a master carver. Yet the tiny animals he creates from ivory lack life. Not till he spends days alone, nursing a dying killer whale, does he learn the secret of patience needed to make his carvings come alive. Illustrations rich in color and contrast depict the ocean setting and Omu's friends, the whales.

11.27 Turner, Ann. **Dakota Dugout.** Illustrated by Ronald Himler. Macmillan, 1985. Ages 4–10. (Picture book)

A narrative told by a grandmother explains what it was like to live in a sod house on the Dakota plains. The drawings are simple but convey much feeling. The poetic text combines with these drawings to portray life on the prairie. *ALA Notable Children's Book.*

11.28 Turner, Ann. **Nettie's Trip South.** Illustrated by Ronald Himler. Macmillan, 1987. Ages 7–10.

In this story based on the real diary of the author's great-grandmother, Nettie travels from Albany, New York, to Virginia and experiences firsthand the treatment of blacks in the pre–Civil War South. Illustrations bring to life the message that "If we slipped into a Black skin like a tight coat, everything would change."

11.29 Whelan, Gloria. **Next Spring an Oriole.** Illustrated by Pamela Johnson. Random House/Stepping Stone Books, 1987. Ages 8–10.

This book could easily serve as an introduction to Laura Ingalls Wilder's Little House books. When Libby and her parents travel by covered wagon to the Michigan frontier in the

1830s, she has many new, realistically presented experiences, she becomes friends with a small Native American girl, and she learns about the true meaning of sharing.

11.30   Winter, Jeanette. **Follow the Drinking Gourd.** Illustrated by the author. Alfred A. Knopf/Borzoi Books, 1988. Ages 5–10. (Picture book)

"Follow the drinking gourd" is the refrain to a song that was sung by slaves in the United States before the Civil War. Hidden in the lyrics to the song were the directions to the escape route north to freedom. The "drinking gourd," for example, was the Big Dipper, which points to the North Star. This book weaves together the song lyrics with the story of an escape on the Underground Railway. The glowing illustrations echo the rhythm and drama of the song in the style of American folk art.

Intermediate

11.31   Angell, Judie. **One-way to Ansonia.** Bradbury Press, 1985. Ages 9–13.

Ten-year-old Rose and her four brothers and sisters have just emigrated from Russia to the United States. During the next six years, each family member learns to cope with the realities of ghetto life in New York City's Lower East Side in the late 1890s. Rose, determined to be master of her own life, overrides her father's choice of a husband and chooses her own. After her son is born, Rose takes her life's savings and sets out to build a better life for her small family—away from the troubles of the city.

11.32   Beatty, Patricia. **The Coach That Never Came.** William Morrow, 1985. Ages 10 and up.

Here is a peppy adventure story with a good dollop of mystery and intrigue thrown in. That the mystery is 110 years old and based on an actual historical event in the American Old West both enhances the story and reveals that history (and historical research) need not be dull. Thirteen-year-old Paul Braun gets involved with the mystery while visiting his grandmother in Colorado. She gives him a jeweled belt buckle once owned by a distant relative. As Paul tries to discover more about this relative, he learns of the still-unsolved disappearance of a stage coach and its cargo of gold. The story involves a developing friendship between Paul and a Native American boy and, without preaching, sets a small part of our history right.

11.33   Bohner, Charles. **Bold Journey: West with Lewis and Clark.** Houghton Mifflin, 1985. Ages 12 and up.

Charles Bohner brings to life the expedition of Lewis and Clark as they search for a northwest passage to the Pacific in the early 1800s. In the novel, Private Hugh McNeal relates his role in the journey and captures the spirit of this remarkable expedition. *Notable Children's Trade Book in the Field of Social Studies.*

11.34   Brown, Drollene P. **Sybil Rides for Independence.** Illustrated by Margot Apple. Albert Whitman, 1985. Ages 7–12. (Picture book)

On April 26, 1777, Colonel Ludington sends his sixteen-year-old daughter, Sybil, on a dangerous night ride to warn the minutemen of the British attack on Danbury, Connecticut. A four-page historical overview of the Revolutionary War is found at the end of the book, but more documentation of historical information would make this a stronger research resource. Few words per page and illustrations on most pages make this easy-to-read book accessible for older, less skilled readers.

11.35   Carrick, Carol. **Stay Away from Simon!** Illustrated by Donald Carrick. Clarion Books, 1985. Ages 8–12.

This story, set in Massachusetts in the 1830s, portrays a view of the feelings about handicapped people during that era. Lucy is told to stay away from Simon, who is mentally disabled. Then one snowy evening Simon, Lucy, and her brother Josiah learn about tolerance and believing in each other and in oneself. This well-written book presents a lesson to youngsters that can stand to be repeated many times over. Well-done black-and-white drawings grace the story. *ALA Notable Children's Book.*

11.36   Conrad, Pam. **Prairie Songs.** Illustrated by Darryl S. Zudeck. Harper and Row, 1985. Ages 10–12.

The solitude and loneliness of life on the Nebraska prairie during the early part of the westward movement is portrayed in this book. The stark living conditions of Louisa and her family are realistically yet sympathetically depicted. The arrival of a doctor and his beautiful but frail wife brings some changes to Louisa's life. *IRA Children's Book Award* and *Notable Children's Trade Book in the Field of Social Studies.*

11.37 Donahue, Marilyn Cram. **Straight along a Crooked Road.** Walker/American History Series for Young People, 1985. Ages 10–12.

This absorbing story of a family's long trek from Vermont to California, part of it along the Oregon Trail, is set during the westward expansion of the United States between 1850 and 1853. Because the reader rapidly cares about the characters, and because the book reinforces many traditional stereotypes, it could make an intriguing instrument for stimulating class discussions about differing views regarding social realities in nineteenth-century America.

11.38 Donahue, Marilyn Cram. **The Valley in Between.** Walker, 1987. Ages 10–13.

In this sequel to *Straight along a Crooked Road*, Emmie, now thirteen, lives in the San Bernardino Valley of California in the 1850s. Can she come to understand her aunt, and what will she do about Tad? The book contains a bibliography, index, map, and a chronology of important dates in the history of the middle 1800s in California. Many of these historical events, such as the discovery of gold, are mentioned in the novel.

11.39 Hansen, Joyce. **Out from This Place.** Walker/American History Series for Young People, 1988. Ages 10–14.

In this sequel to *Which Way Freedom?* (no. 11.40), fourteen-year-old Easter rescues young Jason and returns to the coastal islands, still hoping to find Obi. After the end of the Civil War, Easter decides to attend school in Philadelphia to become a teacher. Obi continues to look for Easter and Jason.

11.40 Hansen, Joyce. **Which Way Freedom?** Walker/American History Series for Young People, 1986. Ages 10–14.

Obi, one of three slave children on a plantation, makes his way to the coast and joins a black regiment of the Union Army in 1864. Soon he is involved in the massacre at Fort Pillow, Tennessee, and is one of the few survivors. He is determined to return to the plantation and rescue the other two children. *Coretta Scott King Honor Book* (for writing) and *Notable Children's Trade Book in the Field of Social Studies.*

11.41   Harvey, Brett. **Cassie's Journey: Going West in the 1860s.** Illustrated by Deborah Kogan Ray. Holiday House, 1988. Ages 8–10. (Picture book)

Based on actual accounts of wagon trips, the story describes, in Cassie's words, the trip that she and her family take from Illinois to California. The bleak, soft-pencil illustrations are just right for the diary style of prose that tells of the dramatic journey. A map is included.

11.42   Hilts, Len. **Timmy O'Dowd and the Big Ditch: A Story of the Glory Days on the Old Erie Canal.** Harcourt Brace Jovanovich/Gulliver Books, 1988. Ages 9–12.

Len Hilts presents a fascinating picture of life along the Erie Canal in the 1840s. Although this is a work of fiction, the author weaves historical details into this account of the O'Dowd family and the challenges they face when the Erie Canal is damaged by storms. This would be a good supplementary book during a social studies unit on the Erie Canal. A glossary, bibliography, and recommended reading list are included.

11.43   Howard, Ellen. **Edith Herself.** Illustrated by Ronald Himler. Atheneum/Jean Karl Books, 1987. Ages 10–12.

When Edith's mother dies, Edith is sent to live with an older married sister. Edith's problems of adjusting to her new, strict home are further hampered when she begins having epileptic seizures, or "fits," as they were commonly known in the late 1800s. In learning to live with her disease, Edith also learns to live with her new family.

11.44   Josephs, Anna Catherine. **Mountain Boy.** Illustrated by Bill Ersland. Raintree Publishers/Carnival Press Books, 1985. Ages 9–12.

This fictionalized account is based on the true adventures of a young Southern boy who helped a group of escaped Union prisoners elude the Confederate soldiers in the mountains of North Carolina and reach freedom during the Civil War. The colorful illustrations support this portrayal of the dilemma of a young boy torn between two loves. *Children's Choice.*

11.45 Lawlow, Laurie. **Addie across the Prairie.** Illustrated by Gail Owens. Albert Whitman, 1986. Ages 9–11.

Addie unhappily accompanies her family to their new home in the Dakota Territory. She is reluctant at first to make any adjustments to her new life, but her attitude gradually changes as she develops relationships with many supportive people.

11.46 Luenn, Nancy. **Arctic Unicorn.** Atheneum/Argo Books, 1986. Ages 10–12.

Thirteen-year-old Kala, who lives in a small Eskimo village on Baffin Island, discovers that she has been gifted with the power to become a shaman. She resists because she wants only a life like that of her friends. But even as she resists the power, she is drawn closer to accepting it so that she can save the seals and, ultimately, her people.

11.47 McCall, Edith. **Message from the Mountains.** Walker/American History Series for Young People, 1985. Ages 9–12.

Starting with a little-known fact of Kit Carson's life, this fictionalized version of one summer in the life of Carson and his friend Jim Mathews paints a realistic portrayal of life on the Western frontier in Missouri during the 1800s. The book can be used for drawing implications about responsibility.

11.48 Rappaport, Doreen. **Trouble at the Mines.** Illustrated by Joan Sandin. Thomas Y. Crowell, 1987. Ages 10–12.

This historical fiction portrays a family's struggle to survive during a mining strike in Pennsylvania in the late 1890s. Mother Jones arrives to support the strikers and their families. The brief descriptions and brisk invented dialogue of Mother Jones and the members of the Wilson family move the plot quickly. The typeface is large and generously spaced. Black-and-white drawings punctuate each chapter.

11.49   Wallace, Bill. **Red Dog.** Holiday House, 1987. Ages 9–12.

In an isolated valley in the Wyoming Territory in the 1860s, twelve-year-old Adam depends on his red-haired dog, Ruff, for consolation in adjusting to his new stepfather, Sam. When Sam goes to file a gold claim, gold speculators hold the family hostage. Adam's escape is filled with heroic action and shows people and animals working together. A well-paced portrayal of life on the western frontier.

World

Primary

11.50   Alderson, Sue Ann. **Ida and the Wool Smugglers.** Illustrated by Ann Blades. Margaret K. McElderry Books, 1988. Ages 6–9. (Picture book)

In a story set in frontier Canada, little Ida is to take bread to neighbors who have just had a new baby. She is warned by her mother to stay in the meadow to avoid smugglers who are stealing the sheep. When Ida hears the smugglers, she cleverly herds her pet lamb and the twin baby lambs to the neighbors. Children will relate to this "growing-up" story. Watercolor illustrations provide a happy look at the early days in Canada.

Intermediate

11.51   Alexander, Lloyd. **The Drackenberg Adventure.** E. P. Dutton, 1988. Ages 10–13.

Vesper Holly, the extraordinary heroine and adventurer, travels to the obscure European territory of Drackenberg with her guardians, Brinnie and Mary. There they encounter archenemy Dr. Helvitius. But with finesse, Vesper makes her way through the complexities of the politics and mystery of Drackenberg and solves the problems satisfactorily. Lloyd Alexander's style and great adventure make this an enjoyable book to read. Sequel to *The Illyrian Adventure* and *The El Dorado Adventure.*

11.52   Alexander, Lloyd. **The El Dorado Adventure.** E. P. Dutton, 1987. Ages 10–13.

Vesper Holly travels to the Central American republic of El Dorado to inspect her estate holdings. She works feverishly to foil the canal-building scheme of dastardly Dr. Helvitius and save the homeland of the Chirica tribe.

11.53 Garfield, Leon. **The December Rose.** Viking Kestrel, 1987. Ages 10–14.

Victorian London comes alive as the canny chimney sweep's boy, Barnacle, is pursued by relentless Inspector Creaker. The small, indomitable urchin, accidently involved in murder, finds firm friends in bargeman Tom Gosling and the McDippers, but author Leon Garfield keeps the reader in suspense and well aware of the harshness of life in perilous times.

11.54 Law, Felicia. **Darwin and the Voyage of the Beagle.** Illustrated by Judy Brook. André Deutsch, 1985. Ages 9–12. (Picture book)

Charles Darwin's five-year exploratory journey aboard the ship *Beagle* is presented in this fictionalized account featuring Darwin and the purely fictional Ben Sweet, a cabin boy. Lively narration, an oversized format, and numerous pen-and-ink maps and nature drawings will attract the reluctant science and history student, while offering enough solid information to please the serious biology buff. The book is a natural model and inspiration for journal writing.

Twentieth Century

United States

Primary

11.55 Bragg, Michael. **Betty's Wedding: A Photograph Album of My Big Sister's Wedding.** Illustrated by the author. Macmillan, 1988. Ages 4–9. (Picture book)

The hand-lettered text and nostalgic paintings of photographs combine to produce a 1920s photograph album of the six months of preparation for an older sister's wedding. Included are making and fitting the dresses, buying parcels, and baking the cake.

11.56   Hartley, Deborah. **Up North in Winter.** Illustrated by Lydia
Dabcovich. E. P. Dutton, 1986. Ages 4–9. (Picture book)

As Dad tells the story, it was a fox that saved Grandpa's life
as he trudged miles across a frozen lake one cold winter night
long ago. Softly shaded illustrations add warmth to this
nostalgic family tale.

11.57   Hendershot, Judith. **In Coal Country.** Illustrated by Thomas
B. Allen. Alfred A. Knopf/Borzoi Books, 1987. Ages 6–9.

A young girl observes the details of daily life in an Ohio coal-
mining town. The sparse text evokes the elegance and agony,
and the joys and pains of the family's life. The richly textured
pastel illustrations and colored paper punctuate the emotional
vignettes.

11.58   Howard, Elizabeth Fitzgerald. **The Train to Lulu's.** Illustrated
by Robert Casilla. Bradbury Press, 1988. Ages 5–9. (Picture
book)

Bright watercolor paintings accompany this story of two
young sisters who make the nine-hour train trip alone from
Boston to Baltimore during the late 1930s in order to stay
with their great-aunt Lulu for the summer. Their adventures
en route make for an exciting story.

11.59   Levinson, Riki. **Dinnie Abbie Sister-r-r!** Illustrated by Helen
Cogancherry. Bradbury Press, 1987. Ages 7–9.

This is a gentle picture of a loving Jewish family in Brooklyn
during the 1930s as seen through the eyes of five-year-old
Jennie. Episodic chapters, simple narration, and softly
shaded drawings introduce middle-grade readers to the pleasures of a simpler time—dancing in the rain, baking cookies,
sledding, and train rides.

11.60   Levinson, Riki. **I Go with My Family to Grandma's.** Illustrated by Diane Goode. E. P. Dutton, 1986. Ages 4–8. (Picture book)

Whimsical and riotous color illustrations create a lovingly
drawn, nostalgic portrait of the treks of five families of cousins who arrive by different means of transportation at Grandma's house during the early 1900s. Children and grownups
alike should be drawn to the story by the wonderful facial ex-

pressions and body language evoked by Diane Goode's illustrations. *Notable Children's Trade Book in the Field of Social Studies.*

11.61   Polacco, Patricia. **Meteor!** Illustrated by the author. Dodd, Mead, 1987. Ages 5–9.

Motivated by a real event, the fall of a meteor near the family home in Union City, Michigan, Patricia Polacco develops a story about the effects of "meteor madness" on the people of a rural community before the meteor is taken to a final resting place. Colorful comic illustrations support the humor of the story.

11.62   Rosenblum, Richard. **My Block.** Illustrated by the author. Atheneum, 1988. Ages 4–8. (Picture book)

Students who think of "the olden days" as alien will delight in Rosenblum's cozy, nostalgic world of the 1930s, which shows children as fundamentally the same regardless of the times. A respect for the old trades and small neighborhoods combines with a cartoon style of illustration to make this a painless peek into an idealized past, as a young boy tries to think of an appropriate career so that he can stay on his New York block forever.

11.63   Teitelbaum, Michael. **An American Tail: A Steven Spielberg Presentation of a Don Bluth Film.** Illustrations from the Don Bluth film. Grosset and Dunlop/PlayValue Books, 1986. Ages 7–10.

Fievel Mousekewitz, a seven-year-old Russian mouse, flees with his family from their homeland for the promise of a better, cat-free life in America. They find New York City full of adventure, danger, and excitement as they begin their new life in America. Each of the four read-aloud storybooks—*Escape from the Catsacks*, *Fievel's New York Adventure*, *Little Lost Fievel*, and *The Mott Street Maulers*—re-creates a special episode from the film, with actual movie art reproduced in full color.

11.64   Wallace, Ian. **The Sparrow's Song.** Illustrated by the author. Viking Kestrel, 1986. Ages 7–9. (Picture book)

In the early 1900s at Niagara Falls, Katie discovers an orphaned sparrow at the creek. Her brother, Charles, has killed the mother sparrow with his slingshot. Now both children attempt to keep the bird alive and finally to release it.

Intermediate

11.65   Boutis, Victoria. **Looking Out.** Four Winds Press, 1988. Ages 10–14.

Inner convictions and outer appearances are contrasted in this thoughtful novel set in 1953. Ellen Gerson's parents are Communists and incensed by the treatment of the Rosenbergs. Her family has moved often, and Ellen has always been an outsider at school. She is afraid that she will do something to betray her parents' secret. Finally it looks as though Ellen will be popular, but is the price—conformity—too high?

11.66   Cannon, Bettie. **A Bellsong for Sarah Raines.** Charles Scribner's Sons, 1987. Ages 11 and up.

Sarah moves back to Kentucky after the suicide of her father during the Depression. She must come to terms with her father's death, a new home, and many new friends and relatives in this story with a gripping conclusion.

11.67   Clifford, Eth. **The Man Who Sang in the Dark.** Illustrated by Mary Beth Owens. Houghton Mifflin, 1987. Ages 9–11.

This warm, extended-family story set in a bleak Philadelphia apartment during the Depression centers on ten-year-old Leah, her four-year-old brother, and her recently widowed mother. The family has just moved to the third floor of the building owned by Mr. and Mrs. Safer. Leah gets to know the Safers' blind nephew, Gideon Brown, who recently moved to the second floor. In episodic chapters, the reader sees this extended family adjust to hard times and watches the development of active characters. A good read-aloud period piece.

11.68   Corcoran, Barbara. **The Sky Is Falling.** Atheneum/Jean Karl Books, 1988. Ages 11–12.

In fall of 1931, Annah's world shatters when her father loses his job and the family must leave their comfortable home and well-to-do lifestyle. Annah goes to live with her Aunt Ed in a cottage on a remote New Hampshire lake where she befriends an impoverished, but scrappy, girl. Annah learns that change can bring with it opportunities for growth and adventure. For a good reader, this book offers an engrossing and thoughtful picture of what life was like for many families during the Depression.

11.69 Delton, Judy. **Kitty from the Start.** Houghton Mifflin, 1987. Ages 8–10.

Set in Minneapolis–St. Paul during the Depression, this sequel to three other books about Kitty finds the third grader adjusting to a new Catholic school. Her best friends, the proper Margaret Mary and the more free-spirited Eileen, provide a background for solving childhood concerns in an honest, humorous manner.

11.70 Edwards, Pat. **Nelda.** Houghton Mifflin, 1987. Ages 10–13.

Nelda Shanks, the spunky eleven-year-old daughter of an itinerant Mississippi farm family, experiences hard times during the Depression, but she is determined to be rich. She sees her chance when she becomes the live-in companion of Miss Mattie May Wynn. The conflicts Nelda experiences in lifestyles, values, and attitudes are described with insight and humor.

11.71 Herman, Charlotte. **Millie Cooper, 3B.** Illustrated by Helen Cogancherry. E. P. Dutton, 1985. Ages 8–10.

Third-grader Millie, an only child, is a terrific speller and desperately wants a Reynolds Rocket ballpoint pen so she will not smudge her papers with ink blots. But these things do not help her with her composition on the topic "Why I'm Special!" Millie's problems with school are universal even though the story takes place in 1946. Black-and-white full-page drawings throughout the book evoke the setting. Intermediate readers will identify with this heroine.

11.72 Lord, Athena V. **The Luck of Z.A.P. and Zoe.** Illustrated by Jean Jenkins. Macmillan, 1987. Ages 10–12.

Wherever Zachary is, there is sure to be adventure and fun. Eleven-year-old Zach and his four-year-old sister, Zoe, are children of Greek descent living in upstate New York in the 1940s. Zach decides to start a club with members who have the initials of Z.A.P. This book continues the story began in *Today's Special: Z.A.P. and Zoe.*

11.73   Lyon, George Ella. **Borrowed Children.** Orchard Books, 1988. Ages 11 and up.

During the hard times of the Depression, twelve-year-old Amanda is forced to give up her treasured schooling and assume full-time mothering and housekeeping duties for her family, including the newborn brother whose birth almost cost their mother her life. George Ella Lyon has provided a wonderfully moving exploration of Amanda's search for herself, her place in the family, and her efforts to cope with her feelings. It is an engaging narrative about coming to terms with a bewildering world.

11.74   MacLachlan, Patricia. **Sarah, Plain and Tall.** Harper and Row Junior Books, 1985. Ages 8–10.

Anna, Caleb, and Papa are a prairie frontier family, loving, but lonely for the special warmth of a wife and mother. Papa's advertisement for a wife is answered by Sarah, whose trial visit offers contented fulfillment and the promise of happiness. Simple, direct language breathes life into history, portraying human needs and emotions as timeless. The place, time, and characters are developed vividly. *Children's Choice, Newbery Medal, Notable Children's Trade Book in the Field of Social Studies,* and *Scott O'Dell Award.*

11.75   Naylor, Phyllis Reynolds, and Lura Schield Reynolds. **Maudie in the Middle.** Illustrated by Judith Gwyn Brown. Atheneum/Jean Karl Books, 1988. Ages 10–13.

The middle of seven children, Maudie feels that she just does not matter to anyone. Growing up on an Iowa farm in the early 1900s, Maudie learns to accept herself as she is, as someone special with her own unique gifts and ability to help her family in a crisis. This is a charming return to the older days of ice cream socials and hayrides, a time of strong family values and love.

11.76   Olsen, Violet. **View from the Pighouse Roof.** Atheneum, 1987. Ages 10–13.

A unique coming-of-age story describes a crucial year in thirteen-year-old Marie's life as she comes to terms with death and the ultimate tenacity of life in Depression-stricken Iowa. A vivid setting, thematic richness, and fully realized characters create a heartwarming family novel.

11.77 Pendergraft, Patricia. **Hear the Wind Blow.** Philomel Books, 1988. Ages 10–12.

The narrator of this story is twelve-year-old Isadora, who dreams of becoming a dancer. Others in her poor rural community also have dreams; some are achieved, while others end in disaster. The story focuses on Isadora's daily life at home and in school, where her best friend dreams of reforming the school bully. The reader quickly becomes immersed in this story of a rural community in the unspecified past through the characters, who are rendered unforgettable by the author's vivid descriptions and through events in the story. Religious themes are explored when a revival comes to the valley town.

11.78 Snyder, Carol. **Ike and Mama and the Seven Surprises.** Illustrated by Charles Robinson. Lothrop, Lee and Shepard Books, 1985. Ages 10–13.

A boy, a dog, a father ill with tuberculosis, and a bar mitzvah are the key ingredients to this new book about Ike and Mama and their life during the Depression. Because Ike saves the life of an another living thing, Mama promises that he will receive seven surprises in the five weeks before his bar mitzvah. Fans of Ike and Mama will want to read about their latest experiences in this fifth book in a series.

11.79 Snyder, Zilpha Keatley. **And Condors Danced.** Delacorte Press, 1987. Ages 10–12.

This readable coming-of-age story includes engaging characters and a detailed picture of life on a California ranch in the early twentieth century as eleven-year-old Carly learns to cope with unexpected tragedies. While the plot moves along at a leisurely pace, the interaction of the characters should be sufficient to hold the reader's interests.

11.80 Taylor, Mildred D. **The Friendship.** Illustrated by Max Ginsburg. Dial Books for Young Readers, 1987. Ages 8–11.

Set in rural Mississippi during the Depression, this short story is narrated by Cassie Logan and her brother, who have appeared in previous books by Mildred D. Taylor. It focuses on a confrontation between an elderly black man and a white store owner. The strong characterization and poignant pen-and-ink drawings make this book a good starter for discussion of racial injustice. *ALA Notable Children's Book, Boston Globe–Horn Book Award*, and *Coretta Scott King Award* (for writing).

World

Primary

11.81   Ziefert, Harriet. **A New Coat for Anna.** Illustrated by Anita Lobel. Alfred A. Knopf/Borzoi Books, 1986. Ages 6–11.

Anna needs a new coat, and her mother, who has no money, devises a barter scheme to get one. She gives a gold watch for wool, a lamp for getting the wool spun, a necklace for weaving the cloth, and a porcelain teapot to the tailor. Anna gets her beautiful new red coat in time for the next Christmas. Anita Lobel's illustrations depict life in postwar Europe, as well as the coat making. *ALA Notable Children's Book* and *Notable Children's Trade Book in the Field of Social Studies.*

Intermediate

11.82   Carey, Mary. **A Place for Allie.** Dodd, Mead, 1985. Ages 10–13.

Turn-of-the-century Novia Scotia is the setting for this coming-of-age novel in which twelve-year-old Allie faces trials that test her independence. Her father's death changes the family circumstances and deepens the conflict with her mother. Allie and her sister run away, forcing a compromise with her family. The book presents a good portrayal of family relationships for thoughtful readers.

11.83   Gallaz, Christophe, and Roberto Innocenti. **Rose Blanche.** Illustrated by Roberto Innocenti. Creative Education, 1985. Ages 9 and up.

Nazi occupation of her German town causes young Rose Blanche to observe the changes brought by the noisy tanks and soldiers. After following a truck to a concentration camp in the woods nearby, Rose Blanche secretly shares food with the prisoners until the war ends. The child is a luminous, hopeful image in the midst of predominating sombre colors in the haunting, surrealistic paintings. The narrative voice shifts from first to third person midway, underscoring an innocent's odyssey as she witnesses and responds to individual and corporate evils of the Hitler regime. Symbolic references to the actual White Rose Movement increase the book's power and may lead older students to *The Short Life of Sophie Scholl* by Hermann Vinke. This is a sad, provocative, unusual book. *ALA Notable Children's Book* and *Mildred L. Batchelder Award.*

11.84   Garrigue, Sheila. **The Eternal Spring of Mr. Ito.** Bradbury Press, 1985. Ages 10 and up.

Occasionally a book appears that transcends easy age classification and captivates adults and children alike. This is such a book. In the aftermath of the Japanese bombing of Pearl Harbor and Hong Kong, a wave of anti-Japanese hysteria swept the United States and Canada. Against this backdrop, Sheila Garrigue has woven a many-textured drama involving two different Canadian families caught up in the ensuing social turbulence. This story of a special friendship, its consequences, and its implications illuminates far more than its parochial setting or its individual characters, and reaches beyond the particular cultures involved. *Notable Children's Trade Book in the Field of Social Studies.*

11.85   Heuck, Sigrid (translated by Rika Lesser). **The Hideout.** E. P. Dutton, 1988. Ages 10–12.

Rebecca loses her parents and her memory in the bomb blasts in Germany during World War II. She is sent away to an orphanage, where she meets Sami, a boy who lives in a hideout in a nearby cornfield. Together they cope with loneliness, hunger, and fear by creating a fantasy world. The interplay between their fantasy and the real war brings understanding of the nature of war and peace. This book, written by an author who experienced similar events, makes the everyday details of wartime life from a child's point of view seem very real. The book is best read individually with an adult nearby for discussion.

11.86   Mattingley, Christobel. **The Angel with a Mouth-Organ.** Illustrated by Astra Lacis. Holiday House, 1986. Ages 10–12.

Bordering on the sentimental, this emotional tale relates, through the eyes of a ten year old, a family's saga of displacement hardships, including starvation, death, long marches, and separation from the father. The glass Christmas angel becomes a symbol of hope for the family. This is a book to share with a class as a strong anti-war statement. Although it is an illustrated book, it is not intended for younger children.

11.87   Ossowski, Leonie (translated by Ruth Crowley). **Star without a Sky.** Lerner Publications, 1985. Ages 9 and up.

In a story set in World War II Germany, five young friends must make choices about their relationship with a Jewish boy. What is really important? His life? Their values? Are things really the way they seem to be? The riveting story will hold the reader's attention to the end.

11.88   Tsuchiya, Yukio (translated by Tomoko Tsuchiya Dykes). **Faithful Elephants: A True Story of Animals, People and War.** Illustrated by Ted Lewin. Houghton Mifflin, 1988. Ages 10–12. (Picture book)

This translated story is based on the killing of the animals in Tokyo's Ueno Zoo, which took place during World War II in order to protect the people from the animals in case the zoo was bombed and the animals got loose. This stark tale of war's tragedy focuses on starving the elephants as the only way to kill them. Although this is a picture story, the audience is upper elementary children. Allow plenty of time to talk about the book, perhaps as part of a discussion or unit on peace.

11.89   Vander Els, Betty. **The Bombers' Moon.** Farrar, Straus and Giroux, 1985. Ages 10–12.

Ruth and Simeon are missionary children living in China at the outset of World War II. They must leave their home and parents when the fighting reaches Asia. Ruth becomes the "big sister" and takes care of Simeon. The story takes the reader from the interior of China, to India, and back to Shanghai as the children travel from one place of safety to another.

Recommended Books Published before 1985

Aiken, Joan. *Midnight Is a Place.* Viking Press, 1974. 10 and up.
Bawden, Nina. *Carrie's War.* J. B. Lippincott, 1973. 9–12.
Beatty, Patricia. *Hail Columbia.* Illustrated by Liz Dauber. William Morrow, 1970. 10–12.

Behn, Harry. *The Faraway Lurs*. World, 1963. 11 and up.

Benchley, Nathaniel. *Sam the Minuteman*. Illustrated by Arnold Lobel. Harper and Row, 1969. 5–8.

Bishop, Claire Huchet, and Janet Joly. *Twenty and Ten*. Illustrated by William Pène du Bois. Viking Press, 1952. 8–11.

Blos, Joan W. *A Gathering of Days: A New England Girl's Journal, 1830–32; A Novel*. Charles Scribner's Sons, 1979. 10 and up.

Brink, Carol Ryrie. *Caddie Woodlawn*. Rev. ed. Illustrated by Trina Schart Hyman. Macmillan, 1973. 9–12.

Burch, Robert. *Queenie Peavy*. Illustrated by Jerry Lazare. Viking Press, 1966. 10 and up.

Burnett, Frances Hodgson. *The Secret Garden*. Illustrated by Tasha Tudor. Harper and Row, 1962. 10–12.

Burton, Hester. *Time of Trial*. Illustrated by Victor G. Ambrus. Collins, World, 1964. 10 and up.

Clapp, Patricia. *Witches' Children: A Novel of Salem*. Lothrop, Lee and Shepard Books, 1982. 10 and up.

Collier, James Lincoln, and Christopher Collier. *My Brother Sam Is Dead*. Four Winds Press, 1974. 11 and up.

Dalgliesch, Alice. *The Courage of Sarah Noble*. Illustrated by Leonard Weisgard. Charles Scribner's Sons, 1954. 7–9.

De Angeli, Marguerite. *The Door in the Wall*. Doubleday, 1949. 10–12.

Forbes, Esther. *Johnny Tremain*. Illustrated by Lynd Ward. Houghton Mifflin, 1943. 10 and up.

Fox, Paula. *The Slave Dancer*. Illustrated by Eros Keither. Bradbury Press, 1973. 11 and up.

Fritz, Jean. *The Cabin Faced West*. Illustrated by Feodor Rojankovsky. Coward, McCann and Geoghegan, 1958. 8–11.

Garfield, Leon. *Footsteps*. Delacorte Press, 1980. 11 and up.

Hall, Donald. *Ox-cart Man*. Illustrated by Barbara Cooney. Viking Press, 1979. 6–9.

Haugaard, Erik Christian. *Hakon of Rogen's Saga*. Illustrated by Leo and Diane Dillon. Houghton Mifflin, 1963. 10 and up.

Highwater, Majake. *Anpao: An American Indian Odyssey*. Illustrated by Fritz Scholder. J. B. Lippincott, 1977. 11 and up.

Hunt, Irene. *Across Five Aprils*. Follett, 1964. 10 and up.

Hunter, Mollie. *The Stronghold*. Harper and Row, 1974. 11–13.

Keith, Harold. *Rifles for Watie*. Thomas Y. Crowell, 1957. 5 and up.

Kelly, Eric P. *The Trumpeter of Krakow*. Illustrated by Janina Domanska. Macmillan, 1966. 10 and up.

Kerr, Judith. *When Hitler Stole Pink Rabbit.* Coward, McCann and Geoghegan, 1972. 9–12.

Konigsburg, E. L. *A Proud Taste for Scarlet and Miniver.* Atheneum, 1973. 10 and up.

Kurelek, William. *A Prairie Boy's Summer.* Houghton Mifflin, 1975. 8–10.

Lenski, Lois. *Strawberry Girl.* J. B. Lippincott, 1945. 8–11.

Lobel, Arnold. *On the Day Peter Stuyvesant Sailed into Town.* Harper and Row, 1971. 6–9.

Lofts, Norah. *The Maude Reed Tale.* Illustrated by Anne and Janet Grahame Johnstone. Thomas Nelson, 1972. 10 and up.

Meigs, Cornelia. *Master Simon's Garden.* Illustrated by John Rae. Macmillan, 1947. 9–12.

Monjo, F. N. *The Drinking Gourd.* Illustrated by Fred Brenner. Harper and Row, 1970. 7–9.

Newman, Robert. *The Case of the Baker Street Irregulars: A Sherlock Holmes Story.* Atheneum, 1978. 10 and up.

North, Sterling. *Rascal.* Avon Books, 1976. 10 and up.

O'Dell, Scott. *Island of the Blue Dolphins.* Houghton Mifflin, 1960. 10 and up.

———. *Sing Down the Moon.* Houghton Mifflin, 1970. 10 and up.

Paterson, Katherine. *The Master Puppeteer.* Illustrated by Haru Wells. Thomas Y. Crowell, 1976. 10 and up.

Peck, Robert Newton. *Soup.* Illustrated by Charles Gehm. Alfred A. Knopf, 1974. 9–12.

Picard, Barbara Leonie. *One Is One.* Illustrated by Victor G. Ambrus. Oxford University Press, 1965. 11 and up.

Polland, Madeleine. *Queen without a Crown.* Illustrated by Herbert Danska. Holt, Rinehart and Winston, 1966. 10 and up.

Rylant, Cynthia. *When I Was Young in the Mountains.* Illustrated by Diane Goode. E. P. Dutton, 1982. 5–8.

Sebestyen, Ouida. *Words by Heart.* Little, Brown, 1979. 10 and up.

Seredy, Kate. *The Good Master.* Viking Press, 1935. 9–11.

Serraillier, Ian. *The Silver Sword.* Illustrated by C. Walter Hodges. Criterion, 1959. 10 and up.

Speare, Elizabeth George. *The Witch of Blackbird Pond.* Houghton Mifflin, 1958. 11 and up.

Sutcliff, Rosemary. *The Eagle of the Ninth.* Illustrated by C. Walter Hodges. Henry Z. Walck, 1954. 10 and up.

Talbot, Charlene Joy. *An Orphan for Nebraska.* Atheneum, 1979. 10 and up.

Taylor, Mildred D. *Roll of Thunder, Hear My Cry*. Illustrated by Jerry Pinkney. Dial Books for Young Readers, 1976. 9–11.

Taylor, Theodore. *The Cay*. Doubleday, 1969. 10 and up.

Thrasher, Crystal. *The Dark Didn't Catch Me*. Atheneum, 1979. 10 and up.

Trease, Geoffrey. *Bows against the Barons*. Hawthorn, 1967. 9–13.

Treece, Henry. *Splintered Sword*. Illustrated by Charles Keeping. Duell, Sloan and Pearce, 1965. 10 and up.

Turkle, Brinton. *Thy Friend, Obadiah*. Viking Press, 1969. 5–8.

Uchida, Yoshiko. *Journey Home*. Illustrated by Charles Robinson. Atheneum, 1978. 10 and up.

Voigt, Cynthia. *The Callender Papers*. Atheneum, 1983. 10 and up.

Wibberley, Leonard. *John Treegate's Musket*. Farrar, Straus and Giroux, 1979. 10 and up.

Wilder, Laura Ingalls. *Little House in the Big Woods*. Illustrated by Garth Williams. Harper and Row, 1953. 9–11.

12 Biography

Artists, Photographers, Poets, and Writers

Intermediate

12.1 Cleary, Beverly. **A Girl from Yamhill: A Memoir.** William Morrow, 1988. Ages 11–13.

Beverly Cleary fans, children and adults alike, will enjoy the account of her childhood growing up in the Pacific Northwest. Her own story has all the warmth, humor, and poignancy of one of her works of fiction. Photographs from the family album enhance the text and add further warmth. This book, Elaine Scott's *Ramona: Behind the Scenes of a Television Show* (15.6), and Cleary's body of work would be an excellent combination for an author-centered literature unit. *ALA Notable Children's Book.*

12.2 Gherman, Beverly. **Georgia O'Keeffe: The "Wideness and Wonder" of Her World.** Atheneum, 1986. Ages 11–14.

This biography of a distinguished American artist shows how she broke conventional rules in several ways: in her use of color and light, her recognition within a male-dominated field, her relationship with photographer Alfred Stieglitz, and her spiritual kinship with New Mexico's landscapes. A few black-and-white photographs are distributed throughout the book.

12.3 Kamen, Gloria. **Kipling: Storyteller of East and West.** Illustrated by the author. Atheneum, 1985. Ages 8–12.

This brief biography brings Rudyard Kipling to life as a man and a writer. His early years in India, his schooling in England, and his success as a writer are presented. Brown-tone illustrations add to the book's appeal. There is also a short glossary.

12.4 Levinson, Nancy Smiler. **I Lift My Lamp: Emma Lazarus and the Statue of Liberty.** E. P. Dutton/Lodestar Books/Jewish Biography Series, 1986. Ages 10–13.

Emma Lazarus, stirred by the plight of Jewish refugees, used her talent as a writer to aid and influence them. Woven into her life story is the building of the Statue of Liberty. The reader will gain insights into its significance and learn that Lazarus's words are inscribed on the pedestal.

12.5 Lewis, C. S. (edited by Lyle W. Dorsett and Marjorie Lamp Mead). **Letters to Children.** Macmillan, 1985. Ages 9 and up.

Of special interest to readers who are already familiar with C. S. Lewis's books, particularly the Narnia series, this collection of letters offers revealing insights into the author and the characters he created. Lewis's responses to his readers' questions are direct, informative, and uncondescending.

12.6 Meltzer, Milton. **Dorothea Lange: Life through the Camera.** Illustrated by Donna Diamond; photographs by Dorothea Lange. Viking Penguin/Puffin Books/Women of Our Time Books, 1985. Ages 10–13.

This is a simpler biography of Dorothea Lange than Milton Meltzer's earlier book about her. It describes the personal and, more importantly, the professional life of Lange, whose photographs of migrant workers and rural America during the Depression made powerful impact on the American public and helped bring about social reforms. A few of Lange's own photographs are included.

12.7 Quackenbush, Robert. **Who Said There's No Man on the Moon? A Story of Jules Verne.** Illustrated by the author. Prentice-Hall, 1985. Ages 7–11.

As a child, Jules Verne dreamed of traveling to exotic lands. He made up his mind to travel in his imagination. This book tells how Verne became one of the world's greatest storytellers and predictors of future events. Entertaining cartoons add to the enjoyment of this humorous, informative biography. *Notable Children's Trade Book in the Field of Social Studies.*

12.8 Sufrin, Mark. **Focus on America: Profiles of Nine Photographers.** Charles Scribner's Sons, 1987. Ages 10–13.

"A picture is worth a thousand words" could have been coined here. This book focuses on nine reknowned photographers who captured historical events in America's past and brought them alive. Included are Berenice Abbott, Margaret Bourke-White, Mathew Brady, Edward Curtis, Walker Evans, Lewis Hine, William Henry Jackson, Dorothea Lange, and W. Eugene Smith. The book presents several examples of their special photographs depicting the strife and hardships during America's growth and its effect on humankind.

Entertainers

Intermediate

12.9   Gish, Lillian (as told to Selma G. Lanes). **An Actor's Life for Me!** Illustrated by Patricia Henderson Lincoln. Viking Kestrel, 1987. Ages 9 and up.

This well-written first-person account covers Lillian Gish's life in the theater from 1902 to 1913. Each short chapter portrays a different situation in her life. Black-and-white and color illustrations accompanied by some original photographs enhance the story.

12.10   Saunders, Susan. **Dolly Parton: Country Goin' to Town.** Illustrated by Rodney Pate. Viking Kestrel/Women of Our Time Books, 1985. Ages 8–12.

In this biography written for the intermediate reader, the author follows Dolly Parton from her childhood in the Smoky Mountains to her success in Nashville. The book portrays not only the glamour of Parton's lifestyle, but also her struggle to become a popular singer.

Explorers

Intermediate

12.11   Brown, Fern G. **Amelia Earhart Takes Off.** Illustrated by Lydia Halverson. Albert Whitman, 1985. Ages 9–13.

This is an intriguing story of an adventurous child, Amelia Earhart, who endured numerous moves, an alcoholic father, and a society with a conservative view of women's roles. As a determined young woman, she took many jobs to finance flying lessons and her own airplanes. When Earhart began to set aviation records, her notoriety paid off, and she was able to plan and execute even more daring flights. After her marriage to publisher George Putnam, Earhart continued to fly and planned a flight around the world. Her disappearance, near the completion of the flight, remains a mystery.

12.12 Lauber, Patricia. **Lost Star: The Story of Amelia Earhart.** Scholastic/Scholastic Hardcover Books, 1988. Ages 10 and up.

The life of the first woman to fly across the Atlantic Ocean is traced from her childhood in the early 1900s to her mysterious last flight and disappearance while trying to fly around the world in 1937. Photographs from Amelia Earhart's private and public life document this appealing biography of a pioneer in aviation history.

12.13 Levinson, Nancy Smiler. **Chuck Yeager: The Man Who Broke the Sound Barrier.** Walker, 1988. Ages 11–13.

Chuck Yeager was the first person to fly faster than the speed of sound. His story as an Air Force test pilot is told here. Children who like to read biographies will enjoy this simply written story. Black-and-white photographs illustrate the book, and a glossary, bibliography, and index provide reference information.

12.14 McClung, Robert M. **The True Adventures of Grizzly Adams.** William Morrow, 1985. Ages 11–14.

John Adams, known today as Grizzly Adams, was one of the more colorful men of the California Gold Rush of 1849. This book dispels many of the tales of Grizzly Adams as portrayed in the media. It tells the story of a unique man who turned his back on his family and society for several years to live among the untamed animals of the West, and who was a legend in his own time. The book contains illustrations, a bibliography, and an index.

12.15 Reynolds, Kathy. **Marco Polo.** Illustrated by Daniel Woods. Raintree Children's Books/Raintree Stories, 1986. Ages 9–11. (Picture book)

Told as if Marco Polo were recounting his journey, this is a simple introduction to the exciting adventures of Polo. Illustrations help the readers learn about the places Polo visited on his thirteenth-century trek from Venice to China and back. The book would be useful for social studies units as well as appropriate for pleasure reading.

Humanitarians

Intermediate

12.16   Brown, Drollene P. **Belva Lockwood Wins Her Case.** Illustrated by James Watling. Albert Whitman, 1987. Ages 9–12.

This well-written book tells about a little-known woman born in the 1830s who became a teacher, suffragette, lawyer, and the first woman to run for president of the United States. The book would make an excellent focus for discussions about the struggles of individuals against mindless sex-role stereotypes.

12.17   Meltzer, Milton. **Mary McLeod Bethune: Voice of Black Hope.** Illustrated by Stephen Marchesi. Viking Kestrel/ Women of Our Time Books, 1987. Ages 10–13.

The life of Mary McLeod Bethune, educator and advocate for the equality of black persons and of women during the first half of the twentieth century, is presented here. This biography is highly recommended for the study of Afro-American history as well as for personal reading.

Political Leaders

Primary

12.18   Adler, David A. **Thomas Jefferson: Father of Our Democracy.** Illustrated by Jacqueline Garrick. Holiday House, 1987. Ages 6–9.

This is better than many biographies written for primary students: the sentences are longer, the chapters are better structured, and there is an index. It should be used with care, however. Adults will need to supplement the book with material from other sources, as there are some inaccuracies. The author, for example, states that slaves lived in houses, while the truth is they lived in cabins and shared quarters in one-room shacks. Also, it should be noted that the illustrations do not solidly enhance the text.

Intermediate

12.19   Dolan, Edward F., Jr. **Famous Builders of California.** Dodd, Mead, 1987. Ages 9–12.

Seven men important in shaping the history of California are introduced in this book. Many anecdotes about Western life liven up the stories of Father Junipero Serra, John Frémont, John Sutter, Henry Wells, William Fargo, John Muir, and Luther Burbank. Included are an index and a list of further readings on each of the men.

12.20 Freedman, Russell. **Lincoln: A Photobiography.** Clarion Books, 1987. Ages 11 and up.

A cogent narrative and nearly one hundred photographs document the life of Abraham Lincoln and the times in which he lived. Through frequent use of direct quotes from Lincoln and the people who loved or hated him, Russell Freedman manages to bring a larger-than-life historical legend down to earth, focusing on his personal ambition and sense of failure, his wit and melancholy. *ALA Notable Children's Book* and *Newbery Medal.*

12.21 Haskins, Jim. **Winnie Mandela: Life of Struggle.** G. P. Putnam's Sons, 1988. Ages 11 and up.

Winnie Mandela has emerged as an activist for racial equality since the imprisonment of her husband, Nelson Mandela, in South Africa. The author traces Winnie's life from childhood to her activities at the present time. The book contains quotations from her own autobiography. Also included are an index and a bibliography.

12.22 Hilton, Suzanne. **The World of Young Tom Jefferson.** Illustrated by William Sauts Bock. Walker, 1986. Ages 10–13.

Black-and-white illustrations add to many details taken from journals, diaries, and newspapers to illuminate the times of Thomas Jefferson. In this way, Suzanne Hilton presents a side of Thomas Jefferson that shows that everything did not come easily to him. An interesting appendix, "What Happened to . . . ," provides additional information. Also included are a time line of the life of Thomas Jefferson and an index.

12.23 Randolph, Sallie G. **Gerald R. Ford, President.** Walker/Presidential Biography Series, 1987. Ages 12 and up.

Although the author's partisanship is evident in this biography, the portrait of former president Gerald R. Ford which

emerges is that of a remarkable man about whom the general
public still knows very little. This book could stimulate discussions about how honorable people can disagree honestly
and still work together, about the rewards and pitfalls of political life, and about how difficult it is for most of us to know
the people and the truths behind our public officials. The
book includes an index.

Scientists and Inventors

Intermediate

12.24 McCall, Edith. **Mississippi Steamboatman: The Story of
Henry Miller Shreve.** Walker, 1986. Ages 10–13.

This book tells the story of the other inventor of the steam-
powered paddleboat, Henry Shreve. Shreve did what Robert
Fulton was unable to do—he built a boat and engine that
could go up the Mississippi River. The book gives historical
details and describes Shreve's successes and failures. It contains copies of illustrations and maps from the 1800s.

12.25 Mitchell, Barbara. **Click! A Story about George Eastman.** Illustrated by Jan Hosking Smith. Carolrhoda Books/Creative
Minds Books, 1986. Ages 8–11.

This biography of George Eastman portrays his curiosity and
self-discipline as he worked to create a camera simple enough
for everyone to use. The text is written in short sentences and
appears in a large typeface; it is highlighted with black-and-
white illustrations on nearly every other page.

12.26 Mitchell, Barbara. **A Pocketful of Goobers: A Story about
George Washington Carver.** Illustrated by Peter E. Hanson.
Carolrhoda Books/Creative Minds Books, 1986. Ages 8–12.

Episodes from the life of George Washington Carver are recreated to portray the challenges he faced as a black child
struggling to get an education in the mid-1800s and as a sensitive, creative scientist committed to improving the conditions of Southern farmers. Short sentences and the large typeface make the text easy reading. Black-and-white illustrations
appear on almost every other page.

12.27 Mitchell, Barbara. **We'll Race You, Henry: A Story about Henry Ford.** Illustrated by Kathy Haubrich. Carolrhoda Books/Creative Minds Books, 1986. Ages 8–12.

This biography of Henry Ford presents a realistic picture of the difficulties and the perseverance needed to be a successful inventor. Many black-and-white full-page illustrations in pencil help the young reader get the feel of the times in which the Model T was invented.

12.28 Saunders, Susan. **Margaret Mead: The World Was Her Family.** Illustrated by Ted Lewin. Viking Kestrel/Women of Our Time Books, 1987. Ages 10–13.

Margaret Mead was a pioneer in anthropology—a pioneer in the sense that she was the first woman to work as an anthropologist studying primitive cultures outside North America and in her popularizing of the field of anthropology. Susan Saunders tells a fascinating story, honest and not entirely adulatory, of Mead's personal as well as professional life.

Others

Intermediate

12.29 Drimmer, Frederick. **The Elephant Man.** G. P. Putnam's Sons, 1985. Ages 11–12.

Joseph Merrick is portrayed honestly and sensitively as a timid, lonely man. During his childhood in England in the mid-1800s, his disfiguring disease began to manifest itself, and he became the pariah of his family and community. As a young man, Merrick agreed to join a freak show in order to earn a living. Dr. Frederic Treves, a young surgeon, befriended the deformed cripple, provided living quarters in a London hospital, and introduced him to compassionate members of London's society. The book includes photographs and an afterword that explains neurofibromatosis and that provides other facts of interest to the curious reader. *Notable Children's Trade Book in the Field of Social Studies.*

12.30 Henry, Sondra, and Emily Taitz. **One Woman's Power: A Biography of Gloria Steinem.** Dillon Press/People in Focus Books, 1987. Ages 10 and up.

Gloria Steinem, a talented writer, used her pen and her determination to further the cause of civil rights for minorities and women. This biography addresses her idealism and commitment by relating her unhappy childhood, her struggle for credibility, and her editorship of *Ms.* magazine, the first national feminist magazine. In the afterword, Steinem notes her hopes for the future. Included are a bibliography and an appendix that briefly recounts the history of the women's rights movement.

12.31 Meltzer, Milton. **Betty Friedan: A Voice for Women's Rights.** Illustrated by Stephen Marchesi. Viking Kestrel/Women of Our Time Books, 1985. Ages 8–12.

Betty Friedan became well known after the publication of her book *The Feminine Mystique* in 1963. This biography focuses on her childhood and youth and how these early years influenced her to become a feminist.

12.32 Van Steenwyk, Elizabeth. **Levi Strauss: The Blue Jeans Man.** Walker, 1988. Ages 10–13.

When gold was discovered in California, Levi Strauss went west—not as a miner but to peddle goods from his brother's store in New York. After seeing how tattered and grubby the miners looked, he decided to try to make trousers for them from heavier material. He went into the business of making blue denim workpants, known today as blue jeans. Included are black-and-white illustrations and photographs, a bibliography, and an index.

12.33 Wulffson, Don L. **Incredible True Adventures.** Dodd, Mead, 1986. Ages 9–13.

Nine true-life adventures that pit individuals against seemingly incredible odds are given dramatic retellings and are enhanced with photographs and prints. South American jungles, a tornado, wartime survival, an Arctic shipwreck, violent seas, and an Iron Curtain escape offer varied settings and touches of human triumph in the face of difficulties.

Recommended Books Published before 1985

Aldis, Dorothy Keeley. *Nothing Is Impossible: The Story of Beatrix Potter.* Illustrated by Richard Cuffari. Atheneum, 1969. 9–12.

Aliki. *The Story of Johnny Appleseed.* Prentice-Hall, 1963. 5–8.

Arkin, David. *The Twenty Children of Johann Sebastian Bach.* W. Ritchie Press, 1968. 7–10.

Barth, Edna. *I'm Nobody! Who Are You? The Story of Emily Dickinson.* Illustrated by Richard Cuffari. Clarion Books, 1971. 10 and up.

Coerr, Eleanor. *Sadako and the Thousand Paper Cranes.* Illustrated by Ronald Himler. G. P. Putnam's Sons, 1977. 8–11.

D'Aulaire, Ingri, and Edgar Parin D'Aulaire. *Abraham Lincoln.* Doubleday, 1957. 6–8.

dePaola, Tomie. *Francis: The Poor Man of Assisi.* Holiday House, 1982. 8–10.

Fritz, Jean. *The Double Life of Pocahontas.* Illustrated by Ed Young. G. P. Putnam's Sons, 1983. 9–12.

———. *Why Don't You Get a Horse, Sam Adams?* Illustrated by Trina Schart Hyman. Coward, McCann and Geoghegan, 1974. 8–10.

Greenfield, Eloise. *Mary McLeod Bethune.* Illustrated by Jerry Pinkney. Thomas Y. Crowell, 1977. 7–9.

Hamilton, Virginia. *Paul Robeson: The Life and Times of a Free Black Man.* Harper and Row, 1974. 10 and up.

———. *W.E.B. DuBois: A Biography.* Thomas Y. Crowell, 1972. 10 and up.

Haskins, James. *The Life and Death of Martin Luther King, Jr.* Lothrop, Lee and Shepard Books, 1977. 10 and up.

Henry, Marguerite, and Wesley Dennis. *Benjamin West and Cat Grimalkin.* Bobbs-Merrill, 1947. 8–10.

Hunter, Edith Fisher. *Child of the Silent Night.* Illustrated by Bea Holmes. Houghton Mifflin, 1963. 8–10.

Hyman, Trina Schart. *Self-Portrait.* Addison-Wesley, 1981. 9–11.

Kherdian, David. *The Road from Home: The Story of an Armenian Girl.* Greenwillow, 1979. 11 and up.

Koehn, Ilse. *Mischling, Second Degree: My Childhood in Nazi Germany.* Greenwillow Books, 1977. 11 and up.

Kroeber, Theodora. *Ishi: Last of His Tribe.* Parnassus Press, 1964. 10 and up.

Lasker, David. *The Boy Who Loved Music.* Illustrated by Joe Lasker. Viking Press, 1979. 7–10.

Lasker, Joe. *The Great Alexander the Great.* Viking Press, 1983. 5–9.

Mathis, Sharon Bell. *Ray Charles.* Thomas Y. Crowell, 1973. 7–9.

Monjo, F. N. *Letters to Horseface: Being the Story of Wolfgang Amadeus Mozart's Journey to Italy, 1769–1770, When He Was a Boy of Fourteen.* Illustrated by Don Bolognese and Elaine Raphael. Viking Press, 1975. 9–12.

———. *The One Bad Thing about Father.* Illustrated by Rocco Negri. Harper and Row, 1970. 6–9.

Ortiz, Victoria. *Sojourner Truth: A Self-Made Woman.* J. B. Lippincott, 1974. 10 and up.

Peare, Catherine Owens. *The Helen Keller Story.* Thomas Y. Crowell, 1959. 9–11.

Provensen, Alice, and Martin Provensen. *The Glorious Flight across the Channel with Louis Bleriot, July 25, 1909.* Viking Kestrel, 1983. 6–9.

Quackenbush, Robert. *Ahoy! Ahoy! Are You There? A Story of Alexander Graham Bell.* Prentice-Hall, 1981. 7–9.

Reiss, Johanna. *The Upstairs Room.* Thomas Y. Crowell, 1972. 9–12.

Tobias, Tobi. *Marian Anderson.* Illustrated by Symeon Shimin. Thomas Y. Crowell, 1972. 7–10.

Walker, Alice. *Langston Hughes: American Poet.* Illustrated by Don Miller. Thomas Y. Crowell, 1974. 7–10.

Wibberley, Leonard. *Young Man from the Piedmont: The Youth of Thomas Jefferson.* Farrar, Straus, and Giroux, 1973. 10 and up.

Wilder, Laura Ingalls. *West from Home: Letters of Laura Ingalls Wilder to Almanzo Wilder, San Francisco, 1915.* Harper and Row, 1974. 10 and up.

Yates, Elizabeth. *Amos Fortune: Free Man.* Illustrated by Nora S. Unwin. E. P. Dutton, 1950. 9–12.

Zemach, Margot. *Self-Portrait.* Addison-Wesley, 1978. 9–11.

13 Social Studies: Nonfiction

Careers

Primary

13.1   Gibbons, Gail. **Farming.** Illustrated by the author. Holiday House, 1988. Ages 3–8. (Picture book)

Readers are taken to a farm during the four seasons of the year, with all the indoor and outdoor farm chores explained in easy-to-understand language. Bright, colorful illustrations highlight the text.

13.2   Johnson, Jean. **Fire Fighters: A to Z.** Photographs by the author. Walker, 1985. Ages 4–7. (Picture book)

Black-and-white photographs illustrate firefighters engaged in various duties for each letter of the alphabet, from A, "alarm," to Z, "zone." A final section, "More about Fire Fighters," provides more information about the fire-fighting profession and raises readers' awareness of firefighters.

13.3   Johnson, Jean. **Police Officers: A to Z.** Illustrated by the author. Walker, 1986. Ages 4–8. (Picture book)

Black-and-white photographs, a brief text, and an alphabetical arrangement of terms are used to show the varied responsibilities of law enforcement officials. This is an excellent introduction to the role of police officer as community helper and peacekeeper, in contrast to the violent media image that children are used to seeing. Photographs depict female, male, black, white, young, and old officers.

Intermediate

13.4   Bellville, Cheryl Walsh. **Rodeo.** Photographs by the author. Carolrhoda Books, 1985. Ages 9–12. (Picture book)

The thrill of a rodeo builds through informative descriptions of bareback bronc riding, calf roping, bronc riding, barrel racing, steer wrestling, and bull riding. Action-packed color photographs are used on every page. The author, formerly a professional rodeo rider, writes with conviction.

13.5 Hewett, Joan. **Motorcycle on Patrol: The Story of a Highway Officer.** Photographs by Richard Hewett. Clarion Books, 1986. Ages 10–12.

Policeman Fermin Piol is a patrol officer who decides to become a member of the motorcycle corps of the California Highway Patrol. This book follows him through his training and his first few weeks on the job.

13.6 Wolf, Bernard. **Cowboy.** Photographs by the author. William Morrow, 1985. Ages 10–12. (Picture book)

Wally McRae, a rancher in Rosebud County, Montana, is featured in this day-by-day account of the life of a cowboy. It describes the work he does, including branding cattle and horses, rounding up cattle in the spring, and gathering and storing hay, and what he does for recreation. Today's cowboys are trying to exist in a modern world doing things the way they did them one hundred years ago, but they are experiencing many challenges to their traditional lifestyle. Black-and-white photographs greatly enhance this book.

Communication

Primary

13.7 Aliki. **How a Book Is Made.** Illustrated by the author. Thomas Y. Crowell, 1986. Ages 5–9. (Picture book)

Step-by-step book production—from the author's inspiration to the technical processing to purchase of the book in a book store—is explained in this unique and fascinating picture book. The concise, accurate text, cheerful line-and-wash comic-strip-style illustrations, and supplementary detailed information within the illustrations make this book accessible and interesting to a wide age group. *Children's Choice, Notable Children's Trade Book in the Field of Social Studies,* and *Notable Children's Trade Book in the Language Arts.*

Intermediate

13.8   Adorjan, Carol, and Yuri Rasovsky. **WKID: Easy Radio Plays.** Illustrated by Ann Iosa. Albert Whitman, 1988. Ages 8–12.

Would-be actors will enjoy the practical tips given along with four scripts for radio plays that demonstrate the genres of horror, science fiction, comedy, and literary fantasy. A glossary of radio terms, suggestions for sound effects and music, and line drawings of directors' hand signals add to this lively informal presentation.

Community Life

Primary

13.9   Provensen, Alice, and Martin Provensen. **Town and Country.** Illustrated by the authors. Crown, 1985. Ages 5–9. (Picture book)

Detailed full-page illustrations add much to this informational book about life in the city and on a farm near a village. The sights and sounds and the activities of both locations make each one appealing for different reasons.

Intermediate

13.10   Ashabranner, Brent. **Dark Harvest: Migrant Farmworkers in America.** Photographs by Paul Conklin. Dodd, Mead, 1985. Ages 9–12.

Following the crops, migrant workers travel the United States to harvest the nation's fruits and vegetables—doing work that is necessary to agriculture where machines cannot replace human hands. Sensitive photography, research, and interviews are effectively combined in this presentation of migrant workers' lives and serve to diffuse myths as well as give important insights. Social studies classes will find this book an important addition to the curriculum. *ALA Notable Children's Book, Boston Globe–Horn Book Award,* and *Notable Trade Book in the Field of Social Studies.*

13.11   Foster, Sally. **Where Time Stands Still.** Photographs by the author. Dodd, Mead, 1987. Ages 7–12. (Picture book)

Black-and-white photographs graphically describe the day-to-day social life and customs of a typical Amish family living on a farm in Lancaster County, Pennsylvania.

Disabilities

Intermediate

13.12   Butler, Beverly. **Maggie by My Side.** Dodd, Mead, 1987. Ages 8–12.

Beverly Butler, blind since she was fourteen, describes the information, training, and discipline required when she got her fifth guide dog, Maggie. The personal narrative honestly conveys the joys and sorrows experienced as a blind person and a guide dog learn to respect and depend upon each other. Black-and-white photographs of the author, several of her guide dogs, and the training center are included. *ALA Notable Children's Book.*

13.13   Roy, Ron. **Move Over, Wheelchairs Coming Through! Seven Young People in Wheelchairs Talk about Their Lives.** Photographs by Rosmarie Hausherr. Clarion Books, 1985. Ages 9–12.

Typical days in the lives of seven disabled young people are described. Readers can learn how these people, aged nine through nineteen, have adapted to their disabilities to lead active lives at home and in school. Quotes from each person punctuate the emotional impact of the disabilities, from the humor of some situations to the frustrations of the smallest task. Black-and-white photographs illustrate the range of experiences described in the text. *Notable Children's Trade Book in the Field of Social Studies.*

13.14   Walker, Lou Ann. **Amy: The Story of a Deaf Child.** Photographs by Michael Abramson. E. P. Dutton/Lodestar Books, 1985. Ages 7–11. (Picture book)

The first-person narrative and candid black-and-white photographs effectively show how eleven-year-old Amy copes with her deafness and enjoys a wide range of activities, aided by hearing aids and sign language. The photographs go even further in developing readers' interest in this plucky child. *Children's Choice* and *Notable Children's Trade Book in the Field of Social Studies.*

Ethnic and Racial Groups

Primary

13.15 Snowdon, Lynda. **Children around the World.** Dillon Press/ International Picture Library, 1986. Ages 6–9. (Picture book)

Children from Austria, Holland, Mexico, Bolivia, Brazil, Morocco, Nepal, Japan, India, China, Tunisia, and other African countries are shown in full-color photographs as they work and play.

Intermediate

13.16 Ashabranner, Brent. **Children of the Maya: A Guatemalan Indian Odyssey.** Photographs by Paul Conklin. Dodd, Mead, 1986. Ages 11 and up.

Brent Ashabranner combines historical background and current events in Central America with personal accounts and interviews to show the difficulties faced by Guatemalan refugees before and after they left home. The refugees' mixed emotions and attempts at balancing their new life in a small town in southeastern Florida while still preserving their own cultural traditions is shown in black-and-white photographs and related in the finely written narrative. *ALA Notable Children's Book* and *Notable Children's Trade Book in the Field of Social Studies.*

13.17 Costabel, Eva Deutsch. **The Pennsylvania Dutch: Craftsmen and Farmers.** Illustrated by the author. Atheneum, 1986. Ages 8–11.

Readers are introduced to the Pennsylvania Dutch—German immigrants who began settling in Pennsylvania in the late 1600s. This book describes the daily life of the settlers, focusing on their artistic contributions. The Pennsylvania Dutch are depicted through line-and-wash drawings, mostly done in folk-art colors, involved in such crafts as clock making, quilting, woodworking, tinsmithing, and scissor cutting. A bibliography and index are included.

13.18 Hirschfelder, Arlene. **Happily May I Walk: American Indians and Alaska Natives Today.** Charles Scribner's Sons, 1986. Ages 10–13.

The many erroneous myths and stereotypes surrounding Native Americans are debunked in this concise, comprehensive overview of Native American life today. Topics addressed include education, economics, politics, religion, and culture. The brief historical background, maps, index, and numerous black-and-white photographs make this a useful volume for assignments and for the student interested in America's true natives.

13.19   Katz, William Loren. **Black Indians: A Hidden Heritage.** Atheneum, 1986. Ages 12 and up.

This is an important addition to an aspect of American history that is little known by Americans—the existence of black Indians. The author gives an enlightening account of blacks in America, from the time they arrived as slaves until the era of Bill Pickett, one of the best cowboys in the West, and looks at relations between blacks and Native Americans. The text is complemented by photographs and prints. There is a lengthy bibliography, but not all the authors whose works are quoted appear in the bibliography. *Notable Children's Trade Book in the Field of Social Studies.*

13.20   Marston, Elsa. **Mysteries in American Archeology.** Walker/ American History Series for Young People, 1986. Ages 10–13.

Who were the Mound Builders? Why did they disappear? Why was Mesa Verde abandoned? What did sun spirals and medicine wheels mean? What we know about America's earliest people emerges through an investigation of clues found at forty-one archaeological sites from New Hampshire to California. Some intriguing questions, however, remain unanswered. Appendixes, a glossary, and an index are included along with black-and-white drawings and photographs in each of the eleven chapters.

13.21   Moran, Tom. **A Family in Ireland.** Photographs by the author. Lerner Publications, 1986. Ages 8–12.

One in a series of books about families in other countries, this photographic story of a family living in County Galway, Ireland, portrays the family on their farm, at school, and involved in recreational activities. A pronunciation guide for the Gaelic names and terms and facts about the Republic of Ireland accompany this story of the O'Neachtain family.

13.22　Wolfson, Evelyn. **From Abenaki to Zuni: A Dictionary of Native American Tribes.** Illustrated by William Sauts Bock. Walker, 1988. Ages 10–12.

This lengthy book is more than a dictionary. Sixty-eight of the larger North American Indian tribes are described. Information about clothing, homes, food, tools, habitats, social life and customs, and modern descendants is included for each tribe. The book would serve as a valuable classroom resource for a unit on Native Americans.

13.23　Yue, Charlotte, and David Yue. **The Pueblo.** Houghton Mifflin, 1986. Ages 9–12.

Soft pencil drawings illustrate a detailed account of Pueblo Indian daily life, customs, history, and dwellings from ancient times to the present day. Information is well organized and accessible through the table of contents or the index. A substantial bibliography suggests further reading. *Notable Children's Trade Book in the Field of Social Studies.*

Food, Clothing, and Shelter

Primary

13.24　Carrick, Donald. **Milk.** Illustrated by the author. Greenwillow Books, 1986. Ages 3–7. (Picture book)

With sparse text and full-page watercolor illustrations, this book identifies the steps involved in transporting milk from the cow on the farm to the consumer in the grocery store. *Outstanding Science Trade Book for Children.*

13.25　Gibbons, Gail. **The Milk Makers.** Illustrated by the author. Macmillan, 1985. Ages 5–8. (Picture book)

Milk production and processing is described from cow to carton in a simple, straightforward manner. Terms are defined and pronunciations given. The flat, coloring-book-style illustrations make the subject accessible to young readers. *ALA Notable Children's Book* and *Outstanding Science Trade Book for Children.*

13.26　Gibbons, Gail. **Up Goes the Skyscraper!** Illustrated by the author. Four Winds Press, 1986. Ages 5–8. (Picture book)

Children interested in construction will learn how a sky-scraper grows from bottom to top. Gail Gibbons's precise, boldly colored drawings illustrate each step in detail appropri-ate to primary-grade readers. The text is brief and easy to read, while captions and labels add information to the illustra-tions, which dominate each page.

13.27   Goodall, John S. **The Story of a Castle.** Illustrated by the au-thor. Margaret K. McElderry Books, 1986. Ages 4–11. (Pic-ture book)

A wordless presentation of the uses of a castle during the past eight hundred years utilizes half pages interspersed with full-page spreads, all in full color.

13.28   Rogow, Zack. **Oranges.** Illustrated by Mary Szilagyi. Orchard Books, 1988. Ages 3–7. (Picture book)

Oranges have never looked richer and more luscious than they do in these vivid, glowing illustrations. The progress of the orange from seedling to big-city market, aided by workers of many nationalities, is simply described in text easy enough for beginning readers.

Intermediate

13.29   Giblin, James Cross. **From Hand to Mouth; Or, How We In-vented Knives, Forks, Spoons, and Chopsticks and the Table Manners to Go with Them.** Thomas Y. Crowell, 1987. Ages 10–12.

The captivating expository text traces the development of eating utensils from flint knives through specific cultural inno-vations to the cross-cultural uses being made today. The text is punctuated with photographs and reproductions of historic engravings. An index is included. *ALA Notable Children's Book.*

13.30   Giblin, James Cross. **Milk: The Fight for Purity.** Thomas Y. Crowell, 1986. Ages 9–14.

The history of milk production exemplifies the struggle for consumer rights and safety. James Cross Giblin wisely chose a product familiar to children and engages the young reader as both a primary consumer and a potential activist. An out-standing book design makes the topic even more appealing. *ALA Notable Children's Book.*

13.31 Weil, Lisl. **New Clothes: What People Wore—From Cavemen to Astronauts.** Illustrated by the author. Atheneum/Jean Karl Books, 1987. Ages 7–10.

This survey of Americans' and Europeans' use of clothing is sound on several points. The writing is direct, laced with flashes of humor. A smattering of history can be picked up along the way, allowing children to strengthen their grasp of time. Most importantly, the book suggests intelligent reasons for the changes in clothing styles, showing that they don't evolve in a vacuum, but are the result of direct external events.

13.32 Weiss, Harvey. **Shelters: From Tepee to Igloo.** Illustrated by the author. Thomas Y. Crowell, 1988. Ages 10–12.

Men and women have always wanted some kind of shelter to protect them from the extremes of weather, from wild animals, or from other people. This book creatively presents the variety of shelters that have been constructed by people around the world and in all walks of life. It describes the materials available from nature and how people utilized those gifts to build dwellings, including tepees, yurts, log cabins, stone houses, and igloos. Extra care is taken to illustrate the construction of the shelters so that a future architect will learn how they were built.

13.33 Yue, Charlotte, and David Yue. **The Igloo.** Houghton Mifflin, 1988. Ages 10–13.

How people survive in the Arctic, with its crackling cold, months of darkness, and wind-swept ice deserts, is described in this account of the igloo and the role it plays in the Inuit lifestyle. The Inuits' traditional way of life and culture is respectfully treated here. Methods of home building, hunting, and travel are described in fascinating detail with many useful and interesting sketches. An index, bibliography, and lists of books for further reading are included.

Government

Intermediate

13.34 Fritz, Jean. **Shh! We're Writing the Constitution.** Illustrated by Tomie dePaola. G. P. Putnam's Sons, 1987. Ages 7–11.

Drawings enliven every page of a relatively easy-to-read rendition of the events and people of the Constitutional Convention in 1787. The full text of the Constitution is included. *ALA Notable Children's Book.*

13.35 Levy, Elizabeth. **. . . If You Were There When They Signed the Constitution.** Illustrated by Richard Rosenblum. Scholastic, 1987. Ages 10–12.

This book answers the questions that are frequently asked about the Constitution. Although these answers are not given in great depth or detail, basic information about the Constitution is presented in a format that is easy to read and understand.

History and Geography

United States

Primary

13.36 Gibbons, Gail. **From Path to Highway: The Story of the Boston Post Road.** Illustrated by the author. Thomas Y. Crowell, 1986. Ages 6–9. (Picture book)

It was once an Indian path, widened by colonists. A person on horseback carried mail—"the post"—from New York City to Boston. The road actually consisted of three separate roads: a northern route through Massachusetts, a middle route through central Connecticut, and a southern route near the coast of southern Connecticut. The story of the Boston Post Road continues through the era of trains to the present four-lane highway. The easy text is supported by interesting maps, lively folk art, and a list of famous travelers of the road.

13.37 Knowlton, Jack. **Maps and Globes.** Illustrated by Harriett Barton. Thomas Y. Crowell, 1985. Ages 6–12.

This is an inviting introduction to the many types of maps, how they are made, and how they are used. The vocabulary of map reading is presented in italics and clearly defined. Each two-page spread presents one concept introduced by a boldface headline and illustrated with bright, uncluttered maps, charts, and pictures. *Notable Children's Trade Book in the Field of Social Studies.*

Intermediate

13.38   Anderson, Joan. **Pioneer Children of Appalachia.** Photographs by George Ancona. Clarion Books, 1986. Ages 9–12.

This third "living history" book takes a look at pioneer life in nineteenth-century West Virginia. Through black-and-white photographs, members of the fictional Davis family are seen making soap, candles, and baskets, drying fruit, and involved in other cooperative chores. Thrift and ingenuity are demonstrated as the pioneers work and play hard in their everyday tasks. *Notable Children's Trade Book in the Field of Social Studies.*

13.39   Ashabranner, Brent. **Always to Remember: The Story of the Vietnam Veterans Memorial.** Photographs by Jennifer Ashabranner. Dodd, Mead, 1988. Ages 10 and up.

The difficulties and drama involved in the struggle to build the Vietnam Veterans Memorial are clearly presented in this moving documentary. Supported with black-and-white photographs, the text presents detailed information for report writing about the Vietnam War and the national tribute to those who died in it.

13.40   Blumberg, Rhoda. **Commodore Perry in the Land of the Shogun.** Lothrop, Lee and Shepard Books, 1985. Ages 8–12.

Here is an examination of Commodore Matthew Perry's role in opening Japan to world trade in the 1850s. The appendixes, bibliography, and index make this an excellent classroom reference book to illustrate how East met West. *ALA Notable Children's Book, Boston Globe–Horn Book Award, Notable Children's Trade Book in the Field of Social Studies,* and *Newbery Honor Book.*

13.41   Blumberg, Rhoda. **The Incredible Journey of Lewis and Clark.** Lothrop, Lee and Shepard Books, 1987. Ages 11 and up.

This well-written account of the Lewis and Clark expedition, from its origins to its aftermath, has been derived from original sources and secondary scholarship. The tone is balanced and informative, yet Rhoda Blumberg also manages to note some foibles associated with the expedition. The book is well illustrated with maps and large reproductions of works by nineteenth-century artists.

13.42   Fisher, Leonard Everett. **The Alamo.** Illustrated by the author. Holiday House, 1987. Ages 8–11.

This book details the history of the Alamo, from a mission built in the mid-1700s to the siege of 1836, when it became a shrine of Texas liberty. Actual photographs as well as maps and drawings add to this historical documentation.

13.43   Fisher, Leonard Everett. **Monticello.** Holiday House, 1988. Ages 8 and up.

Well-chosen photographs, diagrams, and illustrations in black-and-white dominate this slender volume on a unique work of architecture—Monticello, Thomas Jefferson's home. These visuals combine with a clearly written text to give the reader not only an understanding of the architecture itself, but also a sense of the brilliant man behind it.

13.44   Fleming, Alice. **The King of Prussia and a Peanut Butter Sandwich.** Illustrated by Ronald Himler. Charles Scribner's Sons, 1988. Ages 8–12.

Many strands are woven together in this book to tell a lively true story about the Mennonites' immigration to the United States and their contribution of Turkey Red winter wheat to America's breadbasket. The story is interesting in itself, but even more fascinating is how the author's historical investigation is based on the untangling of the various events. The Mennonites' abandonment of warlike Prussia, their encounters with a Russian queen and Turkish farmers, the children's packing seeds to bring to America, the locust invasion in Kansas—all these events come together to tell how we come to eat our peanut butter on bread from Turkey Red wheat.

13.45   Freedman, Russell. **Cowboys of the Wild West.** Clarion Books, 1985. Ages 10 and up.

Russell Freedman provides a vivid picture of the real life of cowboys—their clothing and equipment, life on the trail and on the ranch, and what happened to the last of the old-time cowboys. The author used recollections of cowboys themselves and over fifty photographs to separate the real life of the cowboy from the legend. The book includes a bibliography for additional reading and an excellent index. *ALA Notable Children's Book* and *Notable Children's Trade Book in the Field of Social Studies.*

13.46 Freedman, Russell. **Indian Chiefs.** Holiday House, 1987. Ages 10–12.

Biographies of six Indian chiefs are presented as they faced the crucial question—should they resist the encroaching white settlers and make war, or should they cooperate with the whites and try to save their land and traditions? Included are biographies of Red Cloud of the Sioux, Santanta, Quanah, Washakie, Joseph, and Sitting Bull as each faced this moment of crisis. Excellent photographs and a bibliography make this a useful text for both teachers and students.

13.47 Haskins, Jim. **The Statue of Liberty: America's Proud Lady.** Lerner Publications, 1986. Ages 9–14.

Unique to this account of the Statue of Liberty is an interpretation of the symbolic importance of the statue, which now represents liberty for all. Jim Haskins points out that even though the ancestors of most of today's black Americans arrived here in chains, one of the reasons for France's gift to the United States was to honor America's abolition of slavery while preserving the union.

13.48 Mercer, Charles. **Statue of Liberty.** Rev. ed. G. P. Putnam's Sons, 1985. Ages 10–12.

This updated centennial edition tells the story behind the building of the Statue of Liberty, including the renovation work done in honor of the centennial. Photographs and an index make this a valuable reference.

13.49 Sewall, Marcia. **The Pilgrims of Plimoth.** Illustrated by the author. Atheneum, 1986. Ages 8–12. (Picture book)

A first-person narrative in language simulating that of the Pilgrims recounts the trials and accomplishments of their first difficult years at Plymouth. Beautiful light-toned oil paintings add meaning to the text. A glossary explains terms unfamiliar to today's readers. *Boston Globe–Horn Book Award* and *Notable Children's Trade Book in the Field of Social Studies.*

13.50 Shapiro, Mary J. **How They Built the Statue of Liberty.** Illustrated by Huck Scarry. Random House, 1985. Ages 10–13.

Budding architects and engineers will be intrigued with this book, which details the step-by-step descriptions of the methods used to build the Statue of Liberty. Information collected from the restoration team, which rebuilt the statue using the same techniques Frederic Bartholdi used in the original construction, is the source for the text and detailed drawings, which clarify the building procedures.

World

Primary

13.51 Kuskin, Karla. **Jerusalem, Shining Still.** Illustrated by David Frampton. Harper and Row/Charlotte Zolotow Books, 1987. Ages 6–10.

Karla Kuskin simply but effectively tells the history of Jerusalem, a story of three thousand years and one that involves great turmoil and rebuilding. It is a history that includes David, Nebuchadnezzar, Herod, Hadrian, Constantine, Saladin, Suleiman, and many groups that came to conquer. The colorful woodcuts enhance the simple, beautiful text.

Intermediate

13.52 Abells, Chana Byers. **The Children We Remember.** Greenwillow Books, 1986. Ages 11 and up.

A brief text accompanied by unforgettable black-and-white photographs documents the fate of Jewish children during the Holocaust, telling the stories of children killed by the Nazis and the stories of survivors. The simple declarative sentences have a tremendous impact, making the reading and viewing of the book a powerful emotional experience, as well as a fitting tribute to the lives that were lost. *Children's Choice* and *Notable Children's Trade Book in the Field of Social Studies.*

13.53 Ballard, Robert D. (edited by Patrick Crean). **Exploring the Titanic.** Illustrated by Ken Marschall. Scholastic/Madison Press Books, 1988. Ages 9–12.

Richly illustrated with actual photographs of the search for and discovery of the *Titanic*, the story of the sinking of the luxury liner in 1912 will be of interest to all age levels. A glossary, time line, and list of recommended further reading are included.

13.54 Fisher, Leonard Everett. **Pyramid of the Sun, Pyramid of the Moon.** Illustrated by the author. Macmillan, 1988. Ages 9 and up.

The richness of Mexico's history is captured through a concise text and starkly dramatic black-and-white paintings. In this short book, Leonard Everett Fisher tells us about the Teotihuacans and the massive adobe pyramids they built to the sun and moon in A.D. 100. We learn that the pyramids are constants through the rise and fall of subsequent civilizations—the Toltec, Chichimec, and Aztec—and through the invasion of Cortez and his armies in 1520. This is a historical overview at its best.

13.55 Goor, Ron, and Nancy Goor. **Pompeii: Exploring a Roman Ghost Town.** Thomas Y. Crowell, 1986. Ages 9–12.

The photodocumentary format of this book shows life in ancient Pompeii through artifacts, existing buildings and ruins, and graffiti. The book describes the destruction of the city by volcano, what the city looked like, and aspects of social, political, cultural, and religious life. It provides useful supplementary material for studies of Roman history. *Notable Children's Trade Book in the Field of Social Studies* and *Notable Children's Trade Book in the Language Arts.*

13.56 Knowlton, Jack. **Geography from A to Z: A Picture History.** Illustrated by Harriett Barton. Thomas Y. Crowell, 1988. Ages 7–10. (Picture book)

Physical geography terms from A, "archipelago," to Z, "zones," are explained. Each of the sixty-three entries in this dictionary is fully illustrated and is stated in terms that the youngest child will be able to understand.

13.57 Sullivan, George. **Treasure Hunt: The Sixteen-Year Search for the Lost Treasure Ship *Atocha*.** Henry Holt, 1987. Ages 10–12.

The successes and frustrations encountered by the people searching for the remains of the shipwrecked Spanish treasure ship *Atocha*, sunk in a storm at sea in 1622, are detailed in lengthy chapters. Occasional black-and-white photographs and maps extend the text. An index is included.

13.58 Sullivan, Jo M. **Liberia . . . in Pictures.** Lerner Publications/ Visual Geography Series, 1988. Ages 11–12.

Sixth-grade social studies teachers will want a copy of this book in their personal library, in their classroom, or in the school library. The text and photographs provide the latest information on the geography, climate, history, government, economy, culture, and people of Liberia, the west African country settled by freed American slaves. This is a revised edition of *Liberia in Pictures* by Camille Mirepoix.

13.59   The Viking Student World Atlas. Viking Kestrel, 1986. Ages 10–12.

This beautifully illustrated reference book contains not only maps but also color photographs and "Did You Know?" sections with interesting geographic facts. Small globes on each map enable the reader to see where a country is located in relation to the rest of the world. The book begins with general information about the world and maps and ends with a complete index.

13.60   Watson, R. L. South Africa . . . in Pictures. Lerner Publications/Visual Geography Series, 1988. Ages 11–12.

Readers are introduced to current information on the geography, history, government, economy, people, and culture of the troubled Republic of South Africa. The book is thoroughly illustrated with photographs, maps, and charts. This is a revised edition of *South Africa in Pictures* by Peter English.

13.61   Winter, Frank H. The Filipinos in America. Lerner Publications/In America Books, 1988. Ages 8–11.

Frank H. Winter discusses the land and people of the Philippines, traces Filipino immigration to the United States, explores the Filipino role in World War II, and presents Filipino contributions to American life. Black-and-white photographs enhance the text. The book contains an index and provides information about a topic for which there are few resources.

Human Relationships

Primary

13.62   Ancona, George. Helping Out. Photographs by the author. Clarion Books, 1985. Ages 5–10. (Picture book)

The author-photographer explains that some of the best times of his youth were spent entering the adult world as a helper.

This book of black-and-white photographs shows children side by side with adults doing important work in many settings. Work is shown as rewarding and fun.

13.63 Bahr, Amy C. **It's OK to Say No: A Book for Parents and Children to Read Together.** Illustrated by Frederick Bennett Green. Grosset and Dunlap/It's OK to Say No Books, 1986. Ages 4–7.

Children are helped to recognize a possibly threatening situation and to remove themselves from it. In this book, children are directed to say "No!"—even to an adult if necessary.

13.64 Bahr, Amy C. **Sometimes It's OK to Tell Secrets: A Book for Parents and Children to Read Together.** Illustrated by Frederick Bennett Green. Grosset and Dunlap/It's OK to Say No Books, 1986. Ages 4–7.

Children are encouraged to tell their parents or another responsible adult if something is wrong, even if it means telling a secret. Some secrets should always be told, and this book presents several situations that illustrate that point.

13.65 Bahr, Amy C. **What Should You Do When . . . ? A Book for Parents and Children to Read Together.** Illustrated by Frederick Bennett Green. Grosset and Dunlap/It's OK to Say No Books, 1986. Ages 4–7.

This book accomplishes just what it sets out to do—to sit an adult and a child down together to discuss what the child should do in case of a confusing or frightening situation. In a nonthreatening way, it presents possible situations, such as being approached by a stranger, receiving a scary phone call, or being inappropriately touched. Children are given the information they need to respond emphatically in such cases. In a "Note to Parents," adults are encouraged to discuss and practice responses with children. Text and illustrations are simple and straightforward. The four books in the series are similar and serve to reinforce each other.

13.66 Bahr, Amy C. **Your Body Is Your Own: A Book for Parents and Children to Read Together.** Illustrated by Frederick Bennett Green. Grosset and Dunlap/It's OK to Say No Books, 1986. Ages 4–7.

In this book, "good touches" are distinguished from "bad touches," and children are directed to remember the differences. Private parts are defined as those parts of their bodies covered by a bathing suit. Children are left with the clear message that their bodies are their own, and that they should speak up loud and clear if anyone violates their privacy.

13.67 Girard, Linda Walvoord. **Who Is a Stranger and What Should I Do?** Illustrated by Helen Cogancherry. Albert Whitman, 1985. Ages 6–8. (Picture book)

This is a thorough discussion of the problem of being approached by a stranger. Each chapter describes a potential danger and how to deal with it in this good book for parents or teachers to share and discuss with children. The book concludes with ten suggestions for review and practice. The realistic pencil drawings add to the understanding of the text.

13.68 Simon, Norma. **Wedding Days.** Illustrated by Christa Kieffer. Albert Whitman, 1988. Ages 6–10. (Picture book)

This attractively illustrated book discusses with honesty and simplicity decisions to marry, plans for the wedding, first and second marriages, formation of new families, anniversaries, and places where the event may be held.

Intermediate

13.69 Kaufman, Curt, and Gita Kaufman. **Hotel Boy.** Photographs by Curt Kaufman. Atheneum, 1988. Ages 8–12.

Poignant black-and-white photographs and the first-person narrative present dramatically what life is like for one of the more than a million children in this country whose families are homeless and dependent on public and private assistance for food and shelter. Henri describes what it is like to live in a hotel in New York City with his brother and his mother while she looks for a job and an apartment.

Transportation

Primary

13.70 Bushey, Jerry. **Monster Trucks and Other Giant Machines on Wheels.** Carolrhoda Books, 1985. Ages 6–9. (Picture book)

A concise, readable text and crisp color photographs are used to introduce young readers to twelve machines on wheels, ranging from the familiar bulldozer to the highly specialized crawler transporter. The basic information supplied makes this a good choice for the avid truck fan as well as the casual browser.

13.71 Gibbons, Gail. **Fill It Up! All about Service Stations.** Illustrated by the author. Thomas Y. Crowell, 1985. Ages 4–8. (Picture book)

A simple text and brightly colored cartoonlike illustrations treat preschoolers and beginning readers to a behind-the-scenes look at an average service station. A busy day is described, with cars stopping at the station for gas or repairs.

13.72 Lyon, David. **The Biggest Truck.** Illustrated by the author. Lothrop, Lee and Shepard Books, 1988. Ages 4–8. (Picture book)

Jim drives the big red truck all night to deliver twenty tons of strawberries to Woosterville, seven hours away. The text is filled with truck-noise words that beg to be read aloud by the truck enthusiasts in the group. The full-color illustrations extol the enormity of the truck, the strength of its propulsion, and the commitment of its driver.

13.73 Maestro, Betsy. **Ferryboat.** Illustrated by Giulio Maestro. Thomas Y. Crowell, 1986. Ages 6–8. (Picture book)

Vibrant watercolor illustrations immerse the reader in the sensations and delights of a ferryboat's journey as it crosses the river with its valuable cargo. The illustrations enhance the text as the vocabulary skillfully teaches about ferryboats. *Notable Children's Trade Book in the Field of Social Studies.*

13.74 Robbins, Ken. **City/Country: A Car Trip in Photographs.** Photographs by the author. Viking Kestrel, 1985. Ages 3–6. (Picture book)

The simple rhythmic text and muted color photographs treat readers to a car trip from the urban bustle of New York City through the ordered suburban landscape to the rustic serenity of the countryside. The scenery is that viewed from a child's backseat perspective.

13.75 Rockwell, Anne. **Fire Engines.** Illustrated by the author. E. P. Dutton, 1986. Ages 3–6. (Picture book)

Colorful pictures that are simple but accurate in detail amplify a text that is brief but informative. In this appealing book for young fire-engine fans, there is a surprise—all the equipment is operated by Dalmation dogs in fire-fighting gear.

13.76 Sattler, Helen Roney. **Train Whistles: A Language in Code.** Rev. ed. Illustrated by Giulio Maestro. Lothrop, Lee and Shepard Books, 1985. Ages 5–8.

Those who lie in bed at night listening to distant train whistles will value this book as it explains what those signals mean. The train's special language is interpreted as the reader follows a freight train cross-country. The common signals are listed again in a chart at the back of the book. Illustrations give further details of trains.

Intermediate

13.77 Boyer, Edward. **River and Canal.** Illustrated by the author. Holiday House, 1986. Ages 11 and up.

The building, mechanics, and history of an imaginary canal reflect the history of American canals. The architect-author has created a book in which the illustrations and text are equally important in providing information. For full benefit, the reader must carefully study both text and illustrations. *Notable Children's Trade Book in the Field of Social Studies.*

Other

Primary

13.78 Turner, Dorothy. **The Man-Made Wonders of the World.** Dillon Press/International Picture Library, 1986. Ages 4–7.

Fascinating double-page full-color photographs illustrate fourteen spectacular man-made structures, including the Great Wall of China, the Sphinx, the Taj Mahal, and the Golden Gate Bridge. Brief captions and an appended map of places featured provide just enough information to send young readers scurrying for more.

Intermediate

13.79   Dolan, Edward F., Jr. **Great Mysteries of the Ice and Snow.**
Dodd, Mead, 1985. Ages 10–13.

Abominable Snowman—fact or fiction? Disappearing and re-
appearing Dougherty Island—fact or fiction? Will we ever
know? Several unsolved mysteries of the ice and snow are
presented with actual accounts, enhanced with photographs
and maps. This book will stimulate the reader's curiosity
about these mysterious occurrences that have never been
solved.

13.80   Fritz, Jean. **China Homecoming.** Photographs by Michael
Fritz. G. P. Putnam's Sons, 1985. Ages 9–14.

In a companion volume to *Homesick: My Own Story,* Jean
Fritz gives a sensitive, moving account of her return to
Wuhan, China, the city where she was born and lived her first
thirteen years. Her skillfully constructed narrative inter-
weaves details of Chinese history and culture with personal
memories and impressions, giving readers a strong sense of
contemporary China. The book includes seventy photographs, thirty of which are in full color. *Notable Children's
Trade Book in the Field of Social Studies.*

13.81   Giblin, James Cross. **Let There Be Light: A Book about Windows.** Thomas Y. Crowell, 1988. Ages 11–13.

In writing about the history of windows, James Cross Giblin
also uniquely introduces young readers to many facets of
world history and of architectural history. The photographs
and prints aid in the understanding of all three histories. *ALA
Notable Children's Book.*

13.82   Graham, Ada, and Frank Graham. **The Big Stretch: The Complete Book of the Amazing Rubber Band.** Illustrated by Richard Rosenblum. Alfred A. Knopf/Borzoi Books, 1985. Ages
9–12.

Here is a browser's delight and a trivia lover's treasure trove.
The book combines entertaining activities with solid science
to stretch a familiar object, the rubber band, into hours of
fun. The black-and-white sketches help to describe the activities and add additional humor to the explanations. Included

are an explanation of how rubber bands are made, a discussion of the rubber band industry, and a list of some of the two thousand modern uses for rubber bands.

13.83 Hausherr, Rosmarie. **The One-Room School at Squabble Hollow.** Photographs by the author. Four Winds Press, 1988. Ages 10–12.

This fascinating photodocumentary of school and community life in the rural town of Squabble Hollow, Vermont, points out how similar the basic elements in life are, no matter how different the situations might seem on first glance. The strong black-and-white photographs are supported by brief explanatory paragraphs in narrative prose style.

Recommended Books Published before 1985

Adams, Barbara. *Like It Is: Facts and Feelings about Handicaps from Kids Who Know.* Illustrated by James Stanfield. Walker, 1979. 9–12.

Adkins, Jan. *Symbols: A Silent Language.* Walker, 1978. 9–11.

Aliki. *A Medieval Feast.* Thomas Y. Crowell, 1983. 7–9.

———. *Mummies Made in Egypt.* Thomas Y. Crowell, 1979. 7–10.

Anno, Mitsumasa. *Anno's U.S.A.* Philomel Books, 1983. 6 and up.

Asimov, Isaac. *The Greeks: A Great Adventure.* Houghton Mifflin, 1965. 10 and up.

Barton, Byron. *Building a House.* Greenwillow Books, 1981. 5–7.

Baylor, Byrd. *The Way to Start a Day.* Illustrated by Peter Parnall. Charles Scribner's Sons, 1978. 7–9.

Bernstein, Joanne E., and Stephen V. Gullo. *When People Die.* Illustrated by Rosmarie Hausherr. E. P. Dutton, 1977. 5–9.

Branley, Franklyn M. *The Mystery of Stonehenge.* Illustrated by Victor G. Ambrus. Thomas Y. Crowell, 1969. 9–12.

Burton, Virginia Lee. *The Little House.* Houghton Mifflin, 1952. 4–7.

———. *Mike Mulligan and His Steam Shovel.* Houghton Mifflin, 1939. 4–8.

Crews, Donald. *Freight Train.* Greenwillow Books, 1978. 3–6.

dePaola, Tomie. *Charlie Needs a Cloak.* Prentice-Hall, 1973. 5–8.

———. *The Lady of Guadalupe.* Holiday House, 1980. 6–9.

———. *The Popcorn Book.* Holiday House, 1978. 6–9.

Epstein, Sam, and Beryl Epstein. *She Never Looked Back: Margaret Mead in Samoa.* Illustrated by Victor Juhasz. Coward, McCann and Geoghegan, 1980. 9–11.

Field, Rachel. *Prayer for a Child*. Illustrated by Elizabeth Orton Jones. Macmillan, 1944. 4–7.

Fisher, Leonard Everett. *The Newspapers*. Holiday House, 1981. 10 and up.

———. *The Railroads*. Holiday House, 1979. 10 and up.

Foster, Genevieve. *Year of Independence, 1776*. Charles Scribner's Sons, 1970. 9–11.

Gardner, Richard A. *The Boys and Girls Book about Divorce*. Illustrated by Alfred Lowenheim. Bantam, 1971. 9–12.

Gibbons, Gail. *Boat Book*. Holiday House, 1983. 4–7.

———. *Department Store*. Thomas Y. Crowell, 1984. 4–7.

———. *New Road!* Thomas Y. Crowell, 1983. 4–7.

———. *The Post Office Book: Mail and How It Moves*. Thomas Y. Crowell, 1982. 4–7.

Giblin, James Cross. *The Skyscraper Book*. Illustrated by Anthony Kramer and David Anderson. Thomas Y. Crowell, 1981. 9–12.

Goodall, John S. *The Story of an English Village*. Atheneum, 1979. 8–10.

Haskins, James (with J. M. Stifle). *The Quiet Revolution: The Struggle for the Rights of Disabled Americans*. Thomas Y. Crowell, 1979. 10 and up.

Hoobler, Dorothy, and Thomas Hoobler. *An Album of World War I*. Franklin Watts, 1976. 9–12.

James, Elizabeth, and Carol Barkin. *How to Keep a Secret: Writing and Talking in Code*. Illustrated by Joel Schick. Lothrop, Lee and Shepard Books, 1978. 9–12.

Jaspersohn, William. *A Day in the Life of a Television News Reporter*. Little, Brown, 1981. 9–12.

Kurelek, William. *Lumberjack*. Houghton Mifflin, 1974. 8–10.

Lasker, Joe. *Merry Ever After: The Story of Two Medieval Weddings*. Viking Press, 1979. 7–9.

Lasky, Kathryn. *Sugaring Time*. Illustrated by Christopher G. Knight. Macmillan, 1983. 8 and up.

———. *Tall Ships*. Illustrated by Christopher G. Knight. Charles Scribner's Sons, 1978. 10 and up.

———. *The Weaver's Gift*. Illustrated by Christopher G. Knight. Frederick Warne, 1980. 10 and up.

LeShan, Eda. *Grandparents: A Special Kind of Love*. Illustrated by Tricia Taggert. Macmillan, 1984. 9–12.

Macaulay, David. *Castle: The Story of Its Construction*. Houghton Mifflin, 1973. 9 and up.

———. *Pyramid*. Houghton Mifflin, 1975. 9 and up.

MacGregor, Anne, and Scott MacGregor. *Domes: A Project Book.* Lothrop, Lee and Shepard Books, 1981. 9–11.

Maestro, Betsy, and Giulio Maestro. *On the Town: A Book of Clothing Words.* Crown, 1983. 4–6.

Mango, Karin N. *Mapmaking.* Illustrated by Judith Hoffman Corwin. Julian Messner, 1984. 9–12.

Maruki, Toshi. *Hiroshima No Pika.* Lothrop, Lee and Shepard Books, 1982. 9 and up.

Meltzer, Milton. *The Black Americans: A History in Their Own Words, 1619–1983.* Thomas Y. Crowell, 1984. 10 and up.

———. *Never to Forget: The Jews of the Holocaust.* Harper and Row, 1976. 10 and up.

Moskin, Marietta D. *In Search of God: The Story of Religion.* Atheneum, 1979. 10 and up.

Musgrove, Margaret. *Ashanti to Zulu: African Traditions.* Illustrated by Leo and Diane Dillon. Dial Books for Young Readers/E. P. Dutton, 1976. 7–9.

Rau, Margaret. *The Minority Peoples of China.* Julian Messner, 1982. 9–12.

Rockwell, Anne. *When We Grow Up.* E. P. Dutton, 1981. 4–6.

Rockwell, Harlow. *My Doctor.* Macmillan, 1973. 3–6.

Rosenberg, Maxine. *Being Adopted.* Illustrated by George Ancona. Lothrop, Lee and Shepard Books, 1984. 8–10.

Rounds, Glen. *The Prairie Schooners.* Holiday House, 1968. 9–10.

Scarry, Huck. *Life on a Barge: A Sketchbook.* Prentice-Hall, 1982. 8–10.

Shapiro, Rebecca. *A Whole World of Cooking.* Little, Brown, 1972. 10 and up.

Shirer, William L. *The Rise and Fall of Adolph Hitler.* Random House, 1961. 10 and up.

Simon, Norma. *All Kinds of Families.* Illustrated by Joe Lasker. Albert Whitman, 1976. 4–7.

Sobol, Harriet Langsam. *Pete's House.* Illustrated by Patricia Agre. Macmillan, 1978. 7–9.

Stein, Sara Bennett, et al. *About Handicaps: An Open Family Book for Parents and Children Together.* Illustrated by Dick Frank. Walker, 1974. 4–8.

Sullivan, George. *Supertanker! The Story of the World's Biggest Ships.* Dodd, Mead, 1978. 9–12.

Tunis, Edwin. *Wheels: A Pictorial History.* Thomas Y. Crowell, 1955. 9–12.

Walker, Barbara Muhs. *The Little House Cookbook: Frontier Foods from Laura Ingalls Wilder's Classic Stories.* Illustrated by Garth Williams. Harper and Row, 1979. 10–12.

Watanabe, Shigeo. *How Do I Put It On? Getting Dressed.* Illustrated by Yasuo Ohtomo. Philomel Books, 1979. 3–5.

Weitzman, David. *My Backyard History Book.* Illustrated by James Robertson. Little, Brown, 1975. 9–12.

Wolf, Bernard. *Anna's Silent World.* J. B. Lippincott, 1977. 7–9.

———. *In This Proud Land: The Story of a Mexican American Family.* J. B. Lippincott, 1978. 9–12.

Yolen, Jane. *Simple Gifts: The Story of the Shakers.* Illustrated by Betty Fraser. Viking Press, 1976. 10–12.

14 Science and Mathematics: Nonfiction

Aeronautics and Space

Primary

14.1 Ride, Sally (with Susan Okie). **To Space and Back.** Lothrop, Lee and Shepard Books, 1986. Ages 5–12.

This fascinating firsthand account of life aboard a space shuttle gives insights into daily routines as well as the kind of work astronauts do. Sally Ride's amiable tone throughout the text makes descriptions of such things as weightlessness and launching a satellite highly readable. The fifty full-color photographs are always informative and often breathtaking. *Outstanding Science Trade Book for Children.*

Intermediate

14.2 Berliner, Don. **Research Airplanes: Testing the Boundaries of Flight.** Lerner Publications, 1988. Ages 9–12.

Don Berliner details how a research airplane is designed and flown. Subsequent chapters deal with specific kinds of research planes, including subsonic, supersonic, and V/STOL (vertical short takeoff and landing) planes. Numerous photographs and an index are provided.

14.3 Branley, Franklyn M. **Mysteries of Outer Space.** Illustrated by Sally J. Bensusen. E. P. Dutton/Lodestar Books/Mysteries of the Universe Series, 1985. Ages 9–12.

In a question-and-answer format, information about forces operating in space and about the ways humans are using and exploring outer space is presented in easily read, succinct paragraphs. Diagrams are included to illustrate the more abstract concepts. The book discusses such topics as the sky in outer space, time in outer space, survival in space, uses of space, and mining the asteroids. Included is a comprehensive index.

14.4   Briggs, Carole S. **Research Balloons: Exploring Hidden Worlds.** Lerner Publications, 1988. Ages 10–13.

Carole S. Briggs traces the history of balloon flight and explains how balloon research has enhanced the history of space exploration. Through photographs, drawings, illustrations, and lively text, the author explains balloon research and its place in scientific research. A glossary and index are provided.

14.5   Dwiggins, Don. **Flying the Space Shuttles.** Dodd, Mead, 1985. Ages 10–12.

The history and purposes of the U.S. space shuttle program are presented, accented by color photographs taken during various missions. The numerous procedures that are used on flights are adequately explained in this stimulating book for space enthusiasts. *Outstanding Science Trade Book for Children.*

14.6   Marshall, Ray. **The Plane.** Illustrated by John Bradley. Viking Kestrel/Watch It Work Books, 1985. Ages 6–10.

Lift-up flaps, pop-ups, and moving diagrams illustrate the principles of flight and the internal and external workings of an airplane. Brief but informative, this pop-up book includes a paper model plane, drawn to scale and ready for assembly.

14.7   Maurer, Richard. **The NOVA Space Explorer's Guide: Where to Go and What to See.** Clarkson N. Potter, 1985. Ages 8–12.

As if participating in a fictional voyage through space, the reader is presented with information about rockets, planets, moons, stars, and galaxies. The major portion of each page contains black-and-white and color photographs or inserts of pertinent charts or historical information. The text moves quickly and blends the fictional account of the journey with factual information about the particular sights along the way. The layout invites browsing, or the reader can focus on the text of each chapter in this oversize, intriguing book. *ALA Notable Children's Book.*

14.8   Schulke, Flip, Debra Schulke, Penelope McPhee, and Raymond McPhee. **Your Future in Space: The U.S. Space Camp
Training Program.** Crown, 1986. Ages 10 and up.

Here is a description of the U.S. Space Camp Training Program for students in fifth through tenth grade. The reader will
learn about the physics of space travel, the training of astronauts, and the probable daily routines onboard a space station. The major portion of each page is devoted to full-color
photographs of the training equipment and simulated spacecraft experiences at the camp, as well as to photographs of
actual NASA astronauts training and practicing the use of
space technology.

14.9   Stoff, Joshua. **Dirigible.** Illustrated by the author. Atheneum,
1985. Ages 10–13. (Picture book)

Joshua Stoff tells of the construction, launching, and operation of a dirigible during the 1930s. Although the airship is fictional, the author includes realistic details and technically accurate illustrations to describe the process of building and
flying a dirigible. An index and bibliography are included.

14.10   Stoff, Joshua. **The Voyage of the *Ruslan:* The First Manned
Exploration of Mars.** Illustrated by the author. Atheneum,
1986. Ages 10–14.

Come aboard the *Ruslan* in the 1990s as its Russian crew explores Mars. Using current data from American and Soviet
space research and development, the author speculates about
the conditions of future flight and the nature of discoveries to
be made on the red planet.

14.11   Sullivan, George. **Famous Air Force Bombers.** Dodd, Mead,
1985. Ages 9–12.

Air Force bombers, essential to American military defense
since World War II, are described and pictured, from the
B-17 Flying Fortress to the Stealth bomber. George Sullivan
describes the history of each plane and provides statistics for
the most avid of airplane buffs.

14.12   Sullivan, George. **Famous Navy Fighter Planes.** Dodd, Mead,
1986. Ages 10–12.

This book examines the progression of the navy's fighting air
machines from World War I to the present. Statistical data

are given for each plane, and the history and significance of each plane are discussed, with any technical words explained in the text. The book is filled with black-and-white photographs, and information is provided on where the aircraft are displayed.

14.13　Sullivan, George. **Famous U.S. Spy Planes.** Dodd, Mead, 1987. Ages 9–12.

George Sullivan details the most significant intelligence-gathering planes used by the United States. The account is arranged in chronological order, from the first spy plane of World War I, the Curtiss JN, to the Lockheed SR-71 Blackbird, and provides a description and brief history of each of twenty-four famous U.S. spy planes. Numerous photographs are also included.

14.14　Sullivan, George. **The Thunderbirds.** Dodd, Mead, 1986. Ages 9–12.

Here is a thorough and detailed account of the U.S. Air Force's famous crack aerial demonstration squadron. The history of the unit, planning and executing an air show, and becoming a member of the Thunderbirds are explained. Numerous color photographs and diagrams of flight patterns add clarity to the text.

The Animal Kingdom

Animal Behaviors

Primary

14.15　Oxford Scientific Films (edited by Miranda MacQuitty). **Side by Side.** G. P. Putnam's Sons, 1988. Ages 5–12. (Picture book)

Fascinating full-color photographs present animals and plants that use each other in harmful or helpful ways. A brief text identifies each animal or plant in the partnership and how it affects the other.

Intermediate

14.16　Hirschi, Ron. **One Day on Pika's Peak.** Photographs by Galen Burrell. Dodd, Mead, 1986. Ages 8–10.

On a summer day in the Rocky Mountains, the lives of a weasel and a pika family entwine through their roles as predator and prey. From one to three closeup color photographs on each page enhance the informative text. An index and appendix are included.

14.17   Patterson, Francine. **Koko's Story.** Photographs by Ronald H. Cohn. Scholastic, 1987. Ages 6–12.

Readers who liked *Koko's Kitten* will enjoy a second photodocumentary about the remarkable lowland gorilla who has been taught to communicate with humans through sign language. Koko presently is being studied at Stanford University, where she has acquired several new friends, including Michael, a young male gorilla, and Lipstick, her latest kitten. *Children's Choice.*

14.18   Silverstein, Alvin, and Virginia Silverstein. **Nature's Living Lights: Fireflies and Other Bioluminescent Creatures.** Illustrated by Pamela and Walter Carroll. Little, Brown, 1988. Ages 10–13.

Bioluminescence is the scientific term for the chemical reaction that produces light in certain insects, plants, and sea animals for the purposes of communication, finding food, and attracting mates. Simplified explanantions in easy-to-read prose are given for one of nature's mysteries. Photographs in place of the illustrations would have enhanced this well-written material.

Birds

Primary

14.19   Featherly, Jay. **Ko-hoh: The Call of the Trumpeter Swan.** Photographs by the author. Carolrhoda Books/Nature Watch Books, 1986. Ages 5–12.

The life cycle, nest building, mating, raising of young, and other behaviors of the trumpeter swan are clearly explained in this book with beautiful photographs showing the swan in its North American habitat.

14.20   Hirschi, Ron. **What Is a Bird?** Photographs by Galen Burrell. Walker, 1987. Ages 4–7. (Picture book)

A simple, lyrical text and crisp full-color photographs introduce traits of birds to the very young child. The book depicts a variety of familiar and exotic winged creatures in such activities as nest sitting, flying, balancing on a wire, leaping, diving, dancing, and sleeping. This title is useful for its elegant appreciation of birds and also as a model for children's own catalogs of animal characteristics.

14.21   Hirschi, Ron. **Where Do Birds Live?** Photographs by Galen Burrell. Walker, 1987. Ages 6–8.

Each wide-angle, full-color photograph introduces readers to the habitats of specific groups of birds, including ponds, rivers, old trees, mountains, and backyards. Closeup individual photographs of different kinds of birds provide contrasts and extend the reader's experience. Adults may refer to the afterword for answers to potential questions from children.

14.22   Selsam, Millicent E., and Joyce Hunt. **A First Look at Owls, Eagles, and Other Hunters of the Sky.** Illustrated by Harriett Springer. Walker, 1986. Ages 5–10. (Picture book)

The conversational style used by the authors invites readers and listeners to interact with this book. Questions asked in the text about birds of prey are answered in the detailed black-and-white illustrations. An emphasis on classification makes this book especially useful in science classes and also in developing thinking skills.

Intermediate

14.23   Billings, Charlene W. **The Loon: Voice of the Wilderness.** Dodd, Mead/Skylight Books, 1988. Ages 10–13.

Information is given about the loon's habitats, habits, migrations, and the current threats to its existence. Outstanding color photographs of this elusive bird supplement the text. The book is indexed.

14.24   McNulty, Faith. **Peeping in the Shell: A Whooping Crane Is Hatched.** Illustrated by Irene Brady. Harper and Row, 1986. Ages 8–12.

The plight of the endangered whooping crane is emphasized through the true story of a scientist who mimicked crane behavior, courted and artificially inseminated a female crane, and then cared for her and the egg until the chick hatched. A lively telling of this fascinating event and numerous pencil drawings make this a unique and welcome addition to all science collections. *ALA Notable Children's Book* and *Outstanding Science Trade Book for Children.*

14.25   Ryden, Hope. **America's Bald Eagle.** Photographs by the author. G. P. Putnam's Sons, 1985. Ages 8–12.

The grandeur of the bald eagle, as well as its precarious existence, is detailed in the narrative prose text and the closeup black-and-white photographs. Information is given about nest building and the lengthy time during which the eagle parents feed, care for, and protect the eaglets until they can care for themselves. Situations threatening the eagle's survival and the various efforts to save our national bird are described. An index is included.

14.26   Scott, Jack Denton. **Swans.** Photographs by Ozzie Sweet. G. P. Putnam's Sons, 1987. Ages 8–10.

Information about swans' habitats, eating and nesting practices, and flight patterns is set forth in black-and-white closeup photographs that fill or almost fill each page. The text adds details and vocabulary specific to each of the seven species of swans. An index is included.

14.27   Singer, Arthur, and Alan Singer, illustrators (text by Virginia Buckley). **State Birds.** E. P. Dutton/Lodestar Books, 1986. Ages 9–12.

Arthur Singer, one of the most respected bird artists, and his son Alan portray the birds honored by each state. Their brilliant illustrations depict the birds, both male and female, in typical habitats. Virginia Buckley's text gives details of the birds' origins, characteristics, and habits. She also lists the dates of the state resolutions and the methods of selection that led to the choices. The book is recommended by the National Audubon Society and the National Wildlife Federation. *Outstanding Science Trade Book for Children.*

Fish

Intermediate

14.28   Reed, Don C. **Sevengill: The Shark and Me.** Illustrated by Pamela Ford Johnson. Alfred A. Knopf and Sierra Club/Borzoi Books, 1986. Ages 10–12.

Here is a realistic portrayal of sharks as told from the perspective of diver Don C. Reed. He recounts the birth and early life of Sevengill the shark and dispels some common myths about sharks. A sense of mystery and a reverence for life surround Reed's depictions of sharks as predators.

14.29 Schlein, Miriam. **The Dangerous Life of the Sea Horse.** Illustrated by Gwen Cole. Atheneum, 1986. Ages 7–10.

Sepia drawings amplify the simple text which describes the life cycle of this intriguing creature. Pronunciations, metric and standard measurements, an index, and a lack of anthropomorphism enhance the presentation of the sea horse's life.

General Information

Primary

14.30 Cole, Sheila. **When the Tide Is Low.** Illustrated by Virginia Wright-Frierson. Lothrop, Lee and Shepard Books, 1985. Ages 3–8.

Realistic full-color watercolors illustrate the story of a mother and her young child as they plan a visit to the beach at low tide. At the end of the book is an illustrated and detailed glossary of the animals they expect to find at the beach. *Outstanding Science Trade Book for Children.*

14.31 Gibbons, Gail. **Zoo.** Illustrated by the author. Thomas Y. Crowell, 1987. Ages 3–7. (Picture book)

Gail Gibbons lets children behind the scenes at a zoo and answers questions they would be likely to ask: How do animals get to the zoo? Who takes care of them? What do they eat? With simple text and brightly colored illustrations, she invites readers to come in and find out about the zoo kitchen, nursery, and hospital and to get an idea of how much work is needed to keep the zoo running and the animals comfortable.

14.32 Heller, Ruth. **How to Hide a Butterfly and Other Insects.** Illustrated by the author. Grosset and Dunlap, 1985. Ages 4–7.

This is one in a series of six books explaining the concept of camouflage to young readers. Text in verse and full-color illustrations show how insects can nearly vanish when predators approach.

14.33   Heller, Ruth. **How to Hide a Polar Bear and Other Mammals.**
Illustrated by the author. Grosset and Dunlap, 1985. Ages
4–7. (Picture book)

Even the huge polar bear uses camouflage for protection.
This book depicts how some mammals conceal themselves.

14.34   Heller, Ruth. **How to Hide an Octopus and Other Sea Creatures.** Illustrated by the author. Grosset and Dunlap, 1985.
Ages 4–7.

Eight sea creatures, including an octopus, demonstrate how
they use camouflage to "disappear" from view.

14.35   Heller, Ruth. **Ruth Heller's How to Hide a Crocodile and
Other Reptiles.** Illustrated by the author. Grosset and Dunlap, 1986. Ages 4–7.

Reptiles are often undiscovered in their surroundings. In this
book about camouflage, young readers will enjoy seeing the
reptiles alone and then searching for them in their natural settings. Full-color drawings are accompanied by a cleverly written poem for each reptile.

14.36   Heller, Ruth. **Ruth Heller's How to Hide a Gray Treefrog and
Other Amphibians.** Illustrated by the author. Grosset and
Dunlap, 1986. Ages 4–7.

Light verse and full-color illustrations combine to demonstrate how amphibians can use camouflage to deceive their
enemies.

14.37   Heller, Ruth. **Ruth Heller's How to Hide a Whippoorwill and
Other Birds.** Illustrated by the author. Grosset and Dunlap,
1986. Ages 4–7.

Whippoorwills and other birds use their own markings and
colorings for protection from predators. This is another in a
series about animal camouflage.

14.38   Hoban, Tana. **A Children's Zoo.** Photographs by the author.
Greenwillow Books, 1985. Ages 5–7. (Picture book)

Tana Hoban's fresh photographs invite the youngest reader to
tour the zoo. Descriptive words boldly enhance each page. A
special feature of this book is a glossary that includes animal
habitats and eating habits. *Outstanding Science Trade Book
for Children.*

14.39 Lauber, Patricia. **What Big Teeth You Have!** Illustrated by Martha Weston. Thomas Y. Crowell, 1986. Ages 7–11.

Teeth get special attention in this book because they offer clues to an animal's lifestyle and classification. Each section describes the teeth of a different group of animals, even dinosaurs. The text reads easily, with unfamiliar words defined in context. Black-and-white sketches add interest and information. An index is included.

14.40 Oxford Scientific Films (edited by Jennifer Coldrey and Karen Goldie-Morrison). **Hide and Seek.** G. P. Putnam's Sons, 1986. Ages 6–11.

Full-color photographs document thirty-seven animals camouflaged in twelve different kinds of habitats, including grasslands, snow, bark, living or dead leaves, and flowers. Brief sentences point out specific observations about each photograph. Following the photographs are several pages of additional information about these animals, including how camouflage can aid the predator and protect the prey.

14.41 Robinson, Marlene M. **What Good Is a Tail?** Dodd, Mead, 1985. Ages 5–9. (Picture book)

The physical appearances and functions of twenty-three tails are detailed in sparse text and distinctive black-and-white photographs. After learning about each tail, the reader turns the page to associate the tail with the complete animal. The information is organized to explain the functions of tails, citing examples for each function from a variety of animals, including mammals, reptiles, fish, amphibians, and birds. An index is included. *Outstanding Science Trade Book for Children.*

14.42 Seymour, Peter. **How Things Are Made.** Illustrated by Linda Griffith; designed by David A. Carter. E. P. Dutton/Lodestar Books/Turn-the-Wheel Books, 1988. Ages 6–8. (Picture book)

How does a beaver build a dam or a spider spin a web? Various animal tasks are explained in a five-step process for each of eight animals: beavers, cows, bees, sheep, spiders, prairie dogs, birds, and silkworms. After reading each step, the reader can turn a wheel on the page that depicts the animal's activity during that step. Sturdy construction and clearly drawn pictures provide interesting information at a beginning level.

14.43 Silver, Donald M. **The Animal World.** Illustrated by Patricia J. Wynne. Random House/Library of Knowledge, 1987. Ages 6–10.

Donald M. Silver provides a catalog of information about the animal world, ranging from single-celled creatures through mammals. The information is clearly organized and presented with a profusion of full-color drawings of the animals and their habitats. An extensive index is included.

14.44 Tison, Annette, and Talus Taylor. **The Big Book of Animal Records.** Illustrated by the authors. Grossett and Dunlap, 1985. Ages 5–11.

The biggest, smallest, strangest, most wonderful animals and other record holders of the animal world are all colorfully presented in this ninety-page reference book for children.

14.45 Yabuuchi, Masayuki. **Whose Baby?** Illustrated by the author. Philomel Books, 1985. Ages 4–6.

The captivating world of animal families is simply but accurately presented in this book. It offers realistic and colorful paintings of animals and their young and introduces the proper terminology for animal babies.

14.46 Yabuuchi, Masayuki. **Whose Footprints?** Illustrated by the author. Philomel Books, 1985. Ages 4–6. (Picture book)

The smallest of nature lovers will be intrigued by the variety of animal footprints shown here and the animals that make them. Included are footprints of a duck, cat, bear, horse, hippopotamus, and goat. Simple yet bold paintings accompany thought-provoking questions. The technique of questioning prior to giving information encourages predictions and group discussion.

Intermediate

14.47 Curtis, Patricia. **All Wild Creatures Welcome: The Story of a Wildlife Rehabilitation Center.** Photographs by David Cupp. E. P. Dutton/Lodestar Books, 1985. Ages 10–13.

Children intrigued with the rehabilitation of wounded wild animals, such as birds, rabbits, deer, opossums, raccoons, and skunks, will be fascinated with this description of a wildlife rehabilitation center, where animals are nursed back to health so they can return to the wild. Useful information is provided about what readers should do if they find orphaned, injured, or sick animals. A reference section of books and brochures and locations of rehabilitation centers is included. *Outstanding Science Trade Book for Children.*

14.48   Hoffman, Stephen M. **What's under That Rock?** Illustrated by Diane Dollar. Atheneum, 1985. Ages 10–12.

The inquisitive, science-minded person has a chance to investigate insects, amphibians, reptiles, and other animals that live under rocks, stones, logs, and other objects on the ground. Black-and-white illustrations accompany the descriptions of the animals and their habitats. Included are a glossary of terms and maps showing the range of each animal.

14.49   Thomson, Peggy. **Keepers and Creatures at the National Zoo.** Photographs by Paul S. Conklin. Thomas Y. Crowell, 1988. Ages 10–12.

The narrative prose provides specific information about the care and feeding of a variety of animals at the National Zoo in Washington, D.C., and describes the energy and understanding of the animals' keepers. Numerous black-and-white photographs and captions supply additional information. A detailed index makes the information readily accessible.

14.50   Wood, John Norris. **Nature Hide and Seek: Jungles.** Illustrated by Kevin Dean and the author. Alfred A. Knopf/Borzoi Books, 1987. Ages 9–12. (Picture book)

This unique and facinating book allows children to test their powers of observation. Folds and flaps hide many jungle animals from various regions. After children find as many creatures as possible, they can check their results with the answers on the top of the page. Many unfamiliar animals are introduced in this text.

Insects and Spiders

Primary

14.51   Dorros, Arthur. **Ant Cities.** Illustrated by the author. Thomas Y. Crowell/Let's-Read-and-Find-Out Science Books, 1987. Ages 5–10.

Fascinating details about a common insect, the ant, are presented in a simple, understandable text. Illustrations give the reader an inside view of the intricacy of an ant city and demonstrate how the work of keeping the city operating is shared among the ants. Directions are included for making an ant farm.

14.52   Fischer-Nagel, Heiderose, and Andreas Fischer-Nagel. **Life of the Honeybee.** Photographs by the authors. Carolrhoda Books/Nature Watch Books, 1986. Ages 5–10. (Picture book)

This book presents a range of topics about honeybees, including their colonies, reproduction of the species, and the production and collection of honey. The narrative prose also provides an explanation of the ways that the worker bees communicate while finding food. The full-color photographs help the reader locate specific information in the text since there is no index. A glossary of sixteen words is included. *Outstanding Science Trade Book for Children.*

14.53   Fischer-Nagel, Heiderose, and Andreas Fischer-Nagel. **Life of the Ladybug.** Photographs by the authors. Carolrhoda Books/Nature Watch Books, 1986. Ages 5–10. (Picture book)

This explanation of the life cycle of the ladybug begins with the mating of male and female and covers the metamorphosis from egg to larva, to pupa, to adult. The brief text uses scientific terms, which are highlighted in dark print, and is complemented by full-color photographs on each page. A sixteen-word glossary is included, but there is no index. *Outstanding Science Trade Book for Children.*

Intermediate

14.54   Patent, Dorothy Hinshaw. **Mosquitoes.** Holiday House, 1986. Ages 9–12.

This informative research book discusses the mosquito's feeding habits, how and where it breeds, and diseases that it carries. The information in the text is routine, but the black-and-white photographs greatly enhance the book, making it more than just another insect book. *Outstanding Science Trade Book for Children.*

14.55 Settel, Joanne, and Nancy Baggett. **How Do Ants Know When You're Having a Picnic? (And Other Questions Kids Ask about Insects and Other Crawly Things).** Illustrated by Linda Tunney. Atheneum, 1986. Ages 9–12.

Informative but brief explanations are presented for many aspects of nature that you always have wondered about—and many things that you have no doubt never thought about before. Why do fireflies flicker? Why do inchworms inch? How do flies walk on walls? Readers can browse and read answers to questions that catch their attention, or they can use the index to find desired information. Black-and-white drawings illustrate some of the information. *Outstanding Science Trade Book for Children.*

14.56 Shepherd, Elizabeth. **No Bones: A Key to Bugs and Slugs, Worms and Ticks, Spiders and Centipedes, and Other Creepy Crawlies.** Illustrated by Ippy Patterson. Macmillan, 1988. Ages 10–12.

Readers are introduced to the beginnings of insect classification by using a simplified key and "clues." Once a particular insect has been identified, readers are directed to a section that provides detailed information about the insect. The simple black-and-white drawings further aid in the identification process. An index and suggested reading list are also included.

Mammals

Primary

14.57 Arnosky, Jim. **Watching Foxes.** Illustrated by the author. Lothrop, Lee and Shepard Books, 1985. Ages 2–6. (Picture book)

Jim Arnosky records the activities of four baby red foxes and their mother as they frolic in the early spring sunshine just outside their den. His watercolor and colored-pencil illustrations capture motion and life and are accompanied by a text of less than a hundred words, written in short sentences and printed in a large typeface.

14.58 Casey, Denise. **The Friendly Prairie Dog.** Photographs by Tim W. Clark and others. Dodd, Mead, 1987. Ages 5–10.

This simple text briefly covers the physical characteristics, habits, behavior, and natural environment of the prairie dog. Excellent color photographs and a useful index are included.

14.59 Dabcovich, Lydia. **Busy Beavers.** Illustrated by the author. E. P. Dutton, 1988. Ages 4–9. (Picture book)

A simple text, large print, and full-page illustrations describe a beaver family in their day-to-day activities of building a dam, swimming, playing, and getting away from danger.

14.60 Fischer-Nagel, Heiderose, and Andreas Fischer-Nagel. **Inside the Burrow: The Life of the Golden Hamster.** Illustrated by the authors. Carolrhoda Books/Nature Watch Books, 1986. Ages 5–10.

Sharply focused color photographs depict the golden hamster in the wild and as a pet. The informative text is clearly written, making this useful for reports as well as for browsing. The book includes tips on caring for pet hamsters.

14.61 Graham, Ada, and Frank Graham. **We Watch Squirrels.** Illustrated by D. D. Tyler. Dodd, Mead, 1985. Ages 5–9. (Picture book)

The reader is encouraged to observe the physical attributes, the habits and actions, and the habitat of the common gray squirrel. Detailed pencil and pen-and-ink drawings focus the reader's attention precisely on what the text explains.

14.62 Hall, Derek. **Elephant Bathes.** Illustrated by John Butler. Alfred A. Knopf and Sierra Club/Growing Up Books, 1985. Ages 2–5. (Picture book)

An unwelcome hornet sting leads a young elephant to learn that a bath and dust shower will protect his skin from insects. Precise watercolor illustrations complement and amplify information in the simply written text.

14.63 Isenbart, Hans-Heinrich. **Birth of a Foal.** Photographs by Thomas David. Carolrhoda Books/Nature Watch Books, 1986. Ages 5–10. (Picture book)

The birth and growth of a foal are explained in a brief, factual text and illustrated with full-color photographs. A glossary is included as well as two line-drawing charts illustrating the development of the foal fetus and the birth process. *Outstanding Science Trade Book for Children.*

14.64 Johnston, Ginny, and Judy Cutchins. **Andy Bear: A Polar Cub Grows Up at the Zoo.** Photographs by Constance Noble. William Morrow, 1985. Ages 5–9.

The first year in the life of Andy Bear, a polar bear born at the Atlanta zoo, makes a fascinating tale. Photographs taken by the zookeeper who first saved and then cared for Andy as he grew from a 1.5-pound baby to a 150-pound cub complement the text. Facts about polar bears, their natural habitat, and their traits are woven smoothly into Andy's story. *Children's Choice.*

14.65 Leighner, Alice Mills. **Reynard: The Story of a Fox Returned to the Wild.** Photographs by the author. Atheneum, 1986. Ages 7–10.

This photo-essay tells the fascinating true story of an abandoned red fox cub who is cared for by humans and trained to return to the wild. Much factual information about the red fox is included in this concise, readable account, making it useful for school projects as well as pleasure reading.

14.66 Patent, Dorothy Hinshaw. **All about Whales.** Holiday House, 1987. Ages 5–9.

An interesting, brief text describes the various kinds of whales, their physical characteristics, their feeding habits, how they communicate with other whales, and how people have hunted and protected whales. Particular points of the text are expanded through the black-and-white photographs on each page. An index is included.

14.67 Selsam, Millicent E., and Joyce Hunt. **A First Look at Seals, Sea Lions, and Walruses.** Illustrated by Harriett Springer. Walker/First Look at Series, 1988. Ages 6–8. (Picture book)

Do you know the difference between eared seals and true seals, or between sea lions and walruses? Specific body markings and characteristics are noted in the simple text and detailed black-and-white drawings on each page. A summary of what to look for is at the end of the book, along with a world map that shows the habitat of each of the fifteen animals discussed in the book.

14.68 Stein, Sara Bonnett. **Mouse.** Illustrated by Manuel Garcia. Harcourt Brace Jovanovich, 1985. Ages 3–7.

This book depicts the life cycle and habits of a mouse who raises her family in the back of a closet. Accurate full-color paintings enhance the basic information in the text.

Intermediate

14.69   Anderson, Lucia. **Mammals and Their Milk.** Illustrated by Jennifer Dewey. Dodd, Mead, 1985. Ages 9–12.

A descriptive, straightforward text informs the reader about how mammal babies receive nourishment from their mothers' bodies. The definitions of terms like *lactose, casein,* and *antibodies* are developed carefully. Mammals ranging from mice to elephants are depicted in warm, colorful pencil drawings that occupy about half of each page. Simple experiments described at the end of the book should lead to an understanding of the properties of milk. The book is good for discussion with young children and can be read independently by older children.

14.70   Featherly, Jay. **Mustangs: Wild Horses of the American West.** Illustrated by the author. Carolrhoda Books/Nature Watch Books, 1986. Ages 8–10.

The narrative prose presents intriguing information about the behavior, habitat, unique physical features, and history of the mustangs that roam wild in areas of the western United States. Full-color photographs cover more than half of each page. A glossary of specific vocabulary is helpful.

14.71   Hopf, Alice L. **Bats.** Photographs by Merlin D. Tuttle. Dodd, Mead/Skylight Books, 1985. Ages 8–12.

The unique characteristics and behaviors of many types of bats are examined in eight clearly written chapters and in the fascinating black-and-white photographs that appear on about every other page. This sensitive portrayal of bats is sure to dispel some irrational beliefs about this unpopular mammal.

14.72   Johnson, Sylvia A. **Bats.** Photographs by Modoki Masuda. Lerner Publications/Natural Science Books, 1985. Ages 8–12.

The narrative prose explains some of the most intriguing characteristics of bats: their wing structure and how it enables flight, echolocation, their feeding habits, and the birth and care of the young. Information about hibernation and bats living in tropical areas is included as well as a discussion of the ways people and bats interact. Almost every page includes a full-color photograph illustrating specific points in the text. An index is included. *Special Award of the New York Academy of Sciences: Children's Science Book Award.*

14.73 Johnson, Sylvia A., and Alice Aamodt. **Wolf Pack: Tracking Wolves in the Wild.** Lerner Publications, 1985. Ages 8–12.

Facts about the wolf's size, feeding habits, habitats, life cycle, communication, and social behavior are explained, encouraging a sense of respect for this often-maligned species. The reader will learn how wolves in a pack work together to hunt, maintain their territory, and raise their young. Full-color photographs throughout the book extend the reader's understanding of points made in the text. A glossary and an index are included. *ALA Notable Children's Book.*

14.74 Lavine, Sigmund A. **Wonders of Tigers.** Dodd, Mead, 1987. Ages 12 and up.

The behavior and characteristics of tigers are explored in this book. It explains why big cats are able to roar and little cats purr, why tigers walk on their toes, and why they crush their food before they swallow. The book is illustrated with black-and-white photographs, drawings, and old prints.

14.75 McDearmon, Kay. **Giant Pandas.** Dodd, Mead/Skylight Books, 1986. Ages 10–12.

Readers will enjoy a close look at the lovable giant panda. The book describes the giant panda's characteristics and habits, its life in the wild and in captivity, efforts to hunt it, and attempts to save this endangered species. Black-and-white photographs provide additional information. *Outstanding Science Trade Book for Children.*

14.76 Minta, Kathryn A. **The Digging Badger.** Dodd, Mead/Skylight Books, 1985. Ages 10–12.

North America's fastest digger is featured in this book. The badger's physical appearance, behavior, and habitat are described in this thoroughly researched work. Photographs convey further information about the badger's life. *Outstanding Science Trade Book for Children.*

14.77   Patent, Dorothy Hinshaw. **Buffalo: The American Bison Today.** Photographs by William Muñoz. Clarion Books, 1986. Ages 10–12.

The buffalo, a symbol of strength in America, today owes its survival to careful management in national parks, on preserves, and on privately owned ranch land. The life of the buffalo, including courtship, birth, and winter survival, is depicted here in dynamic black-and-white photographs. An interesting added feature is a directory for herd locations. *Outstanding Science Trade Book for Children.*

14.78   Patent, Dorothy Hinshaw. **Dolphins and Porpoises.** Holiday House, 1987. Ages 9–12.

Dolphin and porpoise anatomy, living habits, and communication abilities are explained in a straightforward text with minimal scientific vocabulary. The text is supported by sixty-five black-and-white photographs. An index is included. *Outstanding Science Trade Book for Children.*

14.79   Patent, Dorothy Hinshaw. **The Sheep Book.** Photographs by William Muñoz. Dodd, Mead, 1985. Ages 9–12.

The world of sheep, from birth to shearing, is simply and clearly presented. Included is information about the different breeds and about the uses of sheep. Clear black-and-white photographs aid the reader in understanding the material. *Outstanding Science Trade Book for Children.*

14.80   Patent, Dorothy Hinshaw. **Thoroughbred Horses.** Holiday House, 1985. Ages 9–12.

Readers, particularly horse lovers, will enjoy learning about the history of thoroughbred horses and how they are trained, primarily as racehorses. Also included are descriptions of breeding practices and such competitive sports as polo and fox hunting. Black-and-white photographs highlight well-known horses and jockeys and emphasize the versatility of the breed. A bibliography, glossary, and index add to the usefulness of this book, which is an appropriate companion to Dr. Patent's *Horses of America* and *Arabian Horses.*

14.81   Powzyk, Joyce. **Wallaby Creek.** Illustrated by the author. Lothrop, Lee and Shepard Books, 1985. Ages 8–12.

The laughing kookaburra, platypus, and wallaby are just three of the twelve animals observed and studied by the author during a stay at Wallaby Creek, Australia. Detailed watercolor paintings show each animal in its natural setting. The descriptions are so well written that the reader will want to do further research on these animals. *ALA Notable Children's Book* and *Outstanding Science Trade Book for Children.*

14.82 Rue, Leonard Lee III (with William Owen). **Meet the Beaver.** Illustrated by the author. Dodd, Mead, 1986. Ages 9–12.

In a first-person narrative, a noted wildlife photographer offers information about the life and habitat of the beaver. Specific facts about a beaver's body, swimming skills, and dam building are combined with personal observations made by the author over the years. Black-and-white photographs on every other page clarify specific information. An index is included. *Outstanding Science Trade Book for Children.*

14.83 Schnieper, Claudia. **On the Trail of the Fox.** Photographs by Felix Labhardt. Carolrhoda Books/Nature Watch Books, 1986. Ages 10 and up.

The habits of the elusive red fox are carefully detailed in closeup color photographs, one to three on each page, of life in the den and outside it. The informative accompanying text provides additional information about the fox's birth, mating, raising of young, hunting, fighting, and playing. Terminology that is defined in context is highlighted in boldface type. A glossary and index are included.

Pets

Primary

14.84 Bare, Colleen Stanley. **Guinea Pigs Don't Read Books.** Photographs by the author. Dodd, Mead, 1985. Ages 3–8. (Picture book)

Information about this cuddly pet is presented humorously in simple, oversized print and in full-color closeup photographs of various kinds of guinea pigs. Readers will learn that guinea pigs make good pets and are gentle and lovable. *Children's Choice* and *Outstanding Science Trade Book for Children.*

14.85　　Bare, Colleen Stanley. **To Love a Dog.** Photographs by the author. Dodd, Mead, 1987. Ages 2–6. (Picture book)

Through clear, bright, full-color photographs and a simple, rhythmic text in large print, young children are introduced to the numerous sizes, colors, and shapes of dogs. The book emphasizes dogs' need for human care and love.

14.86　　Hausherr, Rosmarie. **My First Kitten.** Photographs by the author. Four Winds Press, 1985. Ages 5–9.

With guidance from his parents and a veterinarian, seven-year-old Adam learns how to provide a loving and comfortable home and proper care for his new kitten. Black-and-white photographs illustrate every page. Specific information for parents is included on the last page. *Outstanding Science Trade Book for Children.*

14.87　　Hausherr, Rosmarie. **My First Puppy.** Photographs by the author. Four Winds Press, 1986. Ages 7–10.

Thorough and detailed, this book gives readers a realistic idea of the responsibilities and pleasures of pet ownership. Close-up photographs of Jenny and her first puppy are integrated with a clear text. The result is an interesting and informative book that will be of use to the entire family. *Notable Children's Trade Book in the Field of Social Studies* and *Outstanding Science Trade Book for Children.*

14.88　　McPherson, Mark. **Choosing Your Pet.** Photographs by Marianne Bernstein. Troll Associates, 1985. Ages 10–12.

It is fun to choose a pet, once one knows *how* to choose one. Pets ranging from mice to snakes and including everything in between are discussed. A brief background is given for each pet, including eating habits, living conditions, and supplies needed. This is a book that offers valuable information in selecting a suitable pet.

14.89　　Simon, Norma. **Cats Do, Dogs Don't.** Illustrated by Dora Leder. Albert Whitman, 1986. Ages 4–6. (Picture book)

Warm, ethnically diverse illustrations depict the many differences between dogs and cats. The illustrations are in bright colors and complement the slight text. The large print and illustrations make this useful for working with groups of young children.

Intermediate

14.90 McPherson, Mark. **Caring for Your Cat.** Photographs by Marianne Bernstein. Troll Associates, 1985. Ages 8–11.

This is one in a series of books aimed at young pet owners. It describes how to choose a cat from the many breeds available, how to care for a young kitten, feeding and grooming a cat, veterinary care, and neutering a cat. High-quality photographs show children caring for their cats.

14.91 McPherson, Mark. **Caring for Your Dog.** Photographs by Marianne Bernstein. Troll Associates, 1985. Ages 8–11.

Bringing home a new puppy requires love, attention, and knowledge. This book will provide the knowledge. It explains how to select the right puppy, how to care for a puppy, how to housebreak and train a dog, how to feed and groom a dog, how to keep your dog healthy, and how to care for your dog when she has puppies. Photographs of children and their dogs demonstrate the pleasures of being responsible for a pet.

14.92 McPherson, Mark. **Caring for Your Fish.** Photographs by Marianne Bernstein. Troll Associates, 1985. Ages 8–11.

Here is a handbook for setting up a tropical fish tank. The book describes the necessary equipment and discusses both freshwater fish (such as goldfish and guppies) and saltwater fish. Photographs depict different species of fish and children tending their fish.

Reptiles and Amphibians

Primary

14.93 Ancona, George. **Turtle Watch.** Photographs by the author. Macmillan, 1987. Ages 6–10.

Information on how a female sea turtle climbs beyond the tidewater level, digs an egg chamber in the sand, lays her leathery eggs, and returns to the sea is blended with the presentation of how two young children in Praia do Forte, Brazil, take part in providing a safe environment for the hatching of the sea turtle's eggs and the returning of the hatchlings to the sea. The text and the black-and-white photographs focus the reader's attention on the protection of the sea turtle. *ALA Notable Children's Book.*

14.94   Florian, Douglas. **Discovering Frogs.** Illustrated by the author. Charles Scribner's Sons, 1986. Ages 5–10.

The behavior and development of several kinds of frogs are explained in colored drawings and in the carefully worded text. Each drawing is labeled as to its correspondence to the frog's actual size.

14.95   Lauber, Patricia. **Snakes Are Hunters.** Illustrated by Holly Keller. Thomas Y. Crowell/Let's-Read-and-Find-Out Science Books, 1988. Ages 5–10.

Information about how snakes hunt, catch, and eat their prey is included with more general information about various common and not-so-common snakes. The clearly written text, which comprises about one-third of most pages, is supplemented with color drawings, some of which have labels for easy identification.

Archaeology

Primary

14.96   Gibbons, Gail. **Sunken Treasure.** Illustrated by the author. Thomas Y. Crowell, 1988. Ages 7–10. (Picture book)

The topic of sunken treasure is fascinating to readers of all ages. In a book for young readers, Gail Gibbons describes the many years of searching for the *Atocha*, a Spanish galleon that sank off the coast of Florida in 1622. Color illustrations enhance the story of the sinking of the *Atocha* and the search for its treasures.

Intermediate

14.97   Dunrea, Olivier. **Skara Brae: The Story of a Prehistoric Village.** Illustrated by the author. Holiday House, 1985. Ages 9–12.

This imaginative re-creation of the history and culture of a neolithic village from its founding to its abandonment four thousand years ago is based on real archaeological evidence unearthed in the sand dunes of Scotland's Orkney Islands in the mid-nineteenth century. The book whets interest not only in the Skara Brae village itself, but also in the painstaking work of the archaeologist. Diagrams and drawings of the site provide additional information. *Notable Children's Trade Book in the Field of Social Studies.*

14.98 Hackwell, W. John. **Digging to the Past: Excavations in Ancient Lands.** Illustrated by the author. Charles Scribner's Sons, 1986. Ages 10 and up.

How does an archaeologist work in the field to learn about the past? What happens in a dig? Using his firsthand experience with an expedition in the Middle East, the author describes many stages of an excavation. The book is graphically illustrated on each page with brilliant watercolor or black-and-white drawings. An index is included.

14.99 Lauber, Patricia. **Tales Mummies Tell.** Thomas Y. Crowell, 1985. Ages 10–12.

Readers will be fascinated by the intriguing photographs of human and animal mummies and the wealth of information they reveal about the beliefs, customs, and health of ancient civilizations and prehistoric life. The book examines naturally occurring mummies and those preserved by humans. Included are a frozen baby mammoth found in Siberia and human mummies found in Egypt, Peru, and Denmark. *ALA Notable Children's Book* and *Outstanding Science Trade Book for Children.*

Astronomy

Primary

14.100 Branley, Franklyn M. **Journey into a Black Hole.** Illustrated by Marc Simont. Thomas Y. Crowell/Let's-Read-and-Find-Out Science Books, 1986. Ages 7–9.

An exciting imaginary trip to a black hole is described, providing readers with current scientific information. The text is supported with full-color illustrations.

14.101 Branley, Franklyn M. **What the Moon Is Like.** Illustrated by True Kelley. Thomas Y. Crowell/Let's-Read-and-Find-Out Science Books, 1986. Ages 5–7.

Cartoon-style drawings, black-and-white photographs, and an elementary conversational text introduce readers to the basics of lunar life. Much of the information presented is based on experiences of the Apollo astronauts. *Outstanding Science Trade Book for Children.*

14.102 Wandelmaier, Roy. **Stars.** Illustrated by Irene Trivas. Troll Associates/Now I Know Books, 1985. Ages 5–7. (Picture book)

A curious bear talks about what he knows about stars. The birth of a star is explained, and such stars as red giants, dwarfs, and supernovas are discussed. Bright, colorful illustrations make the book enjoyable.

Intermediate

14.103 Apfel, Necia H. **Nebulae: The Birth and Death of Stars.** Lothrop, Lee and Shepard Books, 1988. Ages 10–12. (Picture book)

Complex concepts about the formation and characteristics of nebulae, or clouds of dust particles and gases in space, are clearly presented in large print. The text explains how nebulae form from the residue of dying stars and how some nebulae contain matter from which new stars are born. Breathtaking full-page color photographs from powerful telescopes show many examples of these outer-space phenomena. The younger reader who has some background knowledge would find this an exciting book.

14.104 Branley, Franklyn M. **Mysteries of the Satellites.** Illustrated by Sally J. Bensusen. E. P. Dutton/Lodestar Books/Mysteries of the Universe Series, 1986. Ages 10–14.

This carefully organized book provides a thorough discussion of the natural satellites, or moons, orbiting seven of the planets in our solar system. Information on our moon is particularly detailed. Pen-and-ink diagrams together with black-and-white photographs extend the text. The book will best serve those with a special interest in space or those seeking a research resource.

14.105 Branley, Franklyn M. **Space Telescope.** Illustrated by Giulio Maestro. Thomas Y. Crowell/Voyage into Space Books, 1985. Ages 10–12.

The space telescope, designed to probe areas of outer space not yet seen or explored, is carefully described, not only in the text but also through diagrams and photographs. New information is made understandable through comparison with familiar concepts. The extensive index broadens the book's usefulness. Though the book mentions that the launching of the space telescope was scheduled for 1986, the *Challenger* accident postponed use of a space shuttle for this purpose.

14.106   Gallant, Roy A. **The Macmillan Book of Astronomy.** Illustrated by Ron Miller, Don Dixon, Davis Meltzer, and Brian Sullivan. Macmillan, 1986. Ages 8–12.

Current basic information about the size, temperature, and orbits of the nine planets and their moons, and about the sun and other elements of the solar system is presented in clear, concise text. Full-page, color-enhanced NASA photographs taken during space flights are included for most of the planets, making this oversized book fascinating for browsers. An index assists the reader in finding specific information.

14.107   Lauber, Patricia. **Journey to the Planets.** Rev. ed. Crown, 1987. Ages 8–12.

Geographic and atmospheric information about the planets and their moons is presented in an interpretive narrative. The intriguing text is expanded on almost every page with black-and-white NASA photographs taken on recent space flights. An index is included.

14.108   Simon, Seymour. **Jupiter.** William Morrow, 1985. Ages 8–12.

This is one in a series of books by Seymour Simon about the planets and their moons. The text about Jupiter is enhanced by spectacular full-color NASA photographs that were sent back by the two unmanned Voyager spaceships. We have only begun to explore Jupiter, Simon says, but what we do know about this planet is presented in a detailed and exciting way. *ALA Notable Children's Book.*

14.109   Simon, Seymour. **Saturn.** William Morrow, 1985. Ages 8–12.

This excellent book introduces readers to the planet Saturn. Full-color NASA photographs sent back by the Voyager spacecraft show Saturn, its rings, and its moons. The text gives the history of Saturn and up-to-date information in a straightforward, brief manner. *ALA Notable Children's Book* and *Outstanding Science Trade Book for Children.*

Computers

Primary

14.110 Simon, Seymour. **The BASIC Book.** Illustrated by Barbara and Ed Emberley. Thomas Y. Crowell/Let's-Read-and-Find-Out Science Books, 1985. Ages 7–9.

A reader paying close attention to the page-by-page sequence of information can learn the programming concepts presented and can actually write a simple program. Each page is partitioned into a section presenting BASIC programming information and a section telling the story of how a group of children write a program to use at a birthday party. Comical characters and primary colors add humor and underscore particular vocabulary words. A glossary is included.

14.111 Simon, Seymour. **Bits and Bytes: A Computer Dictionary for Beginners.** Illustrated by Barbara and Ed Emberley. Thomas Y. Crowell/Let's-Read-and-Find-Out Science Books, 1985. Ages 7–9.

Fifty computer words are presented, each with a clear, concise definition. Words describing hardware, software, electronic aspects of the computer, and programming are included. Each word is illustrated with lively drawings that support and extend the definitions, strengthening the reader's understanding.

14.112 Simon, Seymour. **How to Talk to Your Computer.** Illustrated by Barbara and Ed Emberley. Thomas Y. Crowell/Let's-Read-and-Find-Out Science Book/Computer Books, 1985. Ages 5–7. (Picture book)

Easy-to-read vocabulary and cartoonlike illustrations depicting minority and disabled students make this an easy-to-follow book. The book uses the programming languages of BASIC and LOGO to illustrate home computer programs and languages.

14.113 Simon, Seymour. **Meet the Computer.** Illustrated by Barbara and Ed Emberley. Thomas Y. Crowell/Let's-Read-and-Find-Out Science Books/Computer Books, 1985. Ages 5–9. (Picture book)

This book is similar in format and writing style to other titles in this science series. The text is clearly written and easy to understand in its discussion of the parts of a computer and how it works. The cartoonlike illustrations follow and expand upon the text. The vocabulary is geared to first and second graders, but they would need an explanation of the term *load*.

14.114 Simon, Seymour. **Turtle Talk: A Beginner's Book of LOGO.** Illustrated by Barbara and Ed Emberley. Thomas Y. Crowell/ Let's-Read-and-Find-Out Science Books/Computer Books, 1986. Ages 7–9. (Picture book)

With cheerful cartoonlike characters, including a few personable green turtles, a step-by-step introduction to LOGO is made easy for the reader with a home computer. Some basic computer terms and graphics procedures are presented in the context of having fun creating pictures and shapes on the screen.

Conservation and Ecology

Primary

14.115 Arnold, Caroline. **Saving the Peregrine Falcon.** Photographs by Richard R. Hewett. Carolrhoda Books/Nature Watch Books, 1985. Ages 6–10.

The narrative prose presents information about the peregrine falcon and its endangered status. Scientists have intervened in the life cycle of the peregrine by removing the fragile eggs from nests, hatching the eggs, raising the chicks, and returning the birds to wild habitats. Half-page or full-page full-color photographs show each step in the restoration program. *Outstanding Science Trade Book for Children.*

14.116 Arnosky, Jim. **I Was Born in a Tree and Raised by Bees.** Rev. ed. Illustrated by the author. Bradbury Press, 1988. Ages 7–11. (Picture book)

Crinkleroot, a friendly old woodsman, guides readers on this book's tour of the forest through the seasons. Although

Crinkleroot is an exaggerated figure, there is much to learn from his observations about the forest plants and animals. Tidbits of accurate science information are tucked into the text as well as into the detailed illustrations, which invite careful exploration.

14.117 Coats, Laura Jane. **The Oak Tree.** Illustrated by the author. Macmillan, 1987. Ages 3–7.

During a period of twenty-four hours, while a mother robin tends her babies in their nest in an oak tree, we can see the ever-changing natural events around the tree involving the sun, rain, a rainbow, children, and animals.

14.118 Goffstein, M. B. **School of Names.** Illustrated by the author. Harper and Row/Charlotte Zolotow Books, 1986. Ages 6–9. (Picture book)

In sparse text and abstract pastel drawings, M. B. Goffstein portrays the harmony of the universe. The narrator wants to name all objects in the universe. "I would like to recognize and greet everyone by name. For all the years I may live, no place but the earth is my home." Teachers will find this book perfectly conveys the concept of peace to young children. *Notable Children's Trade Book in the Language Arts.*

14.119 Hirschi, Ron. **Who Lives in . . . Alligator Swamp?** Photographs by Galen Burrell. Dodd, Mead/Where Animals Live Books, 1987. Ages 3–7. (Picture book)

A walk through a swamp on a summer day is replicated in full-color closeup photographs of the animals and plants commonly seen. The text invites the reader to look more closely or to listen for specific sounds, guiding the young person's senses on a satisfying, safe journey through a fascinating environment.

14.120 Hirschi, Ron. **Who Lives in . . . the Forest?** Photographs by Galen Burrell. Dodd, Mead/Where Animals Live Books, 1987. Ages 3–7. (Picture book)

Full-color photographs introduce forest plants and the animals that might be seen on an early spring walk through a forest—rabbits, chipmunks, owls, squirrels, bears, and fish. Readers are encouraged to stay alert and to use their senses fully as they explore the natural world. *Outstanding Science Trade Book for Children.*

14.121 Kuhn, Dwight, photographer (text by David M. Schwartz). **The Hidden Life of the Forest.** Crown, 1988. Ages 4–10. (Picture book)

This would be a good book to examine before a field trip to the nature center or school forest, not only because it points out the plants, insects, and animals to be found in a woodland environment, but also because it awakens observers to the beauty of nature. Magnificent photographs freeze on paper sights that many of us miss, such as an owl flying at night, a wolf spider's babies, and a wasp laying eggs in bark. The text adds interesting observations about each subject. There is no index.

14.122 Kuhn, Dwight, photographer (text by David M. Schwartz). **The Hidden Life of the Meadow.** Crown, 1988. Ages 4–10. (Picture book)

These color photographs of the plants and animals in a meadow community increase an observer's appreciation for nature's diversity, complexity, and beauty. There are photographs of a bee sipping, a praying mantis eating a grasshopper, dandelion parachutes in the sunlight, newborn mice, and other sights normally missed on a walk through a field. The book is good for browsing and can be read in any order. There is no index.

14.123 Kuhn, Dwight, photographer (text by David M. Schwartz). **The Hidden Life of the Pond.** Crown, 1988. Ages 4–10. (Picture book)

A mosquito developing from the egg, a hydra catching a waterflea, a star-nosed mole hunting, a perfect water lily: these sights and more are captured in fascinating color photographs of the life of a pond throughout the year. A pond will never look the same to anyone who has browsed through this book. Interesting facts and observations about the animals, insects, and plants in a pond are given in the text.

14.124 Romanova, Natalia. **Once There Was a Tree.** Illustrated by Gennady Spirin. Dial Books for Young Readers, 1985. Ages 5–9.

This beautifully illustrated book is about a stump that remains after a tree is struck by lightning and felled by a woodsman. Many living creatures use this stump to survive and feel that it belongs to them. The book deeply communicates the feeling that this stump belongs to the Earth, which in turn belongs to everyone and everything in nature. *Outstanding Science Trade Book for Children.*

Intermediate

14.125 George, Jean Craighead. **One Day in the Prairie.** Illustrated by Bob Marstall. Thomas Y. Crowell, 1986. Ages 8–12.

Spend one day on an Oklahoma wildlife refuge with a young photographer, and you get a feeling for prairie ecology. Black-and-white pencil drawings show a tornado forming and its effect on the buffalo herd, the prairie dogs, and the other animals. The narrative style makes this book good for browsing, while the short bibliography and index make it suitable for a research assignment. *Outstanding Science Trade Book for Children.*

14.126 Hess, Lilo. **Secrets in the Meadow.** Photographs by the author. Charles Scribner's Sons, 1986. Ages 10–12.

After reading this book, one will never look at a meadow in the same offhand manner. Lilo Hess very simply, yet adequately, describes the many forms of animal life found in a meadow. Its inhabitants take on the roles of builders, weavers, herdsmen, hunters, assassins, soldiers, actors, and musicians. Black-and-white photographs depict some of the animals that can be found in a meadow. Difficult vocabulary words are defined at the back of the book.

14.127 McLaughlin, Molly. **Earthworms, Dirt, and Rotten Leaves: An Exploration in Ecology.** Illustrated by Robert Shetterly. Atheneum, 1986. Ages 9–14.

A basic introduction to ecology invites young readers to participate actively in scientific investigation with several simple experiments involving careful observation of earthworm behavior. The excellently written text imparts much information, not only about ecology and earthworms, but about science as a discipline. *ALA Notable Children's Book* and *Outstanding Science Trade Book.*

14.128 Smith, Howard E., Jr. **Small Worlds: Communities of Living Things.** Illustrated by the author. Charles Scribner's Sons, 1987. Ages 10 and up.

Plant and animal communities form unique relationships with their environments and can be found everywhere—in vacant city lots, inside old houses, on sand dunes, and in trees. A well-written, lively text describes eleven such ecosystems for young naturalists, who may be inspired to explore these small worlds for themselves.

Earth Science, Meteorology, and Oceanography

Primary

14.129 Branley, Franklyn M. **Snow Is Falling.** Rev. ed. Illustrated by Holly Keller. Thomas Y. Crowell/Let's-Read-and-Find-Out Science Books, 1986. Ages 3–9.

How can snow be both helpful and harmful to people, plants, and animals? Answers are provided in a brief easy-to-understand text with full-color illustrations.

14.130 Branley, Franklyn M. **Tornado Alert.** Illustrated by Giulio Maestro. Thomas Y. Crowell/Let's-Read-and-Find-Out Science Books, 1988. Ages 6–10. (Picture book)

Tornadoes, the fastest blowing wind on Earth, are sometimes called twisters or cyclones. Readers of this book will learn what a tornado is, how it develops and moves along, and how to protect themselves during a tornado. The text is written in simple, easy-to-understand language, and numerous illustrations help convey information.

14.131 Branley, Franklyn M. **Volcanoes.** Illustrated by Marc Simont. Thomas Y. Crowell/Let's-Read-and-Find-Out Science Books, 1985. Ages 4–9. (Picture book)

Examples of ancient and recent volcanic eruptions introduce this simple and clear explanation of why and where volcanoes occur. The work of geologists to study and predict eruptions is stressed. Bold illustrations, many of them double page, include a map of the Earth's plates, cross-section views, and dramatic representations of volcanic eruptions.

14.132 Branley, Franklyn M. **What Makes Day and Night.** Rev. ed. Illustrated by Arthur Dorros. Thomas Y. Crowell/Let's-Read-and-Find-Out Science Books, 1986. Ages 4–8.

Cheerful colored illustrations depict for young children the concept of the Earth's rotation and why we have day and night. A simple experiment to demonstrate how daylight turns to darkness allows child participation.

14.133 Cole, Joanna. **The Magic School Bus inside the Earth.** Illustrated by Bruce Degen. Scholastic/Hardcover Books, 1987. Ages 6–9. (Picture book)

In another winning combination of fantasy, fun, and fact, the Magic School Bus transports Ms. Frizzle's class on a second field trip—this time underground, where the class and the reader gain firsthand knowledge of rocks and volcanoes. Zany cartoon-style illustrations and a lively informative text prove nonfiction can be enjoyable. Sequel to *The Magic School Bus at the Waterworks.*

14.134 Florian, Douglas. **Discovering Seashells.** Illustrated by the author. Charles Scribner's Sons, 1986. Ages 4–9.

The habitat, inhabitants, and categories of seashells are introduced. The colored drawings include information about how the illustrations relate to the actual size of the shells.

14.135 Gans, Roma. **Danger—Icebergs!** Rev. ed. Illustrated by Richard Rosenblum. Thomas Y. Crowell/Let's-Read-and-Find-Out Science Books, 1987. Ages 6–8. (Picture book)

Basic information about the formation, structure, and location of icebergs and the dangers they present to ships is conveyed effectively in an easy-to-read text and format. Each page is illustrated with large, full-color drawings which capture the movement and drama of the massive floating hunks of glaciers.

14.136 Gibbons, Gail. **Weather Forecasting.** Illustrated by the author. Four Winds Press, 1987. Ages 5–10. (Picture book)

Modern, sophisticated equipment used to predict the weather as well as the professionals behind the scenes are clearly and carefully shown and explained in this brightly illustrated book which tells about weather and forecasting during the four seasons.

14.137 Naylor, Sue. **The Natural Wonders of the World.** Dillon Press/International Picture Library, 1986. Ages 7–10. (Picture book)

Stunning two-page color photographs of fourteen natural wonders of the world are featured. The five or six sentences accompanying the photographs of such places as the Grand Canyon, an erupting volcano in New Guinea, and Table Mountain, South Africa, provide some facts while inviting the reader to think more about the picture. Both photographs and text should stimulate many more questions for further exploration and discussion. A map showing the location of each wonder is also included.

14.138 Peters, Lisa Westberg. **The Sun, the Wind, and the Rain.** Illustrated by Ted Rand. Henry Holt, 1988. Ages 4–9. (Picture book)

This is a wonderful book for a first lesson in geology. It is the story of two mountains, one made by the Earth and the other made by Elizabeth. The marvelous illustrations juxtapose the two stories as we learn how mountains, large and small, are transformed by sun, wind, and rain.

14.139 Tangborn, Wendell V. **Glaciers.** Rev. ed. Illustrated by Marc Simont. Thomas Y. Crowell/Let's-Read-and-Find-Out Science Books, 1988. Ages 5–9. (Picture book)

A clear, easy-to-understand text explains the formation and movement of glaciers, which today are found primarily near the poles. The impact of these giant ice fields on shaping the land thousands of years ago and their receding patterns of today are also discussed.

Intermediate

14.140 Anno, Mitsumasa. **Anno's Sundial.** Illustrated by the author. Philomel Books, 1985. Ages 11 and up.

Complex concepts of time related to the rotation of the Earth around the sun are described and presented in diagrams and drawings in this challenging book. Three-dimensional pop-up objects, such as a tower, house, and sphere, appear every three or four pages and invite the reader to experiment with the sun and shadows for better understanding. For the determined reader, the meaning of such terms as *latitude* and *longitude* will be developed, as will comprehension of the sundial and why it works.

14.141 Arnold, Caroline. **A Walk on the Great Barrier Reef.** Photographs by Arthur Arnold. Carolrhoda Books/Nature Watch Books, 1988. Ages 9–12.

The fascinating undersea world along Australia's Great Barrier Reef is explored in color photographs showing fish, coral, and other sea life in great detail. The text is full of information about the formation of reefs and the plants and animals that live on reefs. The book contains a glossary and index, but chapters would have provided a helpful organization. The book is for that curious reader who thrives on detailed information about faraway places.

14.142 Blair, Carvel Hall. **Exploring the Sea: Oceanography Today.** Illustrated by Harry McNaught. Random House/Library of Knowledge, 1986. Ages 10–12.

The formation of the world's major oceans and the changes that are constantly taking place on the ocean floor and along the coastlines are the focus of this book. Colored illustrations highlight the technical information about oceans as well as the marine life in the oceans, making the book a good resource for the study of oceanography.

14.143 Branley, Franklyn M. **It's Raining Cats and Dogs: All Kinds of Weather and Why We Have It.** Illustrated by True Kelley. Houghton Mifflin, 1987. Ages 8–12.

Information and folklore about rain, snow, smog, lightning, hurricanes, tornadoes, and clouds are presented in a lively narrative with black-and-white illustrations and charts on every page. A bibliography and index are included.

14.144 Catchpole, Clive. **Deserts.** Illustrated by Brian McIntyre. Dial Books for Young Readers/Pied Piper Books/The Living World Series, 1985. Ages 8–11.

Desert plants and animal life are featured in this book about the world's deserts. Colored drawings provide additional information, and world maps pinpoint desert locations.

14.145 Lauber, Patricia. **Volcano: The Eruption and Healing of Mount St. Helens.** Bradbury Press, 1986. Ages 10–12.

Beautiful photographs as well as scientific descriptions carefully re-create the eruption of Mount St. Helens in 1980. After the destruction, the area around the volcano became a science laboratory for the study of new life. *ALA Notable Children's Book, Newbery Honor Book,* and *Outstanding Science Trade Book for Children.*

14.146 Milne, Lorus J., and Margery Milne. **A Shovelful of Earth.** Illustrated by Margaret La Farge. Henry Holt, 1987. Ages 9–13.

Each chapter presents fascinating information about the composition of earth. The book encourages the reader to go outside, dig, observe closely, and perform the investigations described in order to find out more about the abundance of plant and animal life in a part of the world that is often ignored or taken for granted—the soil beneath our feet. Soils from forest, desert, and grassland habitats are contrasted and compared. Finely detailed black-and-white drawings illustrate aspects of each chapter. An extensive glossary and index are included.

14.147 Siebert, Diane. **Mojave.** Illustrated by Wendell Minor. Thomas Y. Crowell, 1988. Ages 8–12. (Picture book)

The lyrical poetry and the elegant paintings celebrate the striking details of the flora and fauna living together in the Mojave Desert. The horizontal layout of each page, with text on the left and paintings on the right, strengthens the broad sweep of the reader's attention as it is guided to focus on one detail at a time.

14.148 Tayntor, Elizabeth, Paul Erickson, and Les Kaufman. **Dive to the Coral Reefs.** Crown/New England Aquarium Books, 1986. All ages.

Information about the plants and animals of the Jamaican Pear Tree and Rio Bueno reefs is presented with stunning full-color photographs and brief, clearly written text. The book is large, and the text and photographs are arranged so each piece of information is easily understood. No index is included. *Outstanding Science Trade Book for Children.*

Energy

Intermediate

14.149 Math, Irwin. **More Wires and Watts: Understanding and Using Electricity.** Illustrations by Hal Keith. Charles Scribner's Sons, 1988. Ages 11–13.

The nature of electricity is demonstrated through informative illustrations and through models that a young person can construct using readily available materials. The projects range from simple demonstrations (a lemon battery to reproduce Volta's energy discovery) to more complex working models (a weather station or tilt game). Vocabulary, symbols, and concepts are clearly explained. Directions are given step-by-step and in detail so that even a beginner will not get lost; however, adult assistance is required.

General Science Concepts

Primary

14.150 Branley, Franklyn M. **Air Is All around You.** Rev. ed. Illustrated by Holly Keller. Thomas Y. Crowell/Let's-Read-and-Find-Out Science Books, 1986. Ages 5–8.

How can you prove air is in an empty glass, or that air is in water? Two simple experiments give the young reader a way to learn some basic concepts about air. Full-page color drawings and the straightforward text present the information simply.

14.151 Branley, Franklyn M. **Gravity Is a Mystery.** Illustrated by Don Madden. Thomas Y. Crowell/Let's-Read-and-Find-Out Science Books, 1986. Ages 4–8.

Young readers can respond to this simple description of the force of gravity. Each idea is supported by full-color humorous drawings detailing typical experiences that will be familiar to many children. A chart shows how a child's weight changes if measured on different planets in the solar system. The text makes it clear that although much is known about the effects of gravity, no one yet knows exactly what gravity is.

14.152 Cole, Joanna. **Evolution.** Illustrated by Aliki. Thomas Y. Crowell/Let's-Read-and-Find-Out Science Books, 1987. Ages 5–8.

What fossils tell scientists about the earliest organisms on Earth and how they evolved into complex plants and animals are explained in simplified text and colored-pencil drawings on each page. Several charts clarify the various stages of evolution. Although complex concepts receive scant treatment, the book provides a good basic introduction to evolution. It can be read by a child alone, but the concepts would be better understood if discussed with adults. *Outstanding Science Trade Book for Children.*

14.153 Gibbons, Gail. **Dinosaurs, Dragonflies and Diamonds: All about Natural History Museums.** Illustrated by the author. Four Winds Press, 1988. Ages 4–9. (Picture book)

Here is a description of what can be found in a natural history museum, from the personnel who work there to the exhibits themselves. The book is brightly and carefully illustrated and perfect for the young child.

14.154 Simon, Seymour. **Shadow Magic.** Illustrated by Stella Ormai. Lothrop, Lee and Shepard Books, 1985. Ages 5–7. (Picture book)

This is a simple introduction to shadows, including how the Earth casts its shadow. Several simple experiments include making a sundial and producing shadow shows on the wall. The author employs the question technique (What does your shadow do?), which gives the text a condescending air. Illustrations in pencil with pastel shades depict a group of multiracial children engaged in activities with shadows.

Intermediate

14.155 Asimov, Isaac. **How Did We Find Out about Sunshine?** Illustrated by David Wool. Walker/How Did We Find Out Series, 1987. Ages 9–12.

An esteemed science writer presents a historical overview of the research and discoveries that led to our current knowledge about the sun. Topics presented include the sun's age, its composition, and its relationship to energy, radioactivity, and fusion. Clear, straightforward writing and frequent black-and-white drawings make a complex subject accessible to intermediate-age science students.

14.156 Cobb, Vicki. **The Secret Life of Cosmetics: A Science Experiment Book.** Illustrated by Theo Cobb. J. B. Lippincott, 1985. Ages 10 and up.

Vicki Cobb skillfully turns an examination of everyday products—soap, toothpaste, perfume, and cosmetics—into an exciting series of scientific explorations. She begins with a brief history of each product and follows with interesting experiments that show how and why the products work. The well-presented experiments include a listing of needed materials and equipment, a description of the procedures, and follow-up observations and suggestions.

14.157 Macaulay, David. **The Way Things Work.** Illustrated by the author. Houghton Mifflin, 1988. All ages.

David Macaulay "offers the least mechanically minded reader a window of understanding into the complexities of today's technology." This widely acclaimed book uses a woolly mammoth to illustrate the most complex principles of the workings of all machines, from mechanical clocks to the record player to the radio telescope. A glossary of technical terms is included. *ALA Notable Children's Book.*

14.158 Markle, Sandra. **Exploring Summer.** Illustrated by the author. Atheneum, 1987. Ages 10–13.

"Mom, I'm bored," is the normal cry from children during summer vacation. Engaging in these science activities can cure boredom as well as educate the curious mind. Puzzles, games, crafts, jokes, and scientific facts could bring out the explorer in any young child or adult. Creatively written, this book is a good resource for teachers and parents.

14.159 Thomson, Peggy. **Auks, Rocks and the Odd Dinosaur: Inside Stories from the Smithsonian's Museum of Natural History.** Thomas Y. Crowell, 1986. Ages 8–12.

The lively text reveals behind-the-scenes details of fascinating exhibits at the Smithsonian's Museum of Natural History, including a five-foot giant rift worm, the fabulous forty-five-carat Hope diamond, a giraffe bagged by President Theodore Roosevelt, and a model kitchen covered with 130,000 cockroaches. Illustrated with black-and-white photographs, the book will satisfy the curiosity of those interested in the unique. *Boston Globe–Horn Book Award* and *ALA Notable Children's Book.*

14.160 Walpole, Brenda. **175 Science Experiments to Amuse and Amaze Your Friends. Experiments! Tricks! Things to Make!** Illustrated by Kuo Kang Chen and Peter Bull. Random House, 1988. Ages 10–13. (Picture book)

The simple experiments, tricks, and creations illustrate the principles of light, water, movement, and air. Clear full-color drawings provide the visual information needed to make the written directions specific and easily understood. Photographs are included to show the real-world applications of the science concepts that are demonstrated in the simple experiments. The four categories of experiments and the detailed index make this an easy-to-use reference book.

Human Health and Development

Primary

14.161 Banish, Roslyn. **Let Me Tell You about My Baby.** Photographs by the author. Harper and Row, 1988. Ages 2–5. (Picture book)

A young boy tells about the arrival of his baby brother. He describes events in his mother's pregnancy, the baby's birth, postnatal care, his brother's first smile, and his own feelings about the baby. Charming black-and-white photographs carry most of the story. This is a good choice when preparing a preschooler for a first sibling.

14.162 Berger, Melvin. **Germs Make Me Sick!** Illustrated by Marylin Hafner. Thomas Y. Crowell/Let's-Read-and-Find-Out Science Books, 1985. Ages 4–7.

Germs, primarily bacteria and viruses, make us sick. In simple terms and short paragraphs, this book shows a beginning reader how they do it. Our bodies' natural defenses are also described as they fight to make us well. Cartoonlike illustrations occupy much of each page and make it easier to visualize the tiny culprits and their effects.

14.163 Cole, Joanna. **The New Baby at Your House.** Photographs by Hella Hammid. William Morrow, 1985. Ages 3–9.

Excitement, jealousy, worry, and the fear of losing personal attention, space, or possessions are all emotions an older sibling may experience when a new baby is brought into a family. All these feelings are addressed in ways that will encourage an older sibling to talk about his or her own feelings. Over fifty black-and-white photographs present situations in a variety of families. A five-page message to parents is included.

14.164 DeSantis, Kenny. **A Doctor's Tools.** Photographs by Patricia A. Agre. Dodd, Mead, 1985. Ages 4–6. (Picture book)

Visiting a doctor is a common occurrence for many young children. It can bring about feelings of anxiety for the child as well as the parent. This book can alleviate children's fears by familiarizing them with tools the doctor uses for examinations. Black-and-white photographs with pronunciation keys for correct identification are included.

14.165 Kitzinger, Sheila. **Being Born.** Photographs by Lennart Nilsson. Grosset and Dunlap, 1986. Ages 5–12.

Using a second-person narrative, Sheila Kitzinger explains prenatal developments from fertilization through birth. The fetal development and the birth are documented with striking full-color photographs on every page. The text style and vocabulary are simplified but straightforward, providing young readers accurate information. *ALA Notable Children's Book* and *Outstanding Science Trade Book for Children.*

14.166 Kuklin, Susan. **When I See My Dentist. . . .** Photographs by the author. Bradbury Press, 1988. Ages 4–8. (Picture book)

The information and reassurance needed by four year olds prior to a dental checkup are presented in a brief, casual account told in the first person by Erica. The author photographed and audiotaped the checkup and worked with Erica's preschool to ensure an accurate and appropriate book.

14.167 Kuklin, Susan. **When I See My Doctor. . . .** Photographs by the author. Bradbury Press, 1988. Ages 4–8. (Picture book)

Four-year-old Thomas describes the usual procedures of a physical examination, thus reassuring youngsters who are nervous about a doctor's appointment. Photographs convey additional information about Thomas's visit to the doctor.

14.168 Patent, Dorothy Hinshaw. **Babies!** Holiday House, 1988. Ages 5–8. (Picture book)

Physical, mental, and social developmental milestones in a baby's first two years of life are described. The text is brief and straightforward. Full-color photographs of babies appear on every page.

14.169 Showers, Paul. **What Happens to a Hamburger?** Rev. ed. Illustrated by Anne Rockwell. Thomas Y. Crowell/Let's-Read-and-Find-Out Science Books, 1985. Ages 4–8.

Easy experiments and simple diagrams explain to children why our bodies need good food to grow and develop and what happens to each area of the digestive system as food passes through.

Intermediate

14.170 Asimov, Isaac. **How Did We Find Out about the Brain?** Illustrated by Erika W. Kors. Walker/How Did We Find Out Series, 1987. Ages 10–12.

Isaac Asimov clearly explains the development of scientific knowledge about the brain in simple, direct language and black-and-white illustrations. Included are pronunciation keys and the etymology of the terms that are used to describe parts of the brain. This is a good reference book that independent researchers will find easy to use.

14.171 Elting, Mary. **The Macmillan Book of the Human Body.** Illustrated by Kirk Moldoff. Macmillan, 1986. Ages 10–12.

This book investigates the various systems of the human body and describes the function, purpose, and organs that are involved. The bodily functions are presented in a candid way with a personal perspective. Bright illustrations and descriptive comparisons make this a readable book that will help young people understand the human body.

14.172 Johnson, Eric W. **People, Love, Sex, and Families: Answers to Questions That Preteens Ask.** Illustrated by David Wool. Walker, 1985. Ages 9–12.

Eric W. Johnson has written another excellent book on sex education. This book for preteens is a compilation of answers to questions asked by about one thousand fourth, fifth, and sixth graders. In addition to presenting facts about the human body and people's feelings, he examines how people behave in different situations dealing with love, sex, and family relationships.

14.173 Phifer, Kate Gilbert. **Tall and Small: A Book about Height.** Illustrated by Dennis Kendrick. Walker, 1987. Ages 9–12.

Children or teens who feel vulnerable because of discomfort with their body image may be reassured by this commonsensical and straightforward look at height. Genetic and environmental causes of growth are examined in sufficient depth to give information, but not kill the reader's interest. The underlying theme—that all people are worthy of respect, regardless of their outward packaging—is as valuable as the informative text.

14.174 Settel, Joanne, and Nancy Baggett. **Why Does My Nose Run? (And Other Questions Kids Ask about Their Bodies).** Illustrated by Linda Tunney. Atheneum, 1985. Ages 9–12.

Children wonder about the everyday workings of their bodies. "Why do I get goose bumps?" "Why do I yawn?" "Why does my stomach growl?" These three are a sample of the many questions that the authors answer clearly, accurately, and with humor. The diagrams are useful and the question-and-answer format invites browsing.

14.175 Woods, Geraldine, and Harold Woods. **Cocaine.** Franklin Watts/First Books, 1985. Ages 12 and up.

This exploration of the drug cocaine presents theoretical causes and factual effects of cocaine abuse. Poignant black-and-white photographs add to this examination of the historical background of cocaine, how it is grown and processed, and the trade of this drug. Treatment programs are discussed. A glossary is included with easy reference for people who need help for themselves or others.

Machines

Primary

14.176 Lauber, Patricia. **Get Ready for Robots!** Illustrated by True Kelley. Thomas Y. Crowell/Let's-Read-and-Find-Out Science Books, 1987. Ages 4–9.

How does a robot help construct a family's refrigerator or washing machine? What jobs might robots do in the future? Colorful, cartoonlike, detailed drawings on each page complement the text, which presents complex ideas in a straightforward, clear manner. *Outstanding Science Trade Book for Children.*

Intermediate

14.177 Ford, Barbara. **Keeping Things Cool: The Story of Refrigeration and Air Conditioning.** Walker/Inventions That Changed Our Lives Series, 1986. Ages 10–12.

This historical account discusses cooling devices from ancient times to such modern mechanical devices as freezers, refrigerators, and air conditioners. Unusual uses of cooling substances are included. The historical photographs and an index make this useful for school reports.

14.178 Lindblom, Steven. **How to Build a Robot.** Illustrated by the author. Thomas Y. Crowell, 1985. Ages 9–12.

Defining a robot as a device which can "think," move, and sense, Steven Lindblom examines each of these three criteria, assembling a fascinating blend of information about historic attempts to build robots, about movie robots, and about how such devices can be made using current technology. Black-and-white photographs and drawings illustrate each page. An index is included.

14.179 Lovitt, Chip. **Inventions No One Mentions.** Scholastic, 1987. Ages 10–12.

With short, cleverly written paragraphs and black-and-white illustrations, the author has created a hilarious look at actual patented inventions of the late nineteenth and early twentieth centuries that did not work.

14.180 Silverstein, Herma. **Scream Machines: Roller Coasters Past, Present and Future.** Walker, 1986. Ages 9–12.

The history and development of America's most sensational and thrilling amusement park ride, the roller coaster, is thoroughly explored. Enough physics to clarify the operation of the ride is presented, and the book concludes with a list of "America's best" roller coasters.

Mathematics

Primary

14.181 Anno, Mitsumasa. **Anno's Math Games.** Illustrated by the author. Philomel Books, 1987. Ages 6–11.

Two whimsical problem solvers, Kriss and Kross, pose problems that guide the reader to compare, contrast, take apart into smaller pieces, and combine elements to make a different kind of whole. The problems introduce the mathematical concepts of multiplication, sequence and ordinal numbering, measurement, and direction. The brief text presents the problems, but the reader must search the illustration on each page to find the solution. *ALA Notable Children's Book.*

14.182 Schwartz, David M. **How Much Is a Million?** Illustrated by Steven Kellogg. Lothrop, Lee and Shepard Books, 1985. Ages 5–10.

To count from one to one million would take twenty-three days. A trillion kids standing on each other's shoulders would reach beyond Jupiter. Through several other concrete examples, illustrated with painstaking, mind-bending, full-page drawings, children are invited to develop an understanding of numerical concepts as immense as a billion and a trillion. *ALA Notable Children's Book* and *Children's Choice.*

Intermediate

14.183 Nozaki, Akihiro. **Anno's Hat Tricks.** Illustrated by Mitsumasa Anno. Philomel Books, 1985. Ages 7–11.

An introduction to binary logic is provided to two children and Shadowchild, who represents the reader, as they attempt to solve illustrated word puzzles. A note to parents and older readers offers helpful information for understanding the complex problems presented. *Outstanding Science Trade Book for Children.*

Physics and Chemistry

Primary

14.184 Simon, Seymour. **Soap Bubble Magic.** Illustrated by Stella Ormai. Lothrop, Lee and Shepard Books, 1985. Ages 5–9. (Picture book)

A bit of dishwashing soap and a piece of bent wire teach basic physical laws and foster active enjoyment. These simple experiments allow discovery by posing questions, awaiting reader input, and then answering them. The multiethnic drawings also answer questions after the fact, so the young child is encouraged to think. The directions are clear, and safety is stressed where necessary. *Outstanding Science Trade Book for Children.*

Intermediate

14.185 Berger, Melvin. **Atoms, Molecules and Quarks.** Illustrated by Greg Wenzel. G. P. Putnam's Sons, 1986. Ages 11–14.

A description of the composition, behavior, and uses of atoms, molecules, and quarks is presented with a variety of applications and examples, including experiments. In this challenging resource book, specific terms are carefully defined.

14.186 Cobb, Vicki. **Chemically Active! Experiments You Can Do at Home.** Illustrated by Theo Cobb. J. B. Lippincott, 1985. Ages 9–12.

Readers begin to learn some basic principles of chemistry by investigating solutions and their attributes. By following explicit directions, they learn increasingly complex information about chemical reactions. Safety precautions are described in the preface, and reminders are included in every investigation. A detailed index is included.

14.187 Markle, Sandra. **Science Mini-Mysteries.** Atheneum, 1988. Ages 8–12.

Each of the twenty-nine mysteries is introduced with a paragraph of text and a black-and-white photograph. The steps which lead to a solution are outlined on the following page, and answers are printed upside down at the bottom of the page, just in case frustration overcomes curiosity. The majority of experiments are based on chemistry and physics. An index is included.

14.188 White, Jack R. **The Hidden World of Forces.** Illustrated with diagrams and photographs by the author. Dodd, Mead, 1987. Ages 10 and up.

There are constant forces all around us, including gravitation, friction, and electromagnetism. For many, it is difficult to recognize these forces and to associate our daily activities with them. Photographs, diagrams, and experiments are presented to bring the knowledge of forces to a level that is easy for even the novice scientist to understand.

Plants

Intermediate

14.189 Arnow, Jan. **Hay from Seed to Feed.** Photographs by the author. Alfred A. Knopf/Borzoi Books, 1986. Ages 10–12.

The cycle of alfalfa's growing season in Kentucky is closely detailed in half-page and full-page black-and-white photographs and the clearly written, informative text. From preparing the soil to harvesting the alfalfa to feeding livestock, the farmer's activities are carefully explained. *Outstanding Science Trade Book for Children.*

14.190 Lauber, Patricia. **From Flower to Flower: Animals and Pollination.** Photographs by Jerome Wexler. Crown, 1986. Ages 7–12.

A unique, intriguing look at pollination is presented with a brief text and precise black-and-white photographs on every page. The book is large, allowing for a dramatic arrangement of photographs, text, and white space. The roles of bees, other insects, birds, other animals, and the wind are described. An index is included.

14.191 Oechsli, Helen, and Kelly Oechsli. **In My Garden: A Child's Gardening Book.** Illustrated by Kelly Oechsli. Macmillan, 1985. Ages 7–12.

The joy of gardening is conveyed in step-by-step directions on how to begin a vegetable garden, select the type of seeds, care for the garden, and make a compost pile. Children should delight in the informative, colorful drawings that dominate every page. An index and charts are included, and drawings are frequently labeled. *Outstanding Science Trade Book for Children.*

14.192 Patent, Dorothy Hinshaw. **Wheat: The Golden Harvest.** Photographs by William Muñoz. Dodd, Mead, 1987. Ages 8–12.

The concise text presents basic information about the planting and harvesting of winter and spring wheat. Also described are the various uses for wheat and the exceptional nutritional value of wheat kernels. Full-color photographs on each page enhance the text. A glossary and an index are included. *Outstanding Science Trade Book for Children.*

14.193 Wexler, Jerome. **From Spore to Spore: Ferns and How They Grow.** Photographs by the author. Dodd, Mead, 1985. Ages 9–12. (Picture book)

Jerome Wexler's thorough and detailed treatment of the life cycle of the fern is enhanced by photographs that illustrate the many new terms necessary to understand the complexity of this specialized subject. Tips on raising the plant are also included.

Prehistoric Life

Primary

14.194 Aliki. **Dinosaur Bones.** Illustrated by the author. Thomas Y. Crowell/Let's-Read-and-Find-Out Science Books, 1988. Ages 7–9. (Picture book)

How has scientists' thinking about dinosaur bones changed since early discoveries in the 1800s? The clear, concise text explains the story of bones and what they tell us about dinosaurs. Color drawings with extensive captions present much of the information. This book is for the reader who likes detail.

14.195 Aliki. **Dinosaurs Are Different.** Illustrated by the author. Thomas Y. Crowell/Let's-Read-and-Find-Out Science Books, 1985. Ages 7–10.

The scientific classification of orders and suborders of dinosaurs is presented with specific attention given to differences and similarities in the hip, the jaw, and the skull structures of dinosaur skeletons. The scientific information is made lively with full-color drawings of children responding to huge skeletons and the classification information.

14.196 Gibbons, Gail. **Dinosaurs.** Illustrated by the author. Holiday House, 1987. Ages 5–9.

Brief information about the size, weight, and feeding habits of fifteen dinosaurs is presented with full-color illustrations on every page. Pronunciation hints are included. References are made to the work of paleontologists in finding out about dinosaurs and to possible theories for the disappearance of the dinosaurs.

Intermediate

14.197 Knight, David C. **"Dinosaurs" That Swam and Flew.** Illustrated by Lee J. Ames. Prentice-Hall, 1985. Ages 8–12.

The short, factual text on each page details the physical appearance and living habits of the flying and swimming reptile ancestors of the giant land dinosaurs. Several theories concerning the disappearance of the giant reptiles are presented. Pronunciation guides within the text and black-and-white drawings on each page aid the reader. An index and a list of museums where remains of these reptiles may be found are also included. *Outstanding Science Trade Book for Children.*

14.198 Lauber, Patricia. **Dinosaurs Walked Here, and Other Stories Fossils Tell.** Bradbury Press, 1987. Ages 8–12.

The clear, explanatory text offers information and insight into the wonders, beauty, and importance of the fossil records of plants and animals of the prehistoric world. The excitement of the text is heightened by the large full-color photographs and drawings on almost every page. An index is included. *ALA Notable Children's Book.*

14.199 Peters, David. **Giants of Land, Sea and Air: Past and Present.** Illustrated by the author. Alfred A. Knopf and Sierra Club/ Borzoi Books, 1986. Ages 9–13.

Specific information about over seventy animals, all of which are the largest of their kind, is presented in one or two paragraphs per animal. Many of the animals are from prehistoric eras. The detailed illustrations are drawn to the same scale, which invites comparisons between animals. Included are fold out pages depicting the largest animals and an index. *Outstanding Science Trade Book for Children.*

14.200 Sattler, Helen Roney. **Pterosaurs, the Flying Reptiles.** Illustrated by Christopher Santoro. Lothrop, Lee and Shepard Books, 1985. Ages 7–10. (Picture book)

Scientifically accurate watercolor illustrations add impact to a well-researched study of pterosaurs, the flying reptiles that flourished for 120 million years during the Mesozoic Era. A time-line, pronunciation guide, and index give validity to an attractive and accessible source of scientific information for middle-grade students.

14.201 Wilson, Ron. **100 Dinosaurs from A to Z.** Illustrated by Cecilia Fitzsimons. Grosset and Dunlap, 1986. All ages.

Information is presented for each of one hundred dinosaurs, ranging from the well known to those that are rarely cited. Included is a description of the foods eaten, the defenses used, and the significant features of each dinosaur. The animal's weight, length, location, and time period are easily found at the end of each entry. Every dinosaur is drawn as it might have looked when alive.

Recommended Books Published before 1985

Aliki. *Digging Up Dinosaurs.* Thomas Y. Crowell, 1981. 4–7.

Arnosky, Jim. *Secrets of a Wildlife Watcher.* Lothrop, Lee and Shepard Books, 1983. 8 and up.

Baylor, Byrd. *The Desert Is Theirs.* Illustrated by Peter Parnall. Charles Scribner's Sons, 1975. 5–8.

Branley, Franklyn M. *Air Is All around You.* Illustrated by Robert Galster. Thomas Y. Crowell, 1962. 6–8.

Burton, Marilyn. *The I Hate Mathematics! Book.* Illustrated by Martha Hairston. Little, Brown, 1975. 10 and up.

Carrick, Carol. *The Crocodiles Still Wait.* Illustrated by Donald Carrick. Houghton Mifflin, 1980. 7–9.

Cobb, Vicki. *How to Really Fool Yourself: Illustrations for All Your Senses.* Illustrated by Leslie Morrill. J. B. Lippincott, 1981. 9–12.

———. *Science Experiments You Can Eat.* Illustrated by Peter Lippman. J. B. Lippincott, 1972. 9–12.

Cole, Joanna. *A Frog's Body.* Illustrated by Jerome Wexler. William Morrow, 1980. 4–8.

dePaola, Tomie. *The Quicksand Book.* Holiday House, 1977. 7–10.

Flanagan, Geraldine Lux, and Sean Morris. *Window into a Nest.* Houghton Mifflin, 1975. 8–12.

George, Jean Craighead. *One Day in the Alpine Tundra.* Illustrated by Walter Gaffney-Kessel. Thomas Y. Crowell, 1984. 9–12.

———. *All upon a Sidewalk.* Illustrated by Don Bolognese. E. P. Dutton, 1974. 4–9.

Gibbons, Gail. *The Tool Book.* Holiday House, 1982. 4–7.

Goor, Nancy, and Ron Goor. *Shadows: Here, There and Everywhere.* Thomas Y. Crowell, 1981. 5–8.

Grillone, Lisa, and Joseph Gennaro. *Small Worlds Close Up.* Crown, 1978. 8–12.

Herzig, Alison Cragin, and Jane Lawrence Mali. *Oh Boy! Babies!* Illustrated by Katrina Thomas. Little, Brown, 1980. 8–11.

Holling, Holling Clancy. *Pagoo.* Illustrated by the author and Lucille Webster Holling. Houghton Mifflin, 1957. 8–10.

Kohl, Judith, and Herbert Kohl. *View from the Oak: The Private Worlds of Other Creatures.* Illustrated by Roger Bayless. Sierra Club/Charles Scribner's Sons, 1977. 10 and up.

Macaulay, David. *Underground.* Houghton Mifflin, 1976. 10 and up.

Selsam, Millicent. *Greg's Microscope.* Illustrated by Arnold Lobel. Harper and Row, 1963. 4–7.

Simon, Seymour. *The Moon.* Four Winds Press, 1984. 5–9.

———. *The Optical Illusion Book.* Illustrated by Constance Ftera. William Morrow, 1984. 9–11.

15 Fine Arts: Nonfiction

Drama

Primary

15.1 Goffstein, Brooke. **An Actor.** Illustrated by the author. Harper and Row/Charlotte Zolotow Books, 1987. Ages 5–7. (Picture book)

In this companion to *An Artist* and *A Writer*, a young girl explores the varied and exciting identities possible for actors in the theater. Childlike crayon drawings and minimal text offer almost a meditation on an actor's life, appropriate for quiet individual reading or as a discussion starter.

Intermediate

15.2 Bellville, Cheryl Walsh. **Theater Magic: Behind the Scenes at a Children's Theater.** Carolrhoda Books, 1986. Ages 9–12.

Milwaukee artist Nancy Ekholm Burkert's illustrations for Hans Christian Andersen's "The Nightingale" inspired the set and costume designs for the Minneapolis Children's Theatre Company's dramatic adaptation of the tale. Color and black-and-white photographs document the many steps involved in a full-scale theater production, including planning and designing the play, selecting the cast, rehearsing, and the opening performance. *Notable Children's Trade Book in the Field of Social Studies.*

15.3 Kamerman, Sylvia E., editor. **Patriotic and Historical Plays for Young People: One-Act Plays and Programs about the People and Events That Made Our Country Great.** Plays, 1987. Ages 10–12.

Twenty-five plays and choral readings make events of the American Revolution, such as the Boston Tea Party, Paul Revere's ride, and Molly Pitcher's heroic actions, come alive for students. The appendix includes production notes and the historical documents referred to in the plays. The full text of the Constitution and Bill of Rights are also included.

15.4   Kamerman, Sylvia E., editor. **Plays of Black Americans.** Plays, 1987. Ages 10–12.

These plays and choral readings focus on the achievements of black Americans and their fight for equal rights. Included are Harriet Tubman, Crispus Attucks, Daniel Hale Williams, and Martin Luther King, Jr. An appendix contains production notes. The plays and choral readings would be appropriate for the history classroom and also for the celebration of Black History Month.

15.5   Miller, Helen Louise, editor. **Special Plays for Holidays.** Plays, 1986. Ages 7–11.

This collection of fifteen one-act plays celebrates children's favorite school-year holidays, as well as the less-often acknowledged Book Week and Mother's Day. Story lines feature a variety of realistic situations and animal fantasies. Mixed-gender casts, simple props, and limited performance time (all are twenty-five minutes or less) make these plays well suited for classroom or club use.

15.6   Scott, Elaine. **Ramona: Behind the Scenes of a Television Show.** Photographs by Margaret Miller. William Morrow, 1988. Ages 9–12.

The making of a television show—from inception through casting, production, and, finally, airing—is presented using the acclaimed "Ramona" series as an example. An abundance of well-chosen black-and-white photographs enhance an entertaining, straightforward, and informative text. The combined appeal of television and Beverly Cleary's Quimby family will attract readers even if they are unfamiliar with the particular series. *ALA Notable Children's Book.*

15.7   Spruyt, E. Lee. **Behind the Golden Curtain: "Hansel and Gretel" at the Great Opera House.** Illustrated by the author. Four Winds Press, 1986. Ages 10–12.

The Metropolitan Opera comes to life through a behind-the-scenes look at the opera *Hansel and Gretel.* A brief synopsis of the story line precedes the description of step-by-step preparations for opening day at the Met. The text will be easily understood by the reader and includes definitions for those unfamiliar with operatic productions. For many readers, this book may be the closest they will ever get to seeing an opera at the Met.

Music

Primary

15.8   Fox, Dan (music), and Claude Marks (commentary). **Go in and out the Window: An Illustrated Songbook for Young People.** Metropolitan Museum of Art and Henry Holt, 1987. All ages.

It is difficult to find fault with a songbook illustrated by the likes of Renoir, Homer, Boucher, Lewis Hines, and numerous other fine artists whose works are in the collection of the Metropolitan Museum of Art. In this unique and elegant songbook, each piece of music is accompanied by one to three fine reproductions and a brief commentary specifically geared to a younger audience. These traditional children's songs cover a wide range of genres, from ballads to spirituals. The easy-to-play arrangements are for piano or guitar. Children will be intrigued not only by the music, but by the artwork as well. *ALA Notable Children's Book.*

15.9   Paxton, Arthur K. **Making Music.** Photographs by the author. Atheneum, 1986. Ages 6–10. (Picture book)

Clear black-and-white photographs and a straightforward text show how David Amram, a well-known American composer, develops a musical composition, from its inception to its performance.

15.10   Raffi. **Down by the Bay.** Illustrated by Nadine Bernard Westcott. Crown/Raffi Songs to Read, 1987. Ages 2–8. (Picture book)

The children's song "Down by the Bay" from Raffi's album *Singable Songs* is illustrated with simple but rich watercolors. Readers are introduced to such animals as a goose kissing a moose, a whale with a polka-dot tail, and llamas eating their pajamas. For children and adults who wish to sing the song, the words and music are printed on the final two pages of the book.

15.11   Raffi. **One Light, One Sun.** Illustrated by Eugenie Fernandes. Crown/Raffi Songs to Read, 1988. Ages 3–6. (Picture book)

The activities of three diverse, neighboring families are detailed for one day in this read-along, sing-along book taken from a Raffi record album by the same name. Bold full-page illustrations and only three or four words for each double-page spread cheerfully show how the sun, warming everyone as the world turns, connects people together.

15.12   Raffi. **The Raffi Singable Songbook: A Collection of 51 Songs from Raffi's First Three Records for Young Children.** Illustrated by Joyce Yamamoto. Crown, 1987. Ages 3–6.

Children and adults will recognize the varied songs in this collection by popular Canadian songwriter Raffi. Lyrics and both guitar and piano arrangements are provided. The book features watercolors by Joyce Yamamoto and other illustrations by Canadian children.

15.13   Raffi. **The Second Raffi Songbook: 42 Songs from Raffi's Albums "Baby Beluga," "Rise and Shine," and "One Light, One Sun."** Illustrated by Joyce Yamamoto. Crown, 1987. Ages 3–6.

Additional songs from Raffi's record albums are featured in this collection, along with piano arrangements and suggestions for rhythmic accompaniment.

15.14   Raffi. **Shake My Sillies Out.** Illustrated by David Allender. Crown/Raffi Songs to Read, 1987. Ages 2–8. (Picture book)

This is an illustrated version of Raffi's song "Shake My Sillies Out" from one of his record albums. Children will be eager to clap their crazzies out, jump their jiggles out, and wiggle their waggles away. The simple, childlike watercolors are rich in color, endearing, and expressive. The music and words appear on the last two pages of text so readers can sing along.

15.15   Raffi. **Wheels on the Bus.** Illustrated by Sylvie Kantorovitz Wickstrom. Crown/Raffi Songs to Read, 1988. Ages 3–6. (Picture book)

The popular children's song about the bus with wheels that go round and round is beautifully illustrated in bright, detailed watercolor pictures that follow the activities of the passengers

as the bus winds around a French village. Readers and listeners will want to join in with the sounds of the bus and the
motions of the driver and the passengers. The full lyrics, with
music, are included on the last page.

Intermediate

15.16   Arnold, Caroline. **Music Lessons for Alex.** Photographs by
Richard Hewett. Clarion Books, 1985. Ages 9–11. (Picture
book)

The successes and frustrations of learning to play the violin
are realistically conveyed in this photodocumentary of a
young girl's first year of lessons. Information about selecting
an instrument, musical notation, and specific methods used in
lessons adds a factual component to this personal account.
Black-and-white photographs heighten the emotional impact
of the text. The index makes this a useful book for beginning
string players and parents.

Visual Arts

Primary

15.17   Anno, Mitsumasa. **Upside-Downers.** Illustrated by the author. Philomel Books, 1988. Ages 6–10. (Picture book)

In the land of cards, which way is "upside downside up"? As
he has in other visually exciting and intriguing books, Mitsumasa Anno approaches his subject in a unique and challenging manner. In this book, figures from two sets of playing
cards, each upside-down to the other, quarrel. The book can
be read simultaneously by two readers sitting opposite one
another, or a single reader can read through the book in one
direction, turn it around, and read in the other direction. This
is a beautiful book for browsing, and it will be useful in art
classes for a wide range of ages.

15.18   Brown, Laurene Krasny, and Marc Brown. **Visiting the Art
Museum.** Illustrated by Marc Brown. E. P. Dutton, 1986.
Ages 4–10. (Picture book)

This amusing yet fact-filled tour of an art museum will prepare children for a museum visit of their own. Softly colored,

full-page illustrations surround reproductions of artwork representing various styles, from primitive to twentieth-century pop art.

15.19 Harris, Steven Michael. **This Is My Trunk.** Illustrated by Norma Welliver. Atheneum, 1985. Ages 4–8.

A circus clown's life, filled with hard work and demanding agility and skill, is the focus of this book. The clown's costume and makeup and the behind-the-scenes activity at the circus are described with the kind of specific detail that children will enjoy. The cheerful drawings and economical text portray a performer who enjoys his work as a pantomime artist.

15.20 Kinnealy, Janice. **How to Draw Flowers.** Illustrated by the author. Watermill Press, 1987. Ages 6–8.

Step-by-step instructions for drawing flowers are given for the budding artist. The book is illustrated with black-and-white illustrations with a blue wash background to give a progressive idea of how to draw each flower.

15.21 Prokofiev, Sergei. **Peter and the Wolf.** Illustrated by Barbara Cooney. Viking Kestrel, 1985. Ages 5–8.

This book contains five pop-up Russian scenes, all of which have layers to give a three-dimensional look and three of which have movable parts. String and acetate embellish some of the scenes for further realism, all done in Barbara Cooney's usual pleasant pastel painting style, which never becomes cloying. The text is a simple retelling of this classic story, and the book provides a visual way for young readers or listeners to enjoy "Peter and the Wolf." *Children's Choice.*

Intermediate

15.22 Clise, Rick. **Special Effects: A Look behind the Scenes at Tricks of the Movie Trade.** Illustrated by Peter Thomson. Viking Kestrel, 1986. Ages 12 and up.

This book is profusely illustrated with photographs and drawings to show the behind-the-scenes tricks of the movie trade. Readers who have ever wondered how the chase, monsters, amazing machines, and many more special effects are accomplished will enjoy this book.

15.23   Goffstein, M. B. **An Artists Album.** Harper and Row/Charlotte Zolotow Books, 1985. Ages 9–13. (Picture book)

Five exquisite prose poems pay tribute to five artists: Vermeer, Boudin, Cézanne, Monet, and an anonymous Woodland Indian woman. Each poem reflects Goffstein's personal impressions of the artist and his or her art, and each is accompanied by two reproductions. Together art and poetry function as a small gallery, encouraging the child to focus on details before stepping back for a broader view.

15.24   Haldane, Suzanne. **Painting Faces.** Photographs by the author. E. P. Dutton, 1988. Ages 6–12.

Children intrigued by face painting will be fascinated to learn that this is an age-old art, practiced by cultures around the world. Straightforward text explains the history of face painting while colorful closeup photography shows traditional designs. Easy-to-follow directions will allow children to adapt ethnic designs or to create their own. *ALA Notable Children's Book.*

Recommended Books Published before 1985

Ancona, George. *Dancing Is.* E. P. Dutton, 1981. 7–9.

Anderson, David. *The Piano Makers.* Pantheon Books, 1982. 9 and up.

Arnosky, Jim. *Drawing Life in Motion.* Lothrop, Lee and Shepard Books, 1984. 9 and up.

Elliott, Donald. *Frogs and Ballet.* Illustrated by Clinton Arrowhead. Gambit, 1976. 6–10.

Glubok, Shirley. *The Art of the North American Indian.* Macmillan, 1964. 9 and up.

Macaulay, David. *Cathedral: The Story of Its Construction.* Houghton Mifflin, 1973. 9 and up.

Powers, Bill. *Behind the Scenes at a Broadway Musical.* Crown, 1981. 9–13.

Schaaf, Peter. *The Violin Close Up.* Four Winds Press, 1980. 6–9.

16 Crafts and Hobbies: Nonfiction

Cooking

Intermediate

16.1 Madavan, Vijay. **Cooking the Indian Way.** Photographs by Robert L. and Diane Wolfe. Lerner Publications/Easy Menu Ethnic Cookbooks, 1985. Ages 10 and up.

This book in a series on easy ethnic menus is an excellent source for learning to appreciate another culture. The introduction includes a map, the Indian flag, and a brief summary of the Indian people, their customs, and the country's resources. The book presents beautiful color photographs of many of the dishes, the Hindi words for various foods, with the phonetic pronunciations, and recipes for such traditional dishes as lamb kebobs, yogurt chicken, and apple chutney.

16.2 Nguyen, Chi, and Judy Monroe. **Cooking the Vietnamese Way.** Photographs by Robert L. and Diane Wolfe. Lerner Publications/Easy Menu Ethnic Cookbooks, 1985. Ages 10 and up.

Here are tantalizing recipes from Vietnam in a book in a series on easy ethnic menus from other cultures. An introduction to the geography, history, and holiday feasts of Vietnam is included. Featured are recipes for such dishes as spring rolls, sweet and sour soup, and Vietnamese fried rice, beautiful full-color photographs and pencil sketches of the dishes, and such information as how to use chopsticks.

Craft Art

Primary

16.3 Blocksma, Mary, and Dewey Blocksma. **Easy-to-Make Water Toys That Really Work.** Illustrated by Art Seiden. Prentice-Hall, 1985. Ages 6–11.

Instructions are given for making twenty-nine water toys from simple items that can be found around the house or in stores. Clear directions are accompanied by an abundance of drawings that illustrate every step. Projects are preceded by tips, a list of supplies, and safety instructions. An epilogue encourages the reader's creativity.

Intermediate

16.4   Botermans, Jack. **Paper Capers: An Amazing Array of Games, Puzzles, and Tricks.** Illustrated by the author. Henry Holt/Owl Books, 1986. Ages 12 and up. (Picture book)

This is a fascinating but often difficult book of paper folding, optical illusions, games, and puzzles. Accurate black-and-white drawings illustrate the how-to instructions.

16.5   Hautzig, Esther. **Make It Special: Cards, Decorations, and Party Favors for Holidays and Other Special Occasions.** Illustrated by Martha Weston. Macmillan, 1986. Ages 8–12.

This how-to book, illustrated with pen-and-ink drawings, presents suggestions and directions for cards, decorations, party favors, and small gifts for parties celebrating holidays, birthdays, and other special times.

Other Projects and Pastimes

Primary

16.6   Dolman, Sue. **The Brambly Hedge Pattern Book.** Illustrated by the author. Philomel Books, 1985. Ages 8–10.

This is a book of detailed instructions and full-size patterns for making fabric versions of the characters in Jill Barklem's Brambly Hedge stories. These mice wear quaint humanlike clothing and are about six inches tall. Constructing the mice will require some sewing expertise.

Intermediate

16.7   Lewis, Shari. **Shari Lewis Presents 101 Things for Kids to Do.** Illustrated by Jon Buller. Random House, 1987. Ages 8 and up.

Shari Lewis provides directions for simple magic tricks, stunts, riddles, games, and more to provide hours and hours of fun for kids. Included are explanations of how to turn a quarter into a dime and how to make a drinking cup from a piece of paper.

16.8 Nakano, Dokuohtei (translated by Eric Kenneway). **Easy Origami.** Illustrated by the author. Viking Kestrel, 1985. Ages 8–12. (Picture book)

Over fifty origami projects are demonstrated with detailed instructions in this book written by a Japanese art teacher to encourage a wider interest in the craft of origami. Included are paper items to play with, to use, and to display. Most items have ten or fewer folds.

16.9 Potter, Beatrix. **The Big Peter Rabbit Book.** Illustrated by the author. Frederick Warne, 1986. Ages 8 and up.

The publisher has compiled drawings and segments of stories from the tales of Beatrix Potter to create a book of things to do, games to play, and presents to make—all with the Peter Rabbit theme.

16.10 Streb, Judith. **Holiday Parties.** Illustrated by Anne Canevari Green. Franklin Watts, 1985. Ages 8–12.

Here is a party planner for Valentine's Day, Halloween, Thanksgiving, Christmas, and Hanukkah. The book, illustrated with line drawings, explains the origins of each holiday and the meaning of the symbols connected with each. There are suggestions for invitations, placemats, place cards, party favors, room and door decorations, refreshments, and games.

16.11 Webster, Harriet. **Winter Book.** Illustrated by Irene Trivas. Charles Scribner's Sons, 1988. Ages 6–12.

This collection of wintertime activities and lore is a sure antidote to cabin fever. There are outdoor games and nature studies to entice families out into the snow as well as indoor cooking and craft projects. A chapter on celebrations includes ideas for making decorations, festive foods, and special games to make holidays joyous and memorable. The illustrations, sketched in black and white, are both attractive and helpful. An index is included.

Recommended Books Published before 1985

Adkins, Jan. *The Art and Industry of Sandcastles.* Walker, 1971. 8–11.

Brown, Marc. *Your First Garden Book.* Little, Brown, 1981. 5–8.

Caney, Steven. *Steven Caney's Kids' America.* Workman, 1978. 8 and up.

Fleischman, Sid. *Mr. Mysterious's Secrets of Magic.* Illustrated by Eric von Schmidt. Little, Brown, 1975. 8–10.

Shapiro, Rebecca. *A Whole World of Cooking.* Little, Brown, 1972. 10 and up.

Walker, Barbara Muhs. *The Little House Cookbook: Frontier Foods from Laura Ingalls Wilder's Classic Stories.* Harper and Row, 1979. 10–12.

17 Sports and Games: Nonfiction

Baseball

Primary

17.1   Fertig, Dennis. **Take Me Out to the Ball Game.** Photographs
by Wm. Franklin McMahon. Albert Whitman, 1987. Ages
7–10. (Picture book)

Black-and-white photographs help transport the reader to a
Chicago Cubs/Atlanta Braves baseball game at Wrigley Field.
The reader accompanies a young boy and his father as they
tour the ball park and are introduced to various players, parts
of the stadium, and other aspects of the game on the boy's
first visit to a major league baseball game.

17.2   Solomon, Chuck. **Our Little League.** Photographs by the author. Crown, 1988. Ages 6–8. (Picture book)

The text and photographs tell the story of the Little Mets as
they practice and prepare for their big game with the Bombers. Little league players especially will find that they can
easily relate to this book.

Intermediate

17.3   Horenstein, Henry. **Spring Training.** Photographs by the author. Macmillan/Pond Press Books, 1988. Ages 6–10. (Picture
book)

Colorful, action-filled photographs reveal the ins and outs of
spring training for the Boston Red Sox as they spend the pre-
season in Winter Haven, Florida. Sports-minded students will
learn what happens on and off the field through the brief, informative text, well placed in relation to the photographs
dominating each page.

17.4   Sullivan, George. **Baseball Backstage.** Holt, Rinehart and
Winston, 1986. Ages 9–12.

This behind-the-scenes look at the New York Yankees is a realistic portrayal of the jobs that are performed off the baseball field in such positions as general manager and clubhouse attendant. Long days and heavy responsibilities do not lessen the fierce competition for a job in baseball. Those who enjoy the sport will be surprised at the amount of support staff needed by a baseball club.

17.5   Sullivan, George. **Pitcher.** Photographs by the author; illustrated by Don Madden. Thomas Y. Crowell, 1986. Ages 9–12.

Clear photographs, direct prose, and humor-filled line drawings create an effective overview of the techniques of baseball pitching. Types of pitches, strategy, body position, and the necessity for team play are all covered in this useful introduction.

Bicycling

Intermediate

17.6   Coombs, Charles. **All-Terrain Bicycling.** Henry Holt, 1987. Ages 9–12.

Charles Coombs provides the bicyclist with comprehensive information about the sport of all-terrain or mountain bicycling. He explains the how-tos of this different form of biking and provides numerous photographs to supplement the comprehensive text. How to buy a bike, how to care for it, and racing techniques are discussed. Also included are a glossary of biking terms and an index.

Football

Intermediate

17.7   Madden, John. **The First Book of Football.** Crown, 1988. Ages 8–12.

Football and television star John Madden advises readers to "put this book down, grab a ball, and go play." The emphasis here is on learning about the game of football and on developing skills while having fun playing with buddies. Being a fan is fun too, so the book provides all the information needed to be an informed observer: offense (neat lockers), defense (messy lockers), plays, special teams, life in the NFL, and what makes greatness. Photographs and diagrams add interest and clarity. An index is included.

17.8   Sullivan, George. **All about Football.** Dodd, Mead, 1987. Ages 9–12.

George Sullivan reviews football's history, rules of play, and strategies in a writing style which is clear, concise, and free of jargon. The book contains a glossary of football terms, brief biographical sketches of eleven recently retired professional players, an appendix of professional football records, and a number of black-and-white photographs of football action, many of them taken by the author.

Games

Intermediate

17.9   Gryski, Camilla. **Many Stars and More String Games.** Illustrated by Tom Sankey. William Morrow, 1985. Ages 9–12. (Picture book)

This book, by the author of *Cat's Cradle, Owl's Eyes*, is another successful presentation of string games. Camilla Gryski introduces the young reader to the basics of string games, gives a short history, and describes how to make the strings for use in the games. Each string game is attributed to a particular culture and is illustrated and described step-by-step. Stories for some of the figures are included. The book works best with two people—one reading the text and the other executing the string movements. It is a wonderful addition to classroom activities.

17.10   Zubrowski, Bernie. **Raceways: Having Fun with Balls and Tracks.** Illustrated by Roy Doty. William Morrow/Boston Children's Museum Activity Books, 1985. Ages 8–11.

Ball-and-track raceways ranging from simple inclined marble tracks to complicated Rube Goldberg machines are used to enhance the reader's understanding of such scientific principles as kinetic energy, acceleration, and momentum. Comprehensive instructions, clarified by diagrams, are given for constructing the games.

Riding

Intermediate

17.11   Johnson, Neil. **Born to Run: A Racehorse Grows Up.** Photographs by the author. Scholastic/Hardcover Books, 1988. Ages 7–9.

Clear full-color photographs show the beauty, grace, and energy of a racehorse from its birth to a victorious first race. The straightforward narrative describes the three-year process of readying a horse for competition, including those people who play crucial roles—grooms, trainers, and jockeys. The text is informative enough to hold the interest of children in third grade and older. Striking photographs will attract even younger children.

17.12   Tinkelman, Murray. **Little Britches Rodeo.** Photographs by the author, with additional photographs by Ronni and Susan B. Tinkelman. Greenwillow Books, 1985. Ages 8–11.

Bareback riding, goat tying, calf roping, and steer wrestling are some of the skills needed by young people who aspire to success in the National Little Britches Rodeo. Lean prose and large, clear black-and-white photographs convey the fun, hard work, and danger involved in this sport for boys and girls from eight to eighteen years old. A glossary is also included.

Other Sports

Intermediate

17.13   Sullivan, George. **Better Tennis for Boys and Girls.** Photographs by the author. Dodd, Mead, 1987. Ages 8–12.

Illustrated with many photographs and diagrams, this book serves as a good introduction to the sport of tennis. Included is a discussion of such topics as rules and scoring, equipment, forehand shots, backhand shots, serving, volleying, and tactics for winning.

17.14   Sullivan, George. **Better Wrestling for Boys.** Photographs by the author. Dodd, Mead, 1986. Ages 10–14.

Beginning wrestlers will benefit from this clearly written introduction to the sport. A bit of history is followed by a lucid

explanation of weight classes, equipment, moves and holds,
floor layout, and scoring. The large, clear photographs support the text, and a glossary is also helpful.

Recommended Books Published before 1985

Adoff, Arnold. *I Am the Running Girl.* Illustrated by Ronald Himler.
Harper and Row, 1979. 8 and up.
Arnosky, Jim. *Freshwater Fish and Fishing.* Four Winds Press, 1982.
9 and up.
Charosh, Mannis. *Mathematical Games for One or Two.* Illustrated
by Lois Ehlert. Thomas Y. Crowell, 1972. 6–9.
Gryski, Camilla. *Cat's Cradle, Owl's Eyes: A Book of String Games.*
Illustrated by Tom Sankey. William Morrow, 1984. 9–12.

18 Holidays: Fiction and Nonfiction

Christian Holidays: Christmas

Fiction

Primary

18.1   Berger, Barbara Helen. **The Donkey's Dream.** Illustrated by the author. Philomel Books, 1985. Ages 5–7. (Picture book)

In this special book, a donkey tells of the long trek before the birth of Jesus and of the dreams that it has during that journey. This tale is clothed in symbolism, which the author explains in the notes. The illustrations are vividly drawn in hues of blues and pinks.

18.2   Cazet, Denys. **December 24th.** Illustrated by the author. Bradbury Press, 1986. Ages 5–8. (Picture book)

On December 24th, rabbits Emily and Louie bring Grandpa a present, but first they ask him to guess what makes the day special. The silliness begins as Grandpa dons various holiday costumes in an attempt to discover the special occasion. The bright and zany illustrations echo the humor of the story.

18.3   Cuyler, Margery. **Fat Santa.** Illustrated by Marsha Winborn. Henry Holt, 1987. Ages 3–7. (Picture book)

Molly wants to see Santa more than anything else. Her wish comes true when Santa gets stuck in her chimney. Fortunately, she is able to help him out.

18.4   dePaola, Tomie. **An Early American Christmas.** Illustrated by the author. Holiday House, 1987. Ages 3–8. (Picture book)

It's nice to see a children's book that offers another side to Christmas. Tomie dePaola re-creates life in an early New England town, before it was acceptable to celebrate Christmas. By following the traditions of a "Christmas family" as they bake and prepare other symbols of the holiday, we learn how the customs we take for granted first caught on. The illustrations are typical of dePaola, allowing children to trace across the page the process of making cookies or candles. Ink, pastels, and watercolors are used in combination against plain white backgrounds.

18.5   Dubanevich, Arlene. **Pigs at Christmas.** Illustrated by the author. Bradbury Press, 1986. Ages 5–8. (Picture book)

Six frenzied pigs rush to prepare for Christmas. The bright cartoon-style illustrations are both detailed and hilarious, while the simple text is revealed in conversation balloons.

18.6   Ehrlich, Amy. **Bunnies at Christmastime.** Illustrated by Marie H. Henry. Dial Books for Young Readers, 1986. Ages 4–7. (Picture book)

Three bunny children are supposed to invite Uncle Jack to their Christmas party. They cannot find him, so they invite Santa instead. This is a warm and realistic story, with a simple plot. The illustrations, done in pencil and watercolor wash, are a perfect complement to the story.

18.7   Godden, Rumer. **The Story of Holly and Ivy.** Illustrated by Barbara Cooney. Viking Kestrel, 1985. Ages 5–8. (Picture book)

In this somewhat sentimental holiday classic, an orphan and a doll each find a home at Christmas. The detailed and exquisite illustrations in this oversized edition befit the theme of wishes coming true. *Notable Children's Trade Book in the Field of Social Studies.*

18.8   Helldorfer, M. C. **Daniel's Gift.** Illustrated by Julie Downing. Bradbury Press, 1987. Ages 4–8. (Picture book)

This is a Christmas story adapted from a fifteenth-century mystery play, which in turn had its source in earlier folklore and ballads. This explanation appears in a note at the end of the book along with historical background notes for the illustrations. It is too bad that the notes do not appear first, for they enhance the reader's appreciation of the story. This tale of shepherds guarding their flocks of sheep reads as if it should be acted out, and it even includes a typical comic interlude. The richly colored illustrations are bordered in a manner similar to a medieval book of hours.

18.9   Holabird, Katharine. **Angelina's Christmas.** Illustrated by Helen Craig. Clarkson N. Potter, 1985. Ages 4–7. (Picture book)

Angelina and Henry Mouseling, concerned about lonely Mr. Bell, bring a basket of holiday goodies to the retired postman. In return, Mr. Bell dons his old Santa suit and shares his own brand of Christmas cheer. Colorfully detailed illustrations add whimsy to a story of friendship and caring.

18.10   Hughes, Shirley. **Lucy and Tom's Christmas.** Illustrated by the author. Viking Penguin/Puffin Books, 1987. Ages 2–5. (Picture book)

Although this book is about one family's Christmas, it conveys the familiar warmth of anyone's holiday, even if customs differ. Preschoolers Lucy and Tom are the central characters in this realistic and humorous picture account of their preparations and celebration.

18.11   Le Tord, Bijou. **The Little Hills of Nazareth.** Illustrated by the author. Bradbury Press, 1988. Ages 2–6. (Picture book)

Small watercolors of people and animals with gentle faces are framed on each page. The story of the birth of Jesus is told in few words with the message of God's love for all creatures—Mary, Joseph, and Naboth the donkey. This is a quiet book, meant for a lap reading rather than in a group.

18.12   Marshall, James. **Merry Christmas, Space Case.** Illustrated by the author. Dial Books for Young Readers, 1986. Ages 5–10. (Picture book)

The "thing" from outer space visited Buddy McGee at Halloween and promised to return. As Christmas approaches, Buddy eagerly awaits the thing's return visit, but the Goober twins are doubtful. Amusing colorful illustrations accompany a crisply told, hilarious story.

18.13   Rogers, Jean. **King Island Christmas.** Illustrated by Rie Muñoz. Greenwillow Books, 1985. Ages 4–8. (Picture book)

King Island's new priest is stranded on a storm-tossed
freighter in the Bering Sea, and the entire island community
must rally together to bring him ashore in time for Christmas
and before ice locks in their Eskimo village. Watercolor illustrations with round shapes and warm colors against white
snow and gray sea complement the text.

18.14   Ross, Pat. **M & M and the Santa Secrets.** Illustrated by
Marylin Hafner. Viking Kestrel, 1985. Ages 6–8. (Picture
book)

To determine the perfect Christmas gifts for each other, best
friends Mimi and Mandy enlist the help of a street-corner
Santa. Humorous black-and-white pencil illustrations accent
this cheerful story, which is the fourth in the "M & M" series.

18.15   Scheidl, Gerda Marie (translated by Anthea Bell). **Four Candles for Simon.** Illustrated by Marcus Pfister. North-South
Books, 1987. Ages 7–9. (Picture book)

Simon the shepherd boy is supposed to watch over one little
lamb. When the lamb disappears one night, Simon must find
it. His friend Jacob gives him four candles to light his way. It
is by sharing these candles with others that Simon is able to
find the lamb. The subdued hues of brown, gray, and rust in
watercolor wash set the tone of this beautifully written and
unusual Christmas story.

18.16   Speare, Jean. **A Candle for Christmas.** Illustrated by Ann
Blades. Margaret K. McElderry Books, 1986. Ages 7–9. (Picture book)

Tomas, who lives on a reservation, is left with a nurse in the
Northwest Territories of Canada while his parents go off to
check on an uncle who has not been heard from in some time.
Will his parents be home for Christmas as they promised?
This is the big question that Tomas asks himself.

18.17   Tompert, Ann. **The Silver Whistle.** Illustrated by Beth Peck.
Macmillan, 1988. Ages 5–9. (Picture book)

As in "The Little Drummer Boy" and "In the Bleak Mid-
winter," it is not the costliness of the gift one lays before the
Christ child that matters, but the kind heart which underlies
it. Richly textured pen-and-ink and watercolor paintings tell
Miguel's story, filled with the true spirit of the season.

18.18　Trivas, Irene. **Emma's Christmas.** Illustrated by the author. Orchard Books/Richard Jackson Books, 1988. Ages 4–10. (Picture book)

To woo Emma, on the first day of Christmas the prince sends her a partridge in a pear tree. Subsequent days bring the calling birds, French hens, and others from the familiar song until Emma's farm is overflowing and she is won over. Cheerful watercolor illustrations on each page detail the addition of each day's worth of gifts.

18.19　Van Allsburg, Chris. **The Polar Express.** Illustrated by the author. Houghton Mifflin, 1985. Ages 5–12. (Picture book)

An adult's memory of one Christmas Eve in his childhood involves a trip on a magical train to the North Pole to choose the first gift. He asks for a silver bell from Santa's sleigh. The bell still rings for the narrator, "as it does for all who truly believe." The distinctive composition of each full-color painting and the skillful use of color mark this fantasy. *ALA Notable Children's Book, Boston Globe–Horn Book Award,* and *Caldecott Medal.*

18.20　Wooding, Sharon L. **Arthur's Christmas Wish.** Illustrated by the author. Atheneum, 1986. Ages 3–7. (Picture book)

Arthur the mouse is an unlikely hero. He eats too much and he is lazy. At first he is helped by his fairy godfather, but by the story's end, Arthur surprises himself by drawing on an unknown inner discipline. The story's clear message is softened by Sharon L. Wooding's warm illustrations and by her subtly humorous writing style.

18.21　Zimelman, Nathan. **The Star of Melvin.** Illustrated by Olivier Dunrea. Macmillan, 1987. Ages 5–8. (Picture book)

Melvin is an unimportant angel who aspires to become a star polisher. Finally given a chance, Melvin polishes his star so faithfully and to such perfection that God chooses Melvin's star to be the Star of Bethlehem. This unique Christmas story is illustrated with lots of heavenly blues.

Intermediate

18.22　Langstaff, John, editor. **What a Morning! The Christmas Story in Black Spirituals.** Illustrated by Ashley Bryan. Margaret K. McElderry Books, 1987. All ages.

Ashley Bryan's paintings not only illustrate each of five spirituals; they also tell the nativity story about a black holy family. The full-color illustrations have a Caribbean look in their design and brilliant use of light and color. The music is easy to sing and rather easy to play. *ALA Notable Children's Book* and *Coretta Scott King Honor Book* (for illustrations).

18.23 Rylant, Cynthia. **Children of Christmas: Stories for the Season.** Illustrated by S. D. Schindler. Orchard Books, 1987. Ages 8–12.

Pencil drawings accompany six sensitive Christmas stories about a Christmas tree man, a stop in a diner on Christmas Eve, a grandfather who visits for the holidays, a poor, solitary child's encounter with a cabdriver, a train that arrives with holiday gifts, and an old woman's search for "the sick place."

Nonfiction

Primary

18.24 Brett, Jan, illustrator. **The Twelve Days of Christmas.** Dodd, Mead, 1986. Ages 5–8. (Picture book)

This old Christmas carol is a counting song celebrating the tradition of gift giving. Each of the famous twelve gifts is exquisitely illustrated, finely drawn, and brilliantly colored. Each page is bordered with scenes from an old-fashioned holiday and with the animals, birds, and symbols of the season. A note provides historical information about the song, said to date back to the thirteenth century.

18.25 Brierley, Louise, illustrator. **The Twelve Days of Christmas.** Henry Holt, 1986. Ages 6–12. (Picture book)

Newly dressed in oddly appealing illustrations placed formally on right-hand pages facing the text, this old counting song is presented without accompanying music. Generous use of white space sets off the small illustrations that share the page with the text; the larger illustrations facing the text are formally framed. The larger illustrations feature an unusual array of human and animal creatures; even the cows are wraithlike.

18.26   dePaola, Tomie, illustrator. **Tomie dePaola's Book of Christmas Carols.** G. P. Putnam's Sons, 1987. Ages 5–12. (Picture book)

Thirty-two familiar Christmas carols are collected here, with large watercolor illustrations for each song. The well-designed selections will be loved by singers of all ages.

18.27   Thomas, Dylan. **A Child's Christmas in Wales.** Illustrated by Trina Schart Hyman. Holiday House, 1985. All ages.

The noted Welsh poet's classic memories of Christmases in his childhood appear in a handsome volume with forty-five illustrations, half of which are in full color. Trina Schart Hyman's art evokes humor and nostalgia. Her illustrations enliven the snow-filled, uncle-filled, escapade-filled reminiscence for an audience younger than that previously able to appreciate this work. *ALA Notable Children's Book and Notable Children's Trade Book in the Field of Social Studies.*

18.28   Weil, Lisl. **Santa Claus around the World.** Illustrated by the author. Holiday House, 1987. Ages 5–8. (Picture book)

In picture-book format, this book explains the history of Santa Claus and describes how people around the world celebrate his arrival. Copious cartoon illustrations in black, white, and red fill each page. This book will be useful for adults who want to explain Santa Claus to young children.

18.29   Windham, Sophie, illustrator. **Twelve Days of Christmas.** G. P. Putnam's Sons/Lift-the-Flap Books, 1986. Ages 5–10. (Picture book)

This is an exquisite edition of the well-known Christmas carol about twelve days of Christmas gifts. Each of the days is introduced on a left-hand page with a large illustration. The reader must lift flaps on the right-hand page to see the gift for that particular day. The detailed, jeweltone illustrations, along with the many flaps to lift, make this a book to linger over.

Intermediate

18.30   Giblin, James Cross. **The Truth about Santa Claus.** Thomas Y. Crowell, 1985. Ages 9–12.

This thorough and engaging history of one of the most adored of mythical figures traces how our familiar Santa Claus devel-

oped from a combination of historical facts, religious mythology, folklore, tradition, and commercial promotion. The
account starts with the legendary life of Saint Nicholas in the
third century and continues through England's Father Christmas, Thomas Moore's St. Nick and his eight reindeer, to the
contemporary sidewalk Santa. *ALA Notable Children's Book*
and *Notable Children's Trade Book in the Field of Social
Studies.*

Christian Holidays: Easter

Fiction

Primary

18.31   Claret, Maria (revised by Jane O'Sullivan). **The Chocolate
Rabbit.** Barron's Educational Series, 1985. Ages 4–7. (Picture
book)

Things go wrong for a young rabbit when he tries to help Pop-
pa. Through a misadventure, he helps create a chocolate rabbit. Intricate illustrations add to the charm of this book.

18.32   Houselander, Caryll. **Petook: An Easter Story.** Illustrated by
Tomie dePaola. Holiday House, 1988. Ages 5–12. (Picture
book)

This Easter message of "new life" written by a religious writer is fully illustrated by a popular contemporary artist. Petook, a rooster, witnesses the crucifixion of Christ. Three
days later he celebrates the birth of new chicks on Easter
morning.

18.33   Kraus, Robert. **How Spider Saved Easter.** Illustrated by the
author. Scholastic, 1988. Ages 3–5. (Picture book)

When Spider visits Ladybug and Fly, he eats all his Easter
basket candy and helps dye eggs. After falling into the dye
and turning multicolored, he spins a new spider-web hat for
Ladybug that wins her first place in the Easter parade. Full-
color illustrations highlight the text.

Halloween

Fiction

Primary

18.34 Bunting, Eve. **Ghost's Hour, Spook's Hour.** Illustrated by Donald Carrick. Clarion Books, 1987. Ages 4–7. (Picture book)

A howling wind, mysterious creaks, and a clock striking midnight send a young boy and his dog on a journey through a dark house in search of parental comfort in this picture book that is ideal for group sharing. Expressive full-color paintings portray the drama of being lost in the dark and the security of a mother's hug.

18.35 Carlson, Natalie Savage. **Spooky and the Ghost Cat.** Illustrated by Andrew Glass. Lothrop, Lee and Shepard Books, 1985. Ages 5–8.

Spooky, the Bascomb family's pet cat, falls for a mysterious white cat and determines that his previous owner, a witch, has put the white cat under a spell. One Halloween night, Spooky, with his powers enhanced, maneuvers the witch onto a wild broom ride, breaks the spell, and releases the white cat, who then becomes the Bascomb family's second pet cat. The illustrations and text evoke sound, mood, and movement. This book will be enjoyed by large groups at story hour.

18.36 Donnelly, Liza. **Dinosaurs' Halloween.** Illustrated by the author. Scholastic/Hardcover Books/Lucas Evans Books, 1987. Ages 5–8. (Picture book)

Some exciting events happen when a boy in a dinosaur costume and his dog go out trick-or-treating. A glossary of the ten dinosaurs appearing in the story is found at the conclusion of this scary-funny fantasy.

18.37 Herman, Emily. **Hubknuckles.** Illustrated by Deborah Kogan Ray. Crown, 1985. Ages 6–8.

Lee, her younger brothers, and her sister are visited by a dancing ghost, Hubknuckles, every Halloween. One year Lee is convinced that either her father or mother must be the ghost, so she decides to go out and dance with Hub-knuckles—only to discover at the end of her dance that both her parents are in the house. Striking black-and-white illustrations enhance this Halloween story.

18.38   Williams, Linda. **The Little Old Lady Who Was Not Afraid of Anything.** Illustrated by Megan Lloyd. Harper and Row/ Harper Trophy Books, 1986. Ages 3–7.

This Halloween story is perfect for telling to young children, who will no doubt join in with the sound effects. An old woman who is not afraid of anything is pursued through the woods by the noisy parts of a spooky character who reassembles himself at her doorstep. This is shivery, but not too scary. The story is good without the illustrations, but they are so bright and humorous that they make the book all the better. *Notable Children's Trade Book in the Language Arts* and *Children's Choice.*

Intermediate

18.39   Stolz, Mary. **The Scarecrows and Their Child.** Illustrated by Amy Schwartz. Harper and Row, 1987. Ages 8–11.

Handy and Miss Blossom are scarecrows who marry and have a cat child named Bohel. Their loving, though unconventional, family is torn apart and then reunited on a magical Halloween. This is a lively story, and the suspense and short chapters are sure to please children newly ready for chapter books.

Jewish Holidays

Fiction

Primary

18.40   Chaikin, Miriam. **Yossi Asks the Angels for Help.** Illustrated by Petra Mathers. Harper and Row, 1985. Ages 8–10.

Yossi has a problem. Forgetful and a dreamer, he has lost the money he intended to use for Hanukkah gifts. Persistence, wise words from the *rebbe*, and some careful thinking teach Yossi that it is fine to pray for divine help, as long as one does not do so to the exclusion of human ingenuity. Yossi is a character that other children will like.

18.41 Hirsh, Marilyn. **I Love Passover.** Illustrated by the author. Holiday House, 1985. Ages 6–9. (Picture book)

Sarah, a young Jewish girl, is inquisitive about the upcoming celebration of Passover. Her mother explains the holiday's historical beginnings, how it is observed, what it means, and the symbolism that is involved. Colorful and realistic illustrations add to this simply told story.

18.42 Zalben, Jane Breskin. **Beni's First Chanukah.** Illustrated by the author. Henry Holt, 1988. Ages 3–5. (Picture book)

The first holiday celebration that a little child will actually be able to remember is always special. This simple but satisfying story is about Beni Bear's first Hanukkah. He enjoys the preparations, the family traditions, and the first-night festivities with relatives and friends. The illustrations are done in warm and loving detail. Mama's latke recipe is included.

Intermediate

18.43 Sussman, Susan. **Hanukkah: Eight Lights around the World.** Illustrated by Judith Friedman. Albert Whitman, 1988. Ages 7–10.

After a general introduction to Hanukkah, eight short stories, each three pages in length, describe how young people in different countries celebrate the holiday. Detailed illustrations in soft hues of blue and gray grace this carefully designed book. A glossary and bibliography are included.

Nonfiction

Primary

18.44 Chaikin, Miriam. **Sound the Shofar: The Story and Meaning of Rosh Hashanah and Yom Kippur.** Illustrated by Erika Weihs. Clarion Books, 1986. Ages 9–12.

The history, symbols, legends, and customs of Rosh Hashanah and Yom Kippur are outlined in detail. Miriam Chaikin first describes the original customs associated with the earliest celebrations of these high holy days and then traces how these customs have changed and evolved to the present. Thorough coverage and the presence of a glossary, a pronunciation guide, and an extensive index add to the book's usefulness. *Notable Children's Trade Book in the Field of Social Studies.*

Thanksgiving

Fiction

Primary

18.45   Kroll, Steven. **Oh, What a Thanksgiving!** Illustrated by S. D. Schindler. Scholastic/Hardcover Books, 1988. Ages 4–9. (Picture book)

David has quite an imagination. He finds modern Thanksgivings boring and wishes he were back at the more exciting first Thanksgiving, only to discover, with the help of his teacher and his parents, that Thanksgiving today is a memorable event, too.

Valentine's Day

Fiction

Primary

18.46   Carlson, Nancy. **Louanne Pig in the Mysterious Valentine.** Illustrated by the author. Viking Penguin/Puffin Books, 1987. Ages 3–5. (Picture book)

When Louanne Pig receives the most beautiful valentine she has ever seen, she sets out to discover who her secret admirer could be. She is relieved to discover it could not have been sent by any of the mean boys in her school, but she never for a moment suspects her father could be the sender.

18.47   Lexau, Joan M. **Don't Be My Valentine.** Illustrated by Syd Hoff. Harper and Row/I Can Read Books, 1985. Ages 4–8.

On Valentine's Day all around the world, situations similar to Sam's might be taking place. Sam's goal is to be independent, but whenever the opportunity presents itself, he experiences difficulty and is always rescued by Amy Lou. Cookies for the party are forgotten, but Sam remembers to make a nasty valentine for Amy Lou—which tragically falls into the hands of the teacher. This is a story to which all children can relate.

18.48 Wittman, Sally. **The Boy Who Hated Valentine's Day.** Illustrated by Chaya Burstein. Harper and Row, 1987. Ages 5–9.

In his third-grade classroom, Ben has some surprises on Valentine's Day when he forges his classmates' signatures on valentines. Little does he realize what might happen when his scheme takes a different slant.

18.49 Ziefert, Harriet. **Where Is Nicky's Valentine?** Illustrated by Richard Brown. Viking Penguin/Puffin Books, 1987. Ages 3–6. (Picture book)

Nicky the kitten makes the rounds delivering valentines to all his friends, who are hidden away behind all sorts of lift-up flaps. The flaps are simple enough for small hands to manipulate without damage, and the story is easy for a small child to follow. *Children's Choice.*

Other Holidays

Fiction

Primary

18.50 Kroll, Steven. **Happy Father's Day.** Illustrated by Marylin Hafner. Holiday House, 1985. Ages 4–8. (Picture book)

A father's large family treats him to one surprise after another, all planned to help him enjoy a family outing to a baseball game. Even the baby participates in this warm story.

18.51 Kroll, Steven. **Happy Mother's Day.** Illustrated by Marylin Hafner. Holiday House, 1985. Ages 4–8. (Picture book)

This story of a planned surprise for a mother is simply bursting with love and warmth. The happiness of the caring family is apparent in the detailed illustrations and exuberant text. Steven Kroll builds suspense with the refrain ''. . . there's another surprise!'' This book will bear repeated readings—and they will be requested.

18.52 Sharmat, Marjorie Weinman. **Hooray for Father's Day!** Illustrated by John Wallner. Holiday House, 1987. Ages 5–9. (Picture book)

Two mule children want to make this a special Father's Day for their father. Sterling plans to fix breakfast and give a bath, while Monica plans to buy a jump rope, sweatband, and tickets for a picnic. A change of events at the end gives Father Mule exactly what he wants.

18.53 Sharmat, Marjorie Weinman. **Hooray for Mother's Day!** Illustrated by John Wallner. Holiday House, 1986. Ages 6–9. (Picture book)

Alaric Chicken is cautious when he attempts to select a perfect gift for his mother on Mother's Day. Slippers, chocolates, perfume, or colorful paintings just don't seem to be right, so he selects another gift. Wait until Mother sees this gift! The bright illustrations convey the contemporary approach of this story.

Nonfiction

Primary

18.54 Gibbons, Gail. **Happy Birthday!** Illustrated by the author. Holiday House, 1986. Ages 6–9. (Picture book)

Why are there birthdays? Why do we celebrate them with parties? This brightly illustrated book examines the historical beliefs, traditions, and activities associated with birthdays.

18.55 Laird, Elizabeth. **Happy Birthday: A Book of Birthday Celebrations.** Illustrated by Satomi Ichikawa. Philomel Books, 1988. Ages 7–9.

In this potpourri of birthday customs, a birthday girl named Julie learns how birthdays are celebrated around the world. Music of the classic song "Happy Birthday to You," the zodiac signs, gems, games, costumes, making cards, and many more ideas are included. The book is illustrated with full-color drawings.

Intermediate

18.56 Brown, Tricia. **Chinese New Year.** Photographs by Fran Ortiz. Henry Holt, 1987. Ages 7–9. (Picture book)

Black-and-white photographs depict the festivities and rituals involved when Chinese Americans in San Francisco's Chinatown celebrate Chinese New Year. A simple paragraph accompanies each photograph to explain the customs and events. Despite the attractive layout, the pictures are too dark. The book's chief value will be for curriculum use when studying the holiday.

Recommended Books Published before 1985

Adshead, Gladys. *Brownies—It's Christmas*. Oxford University Press, 1955. 4–6.

Balian, Lorna. *Bah! Humbug?* Abingdon Press, 1977. 4–7.

———. *Humbug Witch*. Abingdon Press, 1965. 5–7.

Barth, Edna. *Hearts, Cupids and Red Roses: The Story of the Valentine Symbols*. Illustrated by Ursula Arndt. Clarion Books, 1974. 8–10.

Brewton, John E., et al., comps. *In the Witch's Kitchen: Poems for Halloween*. Thomas Y. Crowell, 1980. 8–12.

Bright, Robert. *Georgie's Halloween*. Doubleday, 1971. 4–8.

Brown, Margaret Wise. *Christmas in the Barn*. Illustrated by Barbara Cooney. Thomas Y. Crowell, 1952. 4–7.

Cheng, Hou-tien. *The Chinese New Year*. Holt, Rinehart and Winston, 1976. 6–9.

dePaola, Tomie. *The Clown of God: An Old Story*. Harcourt Brace Jovanovich, 1978. 6–9.

Drucker, Malka. *Hanukkah: Eight Nights, Eight Lights*. Illustrated by Brom Hoban. Holiday House, 1980. 9–12.

Epstein, Morris. *All about Jewish Holidays and Customs*. Illustrated by Arnold Lobel. Ktav, 1970. 8–12.

Fisher, Aileen. *Easter*. Illustrated by Ati Forberg. Thomas Y. Crowell, 1968. 5–8.

Gibbons, Gail. *Thanksgiving*. Holiday House, 1983. 4–7.

Giblin, James Cross. *Fireworks, Picnics, and Flags*. Illustrated by Ursula Arndt. Clarion Books, 1983. 8–12.

Kahl, Virginia. *Plum Pudding for Christmas*. Charles Scribner's Sons, 1956. 4–8.

Keats, Ezra Jack. *The Little Drummer Boy*. Macmillan, 1968. 4 and up.

Kurelek, William. *A Northern Nativity: Christmas Dreams of a Prairie Boy*. Tundra Books, 1976. 8–11.

L'Engle, Madeleine. *The Twenty-Four Days before Christmas: An Austin Family Story*. Illustrated by Joe DeVelasco. Harold Shaw, 1984. 6–8.

Livingston, Myra Cohn, ed. *Callooh! Callay! Holiday Poems for Young Readers*. Illustrated by Janet Stevens. Atheneum, 1978. 9–12.

Meyer, Carolyn. *Christmas Crafts: Things to Make the 24 Days before Christmas*. Illustrated by Anita Lobel. Harper and Row, 1974. 8–10.

Milhous, Katherine. *The Egg Tree*. Charles Scribner's Sons, 1950. 6–9.

Moore, Clement C. *The Night before Christmas*. Illustrated by Tasha Tudor. Rand McNally, 1975. 5–9.

Perl, Lila, and Alma Flor Ada. *Piñatas and Paper Flowers/Piñatas y flores de papel: Holidays of the Americas in English and Spanish*. Illustrated by Victoria de Larrea. Clarion Books, 1983. 8–12.

Prelutsky, Jack. *It's Valentine's Day*. Illustrated by Vossi Abolafia. Greenwillow Books, 1983. 4–8.

19 Professional Books

Authors and Illustrators: Autobiography, Biography, and Essays

Brown, Marcia. *Lotus Seeds: Children, Pictures and Books.* Charles Scribner's Sons, 1985.

Fisher, Margery. *The Bright Face of Danger.* Horn Book, 1986.

———. *Classics for Children and Young People.* Thimble Press, 1986.

Gág, Wanda. *Growing Pains: Diaries and Drawings from the Years 1908–1917.* Minnesota Historical Society Press, 1984.

L'Engle, Madeleine. *Trailing Clouds of Glory: Spiritual Values in Children's Books.* Westminster Press, 1985.

Livingston, Myra Cohn. *The Child as Poet: Myth or Reality?* Horn Book, 1984.

Nodelman, Perry, ed. *Touchstones: Reflections on the Best in Children's Literature.* Vols. 1 and 2. Children's Literature Association Publications (210 Education Building, Purdue University, West Lafayette, IN 47907), 1986.

Once upon a Time: Celebrating the Magic of Children's Books in Honor of the Twentieth Anniversary of "Reading Is Fundamental." G. P. Putnam's Sons, 1986.

Paterson, Katherine. *Gates of Excellence: On Reading and Writing Books for Children.* E. P. Dutton/Lodestar Books, 1981.

Sendak, Maurice. *Caldecott and Company.* Farrar, Straus and Giroux, 1988.

Collections

Bauer, Carolyn Feller. *Celebrations: Read Aloud Holiday and Theme Programs.* H. W. Wilson, 1985.

———. *Windy Day Stories and Poems.* Illustrated by Dirk Zimmer. J. B. Lippincott, 1988.

Kennedy, Richard. *Richard Kennedy: Collected Stories.* Illustrated by Marcia Sewall. Harper and Row, 1987.

Yolen, Jane, Martin Greenberg, and Charles Waugh, eds. *Dragons and Dreams: A Collection of New Fantasy and Science Fiction Stories*. Harper and Row, 1986.

Bettelheim, Bruno. *Uses of Enchantment: The Meaning and Importance of Fairy Tales*. Alfred A. Knopf, 1976.

England, Claire, and Adele M. Fasick. *Childview: Evaluating and Reviewing Materials for Children*. Libraries Unlimited, 1987.

Hearne, Betsy, and Marilyn Kaye, eds. *Celebrating Children's Books: Essays on Children's Literature*. Lothrop, Lee and Shepard Books, 1981.

Heins, Paul. *Crosscurrents of Criticism: Horn Book Essays, 1968–77*. Horn Book, 1977.

Sims, Rudine. *Shadow and Substance: Afro-American Experience in Contemporary Children's Fiction*. National Council of Teachers of English, 1982.

Guides for Parents

American Library Association. *Opening Doors for Preschool Children and Their Parents*. American Library Association, 1981.

Butler, Dorothy. *Babies Need Books*. Atheneum, 1982.

Cascardi, Andrea E. *Good Books to Grow On: A Guide to Building Your Child's Library from Birth to Age Five*. Warner, 1985.

Hearne, Betsy. *Choosing Books for Children: A Commonsense Guide*. Delacorte Press, 1981.

Jett-Simpson, Mary. *Reading Resource Book: Parents and Beginning Reading*. Humanics, 1986.

Kimmel, Margaret Mary, and Elizabeth Segal. *For Reading Out Loud! A Guide to Sharing Books with Children*. Delacorte Press, 1988.

Lamme, Linda Leonard. *Growing Up Reading: Sharing with Your Child the Joys of Reading*. Acropolis Books, 1985.

Larrick, Nancy. *A Parent's Guide to Children's Reading*. Bantam Books, 1982.

Trelease, Jim. *The Read-Aloud Handbook*. Viking Penguin, 1986.

Illustrations

Bader, Barbara. *American Picture Books from Noah's Ark to the Beast Within*. Macmillan, 1976.

Lacy, Lyn Ellen. *Art and Design in Children's Picture Books: An Analysis of Caldecott Award–Winning Books*. American Library Association, 1986.

MacCann, Donnarae, and Olga Richard. *The Child's First Books.* H. W. Wilson, 1973.
Schwarcz, Joseph H. *Ways of the Illustrator: Visual Communication in Children's Literature.* American Library Association, 1982.
Shulevitz, Uri. *Writing with Pictures: How to Write and Illustrate Children's Books.* Watson-Guptill, 1985.

Reference Works and Textbooks

Carpenter, Humphrey, and Mari Prichard. *The Oxford Companion to Children's Literature.* Oxford University Press, 1984.
Dunhouse, Mary Beth, ed. *International Directory of Children's Literature.* Facts on File, 1986.
Field, Carolyn. *Special Collections in Children's Literature.* American Library Association, 1982.
Glazer, Joan. *Literature for Young Children.* 2d ed. Charles E. Merrill, 1986.
Jay, M. Ellen, and Hilda L. Jay. *Building Reference Skills in the Elementary School.* Shoe String Press/Library Professional Publications, 1986.
Junior Book of Authors and Illustrators. H. W. Wilson, 1951–1983.
Kingman, Lee. *Newbery and Caldecott Medal Books: 1976–1987.* Horn Book, 1987.
Kirkpatrick, D. L. *Twentieth-Century Children's Writers.* St. Martin's Press, 1978.
Lukens, Rebecca. *A Critical Handbook of Children's Literature.* Scott Foresman, 1986.
Morris, Christopher, ed. *The Lincoln Writing Dictionary for Children.* Harcourt Brace Jovanovich, 1988.
Newbery and Caldecott Medal Books, 1922–1975. Horn Book, 1955–1986.
Opie, Iona, and Peter Opie. *Oxford Dictionary of Nursery Rhymes.* Oxford University Press, 1973.
Peterson, Carolyn S. *Index to Children's Songs: A Title, First Line, and Subject Index.* H. W. Wilson, 1979.
Sutherland, Zena, and May Hill Arbuthnot. *Children and Books.* Illustrated by Leo and Diane Dillon. Scott, Foresman, 1986.
Stewig, John Warren. *Children and Literature.* Houghton Mifflin, 1988.
Townsend, John Rowe. *Written for Children.* 3d ed. J. B. Lippincott, 1987.

Specialized Bibliographies and Book Selection

Adell, Judith, and Hilary Dole Klein. *A Guide to Non-Sexist Children's Books*. Vol. 1. Academy Press, 1976.

Association for Library Service to Children. *Notable Children's Books, 1976–1980*. American Library Association, 1986.

Baskin, Barbara H. *More Notes from a Different Drummer: A Guide to Juvenile Fiction Portraying the Disabled*. R. R. Bowker, 1984.

Beilke, Patricia F., and Frank J. Sciara. *Selecting Materials for and about Hispanic and East Asian Children and Young People*. Shoe String Press/Library Professional Publications, 1986.

Carr, Jo. *Beyond Fact: Nonfiction for Children and Young People*. American Library Association, 1982.

Carroll, Frances Laverne, and Mary Meacham, eds. *Exciting, Funny, Scary, Short, Different, and Sad Books Kids Like about Animals*. American Library Association, 1985.

Children's Catalog. 15th ed. H. W. Wilson, 1986.

Children's Books Council. *Children's Books: Awards and Prizes*. Children's Book Council, 1986.

Children's Books in Print. R. R. Bowker. Issued annually.

Dreyer, Sharon S. *The Bookfinder: A Guide to Children's Literature about the Needs and Problems of Youth Aged 2 and Up*. Vol. 3. American Guidance Service, 1985. Vols. 1 and 2 also available.

Fiction, Folklore, Fantasy, and Poetry for Children, 1976–1985. R. R. Bowker, 1986.

Field, Carolyn W., and Jaqueline Shackter Weiss. *Values in Selected Children's Books of Fiction and Fantasy*. Shoe String Press/Library Professional Publications, 1987.

Griffin, Barbara K. *Special Needs Bibiliography: Current Books for/ about Children and Young Adults Regarding Social Concerns, Emotional Concerns, the Exceptional Child*. The Griffin (P.O. Box 295, DeWitt, NY 13214), 1986.

Monson, Dianne, ed., and the NCTE Committee on the Elementary School Booklist. *Adventuring with Books: A Booklist for Pre-K–Grade 6*. 8th ed. (for the years 1981–1984). National Council of Teachers of English, 1985.

Moss, Elaine. *Picture Books for Young People, 9–13*. Thimble Press, 1985.

O'Neil, Robert. *Classrooms in the Crossfire*. Indiana University Press, 1981.

Quimby, Harriet B., and Margaret Mary Kimmel. *Building a Children's Literature Collection*. Rev. ed. Choice, 1983.

Rollock, Barbara. *The Black Experience in Children's Books.* New York Public Libraries, 1984.

Roman, Susan. *Sequence: An Annotated Guide to Children's Books in Series.* American Library Association, 1985.

Schon, Isabel. *Books in Spanish for Children and Young Adults: An Annotated Guide, Series III.* Scarecrow Press, 1985.

Tway, Eileen, editor, and the NCTE Committee on Reading Ladders for Human Relations. *Reading Ladders for Human Relations.* 6th ed. National Council of Teachers of English, 1981.

Wilms, Denise, and Ilene Cooper. *A Guide to Non-Sexist Children's Books.* Vol. 2 (1976–1985). Academy Press, 1987.

Storytelling

Baker, Augusta, and Ellin Green. *Storytelling: Art and Technique.* 2d ed. R. R. Bowker, 1987.

Livo, Norma, and Sandra Rietz. *Storytelling: Process and Practice.* Libraries Unlimited, 1986.

MacDonald, Margaret Read, ed. *Twenty Tellable Tales: Audience Participation Folktales for the Beginning Storyteller.* Illustrated by Roxanne Murphy. H. W. Wilson, 1986.

Pellowski, Anne. *Family Storytelling Handbook.* Macmillan, 1987.

————. *The Story Vine: A Source of Unusual and Easy-to-Tell Stories from around the World.* Illustrated by Lynn Sweat. Macmillan, 1984.

Sawyer, Ruth. *The Way of the Story Teller.* Viking Press, 1970 (1942).

Smith, Jimmy Neil. *Homespun.* Crown, 1988.

Teaching Methods

Bosma, Bette. *Fairy Tales, Fables, Legends, and Myths: Using Folk Literature in Your Classroom.* Teachers College Press, 1987.

Burke, Eileen. *Early Childhood Literature: For Love of Child and Book.* Allyn and Bacon, 1987.

Cullinan, Bernice E., ed. *Children's Literature in the Reading Program.* International Reading Association, 1987.

Hopkins, Lee Bennett. *Pass the Poetry, Please!* Harper and Row, 1987.

Leonard, Charlotte. *Tied Together: Topics and Thoughts for Introducing Children's Books.* Scarecrow, 1980.

Livingston, Myra Cohn. *When You Are Alone It Keeps You Capone.* Atheneum, 1973.

Sloan, Glenna. *The Child as Critic: Teaching Literature in Elementary and Middle Schools*. 2d ed. Teachers College Press, 1984.
Stewig, John Warren. *Read to Write*. R. C. Owens Publishers, in press.

Additional Professional Books

Applebee, Arthur N. *The Child's Concept of Story: Ages Two to Seventeen*. University of Chicago Press, 1978.
Ciardi, John, and Miller Williams. *How Does a Poem Mean?* 2d ed. Houghton Mifflin, 1975.
Jenkinson, Edward B. *Censors in the Classroom: The Mind Benders*. Southern Illinois University Press, 1979.
Lanes, Selma G. *The Art of Maurice Sendak*. Harry N. Abrams, 1980.
McCaslin, Nellie, ed. *Children and Drama*. 2d ed. Longman, 1981.
———. *Creative Drama in the Primary and Intermediate Grades*. Longman, 1987.
Wagner, Betty Jane. *Dorothy Heathcote: Drama as a Learning Medium*. National Educational Association, 1976.

20 Teaching with Literature

As teachers consider the academic needs and the focused interests of students, they look for suggestions of titles which might be used for instruction as well as for providing rich literary experiences. The following suggested books, all reviewed in this volume, are rich in four ways: strong characterizations, vivid settings, defined story structures, and striking use of language. Books are also suggested which connect well with writing. Many of the titles could easily be placed in more than one category because they are distinctive in several ways. These suggestions are starting points for teachers who are searching for the right title to fill a need in a language arts program. (The number preceding each author's name indicates the chapter in which the annotation can be found and the placement of the annotation within that chapter.)

Characterization

Primary

10.185 Goffstein, M. B. *Our Snowman.*
11.58   Howard, Fitzgerald. *The Train to Lulu's.* Illus. by Robert Casilla.
10.193 Joosse, Barbara M. *Jam Day.* Illus. by Emily Arnold Mc-Cully.
10.55   Jukes, Mavis. *Blackberries in the Dark.*
10.194 ———. *Like Jake and Me.* Illus. by Lloyd Bloom.
10.18   Little, Jean. *Lost and Found.* Illus. by Leoung O'Young.
10.129 Schwartz, Amy. *Annabelle Swift, Kindergartner.*
10.208 Stevenson, Suçie. *Do I Have to Take Violet?*

Intermediate

10.140 Bauer, Marion. *On My Honor.*
10.266 Blume, Judy. *Just as Long as We're Together.*
10.222 Cleaver, Vera. *Sweetly Sings the Donkey.*
10.145 Duder, Tessa. *Jellybean.*

8.319   Dunlop, Eileen. *The House on the Hill.*
5.59   Merriam, Eve. *Halloween ABC.* Illus. by Lane Smith.
18.23   Rylant, Cynthia. *Children of Christmas.* Illus. by S. D. Schindler.
10.167 Shura, Mary Francis. *The Josie Gambit.*
10.33   Springer, Nancy. *A Horse to Love.*
11.80   Taylor, Mildred D. *The Friendship.* Illus. by Max Ginsburg.

Predictable Books and Strong Story Structure

Primary

8.283   Bang, Molly. *The Paper Crane.*
8.27   Boujon, Claude. *Bon Appétit, Mr. Rabbit!*
8.219   Burningham, John. *John Patrick Norman McHennessy—The Boy Who Was Always Late.*
8.40   Carle, Eric. *The Very Busy Spider.*
8.49   Cherry, Lynne. *Who's Sick Today?*
8.60   Deming, A. G. *Who Is Tapping at My Window?* Illus. by Marcia Wellington.
7.8   Domanska, Janina. *Busy Monday Morning.*
1.84   Hayes, Sarah. *This Is the Bear.* Illus. by Helen Craig.
10.105 Hutchins, Pat. *The Doorbell Rang.*
8.85   Kroll, Steven. *Don't Get Me in Trouble!* Illus. by Marvin Glass.
18.51   ———. *Happy Mother's Day.* Illus. by Marylin Hafner.
4.48   Marshall, Edward. *Four on the Shore.* Illus. by James Marshall.
8.99   Marshall, James. *Wings: A Tale of Two Chickens.*
4.57   O'Connor, Jane. *The Teeny Tiny Woman.* Illus. by R. W. Alley.
8.112   Oppenheim, Joanne. *You Can't Catch Me!* Illus. by Andrew Shachat.
2.17   Peek, Merle. *Mary Wore Her Red Dress, and Henry Wore His Green Sneakers.*
14.81   Powzyk, Joyce. *Wallaby Creek.*
8.132   Stehr, Frédéric. *Quack-Quack.*
8.294   Walter, Mildred Pitts. *Brother to the Wind.* Illus. by Leo and Diane Dillon.
8.152   West, Colin. *"Pardon?" Said the Giraffe.*
1.140   Yektai, Niki. *What's Missing?* Illus. by Susanna Ryan.
4.84   Yep, Laurence. *The Curse of the Squirrel.* Illus. by Dirk Zimmer.

8.8 Yorinks, Arthur. *Company's Coming.* Illus. by David Small.

1.142 Ziefert, Harriet. *Where's the Halloween Treat?* Illus. by Richard Brown.

Intermediate

8.162 Conly, Jane Leslie. *Rasco and the Rats of 1956.* Illus. by Leonard Lubin.

11.7 Fleischman, Sid. *The Whipping Boy.* Illus. by Peter Sis.

9.10 Kurtz, Katherine. *The Legacy of Lehr.*

5.63 Livingston, Myra Cohn. *There Was a Place, and Other Poems.*

9.12 Service, Pamela F. *A Question of Destiny.*

Rich Language

Primary

5.32 Lobel, Arnold. *Whiskers and Rhymes.*

10.20 McNulty, Faith. *The Lady and the Spider.* Illus. by Bob Marstall.

8.291 Mahy, Margaret. *Seventeen Kings and Forty-Two Elephants.*

10.200 Martin, Bill, Jr., and John Archambault. *White Dynamite and Curly Kidd.* Illus. by Ted Rand.

Intermediate

10.40 Baylor, Byrd. *I'm in Charge of Celebrations.* Illus. by Peter Parnall.

5.59 Fleischman, Paul. *I Am Phoenix: Poems for Two Voices.* Illus. by Ken Nutt.

5.60 ———. *Joyful Noise.*

5.6 Janeczko, Paul B. *This Delicious Day: Sixty-Five Poems.*

11.74 MacLachlan, Patricia. *Sarah, Plain and Tall.*

5.64 Ryder, Joanne. *Inside Turtle's Shell, and Other Poems of the Field.* Illus. by Susan Bonners.

8.310 Service, Pamela F. *Tomorrow's Magic.*

Setting

Primary

11.57 Hendershot, Judith. *In Coal Country.* Illus. by Thomas B. Allen.

10.38   Parnall, Peter. *Winter Barn.*
11.25   Roop, Peter, and Connie Roop. *Keep the Lights Burning,*
          Abbie. Illus. by Peter Hanson.
10.212   Yolen, Jane. *Owl Moon.* Illus. by John Schoenherr.

Intermediate

10.371   Fox, Paula. *Lily and the Lost Boy.*
11.53   Garfield, Leon. *The December Rose.*
 8.320   Hearne, Betsy. *Eli's Ghost.* Illus. by Ronald Himler.
10.374   Nilsson, Ulf. *If You Didn't Have Me.* Illus. by Eva
          Ericksson.
10.8   Paulsen, Gary. *Hatchet.*
14.147   Siebert, Diane. *Mojave.* Illus. by Wendell Minor.

Writing Connections

Primary

 4.112   Ahlberg, Janet, and Allan Ahlberg. *The Jolly Postman; or,*
          Other People's Letters.
 8.39   Caple, Kathy. *Harry's Smile.*
10.94   Dupasquier, Phillipe. *Dear Daddy. . . .*
14.20   Hirschi, Ron. *What Is a Bird?* Illus. by Galen Burrell.
 8.107   Moore, Lilian. *I'll Meet You at the Cucumbers.* Illus. by
          Sharon Wooding.
 8.111   Oakley, Graham. *The Diary of a Church Mouse.*
10.136   Williams, Vera B. *Cherries and Cherry Pits.*

Intermediate

 4.113   Benjamin, Carol Lea. *Writing for Kids.*
11.71   Herman, Charlotte. *Millie Cooper, 3B.* Illus. by Helen
          Cogancherry.
 8.166   Lively, Penelope. *A House Inside Out.* Illus. by David
          Parkins.
10.298   Lowry, Lois. *Anastasia Has the Answers.*
 4.114   Mabery, D. L. *Tell Me about Yourself.*
 4.54   Nixon, Joan Lowery. *If You Were a Writer.* Illus. by Bruce
          Degen.
 8.169   Wrightson, Patricia. *Moon-Dark.* Illus. by Noela Young.

21 Book Awards and Booklists

Jane Addams Award

This award is given annually to a book for children that most effectively promotes peace, social justice, world community, and equality of the sexes and of all races. It is given by the Women's International League for Peace and Freedom and the Jane Addams Peace Association. The most recent winners of this award, established in 1953, are listed.

1978 Yep, Laurence; *Child of the Owl*; Harper and Row.
1979 Highwater, Jamake; *Many Smokes, Many Moons*; J. B. Lippincott.
1980 Kherdian, David; *Road from Home: The Story of an Armenian Girl*; Greenwillow Books.
1981 White, Florence M.; *First Woman in Congress: Jeannette Rankin*; Julian Messner.
1982 Lord, Athena V.; *Spirit to Ride the Whirlwind*; Macmillan.
1983 Maruki, Toshi; *Hiroshima No Pika*; Lothrop, Lee and Shepard Books.
1984 Bauer, Marion; *Rain of Fire*; Clarion Books.
1985 Vinke, Herman; trans. by Hedwig Pachter; *Short Life of Sophie Scholl*; Harper and Row.
1986 Meltzer, Milton; *Ain't Gonna Study War No More: The Story of America's Peace Seekers*; Harper and Row.
1987 Vigna, Judith; ed. by Kathleen Tucker; *Nobody Wants a Nuclear War*; Albert Whitman.
1988 Gordon, Sheila; *Waiting for the Rain: A Novel of South Africa;* Orchard Books.

Hans Christian Andersen Award

These awards are given every two years to an author and to an illustrator, living at the time of nomination, who are judged to have made a lasting contribution of outstanding value to literature for children and young people. An international jury selects from nominations made by national organizations. The award is given by the International Board on Books for Young People (IBBY). The author award was established in 1956; the illustrator award was first given in 1966.

1956 Eleanor Farjeon for *The Little Bookroom*; (Henry Z. Walck) Oxford
      University Press
1958 Astrid Lindgren for *Rasmus Pa Luffen*; Raben and Sjogren (Viking
      Press, titled *Rasmus and the Vagabond*)
1960 Erich Kästner (Germany)
1962 Meindert DeJong (United States)
1964 René Guillot (France)
1966 Author: Tove Jansson (Finland)
      Illustrator: Alois Carigiet (Switzerland)
1968 Author: James Krüss (Germany) and Jose Maria Sanchez-Silva
      (Spain)
      Illustrator: Jiri Trnka (Czechoslovakia)
1970 Author: Gianni Rodari (Italy)
      Illustrator: Maurice Sendak (United States)
1972 Author: Scott O'Dell (United States)
      Illustrator: Ib Spang Olsen (Denmark)
1974 Author: Maria Gripe (Sweden)
      Illustrator: Farshid Mesghali (Iran)
1976 Author: Cecil Bodker (Denmark)
      Illustrator: Tatjana Mawrina (U.S.S.R.)
1978 Author: Paula Fox (United States)
      Illustrator: Svend Otto (Denmark)
1980 Author: Bohumil Ríha (Czechoslovakia)
      Illustrator: Suekichi Akaba (Japan)
1982 Author: Lygia Bojunga Nunes (Brazil)
      Illustrator: Zibigniew Rychlicki (Poland)
1984 Author: Christine Nostlinger (Austria)
      Illustrator: Mitsumasa Anno (Japan)
1986 Author: Patricia Wrightson (Australia)
      Illustrator: Robert Ingpen (Australia)
1988 Author: Annie M. G. Schmidt (Holland)
      Illustrator: Dusan Kallay (Yugoslavia)

Mildred L. Batchelder Award

This award is given to a United States publisher for a children's book
considered to be the most outstanding of those books originally published in a foreign language in a foreign country and subsequently
published in English in the United States during the preceding year.
The award, established in 1968, is given annually unless no book during that year is deemed worthy of the honor. It is given by the Association for Library Service for Children of the American Library Association.

1968 Alfred A. Knopf for *The Little Man* by Erich Kästner; trans. from the
      German by James Kirkup; illus. by Rick Schreiter; originally pub-
      lished in Switzerland by Atrium Verlag as *Der Kleine Mann* in
      1963.

1969 Charles Scribner's Sons for *Don't Take Teddy* by Babbis Friis-Boasted; trans. from the Norwegian by Lise Sømme McKinnon.

1970 Holt, Rinehart and Winston for *Wildcat under Glass* by Alki Zei; trans. from the Greek by Edward Fenton; originally published by Editions "Themelio" as *To Kaplani Tis Vitrinas* in 1963.

1971 Pantheon Books for *In the Land of Ur: The Discovery of Ancient Mesopotamia* by Hans Baumann; trans. from the German by Stella Humphries; originally published in Germany by Sigbert Mohn Verlag as *Im Lande Ur* in 1968.

1972 Holt, Rinehart and Winston for *Friedrich* by Hans Peter Richter; trans. from the German by Edite Kroll; originally published in Germany by Sebaldus-Verlag as *Damals War Es Friedrich* in 1961.

1973 William Morrow for *Pulga* by S. R. van Iterson; trans. from the Dutch by Alexander and Alison Gode; originally published in Holland by Vitgeverij Leopold as *De Adjudant Van de Vrachtwagen*.

1974 E. P. Dutton for *Petros' War* by Alki Zei; trans. from the Greek by Edward Fenton; originally published in Greece by Editions "Kedros" as *O Megalos Peripatos Tou Petrou* in 1971.

1975 Crown for *An Old Tale Carved out of Stone* by A. Linevski; trans. from the Russian by Maria Polushkin.

1976 Henry Z. Walck for *The Cat and Mouse Who Shared a House*, retold from the Brothers Grimm by Ruth Hürlimann; trans. from the German by Anthea Bell; originally published in Switzerland by Atlantis Verlag as *Katze und Maus in Gesellschaft* in 1973.

1977 Atheneum for *The Leopard* by Cecil Bodker; trans. from the Danish by Gunnar Poulsen; originally published in Denmark by Branner and Korch as *Leoparden* in 1970.

1978 Franklin Watts for *Konrad* by Christine Nöstlinger; trans. from the German by Anthea Bell; illus. by Carol Nicklaus; originally published in Germany by Verlag Friedrich Oetinger as *Konrad* in 1975.

1979 Harcourt Brace Jovanovich for *Rabbit Island* by Jörg Steiner; trans. from the German by Ann Conrad Lammers; illus. by Jörg Müller; originally published in Switzerland by Verlag Sauerlander AG as *Die Kanincheninsel* in 1977.

1980 E. P. Dutton for *The Sound of the Dragon's Feet* by Alki Zei; trans. from the Greek by Edward Fenton; originally published in Greece by Editions "Kedros" as *Konda Stis Raghes* in 1977.

1981 William Morrow for *The Winter When Time Was Frozen* by Els Pelgrom; trans. from the Dutch by Maryka and Raphael Rudnik; originally published in Holland by Uitgeverij as *De Kinderen Van Het Achtste Woud* in 1977.

1982 Bradbury Press for *The Battle Horse* by Harry Kullman; trans. from the Swedish by George Blecher and Lone Thygesen-Blecher; originally published in Sweden as *Stridshästen* in 1977.

1983 Lothrop, Lee and Shepard Books for *Hiroshima No Pika* by Toshi Maruki; trans. from the Japanese; originally published in Japan by Komine Shoten as *Hiroshima No Pika* in 1980.

1984 Viking Penguin for *Ronia, the Robber's Daughter* by Astrid Lindgren; trans. from the Swedish by Patricia Crampton; originally published in Sweden by Rabén and Sjögren Bokforlag as *Ronja Rovardotter* in 1981.

1985 Houghton Mifflin for *The Island on Bird Street* by Uri Orlev; trans. from the Hebrew by Hillel Halkin; originally published in Israel by Keter Publishing House as *Ha-I-Bi-Rehovha-Tsiporim* in 1981.

1986 Creative Education for *Rose Blanche* by Christophe Gallaz and Roberto Innocenti; trans. from the Italian by Martha Coventry and Richard Graglia; illus. by Roberto Innocenti; originally published in Switzerland in 1985.

1987 Lothrop, Lee and Shepard Books for *No Hero for the Kaiser* by Rudolf Frank; trans. from the German by Patricia Crampton; illus. by Klaus Steffens; originally published in Germany by Müller and I. Kiepenheuer Verlag as *Der Schadel des Neger Haüptlings Makaua* in 1931; published in Germany by Otto Maier Verlag as *Der Junge, der Seinen Geburtstag Vergass* in 1983.

1988 Margaret K. McElderry Books for *If You Didn't Have Me* by Ulf Nilsson; trans. from the Swedish by Lone Thygesen-Blecher and George Blecher; illus. by Eva Eriksson.

1989 Lothrop, Lee and Shepard Books for *Crutches* by Peter Hartling; trans. from the German by Elizabeth D. Crawford.

Boston Globe–Horn Book Award

This award has been given annually in the fall since 1967 by *The Boston Globe* and *The Horn Book Magazine*. Through 1975, two awards were given—for outstanding text and for outstanding illustration; in 1976 the award categories were changed to outstanding fiction or poetry, outstanding nonfiction, and outstanding illustration; in 1988 the illustration category was changed to picture book.

1967 Text: Haugaard, Erik Christian; *The Little Fishes*; Houghton Mifflin.
       Illustration: Spier, Peter; *London Bridge Is Falling Down*; Doubleday.
1968 Text: Lawson, John; *The Spring Rider*; Thomas Y. Crowell.
       Illustration: Mosel, Arlene; *Tikki Tikki Tembo*; illus. by Blair Lent; Holt.
1969 Text: Le Guin, Ursula K.; *A Wizard of Earthsea*; Houghton Mifflin.
       Illustration: Goodall, John S.; *The Adventures of Paddy Pork*; Harcourt, Brace and World.
1970 Text: Townsend, John Rowe; *The Intruder*; J. B. Lippincott.
       Illustration: Keats, Ezra Jack; *Hi, Cat!*; Macmillan.
1971 Text: Cameron, Eleanor; *A Room Made of Windows*; Atlantic Monthly Press.
       Illustration: Mizumura, Kazue; *If I Built a Village*; Thomas Y. Crowell.
1972 Text: Sutcliff, Rosemary; *Tristan and Iseult*; E. P. Dutton.
       Illustration: Burningham, John; *Mr. Gumpy's Outing*; Holt.
1973 Text: Cooper, Susan; *The Dark Is Rising*; Margaret K. McElderry Books.
       Illustration: Hyman, Trina Schart; *King Stork*; Little, Brown.
1974 Text: Hamilton, Virginia; *M. C. Higgins, the Great*; Macmillan.
       Illustration: Feelings, Muriel; *Jambo Means Hello*; illus. by Tom Feelings; Dial Press.

1975 Text: Degens, T.; *Transport 7-41*; Viking Press.
Illustration: Anno, Mitsumasa; *Anno's Alphabet*; Thomas Y. Crowell.
1976 Fiction: Walsh, Jill Paton; *Unleaving*; Farrar, Straus and Giroux.
Nonfiction: Tamarin, Alfred, and Shirley Glubok; *Voyaging to Cathay: Americans in the China Trade*; Viking Press.
Illustration: Charlip, Remy, and Jery Joyner; *Thirteen*; Parents Magazine Press.
1977 Fiction: Yep, Laurence; *Child of the Owl*; Harper and Row.
Nonfiction: Dickinson, Peter; *Chance, Luck and Destiny*; Atlantic Monthly Press.
Illustration: Tripp, Wallace; *Granfa' Grig Had a Pig, and Other Rhymes*; Little, Brown.
1978 Fiction: Raskin, Ellen; *The Westing Game*; E. P. Dutton.
Nonfiction: Koehn, Ilse; *Mischling, Second Degree: My Childhood in Nazi Germany*; Greenwillow Books.
Illustration: Anno, Mitsumasa; *Anno's Journey*; Philomel Books.
1979 Fiction: Fleischman, Sid; *Humbug Mountain*; Atlantic Monthly Press.
Nonfiction: Kherdian, David; *The Road from Home: The Story of an Armenian Girl*; Greenwillow Books.
Illustration: Briggs, Raymond; *The Snowman*; Random House.
1980 Fiction: Davies, Andrew; *Conrad's War*; Crown.
Nonfiction: Salvadori, Mario; *Building: The Fight against Gravity*; Margaret K. McElderry Books.
Illustration: Van Allsburg, Chris; *The Garden of Abdul Gasazi*; Houghton Mifflin.
1981 Fiction: Hall, Lynn; *The Leaving*; Charles Scribner's Sons.
Nonfiction: Lasky, Kathryn; *The Weaver's Gift*; Frederick Warne.
Illustration: Sendak, Maurice; *Outside Over There*; Harper and Row.
1982 Fiction: Park, Ruth; *Playing Beatie Bow*; Atheneum.
Nonfiction: Siegal, Aranka; *Upon the Head of the Goat: A Childhood in Hungary, 1939–1944*; Farrar, Straus and Giroux.
Illustration: Willard, Nancy; *A Visit to William Blake's Inn: Poems for Innocent and Experienced Travelers*; illus. by Alice and Martin Provensen; Harcourt Brace Jovanovich.
1983 Fiction: Hamilton, Virginia; *Sweet Whispers, Brother Rush*; Philomel Books.
Nonfiction: Davis, Daniel S.; *Behind Barbed Wire: The Imprisonment of Japanese Americans during World War II*; E. P. Dutton.
Illustration: Williams, Vera B.; *A Chair for My Mother*; Greenwillow Books.
1984 Fiction: Wrightson, Patricia; *A Little Fear*; Margaret K. McElderry Books.
Nonfiction: Fritz, Jean; *The Double Life of Pocahontas*; G. P. Putnam's Sons.
Illustration: *Jonah and the Great Fish*; Hutton, Warwick, reteller and illus.; Margaret K. McElderry Books.
1985 Fiction: Brooks, Bruce; *The Moves Make the Man*; Harper and Row.
Nonfiction: Blumberg, Rhoda; *Commodore Perry in the Land of the Shogun*; Lothrop, Lee and Shepard Books.
Illustration: Hurd, Thacher; *Mama Don't Allow*; Harper and Row.

1986   Fiction: O'Neal, Zibby; *In Summer Light*; Viking Kestrel.
        Nonfiction: Thomson, Peggy; *Auks, Rocks and the Odd Dinosaur: In-
        side Stories from the Smithsonian's Museum of History*; Thomas
        Y. Crowell.
        Illustration: Bang, Molly; *Paper Crane*; Greenwillow Books.
1987   Fiction: Lowry, Lois; *Rabble Starkey*; Houghton Mifflin.
        Nonfiction: Sewall, Marcia; *Pilgrims of Plimoth*; Atheneum.
        Illustration: Steptoe, John; *Mufaro's Beautiful Daughters: An African
        Tale*; Lothrop, Lee and Shepard Books.
1988   Fiction Award: Taylor, Mildred D.; *The Friendship*; Dial Books for
        Young Children.
        Fiction Honor Books: Doherty, Berlie; *Granny Was a Buffer Girl*; Or-
        chard Books. Fleischman, Paul; *Joyful Noise: Poems for Two
        Voices*; Charlotte Zolotow Books. Mahy, Margaret; *Memory*; Mar-
        garet K. McElderry Books.
        Nonfiction Award: Hamilton, Virginia; *Anthony Burns: The Defeat
        and Triumph of a Fugitive Slave*; Alfred A. Knopf.
        Nonfiction Honor Books: Chiasson, John; *African Journey*; Bradbury
        Press. Little, Jean; *Little by Little: A Writer's Education*; Viking
        Kestrel.
        Picture Book Award: Snyder, Dianne; *The Boy of the Three-Year
        Nap*; Houghton Mifflin.
        Picture Book Honor Books: Baker, Jeannie; *Where the Forest Meets
        the Sea*; Greenwillow Books. Williams, Vera B.; *Stringbean's Trip
        to the Shining Sea*; Greenwillow Books.

Randolph Caldecott Award

The Caldecott Medal, first awarded in 1938, is given to the illustrator
of the most distinguished American picture book for children published in the United States in the preceding year. The illustrator must
be a citizen or resident of the United States. Honor books may be
named. The award is administered by the Association for Library
Services for Children of the American Library Association.

1938   Medal: Fish, Helen Dean; illus. by Dorothy O. Lathrop; *Animals of
        the Bible: A Picture Book*; Stokes (J. B. Lippincott).
        Honor Books: Artzybasheff, Boris; *Seven Simeons*; Viking Press.
        Fish, Helen Dean; illus. by Robert Lawson; *Four and Twenty
        Blackbirds*; Stokes (J. B. Lippincott).
1939   Medal: Handforth, Thomas; *Mei Li*; Doubleday.
        Honor Books: Armer, Laura Adams; *The Forest Pool*; Longmans,
        Green (David McKay). Leaf, Munro; illus. by Robert Lawson;
        Wee Gillis; Viking Press. Gág, Wanda, trans. and illus.; *Snow
        White and the Seven Dwarfs*; Coward-McCann. Newberry, Clare
        Turlay; *Barkis*; Harper (Harper and Row). Daugherty, James;
        Andy and the Lion; Viking Press.

1940   Medal: d'Aulaire, Ingri, and Edgar Parin d'Aulaire; *Abraham Lincoln*; Doubleday.
     Honor Books: Hader, Berta, and Elmer Hader; *Cock-a-Doodle-Doo*; Macmillan. Bemelmans, Ludwig; *Madeline*; Simon and Schuster. Ford, Lauren; *The Ageless Story*; Dodd, Mead.

1941   Medal: Lawson, Robert; *They Were Strong and Good*; Viking Press.
     Honor Book: Newberry, Clare Turlay; *April's Kittens*; Harper (Harper and Row).

1942   Medal: McCloskey, Robert; *Make Way for Ducklings*; Viking Press.
     Honor Books: Petersham, Maud, and Miska Petersham; *An American ABC*; Macmillan. Clark, Ann Nolan; illus. by Velino Herrera; *In My Mother's House*; Viking Press. Holling, Holling Clancy; *Paddle-to-the-Sea*; Houghton Mifflin. Gág, Wanda; *Nothing at All*; Coward-McCann.

1943   Medal: Burton, Virginia Lee; *The Little House*; Houghton Mifflin.
     Honor Books: Buff, Mary, and Conrad Buff; *Dash and Dart*; Viking Press. Newberry, Clare Turlay; *Marshmallow*; Harper (Harper and Row).

1944   Medal: Thurber, James; illus. by Louis Slobodkin; *Many Moons*; Harcourt, Brace and World.
     Honor Books: Text arranged from the Bible by Jessie Orton Jones; illus. by Elizabeth Orton Jones; *Small Rain*; Viking Press. Kingman, Lee; illus. by Arnold Edwin Bare; *Pierre Pidgeon*; Houghton Mifflin. Chan, Chih-Yi; illus. by Plato Chan; *Good-Luck Horse*; Whittlesey. Hader, Berta, and Elmer Hader; *Mighty Hunter*; Macmillan. Brown, Margaret Wise; illus. by Jean Charlot; *A Child's Good Night Book*; W. R. Scott.

1945   Medal: Field, Rachel; illus. by Elizabeth Orton Jones; *Prayer for a Child*; Macmillan.
     Honor Books: Tudor, Tasha, comp. and illus.; *Mother Goose*; Oxford University Press. Ets, Marie Hall; *In the Forest*; Viking Press. de Angeli, Marguerite; *Yonie Wondernose*; Doubleday. Sawyer, Ruth; illus. by Kate Seredy; *The Christmas Anna Angel*; Viking Press.

1946   Medal: Petersham, Maud, and Miska Petersham; *The Rooster Crows*; Macmillan.
     Honor Books: Brown, Margaret Wise; illus. by Leonard Weisgard; *Little Lost Lamb*; Doubleday. Wheeler, Opal, music; illus. by Marjorie Torrey; *Sing Mother Goose*; E. P. Dutton. Reyher, Becky; illus. by Ruth C. Gannett; *My Mother Is the Most Beautiful Woman in the World*; Lothrop, Lee and Shepard Books. Wiese, Kurt; *You Can Write Chinese*; Viking Press.

1947   Medal: MacDonald, Golden; illus. by Leonard Weisgard; *The Little Island*; Doubleday.
     Honor Books: Tresselt, Alvin R.; illus. by Leonard Weisgard; *Rain Drop Splash*; Lothrop, Lee and Shepard Books. Flack, Marjorie; illus. by Jay Hyde Barnum; *Boats on the River*; Viking Press. Graham, Al; illus. by Tony Palazzo; *Timothy Turtle*; Robert Welch (Viking Press). Politi, Leo; *Pedro: Angel of Olvera Street*; Charles Scribner's Sons. Wheeler, Opal; illus. by Marjorie Torrey; *Sing in Praise*; E. P. Dutton.

1948   Medal: Tresselt, Alvin; illus. by Roger Duvoisin; *White Snow, Bright Snow*; Lothrop, Lee and Shepard Books.
        Honor Books: Brown, Marcia; *Stone Soup*; Charles Scribner's Sons. Geisel, Theodor S. (Dr. Seuss); *McElligot's Pool*; Random House. Schreiber, George; *Bambino the Clown*; Viking Press. Davis, Lavinia R.; illus. by Hildegard Woodward; *Roger and the Fox*; Doubleday. Malcolmson, Anne, ed.; illus. by Virginia Lee Burton; *Song of Robin Hood*; Houghton Mifflin.
1949   Medal: Hader, Berta, and Elmer Hader; *The Big Snow*; Macmillan.
        Honor Books: McCloskey, Robert; *Blueberries for Sal*; Viking Press. McGinley, Phyllis; illus. by Helen Stone; *All around the Town*; J. B. Lippincott. Politi, Leo; *Juanita*; Charles Scribner's Sons. Wiese, Kurt; *Fish in the Air*; Viking Press.
1950   Medal: Politi, Leo; *Song of the Swallows*; Charles Scribner's Sons.
        Honor Books: Holbrook, Stewart; illus. by Lynd Ward; *America's Ethan Allen*; Houghton Mifflin. Davis, Lavinia R.; illus. by Hildegard Woodward; *The Wild Birthday Cake*; Doubleday. Krauss, Ruth; illus. by Marc Simont; *Happy Day*; Harper (Harper and Row). Brown, Marcia; *Henry-Fisherman*; Charles Scribner's Sons. Geisel, Theodor S. (Dr. Seuss); *Bartholomew and the Oobleck*; Random House.
1951   Medal: Milhous, Katherine; *The Egg Tree*; Charles Scribner's Sons.
        Honor Books: Brown, Marcia; *Dick Whittington and His Cat*; Charles Scribner's Sons. Will (William Lipkind); illus. by Nicolas (Mordvinoff); *The Two Reds*; Harcourt, Brace and World. Geisel, Theodor S. (Dr. Seuss); *If I Ran the Zoo*; Random House. Newberry, Clare Turlay; *T-Bone the Baby-Sitter*; Harper (Harper and Row). McGinley, Phyllis; illus. by Helen Stone; *The Most Wonderful Doll in the World*; Lippincott.
1952   Medal: Will (William Lipkind); illus. by Nicolas (Mordvinoff); *Finders Keepers*; Harcourt, Brace and World.
        Honor Books: Ets, Marie Hall; *Mr. T. W. Anthony Woo*; Viking Press. Brown, Marcia; *Skipper John's Cook*; Charles Scribner's Sons. Zion, Gene; illus. by Margaret Bloy Graham; *All Falling Down*; Harper (Harper and Row). du Bois, William Pène; *Bear Party*; Viking Press. Olds, Elizabeth; *Feather Mountain*; Houghton Mifflin.
1953   Medal: Ward, Lynd; *The Biggest Bear*; Houghton Mifflin.
        Honor Books: Brown, Marcia; *Puss in Boots*; Charles Scribner's Sons. McCloskey, Robert; *One Morning in Maine*; Viking Press. Eichenberg, Fritz; *Ape in a Cape*; Harcourt, Brace and World. Zolotow, Charlotte; illus. by Margaret Bloy Graham; *The Storm Book*; Harper (Harper and Row). Kepes, Juliet; *Five Little Monkeys*; Houghton Mifflin.
1954   Medal: Bemelmans, Ludwig; *Madeline's Rescue*; Viking Press.
        Honor Books: Sawyer, Ruth; illus. by Robert McCloskey; *Journey Cake, Ho!*; Viking Press. Schlein, Miriam; illus. by Jean Charlot; *When Will the World Be Mine?*; W. R. Scott. Adapted from Andersen, Hans Christian; trans. by M. R. James; illus. by Marcia

Brown; *The Steadfast Tin Soldier*; Charles Scribner's Sons.
Krauss, Ruth; illus. by Maurice Sendak; *A Very Special House*;
Harper (Harper and Row). Birnbaum, Abe; *Green Eyes*; Capitol.

1955 Medal: Perrault, Charles; illus. by Marcia Brown; *Cinderella*; Harper
(Harper and Row).
Honor Books: de Angeli, Marguerite, comp. and illus.; *Book of Nursery and Mother Goose Rhymes*; Doubleday. Brown, Margaret
Wise; illus. by Tibor Gergely; *Wheel on the Chimney*; J. B. Lippincott.

1956 Medal: Langstaff, John; illus. by Feodor Rojankovsky; *Frog Went A-Courtin'*; Harcourt, Brace and World.
Honor Books: Ets, Marie Hall; *Play with Me*; Viking Press. Yashima,
Taro; *Crow Boy*; Viking Press.

1957 Medal: Udry, Janice May; illus. by Marc Simont; *A Tree Is Nice*;
Harper (Harper and Row).
Honor Books: Ets, Marie Hall; *Mr. Penny's Race Horse*; Viking
Press. Tudor, Tasha; *1 Is One*; Oxford (Henry Z. Walck). Titus,
Eve; illus. by Paul Galdone; *Anatole*; Whittlesey (McGraw Hill).
Elkin, Benjamin; illus. by James Daugherty; *Gillespie and the
Guards*; Viking Press. du Bois, William Pène; *Lion*; Viking Press.

1958 Medal: McCloskey, Robert; *Time of Wonder*; Viking Press.
Honor Books: Freeman, Don; *Fly High, Fly Low*; Viking Press.
Titus, Eve; illus. by Paul Galdone; *Anatole and the Cat*; Whittlesey (McGraw Hill).

1959 Medal: Cooney, Barbara, ed. and illus.; *Chanticleer and the Fox*;
Thomas Y. Crowell.
Honor Books: Frasconi, Antonio; *The House That Jack Built*;
Thomas Y. Crowell. Joslin, Sesyl; illus. by Maurice Sendak; *What
Do You Say, Dear?*; W. R. Scott. Yashima, Taro; *Umbrella*; Viking Press.

1960 Medal: Ets, Marie Hall, and Aurora Labastida; *Nine Days to Christmas*; Viking Press.
Honor Books: Goudey, Alice E.; illus. by Adrienne Adams; *Houses
from the Sea*; Charles Scribner's Sons. Udry, Janice May; illus. by
Maurice Sendak; *The Moon Jumpers*; Harper (Harper and Row).

1961 Medal: Robbins, Ruth; illus. by Nicolas Sidjakov; *Baboushka and the
Three Kings*; Parnassus Press.
Honor Book: Lionni, Leo; *Inch by Inch*; Obolensky.

1962 Medal: Brown, Marcia; *Once a Mouse*; Charles Scribner's Sons.
Honor Books: Spier, Peter; *The Fox Went Out on a Chilly Night*;
Doubleday. Minarik, Else; illus. by Maurice Sendak; *Little Bear's
Visit*; Harper (Harper and Row). Goudey, Alice; illus. by Adrienne
Adams; *The Day We Saw the Sun Come Up*; Charles Scribner's
Sons.

1963 Medal: Keats, Ezra Jack; *The Snowy Day*; Viking Press.
Honor Books: Belting, Natalia; illus. by Bernarda Bryson; *The Sun Is
a Golden Earring*; Holt, Rinehart and Winston. Zolotow, Charlotte; illus. by Maurice Sendak; *Mr. Rabbit and the Lovely Present*; Harper and Row.

1964   Medal: Sendak, Maurice; *Where the Wild Things Are*; Harper and
        Row.
        Honor Books: Lionni, Leo; *Swimmy*; Pantheon Books. Nic Leodhas,
        Sorché; illus. by Evaline Ness; *All in the Morning Early*; Holt,
        Rinehart and Winston. Reed, Philip; *Mother Goose and Nursery
        Rhymes*; Atheneum.
1965   Medal: de Regniers, Beatrice Schenk; illus. by Beni Montresor; *May I
        Bring a Friend?*; Atheneum.
        Honor Books: Scheer, Julian; illus. by Marvin Bileck; *Rain Makes
        Applesauce*; Holiday House. Hodges, Margaret; illus. by Blair
        Lent; *The Wave*; Houghton Mifflin. Caudill, Rebecca; illus. by
        Evaline Ness; *A Pocketful of Cricket*; Holt, Rinehart and Winston.
1966   Medal: Nic Leodhas, Sorché; illus. by Nonny Hogrogian; *Always
        Room for One More*; Holt, Rinehart and Winston.
        Honor Books: Tresselt, Alvin; illus. by Roger Duvoisin; *Hide and
        Seek Fog*; Lothrop, Lee and Shepard Books. Ets, Marie Hall; *Just
        Me*; Viking Press. Jacobs, Joseph, ed.; illus. by Evaline Ness; *Tom
        Tit Tot*; Charles Scribner's Sons.
1967   Medal: Ness, Evaline; *Sam, Bangs and Moonshine*; Holt, Rinehart
        and Winston.
        Honor Book: Emberley, Barbara; illus. by Ed Emberley; *One Wide
        River to Cross*; Prentice-Hall.
1968   Medal: Emberley, Barbara; illus. by Ed Emberley; *Drummer Hoff*;
        Prentice-Hall.
        Honor Books: Lionni, Leo; *Frederick*; Pantheon Books. Yashima,
        Taro; *Seashore Story*; Viking Press. Yolen, Jane; illus. by Ed
        Young; *The Emperor and the Kite*; World Publishing.
1969   Medal: Ransome, Arthur; illus. by Uri Shulevitz; *The Fool of the
        World and the Flying Ship*; Farrar, Straus and Giroux.
        Honor Book: Dayrell, Elphinstone; illus. by Blair Lent; *Why the Sun
        and the Moon Live in the Sky*; Houghton Mifflin.
1970   Medal: Steig, William; *Sylvester and the Magic Pebble*; Simon and
        Schuster.
        Honor Books: Keats, Ezra Jack; *Goggles*; Macmillan. Lionni, Leo;
        Alexander and the Wind-up Mouse; Pantheon Books. Preston,
        Edna Mitchell; illus. by Robert Andrew Parker; *Pop Corn and Ma
        Goodness*; Viking Press. Turkle, Brinton; *Thy Friend, Obadiah*;
        Viking Press. Zemach, Harve; illus. by Margot Zemach; *The
        Judge*; Farrar, Straus and Giroux.
1971   Medal: Haley, Gail E.; *A Story, A Story*; Atheneum.
        Honor Books: Sleator, William; illus. by Blair Lent; *The Angry
        Moon*; Atlantic Monthly Press. Lobel, Arnold; *Frog and Toad Are
        Friends*; Harper and Row. Sendak, Maurice; *In the Night Kitchen*;
        Harper and Row.
1972   Medal: Hogrogian, Nonny; *One Fine Day*; Macmillan.
        Honor Books: Domanska, Janina; *If All the Seas Were One Sea*; Mac-
        millan. Feelings, Muriel; illus. by Tom Feelings; *Moja Means One:
        Swahili Counting Book*; Dial Press. Ryan, Cheli Duran; illus. by
        Arnold Lobel; *Hildilid's Night*; Macmillan.
1973   Medal: Mosel, Arlene; illus. by Blair Lent; *The Funny Little Woman*;
        E. P. Dutton.

Honor Books: Baskin, Hosea, Tobias Baskin, and Lisa Baskin; illus. by Leonard Baskin; *Hosie's Alphabet*; Viking Press. Baylor, Byrd; illus. by Tom Bahti; *When Clay Sings*; Charles Scribner's Sons. Grimm, Jakob, and Wilhelm Grimm; trans. by Randall Jarrell; illus. by Nancy Ekholm Burkert; *Snow-White and the Seven Dwarfs*; Farrar, Straus and Giroux. McDermott, Gerald; *Anansi the Spider*; Holt, Rinehart and Winston.

1974   Medal: Zemach, Harve; illus. by Margot Zemach; *Duffy and the Devil*; Farrar, Straus and Giroux.
Honor Books: Jeffers, Susan; *The Three Jovial Huntsmen*; Bradbury Press. Macaulay, David; *Cathedral*; Houghton Mifflin.

1975   Medal: McDermott, Gerald; *Arrow to the Sun*; Viking Press.
Honor Book: Feelings, Muriel; illus. by Tom Feelings; *Jambo Means Hello: Swahili Alphabet Book*; Dial Press.

1976   Medal: Aardema, Verna; illus. by Leo and Diane Dillon; *Why Mosquitoes Buzz in People's Ears*; Dial Books for Young Readers.
Honor Books: Baylor, Byrd; illus. by Peter Parnell; *The Desert Is Theirs*; Charles Scribner's Sons; dePaola, Tomie; *Strega Nona: An Old Tale Retold*; Prentice-Hall.

1977   Medal: Musgrove, Margaret; illus. by Leo and Diane Dillon; *Ashanti to Zulu: African Traditions*; Dial Books for Young Readers.
Honor Books: Steig, William; *The Amazing Bone*; Farrar, Straus and Giroux. Hogrogian, Nonny; *The Contest*; Greenwillow Books. Goffstein, M. B.; *Fish for Supper*; Dial. McDermott, Beverly Brodsky; *The Golem*; J. B. Lippincott. Baylor, Byrd; illus. by Peter Parnall; *Hawk, I'm Your Brother*; Charles Scribner's Sons.

1978   Medal: Spier, Peter; *Noah's Ark*; Doubleday.
Honor Books: Macaulay, David; *Castle*; Houghton Mifflin. Zemach, Margot; *It Could Always Be Worse*; Farrar, Straus and Giroux.

1979   Medal: Goble, Paul; *The Girl Who Loved Wild Horses*; Bradbury Press.
Honor Books: Crews, Donald; *Freight Train*; Greenwillow Books. Baylor, Byrd; illus. by Peter Parnall; *The Way to Start a Day*; Charles Scribner's Sons.

1980   Medal: Hall, Donald; illus. by Barbara Cooney; *Ox-Cart Man*; Viking Press.
Honor Books: Isadora, Rachel; *Ben's Trumpet*; Greenwillow Books. Shulevitz, Uri; *The Treasure*; Farrar, Straus and Giroux. Van Allsburg, Chris; *The Garden of Abdul Gasazi*; Houghton Mifflin.

1981   Medal: Lobel, Arnold; *Fables*; Harper and Row.
Honor Books: Plume, Ilse; *The Bremen-Town Musicians*; Doubleday. Bang, Molly; *The Grey Lady and the Strawberry Snatcher*; Four Winds Press. Low, Joseph; *Mice Twice*; Atheneum. Crews, Donald; *Truck*; Greenwillow Books.

1982   Medal: Van Allsburg, Chris; *Jumanji*; Houghton Mifflin.
Honor Books: Willard, Nancy; illus. by Alice and Martin Provensen; *A Visit to William Blake's Inn: Poems for Innocent and Experienced Travelers*; Harcourt Brace Jovanovich. Baker, Olaf; illus. by Stephen Gammell; *Where the Buffaloes Began*; Frederick Warne. Lobel, Arnold; illus. by Anita Lobel; *On Market Street*; Greenwillow Books. Sendak, Maurice; *Outside Over There*; Harper and Row.

1983   Medal: Cendrars, Blaise; illus. by Marcia Brown; *Shadow*; Charles
        Scribner's Sons.
        Honor Books: Rylant, Cynthia; illus. by Diane Goode; *When I Was
        Young in the Mountains*; E. P. Dutton. Williams, Vera B.; *A Chair
        for My Mother*; William Morrow.
1984   Medal: Provensen, Alice, and Martin Provensen; *The Glorious Flight:
        Across the Channel with Louis Bleriot, July 25, 1909*; Viking Kes-
        trel.
        Honor Books: Bang, Molly; *Ten, Nine, Eight*; Greenwillow Books.
        Hyman, Trina Schart; *Little Red Riding Hood*; Holiday House.
1985   Medal: Hodges, Margaret; illus. by Trina Schart Hyman; *Saint
        George and the Dragon*; Little, Brown.
        Honor Books: Lesser, Rika; illus. by Paul O. Zelinsky; *Hansel and
        Gretel*; Dodd, Mead. Steptoe, John; *The Story of Jumping Mouse*;
        Lothrop, Lee and Shepard Books. Tafuri, Nancy; *Have You Seen
        My Duckling?*; Greenwillow Books.
1986   Medal: Van Allsburg, Chris; *Polar Express*; Houghton Mifflin.
        Honor Books: Rylant, Cynthia; illus. by Stephen Gammell; *The Rela-
        tives Came*; Bradbury Press. Wood, Audrey; illus. by Don Wood;
        King Bidgood's in the Bathtub; Harcourt Brace Jovanovich.
1987   Medal: Yorinks, Arthur; illus. by Richard Egielski; *Hey, Al*; Farrar,
        Straus and Giroux.
        Honor Books: MacDonald, Suse; *Alphabatics*; Bradbury Press.
        Zelinsky, Paul O.; *Rumplestiltskin*; E. P. Dutton. Grifalconi, Ann;
        The Village of Round and Square Houses; Little, Brown.
1988   Medal: Yolen, Jane; illus. by John Schoenherr; *Owl Moon*; Philomel
        Books.
        Honor Book: Steptoe, John; *Mufaro's Beautiful Daughters: An Af-
        rican Tale*; William Morrow.
1989   Medal: Ackerman, Karen; illus. by Stephen Gammell; *Song and
        Dance Man*; Alfred A. Knopf.
        Honor Books: Snyder, Dianne; illus. by Allen Say; *The Boy of the
        Three-Year Nap*; Houghton Mifflin. Wiesner, David; *Free Fall*;
        Lothrop, Lee and Shepard Books. Marshall, James; *Goldilocks
        and the Three Bears*; Dial Books for Young Readers. McKissack,
        Patricia; illus. by Jerry Pinkney; *Mirandy and Brother Wind*; Al-
        fred A. Knopf.

International Reading Association Children's Book Award

This award is given annually for a first or second book by an author
from any country who shows unusual promise in the children's book
field. It was established in 1975; the illustrator award was added in
1987.

1975   Degens, T.; *Transport 7-41*; Viking Press.
1976   Yep, Laurence; *Dragonwings*; Harper and Row.
1977   Bond, Nancy; *A String in the Harp*; Margaret K. McElderry Books.

1978   Lowry, Lois; illus. by Jenni Oliver; *Summer to Die*; Houghton Mifflin.
1979   Smith, Alison; *Reserved for Mark Anthony Crowder*; E. P. Dutton.
1980   Sebestyen, Ouida; *Words by Heart*; Atlantic Monthly Press.
1981   Beckman, Delores; *My Own Private Sky*; E. P. Dutton.
1982   Magorian, Michelle; *Good Night, Mr. Tom*; Viking Kestrel.
1983   Pierce, Meredith; *Darkangel*; Atlantic Monthly Press.
1984   Bell, Clare; *Ratha's Creature*; Macmillan.
1985   Howker, Janni; *Badger on the Barge, and Other Stories*; Julia MacRae.
1986   Conrad, Pam; illus. by Darryl S. Zudeck; *Prairie Songs*; Harper and Row.
1987   Writing: Rostkowski, Margaret I.; *After the Dancing Days*; Harper and Row.
       Illustration: Russo, Marisabina; *Line Up Book*; Greenwillow Books.
1988   Baker, Leslie; *Third Story Cat*; Little, Brown.
1989   Writing: Wolff, Virginia Euwer; *Probably Still Nick Swansen*; Henry Holt.
       Illustration: Polacco, Patricia; *Rechenka's Eggs*; Philomel Books.

Coretta Scott King Award

These awards, established in 1969, are given annually to a black author and to a black illustrator for books that are outstanding inspirational and educational contributions to literature for children and young people. They are given by the Social Responsibilities Round Table of the American Library Association. Honor books for the past three years are included.

1970   Patterson, Lillie; *Martin Luther King, Jr.*; Garrard.
1971   Rollins, Charlemae H.; *Black Troubador: Langston Hughes*; Rand McNally.
1972   Fax, Elton C.; *Seventeen Black Artists*; Dodd, Mead.
1973   Duckett, Alfred; *I Never Had It Made*; G. P. Putnam's Sons.
1974   Mathis, Sharon B.; illus. by George Ford; *Ray Charles*; Thomas Y. Crowell.
1975   Robinson, Dorothy W.; illus. by Herbert Temple; *The Legend of Africania*; Johnson.
1976   Bailey, Pearl; *Duey's Tale*; Harcourt Brace Jovanovich.
1977   Haskins, James; *The Story of Stevie Wonder*; Lothrop, Lee and Shepard Books.
1978   Greenfield, Eloise; illus. by Carole Byard; *Africa Dream*; John Day.
1979   Writing: Davis, Ossie; *Escape to Freedom: A Play about Young Frederick Douglass*; Viking Press.
       Illustration: Feelings, Tom; *Something on My Mind*; Dial Press.

1980   Writing: Myers, Walter Dean; *The Young Landlords*; Viking Press.
        Illustration: Yarbrough, Camille; illus. by Carole Byard; *Cornrows*;
        Coward, McCann and Geoghegan.

1981   Writing: Poitier, Sidney; *This Life*; Alfred A. Knopf.
        Illustration: Bryan, Ashley; *Beat the Story Drum, Pum Pum*; Athe-
        neum.

1982   Writing: Taylor, Mildred D.; *Let the Circle Be Unbroken*; Dial Books
        for Young Readers.
        Illustration: Steptoe, John; *Mother Crocodile*; Delacorte Press.

1983   Writing: Hamilton, Virginia; *Sweet Whispers, Brothers Rush*; Phil-
        omel Books.
        Illustration: Magubane, Peter; *Black Child*; Alfred A. Knopf.

1984   Writing: Clifton, Lucille; *Everett Anderson's Goodbye*; Holt, Rinehart
        and Winston.
        Illustration: Walter, Mildred Pitts; illus. by Pat Cummings; *My Mama
        Needs Me*; Lothrop, Lee and Shepard Books.

1985   Writing: Myers, Walter Dean; *Motown and Didi: A Love Story*; Vi-
        king Kestrel.

1986   Writing: Hamilton, Virginia; *The People Could Fly: American Black
        Folktales*; Alfred A. Knopf.
        Illustration: Flournoy, Valerie; illus. by Jerry Pinkney; *Patchwork
        Quilt*; Dial Books for Young Readers.

1987   Writing Award: Walter, Mildred Pitts; *Justin and the Best Biscuits in
        the World*; Lothrop, Lee and Shepard Books.
        Writing Honor Books: Bryan, Ashley; *Lion and the Ostrich Chicks,
        and Other African Tales*; Atheneum. Hansen, Joyce; *Which Way
        Freedom?*; Walker.
        Illustration Award: Dragonwagon, Crescent; illus. by Jerry Pinkney;
        Half a Moon and One Whole Star; Macmillan.
        Illustration Honor Book: Cummings, Pat; *C.L.O.U.D.S.*; Lothrop,
        Lee and Shepard Books.

1988   Writing Award: Taylor, Mildred D.; *The Friendship*; Dial Books for
        Young Readers.
        Writing Honor Books: Lester, Julius; *The Tales of Uncle Remus: The
        Adventures of Brer Rabbit*; Dial Books for Young Readers. De
        Veaux, Alexis; illus. by Cheryl Hanna; *An Enchanted Hair Tale*;
        Harper and Row.
        Illustration Award: Steptoe, John; *Mufaro's Beautiful Daughters: An
        African Tale*; Lothrop, Lee and Shepard Books.
        Illustration Honor Books: Bryan, Ashley; *What a Morning: The
        Christmas Story in Black Spirituals*; Macmillan. Rohmer, Harriet;
        Invisible Hunters; Children's Press.

1989   Writing Award: Myers, Walter Dean; *Fallen Angels*; Scholastic.
        Writing Honor Books: Berry, James; *A Thief in the Village, and
        Other Stories*; Orchard Books. Hamilton, Virginia; *Anthony Burns:
        The Defeat and Triumph of a Fugitive Slave*; Alfred A. Knopf.
        Illustration Award: McKissack, Patricia; illus. by Jerry Pinkney; *Mi-
        randy and Brother Wind*; Alfred A. Knopf.
        Illustration Honor Books: Greenfield, Eloise; illus. by Amos Fer-
        guson; *Under the Sunday Tree*; Harper and Row. Stolz, Mary;
        illus. by Pat Cummings; *Storm in the Night*; Harper and Row.

National Council of Teachers of English Award for Excellence in Poetry for Children

The award is given every three years to a living American poet in recognition of his or her aggregate body of poetry for children ages three to thirteen. Established in 1977, the award was given annually until 1982; now it is presented every three years.

1977	David McCord
1978	Aileen Fisher
1979	Karla Kuskin
1980	Myra Cohn Livingston
1981	Eve Merriam
1982	John Ciardi
1985	Lilian Moore
1988	Arnold Adoff

John Newbery Medal

The Newbery Medal, first awarded in 1922, is given annually to the author of the most distinguished contribution to literature for children published in the United States during the preceding year. The author must be a citizen or resident of the United States. Honor books may be named. The award is administered by the Association for Library Service to Children of the American Library Association.

1922   Medal: Van Loon, Hendrik; *The Story of Mankind*; Boni and Liveright (Liveright).
      Honor Books: Hawes, Charles Boardman; *The Great Quest*; Little, Brown. Marshall, Bernard G.; *Cedric the Forester* Appleton, Century, Crofts. Bowen, William; *The Old Tobacco Shop*; Macmillan. Colum, Padraic; *The Golden Fleece*; Macmillan. Meigs, Cornelia; *Windy Hill*; Macmillan.

1923   Medal: Lofting, Hugh; *The Voyages of Doctor Dolittle*; Stokes (J. B. Lippincott).

1924   Medal: Hawes, Charles Boardman; *The Dark Frigate*; Little, Brown.

1925   Medal: Finger, Charles J.; illus. by Paul Honoré; *Tales from Silver Lands*; Doubleday.
      Honor Books: Moore, Anne Carroll; *Nicholas*; G. P. Putnam's Sons. Parrish, Anne, and Dillwyn Parrish; *Dream Coach*; Macmillan.

1926   Medal: Chrisman, Arthur Bowie; illus. by Else Hasselriis; *Shen of the Sea*; E. P. Dutton.
      Honor Book: Colum, Padraic; *The Voyagers*; Macmillan.

1927   Medal: James, Will; *Smoky, the Cowhorse*; Charles Scribner's Sons.

1928   Medal: Mukerji, Dhan Gopal; illus. by Boris Artzybasheff; *Gay Neck*; E. P. Dutton.
      Honor Books: Young, Ella; *The Wonder-Smith and His Son*; Longmans, Green (David McKay). Snedeker, Caroline Dale; *Downright Dencey*; Doubleday.

1929   Medal: Kelly, Eric P.; illus. by Angela Pruszynska; *Trumpeter of Krakow*; Macmillan.
Honor Books: Bennett, John; *The Pigtail of Ah Lee Ben Loo*; Longmans, Green (David McKay). Gág, Wanda; *Millions of Cats*; Coward-McCann. Hallock, Grace T.; *The Boy Who Was*; E. P. Dutton. Meigs, Cornelia; *Clearing Weather*; Little, Brown. Moon, Grace P.; *The Runaway Papoose*; Doubleday. Whitney, Eleanor; *Tod of the Fens*; Macmillan.

1930   Medal: Field, Rachel; illus. by Dorothy P. Lathrop; *Hitty, Her First Hundred Years*; Macmillan.
Honor Books: Miller, Elizabeth C.; *Pran of Albania*; Doubleday. McNeely, Marian Hurd; *The Jumping-Off Place*; Longmans, Green (David McKay). Eaton, Jeanette; *A Daughter of the Seine*; Harper (Harper and Row).

1931   Medal: Coatsworth, Elizabeth; illus. by Lynd Ward; *The Cat Who Went to Heaven*; Macmillan.
Honor Books: Parrish, Anne; *Floating Island*; Harper (Harper and Row). Malkus, Alida; *The Dark Star of Itza*; Harcourt, Brace and World. Hubbard, Ralph; *Queer Person*; Doubleday. Adams, Julia Davis; *Mountains Are Free*; E. P. Dutton. Hewes, Agnes D.; *Spice and the Devil's Cave*; Alfred A. Knopf. Gray, Elizabeth Janet; *Meggy McIntosh*; Doubleday.

1932   Medal: Armer, Laura Adams; illus. by Sidney Armer and the author; *Waterless Mountain*; Longmans, Green (David McKay).
Honor Books: Lathrop, Dorothy; *The Fairy Circus*; Macmillan. Field, Rachel; *Calico Bush*; Macmillan. Tietjens, Eunice; *Boy of the South Seas*; Coward-McCann. Lounsbery, Eloise; *Out of the Flame*; Longmans, Green (David McKay). Alee, Marjorie Hill; *Jane's Island*; Houghton Mifflin. Davis, Mary Gould; *Truce of the Wolf*; Harcourt, Brace and World.

1933   Medal: Lewis, Elizabeth Foreman; illus. by Kurt Wiese; *Young Fu of the Upper Yangtze*; Winston (Holt, Rinehart and Winston).
Honor Books: Meigs, Cornelia; *Swift River*; Little (Little, Brown). Swift, Hildegarde; *The Railroad to Freedom*; Harcourt, Brace and World. Burglon, Nora; *Children of the Soil*; Doubleday.

1934   Medal: Meigs, Cornelia; *Invincible Louisa*; Little, Brown.
Honor Books: Snedeker, Caroline Dale; *Forgotten Daughter*; Doubleday. Singmaster, Elsie; *Swords of Steel*; Houghton Mifflin. Gág, Wanda; *ABC Bunny*; Coward-McCann. Berry, Erick; *Winged Girl of Knossos*; Appleton. Schmidt, Sarah L.; *New Land*; McBride. Kyle, Anne; *Apprentices of Florence*; Houghton Mifflin.

1935   Medal: Shannon, Monica; illus. by Atanas Katchamakoff; *Dobry*; Viking Press.
Honor Books: Seeger, Elizabeth; *The Pageant of Chinese History*; Longmans, Green (David McKay). Rourke, Constance; *Davy Crockett*; Harcourt, Brace and World. Van Stockum, Hilda; *A Day on Skates*; Harper (Harper and Row).

1936   Medal: Brink, Carol Ryrie; illus. by Kate Seredy; *Caddie Woodlawn*; Macmillan.
       Honor Books: Stong, Phil; *Honk the Moose*; Dodd, Mead. Seredy, Kate; *The Good Master*; Viking Press. Gray, Elizabeth Janet; *Young Walter Scott*; Viking Press. Sperry, Armstrong; *All Sail Set*; Winston (Holt, Rinehart and Winston).

1937   Medal: Sawyer, Ruth; illus. by Valenti Angelo; *Roller Skates*; Viking Press.
       Honor Books: Lenski, Lois; *Phoebe Fairchild: Her Book*; Stokes (J. B. Lippincott). Jones, Idwal; *Whistler's Van*; Viking Press. Bemelmans, Ludwig; *The Golden Basket*; Viking Press. Bianco, Margery; *Winterbound*; Viking Press. Rourke, Constance; *Audubon*; Harcourt, Brace and World. Hewes, Agnes D.; *The Codfish Musket*; Doubleday.

1938   Medal: Seredy, Kate; *The White Stag*; Viking Press.
       Honor Books: Robinson, Mabel L.; *Bright Island*; Random House. Bowman, James Cloyd; *Pecos Bill*; Albert C. Whitman. Wilder, Laura Ingalls; *On the Banks of Plum Creek*; Harper (Harper and Row).

1939   Medal: Enright, Elizabeth; *Thimble Summer*; Farrar and Rinehart (Holt, Rinehart and Winston).
       Honor Books: Eaton, Jeanette; *Leader by Destiny*; Harcourt, Brace and World. Gray, Elizabeth Janet; *Penn*; Viking Press. Angelo, Valenti; *Nino*; Viking Press. Crawford, Phyllis; *"Hello, the Boat!"*; Holt (Holt, Rinehart and Winston). Atwater, Richard, and Florence Atwater; *Mr. Popper's Penguins*; Little, Brown.

1940   Medal: Daugherty, James H.; *Daniel Boone*; Viking Press.
       Honor Books: Seredy, Kate; *The Singing Tree*; Viking Press. Robinson, Mabel L.; *Runner of the Mountain Tops*; Random House. Wilder, Laura Ingalls; *By the Shores of Silver Lake*; Harper (Harper and Row). Meader, Stephen W.; *Boy with a Pack*; Harcourt, Brace and World.

1941   Medal: Sperry, Armstrong; *Call It Courage*; Macmillan.
       Honor Books: Gates, Doris; *Blue Willow*; Viking Press. Carr, Mary Jane; *Young Mac of Fort Vancouver*; Thomas Y. Crowell. Wilder, Laura Ingalls; *The Long Winter*; Harper (Harper and Row). Hall, Anna Gertrude; *Nansen*; Viking Press.

1942   Medal: Edmonds, Walter D.; illus. by Paul Lantz; *The Matchlook Gun*; Dodd, Mead.
       Honor Books: Wilder, Laura Ingalls; *Little Town on the Prairie*; Harper (Harper and Row). Foster, G.; *George Washington's World*; Charles Scribner's Sons. Lenski, Lois; *Indian Captive*; Stokes (J. B. Lippincott). Gaggin, E. R.; *Down Ryton Water*; Viking Press.

1943   Medal: Gray, Elizabeth Janet; illus. by Robert Lawson; *Adam of the Road*; Viking Press.
       Honor Books: Estes, Eleanor; *The Middle Moffat*; Harcourt, Brace and World. Hunt, Mabel Leigh; *"Have You Seen Tom Thumb?"*; Stokes (J. B. Lippincott).

1944   Medal: Forbes, Esther; illus. by Lynd Ward; *Johnny Tremain*;
        Houghton Mifflin.
        Honor Books: Wilder, Laura Ingalls; *These Happy Golden Years*;
        Harper (Harper and Row). Sauer, Julia L.; *Fog Magic*; Viking
        Press. Estes, Eleanor; *Rufus M.*; Harcourt, Brace and World.
        Yates, Elizabeth; *Mountain Born*; Coward-McCann.
1945   Medal: Lawson, Robert; *Rabbit Hill*; Viking Press.
        Honor Books: Estes, Eleanor; *The Hundred Dresses*; Harcourt,
        Brace and World. Dalgliesh, Alice; *The Silver Pencil*; Charles
        Scribner's Sons. Foster, Genevieve; *Abraham Lincoln's World*;
        Charles Scribner's Sons. Eaton, Jeanette; *Lone Journey*; Harcourt,
        Brace and World.
1946   Medal: Lenski, Lois; *Strawberry Girl*; J. B. Lippincott.
        Honor Books: Henry, Marguerite; *Justin Morgan Had a Horse*;
        Wilcox and Follett (Follett). Means, Florence Crannell; *The
        Moved-Outers*; Houghton Mifflin. Weston, Christine; *Bhimsa, the
        Dancing Bear*; Charles Scribner's Sons. Shippen, Katherine B.;
        New Found World; Viking Press.
1947   Medal: Bailey, Carolyn Sherwin; illus. by Ruth Gannett; *Miss Hicko-
        ry*; Viking Press.
        Honor Books: Barnes, Nancy; *The Wonderful Year*; Julian Messner.
        Buff, Mary, and Conrad Buff; *Big Tree*; Viking Press. Maxwell,
        William; *The Heavenly Tenants*; Harper (Harper and Row). Fisher,
        Cyrus; *The Avion My Uncle Flew*; Appleton, Century, Crofts. Jew-
        ett, Eleanore M.; *The Hidden Treasure of Glaston*; Viking Press.
1948   Medal: du Bois, William Pène; *The Twenty-one Balloons*; Viking
        Press.
        Honor Books: Bishop, Claire Huchet; *Pancakes-Paris*; Viking Press.
        Treffinger, Carolyn; *Li Lun, Lad of Courage*; Abingdon-Cokes-
        bury (Abingdon Press). Besterman, Catherine; *The Quaint and Cu-
        rious Quest of Johnny Longfoot*; Bobbs-Merrill. Courlander,
        Harold, and George Herzog; *The Cow-Tail Switch*; Holt (Holt,
        Rinehart and Winston). Henry, Marguerite; *Misty of Chin-
        coteague*; Rand McNally.
1949   Medal: Henry, Marguerite; illus. by Wesley Dennis; *King of the
        Wind*; Rand McNally.
        Honor Books: Holling, Holling Clancy; *Seabird*; Houghton Mifflin.
        Rankin, Louise; *Daughter of the Mountains*; Viking Press. Gan-
        nett, Ruth S.; *My Father's Dragon*; Random House. Bontemps,
        Arna; *Story of the Negro*; Alfred A. Knopf.
1950   Medal: de Angeli, Marguerite; *The Door in the Wall*; Doubleday.
        Honor Books: Caudill, Rebecca; *Tree of Freedom*; Viking Press.
        Coblentz, Catherine; *Blue Cat of Castle Town*; Longmans, Green
        (David McKay). Montgomery, Rutherford; *Kildee House*; Double-
        day. Foster, Genevieve; *George Washington*; Charles Scribner's
        Sons. Havighurst, Walter, and Marion Havighurst; *Song of the
        Pines*; Winston (Holt, Rinehart and Winston).
1951   Medal: Yates, Elizabeth; illus. by Nora Unwin; *Amos Fortune, Free
        Man*; Aladdin Books (E. P. Dutton).

Honor Books: Hunt, Mabel Leigh; *Better Known as Johnny Appleseed*; J. B. Lippincott. Eaton, Jeanette; *Gandhi, Fighter without a Sword*; William Morrow. Judson, Clara I.; *Abraham Lincoln, Friend of the People*; Wilcox and Follett (Follett). Parrish, Anne; *The Story of Appleby Capple*; Harper (Harper and Row).

1952   Medal: Estes, Eleanor; *Ginger Pye*; Harcourt, Brace and World.
Honor Books: Baity, Elizabeth Chesley; *Americans before Columbus*; Viking Press. Holling, Holling Clancy; *Minn of the Mississippi*; Houghton Mifflin. Kalashnikoff, Nicholas; *The Defender*; Charles Scribner's Sons. Sauer, Julia L.; *The Light at Tern Rock*; Viking Press. Buff, Mary; *The Apple and the Arrow*; Houghton Mifflin.

1953   Medal: Clark, Ann Nolan; illus. by Jean Charlot; *Secret of the Andes*; Viking Press.
Honor Books: White, E. B.; *Charlotte's Web*; Harper (Harper and Row). McGraw, Eloise J.; *Moccasin Trail*; Coward-McCann. Weil, Ann; *Red Sails for Capri*; Viking Press; Dalgliesh, Alice; *The Bears on Hemlock Mountain*; Charles Scribner's Sons. Foster, Genevieve; *Birthdays of Freedom*; Charles Scribner's Sons.

1954   Medal: Krumgold, Joseph; illus. by Jean Charlot; *And Now Miguel*; Thomas Y. Crowell.
Honor Books: Bishop, Claire Huchet; *All Alone*; Viking Press. DeJong, Meindert; *Shadrach*; Harper (Harper and Row). DeJong, Meindert; *Hurry Home, Candy*; Harper (Harper and Row). Judson, Clara I.; *Theodore Roosevelt, Fighting Patriot*; Follett. Buff, Mary; *Magic Maize*; Houghton Mifflin.

1955   Medal: DeJong, Meindert; illus. by Maurice Sendak; *The Wheel on the School*; Harper (Harper and Row).
Honor Books: Dalgliesh, Alice; *The Courage of Sarah Noble*; Charles Scribner's Sons. Ullman, James Ramsey; *Banner in the Sky*; J. B. Lippincott.

1956   Medal: Latham, Jean Lee; *Carry on, Mr. Bowditch*; Houghton Mifflin.
Honor Books: Lindquist, Jennie D.; *The Golden Name Day*; Harper (Harper and Row). Rawlings, Marjorie Kinnan; *The Secret River*; Charles Scribner's Sons. Shippen, Katherine B.; *Men, Microscopes and Living Things*; Viking Press.

1957   Medal: Sorensen, Virginia; illus. by Beth Krush and Joe Krush; *Miracles on Maple Hill*; Harcourt, Brace and World.
Honor Books: Gipson, Fred; *Old Yeller*; Harper (Harper and Row). DeJong, Meindert; *The House of Sixty Fathers*; Harper (Harper and Row). Judson, Clara I.; *Mr. Justice Holmes*; Follett. Rhoads, Dorothy; *The Corn Grows Ripe*; Viking Press. de Angeli, Marguerite; *The Black Fox of Lorne*; Doubleday.

1958   Medal: Keith, Harold; illus. by Peter Burchard; *Rifles for Watie*; Thomas Y. Crowell.
Honor Books: Sandoz, Mari; *The Horsecatcher*; Westminster Press. Enright, Elizabeth; *Gone-away Lake*; Harcourt, Brace and World. Lawson, Robert; *The Great Wheel*; Viking Press. Gurko, Leo; *Tom Paine, Freedom's Apostle*; Thomas Y. Crowell.

1959　Medal: Speare, Elizabeth George; *The Witch of Blackbird Pond*; Houghton Mifflin.

　　　Honor Books: Carlson, Natalie S.; *The Family under the Bridge*; Harper (Harper and Row). DeJong, Meindert; *Along Came a Dog*; Harper (Harper and Row). Kalnay, Francis; *Chucaro*; Harcourt, Brace and World. Steele, William O.; *The Perilous Road*; Harcourt, Brace and World.

1960　Medal: Krumgold, Joseph; illus. by Symeon Shimin; *Onion John*; Thomas Y. Crowell.

　　　Honor Books: George, Jean; *My Side of the Mountain*; E. P. Dutton. Johnson, Gerald; *America Is Born*; William Morrow. Kendall, Carol; *The Gammage Cup*; Harcourt, Brace and World.

1961　Medal: O'Dell, Scott; *Island of the Blue Dolphins*; Houghton Mifflin.

　　　Honor Books: Johnson, Gerald; *America Moves Forward*; William Morrow. Schaefer, Jack; *Old Ramon*; Houghton Mifflin. Selden, George; *The Cricket in Times Square*; Farrar (Farrar, Straus and Giroux).

1962　Medal: Speare, Elizabeth George; *The Bronze Bow*; Houghton Mifflin.

　　　Honor Books: Tunis, Edwin; *Frontier Living*; World Publishing. McGraw, Eloise J.; *The Golden Goblet*; Coward-McCann. Stolz, Mary; *Belling the Tiger*; Harper and Row.

1963　Medal: L'Engle, Madeleine; *A Wrinkle in Time*; Farrar (Farrar, Straus and Giroux).

　　　Honor Books: Nic Leodhas, Sorché; *Thistle and Thyme*; Holt, Rinehart and Winston. Coolidge, Olivia; *Men of Athens*; Houghton Mifflin.

1964　Medal: Neville, Emily; illus. by Emil Weiss; *It's Like This, Cat*; Harper and Row.

　　　Honor Books: North, Sterling; *Rascal*; E. P. Dutton. Wier, Ester; *The Loner*; David McKay.

1965　Medal: Wojciechowska, Maia; illus. by Alvin Smith; *Shadow of a Bull*; Atheneum.

　　　Honor Book: Hunt, Irene; *Across Five Aprils*; Follett.

1966　Medal: de Treviño, Elizabeth Borten; *I, Juan de Pareja*; Farrar, Straus and Giroux.

　　　Honor Books: Alexander, Lloyd; *The Black Cauldron*; Holt, Rinehart and Winston. Jarrell, Randall; *The Animal Family*; Pantheon Books. Stolz, Mary; *The Noonday Friends*; Harper and Row.

1967　Medal: Hunt, Irene; *Up a Road Slowly*; Follett.

　　　Honor Books: O'Dell, Scott; *The King's Fifth*; Houghton Mifflin. Singer, Isaac Bashevis; *Zlateh the Goat, and Other Stories*; Harper and Row. Weik, Mary Hays; *The Jazz Man*; Atheneum.

1968　Medal: Konigsburg, E. L.; *From the Mixed-up Files of Mrs. Basil E. Frankweiler*; Atheneum.

　　　Honor Books: Konigsburg, E. L.; *Jennifer, Hecate, Macbeth, William McKinley, and Me, Elizabeth*; Atheneum. O'Dell, Scott; *The Black Pearl*; Houghton Mifflin. Singer, Isaac Bashevis; *The Fearsome Inn*; Charles Scribner's Sons. Snyder, Zilpha Keatley; *The Egypt Game*; Atheneum.

1969 Medal: Alexander, Lloyd; *The High King*; Holt, Rinehart and Winston.
Honor Books: Lester, Julius; *To Be a Slave*; Dial Press. Singer, Isaac Bashevis; *When Shlemiel Went to Warsaw, and Other Stories*; Farrar, Straus and Giroux.

1970 Medal: Armstrong, William H.; *Sounder*; Harper and Row.
Honor Books: Ish-Kishor, Sulamith; *Our Eddie*; Pantheon Books. Moore, Janet Gaylord; *The Many Ways of Seeing: An Introduction to the Pleasures of Art*; World. Steele, Mary Q.; *Journey Outside*; Viking Press.

1971 Medal: Byars, Betsy; *Summer of the Swans*; Viking Press.
Honor Books: Babbitt, Natalie; *Kneeknock Rise*; Farrar, Straus and Giroux. Engdahl, Sylvia Louise; *Enchantress from the Stars*; Atheneum. O'Dell, Scott; *Sing Down the Moon*; Houghton Mifflin.

1972 Medal: O'Brien, Robert C.; *Mrs. Frisby and the Rats of NIMH*; Atheneum.
Honor Books: Eckert, Allan W.; *Incident at Hawk's Hill*; Little, Brown. Hamilton, Virginia; *The Planet of Junior Brown*; Macmillan. LeGuin, Ursula K.; *The Tombs of Atuan*; Atheneum. Miles, Miska; *Annie and the Old One*; Atlantic Monthly Press Books. Snyder, Zilpha Keatley; *The Headless Cupid*; Atheneum.

1973 Medal: George, Jean Craighead; *Julie of the Wolves*; Harper and Row.
Honor Books: Lobel, Arnold; *Frog and Toad Together*; Harper and Row. Reiss, Johanna; *The Upstairs Room*; Thomas Y. Crowell. Snyder, Zilpha Keatley; *The Witches of Worm*; Atheneum.

1974 Medal: Fox, Paula; *The Slave Dancer*; Bradbury Press.
Honor Book: Cooper, Susan; *The Dark Is Rising*; Atheneum.

1975 Medal: Hamilton, Virginia; *M. C. Higgins, the Great*; Macmillan.
Honor Books: Collier, James, and Christopher Collier; *My Brother Sam Is Dead*; Four Winds Press. Greene, Bette; *Philip Hall Likes Me, I Reckon Maybe*; Dial Press. Pope, Elizabeth; *The Perilous Gard*; Houghton Mifflin. Raskin, Ellen; *Figgs and Phantoms*; E. P. Dutton.

1976 Medal: Cooper, Susan; *The Grey King*; Atheneum.
Honor Books: Yep, Laurence; *Dragonwings*; Harper and Row. Mathis, Sharon; *The Hundred Penny Box*; Viking Press.

1977 Medal: Taylor, Mildred D.; *Roll of Thunder, Hear My Cry*; Dial Books for Young Readers.
Honor Books: Steig, William; *Abel's Island*; Farrar, Straus and Giroux. Bond, Nancy; *A String in the Harp*; Atheneum.

1978 Medal: Paterson, Katherine; *Bridge to Terabithia*; Thomas Y. Crowell.
Honor Books: Highwater, Jamake; *Anpao: An American Indian Odyssey*; J. B. Lippincott. Cleary, Beverly; *Ramona and Her Father*; William Morrow.

1979 Medal: Raskin, Ellen; *The Westing Game*; E. P. Dutton.
Honor Book: Paterson, Katherine; *The Great Gilly Hopkins*; Thomas Y. Crowell.

1980 Medal: Blos, Joan W.; *A Gathering of Days: A New England Girl's Journal, 1830–32*; Charles Scribner's Sons.
Honor Book: Kherdian, David; *The Road from Home: The Story of an American Girl*; Greenwillow Books.
1981 Medal: Paterson, Katherine; *Jacob Have I Loved*; Thomas Y. Crowell.
Honor Books: Langton, Jane; *The Fledgling*; Harper and Row. L'Engle, Madeleine; *Ring of Endless Light*; Farrar, Straus and Giroux.
1982 Medal: Willard, Nancy; illus. by Alice and Martin Provensen; *A Visit to William Blake's Inn: Poems for Innocent and Experienced Travelers*. Harcourt Brace Jovanovich.
Honor Books: Cleary, Beverly; *Ramona Quimby, Age 8*; William Morrow. Siegal, Aranka; *Upon the Head of the Goat: A Childhood in Hungary, 1939–1944*; Farrar, Straus and Giroux.
1983 Medal: Voigt, Cynthia; *Dicey's Song*; Atheneum.
Honor Books: McKinley, Robin; *The Blue Sword*; Greenwillow Books. Steig, William; *Dr. Desoto*; Farrar, Straus and Giroux. Fleischman, Paul; *Graven Images*; Harper and Row. Fritz, Jean; *Homesick: My Own Story*; G. P. Putnam's Sons. Hamilton, Virginia; *Sweet Whispers, Brother Rush*; Philomel Books.
1984 Medal: Cleary, Beverly; *Dear Mr. Henshaw*; William Morrow.
Honor Books: Brittain, Bill; *The Wish-Giver*; Harper and Row. Voigt, Cynthia; *A Solitary Blue*; Atheneum. Speare, Elizabeth George; *The Sign of the Beaver*; Houghton Mifflin. Lasky, Kathryn; photographs by Christopher Knight; *Sugaring Time*; Macmillan.
1985 Medal: McKinley, Robin; *The Hero and the Crown*; Greenwillow Books.
Honor Books: Brooks, Bruce; *The Moves Make the Man*; Harper and Row. Fox, Paula; *One-Eyed Cat*; Bradbury Press. Jukes, Mavis; illus. by Lloyd Bloom; *Like Jake and Me*; Alfred A. Knopf.
1986 Medal: MacLachlan, Patricia; *Sarah, Plain and Tall*; Harper and Row.
Honor Books: Blumberg, Rhoda; *Commodore Perry in the Land of the Shogun*; Lothrop, Lee and Shepard Books. Paulsen, Gary; *Dogsong*; Bradbury Press.
1987 Medal: Fleischman, Sid; *The Whipping Boy*; Greenwillow Books.
Honor Books: Rylant, Cynthia; *A Fine White Dust*; Bradbury Press. Bauer, Marion Dane; *On My Honor*; Clarion Books. Lauber, Patricia; *Volcano: The Eruption and Healing of Mount St. Helens*; Bradbury Press.
1988 Medal: Freedman, Russell; *Lincoln: A Photobiography*; Clarion Books.
Honor Books: Mazer, Norma Fox; *After the Rain*; William Morrow. Paulsen, Gary; *Hatchet*; Bradbury Press.
1989 Medal: Fleischman, Paul; illus. by Eric Beddows; *Joyful Noise: Poems for Two Voices*; Charlotte Zolotow Books.
Honor Books: Myers, Walter Dean; *Scorpions*; Harper and Row. Hamilton, Virginia; *In the Beginning: Creation Stories from around the World*; Harcourt Brace Jovanovich.

Scott O'Dell Award for Historical Fiction

This award, established in 1981, is given to a distinguished work of historical fiction for children or young adults. The book must be by a United States author, written in English, published in the United States, and set in the New World (North, South, or Central America). The award is given annually if a worthy book has been published. It is administered by the Advisory Committee of the Bulletin of the Center for Children's Books.

1984 Speare, Elizabeth G.; *Sign of the Beaver*; Houghton Mifflin.
1985 Avi; illus. by Ellen Thompson; *Fighting Ground*; J. B. Lippincott.
1986 MacLachlan, Patricia; *Sarah, Plain and Tall*; Harper and Row.
1987 O'Dell, Scott; *Streams to the River, River to the Sea: A Novel of Sacagawea*; Houghton Mifflin.
1988 Beatty, Patricia; *Charley Skedaddle*; William Morrow.

Edgar Allan Poe Award

This annual award was established in 1945 and is sponsored by the Mystery Writers of America. The "Edgar" is given for the best juvenile mystery of the year. The most recent winners are listed.

1980 Nixon, Joan Lowery; *The Seance*; Harper and Row.
1981 Mazer, Norma F.; *Taking Terri Mueller*; Avon Books.
1982 Branscum, Robbie; *The Murder of Hound Dog Bates*; Viking Press.
1983 Voigt, Cynthia; *The Callender Papers*; Macmillan.
1984 Naylor, Phyllis R.; *Night Cry*; Macmillan.
1985 Windsor, Patricia; *The Sandman's Eyes*; Delacorte Press.
1986 Nixon, Joan Lowery; *The Other Side of Dark*; Delacorte Press.
1987 Shreve, Susan; *Lucy Forever and Miss Rosetree, Shrinks*; Henry Holt.
1988 Roberts, Willo Davis; *Megan's Island*; Atheneum.

Laura Ingalls Wilder Award

This award was given every five years from 1954 through 1980 and as of 1983 has been given every three years to an author or illustrator who has made a substantial and lasting contribution to literature for children in the United States. It is administered by the Association for Library Service to Children of the American Library Association.

1954 Laura Ingalls Wilder
1960 Clara Ingram Judson
1965 Ruth Sawyer
1970 E. B. White
1975 Beverly Cleary

1980   Theodor S. Geisel (Dr. Seuss)
1983   Maurice Sendak
1986   Jean Fritz
1989   Elizabeth George Speare

Booklists

American Library Association Notable Children's Books

The Notable Children's Book Committee of the Association for Library Service to Children, a division of the American Library Association, selects notable books each year on the basis of literary quality, originality of text and illustrations, design, format, subject matter of interest and value to children, and likelihood of acceptance by children. The complete list of Notable Children's Books appears yearly in a spring issue of *Booklist*, a journal published by the American Library Association.

International Reading Association Children's Choices

The Children's Choices Committee of the International Reading Association–Children's Book Council Joint Committee selects a group of children's books each year to be presented to children for their consideration and vote. The list comprises those books receiving the highest number of children's votes. The complete list of Children's Choices appears yearly in a fall issue of *The Reading Teacher*, a journal published by the International Reading Association. Single copies are available at no charge by sending a stamped (3 oz.), self-addressed #10 envelope to the Children's Book Council, 67 Irving Place, New York, NY 10003.

Notable Children's Trade Books in the Field of Social Studies

The Book Review Subcommittee of the National Council of the Social Studies–Children's Book Council Joint Committee selects books published in the United States each year that (1) are written primarily for children in grades K–8; (2) emphasize human relations; (3) present an original theme or a fresh slant on a traditional topic; (4) are highly readable; and, when appropriate, (5) include maps and illustrations. The complete list of these notable books appears yearly in a spring issue of *Social Education*, the journal of the National Council of the Social Studies. Single copies are available at no charge by sending a stamped (3 oz.), self-addressed #10 envelope to the Children's Book Council, 67 Irving Place, New York, NY 10003.

Outstanding Science Trade Books for Children

The Book Review Committee of the National Science Teachers Association, in cooperation with the Children's Book Council, selects books each year that (1) are readable; (2) contain information consistent with current scientific knowledge; (3) are pleasing in format and illustrations; and (4) are nonsexist, nonracist, and nonviolent. The complete list of these outstanding books appears yearly in a spring issue of *Science and Children*, the journal of the National Science Teachers Association. Single copies are available at no charge by sending a stamped (3 oz.), self-addressed #10 envelope to the Children's Book Council, 67 Irving Place, New York, NY 10003.

Lists and descriptions of other awards, prizes, and booklists can be located at the front of recent editions of Children's Books in Print, *an annual publication of R. R. Bowker.*

Directory of Publishers

Since there has been a great deal of mobility and change in publishing houses in the last few years, the most accurate and up-to-date listing of publishers and their ordering addresses will be located in the most recent annual copy of *Children's Books in Print*, which can be found in the children's section of most libraries, or in *Books in Print*, which is issued semi-annually. Both publications are issued by R. R. Bowker. A recent list of publishers can also be obtained from the Children's Book Council, 67 Irving Place, New York, NY 10003.

Atheneum Publishers. Distributed by Macmillan Publishing Company. Attention: Mail Order Dept., Riverside Distribution Center, Front and Brown Streets, Riverside, NJ 08075.

Atlantic Monthly Press. Distributed by Little, Brown and Company. Division of Time. Orders to: 200 West Street, Waltham, MA 02154.

Avon Books. Division of the Hearst Corporation. Orders to: P.O. Box 767, Dresden, TN 38225.

Bantam Books. Division of Bantam Doubleday Dell Publishing Group. Orders to: 414 E. Golf Road, Des Plaines, IL 60016.

Barron's Educational Series, P.O. Box 8040, 250 Wireless Boulevard, Hauppauge, NY 11788.

Bradbury Press. Distributed by Macmillan Publishing Company. Attention: Mail Order Dept., Riverside Distribution Center, Front and Brown Streets, Riverside, NJ 08075.

Carolrhoda Books, 241 First Avenue North, Minneapolis, MN 55401.

Clarion Books. Division of Ticknor and Fields. Distributed by Houghton Mifflin. Orders to: Wayside Road, Burlington, MA 01803.

Coward-McCann. Distributed by the Putnam Publishing Group. Orders to: P.O. Box 506, Department B, East Rutherford, NJ 07073.

Creative Education, 123 S. Broad Street, P.O. Box 227, Mankato, MN 56001.

Thomas Y. Crowell. Distributed by Harper and Row. Orders to: Keystone Industrial Park, Scranton, PA 18512.

Crown Publishers, 225 Park Avenue South, New York, NY 10003.

Delacorte Press. Imprint of Dell Publishing Company. Division of Bantam Doubleday Dell Publishing Group, One Dag Hammarskjold Plaza, 245 E. 47th Street, New York, NY 10017.

Dell Books. Imprint of Dell Publishing Company. Division of Bantam Doubleday Dell Publishing Group, One Dag Hammarskjold Plaza, 245 E. 47th Street, New York, NY 10017.

André Deutsch. Distributed by E. P. Dutton. Division of NAL Penguin. Orders to: New American Library, 120 Woodbine Street, Bergenfield, NJ 07261.

Dial Books for Young Readers. Imprint of E. P. Dutton. Division of NAL Penguin. Orders to: New American Library, 120 Woodbine Street, Bergenfield, NJ 07261.

Dial Press. Imprint of Doubleday and Company. Division of Bantam Doubleday Dell Publishing Group. Orders to: 501 Franklin Avenue, Garden City, NY 11530.

Dillon Press, 242 Portland Avenue South, Minneapolis, MN 55415.

Dodd, Mead and Company. Orders to: 6 Ram Ridge Road, Spring Valley, NY 10977.

E. P. Dutton. Division of NAL Penguin. Orders to: New American Library, 120 Woodbine Street, Bergenfield, NJ 07261.

Farrar, Straus and Giroux. Distributed by Harper and Row. Orders to: Keystone Industrial Park, Scranton, PA 18512.

Four Winds Press. Imprint of Macmillan Publishing Company. Attention: Mail Order Dept., Riverside Distribution Center, Front and Brown Streets, Riverside, NJ 08075.

Greenwillow Books. Division of William Morrow and Company. Orders to: 39 Plymouth Street, P.O. Box 1219, Fairfield, NJ 07007.

Grosset and Dunlap, 200 Madison Avenue, New York, NY 10016.

Harcourt Brace Jovanovich. Orders to: 465 S. Lincoln Drive, Troy, MO 63379.

Harper and Row. Orders to: Keystone Industrial Park, Scranton, PA 18512.

Harper Junior Books. Imprint of Harper and Row. Orders to: Keystone Industrial Park, Scranton, PA 18512.

Hill and Wang. Division of Farrar, Straus and Giroux. Distributed by Harper and Row. Orders to: Keystone Industrial Park, Scranton, PA 18512.

Holiday House, 18 E. 53rd Street, New York, NY 10022.

Henry Holt and Company, 4375 W. 1980 South, P.O. Box 30135, Salt Lake City, UT 84104.

Holt, Rinehart and Winston. Division of Harcourt Brace Jovanovich. Attention: Order Fulfillment Dept., 6277 Sea Harbor Drive, Orlando, FL 32887.

Houghton Mifflin Company. Orders to: Wayside Road, Burlington, MA 01803.

Alfred A. Knopf. Subsidiary of Random House. Orders to: 400 Hahn Road, Westminster, MD 21157.

Lerner Publications Company, 241 First Avenue North, Minneapolis, MN 55401.

J. B. Lippincott Company. Subsidiary of Harper and Row. Orders to: Keystone Industrial Park, Scranton, PA 18512.

Little, Brown and Company. Orders to: 200 West Street, Waltham, MA 02154.

Lothrop, Lee and Shepard Books. Subsidiary of William Morrow and Company. Orders to: 39 Plymouth Street, P.O. Box 1219, Fairfield, NJ 07007.

Margaret K. McElderry Books. Division of Macmillan Publishing Company. Attention: Mail Order Dept., Riverside Distribution Center, Front and Brown Streets, Riverside, NJ 08075.

Macmillan Publishing Company. Attention: Mail Order Dept., Riverside Distribution Center, Front and Brown Streets, Riverside, NJ 08075.

William Morrow and Company. Subsidiary of the Hearst Corporation. Orders to: 39 Plymouth Street, P.O. Box 1219, Fairfield, NJ 07007.

North-South Books. Distributed by Henry Holt and Company, 4375 W. 1980 South, P.O. Box 30135, Salt Lake City, UT 84104.

Orchard Books. Division of Franklin Watts. Orders to: Sherman Turnpike, Danbury, CT 06816.

Pantheon Books. Division of Random House. Orders to: 400 Hahn Road, Westminster, MD 21157.

Philomel Books. Imprint of the Putnam Publishing Group. Orders to: P.O. Box 506, Department B, East Rutherford, NJ 07073.

Platt and Munk Publishers. Division of Grosset and Dunlap, 200 Madison Avenue, New York, NY 10010.

Plays, Inc., 120 Boylston Street, Boston, MA 02116.

Clarkson N. Potter Books. Distributed by the Putnam Publishing Group. Orders to: P.O. Box 506, Department B, East Rutherford, NJ 07073.

Prentice-Hall. Division of Simon and Schuster. Orders to: 200 Old Tappan Road, Old Tappan, NJ 07675.

G. P. Putnam's Sons. Imprint of the Putnam Publishing Group. Orders to: P.O. Box 506, Department B, East Rutherford, NJ 07073.

Raintree Children's Books. Subsidiary of Somerset House Corporation. Orders to: 310 W. Wisconsin Avenue, Mezzanine Level, Milwaukee, WI 53203.

Random House. Orders to: 400 Hahn Road, Westminster, MD 21157.

R and S Books. Distributed by Farrar, Straus and Giroux. Distributed by Harper and Row. Orders to: Keystone Industrial Park, Scranton, PA 18512.

Scholastic. Orders to: P.O. Box 7502, 2931 E. McCarty Street, Jefferson City, MO 65102.

Charles Scribner's Sons. Division of Macmillan Publishing Company. Attention: Mail Order Dept., Riverside Distribution Center, Front and Brown Streets, Riverside, NJ 08075.

Stemmer House, 2627 Caves Road, Owings Mills, MD 21117.

Troll Associates. Subsidiary of Educational Reading Service. Orders to: 100 Corporate Drive, Mahwah, NJ 07430.

Viking Kestrel. Imprint of Viking Penguin. Division of NAL Penguin. Orders to: New American Library, 120 Woodbine Street, Bergenfield, NJ 07261.

Viking Penguin. Division of NAL Penguin. Orders to: New American Library, 120 Woodbine Street, Bergenfield, NJ 07261.

Walker and Company, 720 Fifth Avenue, New York, NY 10019.

Frederick Warne. Division of Viking Penguin. Division of NAL Penguin. Orders to: New American Library, 120 Woodbine Street, Bergenfield, NJ 07261.

Franklin Watts. Subsidiary of Grolier. Orders to: Sherman Turnpike, Danbury, CT 06816.

Westminster Press. Orders to: P.O. Box 718, William Penn Annex, Philadelphia, PA 19105.

Albert Whitman and Company, 5747 W. Howard Street, Niles, IL 60648.

Author Index

Aamodt, Alice, 14.73
Aardema, Verna, 7.12, 7.13
Abells, Chana Byers, 13.52
Ackerman, Karen, 10.172
Adler, David A., 4.98–101, 10.288,
   10.311–315, 12.18
Adoff, Arnold, 5.40, 8.192
Adorjan, Carol, 13.8
Agee, Jon, 8.10
Ahlberg, Allan, 4.112
Ahlberg, Janet, 4.112
Aiken, Joan, 8.1, 8.11, 8.268, 8.298
Alcock, Vivien, 8.184, 10.215
Alderson, Sue Ann, 11.50
Alexander, Lloyd, 8.12, 11.51, 11.52
Alexander, Martha, 10.173
Alexander, Sue, 4.1
Aliki, 13.7, 14.194, 14.195
Allard, Harry, 8.215
Allen, Pamela, 1.51
Amoss, Berthe, 3.1, 10.216
Ancona, George, 13.62, 14.93
Andersen, Hans Christian, 8.276–281,
   8.299, 8.300
Anderson, Joan, 13.38
Anderson, Lucia, 14.69
Anderson, Peggy Perry, 1.52
Andrews, Jan, 10.42
Angell, Judie, 11.31
Anno, Mitsumasa, 1.53, 14.140, 14.181,
   15.17
Apfel, Necia H., 14.103
Archambault, John, 1.107, 4.115, 8.101,
   10.1, 10.47, 10.199, 10.200
Arnold, Caroline, 14.115, 14.141, 15.16
Arnold, Tedd, 10.174
Arnold, Tim, 8.170
Arnosky, Jim, 14.57, 14.116
Arnow, Jan, 14.189
Asch, Frank, 1.54, 8.20
Aseltine, Lorraine, 10.74
Ashabranner, Brent, 13.10, 13.16, 13.39
Asimov, Isaac, 9.2, 14.155, 14.170
Asimov, Janet, 9.2

Auch, Mary Jane, 10.217, 10.218
Aylesworth, Jim, 2.20, 7.137, 8.282

Baggett, Nancy, 14.55, 14.174
Bahr, Amy C., 13.63–66
Baisch, Cris, 10.75
Baker, Barbara, 4.2
Ballard, Robert D., 13.53
Bang, Molly, 8.283, 10.76
Banish, Roslyn, 14.161
Banks, Lynne Reid, 8.185
Barber, Antonia, 8.284
Bare, Colleen Stanley, 14.84, 14.85
Barklem, Jill, 8.21
Barrie, J. M., 6.1
Barton, Byron, 2.37–40
Baskin, Hosie, 7.117
Baskin, Leonard, 7.117
Bates, Betty, 10.71, 10.219
Bauer, Caroline Feller, 5.1, 10.77
Bauer, Marion Dane, 8.13, 10.140
Baum, Arline, 10.78
Baum, Joseph, 10.78
Bawden, Nona, 10.369
Baylor, Byrd, 10.40
Beatty, Patricia, 11.32
Bedard, Michael, 8.315
Beisert, Heide Helene, 1.55
Bellows, Cathy, 8.22
Bellville, Cheryl Walsh, 13.4, 15.2
Bemelmans, Ludwig, 10.362
Benjamin, Alan, 2.41
Benjamin, Carol Lea, 4.113
Bennett, Jill, 7.14
Berenstain, Jan, 4.3, 4.4
Berenstain, Stan, 4.3, 4.4
Berger, Barbara Helen, 8.193, 18.1
Berger, Melvin, 14.162, 14.185
Berliner, Don, 14.2
Bernstein, Joanne E., 4.102, 4.103
Berrill, Margaret, 7.1
Berry, James, 10.370
Bierhorst, John, 7.2
Billings, Charlene W., 14.23

Illustrator Index

Subject Index

Title Index